Time Out

Florence

timeout.com/florence

Published by Time Out Guides Ltd, a wholly owned subsidiary of Time Out Group Ltd.
Time Out and the Time Out logo are trademarks of Time Out Group Ltd.

© **Time Out Group Ltd 2005**
Previous editions 1997, 1999, 2001, 2003.

10 9 8 7 6 5 4 3 2 1

This edition first published in Great Britain in 2005 by Ebury Publishing
Ebury Publishing is a division of The Random House Group Ltd,
20 Vauxhall Bridge Road, London SW1V 2SA

Random House Australia Pty Limited 20 Alfred Street, Milsons Point, Sydney, New South Wales 2061, Australia
Random House New Zealand Limited 18 Poland Road, Glenfield, Auckland 10, New Zealand
Random House South Africa (Pty) Limited Endulini, 5A Jubilee Road, Parktown 2193, South Africa

Random House UK Limited Reg. No. 954009

Distributed in USA by Publishers Group West
1700 Fourth Street, Berkeley, California 94710

Distributed in Canada by Penguin Canada Ltd
10 Alcorn Avenue, Toronto, Ontario, Canada M4V 3B2

For further distribution details, see www.timeout.com

ISBN 1-904978-50-9

A CIP catalogue record for this book is available from the British Library

Colour reprographics by Icon, Crowne House, 56-58 Southwark Street, London SE1 1UN

Printed and bound in Germany by Appl

Papers used by Ebury Publishing are natural, recyclable products made from wood grown in sustainable forests

Time Out Guides Limited
Universal House
251 Tottenham Court Road
London W1T 7AB
Tel + 44 (0)20 7813 3000
Fax + 44 (0)20 7813 6001
Email guides@timeout.com
www.timeout.com

Editorial

Editor Lesley McCave
Deputy Editor Will Fulford-Jones
Consultant Editor Nicky Swallow
Sub Editor Edoardo Albert
Listings Editor Helen Holubov
Proofreader Sylvia Tombesi-Walton
Indexer Jonathan Cox

Editorial/Managing Director Peter Fiennes
Series Editor Ruth Jarvis
Deputy Series Editor Lesley McCave
Business Manager Gareth Garner
Guides Co-ordinator Holly Pick
Accountant Kemi Olufuwa

Design

Art Director Scott Moore
Art Editor Tracey Ridgewell
Designer Josephine Spencer
Junior Designer Pete Ward
Freelance Designer Tessa Kar
Digital Imaging Dan Conway
Ad Make-up Jenni Pritchard

Picture Desk

Picture Editor Jael Marschner
Deputy Picture Editor Tracey Kerrigan
Picture Researcher Helen McFarland

Advertising

Sales Director Mark Phillips
International Sales Manager Ross Canadé
International Sales Executive Simon Davies
Advertising Sales (Florence): MAD & Co. International
Advertising Assistant Lucy Butler

Marketing

Marketing Director Mandy Martinez
Marketing & Publicity Manager, US Rosella Albanese

Production

Production Director Mark Lamond
Production Controller Marie Howell

Time Out Group

Chairman Tony Elliott
Managing Director Mike Hardwick
Group Financial Director Richard Waterlow
Group Commercial Director Lesley Gill
Group General Manager Nichola Coulthard
Group Circulation Director Jim Heinemann
Group Art Director John Oakey
Online Managing Director David Pepper
Group Production Director Steve Proctor
Group IT Director Simon Chappell

Contributors

Introduction Lesley McCave. **History** Anne Hanley (*The Renaissance* Lesley McCave). **Florence Today** Magdalen Nabb. **Art** Danielle Carrabino. **Architecture** Richard Fremantle, Nicky Swallow. **Food in Tuscany** Kate Singleton, Kate Carlisle (*Want food, will travel* Nicky Swallow). **Wine in Tuscany** Kate Singleton. **Where to Stay** Nicky Swallow. **Sightseeing** Julia Burdet (Outside the City Gates, *Garden of earthly delights* Nicky Swallow; *Head for heights* Sam Le Quesne). **Restaurants & Wine Bars** Nicky Swallow. **Cafés & Bars** Julia Burdet. **Shops & Services** Julia Burdet. **Festivals & Events** Nicky Swallow. **Children** Natasha Garland. **Film** Julia Burdet. **Galleries** Julia Burdet. **Gay & Lesbian** Bruno Casini. **Music: Classical & Opera** Nicky Swallow. **Music: Rock, Roots & Jazz** Julia Burdet. **Nightlife** Julia Burdet. **Sport & Fitness** Natasha Garland. **Theatre & Dance** Nicky Swallow. **Florence & Prato Provinces** Nicky Swallow. **Pistoia Province** Nicky Swallow. **Pisa** Kate Singleton. **Pisa & Livorno Provinces** Kate Singleton. **Siena** Kate Singleton. **Siena Province** Kate Singleton. **Lucca** James Mitchell. **Massa-Carrara & Lucca Provinces** Sam Le Quesne. **Arezzo** Kate Singleton. **Arezzo Province** Kate Singleton. **Southern Tuscany** Kate Singleton (*A very big house in the country* Lesley McCave). **Directory** Julia Burdet.

Maps JS Graphics (john@jsgraphics.co.uk).

Photography Jonathan Perugia, except: page 10 Museo de Firenze Com'era, Florence, Italy/www.bridgeman.co.uk; pages 17, 18, 20, 21, 27 akg-images; pages 19, 28 The Art Archives/Galleria degli Uffizi Florence/Dagli Orti (A); page 37 Foster and Partners; page 156 Archives of Agenzia per il Turismo di Siena; page 164 akg-images/Album; page 191 Francesco Martorelli/Studio Portrait; page 263 Photowave; page 274 (bottom) Andrea Vierucci.
The following images were provided by the featured establishments/artists: pages 57, 159, 171, 172, 173, 184, 274 (top).

The Editor would like to thank Fulvia Angelini, Anne Hanley, Rose Magers, and all contributors to previous editions of *Time Out Florence*, whose work forms the basis for parts of this book.

MAD & Co. Advertising & Marketing Director: Margherita Tedone Tel: +39 06 3550 9145 Fax: +39 06 3550 1775. Sales executive (Florence): Donatella Ferrazzano

The photographer's car and scooter were provided by MaxiRent. Tel: (+39 055 2654207 (www.maxirent.com).

Contents

Introduction

If Michelangelo were to reappear in Florence today, he might be surprised at how little had changed in the 500 years since he chipped a huge slab of marble down into the shape of *David*. The monuments that were created by similarly gifted craftsmen before he was even born – Brunelleschi's Duomo, Alberti's façade of Santa Maria Novella church, Masolino and Masaccio's frescoes in the Bracacci Chapel – are still here. The only real difference is that now they're constantly thronging with tourists who've travelled here from all over the world.

And the Florentines themselves? Well, they haven't changed much either. They're still immensely proud of their city, still being accused of aloofness, even arrogance. But they're as welcoming to tourists as they've ever been. Even the entertainment Tuscany provides is the same: centuries-old traditions such as Siena's Palio, boat racing on the Arno and jousting in Arezzo.

That said, Florence does get a bit of a shake-up every now and again, and there's one taking place right now. The developments will improve the city in the end, but with their construction come chaos and infighting. The Tramvia, a tramline designed to link the city centre with the suburbs to the north-west, will ultimately ease vehicle congestion, but in the short term the traffic gridlock is getting worse

as roads and bridges are closed. The Uffizi needs a new exit, and will get one, but for the moment no one can agree on the design. There's also a new Sir Norman Foster-designed train station on the cards as part of a high-speed train link between Milan and Rome, but work on it hadn't even begun as this guide went to press.

As a visitor, you needn't be bothered by all this. Spend your afternoons wandering the backstreets, dipping into alleys, sipping *vino della casa* with the locals or soaking up the sun on Piazza della Signoria. But also make the most of the fact that you're in Florence, the world's greatest living art museum.

If you've chosen to come here in peak season – which, in Florence, rarely ends, but Easter and summer find the town particularly packed – then you'll want to give the city a break for a while. Even if you only make it up to Piazzale Michelangelo or San Miniato al Monte to take in the views, you'll appreciate the space. Better still, stay away for a night or two, and explore the ancient hilltop towns of Volterra and San Gimignano, the grand villas around Lucca, the wineries of Montepulciano or Chianti, or the beaches of the Maremma. If Michelangelo saw the never-ending queues that form daily at the Accademia to see his masterpiece, he'd surely understand.

ABOUT TIME OUT CITY GUIDES

Time Out Florence is one of an expanding series of Time Out guides produced by the people behind the successful listings magazines in London, New York and Chicago. Our guides are all written by resident experts who have striven to provide you with all the most up-to-date information you'll need to explore the city or read up on its background, whether you're a local or a first-time visitor.

THE LOWDOWN ON THE LISTINGS

We have tried to make this book as easy to use as possible. Addresses, phone numbers, opening times and admission prices are all included in the listings. However, businesses can change their arrangements at any time. Before you go out of your way, we would strongly advise you to phone ahead to check opening times and other particulars. While every effort and care has been made to ensure the accuracy of the information

contained in this guide, the publishers cannot accept responsibility for any errors it may contain.

PRICES AND PAYMENT

We have noted where venues such as shops, hotels, bars and restaurants accept the following credit cards: American Express (**AmEx**), Diners Club (**DC**), MasterCard (**MC**) and Visa (**V**). Many hotels and the more salubrious shops and restaurants will also accept travellers' cheques in various denominations; some also take pounds and US dollars.

The prices we've listed in this guide should be treated as guidelines, not gospel. If prices vary wildly from those we've quoted, ask whether there's a good reason. If not, go elsewhere. Then please let us know. We aim to give the best and most up-to-date advice, so we want to know if you've been badly treated or overcharged.

THE LIE OF THE LAND

For convenient orientation, we have divided the city into six areas, most based around their principal church. These areas are clearly marked on the map on pages 318-319 and echoed in the titles of our sightseeing chapters. Bear in mind, however, that central Florence is very compact and it's often easy to walk between destinations. For this reason, we have given bus information only for addresses beyond the old city walls: in the central area, a combination of walking a short distance and using the four electric bus circuits (marked on the maps on pages 318-319) should get you everywhere quickly.

Note that the city's famously complex street numbering system can be confusing. Residential addresses are 'black' numbers (*nero*), while most commercial addresses are 'red' (*rosso*), and take an 'r' suffix – so if there is no suffix you can assume that it is a 'black' number. This system means that on any one street there can be two addresses with the same number in different colours – sometimes far apart.

TELEPHONE NUMBERS

The area code for Florence is 055; which must be dialled in full (including the zero) at all times, whether calling from within Italy (including Florence itself) or from abroad.

The international code for Italy is 39. Numbers preceded by 800 can be called free of charge from Florence. For further details of phone codes, *see p297*.

TUSCANY

A third of this guide is devoted to the highlights of Tuscany. Again, phone numbers are given in their entirety as dialled locally and throughout Italy – when dialling from abroad, preface them with 39, dropping the initial zero. 'Average' prices in the restaurant reviews include an *antipasto* or *primo*, and a *secondo*, *contorno* and *dolce* for one person, but not drinks.

ESSENTIAL INFORMATION

For all the practical information you might need for visiting the area – details of local transport, a listing of emergency numbers, information on local weather and a selection of useful websites – turn to the Directory at the back of this guide. It begins on page 282.

MAPS

We have included a fully indexed colour map of the city at the back of this guide – on pages 318-319. Where possible, we have printed a grid reference against all venues that appear on the map. There's a map of Tuscany on pages 312-313 and individual city maps in the relevant chapters.

LET US KNOW WHAT YOU THINK

We hope you enjoy *Time Out Florence*, and we'd like to know what you think of it. We welcome tips for places that you consider we should include in future editions and take note of your criticism of our choices. You can email us at guides@timeout.com.

Advertisers

We would like to stress that no establishment has been included in this guide because it has advertised in any of our publications and no payment of any kind has influenced any review. The opinions given in this book are those of Time Out writers and entirely independent.

There is an online version of this book, along with guides to over 45 other international cities, at **www.timeout.com**.

Netplan Srl

Italians do it better.

Done by Netplan, done by Italians.

You're going to love the Italian portal **Travelplan.it** because it's just like having a guidebook at hand, free and always up to date.

That's why over 100,000 travelers like yourself log on every month and discover a passion for our country, along with absolutely everything needed to visit it.

Because there's only one way to see Italy: with those who really know it.

www.travelplan.it

In Context

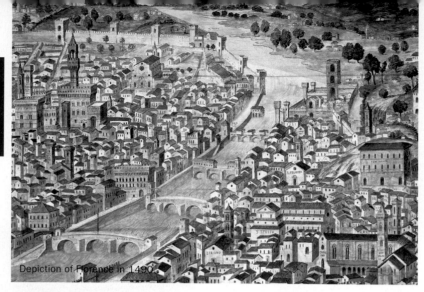

Depiction of Florence in 1490.

History

Renaissance central.

From around the eighth century BC much of central Italy was controlled by the Etruscans, who may have been natives or may have drifted in from Asia Minor. Whatever their origins, they settled in Veio and Cerveteri, close to Rome, and further north – in what is now Tuscany – around Volterra, Populonia, Arezzo, Chiusi and Cortona. They entirely overlooked the site that we now know as Florence, making hilltop Fiesole their northernmost stronghold.

Tantalisingly little evidence remains of Etruscan history and culture before they were clobbered out of existence by the Romans. One of the main reasons we can be sure of so little about them is that they constructed almost everything from wood. Everything, that is, except their tombs. Because of this, their graves and the objects recovered from them constitute most of the evidence on their civilisation. With so little to go on, mythologisers have had a field day. The enchanting frescoes of feasts, dancing and hunting that adorn many of the tombs led DH Lawrence to conclude that 'death to the Etruscan was a pleasant continuance of life'. Others believe that the Etruscans were terrified of mortality, that the seemingly carefree paintings were a desperate plea for the gods to show mercy on the other side.

Historians have come to understand the Etrusican civilisation pretty well. The Etruscans were certainly a religious people, but they were also partial to a good war, against either other tribes or rival Etruscan cities. Their civilisation reached its peak in the seventh and sixth centuries BC, when their loose federation of cities dominated much of what is now southern Tuscany and northern Lazio. Women played an unusually prominent role in society, apparently having as much fun as – if not more than – the lads. Writing in the fourth century BC, Theopompos said: 'Etruscan women take particular care of their bodies and exercise often, sometimes along with the men, and sometimes by themselves. It is not a disgrace for them to be seen naked. They do not share their couches with their husbands but with other men who happen to be present… They are expert drinkers and very attractive.'

Etruscan cities grew wealthy on the proceeds of mining and trading copper and iron. Their art and superbly worked gold jewellery display distinctive oriental influences, adding credence to the theory that the Etruscans migrated to Italy from the East, though such influences could have been due to their extensive trading in the eastern Mediterranean.

At the end of the seventh century BC the Etruscans captured the small town of Rome and ruled it for a century before being expelled. The next few hundred years witnessed city fighting city and tribe battling tribe until the emerging Roman republic overwhelmed all-comers by the third century BC.

ETRUSCAN TO TUSCAN

In 59 BC Julius Caesar established a colony for army veterans along the narrowest stretch of the Arno, and Florentia was born. Strategically located at the heart of Italian territory, it grew into a flourishing commercial centre, becoming the capital of a Roman province in the third century AD. In the fifth century the Roman Empire in the west finally crumbled before the pagan hordes (some of whom were no less cultured than the dissolute Romans they displaced). Italian unity collapsed as Ostrogoths, Visigoths, Huns and Lombards rampaged through the peninsula.

The Goths who swept into central Italy in the fifth century were dislodged by the Byzantine forces of the Eastern emperor in conflicts that left the area badly battle-scarred. The Goth King Totila seized Florence again in 552, only to be ejected two decades later when the Lombards stormed across the Alps and established a regional HQ at Lucca.

In the eighth century Charlemagne and his Frankish forces crushed the last of the Lombard kings of Italy. To thank him for his intervention and ensure his future support (a move that backfired badly, leading to centuries of conflict between pontiff and emperors), Pope Leo III crowned Charlemagne Holy Roman Emperor. Much of the country then came under the (at least nominal) control of the emperor. In practice, local warlords carved out feudal fiefs for themselves and threw their weight around.

The imperial margravate of Tuscany began to emerge as a region of some promise during the tenth and 11th centuries, when it came under the control of the Canossa family. Initially the richest city was Lucca, but it was Pisa's increasingly profitable maritime trade that brought the biggest impetus of ideas and wealth into the region.

As a prosperous merchant class developed in cities all over Tuscany, the region sought to throw off the constraints and demands of its feudal overlords. By 1200 the majority had succeeded (Florence, Siena and Lucca had been established as independent city states, or *comuni*, by the redoutable Matilde di Canossa on her death in 1115). Tuscany became a patchwork of tiny but increasingly self-confident and ambitious independent entities. The potential for conflict was huge, and by the 13th century it crystallised into an intractable and seemingly interminable struggle between Guelphs and Ghibellines.

THE FOREVER WAR

The names Guelph and Ghibelline came from the Italian forms of Welf (the family name of the German emperor Otto IV) and Waiblingen (a castle belonging to the Welfs' rivals for the role of Holy Roman Emperor, the Hohenstaufen) respectively, but by the time the appellations crossed the Alps into Italy (probably in the 12th century) their significance had changed.

'Siena started off Guelph, but couldn't bear being nice to Florence, so swapped to the Ghibelline cause.'

'Guelph' became attached primarily to the increasingly influential merchant classes. In their continuing desire to be free from imperial control, they looked around for a powerful backer. The only viable candidate was the emperor's enemy, the pope, who by this time had recognised the error of creating a rival ruler and was peddling the theory that the fourth-century Roman emperor Constantine (who sat by in his new Eastern capital at Constantinople as the Western Empire fell from the hands of the last Roman emperors into the ruthless ones of barbarian invaders) had assigned not just spiritual but also temporal power in Italy to the papacy. The Guelphs could thus add a patriotic and religious sheen to their own self-interest.

Anyone keen to uphold imperial power and opposed to papal designs and rising commercial interests – mainly the old nobility – became known as Ghibellines. That, at least, was the theory. It soon became clear, however, that self-interest and local rivalries were of far greater importance than theoretical allegiances to emperor or pope.

Although bad feeling had been simmering for decades, the murder of Florentine nobleman Buondelmonte dei Buondelmonti is seen as the spark that ignited flames across Tuscany. On his wedding day in 1215, Buondelmonte was stabbed to death by a member of the Amidei family for having previously jilted an Amidei maiden. The subsequent trial dissolved into a test of wills (and soon of arms) between the pro-Empire Amidei and the pro-*comune* faction mourning the demise of the groom. The Ghibelline Amidei prevailed with help from Emperor Frederick II in 1248, but were ousted with Guelph aid two years later, when a semi-democratic government by the merchant class, known as the *piccolo popolo*, was established.

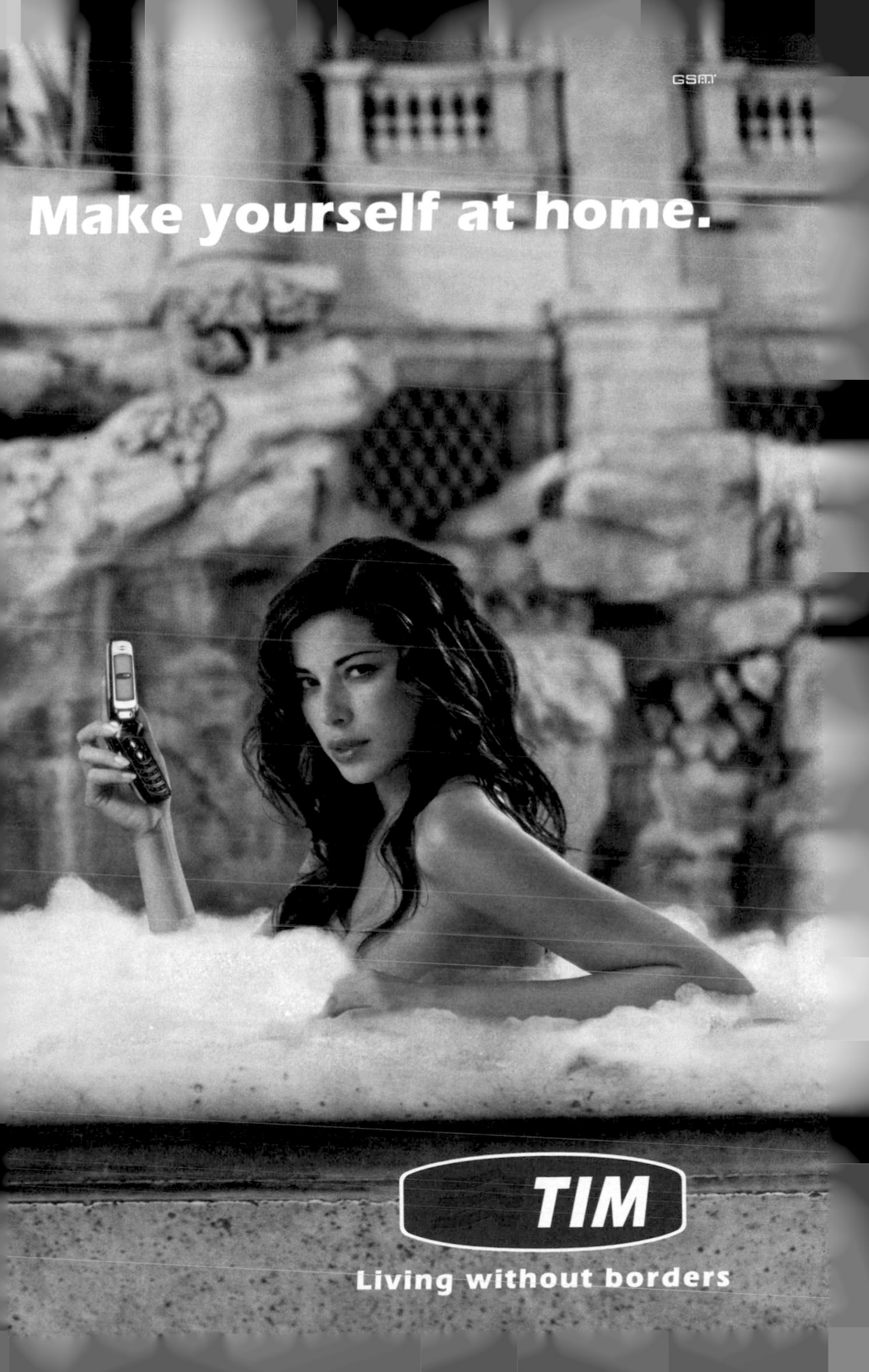
GSM
Make yourself at home.
TIM
Living without borders

The Renaissance

The Renaissance is a massive source of pride for Florence. For centuries the city has basked in its afterglow, and the world has basked with it. The Florentines have learned to live alongside the perennial swarms of tourists and they have grown accustomed to the sight of tour guides marching about their city. Even the most cursory overview of this seminal period in the city's past can substantially increase a visitor's understanding, not just of the history of Florence, but of its architecture, its culture and, above all, its citizens.

The guiding doctrine of the Renaissance (Rinascimento, literally rebirth) was Humanism – the revival of the language and art of the ancient Greeks and Romans and the reconciliation of this pagan heritage with Christianity. Although the most visible manifestation of the Renaissance in Florence was the astonishing outpouring of art in the 15th century, it was classical studies that sparked the new age.

The groundwork had been done by a handful of men: Dante (1265-1321), Petrarch (1304-74) and Boccaccio (1313-75) had all collected Latin manuscripts, which shaped their approach to writing. But it was mounting Florentine wealth that paid for dedicated manuscript detectives such as Poggio Bracciolini (1380-1459) to dig through neglected monastery libraries across Europe.

A few classical works had never been lost, but those that were known were usually corrupt. The volume of unknown works unearthed was incredible. First came the discovery of Quintilian's *The Training of an Orator*, which detailed the Roman education system, Columella's *De Re Rustica* on agriculture, key texts on Roman architecture by Vitruvius and Frontinus, and Cicero's *Brutus* (a justification of Republicanism). And whereas before very few Greek works were known in western Europe, suddenly, almost simultaneously, most of Plato, Homer, Sophocles and many other classics were discovered.

The Renaissance focus on a pre-Christian age didn't mean that God was under threat. Just as the Renaissance artists had no compunction about enhancing the beauty of their forms and compositions with classical features and allusions, so Renaissance Humanists sought explanations beyond the Scriptures that were complementary to accepted religion rather than a challenge to it. Much effort was made to present the wisdom of the ancients as a precursor to the ultimate wisdom of God.

Nor did the Renaissance fascination with things semi-scientific – Leonardo's anatomical drawings, for example, or the widespread obsession with the mathematics of Pythagoras – necessarily mean that this was a scientific age. The 15th century was an era when ideas were still paramount and science, as a process of deduction based on observation and experimentation, didn't really get going until the 17th century. In medicine, the theory of the four humours still held sway. Astronomy and astrology were all but synonymous. Mathematics was an almost mystical art, while alchemy, the attempt to transform base metals into gold, flourished.

It was magnificent while it lasted, but Florence's pre-eminence in art and ideas was abruptly snuffed out on the death of Lorenzo il Magnifico in 1492; the invasion by Charles VIII of France in the 1490s and Savonarola's Bonfire of the Vanities (*see p16*) saw to that. In the early 16th century the cutting edge switched to Rome, where Michelangelo, Bramante and Raphael were in the process of creating their finest works. Thence, after Emperor Charles V sacked Rome in 1527, to Venice, where masters such as Palladio and Titian practised. But the period left Florence with some of the most important masterpieces and artefacts in the world, thankfully still in existence today, and enjoyed by millions of visitors to the city each year.

Ten years on, Ghibellines from Siena dislodged the *piccolo popolo* and came close to razing the town; a decade later, the Guelphs were back in the driving seat, with the major craft guilds running the show through an administration called the *secondo popolo*. In 1293 the body passed a regulation effectively banning the nobility from government in Florence, giving power to a *signoria* (government) made up of representatives of the guilds.

The situation was no less complex in other Tuscan towns: Lucca was generally Guelph-dominated, while Siena and Pisa tended to favour the Ghibellines, but this had as much to do with mutual antagonisms as deeply held beliefs. Siena started off Guelph, but couldn't bear the thought of having to be nice to its traditional enemy, Florence, so swapped to the Ghibelline cause. Similarly, the Guelph/Ghibelline splits within cities were more often class- and grudge-based than ideological.

Throughout the 14th century, power ebbed and flowed between the two (loosely knit) parties across Tuscany and from city to city. When one party was in the ascendant its supporters would tear down its opponents' fortified towers (the Guelphs' with their square crenellations, the Ghibellines' with swallow-tail ones), only to have its own towers levelled as soon as the pendulum swung back.

'Artists willingly threw their works on to the Bonfire of the Vanities.'

Once firmly in command of Florence at the end of the 13th century, the Guelphs started squabbling internally. In around 1300 open conflict broke out between the virulently anti-Imperial 'Blacks' and the more conciliatory 'Whites'. After various toings and froings, the Blacks booted the Whites out for good. Among those sent into exile was Dante Alighieri.

Eventually, the Guelph/Ghibelline conflict ran out of steam. It says much for the energy, innovation, graft and skill of the Tuscans (or for the relative harmlessness of much medieval warfare in Italy) that throughout this stormy period, the region was booming economically.

By the beginning of the 14th century Florence was one of the five biggest cities in Europe, with a population of almost 100,000. It went through a rocky patch in the middle of the century, when England's King Edward III defaulted on his debts (1342), bankrupting several Florentine lenders. Six years later a plague epidemic carried off an estimated half of the city's population. But Florence soon bounced back: its currency – the florin, first minted in 1252 – remained one of Europe's strongest; and with fewer illness-prone poor to employ and feed, Florence may even have benefited economically from the Black Death.

The city's good fortune was due in no small part to its woollen cloth industry. Taxes to finance the costly conflict known as the War of the Eight Saints against Pope Gregory XI in 1375-8 hit the *ciompi* (wool carders) hardest, and they revolted, gaining representation in city government. By the mid 1380s, however, the three guilds formed in the wake of the uprising began to lose ground to the *popolo grasso*, a small group

of the wealthiest merchant families, who had united with the Guelphs to form an oligarchy in 1382. The *popolo grasso* held sway in the *signoria* for 40 years, during which time intellectuals and artists were becoming increasingly involved in political life.

Not all of Florence's business community backed the *popolo grasso*. Banker Cosimo de' Medici's stance against the extremes of the *signoria* gained him the support both of other dissenting merchants and the *popolo minuto* of the less influential guilds. Cosimo's mounting popularity alarmed the *signoria*, and the dominant Albizzi family had him exiled on trumped-up charges in 1433. A year later he returned to Florence by popular consent and, with handy military backing from his allies in Milan, was immediately made first citizen, becoming 'king in all but name'. For most of the next 300 years, the Medici dynasty remained more or less firmly in Florence's driving seat (*see p18* **Take your Medici**).

A FAMILY BUSINESS

Cosimo's habit of giving large sums to charity and endowing religious institutions with artworks helped make Florence a centre of artistic production, while by persuading representatives of the Eastern and Western churches to try to mend their schism at a conference in Florence in 1439, he hosted Greek scholars who could sate his hunger for classical literature.

This artistic and intellectual fervour gathered steam through the long 'reign' of his grandson Lorenzo il Magnifico, which saw Florence become, for a while, the intellectual and artistic centre of the Renaissance that was about to transform Christendom. Under his de facto leadership, Florence enjoyed a long period of relative peace, aided to some extent by Lorenzo's diplomatic skills in minimising squabbles between Italian states.

This isn't to say that all went smoothly: Lorenzo's relations with Pope Sixtus IV were famously bitter, resulting in excommunication and war; the pope also backed the Pazzi Conspiracy, an assault financed by a rival banking clan, the Pazzi, in which Lorenzo was injured and his brother Giuliano killed during Easter Sunday mass in 1478. Moreover, Lorenzo was more scholar-prince than all-round leader: his lack of economic prowess almost bankrupt the family business and come close to doing the same to his city-state. Though his personal popularity endured until his death in 1492, it didn't spill over on to his son Piero di Lorenzo, who in 1494 handed Florence to the French king Charles VIII as he passed through on the way to conquer Naples, then fled.

In a violent backlash against the splendour of Lorenzo's times, Florence turned for inspiration and guidance to a fire-and-brimstone-preaching monk who railed against paintings that made the Blessed Virgin Mary 'look like a harlot' and against Humanist thought, which he said would prompt the wrath of the one true and very vengeful God. Girolamo Savonarola (1452-98) perfectly captured the end-of-century spirit, winning the fanatical devotion not only of the poor and uneducated but of the leading minds of Lorenzo's magnificent court. Artists and art patrons willingly threw their works and finery on to the monk's Bonfire of the Vanities in Piazza della Signoria in 1497.

For Savonarola, Charles VIII represented the 'sword of the Lord': the city's capitulation was a just punishment. Savonarola set up a semi-democratic government, firmly allied to him, then allowed his extremist tendencies to get the better of him, alienating the Borgia pope Alexander VI and getting himself excommunicated. Had Florence been in a better economic state, the pope's gesture may have had little resonance; as it was, the region was devastated by pestilence and starvation. Resentment turned on Savonarola, who was summarily tried and burned at the stake in Piazza della Signoria in May 1498.

The republic created after his death was surprisingly democratic but increasingly ineffective, making stronger leadership look enticing to disaffected Florentines. In 1502 Piero Soderini, from an old noble family, was elected gonfalonier (banner bearer)-for-life, along the model of the Venetian doge. His pro-French policies brought him into conflict with the pro-Spanish pope Julius II, who had Cardinal Giovanni de' Medici whispering policy suggestions in his ear. In 1512 Soderini went into exile. Giuliano de' Medici, Duke of Nemours, was installed as Florence's most prominent citizen, succeeded by his nephew Lorenzo, Duke of Urbino. Their clout was reinforced in 1513 when Giovanni became Pope Leo X.

The Medici clan got a second crack at the papacy in 1524, when Giulio, Lorenzo's illegitimate nephew, became Clement VII. Renowned for his vacillating nature, Clement withdrew his support from Europe's most powerful ruler, the Habsburg emperor Charles V, then dithered for months without reinforcing Rome's fortifications; in 1527 Charles dispatched some troops to show the Medici pope who was who, Rome was sacked and Clement was forced to slink back to Charles's side, crowning him Holy Roman Emperor in 1529. Meanwhile, back in Florence, the local populace had exploited the Medici ignominy in Rome to reinstall the republic. It was short-lived: Clement had agreed to crown Charles in exchange for a promise of help to get Florence back into Medici hands. The city fell in 1530.

When Clement installed Alessandro, his son, in power in Florence in 1530 and Charles V made him hereditary Duke of Florence, the city entered one of its most desperate periods. Buoyed by support from Charles, whose daughter he had married, the authoritarian Alessandro trampled on Florentines' traditional rights and privileges while indulging in some shocking sexual antics.

His successor Cosimo I had different, though no less unpleasant, defects; nor was he much cop at reversing Tuscany's gentle slide into the economic doldrums. Still, this dark horse – whom the pope made the first Grand Duke of Tuscany in 1569 – at least gave the city a patina of action, extending the writ of the *granducato* to all of Tuscany except Lucca, and adorning the city with vast new *palazzi*, including the Uffizi and the Palazzo Pitti.

DECLINE AND FALL

Cosimo's descendants continued to rule for 150 years: they were fittingly poor rulers for what was a very minor statelet in the chessboard of Europe. The *granducato*'s farming methods were backward; the European fulcrum of its core industry, wool-making, like that of its main service industry, banking, had shifted definitively to northern Europe, leaving it to descend inexorably into depression. Its glory – and a very dusty glory it was – hung on its walls and adorned its palaces, with only the occasional spark of intellectual fervour (such as Cosimo II's spirited defence of Galileo Galilei when the astronomer was accused of heresy) to recall what the city had once represented. One 17th-century visitor described Florence as 'much sunk from what it was… one cannot but wonder to find a country that has been a scene of so much action now so forsaken and so poor'.

The male Medici line came to a squalid end in the shape of Gian Gastone, who died in 1737. His pious sister Anna Maria couldn't wait to offload the *granducato*, handing it over to the house of Lorraine, cousins of the Austrian Habsburgs. Grand Duke Francis I and his successors spruced up the city, knocked its administration into shape, introduced new farming methods and generally shook the place out of its torpor.

Napoleon's triumphant romp down the peninsula at the end of the 18th century brought him into possession of Tuscany in 1799, to the joy of liberals and the horror of local peasantry, who drove the French out in the Viva Maria uprising, during which they also wreaked their revenge on unlucky Jews and anyone suspected of Jacobin leanings.

The **Ponte Santa Trinità** takes a pounding in August 1944. *See p22.*

But it wasn't long before the French returned, installing Louis de Bourbon of Parma as head of the Kingdom of Etruria in 1801. Napoleon's sister, Elisa Baciocchi, was made Princess of Piombino and Lucca in 1805, and Grand Duchess of Tuscany from 1809 to 1814 – a time that saw much constitutional reform and much pilfering from Florence's art collections. Many of the works spirited off to Paris were returned to Tuscany after the restoration of the Lorraine dynasty in the shape of Ferdinand III in 1816.

ONE NATION UNDER THE ALPS
By the 1820s and 1830s, under the laid-back if not overly bright Grand Duke Leopold II, Tuscany enjoyed a climate of tolerance that attracted intellectuals, dissidents, artists and writers from all over Italy and Europe. They would meet in the Gabinetto Scientifico-Letterario in the Palazzo Buondelmonti in Piazza Santa Trinità, frequently welcoming prominent foreigners such as Heine and Byron.

For a time Leopold and his ministers kept the influence of the Grand Duke's uncle, Emperor Francis II of Austria, at arm's length while playing down the growing populist cry for Italian unification. But by the 1840s it was clear that the nationalist movement posed a serious threat to the status quo. Even relaxed Florence

was swept up in nationalist enthusiasm, causing Leopold to clamp down on reformers and impose some censorship. And in 1848, a tumultuous year of revolutions, insurrections in Livorno and Pisa forced Leopold to grant concessions to the reformers, including a Tuscan constitution.

When news reached Florence that the Milanese had driven the Austrians out of their city, and that Carlo Alberto, King of Sardinia-Piedmont, was determined to push them out of Italy altogether, thousands of Tuscans joined the cause. In 1849 the pendulum seemed to be swinging back in favour of the better-trained Austrians. But radicals in Florence dug in and bullied the Grand Duke into appointing the activist reformer Giuseppe Montanelli, a professor of law at Pisa University, to head a new government. Montanelli went to Rome to attend a constituent assembly, but the alarmed Pope Pius IX threatened to excommunicate anyone taking part in such a gathering.

Leopold panicked, and fled in disguise to Naples. A provisional government was set up but, in the absence of armed support, collapsed. The Florentines invited Leopold back; he returned in July 1849 but brought Austrian troops to keep order. Grim times followed for

Take your Medici

The name Medici (pronounced with the stress on the 'e') is all but synonymous with Florence and Tuscany. It suggests that the family's origins probably lie in the medical profession, though their later wealth was built on banking.

Giovanni di Bicci (1360-1429)

The fortune Giovanni di Bicci quietly built up through his banking business – boosted immensely by the fact that it handled the papal account – provided the basis for the Medici's later clout.

Cosimo 'Il Vecchio' (1389-1464)

Cosimo, Giovanni di Bicci's son, ran Florence informally from 1434, presiding over one of its most prosperous and prestigious eras. An even more astute banker than his father, he spent lavishly on charities and public building projects, introducing a progressive income tax system and balancing the interests of the volatile Florentine classes relatively successfully. In addition to all these achievements, Cosimo was also an intellectual: he encouraged new Humanist learning and developments in art, built up a wonderful public library (the first in Europe) and financed scholars and artists. The name *Il Vecchio* ('The Elder') was a mark of respect.

Piero 'Il Gottoso' (1416-69)

All the Medici suffered from gout, but poor Piero the Gouty's joints gave him such gyp that he had to be carried around for half his life. During his short spell at the helm he proved a surprisingly able ruler: he crushed an anti-Medici conspiracy, maintained the success of the Medici bank and patronised the city's best artists and architects.

Lorenzo 'Il Magnifico' (1449-92)

Cosimo's grandson Lorenzo was the big Medici, famous in his own time and legendary

Cosimo 'Il Vecchio'.

in later centuries. His rule marked the peak of the Florentine Renaissance, with artists such as Botticelli and the young Michelangelo producing superlative works. Lorenzo was a gifted poet, and gathered round him a supremely talented group of scholars and artists. The climate of intellectual freedom he fostered was a major factor in some of the Renaissance's greatest achievements. As a businessman, however, he wasn't a patch on his predecessors and the Medici bank suffered a severe decline. Lorenzo

a city just recovering from one of its worst ever floods. On his return, Leopold seemed content to be an Austrian puppet and clamped down on the press and dissent; his popularity vanished.

In April 1859 Piedmont's Count Camillo Cavour persuaded Napoleon III's France to join him in expelling the Austrians. The French and Piedmontese swept the Austrian armies before them, while in Florence nationalist demos forced the government to resign. On 27 April Leopold

left Florence and his family for the last time. The following year the Tuscan people voted for unification with the Kingdom of Piedmont.

A NEW ROME

Five years later, with Rome holding out against the forces of unification, Florence was declared capital of Italy, much to the annoyance of the Piedmontese capital of Turin – 200 people died in riots there when the shift was announced. The Florentines greeted their new king with

Giovanni; Pope Leo X.

skulking around Italy, trying to persuade unenthusiastic states to help him regain power in a Florence that had no wish to see his mug again.

Giovanni; Pope Leo X (1475-1521)

Lorenzo Il Magnifico's second son wasn't such a loser as his brothers, perhaps because the night before his birth his mother dreamed she would have not a baby but a huge lion. Lorenzo decided early on that Giovanni was destined for a glittering ecclesiastical career, and serious papal ear-bending ensured that he became a monk at eight and a cardinal aged 16. He elbowed his way into the papacy in 1513. Pope Leo (spot the lion reference) was a likeable, open character, and though lazy, he was a generous host and politically conciliatory. But his exploitation of the sale of indulgences to ease his debts added fuel to the fires of critics of papal corruption.

Giuliano, Duke of Nemours (1478-1516)

The third son of Lorenzo Il Magnifico and an improvement on his brother Piero only in the sense that he was more nonentity than swine, Giuliano was ruler of Florence in name only, being little more than a puppet of his brother, Cardinal Giovanni, who went on to become Pope Leo X.

Giulio; Pope Clement VII (1478-1534)

Lorenzo Il Magnifico's illegitimate nephew, Giulio had honours heaped on him by his cousin, Pope Leo. Though this didn't endear him to other cardinals (his disagreeable personality didn't help much either), he swung the papacy in 1524. Pope Clement was notorious for his indecision, irresolution and disloyalty. He abandoned his alliance with Charles V only to regret it when the emperor's troops sacked Rome in 1527. ▶

maintained a façade of being no more than *primus inter pares* ('first among equals'), but he could be ruthless with his enemies.

Piero di Lorenzo (1471-1503)

Piero couldn't live up to his father Lorenzo: ruthless, charmless and tactless, he had a violent temper, no sense of loyalty and a haughty wife. His father described him as foolish, and he did nothing to help his cause when he surrendered the city to the French in 1494. He spent the rest of his days

enthusiasm when he arrived in February 1865 to take up residence in the Palazzo Pitti, but the influx of northerners was met with mixed feelings: business boomed, but the Florentines didn't take to Piedmontese flashiness.

Huge changes were wrought to the city. Ring roads encircled the old centre, avenues, squares (such as Piazza della Repubblica) and suburbs were built and parks were laid out. Intellectuals and socialites crowded the salons and cafés.

When war with Prussia forced the French (who had swapped sides) to withdraw their troops from Italy in 1870, Rome finally fell to Vittorio Emanuele's troops and Italy was united for the first time since the fall of the Roman Empire. Florence's brief reign as capital ended.

WAR AND HARDSHIP

Florence began the 20th century much as it ended it – as a thriving tourist centre. In the early 1900s it drew an exclusive coterie of

► Take your Medici (continued)

Lorenzo, Duke of Urbino (1492-1519)

Son of Piero di Lorenzo, Lorenzo was puny, arrogant, high-handed and corrupt. No one was anything but relieved when he succumbed to tuberculosis, aggravated by syphilis. His only significant legacy was his daughter, Catherine, who, as wife and then widow of Henri II, wielded considerable power in France.

Alessandro (1511-37)

Thought to be Clement's illegitimate son, Alessandro proved to be a bastard by nature as well as by name, abandoning all pretence of respecting the Florentines' treasured institutions and freedoms. Increasingly authoritarian, he tortured and executed his opponents, while managing to outrage the good Florentine burghers by his appalling rudeness and sexual antics. He had a penchant for dressing in women's clothes and riding about town with his bosom buddy and distant cousin, the equally alarming Lorenzaccio. A deputation of senior figures complained to Charles V, to no avail. It was left to Lorenzaccio to stab Alessandro to death.

Cosimo I (1519-74)

With no heir in the direct Medici line, the Florentines chose this obscure 18-year-old, the grandson of Lorenzo II Magnifico's daughter Lucrezia, thinking they could manipulate him. But they could not have been more wrong: cold, secretive and cunning, Cosimo set about ruling with merciless efficiency. His general unpleasantness, however, did not stop him from restoring stability in Florence and boosting the city's international image. He was granted the title Grand Duke of Tuscany by Pope Paul V in 1569.

Alessandro.

Francesco I (1541-87)

Short, skinny, graceless and sulky, Francesco had little in common with his father Cosimo. He retreated into his own little world at any opportunity, to play with his pet reindeer, dabble in alchemy and invent a new process for porcelain production.

Ferdinando I (1549-1609)

Ferdinando was an improvement on his brother Francesco. He reduced corruption, improved trade and farming, encouraged

writers, artists, aesthetes and the upper-middle classes. An English-speaking industry sprang up to cater for the needs of these wealthy foreigners.

The city was neither occupied nor attacked in World War I, though it suffered. Post-war hardship inspired a fierce middle-class rage for order that found expression in the black shirt of Fascism. Groups of *squadristi* were already forming in 1919, organising parades and demonstrations in the streets of Florence.

When Mussolini was elected in 1923, there began in Florence a campaign to expunge the city of foreign elements and influences. Hotels and shops with English names were put under pressure to sever their Anglo-Saxon affiliations. The Florence that had been described as a *ville toute anglaise* by the French social-historian Goncourt brothers was under threat.

Italy entered the war at Germany's side on 10 June 1940, and the Florentines were confident

Gian Gastone.

Ferdinando II (1610-70)
Porky, laid-back, moustachioed Ferdinando did little to pull Florence from the backwater into which it had sunk. He loved to hunt, eye up boys and collect bric-a-brac.

Cosimo III (1642-1723)
Though trade was drying up and plague and famine stalked the land, Cosimo – a joyless, gluttonous, anti-Semitic loner who hung out with monks (his sulky wife Marguerite-Louise must take some blame for this) – did nothing to improve Tuscany's lot during his 53 years at the helm. Instead, intellectual freedom took a nosedive, taxes soared and public executions were a more or less daily occurrence.

Gian Gastone (1671-1737)
Cosimo's disaster of a son was forcibly married to Anna Maria Francesca of Saxe-Lauenberg, who dragged him off to her gloomy castle near Prague, where he drowned his sorrows in taverns before escaping back to Florence in 1708. He was shocked to find himself Grand Duke in 1723. In the coherent early years of his rule he tried to relieve the tax burden and reinstate citizens' rights but quickly lapsed into chronic apathy and dissolution. Eventually he wouldn't even get out of bed and was reduced to having boys entertain him by cavorting about.

Anna Maria (died 1743)
Every visitor to Florence since the mid 18th century has reason to be grateful to the straight-laced, pious Anna Maria, who was Gian Gastone's sister and the very last surviving Medici. In her will she bequeathed all Medici property and treasures to the Grand Duchy in perpetuity, on the sole condition that they never leave Florence.

learning, and developed both the navy and the port of Livorno. By staging a variety of lavish popular entertainments and giving dowries to poor girls, he became the most loved Medici since Lorenzo Il Magnifico, who – coincidentally – had been born exactly one century before Ferdinando.

Cosimo II (1590-1621)
The son of Ferdinando I, Cosimo protected Galileo from a hostile Catholic Church – the only worthwhile thing he would ever do.

that the Allies would never attack their city from the air: Florence was a museum, a testament to artistic evolution, and its monuments were surely its best protection. Nevertheless, the Fascist regime, perhaps for propaganda reasons, began protecting the city's art. Photos of the period show statuary disappearing inside comically inefficient wooden sheds, while the Baptistery doors were bricked up and many main treasures

from the Uffizi and the Palazzo Pitti were taken to the Castello di Montegufoni – owned by the British Sitwell family – in the Tuscan countryside for safekeeping.

The Germans occupied Florence on 11 September 1943, just weeks after Mussolini's arrest and the armistice was signed. Only when it became necessary to hinder the Nazis' communication lines to Rome were aesthetic scruples set aside. In September 1943 a formation of American bombers swooped in to destroy Florence's Campo di Marte station: the operation was bungled, leaving 218 civilians dead, while the station remained in perfect working order. Further air raids were banned by orders from the highest levels.

'Within hours of the Germans' departure, work started to put the bridges back into place. The Ponte Santa Trinità was rebuilt, stone by stone, in exactly the same location.'

At the beginning of the war Florence had a Jewish population of more than 2,000. The chief rabbi saved the lives of many Jews in the city by advising them to hide in convents or little villages under false names. Three raids were carried out by Nazis and Fascists on the night of 27 November 1943. The largest of them was on the Franciscan Sisters of Mary in Piazza del Carmine, where dozens of Jews were concealed. The second train to leave Italy bound for the gas chambers set out from Florence, carrying at least 400 Jews from Florence, Siena and Bologna; not one of them is known to have returned.

By 1944 allied commanding officers had extracted permission from their leaders to attack Florence using only the most experienced squadrons, in ideal weather conditions. On 11 March the Americans began unleashing their bombers on the city, causing casualties but leaving the *centro storico* and its art intact. On 1 August 1944 fighting broke out in various parts of the city, but poorly armed Florentine patriots couldn't prevent the Germans from destroying all the Arno bridges except the Ponte Vecchio. Along with the bridges, the old quarter around the Ponte Vecchio was razed to the ground.

The Val d'Orcia and Monte Amiata areas in southern Tuscany were key theatres for partisans, who held out with considerable loss of life until British and US infantry reinforced their lines on the Arno on 1 September 1944. The German army abandoned Fiesole a week later. When the Allies eventually reached Florence, they discovered a functioning government formed by the partisan Comitati di Liberazione Nazionale (CLN). Within hours of the Germans' departure, work started to put the bridges back into place. The Ponte Santa Trinità was rebuilt, stone by stone, in exactly the same location.

1966 AND ALL THAT

Two decades later the Florentine skill at restoration was required again, this time for a calamity of an altogether different nature: in the early hours of the morning of 4 November 1966 citizens awoke to find their homes flooded by the Arno, which had broken its banks, and soon all the main *piazze* were under water. An estimated 15,000 cars were destroyed, 6,000 shops put out of business and almost 14,000 families left homeless. Many artworks, books and archives were damaged, treasures in the refectory of Santa Croce were blackened by mud, and in the church's nave Donatello's *Cavalcanti Annunciation* was soaked with oil up to the Virgin's knees. As word of the disaster spread around the world, public and private funds were pumped into repairs and restoration.

The city's cultural heritage took another direct hit in May 1993, when a bomb planted by the Mafia exploded in the city centre, killing five people. It caused structural damage to the Uffizi, destroying the Georgofile library and damaging the Vasari Corridor. Not that you'd know it now: in a restoration job carried out in record time, one of the world's most-visited art repositories was returned to its pristine state and tourists began queuing outside again, confirming the modern city's vocation for living off its past.

Florence solemnly commemorated the tenth anniversary of the Uffizi bomb in 2003 and seems to have moved on. The past few years, however, have been blighted by a considerable drop in tourist revenue. For a city that relies heavily on the income generated by its millions of visitors every year, a combination of 9/11, SARS and the general economic recession has made its mark and local hoteliers, restaurateurs and shopkeepers have had much to be glum about. Florentines and tourists alike continue to complain – with reason – about the steep rise in prices resulting from the change to the euro.

In spite of this, the exciting urban planning and architectural projects that were under way at the time of publishing the last edition of this guide are forging ahead. The new traffic system around Porta Il Prato and the Fortezza da Basso has alleviated the terrible jams that were part and parcel of any journey to the north-west of the city (although there is still no evidence of the promised park), and work is ongoing on a tram system set to revolutionise commuter travel, with a bridge in the process of being constructed over the Arno at the Parco delle Cascine. There are bound to be delays along the way, but these and other building projects are definitely well on the path to fruition (*see also pp36-37*).

Key events

7th-6th centuries BC Height of Etruscan civilisation.
3rd century BC Etruria under Roman control.
59 BC Foundation of Florentia by Julius Caesar.
56 BC Caesar, Crassus and Pompey form first triumvirate at Lucca.
AD 540s Tuscany contested in Goth vs Byzantine campaigns.
552 Florence falls to the Goths under Totila.
c800 New walls erected around Florence.
10th-12th centuries Pisa becomes wealthy port; Lucca, seat of margraves of Tuscany, is region's most important city.
1076 Matilde becomes Countess of Tuscany.
1115 Matilde bequeaths all her lands to the pope except Florence, Lucca and Siena, which become independent *comuni*.
1125 Florence captures Fiesole.
1173-5 More new walls for Florence.
1215 Murder of Buondelmonte ignites Guelph/Ghibelline conflict.
1252 First gold florin minted.
1289 Florence defeats Arezzo at Campaldino.
1293 Nobility excluded from government, *signoria* created.
1296 Foundations laid for new Duomo.
1329 Florence takes over Pistoia.
1342 Florence's biggest banks collapse when English king Edward III defaults on debts.
1348 Black Death ravages Tuscany.
1351 Florence buys Prato from Naples.
1375-8 War of the Eight Saints frees Florence from papal influence. Guelphs join with *popolo grasso* to exclude guilds from power.
1406 Florence captures Pisa.
1411 Florence gains Cortona.
1421 Florence buys Livorno from Genova.
1428 War between Florence and Lucca.
1432 Florence beats Siena at San Romano, a battle immortalised by artist Paolo Uccello.
1433 Cosimo de' Medici exiled by Albizzi clan during unpopular Lucchese war.
1434 Return of Cosimo from exile; overthrow and exile of the Albizzi.
1436 Brunelleschi finishes the Duomo dome.
1437 Florence defeats Milan at Barga.
1452 Naples and Venice declare war on Milan and Florence.
1454 Threat of the Turks brings pope, Venice, Florence and Milan together in Holy League.
1466 Piero quashes conspiracy to oust Medici.
1478 Piero's son Lorenzo escapes murder in Pazzi conspiracy. Papacy and Naples declare war on Florence.

1479 Lorenzo goes alone to Naples to negotiate peace treaty with King Ferrante.
1494 Wars of Italy begin – France's Charles VIII invades Italy.
1512 Papal and Spanish armies sack Prato and force return of Medici to Florence.
1524 Giulio de' Medici becomes Pope Clement VII; continues to run Florence from Rome.
1527 Horrific sacking of Rome by Habsburg emperor Charles V's army. Medici expelled; new republic declared.
1529 Charles V, now allied with Clement VII, besieges and takes Florence.
1530 Alessandro de' Medici installed as head of government, then Duke, by Charles V.
1537 Alessandro murdered. Cosimo defeats Florentine rebels at Montemurlo.
1555 With imperial help, Cosimo crushes Siena after a devastating war.
16th-17th centuries Steady decline of Tuscan agriculture and industry overseen by succession of Medici Grand Dukes.
1723 Gian Gastone now the last Medici ruler.
1735 Grand Duchy of Tuscany given to Francis, Duke of Lorraine. Enlightened regime begins.
1737 Death of Gian Gastone's sister, Anna Maria, who leaves all Medici art and treasures to Florence in perpetuity.
1799 French troops enter Florence. Revival of interest in Tuscany, which becomes major stop on the 'Grand Tour'.
1801-7 Grand Duchy absorbed into Kingdom of Etruria.
1809 Napoleon installs his sister Elisa Baciocchi as Grand Duchess of Tuscany.
1816 Grand Duke Ferdinando III returns to Tuscany on defeat of Napoleon.
1824 Genial Leopold II succeeds father.
1859 Leopold allows himself to be overthrown in the *Risorgimento*.
1865-70 Florence becomes first capital of united Italy.
1943 Germans enter Florence, establish Gothic Line on the Arno.
1944 Germans blow up all Pisa's bridges and all but the Ponte Vecchio in Florence. Allies liberate Florence.
1966 The Arno floods, causing huge damage.
1993 Bomb destroys Georgofile library and damages Vasari Corridor.
2002 The lira is withdrawn, euro coins and notes come into circulation.
2005 Work begins on new tramline, and initial designs for new Uffizi exit are rejected.

Florence Today

Novelist Magdalen Nabb takes the pulse of a city that, for all its history, has a curious present and an exciting future.

'The world is made up of five elements: earth, air, fire, water and the Florentines.'
Pope Alexander VI (1492-1503)

No change there, then. Loud and polemical, ironic and often bloody-minded, the Florentine doesn't fit any foreigner's idea of what Italians are like. When an English TV producer came looking for someone about to be evicted from his home so that the event could be filmed for a documentary, the researcher provided the man, along with all the background to his story. 'Yes,' said the producer, 'but will he wave his arms about and cry on camera?' Well, no. He might stab at you with a stiffened hand and yell political slogans in your face, but he won't cry.

Once, a very old Florentine man committed suicide by jumping off the Duomo's beautiful bell tower. How long and how difficult must the climb have been, how heartbreaking that last view of red roofs and marble façades. Later, when neighbours broke into his flat, they found it empty of food and money. They could hear his small dog whining. But they had never heard the old man whine. He had been too proud to tell them that he was too poor to live. The choice of suicides in this city always seems to be the bell tower or the Arno, a choice symptomatic of the Florentine's relationship with his city.

His relationship with God and religion is very particular. Florentines have been called priest-haters, and it is evident – see above – that the Spanish Pope Alexander VI had problems with them. That independent spirit doesn't have much time for middlemen, let alone foreign ones. They don't go in for cults built around favourite saints, either, for the same reason. There's a firework display for their patron, St John the Baptist, on 24 June – and that's it. If a Florentine has something to say to God, he'll say it himself. The morning after the terrible flood of 1966, which wrecked the entire city, a meat roaster staggered out of his shop through tons of mud and water, bearing in his arms a ruined loin of beef as though it were a dead child. He looked up at the sky and roared, 'Right! This time you've gone too far!'

BACK TO THE FUTURE

If you see, in June, a procession of men, halberdiers and cavalry, judges and guildsmen in medieval costume, followed by football teams, also in medieval costume, and a cow with gilded horns, don't imagine it's a bit of tired folklore. The right to wear these costumes is handed down through families and the rivalry between the teams from the four quarters of the city is so serious as to often end in violence. The cloaked noblemen on horseback are real, too, their horses caparisoned in green velvet and tranquilised because of crowds and cannon fire. They ride with one hand on the reins, loose and casual, the other on their hip, looking proud and arrogant.

Proud and arrogant are the words Italians often use to define the Florentine character. Foreign visitors to the city have also complained, saying that Florentines have been resting on their laurels for centuries, not feeling the need to produce anything after Leonardo and Michelangelo.

'You have to watch the news to find out if you can use your car the next morning.'

But there are signs that the Florentines are thinking of getting up from their laurels. In the past few years plans for a clutch of new, high-profile projects have been set in motion, among them the expansion of the Museo dell'Opera del Duomo and the Uffizi (the latter with a spanking new exit), Norman Foster's underground train terminal and the satellite town being built near Peretola Airport. Suddenly, after decades of no new building in Florence, these things have not only made it to the drawing board, but are very likely to happen. As for completion dates, though, don't hold your breath.

BETTER DEATH THAN PISA

As to the foreign architect: a Sicilian would be considered equally foreign. The Florentines are considered proud and arrogant, but their worst sin, in the eyes of other Italians, is that they are *chiusi* (closed to others). The curator of one of the city's most important museums, a Roman, once complained that in his 30 years there no Florentine colleague had ever invited him home. Non-Florentines are foreigners, with the exception of the English. There is a sound historical basis for this attitude. When Florence was the richest city state in the world she fought bitterly with the other city states in the peninsula, especially her nearest neighbours, particularly Pisa. You can still hear the famous saying, 'Better a death in the house than a Pisan at the door'. But this was originally a Pisan saying, 'Better a death in the house than a Florentine.' The victors always seem to get the best lines.

The English, on the other hand, from their considerable base in 19th-century Florence, helped Tuscany get rid of its Austrian rulers and form part of a unified Italian state, whose first capital was Florence. They even published a revolutionary newspaper that escaped the censorship of the Austrian police because it was printed in English.

FORTRESS FLORENCE

So what kind of city did these Florentines build and what can you expect to find here now? First comes a chicken and egg problem: did living in a fortress produce a defensive mentality? Or did the Florentines build a city that reflected their character? A place of austere, masculine architecture, with great palaces that turn their backs to the street and hide their beautiful façades, gardens and fountains from outsiders, the whole surrounded by a defensive wall?

Both are probably true. A defensive, closed and military mentality produced the architecture, it's true. But now, years after that outlook has ceased to be relevant, the architecture of the city perpetuates, nourishes and provokes it. There is still a city-state feeling about the place, a separateness that can be felt in local government, for example. People regularly vote for one party in municipal elections and another in national elections, and this seems perfectly logical – although at this point, anti-Berlusconi feelings are so strong that the usual disjunction may not operate at the next elections. At local level, heated meetings take place and the same problems come up each time, with the traffic first and foremost. It's easy to complain, but Florence is a Renaissance city with a modern traffic load, and that is an impossible circle to square. If you want to preserve the city you've got to reduce traffic, and reduce it in a drastic and permanent fashion. Superficial interventions each time pollution reaches danger levels – alternating number plates, catalytic and non-catalytic exhausts and so on – don't fix the problem and cause inconvenience and irritation. But any of the ad hoc solutions currently in use might help a bit if applied enduringly. Instead of which, you have to watch the local TV news each evening to find out whether you can use your car the next morning.

One solution often touted is more public transport. But where, in a city whose business is history and whose bones are archaeology, do you put it? In this case, the administration is being helpful. The building of a tramline from the central station out to Scandicci in the west will, it is hoped, encourage commuters to leave their cars at home, as did the little train out to Borgo San Lorenzo. Unlike a railway, the tramline has to be built on roads currently clogged with heavy traffic. To help drivers, alternative routes around the construction areas are not only put out on the local TV news but are sent, in the form of a small map, to every home. However, map or no map, the fact remains that there is going to be a considerable upheaval in the city's traffic system for several years to come.

CURRENT CONCERNS

Crime is not a big election issue. Florence is one of the safest cities in the world. There's some bag-snatching, but a few sensible precautions if you're going to be gazing up open-mouthed at buildings and statuary will deal with that. Violent crime is mainly confined to turf wars among professional criminals, with drug and prostitution rings most likely to produce casualties. These are often run by Albanians, which gives rise to some racism among those who conveniently forget those quiet, invisible Albanians and Romanians doing all the heavy, dirty work that Florentines don't want to do.

One big feature in pre-election debates is the question of the artisans. Bad legislation concerning apprenticeships and the desire of young Florentines to work with computers/go to university/own a big car and wear a Rolex/make a lot of money without working too hard and, most importantly, not dirty their hands and flash clothes all contribute to a situation in which the skills handed down over centuries could die out with the current generation. Those apprentices learning skills like shoemaking, marble inlaying or furniture restoration are now very often foreign youngsters, willing to pay a craftsman for the privilege of being taught. Although it's undoubtedly important that these skills be handed on to somebody rather than lost, it's going to be inconvenient for the future prospects of the city if the only place to get a pair of Florentine handmade shoes is Japan.

Feelings on these matters run high among the citizens of Florence. Their relationship with the city is deep-rooted and pervasive. The politicians down in Rome come and go. The real problem facing Florence as a city, and the one facing you as a visitor, is the same: globalisation. Also known in Italy as Berlusconisation, this is a trend favouring faceless global products and chains over the local specialised culture, which then undergoes a Disneyfication process to provide entertainment for tourists. The Florentines are fighting back. Not for nothing was a world conference on globalisation held in the city in 2002. It might not matter that much when yet another hamburger joint or watery coffee bar opens in London. In Florence, where families run small *trattorie* for generations, the effect is deadly. Everybody knows this, but the buildings that house the local restaurants, the marble cutters, the shoemakers and frame makers are being bought up by massively rich chains, and their rent-paying occupants pushed out. So now you can get a greasy hamburger and watery coffee just like the ones in your local shopping mall, and shop at the same clothing stores as your neighbouring high street, with Florence as a cute tourist backdrop.

THE OTHER SIDE

But there are still parts of the city that are relatively free of tourists, and if you want your visit to Florence to feature something different from what you know back home, it can. Florentines themselves never tire of looking down on their ochre and terracotta city, punctuated by green and white marble, and divided by a smooth, olive-green river. Climb up to see it from Bellosguardo, where you'll hear only birds singing. Then stay on the left bank, the Oltrarno, when you come down. Ramble around the narrow, shady streets and peep into the sawing and hammering darkness of tiny workshops. When you leave, make a wish that all this will still be here next time you come. In the interests of which, if you have money to spend, spend it among these people. They are at risk – they just won't tell you.

● *Magdalen Nabb's latest novel set in Florence is* The Innocent, *published by Heineman.*

Legend of the True Cross,
Piero della Francesca. *See p28.*

Art

The masters and their masterpieces.

The number of artworks to come out of Florence is remarkable. The Renaissance was born thanks to the talents of local artists such as Donatello, Botticelli, Leonardo and Michelangelo. The noble families of Florence such as the Medicis entrusted these artists with adorning their city and palaces with art. Lorenzo il Magnifico, in particular, was a keen patron of the arts and fostered the cultural boom of the 15th century, when Florence was the hub of intellectual and artistic activity, and artists, thinkers and poets intermingled. Afterwards masters such as Giorgio Vasari kept Florence at the forefront of the art scene, before the later lull when Rome took centre stage.

MEDIEVAL MASTERS

But to find art, you need to follow the money. And in the case of Florence the trail takes you back to the medieval cloth and banking businesses that were the foundations of the city's wealth. In the 1320s the Bardi, a powerful banking family, commissioned **Giotto** (1267-1337) to decorate their chapel in the church of Santa Croce (*see p97*). Here, Giotto demonstrates the stylistic shift between medieval and early Renaissance painting. Although obscured by tombs and damaged by the 1966 flood, the figures in the *Funeral of Saint Francis* are set in a believable environment with an outpouring of human emotion. As seen in his design for the

Duomo's bell tower (*see p73*), Giotto's style is characterised by clarity and simplicity, rendering his works legible and accessible.

Also in the church of Santa Croce is a painted Crucifix by Giotto's predecessor, **Cimabue** (1240-1302). Looking at this work, tied to the previous Byzantine tradition, brings Giotto's naturalism into focus. Both artists may be further compared in the Uffizi (*see p82*), where Cimabue's *Maestà* (1285-6) hangs with Giotto's *Ognissanti Madonna* (1300-10).

Ignoring the new naturalism of Giotto, **Andrea Orcagna** (1308-68) fashioned his tabernacle in the church of Orsanmichele (1359; *see p80*) in the more popular Gothic style. This highly decorative structure protected the miracle-working image of the Virgin and is inlaid with marble, lapis lazuli, gold and glass.

THE 'REBIRTH'

The dawning of the Renaissance in Florence was marked by the rediscovery of classical texts and a new appreciation for the world of the ancients. Humanism was at the heart of this 'rebirth' of ideas, where the pagan past was placed in a Christian context and Greek and Roman art upheld as the new model.

The 1401 competition for the east doors of the Baptistery saw **Filippo Brunelleschi** (1377-1446) lose out to **Lorenzo Ghiberti** (1378-1455). In a huff, Brunelleschi left for

Botticelli's magnificent **The Birth of Venus**, in the Uffizi. *See p29.*

Rome to study the art of the ancients. But he had the last laugh: on his return to Florence, he built the majestic cupola for the Duomo (1420-36; *see p71*).

As the demand for art grew, so did the number of workshops, in which apprentices learned to paint and sculpt alongside the masters. For example, the workshop of **Luca della Robbia** (1400-82) generated his signature glazed terracotta reliefs, which grace prominent structures in Florence such as Orsanmichele (*see p79*), Brunelleschi's Spedale degli Innocenti (*see p94*) and the interior of the Duomo (*see p70*). Eventually the collaborative production of art by skilled craftsmen led to individual artistic personalities.

As a young apprentice in the workshop of Ghiberti, **Donatello** (1386-1466) worked on the Baptistery doors. Like Brunelleschi, Donatello studied in Rome, and his Orsanmichele statues of St Mark (1411) and St George (1416), now in the Bargello (*see p96*), demonstrate his ability to create naturalistic drapery over believable bodies in the classical vein. Commissioned by Cosimo I de' Medici, Donatello's *David* (1430), now in the Bargello (*see p96*), was the first free-standing life-size nude bronze since antiquity.

Andrea del Verrocchio (1435-88) eventually replaced Donatello as the leading sculptor in Florence, and his *Christ and Doubting Thomas* (1476-83) takes on a new dimension of dynamism as it steps out of its niche of the Orsanmichele (*see p79*). Verrocchio, like Donatello, worked for the Medici, creating the tomb of Piero and Giovanni in the Old Sacristy of San Lorenzo (1469-72; *see p91*), as well as the charming *Putto with Dolphin* fountain (1470) in the Palazzo Vecchio (*see p101*).

Early Renaissance painting took its cue from sculpture, attempting to create the same sense of naturalism on a two-dimensional scale. Brunelleschi's theory of linear perspective became a tool for the realistic representation of distance and depth. Perspective was first applied to painting by artists such as **Masaccio** (1401-28), particularly in his *Trinità* fresco in Santa Maria Novella (1427; *see p87*) and, with the help of **Masolino** (1400-47), the fresco cycle in the Cappella Brancacci (1425; *see p103*). Similarly, **Paolo Uccello** (1396-1475) experimented with foreshortening and a sense of perspective in works such as *The Battle of San Romano* (1435) in the Uffizi (*see p82*) and the fresco of John Hawkwood (1436) in the Duomo (*see p71*).

Piero della Francesca (1416-92) was active in Florence in the 1430s, both as a painter and author of treatises on perspective and mathematics. His *Legend of the True Cross* fresco cycle (c1453-65) in Arezzo (*see p260*) shows his adherence to mathematical order.

Dominican friar **Fra Angelico** (1400-55) used perspective when creating his frescoes in the monastery (now museum) of San Marco as an extension of reality. His *Annunciation* (1440-41; *see p93*) mirrors the architecture of the monks' cells, adding a new sense of immediacy. The stark style of Fra Angelico reflects the humility of his religious order and the function of the monastery as a place of meditation.

'Cellini's life-size *Perseus* is a chilling reminder of the duke's authority.'

Benozzo Gozzoli (1420-97) also places a Biblical event within the context of contemporary Florence. In his painting of the Cappella dei Magi (1459-60) in the Palazzo Medici Riccardi (*see p91*), Lorenzo de' Medici is painted as one of the participants in this lavish procession and the artist included his own self-portrait among the crowd. This new self-awareness of the artist became more and more common. For instance, **Domenico Ghirlandaio** (1449-94) looks out at us from his frescoes in the Cappella Sassetti in the church of Santa Trinità (1483-85; *see p84*), along with other recognisable Florentine personalities.

Filippo Lippi (1406-69), a Carmelite friar, had little interest in creating an illusion of the real world. In his *Madonna with Child and Angels* (1465) in the Uffizi (*see p82*), he includes a fantastic view of nature in the background of his lovely, pearl-adorned Madonna. Disregarding the laws of perspective and human anatomy, his paintings appear comparatively flat.

Filippo passed his linear style on to his pupil, **Sandro Botticelli** (1445-1510). The figures in both *Primavera*, or *Allegory of Spring* (c1482), and *The Birth of Venus* (1476-87), commissioned by the Medici and now in the Uffizi (*see p82*), are infused with grace and idealised beauty and seem to float just above the ground.

THE 'HIGH RENAISSANCE'

The artists of the 15th century developed the tools and methods that would characterise the artistic period of the following century. These artists would surpass their masters in their quest for ideal beauty, balanced proportions and structured compositions.

Leonardo da Vinci (1452-1519) emerged from the workshop of Verrocchio when he helped his master paint the *Baptism of Christ* (1469-80), now in the Uffizi (*see p82*). A true 'Renaissance man', Leonardo was not only a skilled painter but also a sculptor, architect, engineer and

scientist. His exploration of the natural world as a scientist also manifested itself in his art, which reflects a sensitive observation of nature. The carefully structured *Annunciation* (1472) and *Adoration of the Magi* (1481), both in the Uffizi (*see p80*), also show his experimentation with oil.

Another quintessential Florentine Renaissance artist was Michelangelo Buonarroti, better known as **Michelangelo** (1475-1564). He was catapulted to fame with his idealised male nude statue, *David* (1501-4), quickly lauded as the greatest work of sculpture ever created. Though a copy remains in Piazza della Signoria (*see p75*), the original is now in the Accademia (*see p92*), along with the *Slaves* (1527-8). These half-finished sculptures reveal Michelangelo's method for removing excess material to reveal the pre-existing spirit of the statue.

Where to see it

Unmissable paintings/frescoes

Botticelli: *Birth of Venus* and *Primavera*, Uffizi (*see left and p82*).

Della Francesca: *Legend of the True Cross* fresco cycle, Arezzo (*see p28 and p260*).

Fra Angelico: *Annunciation*, Museo di San Marco (*see left and p93*).

Giotto: frescoes depicting the life of Saint Francis, Cappella Bardi (*see p27 and p97*).

Leonardo (with Verrocchio): *Baptism of Christ*, Uffizi (*see left and p82*).

Masaccio and **Masolino**: series of frescoes, Cappella Brancacci (*see p28 and p103*).

Statues of stature

Cellini: *Perseus*, Loggia dei Lanzi (*see p30 and p77*).

Donatello: *Saint George*, Bargello (*see p28 and p96*).

Giambologna: *Rape of the Sabine Women*, Loggia dei Lanzi (*see p30 and p77*).

Michelangelo: *David*, Galleria dell'Accademia (*see above and p92*).

Verrocchio: *Putto with Dolphin*, Palazzo Vecchio (*see p28 and p101*).

Lesser-known delights

Del Sarto: *Last Supper*, Museo del Cenacolo di Andrea del Sarto (*see p30 and p105*).

Ghirlandaio: Cappella Sassetti, church of Santa Trinità (*see left and p84*).

Gozzoli: frescoes in the Cappella dei Magi, Palazzo Medici Riccardi (*see left and p91*).

Orcagna: tabernacle, Orsanmichele (*see p27 and p80*).

David (copy), Piazza della Signoria. *See p29.*

MANNERISM AND BEYOND

After the Renaissance reached its height in
about 1520, Mannerism, or the 'stylish style',
soon dominated court painting in Florence and
throughout Italy. In reaction to the Renaissance
style, Mannerist paintings included distorted
anatomy, artificial colours and crowded,
asymmetrical scenes as seen in the frescoes of
the Chiostro dello Scalzo (1515-17; *see p90*) by
artists such as **Andrea del Sarto** (1486-1530).
A contemporary of Michelangelo and Raphael,
del Sarto was an equally graceful painter and
skilled draughtsman. His *Madonna of the
Harpies* altarpiece (1517) in the Uffizi (*see p80*)
is a fine example of Mannerist painting, as is
his *Last Supper* (1526-7), in the refectory of the
monastery of San Salvi (*see p105*).

Giorgio Vasari (1511-74) also belonged
to the Mannerist circle of painters. In 1571 he
began the fresco decoration of the interior of the
Duomo's cupola, which was later completed by
the Roman artist Federico Zuccari. Vasari is
also the architect responsible for the Uffizi, but
is perhaps best remembered for his book *The
Lives of the Artists* (1500 and 1568), a collection
of biographies of artists, and for his **Corridoio
Vasariano**, an overhead passageway built for
the Medicis (*see p81* **Corridor of power**).

Florence is also home to a number of pieces
of outstanding Mannerist sculpture – some on
public display in the Piazza della Signoria and
its Loggia dei Lanzi (*see p77*) – reflecting the
military strength of the Medici administration
under the Grand Duke of Tuscany, Cosimo I de'
Medici. **Benvenuto Cellini**'s (1500-71) life-size
Perseus (1545-54) is a chilling reminder of the

duke's authority, combining an appreciation
for Renaissance sculptors with the elegance
of Mannerism. Giovanni da Bologna (or
Giambologna; 1524-1608) provided the
equestrian statue of Cosimo I (1598) and,
in the Loggia, *Hercules and Centaur* (1599)
and *Rape of the Sabine Women* (1582).

ART IN THE 17TH TO 20TH CENTURIES

In the 17th century Rome replaced Florence
as the artistic centre of Europe. Apart from a
few Florentine artists such as Ludovico Cardi
(known as **Cigoli**; 1559-1613), **Cristoforo
Allori** (1577-1621) and **Carlo Dolci** (1616-87),
the most important artists were working in
Rome in the baroque style. The Medici family
imported the new vogue to Florence by inviting
several artists to their court. **Pietro da
Cortona** (1596-1669) decorated the state
apartments in the Palazzo Pitti (*see p101*) in
the 1630s (later finished by his pupil Ciro Ferri).
During this time the *pietra dura* technique of
inlaid marble decoration was a speciality of
Florentine artists and craftsmen.

By the 18th century Florence was a necessary
stop on the Grand Tour and began to attract art
lovers. The Accademia delle Belle Arti (1784)
became the centre of artistic activity in Florence
during the 18th and 19th centuries, when the
Romantic and Naturalist styles prevailed.

Throughout the Napoleonic occupation of
the city between 1799 and 1814, Florence
followed the French art scene of neo-classical
painters. A group of artists known as the
Macchiaioli met while frequenting Florence's
Caffè Michelangelo, united by their social,
political, and artistic discontent. Their name,
'stain-makers', or 'splatterers', refers to their
style, comprised of patches of colour and
inspired by French Impressionism and the
Barbizon School. Leading Macchiaioli include
Giovanni Fattori (1825-1908), **Telemaco
Signorini** (1835-1901) and **Silvestro Lega**
(1826-95), and their works are housed in the
Galleria d'Arte Moderna section of the Pitti
Palace (*see p101*).

Perhaps the most renowned Florentine artist
of the 20th century is **Marino Marini** (1901-
80), whose museum is located in the former
church of San Pancrazio (*see p86*). Marini
painted throughout his life but also devoted
himself to sculpture around the 1920s,
experimenting with terracotta, bronze, and
coloured plaster, among other media. Fans of
contemporary art, meanwhile, might not be able
to sate their hunger in Florence itself, but a trip
to the Centro per l'arte Contemporanea Luigi
Pecci in Prato (*see p198*), which has showcased
important works by international artists for the
past two decades, is highly recommended.

Santo Spirito. *See p33.*

Architecture

How the city was built to last.

The story of Florentine architecture begins in Etruscan times. Around the third or fourth century BC the Etruscans first used the arch, a feature that became important in subsequent architecture; their sense of proportion and colour was later a key element in Florentine architecture finding its form in the Middle Ages. Roman design was also important, but Rome was located on the southern border of Etruria and may even have been an Etruscan city. So when, during the Renaissance, the look of both Imperial and Christian Rome infused Florentine development, it was to a great extent a rebirth.

Fiesole, just north of Florence, was the first major town in the area, and likely would have been settled to protect both the pass coming south out of the Appennines and the crossing point over the Arno (roughly where the Ponte Vecchio now stands). Extensive sections of walls survive, some with the massive blocks of stone for which the Etruscans were famous, but there are many other remains from Etruscan and later Roman times; indeed, the Roman theatre is still used for shows in summer.

Only when the Romans began to absorb Etruscan civilisation was Roman Florence built, most likely on the site of a razed Etruscan village. Laid out in the grid pattern still visible on maps, the town was apparently founded by Julius Caesar in 59 BC. Not much of Roman Florence remains above ground, but it is known that the theatre was just behind the Palazzo Vecchio, while the amphitheatre's shape can still be seen in the layout of the streets and buildings just west of Piazza Santa Croce.

Medieval Florence grew up along one of the main axes of Roman Florence (now Via dei Calzaiuoli). At one end of the axis was the religious centre, with the Baptistery and Santa Reparata, the church that once stood on the site of the current Duomo. At the other, where the Palazzo Vecchio now stands, was the civil centre of Piazza della Signoria. Between the two, just as today, was the commercial centre now known as Piazza della Repubblica. A number of towers from medieval times have survived the years: the oldest is the round **Torre della Pagliazza** in Via Santa Elisabetta (just off Via del Corso), but there are others in Via Dante Alighieri (opposite Dante's house), in Piazza di San Pier Maggiore, and in Borgo San Jacopo (near the Ponte Vecchio).

As Florence expanded, new walls had to be built, principally between 1259 and 1333. The newly enclosed area came to include the *borghi*, service areas for industry and storage that grew along the roads leading out of early medieval towns. The *borghi* soon became fairly straight,

Detail above doorway of **Orsanmichele**.

wide streets, and the owners of industrial property found themselves sitting on prime land. Many moved their commercial premises outside the new walls, knocked down the old ones (now inside the city) and built large townhouses in their place, with ample gardens behind. These were the *palazzi* of the future.

IN THE BEGINNING
Indigenous Florentine architecture can really be said to have began in the 11th century with the completion of the Baptistery of San Giovanni, the green and white structure just in front of the Duomo. The buildings that define the style are simple, balanced, sharp-edged structures with wide, overhanging roofs. Any baroque tendencies you may spot in Florentine buildings are imported from Rome.

The style partly arises from the fact that the prominent architects who worked in Florence were all born in or near the city. Among the more important names were, chronologically, **Arnolfo di Cambio** (c1245-1302); **Giotto** (1266/7-1337); **Filippo Brunelleschi** (1377-1446); **Michelozzo di Bartolomeo Michelozzi** (1396-1472); **Leon Battista Alberti** (1404-72); **Giuliano da Sangallo** (c1445-1535); **Il Cronaca** (1454-1508); **Michelangelo Buonarroti** (1475-1564); **Giorgio Vasari** (1511-74); **Bartolomeo Ammannati** (1511-92); **Bernardo Buontalenti** (1531-1608); and, later, **Giuseppe Poggi** (1811-1901) and **Giovanni Michelucci** (1891-1991).

ROMANESQUE AND GOTHIC
Along with **San Miniato al Monte** (*see p108*), the wonderful green-and-white-faced church that looks down on the city from above Piazzale Michelangelo, and **Santissimi Apostoli** (*see p84*), on the north bank of the Arno, the **Baptistery** (*see p73*) is the main Romanesque church in Florence. The original building was constructed in the sixth or seventh century; remodelling followed in the 11th century, with the mosaics inside and the marble decoration outside thought to have been finished in the late 12th or early 13th century. Construction on San Miniato al Monte was begun in the 11th century and completed at the start of the 13th century; alongside the Baptistery, it's among the finest Romanesque churches in Europe.

> ### 'Early Renaissance buildings embrace human thought more than Christian faith.'

A period of Gothic construction followed, as builders used pointed arches (instead of the earlier half-moon ones favoured by Romans) in order to make higher and wider structures. Of the five major Gothic churches in Florence, four were influenced by one built slightly earlier: **San Remigio**, a French pilgrims' church built in the 12th century and located just behind the Palazzo Vecchio. It retains, as does much Florentine building, an external simplicity that belies its rather livelier interior.

The quartet of notable Gothic churches that followed all paid lip service to San Remigio. First to go up was **Santa Maria Novella** (*see p87*), work on which began in 1278. This vast church is perhaps the loveliest structure ever put up by the Dominican order of monks. Work on Santa Maria del Fiore, better known as the **Duomo** (*see p70*), was begun in 1297, perhaps to a design by Arnolfo di Cambio. It carried medieval construction to a yet higher and larger scale, while retaining the essential Gothic principles.

Santa Croce (*see p97*), the fourth major Gothic church in Florence, was begun in 1298, and has also been attributed to Arnolfo. Although this Franciscan building has wide, pointed arches along both sides of the nave, springing diagonally across it, the flat, timber ceiling inside, supported on two rows of parallel nave arches, means that one's eye is drawn along the nave to the main altar and to the wall of stained glass behind it, rather than upwards.

At the end of the 14th century the grain market and store that was San Michele in Orto (now known as **Orsanmichele**; *see p79*) had its ground-floor loggia closed on all sides in order to create a small, rather gloomy church for the guilds of Florence. Every guild commissioned a statue to place in each of the 14 niches around the building's exterior. These statues, modelled on humans rather than on traditional medieval Christian figures, were an important impetus to the development of the early Renaissance. (Those visible today are replicas of the originals, which are housed in the Museo di Orsanmichele and the Bargello).

A few other Gothic structures merit mention here, the most notable being the **Campanile** (*see p73*), the bell tower of the Duomo. Designed by Giotto in about 1330, it was completed only after his death. The **Bargello** (originally the Palazzo del Popolo, begun in 1250; *see p96*) and the **Palazzo Vecchio** (begun in 1299; *see p80*) are two more civic structures built in the Gothic period, the latter also apparently designed by Arnolfo di Cambio.

EARLY RENAISSANCE
When it comes to early Renaissance architecture in Florence, three names tower above the pack. Chief among them is Brunelleschi, who gave the Duomo its cupola (the largest such construction since ancient Roman times) and went on to design two of the city's finest churches: **San Lorenzo** (built 1422-69; *see p91*), including its almost independent Old Sacristy (1422-29), and **Santo Spirito** (1444-81; *see p103*). Less heralded, but just as notable, is his **Cappella dei Pazzi** (begun 1442; *see p97*), a small private family building in the garden of Santa Croce.

Breaking with the past, these buildings embrace human thought even more than Christian faith. Indeed, they turn to ideas and forms of the pagan world that pre-date Christianity, while their very roots spring from a new, lay Christianity centred on the individual. The cupola of the Duomo is really already the ideal Renaissance central-plan church, built on top of an earlier 14th-century structure. Many later churches, dating from the high Renaissance and even baroque periods, descend directly from this amazing structure. St Peter's cupola in Rome, begun about 100 years later by Michelangelo, has roughly the same interior diameter at 42 metres (546 feet).

Michelozzo, the second great architect of the early Renaissance, worked often for Cosimo de' Medici (Cosimo il Vecchio), the founder of the Medici family's fortunes. His most notable construction was Cosimo's town residence, now called the **Palazzo Medici Riccardi** (1444; *see p91*); it was here he developed the traditional Florentine palazzo so that it had two façades, as well as strongly rusticated orders. He also built for Cosimo a number of castellated villas in 13th-century style.

Completing the trio is Alberti, who was Florentine but worked mostly outside the city. His usual taste tended almost to ape the architectural forms of ancient Rome, but in Florence he completed the façade of Santa Maria Novella (1470) in such a harmonious manner that it's remained a symbol of the city. He also built for the Rucellai family the palazzo in the Via della Vigna Nuova (c1446-51), where they still live, and the lovely loggia opposite (1463). To the palazzo's façade Alberti introduced pilasters and capitals of the three classical orders that appear to support the three storeys, strongly separated with carved friezes. He completed the tribune started by Michelozzo at **Santissima Annunziata** (*see p94*) in an ornate style more compatible with Rome than Florence.

LATER RENAISSANCE
Other architects, carried Brunelleschian and Albertian ideals to the end of the 15th and even the 16th centuries. Il Cronaca (Simone del Pollaiolo) built the Santo Spirito vestibule and sacristy (1489-94), structures that carry the Renaissance imitation of the Ancient World almost to a culmination, and also built the **Museo Horne** (formerly Palazzo Horne, 1495-1502; *see p97*), for which he returned to a less rustic style. Giuliano da Sangallo, meanwhile, could be a builder of great delicacy, as evidenced by his cloister in **Santa Maria Maddalena dei Pazzi** (1492; *see p98*) in Borgo Pinti. The preferred architect of Lorenzo

Don't miss # Architecture

Baptistery
See p32 and p73.

Biblioteca Mediceo-Laurenziana
See p34 and p91.

Cappella dei Pazzi
See left and p97.

Ponte Santa Trinità
See p34 and p84.

San Miniato al Monte
See p32 and p108.

Santa Maria Novella station
See p36 and p85.

Santo Spirito
See left and p103.

Stadio Artemio Franchi
See p36 and p185.

il Magnifico, da Sangallo also built two grand structures outside the city: the beautiful **Medici villa** at Poggio a Caiano (begun 1480), and the tiny church of **Santa Maria delle Carceri** in Prato (1484-95).

These Brunelleschian and Albertian ideals were further developed in both Florence and Rome. The main exponent of them was the great Michelangelo, whose work spanned the years before, during and after Florence's subjugation by Habsburg emperor Charles V in 1530, which marked the beginning of the end of Florence's Renaissance spirit. Michelangelo took the bold, classicising style that da Sangallo and Il Cronaca had inherited from Alberti, and instilled it with a sense of uncertainty, but also with great energy and rhythm.

Rather than making the exteriors of his buildings redolent of ancient Rome, Michelangelo gave his creations a pagan grounding oriented towards man's emotional state rather than his Christianity. It was this characteristic, more than any other, that moved his architecture beyond the Renaissance. Neither of the projects he undertook in Florence, both of them in the church of San Lorenzo – the **New Sacristy** (begun c1520; *see p90*) and the **Biblioteca Mediceo-Laurenziana** (Laurentian Library, begun 1524; *see p91*) – contain characteristics that tally with what was then understood to be Christian architecture. With large areas of cold, white wall, and a cupola reminiscent of the Pantheon in Rome, the former draws a line under the Renaissance belief that resurrecting the Antique would provide a new truth sufficient to supplant God. Similarly, the Laurentian Library, with its inspiring vestibule calculated to raise the spirits of readers before they entered the reading room, is a structure so modern as to be mysterious.

Michelangelo left for Rome in 1534, never to return. While many fine structures went up in Florence during the 16th and 17th centuries (churches, private *palazzi*, gardens, *logge*, villas), nothing continued the essence of Brunelleschi and Michelangelo. The **Fortezza da Basso** (1534; *see p89 and p105*), the strongest side of which symbolically faces the city, and the **Forte di Belvedere** (1590; *see p100*), which dominates from just above the Ponte Vecchio, express the total dominance the Medici had attained over their fellow Florentines at this time. The vast **Palazzo Pitti** (1457; *see p101*), where the Medici moved in the mid 16th century, pays further tribute of sorts to them. That said, the period also threw up a number of marvellous formal gardens laid out by wealthy patrons, who employed Niccolò Pericoli, known as Il Tribolo (1500-58), and his pupils and followers to design them.

Michelangelo was followed in Florence by Vasari, Ammannati and Buontalenti, the three main Medici court architects who all worked for Cosimo I (the first Duke of Tuscany after the siege and conquest of Florence). Vasari built the **Uffizi** (1560; *see p80*) for Cosimo and, with Buontalenti's help, filled it with offices and workshops for the city's administration but left the top floor for the gallery. Also by Vasari is the raised corridor that bears his name (*see p81* **Corridor of power**), running from the office building across the Ponte Vecchio to the Medici home at the Palazzo Pitti. Ammannati built the lovely **Ponte Santa Trinità** (*see p84*) over the Arno to replace an bridge that had collapsed in 1557, and began the 300-year expansion of the Palazzo Pitti, while Buontalenti extended the Palazzo Vecchio to its present eastern limits, designed the Forte di Belvedere, and built for the Medici the lovely villas at Petraia (1587) and Pratolino (1568, later demolished).

THE LONG DECLINE

Not much happened in Florence architecturally between 1600 and 1860, at least not compared with the previous three centuries. The period from 1600 to the death of the last Medici ruler in 1737 was a long decline; even after the Grand Duchy of Tuscany became property of the reforming Habsburgs, the city remained a provincial appendage of the Austrian Empire. Napoleon, who destroyed so much, did little to damage Florence. Perhaps he felt at home? After all, his family had been minor Florentine nobles from the 14th century onwards, until their move to Corsica, when it was still part of Italy.

As time passed, gardens and *palazzi* were enlarged, grottos were fitted into hillsides, *piazze* were decorated with fountains and statues, and the vast, questionable **Cappella dei Principi** in San Lorenzo (c1604; *see p90*) was built. A few fine but unspectacular churches, necessarily in a Roman baroque style, also went up, among them **San Gaetano** (1604) in Via de' Tornabuoni; **San Frediano in Cestello** (1680-9) on Lungarno Soderini; **San Giorgio alla Costa** (1705-8), just up the hill from the Ponte Vecchio; and **San Filippo Neri** (1640-1715) in Piazza San Firenze. Eventually, in the 19th century, the railway arrived in Florence and two stations were built: **Leopolda** (1847) and **Maria Antonia** near Santa Maria Novella (1848). Only the Leopolda, just outside Porta al Prato, still stands; it's now a spectacular performance space (*see p177*).

DEVELOPMENT AND DESTRUCTION

Beginning with the era just before the unification of Italy in 1860, Florence underwent a series of huge architectural changes. To

The style file

Below are some visual aids illustrating four of the city's most common architectural styles, along with some examples of where you might see them.

Romanesque: San Miniato al Monte. *See p32 and p108.*

Gothic: the Duomo's Campanile. *See p33 and p73.*

Renaissance: Santa Maria Novella façade. *See p33 and p87.*

Modernist: Stadio Artemio Franchi. *See p36 and p185.*

begin with, much of the as-yet-undeveloped land inside the city walls was set aside for housing. Then, on the north side of the Arno, the walls were pulled down (1865-69), leaving only some of the gates, standing isolated as they still do today. Where once stood the walls, *viali* (avenues) were built for the carriages of the new householders, and two large open spaces were left as breaks in the *viali*: Piazza Beccaria, by Giuseppe Poggi, and Piazza della Libertà. Both were meant to be elegant openings in a neo-classical and neo-Renaissance style, but today, like so much of Florence (and the *viali* themselves), they're submerged in traffic.

The new avenues were continued on the south side of the river, from what is now Piazza Ferrucci up another tree- and villa-lined *viale* to **Piazzale Michelangelo** (1875; *see p107*), a large open space for carriages where a magnificent panorama of Florence and its valley awaited the visitor. They continued along the side of the hills facing Florence and the Forte di Belvedere, and then came back down again to Porta Romana. This wonderful drive of roughly six kilometres (3.5 miles), one of the prettiest in Italy, is also due in great part to Poggi's vision.

In these same years, parts of the old city were demolished to make way for three covered, cast-iron market buildings. This was followed, from 1890 onwards, by the most thoughtless devastation of all. Piazza della Repubblica and its surrounding streets, which had been the centre of the Roman and medieval city, were pulled down so that the city centre could be redeveloped. Then, soon after World War I, the central government in Rome, with much the same speculative mentality, got rid of yet more large sections of the city, in Santa Maria Novella and Santa Croce.

In 1944, only 50 years after the centre of Florence had been gutted, another large area of destruction took place, once again removing scores of irreplaceable ancient buildings. Partly out of fury with their former allies and partly in a hopeless attempt to stem the Anglo-American advance, the Germans blew up almost all the bridges over the Arno (only the Ponte Vecchio was spared), along with all the buildings to the immediate north and immediate south of the Ponte Vecchio. Ponte Santa Trinità was rebuilt in the 1950s to the original plans, but the other three – **Ponte alle Grazie** (*see p95*), **Ponte alla Carraia** and **Ponte alla Vittoria** – were all replaced by modern designs.

Most of the old centre of Florence was still intact just over a century ago, made up of buildings going back to the early Middle Ages on foundations that went back at least to ancient Rome. Thanks to this period of destruction, you can walk all the way from the Duomo, down Via Roma, across Piazza della Repubblica, through Via Calimala and Via por Santa Maria and all the way down to the Ponte Vecchio without passing more than two or three buildings that are much more than a century old. This in itself wouldn't necessarily be a problem, but the newer buildings are, on the whole, banal at best and ugly at worst. It's hard not to look up at them and pine for the past.

> **'On paper, the outlook is rosy, but financial and political self-interest is never far away.'**

Still, though much of Florence's modern architecture is forgettable, there are exceptions. Take **Santa Maria Novella station** (*see p85*), for example, built in 1936 by Giovanni Michelucci; the **Stadio Artemio Franchi** (*see p185*), another fine functional structure (finished in 1932 but since restructured); and Michelucci's church of **San Giovanni Battista** (1960) at the crossing of the Autostrade del Sole and del Mare, designed with vision and sensitivity. The inter-war Fascist period produced a number of other fine if typically grandiose structures: a reception building for the Italian royal family, attached to Santa Maria Novella train station, called the **Palazzina Reale**; the **Instituto Aeronautica Militare** building in the Cascine park (*see p104*); and the **Cinema Puccini**, in Piazza Puccini. Then there are Guido Spadolini's 1970s **Palazzo degli Affari** (part of the Palazzo dei Congressi complex) and the new buildings at **Amerigo Vespucci Airport**.

BEST FOOT FORWARD

At the moment a major programme of building and redevelopment is under way in the city, much of which the citizens of Florence seem to be almost unaware of. Some projects focus on alterations and improvements to existing buildings in the city centre, such as the new exit to the Uffizi and the extension of the Museo dell'Opera del Duomo, while others are much bigger, longer-term plans involving a number of initiatives designed to improve and rehabilitate large areas of the city, in the form of both public and private developments. Heavyweight names, both Italian and international, have been drawn to these projects, which carry with them money and prestige, but, this being Italy, politics as well.

How Sir Norman Foster's new train terminal should look when completed.

Sir Norman Foster will design the enormous underground terminal of the high-speed Milano–Roma train link, which is due to be completed in 2010-11. So far so good. Arata Isozaki recently had his plans for the new Uffizi exit rejected, officially on the grounds that the structure would interfere with an archaeological site, but the rumour is that his project was too modern for local tastes. Isozaki was given a few more months to revise his plans, otherwise the commission would go elsewhere. Santiago Calatrava was set to build the extension to the Museo dell'Opera del Duomo, but plans were delayed and the project is now in the hands of local architect Adolfo Natalini. Work is expected to begin in mid 2006 and finish by 2008-09.

These projects are headline-grabbers, but a host of other changes are taking place away from the spotlight. In order to try to alleviate the seriously overcrowded and over-polluted *centro storico*, parts of Greater Florence are being reclaimed and set aside for new homes, businesses, parks and public buildings, with many of the developments utilising defunct industrial areas and factories rather than eating into precious agricultural land. The biggest is the satellite town that is being developed on the huge ex-FIAT property in Novoli near Peretola Airport, where the university buildings are up and running, and the enormous law courts building is due for completion by 2008. Then there is the massive Tramvia project, designed to transform public transport in the city, which was started in spring 2005.

Of course, one question remains: who will pay for all of these projects? On paper, the outlook is rosy, but financial and political self-interest is never far away in these parts; will 21st-century Florence be able to steer clear?

Food in Tuscany

Get stuffed.

THE BASICS

The three main staples of the Tuscan diet are bread, olive oil and wine. Wines are famously substantial (*see pp42-45 and pp234-235* **Visiting wineries**) and the olive oil peppery, but bread is deliberately bland. Made without salt, it is a neutral canvas for accompanying food. A worthy intention, but an acquired taste.

Tuscany claims to have Italy's best olive oil. Even within Tuscany, each region claims superiority, though the consensus is that the finest oil comes from the slightly inland groves away from the varying temperatures and high moisture levels of the coast. Be sure to seek out oil from small producers, in particular extra virgin oils that have been cold pressed from estate-grown olives. Many producers offer tours of their groves and tastings of their product.

L'ANTIPASTO

Meals generally start with the *antipasto*: literally, 'before the meal'. In Tuscany the most common *antipasto* is *crostini*, chicken liver pâté on bread or toast. Cured meats are a regional speciality – usually pork and wild boar, which are hunted during the winter. *Prosciutto crudo* comes from a pig haunch buried under salt for three weeks, then swabbed with spicy vinegar, covered with black pepper and hung to dry for a further five months. *Capocollo* is a neck cut cured the same way for three days, covered with pepper and fennel seed, rolled round in

yellow butcher's paper and then tied up with string into a sausage shape. It's ready to eat a few months later. The most typical Tuscan salami is *finocchiona* (pork flavoured with fennel seeds and peppercorns). *Salamini di cinghiale*, or small wild boar salamis, include chilli pepper and a little fatty pork to keep them from going too hard (wild boar is a very lean meat). Look out for *milza*, a delicious pungent pâté made from spleen, herbs, spices and wine.

IL PRIMO

The *primo* (first course) is carbohydrate-based. In most parts of Italy this is pasta or rice, but in Tuscany it's as likely to be a bread-based salad or soup. Old bread is never thrown away, but is mixed with Tuscan staples such as tomatoes, garlic, cabbage and *fagioli* (white beans). These form dishes such as *panzanella* (stale bread soaked in water, squeezed, mixed with raw onion, fresh tomato and basil and dressed with oil, salt and pepper), *ribollita* (rich bean and cabbage soup with bread, made using the local *cavolo nero* or black cabbage), *acqua cotta* (toasted bread rubbed with garlic and covered with crinkly dark green cabbage, then topped with olive oil, sometimes with an egg broken into it), *pappa al pomodoro* (an exquisite porridge-like soup with onion, garlic, tomatoes, basil and chilli pepper). The ultimate winter ritual is *bruschetta* or *fettunta* (toasted bread rubbed with garlic and soaked in freshly pressed olive oil).

Fresh pasta in Tuscany usually takes the form of *tagliatelle* (flat egg-based ribbons), *pappardelle* (wide flat ribbons), *ravioli* (parcels containing ricotta and spinach) and *tordelli* (from around Lucca, stuffed with chard, meat and ricotta). South you'll find *pici* (flour and water extruded into fattish strings) and in the Mugello *tortelli* (stuffed with potato and bacon). Ravioli are best eaten with *burro e salvia* (butter and sage) and a sprinkling of parmesan or pecorino. Flat ribbon-like pastas go well with gamey sauces like *lepre* (hare) and *cinghiale* (wild boar), and also *anatra* (duck), as well as *ragù* (made with tomato and minced beef or, occasionally, lamb) and *salsa di pomodoro* (spicy tomato sauce).

IL SECONDO

Cacciagione (game), *salsicce* (sausages) and *bistecca* (beef steak) are the main regional meats, though there is good lamb about (look out for *agnellino nostrale*, meaning young, locally raised lamb). Also common are *coniglio* (rabbit, usually roasted, sometimes with pine nuts, sometimes rolled around a filling such as egg and bacon) and *pollo* (chicken; go for *ruspante*, free-range). During the winter you'll find plenty of slowly stewed and highly spiced *cinghiale*. This species was cross-bred with the domestic pig about 20 years ago, producing a largely herbivorous creature so prolific that it has to be culled. Other common game includes *lepre* and *fagiano* (pheasant). The famous *bistecca fiorentina* is a vast T-bone steak, usually served very rare and quite enough for two or even three people. Though a *fiorentina*, grilled over a herby wood fire, might seem synonymous with Tuscany, the habit of eating huge beef steaks was, in fact, introduced in the 19th century by English aristocrats homesick for roast beef. Have no qualms, the Chianina breed of cattle found locally are a salubrious lot. The meat is often organic – indeed, in keeping with the times, organic farming is increasing throughout Italy.

IL CONTORNO

To accompany your meat course you're normally offered a side plate of vegetables or a salad. *Bietole* (Swiss chard) is available almost throughout the year. It's scalded in salted water and tossed in the pan with olive oil, garlic and chilli pepper. *Fagiolini* (green beans) are likely to be boiled and dressed with oil and lemon or vinegar. The sublime white Tuscan *fagioli* are served lukewarm with olive oil and a sprinkle of black pepper. *Patatine fritte* (French fries) are available almost everywhere, though boiled potatoes dressed with oil, pepper and capers are often much tastier. *Pomodori* (tomatoes) and *cipolle* (onions) sliced, spiced and baked *al forno* (in the oven) are recommended. To those

accustomed to watery lettuce, *radicchio* salads may seem bitter at first. Cultivate a taste for them and you'll go on to appreciate the many wild salad varieties. In early summer, artichokes are often eaten raw, stripped of their tough outer leaves and dipped into olive oil and salt.

IL FORMAGGIO

The one true Tuscan cheese is pecorino, made with ewe's milk. The sheep grazing on the hillsides are more often than not there for their milk rather than meat or wool.

Thirty years ago each small farm would have enough sheep to provide the household with sufficient rounds of pecorino, which can be eaten *fresco* (up to a month old), *semi-stagionato* (with about a month of ripening) or up to six months later, when the cheese is fully *stagionato*, and thus drier, sharper and tastier. Nowadays sheep farming and cheese-making are mostly done by Sardinians, who came over to work the land abandoned by the Tuscans drawn to towns and factory employment.

Fresh ricotta, which is made from whey and is thus not strictly speaking a cheese, is soft, mild and wet and should be eaten with black pepper and a few drops of olive oil on top.

LA FRUTTA

Cherries, then apricots and peaches, are readily available in the summer, grapes in the late summer, and apples and pears in the early autumn. Although citrus fruits imported from the south now take pride of place in the winter months, the indigenous fruits are quinces (*mele cotogne*, excellent baked, stewed or jellied) and persimmons (*cachi*). However, for visitors to Tuscany, fruit is perhaps most interesting in sweet/savoury combinations: *il cacio con le pere* (cheese with pears), *i fichi con il salame* (figs with salami), *melone*, or *popone, con prosciutto* (melon and cured ham).

IL DOLCE

The Tuscans are not great purveyors of desserts, though things have changed in recent years. Christmas classics such as *panforte* are now available year-round, but these days you'll find tiramisù, *torta della nonna* and basic fruit or jam tarts almost everywhere. In addition, the Tuscans like to conclude festive meals with a glass of a dry raisin wine called *vin santo* into which they dunk *cantucci*, little dry biscuits packed with almonds. *Vin santo* is made with a special white grape variety that's dried out in bunches for a month and then crushed to obtain a sweet juice, which is aged for at least five years. This is highly uneconomical – you could get five bottles of wine out of the grapes you need for one bottle of *vin santo*. So to offer a glass of *vin santo* is to honour a guest with the essence of hospitality.

Want food, will travel

Some of the best food in Tuscany is to be found in remote country restaurants or quiet villages and towns. Any foodie worth their *fagioli* should be prepared to go out of their way for a good meal. The places listed below are all well worth a detour, be it for the quality of their cuisine or for their special setting. Prices given are for a meal for one consisting of *antipasto* or *primo*, *secondo*, *contorno* and *dolce*. Drinks and cover charge will be extra.

Costachiara

Via Santa Maria 129, Località Badiola, Terranuova Bracciolini, Arezzo (055 944318/ www.costachiara.it). **Open** 12.30-2.30pm Mon; 12.30-2.30pm, 7.30-10pm Wed-Sun. Closed 3wks Jan, 3wks Aug. **Average** €30. **Credit** AmEx, MC, V.

Housed in an attractive *casa colonica*, this family-run country restaurant offers wonderful rustic food. A groaning board of *antipasti* will start the mouth watering: help yourself to grilled vegetables, tongue in a piquant *salsa verde*, *crostini*, or a slice of roast ham with a dollop of fabulous red onion marmalade. *Primi* include home-made *pici*, either with a gutsy pigeon and guinea fowl sauce, or *all'aglione*, with chilli and garlic-spiked tomato. *Secondi* are all very traditional, with *arrosto girato* (mixed meats spit-roasted over the huge open fire upstairs) and, in autumn, quail with grapes. The home-made desserts are memorable. Accommodation is available.

Da Delfina

Via della Chiesa 1, Artimino, Florence (055 8718074/www.dadelfina.it). **Open** 12.30-2.30pm, 7.45-10.30pm Tue-Sat; 12.30-2.30pm Sun. Closed Aug. **Average** €40. **No credit cards**.

Simple, seasonal Tuscan food at its best, on a spectacular terrace overlooking a classic landscape. In early summer, starters include a delicate bright green *sformato* of nettles served with a lick of bean purée. Nettles crop up again in the *tagliatelle di ortica* with spinach, while chunks of porcini mushrooms are deep fried in a light batter. *Secondi* include stuffed courgette flowers and rabbit stewed with pine nuts and olives, while local sheep's cheeses are served with *cotognata* (quince jam). The wine list offers a choice of excellent local Carmignano; go for one of the full-bodied *riserve*. This really is a lovely spot; shame the service can be a little churlish.

Gambero Rosso

Piazza della Vittoria 13, San Vincenzo, Livorno (0565 701021). **Open** 12.30-2pm, 8-10pm Wed-Sun. Closed Nov, Dec. **Average** €85. **Credit** AmEx, DC, MC, V.

In spite of the two Michelin stars, Gambero Rosso, where eight or so tables are laid in an airy room overlooking San Vincenzo harbour, is a relaxed place. Fulvio Pierangelini's food is sublime. You can choose the five-course set menu (€85) or eat à la carte, where dishes are more creative. 'I Classici' include the signature dish of *passatina di ceci con crostacei*, a silky cream of chickpeas with sweet shrimp tails, and white and black fish ravioli with a rose-coloured seafood sauce. Main-course catch of the day is served lightly sautéed on a bed of creamy mash topped with artichoke hearts. While fish and seafood reign supreme, there are also some fine meat options; try the *cinta senese* pork, locally reared by Pierangelini's son. The wine list is remarkably well priced. *See also p216.*

Osteria dei Nobili Santi

Via dell'Ospizio 8, Porto Ercole, Grosseto (0564 833015). **Open** 7.30-10.30pm Tue-Sat; noon-2.30pm, 7.30-10.30pm Sun. Closed 1st 2wks Feb, 2wks Oct. **Average** €35. **Credit** AmEx, DC, MC, V.

Moreno Santi's pleasant fish restaurant is tucked down a side street in the seaside town of Porto Ercole, once a quiet fishing village but today the upmarket haunt of yachties. The restaurant is famous for the phenomenal range of *antipasti*: order the *carrellata di antipasti* and around 15 delicious *assaggi* (tastes) will be served. They rotate frequently, but recent highlights have included octopus *soppressata* (a kind of terrine), courgette stuffed with sea bass pâté, a sublime creamed cauliflower with mullet roe, prawns in filo pastry with orange sauce, and squid and porcini mushroom soup. If you still have room for more, try the delicious *spaghetti alle vongole* (clams), a simple but satisfying dish flavoured only with olive oil, garlic, parsley and a slosh of white wine. *See also p278.*

Osteria di Passignano

Via Passignano 33, Badia in Passignano, Chianti (055 8071278). **Open** 12.15-2.15pm, 6.30-10.15pm Mon-Sat. Closed last 3wks Jan, 2wks Aug. **Average** €40. **Credit** AmEx, DC, MC, V.

Set in the midst of the Antinori wine estates, in the shadow of a beautiful old monastery, this *osteria* occupies an elegant-rustic room with graceful brick-vaulted ceilings. Come here to sample Mattia Barciulli's imaginative but not over fussy interpretations of classic Tuscan dishes based on seasonal ingredients of the highest quality. While presentation is modern, flavours are traditional; warm ricotta terrine with wild violets and asparagus, red mullet in an olive crust, chicken liver salad with raisins, pine nuts and *vin santo* apples, *pici* with asparagus, tarragon and saffron, and roast suckling pig with a basket of marinated onion and Calvados apples. Leave room for a wicked dessert and choose one of the wines produced from the vines on the doorstep. The shaded terrace is lovely in summer.

Il Silene

Località Pescina 9, Seggiano, Grosseto (0564 950805/www.ilsilene.it). **Open** 12.45-2pm, 7.45-9.30pm Tue-Sun. **Average** €40. **Credit** AmEx, MC, V.

Among the chestnut groves on the northern slopes of Monte Amiata lies the quiet hamlet of Pescina, where this *albergo-ristorante* has been serving guests since 1830. From the outside it looks basic, but the dining room is elegant. The carefully presented seasonal dishes are characterised by the same mix of rustic and more sophisticated elements. There are two set tasting menus, one of traditional Tuscan fare (€43), and the other featuring local ingredients such as truffles (€48). A typical meal might include creamy *taglierini* with wild asparagus, or spinach *crespelle* (a kind of crêpe) stuffed with walnuts and a hint of truffle bathed in a gorgonzola sauce, and juniper-flavoured wild boar stew. Wines are keenly priced. *See also p236* **Monte Amiata**.

La Tana degli Orsi

Via Roma 1, Pratovecchio, Arezzo (0575 583377). **Average** €28. **Open** 7.45-10.30pm Mon, Wed-Sun. Snacks served until 1am. Closed 1wk Apr, July, Nov. **Credit** AmEx, DC, MC, V.

Deep in the unspoilt Casentino, the cosy, relaxed 'Bear's Den' is run by a young couple (he in the kitchen, she out front). Wine is important here: you can come for a glass and a snack if you don't want a full meal. It's difficult, however, to resist the sophisticated versions of traditional dishes that come from

the kitchen, with seasonal local ingredients such as cheese, prosciutto, wild asparagus, truffles and mushrooms. You may find warm brioche with asparagus, taleggio cheese and prosciutto, pigeon and truffle tortelli, venison with artichokes and fabulous local cheeses served with honey and chutneys. Puddings, such as warm chocolate *tortino* (a bit like a soufflé) with mint ice-cream, don't disappoint.

Trattoria Sagginale

Via Belvedere 23, Località Sagginale, Borgo San Lorenzo, Florence (055 8490130). **Open** 12.30-2pm Mon-Wed; 12.30-2pm, 7.30-9.30pm Fri-Sun. Closed 2wks June. **Average** €16. **Credit** MC, V.

'Big Giorgio' is the affable *padrone* at this modest roadside restaurant in the Mugello, known in these parts as Da Giorgione. The locals come for the superb *tortelli di patate*, the area's most famous dish, which are still hand made here by a team of signoras. Day after day, they lovingly churn out soft pillows of light egg pasta filled with a mix of mashed potato, parmesan, minced garlic, parsley and nutmeg. The *tortelli di ricotta e spinaci* is also divine. *Secondi* include grilled meats and a delicious *coniglio ripieno* – rolled, boned and roasted rabbit stuffed with spinach *frittata* and prosciutto. The house wine is plentiful and cheap. A truly rural experience. *See also p200.*

Il Tufo Allegro

Vicolo della Costituzione 2, Pitigliano, Grosseto (0564 616192). **Open** 12.30-2pm, 7.30-9.30pm Mon, Thur-Sun; 7.30-9.30pm Wed. Closed mid Jan-mid Feb, last wk June, 1st wk July. **Average** €35. **Credit** AmEx, MC, V.

The ancient town of Pitigliano is built on an extraordinary outcrop of tufa rock into which this rustic trattoria is half carved; the two tiny downstairs rooms are virtually underground. The menu is based on traditional local recipes, with an original slant. Begin with chicken liver pâté with red onion marmalade and *vin santo* jelly or a plate of local *salumi di cinghiale* (wild boar salami). Move on to soft *gnudi* (ricotta and spinach dumplings) with truffle sauce, or lasagne with artichokes and rabbit sauce. *Secondi* include superb *cinghiale* stewed in local Ciliegiolo wine, and saddle of rabbit with wild fennel. There's a fabulous selection of cheeses, as well as delicious desserts. The wine list has interesting labels, but mark-ups are high. *See also p276.*

Wine in Tuscany

The region's best cellars.

In years gone by, the renown of Tuscan winemaking was derived almost exclusively from one grape variety: the sangiovese, which goes into famous and often highly priced reds such as Chianti. More recently, however, other grape varieties, both local and international, have begun to emerge as blends and varietals, with interesting results. The scope of Tuscan winemaking is expanding as the quality continues to improve. On the red wine shelves, merlots, syrahs and cabernet sauvignons are all as popular as ever, but there are now some fine wines being made with the local ciliegiolo and alicante varieties, especially towards the coast. Vermentino, meanwhile, is at last lifting a number of Tuscan whites above mediocrity.

During the past 15 years, wine production in Tuscany has evolved to such a huge degree that the changes are as evident in the landscape as in the glass. Look out for orchards of fruit trees interspersed with a few rows of tall, exuberant vines, their tendrils embracing sturdy trees for support: this is viticultural archaeology, destined to disappear entirely before long. With the demise of this sort of vine dressing has gone much of the quaffing wine sold in large bottles. Quality has become the watchword: there's not a traditional winemaker left who feels he can do without an oenologist (a wine technician).

The emphasis these days is on densely planted vineyards. Vibrant green geometries have replaced the softer contours and mixed hues of the sparsely planted orchards tended by yesteryear's sharecrop farmers. Vines need to be 'stressed' by competition: that way, they'll concentrate on survival, focusing energy on seed production and, it follows, on sturdy, healthy fruit. Bunches of grapes grown on vines that are radically pruned in winter and again in the spring will often be thinned out to improve quality and ensure that ripening proceeds evenly. The goal: relatively low yields with high concentrations of sugars and aromas.

The quality of recent wines varies by the year. 1997 was a very good year, while 2002 was the opposite; 2003 was problematic for many areas due to excessive summer heat and drought; and 2004 was also tough because of widespread hail in June. However, such phenomena strike in patches, and not every producer is affected.

ALL IN A NAME

While superstar oenologists fly around the country advising growers on what to do and when to do it, the winemakers themselves have grown more aware of what their particular vineyards could and should produce. Such territorial specificity ensures what is known as *tipicità*: a distinct character pertaining to a given place.

To some extent, *tipicità* is defined by the various DOCs (Denominazione di Origine Controllata), which regulate wines from a specific, controlled area), the ultra-select category of DOCGs (Denominazione di Origine Controllata e Garantita) and IGTs (Indicazione Geografica Tipica, table wines from a well-defined area). These certified names are the equivalent of the French *appellation*: each sets out rules and regulations to which producers must adhere. Tuscany has 39 such names, more than any other region in Italy, of which the most famous are **Chianti Classico**, **Brunello di Montalcino** and **Vino Nobile di Montepulciano**.

The reputation of this trio tends to overshadow some fine younger siblings: **Bolgheri Rosso** DOC, for example, made in the coastal area north of Grosseto; **Montescudaio** DOC, a little further south; and, below, the **Morellino di Scansano** DOC. A little further inland is the **Montecucco** DOC, which also produces well-structured reds, while two other newer southern Tuscan DOCs are **Capalbio**, on the coast, and **Sovana**, between the southern slopes of Monte Amiata and the coast. Due east and slightly north of here is the fairly extensive and variegated area devoted to **Orcia** DOC, whose flagship in its early years has been Donatella Cinelli Colombini at the Fattoria del Colle, near Trequanda. While the denomination itself is more a guarantee of *tipicità* than of excellence, some of the new DOCs are very promising, and still relatively reasonably priced.

The well-established Tuscan whites are the **Vernaccia di San Gimignano** DOC and the **Bianco di Pitigliano** DOC. However, a number of the newer DOCs also embrace white wines, though so far not many can stand up to comparisons with the few Tuscan whites of excellence: **Batàr** pinot bianco, made by Agricola Querciabella at Greve in Chianti, and the **Cabreo La Pietra** chardonnay made by Ruffino at Pontassieve.

RAISING THE STANDARD

To match the changes in the vineyard, more attention is now also paid to the cellar. The peasant winemaker of a few years ago now either sells his grapes to larger wineries or has embarked on a programme of investment in new vineyards and appropriate winemaking facilities: spotless new cellars, temperature-controlled steel fermentation tanks, expensive pumps that shift the deep red liquid from one container to another without bruising it, small

French oak barrels (*barriques*) for oxygenating and ageing the wine, immaculate bottling equipment and, as often as not, a tasting room.

A number of small growers instead sell their grapes to the remaining co-operative wineries, which have had to improve in the last few years: quaffable wines are no longer good enough. With the help of agronomists, who advise the growers, and oenologists, who work in the cellars, the better co-operative winemakers are producing acceptable wines with a good price-to-quality ratio that helps smooth over what might otherwise be perceived as a lack of character. Examples include **Agricoltori del Chianti Geografico**, which produces a fine Chianti Classico (especially the 1998); the **Cantina di Montalcino**, whose Brunello '95 meets with acclaim; the **Cantina Cooperativa del Morellino**, which has a good Morellino di Scansano; Redi, the flagship for the **Vecchia Cantina** co-operative winery at Montepulciano; and **Le Chiantigiane**, producing the white vernaccia di San Gimignano. Such wines are widely distributed, both at supermarket level in Italy and in wine stores and chains abroad.

At the other end of the spectrum sit the great aristocratic wine dynasties, names such as **Antinori**, **Ricasoli**, **Frescobaldi**, **Mazzei** and **Folonari** (the owners of Ruffino). These giants have gradually expanded from the area south of Florence, where they principally produce Chianti Classico, to other parts of Tuscany, as well as further afield to Umbria, Apulia, Sicily, California and Chile.

'Foreign winemakers have settled in the region, adding their own passion, individuality and insight.'

They have the clout, financially and socially, to shape palates in anticipation of market trends, as happened with the development of **Galestro** in the late 1970s. In a region that was then largely identified with reds, these producers saw the time was ripe for a white wine in which the emphasis was more on freshness and lightness than aroma and body. The wine was made up largely of the trebbiano toscano grape variety, with small amounts of malvasia del Chianti, vernaccia di San Gimignano, chardonnay, pinot bianco and Rhine-riesling, and production involved pioneering vinification techniques. In 20 years, Galestro has grown to become if not quite a connoisseur's choice, then an acceptable aperitif or accompaniment to lighter summer cuisine.

SIMPLY THE BEST

Still more impressive and influential has been the development from the mid 1980s of the so-called Super Tuscans, also pioneered by the great wine estates. The idea behind them was to open up the way for wines that could satisfy changing tastes, especially abroad: at the time, Tuscan table wines were seen as poor, and the production of DOC wines was stultified by excessive strictures and regulations. The far-sighted few, who felt there was room for wines that didn't conform to established Tuscan models, began experimenting with the grape varieties that had contributed to the renown of French viticulture: cabernets, merlot, chardonnay and sauvignon.

Alongside these enterprising producers came a new generation of highly trained wine technicians, whose wines were beautifully made, highly priced and, for consumers abroad, initially somewhat perplexing. Why should an 'ordinary' wine cost more than certain DOCs? Was there anything beyond the thick glass of the bottle and the refined label? The British and American wine press decreed that reds such as **Tignanello** (sangiovese and cabernet sauvignon) and **Solaia** (cabernet with a small percentage of sangiovese) made by Marchesi Antinori in Chianti deserved the epithet Super Tuscans, and the name stuck. Similar enthusiasm greeted Nicolò Incisa della Rocchetta's **Sassicaia** (90 per cent cabernet sauvignon, ten per cent cabernet franc) and Lodovico Antinori's **Ornellaia** (90 per cent cabernet sauvignon, ten per cent merlot); both are made at Bolgheri near the northern Maremma coast, an area hitherto devoted entirely to sangiovese and trebbiano.

The new wines soon spread in range, reaching areas as distant from the original Chianti region as the western foothills of Monte Amiata and Montalcino. Several of the Super Tuscans have joined the IGT category, some have continued to call themselves *vini da tavola*, and others still have achieved a more specific geographical identity by associating with the newly created DOCs. Moreover, even the traditional native sangiovese grape variety has proved to have plenty to say for itself, both on its own and in discerning combination with varieties from further afield.

ONES TO WATCH

Tuscan wines are currently more varied and interesting than ever before, at least partly thanks to a generation of younger winemakers who are opening up new vistas by fine-tuning a particular feature within a given DOC. Many of them are the offspring of the sharecrop farmers whose own winemaking methods were pretty much those of their medieval forebears, though these youngsters, better educated and travelled than their fathers, are keen to experiment with new clones, grape varieties, vinification methods and ageing techniques.

'Over 90 per cent of Italy's wine and food tourism focuses on Tuscany.'

At Bolgheri, Eugenio Campolmi's winery (**Le Macchiole**) has made a name for itself with Paleo, Messorio and Scrio, all excellent reds. Not far distant, at Suvereto, is Rita Tua's winery (called **Tua Rita**), which produces Redigaffi and Giusto di Notri. Around Montalcino, the number of *contadini* ('peasant farmers', but the term has no negative connotations in Italian) who have become prestigious producers of Brunello is greater: Giancarlo Pacenti at the winery that bears his father's name (Pelagrilli di Pacenti Siro); Paolo Bartolommei at the Caprili winery; Vincenzo Abbruzzese at Val di Cava; and Giacomo Neri at Casanova di Neri, the Fattoi family and winery. All have transcended their families' horizons, but with touching respect for what their fathers taught them.

Another interesting feature of Tuscan winemaking of late has been the contribution of foreign winemakers who have settled in the region, learned all they could from the locals and then added their own passion, expertise, individuality and insight. Foremost among them is British-born Sèan O'Callaghan at the **Riecine** winery outside Gaiole in Chianti; others include Martin Frölich, a former lawyer from Germany, at the **Castagnoli** winery near

Green growers

Ten years ago organic wines in Italy more or less defined the phrase 'minority interest'. Only militants fired with green fever could discipline their palates to ignore the musty aromas and faulty structure of most eco offerings. Today, though, it's a different story. Even the most demanding oenophiles can reconcile their taste buds with their environmental ethics: Tuscany's excellent organic wines should do much to obviate the throbbing-head syndrome associated with over-indulgence.

Making wines from organically grown grapes means not adding industrially synthesised compounds to the soil or vines to increase fertility. Moreover, wines bearing the organic label are allowed only half the residual sulphites permitted in non-organic wine. Most of Tuscany's organic wine producers are smallish: the **Castagnoli** winery perched on a hilltop near Castellina in Chianti, for instance, or **Karl Egger**, who produces an excellent organic vermentino white wine on the west coast near Orbetello. Only a few of the 220 or so winemakers in Montalcino are organic: the tiny **Fornacella** estate, the **Tenute Loacker** winery and **Salicutti** are cases in point. But the most impressive is surely Lionel Cousin's **Cupano** winery, whose Brunello, Rosso di Montalcino and Sant'Antimo are wonderfully elegant and full of depth. Pricey, of course, but well worth it.

Castellina in Chianti, and the Frenchman Lionel Cousin, who in 2003 bottled his first Brunello at **Cupano**, his small organic winery near Montalcino. All three have an independence of spirit that finds its way into the bottle.

GETTING STARTED

The wine map of Tuscany is far more varied than a visit to a UK or US wine shop would ever lead you to believe. It's so rich, in fact, that Tuscany is at the forefront of *il turismo enogastronomico*, whereby tourists devote part of their holiday to visiting wineries and sampling local foods: over 90 per cent of Italy's wine and food tourism focuses on Tuscany. Such tourism is seen as sustainable, as good for the visitor as it is for the local economy and as a lovely way of getting to know the countryside as well as its products. To lure discerning palates to the lesser-known reaches of Tuscan viticulture, the **Movimento del Turismo del Vino** (www.movimentoturismovino.it) has helped set up a number of offices in most of the wine-producing areas. These **Strade del Vino** organise tasting tours, visits to cellars, meals based on local produce and other events. Another event worth a look is **Cantine Aperte**, held on the last weekend of May, when wineries all over the region – and indeed the country – open their doors (and bottles) to visitors.

Visiting wineries entirely under your own steam can be both interesting and frustrating. While most welcome tourists with advance warning, not all have a proper tasting facility, or staff who speak English; nor, indeed, do they have the time to devote to this sort of PR. However, a little research goes a long way. For our picks of wineries open to the public, *see p234* **Visiting wineries**, but well-run local *enoteche* will be in a position to advise, both by providing tastings on its own premises and having staff phone their contacts in selected wineries. These shops are usually run by *appassionati* who will happily provide you with a number of glasses for a 'vertical' tasting of different vintages of the same wine, or a 'horizontal' tasting (no reference to your final posture) of wines of the same variety and/or year made by different producers. *Enoteche* also sell wine, by the bottle or the case. Prices may be higher than at the wineries, but you may well find that the smaller wineries have no product left to sell or are so far away that it's not worth the time and effort to get there.

DRINKING OUT

The **Strade del Vino di Toscana** organisation is gradually working with restaurateurs to improve the level of wine expertise of their staff. In an expensive gourmet restaurant you're bound to find a waiter who really knows about the listed wines, though this isn't really the case in simpler eateries. Where suggestions are not forthcoming, you have a few choices. You could arm yourself pre-emptively with the annually updated English edition of the generally reliable *Italian Wines Guide*, published by Slow Food and Gambero Rosso, and pick something from the wine list. You could choose a bottle made by one of the old, established wine estates. Or you might do some research into the local DOC and opt for a medium-priced bottle, an approach that often leads to a gratifying discovery.

► For **wine shops**, *see p147 and p150.*
► For **wine bars**, *see pp110-128.*
► For **wine and food tourism**, *see p196.*

VILLA BORDONI
GREVE-IN-CHIANTI

COUNTRY HOUSE HOTEL AND RESTAURANT

Villa Bordoni, an idiosynchratic 16 th century noble villa, nestles in the grey-green hills immediately above the town of Greve, capital of the Chianti Classico region of Tuscany. It was discovered by the Gardner family in the winter of 2002. David and Catherine Gardner, both Scottish-born, are the founders and owners of successful Florentine restaurants 'Baldovino' and 'Beccofino'. For some years they had been searching for the ideal property to realise their ambition of opening a luxurious but unpretentious country house hotel in the Florentine Chianti. When discovered, the villa was in a dire condition and slowly decaying into the poetically beautiful landscape which surrounds it. Now that the house, its Italian garden and its six hectares of olive groves and vines have been lovingly restored to their former splendour, David and Catherine are looking forward to welcoming you to their exclusive and romantic getaway. Villa Bordoni the accomodation comprises 6 double rooms, 3 suites and 1 cottage. All rooms have satellite TV, DVD/CD player, minibar, safe and internet connection. Each room has it's own unique furnishings and character. An open air swimming pool, and gym set within the terraced hills of the estate, provides panoramic views of the surrounding countryside. Bar and restaurant (open also to non-residents) with a well stocked wine cellar. The ideal location for summer lunches or wine tastings in the garden. The villa can be rented in it's entirety with staff for special events such as wedding parties or Christmas and Hogmanay.

Via San Cresci 31/32 - Località Mezzuola - Greve in Chianti - Firenze
Tel. 055 2466684 - Fax 055 2009722 - www.villabordoni.com - info@villabordoni.com

Where to Stay

Where to Stay

Wherever you lay your hat…

Florence's hoteliers continue to have a tough time. Business still hasn't picked up fully since 9/11, with an accumulation of negative factors – the threat of terrorism, the Gulf War, a general recession, the decidedly unfriendly US dollar-to-euro exchange rate – leading to an overall fall in visitor numbers. As a result, many hotels didn't increase their prices for 2005, while some actually lowered them. So while accommodation in Florence is still hardly a bargain these days, it's better value than it has been in the past, not least due to the number of new guesthouses and small hotels, some offering reasonable rates, that have cropped up in recent years.

In between the sleek, chic properties at the top end of the market and the crumbling *palazzi* at the bottom are plenty of comfortable four- and five-star establishments, small boutique hotels, cheap and cheerful one- and two-star places and – a recent trend – a host of B&Bs (for definitions of these types of accommodation, *see p57* **When is a hotel not a hotel?**). Do your research carefully: things are improving, but there are still a great many overpriced, under-serviced establishments in Florence short on both charm and comfort. The hotels in this chapter have all been chosen for the value for money they offer within their respective categories or, more prosaically, just because they're great places to stay.

STAR RATINGS AND FACILITIES

Hotels are given a star rating from one to five (although some lodgings are excluded from this system; *see p57* **When is a hotel not a hotel?**), but the rating is an indication of the facilities on offer rather than the standards. There can be enormous disparity within any given category: while the star system is useful up to a point, it certainly shouldn't be taken as wholly indicative of a hotel's calibre.

Most hotels price their rooms according to size, shape, view, the amount of natural light they receive, the size and type of bathroom and whether rooms have balconies or terraces. Bedrooms in all the hotels listed here that fall within the star system have phones and en suite bathrooms, with the exception of the 'Budget' category; where a 'Budget' hotel does offer en suite facilities, we've mentioned it in the review. Many rooms also have safes and hairdryers. In the case of the other categories, facilities vary, so you'd be advised to check before you book if you require something specific. If you don't like the room you've been given, ask to see another one, and don't be put off by grumpy owners. Hotels are required by law to display official maximum room rates in each room; if you feel you've been taken for a ride, there's an office for complaints (*see p298*).

If you're staying in the centre of the city during the long hot summer, a private terrace or balcony – or some kind of communal outside

The best Hotels

For contemporary art
Gallery Hotel Art (*see p49*); Il Guelfo Bianco (*see p53*).

For expense accounters
Villa San Michele (*see p63*).

For good budget lodgings
B&B Borgo Pinti (*see p60*); Cestelli (*see p54*); Dali (*see p54*); Scoti (*see p54*).

For minimalists
Hotel Continentale (*see p51*); Residence Hilda (*see p57*).

For overall value for money
Antica Dimora Firenze (*see p57*); Casa Howard (*see p55*); Relais Grand Tour (*see p56*); Residenza Johlea Uno & Johlea Due (*see p59*).

For rooms with views
Antica Torre Tornabuoni Uno (*see p52*); Camping Panoramico (*see p60*); Lungarno (*see p60*); Pensione Bencistà (*see p64*).

For that home-from-home feeling
Casa Howard (*see p55*); Dei Mori (*see p54*); Lungarno Suites (*see p51*); Relais Grand Tour (*see p56*).

For the sound of twittering birds
Pensione Bencistà (*see p64*); Relais Marignolle (*see p63*); Villa Poggio San Felice (*see p63*); Villa San Michele (*see p63*).

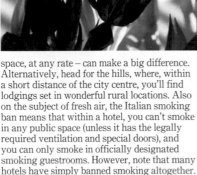

Hotel Continentale. *See p51.*

space, at any rate – can make a big difference. Alternatively, head for the hills, where, within a short distance of the city centre, you'll find lodgings set in wonderful rural locations. Also on the subject of fresh air, the Italian smoking ban means that within a hotel, you can't smoke in any public space (unless it has the legally required ventilation and special doors), and you can only smoke in officially designated smoking guestrooms. However, note that many hotels have simply banned smoking altogether.

Very few hotels in the centre of town have their own parking facilities; most have an arrangement with a nearby private garage, though this will be expensive (we have given rates under each hotel). A law requires hotels with three or more stars to have rooms with disabled access. But the law doesn't extend to all facilities, a fudge that results in the absurd situation where, in some cases, rooms for the disabled are only accessible by a lift that's too narrow to take a wheelchair.

BOOKING AND PRICES

Though it's generally easier to find a hotel room in Florence these days, given the fact that visitor numbers are not yet quite back to their pre-9/11 levels, there is still particularly heavy demand for rooms from Easter (the busiest weekend of the year) to the end of June and in September. Christmas and New Year also pull in the crowds. Book well in advance at these times. However, if you arrive with nowhere to stay, head for the ITA office in the station, which offers a booking service, or to a tourist office (*see p298*), which can provide a list of local hotels. The APT booklet *Guida all'Ospitalità* details hotels,

affittacamere (rooms for rent), residences, campsites and hostels in Florence and its province, as well as listing *case per ferie*, religious institutions that offer a number of beds. The majority are cheap, but are often single-sex only and operate curfews.

Prices given here – which are, of course, subject to change – are for rooms with en suite bathrooms and complimentary breakfast, unless otherwise stated. We have given a range of prices (the minimum and maximum rates) for each type of room. However, bear in mind that many hotels slash their prices by as much as 50 per cent outside of peak season, so our categories are fairly fluid. Times are hard and it's always worth haggling a bit as rates may be lowered if occupancy is down, especially if you're booking at the last minute. Most hotels will put at least one extra bed in a double room for a fee; many provide cots for which you may or may not have to pay extra.

Duomo & Around

Luxury

Gallery Hotel Art

Vicolo dell'Oro 2 (055 27263/fax 055 268557/ www.lungarnohotels.com). **Rates** €242-€352 double for single occupancy; €286-€374 double; €517-€660 suite. **Credit** AmEx, MC, V. **Map** p318 C3.
While its East-meets-West design aesthetic is still refreshingly different from the Florentine norm, the town's original hip hotel (it opened in 1999) is no longer the only trendy kid on the block. Located in a tiny piazza near the Ponte Vecchio, the Gallery has a cosy library with squashy sofas, thoughtfully supplied with cashmere throws for cold evenings,

A CHARMING WELCOME IN THE HEART OF FLORENCE

HOTEL CELLAI

Via 27 Aprile, 14 - Firenze, 50129 - Tel. +39 055 489291 - Fax +39 055 470387
E-mail: info@hotelcellai.it - http://www.hotelcellai.it

and mountains of arty books to browse. Also here is the stylish Fusion Bar, which serves *aperitivi*, brunches, light lunches and dinners (*see p184* **Night nibbles** *and p123* **Hotel cuisine**). The public rooms on the ground floor often double as a show-space for contemporary artists and photographers (*see p167*). The bedrooms are super-comfortable, and the bathrooms are a dream. The penthouse suite has two terraces with stunning views.
Bar. Disabled-adapted rooms. Internet (dataport). No-smoking rooms. Parking (€32/day). Restaurant. Room service. TV (DVD, pay movies).

Helvetia & Bristol
Via dei Pescioni 2 (055 287814/fax 055 288353/ www.royaldemeure.com). **Rates** €180-€230 single; €240-€310 double; €560-€700 suite; €26 breakfast. **Credit** AmEx, DC, MC, V. **Map** p318 B3.
Built in the late 1800s, the Helvetia & Bristol has hosted a distinguished list of guests in the last century: everyone from Igor Stravinsky to Bertrand Russell. Filled with antiques, fine paintings and prints, it retains a historic feel, but manages to be exclusive without being stuffy. In the salon, velvet sofas and armchairs are grouped around a huge fireplace; the belle époque Winter Garden, where breakfast is served until a very civilised 12.30pm, is adorned with potted palms and a tinkling fountain. A new restaurant, done out in vibrant oranges and reds, offers a relaxed atmosphere and an inviting new look at Florentine cooking. The sumptuous decor in the bedrooms will be too opulent for some, but there's no denying the luxury. All in all, this is one of central Florence's best small-ish hotels.
Bar. Business centre. Disabled-adapted rooms. Internet (dataport). No-smoking rooms. Parking (€30/day). Restaurant. Room service. TV.

Hotel Continentale
Vicolo dell'Oro 6r (055 27262/fax 055 283139/ www.lungarnohotels.com). **Rates** €220-€275 single; €319-€407 double; €924-€1,155 suite. **Credit** AmEx, DC, MC, V. **Map** p318 C3.
The last hotel in the Ferragamo family's Lungarno group to be given a make-over, the Continentale is situated across the street from the Gallery (*see p49*), its sister hotel. The hotel has a different feel from its sibling: while both boast a contemporary style, the Continentale is the feminine flipside to the Gallery's more masculine image. Splashes of zingy colour are supplied by some '60s pieces, but otherwise the design is free of fuss: blond woods, creamy fabrics, filmy white curtains, huge glass vases and soft pools of light. Bedrooms have modern four-posters and fabulous bathrooms; 'superiors' have full-on views of the river and the Ponte Vecchio. There's a spectacular roof terrace and bar, but the best place to chill out is the first-floor Relax Room, where light filters through slatted blinds and daybeds afford horizontal views of the crowds milling across the bridge.
Bar. Gym. Internet (dataport). No-smoking rooms. Parking (€32/day). Room service. TV (DVD).

Westin Excelsior. *See p55.*

Lungarno Suites
Lungarno Acciaiuoli 4 (055 27268000/fax 055 27268880/www.lungarnohotels.com). **Rates** €275-€616 apartment. **Credit** AmEx, DC, MC, V. **Map** p318 C3.
Ideal for travellers who want the comforts and levels of service typical of a four-star hotel but a little more independence, the stylish Lungarno Suites – owned by the people behind the Continentale (*see above*) and Gallery Hotel Art (*see p49*), with which it shares a similar style and sensibility – offer fully serviced self-catering apartments of various sizes on the north bank of the Arno. About half the apartments have river views; those on the top floors have terraces. Each unit has a cleverly hidden and fully equipped kitchen, but if you're not willing or able to get everything together, you can have your shopping done for you or order meals from the kitchen at the Gallery.
Internet (high-speed, web TV). No-smoking rooms. Parking (€32/day). Room service.

Savoy
Piazza della Repubblica 7 (055 283313/fax 055 2735666/www.hotelsavoy.com). **Rates** €222-€341 single; €336-€517 double; €822-€1,265 suite. **Credit** AmEx, DC, MC, V. **Map** p318 B3.

Grand Hotel. See p54.

It's located in the shell of the 19th-century hotel of the same name, but the Savoy doesn't bear much of a resemblance to its predecessor. Now one of the city's most popular all-rounders, big with the business, leisure and celebrity brackets, the hotel was added to the Rocco Forte portfolio in the late '90s; Olga Polizzi, Sir Rocco's interior designer sister, has created a characteristically stylish and calm ambience in the old space, setting dark wood, splashes of colour and some modern art against more neutral beiges and creams. The L'Incontro bar and brasserie (*see p123* **Hotel cuisine**) is great for people-watching, especially from the tables in the busy piazza. *Bar. Business centre. Concierge. Disabled-adapted rooms. Gym. Internet (high-speed). No-smoking rooms. Parking (€35-€50/day). Restaurant. Room service. TV (DVD on request).*

Expensive

Albergotto

Via de' Tornabuoni 13 (055 2396464/fax 055 2398108/www.albergotto.com). **Rates** €105-€130 single; €150-€180 double. **Credit** AmEx, DC, MC, V. **Map** p318 C2.
This efficiently run, nicely smart little hotel is right in the middle of the smart shopping haven of Via de' Tornabuoni. The style throughout is fairly traditional (parquet floors, floral fabrics), harking back to the days when the hotel hosted such esteemed guests as Giuseppe Verdi and George Eliot, but it's also elegant and unfussy. There's a nice little breakfast room, plus a cosy living room for reading and relaxing. The suite at the top has rustic beams and great rooftop views through huge windows.
Bar. Disabled-adapted rooms. Internet (high-speed). No-smoking rooms. Parking (€27/day). Room service. TV.

Antica Torre Tornabuoni Uno

Via de' Tornabuoni 1 (055 2658161/fax 055 218841/www.tornabuoni1.com). **Rates** €180-€350 double. **Credit** AmEx, DC, MC, V. **Map** p318 C2.
The roof terrace of this 12-room hotel, which occupies the upper storeys of an ancient tower overlooking Piazza Santa Trinità, has arguably the most spectacular view of any hotel in Florence. Breakfast and drinks are served here in summer to a backdrop of just about every monument in the city. In cooler weather, the glassed-in loggia is almost as good. While undeniably comfortable, even luxurious, the bedrooms (several of which have private terraces) are not terribly inspiring, but the views they all enjoy certainly are.
Business centre. Disabled-adapted rooms. Internet (high-speed). No-smoking rooms. Parking (€20-€30/day). TV (DVD).

Beacci Tornabuoni

Via de' Tornabuoni 3 (055 212645/fax 055 283594/www.bthotel.it). **Rates** €120-€180 single; €200-€260 double; €250-€350 suite. **Credit** AmEx, DC, MC, V. **Map** p318 C2.

The Beacci Tornabuoni is situated on the top two floors of the 15th-century Palazzo Minerbetti Strozzi, but though it's located among Via de' Tornabuoni's designer shops and offers all mod cons, it has a delightful Edwardian feel. The wonderful flower-filled roof garden is used for meals in summer; inside, the old parquet floors creak and groan under the weight of the kind of furniture you might normally expect to find at your grandmother's house. The lovely old reading room smells of a mix of floor wax and wood smoke, the latter from a huge old *pietra serena* fireplace. All in all, comfortable and characterful.

Bar. Business centre. Internet (dataport, high-speed shared terminal). No-smoking rooms. Parking (€20-€30/day). Room service (24hrs). TV.

Il Guelfo Bianco

Via Cavour 29 (055 288330/fax 055 295203/ www.ilguelfobianco.it). **Rates** €100-€135 single; €145-€180 double; €190-€265 triple; €200-€285 family; €320-€420 apartment. **Credit** AmEx, MC, V. **Map** p319 A5.

Inhabiting two 15th century townhouses, this pleasant and efficiently run hotel lies just north of the Duomo. The 43 bedrooms and the two-bed self-catering apartment have been decorated in traditional style; the more capacious rooms allow for an additional two beds, making them a good choice for families. The walls throughout are hung with the owner's impressive contemporary art collection. The rooms that front on to Via Cavour have been soundproofed, but those at the back are still noticeably quieter. Two attractive courtyards offer welcome respite from city noise.

Bar. Disabled-adapted rooms. Internet (dataport, high-speed shared terminal). No-smoking rooms. Parking (€24-€30/day). Room service. TV.

Hermitage

Vicolo Marzio 1, Piazza del Pesce (055 287216/ fax 055 212208/www.hermitagehotel.com). **Rates** €154-€221 single; €163-€245 double; €192-€275 triple. **Credit** MC, V. **Map** p318 C3.

One of the city's most popular three-star hotels, the delightful little Hermitage boasts a superb location practically on top of the Ponte Vecchio. The reception and public rooms are on the top floors, with the bedrooms (all comfortable, some rather small) all located on the lower four floors. Jacuzzi baths or showers have been installed in all the rooms and the decor has been jazzed up a bit: the sitting room is now painted avocado green. The rooms at the front have the views, but they can be noisy. In summer, breakfast on the plant-filled roof terrace is a must.

Bar. Disabled-adapted rooms. Internet (dataport, high-speed). No-smoking rooms. Parking (€21-€34/day). Room service. TV.

Relais degli Uffizi

Chiasso del Buco 16, off Chiasso de' Baroncelli (055 2676239/fax 055 2657909/www.relaisuffizi.it). **Rates** €80-€120 single; €140-€180 double; €160-€200 suite. **Credit** AmEx, MC, V. **Map** p319 C4.

There's no helpful sign to guide you through the warren of narrow passageways that leads off the south side of Piazza della Signoria towards this small hotel: take Chiasso de' Baroncelli and go under the stone arch after around 50 metres on the right. Once you get there, make a beeline for the comfortable sitting room, which has a fabulous view over the piazza. The ten bedrooms are situated on two floors and vary in shape and size, but all are tastefully decorated and furnished: pastel colours, a mix of antique and traditional Florentine painted pieces and original features such as boxed ceilings and creaky parquet floors.

Bar. Disabled-adapted rooms. Internet (dataport). No-smoking rooms. Parking (€28/day). Room service. TV.

Residenza d'Epoca in Piazza della Signoria

Via dei Magazzini 2 (055 2399546/www.inpiazza dellasignoria.it). **Rates** €80-€180 single; €140-€220 double; €300-€350 suite; €1,200-€1,400/wk apartment. **Credit** AmEx, DC, MC, V. **Map** p319 C4.

The location couldn't be more central: this upmarket bed and breakfast sits just on the edge of Florence's most famous square, and most of the rooms on the top three floors, all named after notable Florentines, have views of the piazza. Some are a little oblique; for full-on vistas, ask to be housed in Leonardo or Michelangelo. The rooms are furnished in a fairly traditional, unfussy style: antiques, canopied beds (including two wrought-iron four-posters), oriental rugs on wood floors, elegant fabrics and pastel-coloured walls. Breakfast is served at an enormous oval table on the third floor, but if you don't like socialising first thing, you can order it in your room. Hosts Alessandro and Sonia Pini are two further reasons to stay here: the two enjoy their work, and the welcome you'll receive here will be genuinely warm.

Bar. Business centre. Internet (dataport, high-speed shared terminal). No-smoking rooms. Parking (€24-€30/day). Room service. TV.

Moderate

Casci

Via Cavour 13 (055 211686/fax 055 2396461/ www.hotelcasci.com). **Rates** €70-€110 single; €100-€150 double; €130-€190 triple; €160-€230 quad; €180-€260 family room. Closed 3wks Jan. **Credit** AmEx, DC, MC, V. **Map** p319 A4.

The super-helpful Lombardi family runs this friendly pensione, which occupies a 15th-century palazzo just slightly north of the Duomo. The open-plan bar and breakfast room area have frescoed ceilings and shelves stocked with guidebooks; the 25 bedrooms are functional but quite comfortable and come with up-to-date bathrooms. Bedrooms at the back look on to a beautiful garden; two sizeable family rooms sleep up to five.

Bar. Internet (dataport). No-smoking rooms. Parking (€25/day). Room service. TV.

Cestelli

Borgo SS Apostoli 25 (055 214213/www.hotelcestelli. com). **Rates** €40-€50 single; €75-€85 double; €90-€100 suite. **Credit** AmEx, DC, MC, V. **Map** p318 C3.
When a young Italo-Japanese couple took over the old, one-star Cestelli in 2004, they bought into some wonderful old furniture and a great atmosphere but also, frankly, a bit of a dump. Restoration has improved things a great deal in the eight bright bedrooms (all but three have private baths): the mattresses are now orthopaedic and the bathrooms are equipped with fluffy white towels. However, the owners have taken great care not to destroy the old-fashioned feel: a mix of old and new furniture fills the bedrooms, some of which have original parquet floors. There's no breakfast.
Parking (€20/day).

Dei Mori

Via D Alighieri 12 (055 211438/fax 055 2382216/ www.bnb.it/deimori). **Rates** €80-€100 single; €90-€110 double; reduced rates for longer stays. **Credit** AmEx, MC, V. **Map** p319 B4.
If the rapturous comments in the visitors' book are any indication, this friendly guesthouse in the heart of the medieval city must be one of the best places to stay in Florence. The rooms are keenly priced and comfortable: those on the first floor are more traditional, while those upstairs are quite smart and all en suite. The welcome is exceptionally warm: fresh flowers, bright rugs, cheerful paintings and a comfy sitting room complete with a TV, a stereo and lots of books and magazines. There's a terrace from which you can just see the top of the Duomo.
Internet (dataport). No-smoking rooms. Room service. TV room.

Torre Guelfa

Borgo SS Apostoli 8 (055 2396338/fax 055 2398577/www.hoteltorreguelfa.com). **Rates** €100-€120 single; €150-€185 double; €180-€230 suite. **Credit** AmEx, MC, V. **Map** p318 C3.
Popular with the fashion-show crowd, this very pleasant hotel inhabits three floors of an ancient palazzo and boasts the tallest privately owned tower in the city, from which the 360-degree views are stunning. Breakfast is served in a sunny, glassed-in loggia; there's also an elegant sitting room with a painted box ceiling. The bedrooms are decorated in pastel colours with wrought-iron beds (including several four-posters); No.15 has its own roof garden. The six rooms on the first floor are cheaper, simpler, marginally darker and entirely TV-free.
Bar. Disabled-adapted rooms. Internet (dataport). No-smoking rooms. Parking (€25/day). Room service. TV (some rooms).

Budget

Dali

Via dell'Oriuolo 17 (tel/fax 055 2340706/www. hoteldali.com). **Rates** €40 single; €60-€75 double; €80-€95 triple. **Credit** MC, V. **Map** p319 B4.

Run with genuine care by an enthusiastic young couple, this little gem just east of the Duomo offers spotless, bright and homely rooms at budget prices and – a miracle in central Florence – free car parking in the internal courtyard below. Only four of the ten rooms have private bathrooms, but all are thoughtfully decorated and furnished with hand stencilling, pretty bedcovers and old bedheads. Due to the presence of a pub opposite, the rooms at the front can be a bit noisy, but ear plugs are supplied; rooms at the back overlooking the courtyard are sunny and quiet. Breakfast is not provided, but there are electric kettles and fridges in all the rooms.
No-smoking rooms. Parking (free). TV (some rooms).

Scoti

Via de' Tornabuoni 7 (tel/fax 055 292128/www.hotel scoti.com). **Rates** €70 single; €95 double; €120 triple; €145 quad. **Credit** AmEx, DC, MC, V. **Map** p318 B2.
If you want to secure a room in the wonderful Scoti, housed on the second floor of a 15th-century palazzo, book well ahead: it's popular with visitors from all over the world. After extensive renovation a couple of years back, the lofty bedrooms are simple but bright and sunny and all have their own bathrooms; the frescoed salon has retained its airy of faded glory. Australian hostess Doreen and her Italian husband serve breakfast around a big communal table or in the rooms.
Disabled-adapted rooms. No-smoking rooms. TV room.

Santa Maria Novella

Luxury

Grand Hotel

Piazza Ognissanti 1 (055 27161/fax 055 217400/ www.1starwood.com/grandflorence). **Rates** €423-€563 single; €583-€759 double; €2,275-€3,156 suite; €98 supplement for river view; €39 breakfast. **Credit** AmEx, DC, MC, V. **Map** p318 B1.
While its rooms are no less luxurious than those at its sister hotel across the piazza, the Grand is decidedly different in character to the Westin Excelsior (*see p55*). The reception area is light and airy, while the vast hall, with its stained-glass ceiling, marble floor and *pietra serena* columns, offers old-fashioned opulence; within it are a restaurant, a salon and a piano bar. Less oppressive is new eaterie InCanto, which serves a modern take on Tuscan food in a contemporary setting. Roughly half of the 107 bedrooms and suites are done up in faux-Renaissance Florentine style, complete with frescoes, painted ceilings and heavy traditional fabrics. Humans are greeted warmly, but even furry friends are treated well: if your roommate is canine, you'll be given a dogs' 'welcome kit'.
Bar. Business centre. Concierge. Disabled-adapted rooms. Gym. Internet (dataport, high-speed, wireless in public areas). No-smoking rooms. Parking (€42-€55/day). Restaurants (2). Room service. TV (DVD, pay movies).

Where to Stay

Hotel Santa Maria Novella

*Piazza Santa Maria Novella 1 (055 271840/fax
055 27184199/www.hotelsantamarianovella.it).*
Rates €135-€260 single; €190-€315 double;
€227-€450 suite. **Credit** AmEx, DC, MC, V.
Map p318 B2.
Owned by clothing manufacturer Rifle, this 38-room
hotel is due to double in size by 2006 or 2007. The
property is done out in fairly elaborate Empire style,
with rich colours, painted wood panelling and fancy
marquetry, but contemporary decorative touches
mean it never feels too oppressive. Two cosy sitting
rooms on the ground floor have open fires, velvet
sofas and armchairs, plus original oil paintings on
the walls. The bedrooms, kitted out in bright colours
with modern, country fabrics, come with canopied
beds, silk curtains and plasma-screen TVs; the
grand marble bathrooms are equipped with Santa
Maria Novella goodies. The breakfast room is a
symphony of mirrors, but there's also an intimate
little wood-panelled bar on the ground floor and a
panoramic roof terrace bar at the top.
*Bar. Disabled-adapted rooms. Gym. Internet
(dataport, high-speed). No-smoking rooms. Parking
(€27-€32/day). TV.*

Westin Excelsior

*Piazza Ognissanti 3 (055 27151/fax 055 210278/
www.westin.com/excelsiorflorence).* **Rates** €411-
€543 single; €568-€732 double; €1,900-€4,106 suite;
€98 supplement for river view; €39 breakfast.
Credit AmEx, DC, MC, V. **Map** p318 B1.
While it still offers an element of old-world luxury,
the Westin Excelsior has recently introduced some
contemporary touches to keep pace with the
21st century. There's now a fitness suite, plus two
'wellness' rooms that have been equipped for the
health-conscious guest (yoghurt drinks in the
minibar, a kettle and tisanes, a massage chair, New
Age music on the sound system, even a choice of
pillow types). In addition, the restaurant now offers
a special menu of low-cal dishes. All this, however,
exists within a very traditional framework: the
doormen are dressed in green livery, and the grand
public rooms have polished marble floors, neo-
classical columns, painted wooden ceilings and
stained glass. The 168 rooms and suites are sump-
tuously appointed; some boast terraces with views
over the river to the rooftops of the Oltrarno. Popular
with upmarket tour groups.
*Bar. Business centre. Concierge. Disabled-adapted
rooms. Gym. Internet (dataport, high-speed, wireless
in public areas). No-smoking rooms. Parking (€42-
€55/day). Restaurants (2). Room service. TV (pay
movies, DVD in suites).*

Expensive

Casa Howard

*Via della Scala 18 (06 69924555/fax 06 6794644/
www.casahoward.com).* **Rates** €100-€150 single;
€160-€230 double; €500-€600 suite; €15 breakfast.
Credit AmEx, DC, MC, V. **Map** p318 B2.

The owner of this stylish pied-à-terre sets out to offer
comfortable, upmarket accommodation at reasonable rates in the discreet atmosphere of a handsome
mansion. The 12 rooms are classy and vaguely
eccentric, decorated with strong colours and a mix
of antique and custom-made furniture. Check online
to choose the one you like best: the big, dramatic
Drawing Room, perhaps, or maybe the Black and
White Room, in which a blown-up reproduction of
Monet's *Olympus* covers one wall. Bathrooms are
similarly quirky but well-equipped, and come with
Santa Maria Novella smellies. There's even a
Turkish bath on site, should you have overdone it
on the sightseeing. Bookings are made through the
original Rome branch (contact details above).
*Internet (dataport, high-speed, wireless in public
areas). No-smoking room (1). Parking (€20-€35/
day). TV.*

Grand Hotel Minerva

*Piazza Santa Maria Novella 16 (055 27230/fax
055 26828/www.grandhotelminerva.com).* **Rates**
€189-€270 single; €246-€351 double; €420-€600
suite. **Credit** AmEx, DC, MC, V. **Map** p318 B2.
Once an annexe hosting guests to the adjacent convent, the Minerva has been a hotel since the mid 19th
century. However, the interior was revamped in the
mid 1990s in bright, modern colours; today it's
staffed by a young, dynamic team, and is one of the
nicest hotels in this category that's close to the train
station. Many of the appealing rooms have sunny
views over Piazza Santa Maria Novella (it can get
noisy in summer), while extras include in-room
electric kettles (surprisingly rare in Florence hotels),
a kids' package of videos and games and an in-house
shiatsu masseuse. There's a small pool and a bar on
the panoramic roof garden; the Veranda restaurant
has a terrace on the piazza in summer.
*Bar. Disabled-adapted rooms. Internet (dataport,
high-speed shared terminal). No-smoking rooms.
Parking (€27-€31/day). Pool (outdoor). Restaurant.
Room service. TV.*

JK Place

*Piazza Santa Maria Novella 7 (055 2645181/fax
055 2658387/www.jkplace.com).* **Rates** €255-€285
single; €285-€315 double; €500-€650 suite. **Credit**
AmEx, DC, MC, V. **Map** p318 B2.
This ultra-sophisticated, 20-room hotel is set in an
attractive old town house on Piazza Santa Maria
Novella. The architect/designer is Michele Bonan of
Continentale (*see p51*) and Gallery (*see p49*) fame,
but this property is a little different from her others,
and not just in terms of its diminutive size. The style
is a contemporary take on a neo-classical look:
muted colours beautifully offset fine antiques, old
prints, black-and-white photos and artful flower
arrangements. No two bedrooms look alike: several
of the larger ones overlook the piazza; others are
smaller and don't have views. However, all are
luxurious and lack nothing in the way of facilities.
The bathroom in the top-floor penthouse suite has a
spectacular view; there's also a roof terrace. The

sleek, chic Lounge serves anything from light lunches to cocktails and a full dinner menu (*see p123* **Hotel cuisine**), while the groovy downstairs bar – bright white bathed in fluorescent light – is also worth a look (*see p181* **Designs for (night)life**). *Disabled-adapted rooms. Internet (dataport, high-speed, wireless in public areas). No-smoking rooms. TV (DVD).*

Palazzo del Borgo

Via della Scala 6 (055 216237/289147/fax 055 280947/www.hotelaprile.it). **Rates** €80-€120 single; €120-€180 double; €180-230 triple; €180-€215 suite. **Credit** AmEx, MC, V. **Map** p318 B2.

The three-star Hotel Aprile recently became the four-star Palazzo del Borgo, but happily lost none of its old-world Florentine character in the process. Housed in an ancient palazzo and handily located for the station, it has a comfortable, old-fashioned feel in spite of the recent renovations. The bedrooms vary hugely: some feature frescoes or scraps of 15th-century graffiti, while others have elaborate stucco work. Rooms at the back have superb views over the convent of Santa Maria Novella, and there's a pretty courtyard garden scented with jasmine. Thoughtful extras include free lectures on Florentine art and history in English.
Bar. Disabled-adapted rooms. Internet (dataport, high-speed shared terminal). Parking (€24/day). Room service. TV.

Budget

Abaco

Via dei Banchi 1 (055 2381919/fax 055 282289/ www.abaco-hotel.it). **Rates** €65-€75 double; €5 breakfast. **Credit** AmEx, MC, V. **Map** p318 B2.

There's a bit of a climb up to the second floor of this 550-year-old building; once you've made it, you'll find a modest shell housing a handsome hotel. The friendly owner has painstakingly decorated the place in grand style: the seven bedrooms, each named after a Renaissance artist, are decorated in sumptuous fabrics with reproductions of works by the relevant painter on the walls. Gilding adorns the picture and mirror frames, and most of the beds are canopied. Three rooms have their own full bathrooms, while others have only a shower. Breakfast is free if you pay in cash; there's a further 10% discount in winter.
Bar. Internet (dataport, high-speed shared terminal). No-smoking rooms. Parking (€24/day). TV.

Locanda degli Artisti

Via Faenza 56 (055 213806/www.hotelazzi.it). **Rates** €50-€70 single; €80-€110 double; €90-€130 suite. **Credit** AmEx, MC, V. **Map** p318 A3.

Housed on the first two floors of a rambling old palazzo near the station, the Locanda degli Artisti is an interesting and comfortable little hotel with good prices. The big reception area has a retro vibe; you'll probably be greeted by classical music or jazz on the sound system. Eco-friendly materials and natural colours have been used in the decoration of the bright, sunny bedrooms, and organic produce is served at breakfast. The lovely terrace is great for post-sightseeing relaxation. There's talk that the hotel might begin to host art shows and live music: call or check online for details.
Bar. Disabled-adapted rooms. Internet (dataport, high-speed in suites). No-smoking rooms. Parking (€15/day). TV.

San Lorenzo

Moderate

Relais Grand Tour

Via Santa Reparata 21 (055 283955/fax 055 2676505/www.florencegrandtour.com). **Rates** €87-€95 single; €93-€115 double. **No credit cards.**

The restoration of this 16th-century house and its subsequent transformation into a delightful B&B was a labour of love for owners Cristina and Giuseppe, and it shows. If it seems like the pair treat guests as visitors to their own home, there's a good reason: it is. The couple live on the first floor, where there are three pretty bedrooms; below, on the ground floor, are five quite luxurious (and more expensive) 'suites'. The Mirrors Suite is much loved by honeymooners, while the extraordinary Theatre Suite occupies an authentic private playhouse complete with stage (on which the bed sits) and several rows of seats. Throughout, the bedrooms and bathrooms are done out with carefully chosen antiques, old majolica tiles, pictures and curios. Breakfast is served only in the rooms on the first floor.
Internet (dataport, high-speed in suites, shared terminal). No-smoking rooms. Parking (€23-€27/day). TV (on request).

San Marco

Expensive

Loggiato dei Serviti

Piazza SS Annunziata 3 (055 289592/fax 055 289595/www.loggiatodeiservitihotel.it). **Rates** €90-€140 single; €170-€205 double; €384 suite. **Credit** AmEx, DC, MC, V. **Map** p318 A5.

Housed in a 16th-century convent building, which looks across lovely Piazza SS Annunziata to Brunelleschi's famous portico, this is one of the nicest three-star hotels in Florence. Inside is a tasteful and stylish combination of original architectural features, wonderful antique furniture and the modern comforts of an upmarket hotel. The 48 bedrooms, five of which are housed in an annexe in Via dei Servi, vary in size and style; the four suites are ideal for families. Breakfast is served in a bright, elegant room with vaulted ceilings, while drinks can be ordered in the cosy bar area.
Bar. Disabled-adapted rooms. Internet (dataport). No-smoking rooms. Parking (€24-€30/day). Room service. TV.

When is a hotel not a hotel?

You may find yourself confused about the names given to various categories of accommodation in Florence and Tuscany. Rules about this are established on a regional level, so they vary to some degree throughout Italy.

In Florence, to be officially classed as a hotel (and therefore be subject to a star classification), you must have seven or more rooms. To qualify as an *affittacamere* (literally 'rooms for rent'), you can have no more than six rooms. Some are basically private houses with a couple of rooms for rent (unlike in the UK, most owners don't live on site), while others are, to all intents and purposes, small hotels. Some more upmarket *affittacamere* are now allowed to class themselves as bed and breakfasts. *Residenza d'epoca* is the term used for a listed building with no more than 12 rooms, while to call yourself a residence you must have a minimum of seven self-catering units. To add to the confusion, a number of establishments adopt certain names because they sound nice, but they may officially be classified as something else. There are 'B&Bs' in Florence, for example, that don't actually serve breakfast.

In practice, though, these rules and regulations don't really affect the average traveller – all you need to know is that you don't have to stick to regular hotels if you want something with a bit more character. Our favourites include **Casa Howard** (*see p55*), **Residenza d'Epoca in Piazza della Signoria** (*see p53*), **Le Stanze di Santa Croce** (*see p59*), **Residenza Santo Spirito** (*see p61*), **Villa Poggio San Felice** (*see p63*), **B&B Borgo Pinti** (*see p60*) and **Johlea Uno & Johlea Due** (*see p59*). For shorter-term self-catering options, try **Residence Hilda** (*see below*) or the more luxurious **Lungarno Suites** (*see p51*). In addition to these, there are dozens of others listed in the tourist board's annual accommodation booklet (*see p49*).

Casa Howard.

Residence Hilda

Via dei Servi 40 (055 288021/www.residencehilda.it). **Rates** €195-€306 apartment. **Credit** AmEx DC, MC, V. **Map** p319 A4.

Boasting a prime location just five minutes' walk north of the Duomo, Residence Hilda opened in mid 2005, offering self-catering accommodation. All of the cool, super-modern apartments come with well-equipped kitchen units that can be hidden away behind sliding doors when required. The furnishings throughout the apartments are stylishly spare, with Philippe Starck chairs and other modern classics sitting on blond wood floors. If you're feeling lazy, you can even get the staff to deliver your shopping.

Internet (dataport, high-speed, shared terminal). No-smoking rooms. Parking (€24-€30/day). TV (satellite).

Moderate

Antica Dimora Firenze

Via San Gallo 72n (055 4627296/fax 055 4635450/ www.anticadimorafirenze.it). **Rates** €125-€150 double. **No credit cards.** **Map** p319 A4.

The duo behind the wonderful Residenzas Johlea (*see p59*) have recently added this more upmarket property to their portfolio of small, charming, value-for-money guesthouses. The location is a good one: near Piazza San Marco and just ten minutes' walk north of the Duomo, but away from the worst of the tourist hordes. The six light and airy bedrooms, two of which have four-posters, are all based on different pastel colour schemes, and have been thoughtfully decorated using beautiful fabrics, antiques, oriental rugs and traditional tiled floors.

One room has a private terrace with rooftop views. Breakfast is served in the sitting room, where there are also several coffee-table books that guests are welcome to browse. You can also choose DVDs to watch in your room.
Internet (dataport, high-speed, wireless). Parking (€18/day). TV (DVD).

Hotel delle Arti

Via dei Servi 38A (055 2678553/fax 055 290140/ www.hoteldellearti.it). **Rates** €113-€139 single; €144-€185 double; €180-€215 triple. **Credit** AmEx, DC, MC, V. **Map** p319 A4.

Under the same ownership as the Loggiato dei Serviti (*see p56*), the Hotel delle Arti is done out with just as much taste and style, but it's a simpler property with more of a country look. The nine bedrooms have wooden floors and are painted in restful shades of green and cream; the furniture is mainly made up of pine or wicker pieces, including a couple of four-poster beds, and the upholstery includes some unfussy checked fabrics. The three corner rooms are particularly spacious and light. The pretty breakfast room has an attractive wraparound terrace.
Bar. Disabled-adapted rooms. Internet (dataport, high-speed). No-smoking rooms. Parking (€24-€30/day). Room service. TV.

Morandi alla Crocetta

Via Laura 50 (055 2344747/fax 055 2480954/ www.hotelmorandi.it). **Rates** €115-€140 single; €177-€220 double; €220-€295 triple; €11 breakfast. **Credit** AmEx, DC, MC, V. **Map** p319 A5.

Book well in advance for a bed in this quiet, ten-room hotel, housed in a former 16th-century convent in the university area, especially if you want to stay in one of operation's two rooms with a private terrace. Each room is different from the next, but all are comfortable and reasonably priced. There are antiques, oriental rugs and interesting pictures throughout the place.
Bar. Internet (dataport, high-speed). No-smoking rooms. Parking (€16/day). Room service. TV.

Relais Santa Croce

Via Ghibellina 87 (055 2342230/fax 055 2341195/ www.relaisantacroce.com). **Rates** €195-€245 double for single occupancy; €295-€385 double; €465-€1,150 suite. **Credit** AmEx, DC, MC, V. **Map** p319 C5.

This new hotel offers contemporary style in the shell of a grand, 18th-century palazzo. The public rooms on the first floor are suitably grandiose – especially the vast music room, with its lofty, frescoed ceilings, original creaky parquet floors and stucco panels. The bedrooms on the upper floors, meanwhile, have clean, modern lines with quirky design details (check the amazing collection of light fittings). The rear-facing rooms on the upper floors have views over a jumble of red-tiled rooftops to the façade of the Santa Croce church. The hotel shares its entrance with one of Italy's most celebrated restaurants, the Enoteca Pinchiorri (*see p121*).

Bar. Business centre. Concierge. Disabled-adapted rooms. Internet (dataport, high-speed). No-smoking rooms. Parking (€30/day). Restaurant. Room service. TV (pay movies).

Residenza Johlea Uno & Johlea Due

Via San Gallo 76 & 80 (055 4633292/fax 055 4634552/www.johanna.it). **Rates** €70-€85 single; €95-€115 double. **No credit cards**. **Map** p319 A4.

This mini-chain of what are essentially B&Bs now contains five properties, all striving to achieve high standards at manageable prices. It's an aim that's achieved in admirable fashion at Johlea Uno and Johlea Due: housed in former private apartments two doors apart on the same street, just a ten-minute walk from the Duomo, they share the same phone numbers and booking desk. The standards of comfort and service are similar to those of a three-star hotel: the rooms are decorated in soft pastel colours, furnished partly with antiques and boasting excellent bathrooms. Johlea Uno has a cosy upstairs sitting room with an 'honesty fridge' and a roof terrace.
Internet (dataport). Parking (€18/day). TV.

Le Stanze di Santa Croce

Via delle Pinzochere 6 (055 2001366/www.via pinzochere6.it). **Rates** €130 single; €160 double. **Credit** MC, V. **Map** p319 C5.

JK Place. See p55.

The location of this sweet little three-floor town-house couldn't be better, but you could say the same about the welcoming interior. The four comfortable double bedrooms have been individually furnished with pretty fabrics, lively colours and a mix of old and new furniture; one has a romantic wrought-iron four-poster. Breakfast is served on a lovely flower-filled terrace where guests can hang out all day and help themselves from a well-stocked 'honesty fridge'. Mariangela, the owner, is so good in the kitchen that she even offers cooking courses. A fresh, appealing example of exactly how a B&B should be run. *Internet (dataport). No-smoking rooms. Parking (€18-€24/day).*

Budget

B&B Borgo Pinti
Borgo Pinti 31 (055 2480056/fax 055 2347226/www.bnb.it/beb). **Rates** €40-€45 single; €70-€78 double. **Credit** MC, V. **Map** p319 A6.
Prices continue to be amazingly low at this tiny women-only guesthouse on Borgo Pinti, a simple but stylish retreat from the city heat and dust. The four rooms, located on the top floor of a palazzo and decorated in cool whites and blues, are all airy and quiet, with views over an internal garden and surrounding rooftops. The two communal bath-rooms are spotless. When the sun's up, help yourself to breakfast in the kitchen. *No-smoking rooms.*

Bavaria
Borgo degli Albizi 26 (tel/fax 055 2340313/www.hotelbavariafirenze.it). **Rates** €40-€50 single; €60-€98 double. **Credit** AmEx, MC, V. **Map** p319 B4/5.
Enjoying a marvellously central location, the recently renovated one-star Bavaria occupies the second floor of the grand 16th-century Ramirez Montalvo, the decorated façade of which is attributed to Vasari. The interior is simple and unpretentious but not without style, with fabulous box wood ceilings, sand-coloured walls, terracotta floor tiles and some nice old furniture. Only three rooms have private baths. *No-smoking rooms.*

Hotel Orchidea
Borgo degli Albizi 11 (tel/fax 055 2480346/www.hotelorchideaflorence.it). **Rates** €35-€55 single; €50-€75 double; €75-€100 triple. **No credit cards.** **Map** p318 B5.
Dante's muse Beatrice was born in the 12th-century palazzo that houses the simple, cosy Orchidea. The best of the seven modest but bright and clean rooms overlooks a wonderful overgrown garden. All the rooms are done out in dusty pink and white; only one room has a shower (and no toilet), but all have wash basins and share two communal bathrooms. A pair of rooms on the upper floor, which have their own private bathroom, are good for families or friends sharing.

Luxury

Lungarno
Borgo San Jacopo 14 (055 27261/fax 055 268437/www.lungarnohotels.com). **Rates** €198-€242 single; €297-€385 double; €616-€792 suite. **Credit** AmEx, DC, MC, V. **Map** p318 C3.
The most coveted rooms in this stylish hotel, located in the smart part of the Oltrarno and housed in a 1960s building that incorporates a medieval tower, have terraces overlooking the Arno. However, even if you can't secure a river view, you can enjoy the waterside setting from the breakfast room and lounge/bar, or the outside seating area on the river. More classic in feel than other Ferragamo-owned hotels such as the Gallery Hotel Art (*see p49*) and the Continentale (*see p51*), the Lungarno has been decorated in a cream and navy blue colour scheme, but some lovely mahogany and cherry antique furniture, plus a collection of fine prints, lends a reassuringly traditional touch. Bedrooms are stylish and comfy but, with the exception of a couple of spacious suites, not that big. The Borgo San Jacopo restaurant (*see p123* **Hotel cuisine**) serves excellent food in a calm and elegant setting. *Bar. Disabled-adapted rooms. Internet (dataport). No-smoking rooms. Parking (€35/day). Restaurant. Room service. TV (pay TV).*

Palazzo Magnani Feroni
Borgo San Frediano 5 (055 2399544/fax 055 608908/www.florencepalace.it). **Rates** €210-€750 suite. **Credit** AmEx, DC, MC, V. **Map** p318 C1.
Expect top-class service and facilities at this elegant, grand palazzo just south of the river, with prices to match. The 12 big suites all have separate sitting rooms furnished with squashy sofas, armchairs and antiques. However, the most charming room of all is actually the smallest: a romantic junior suite with floor-to-ceiling frescoes and a little private garden. The bathrooms are super-smart and equipped with slippers, robes and heated towel rails: you can even choose the smell of your soap. The fabulous roof terrace offers views of the whole city. *Bar. Concierge. Gym. Internet (dataport). No-smoking rooms. Parking (€40-€47/day). Room service. TV (DVD).*

Moderate

Annalena
Via Romana 34 (055 222439/fax 055 222403/www.hotelannalena.it). **Rates** €80-€114 single; €95-€166 double; €120-€200 triple. **Credit** AmEx, DC, MC, V. **Map** p318 D1.
The Annalena is housed in a 15th-century building that, at various points in its history, has been used as a refuge for young widows and lodgings for refugees from Mussolini's Fascist police. Today's guests are less desperate, though the hotel retains a

Abaco.
See p56.

link to its past by dint of its pleasantly old-fashioned atmosphere. The huge salon serves as lounge, bar and breakfast room, while the comfortable bedrooms, some of which are very spacious, are furnished mostly with antiques; the best have balconies overlooking the gorgeous gardens.
Bar. Room service. TV.

Hotel Boboli

Via Romana 63 (055 2298645/fax 055 2337169/ www.hotelboboli.com). **Rates** €50-€105 double for single occupancy; €80-€130 double. **Credit** MC, V. **Map** p318 D1.
Although the long-awaited lift has not been put in place (the management hopes to remedy this some time in 2006), this perfectly adequate little hotel near the Boboli Gardens is gradually being spruced up and offers good-value lodgings. The public space on the ground floor has been expanded, and air-conditioning is due to be installed throughout the building. About half the 21 pleasant rooms overlook an interior courtyard and are very quiet; others have views on to the Boboli Gardens or noisy Via Romana. The bathrooms, some of which are tiny,

could do with an update, but that's also on the cards. The sunniest rooms are on the fourth floor, but for now, reaching them requires a steep climb.
Bar. Internet (dataport). TV.

Residenza Santo Spirito

Piazza Santo Spirito 9 (055 2658376/www. residenzasspirito.com). **Rates** €110-€130 double; €180-€210 quad. **Credit** MC, V. **Map** p318 D1.
Housed in the Renaissance palazzo Guardagni, the small Residenza Santo Spirito has three huge rooms furnished largely with antiques. The two doubles have delicately frescoed ceilings and French windows, which give great views over the goings-on in one of Florence's loveliest – and liveliest – squares. The third room sleeps four in two separate rooms and looks on to an internal court-yard. Breakfast is served in the rooms.
No-smoking rooms. Parking (€15-€24/day). TV.

La Scaletta

Via de' Guicciardini 13 (055 283028/214255/fax 055 289562/www.lascaletta.com). **Rates** €65-€90 single; €85-€140 double; €100-€160 triple; €115-€180 quad. **Credit** MC, V. **Map** p318 D3.

Antica Dimora Firenze. *See p57.*

A change of management has offered a new lease of life to the formerly run-down Scaletta, housed in a grand 15th-century palazzo between the Ponte Vecchio and Palazzo Pitti. It's still a two-star spot, but the dreary colours and mishmash of furniture have been swept aside in favour of cleaner – even stylish – lines. The 16 buttermilk-painted bedrooms now have elegant matching curtains and bedspreads, modern wrought-iron bedheads and nice old wardrobes; most are quiet (three overlook the Boboli Gardens), with those on noisy Via Guicciardini boasting double glazing, and two have external bathrooms. The star turns are the two roof gardens, which have breathtaking views of Boboli and the city skyline.
Bar. No-smoking rooms. TV.

Budget

Istituto Gould

Via dei Serragli 49 (055 212576/fax 055 280274).
Open *Office* 8.45am-1pm, 3-7.30pm Mon-Fri; 9am-1.30pm, 2.30-6pm Sat. **Rates** €36-€41 single; €50-€58 double; €63-€72 triple; €84-€92 quad. **Credit** MC, V. **Map** p318 C1.
Run by the Valdese Church, Istituto Gould offers excellent budget accommodation in a well-kept 17th-century palazzo with a serene courtyard, stone staircases, terracotta floors, a tantalisingly lovely garden (unfortunately, not accessible to guests) and lots of atmosphere. There are now some 40 rooms on site: two-thirds are doubles, while the others accommodate a maximum of four. There are plans to add bathrooms to the six rooms that don't already have en suite facilities. If you want to avoid noisy Via dei Serragli, ask for a room at the back; some have access to a terrace. You need to check in during office hours, but once that's done, you get your own key.
No-smoking hotel.

Pensionato Pio X

Via dei Serragli 106 (055 225044/www.hostelpiox.it).
Rates €19 single; €17-€19/person double/triple/quad/quin. **No credit cards. Map** p318 D1.
This Church-owned *pensione*, housed in a 13th-century former convent, is a quiet, pleasant alternative to a youth hostel. The two singles offer amazing value, but most of the rooms contain three or four beds. There's a cheerful sitting room, plus a dining room in which guests are welcome to eat their own food. Only two rooms have private bathrooms (for these you pay the higher rate), but the communal showers are spotless. There's a midnight curfew, but, unlike most hostels, the place is open all day. The minimum stay is two nights, the maximum five.
No-smoking hotel.

Outside the City Gates

Luxury

Villa La Massa

Via della Massa 24 (055 62611/fax 055 633102/ www.villalamassa.it). Complimentary shuttle bus to/ from city centre. **Rates** €210-€260 single; €410-€470 double; €620-€710 suite. **Credit** AmEx, DC, MC, V.
Occupying a mellow Renaissance villa, this luxurious hotel enjoys an exquisite setting on the south bank of the Arno to the east of Florence. Several years ago it was acquired by the proprietors of the legendary Villa d'Este, the luxurious hotel on the shores of Lake Como in northern Italy; a complete and costly overhaul followed. The style is upmarket Tuscan: four-poster beds, antiques, frescoes, opulent fabrics and splendid bathrooms. In warm weather, guests get to dine on a beautiful terrace overlooking the River Arno at the elegant Verrocchio restaurant, which serves appropriately top-class food. Recent additions to the facilities include a fitness centre and a treatment room for massages and other necessary indulgences. There's a complimentary shuttle from Ponte Vecchio, though, not surprisingly, the celebrities who regularly stay here tend to have their means of own transport.
Bar. Business centre. Concierge. Disabled-adapted rooms. Gym. Internet (dataport). No-smoking rooms. Parking (free). Pool (outdoor). Restaurant. Room service. TV (pay movies).

Villa San Michele

Via Doccia 4 (055 5678200/fax 055 5678250/ www.villasanmichele.com). Bus 7. **Rates** €680 single; €892 double; €1,258-€2,629 suite. Closed late Nov-late Mar. **Credit** AmEx, DC, MC, V.
The rooms in this fabulous yet understated hotel, much beloved on the celebrity circuit, are among the most expensive in Italy. Housed in a 15th-century monastery, Villa San Michele enjoys a genuinely superb location, nestled in a beautiful terraced garden on the hillside just below Fiesole. Understated elegance and good taste, combined with subtle nods to the past, inform the style, which is always luxurious but never ostentatious. The views down to the city are splendid: dinner under the loggia at sunset is an unforgettable experience, though the bill will be too. Service throughout the property is immaculate.
Bar. Business centre. Concierge. Gym. Internet (dataport, high-speed). No-smoking rooms. Parking (free). Pool (outdoor). Restaurant. Room service. TV (DVD, pay movies).

Expensive

Relais Marignolle

Via di San Quirichino a Marignolle 16 (055 2286910/fax 055 2047396/www.marignolle.com). No bus. **Rates** €130-€225 double; €275-€345 suite. **Credit** AmEx, MC, V.

Set in rambling grounds on a south-facing hillside at Marignolle (a couple of miles south of Porta Romana), the Bulleri family's classily converted farmhouse is a great base from which to make the most of elegant country living while keeping the city sights within range. Sun pours into the large, bright living room, where comfortable armchairs and sofas, an open fire and an honesty bar encourage lingering. Breakfast is served on a veranda, open in summer and glassed in for colder weather. The seven bedrooms vary in shape and size, but all are decorated along the same tasteful lines: stylish country fabrics, padded bedheads, pristine white paintwork and dark parquet floors. Signora Bulleri serves light meals on request and holds cooking classes. The attractive pool is another nice perk.
Internet (dataport, high-speed shared terminal). No-smoking rooms. Parking (free). Pool (outdoor). Room service. TV.

Villa Poggio San Felice

Via San Matteo in Arcetri 24 (055 220016/ fax 055 2335388/www.villapoggiosanfelice.com). Complimentary shuttle bus to/from city centre. **Rates** €150 single; €200 double; €250 suite. **Credit** AmEx, DC, MC, V.
The hills immediately surrounding Florence are dotted with elegant old houses, of which the 15th-century Villa Poggio San Felice is a prime example. Set in a beautiful, rose-filled garden with a small pool and views of the city, it was rescued from decay by the descendants of a Swiss hotel magnate, who were careful not to spoil it with heavy-handed over-restoration. There are five guest bedrooms; one of them, La Camera dei Nonni, has a big terrace overlooking the city. All in all, it offers peace, quiet and the atmosphere of a cultured private home a ten-minute drive from downtown Florence.
Bar. Concierge. Gym. Internet (dataport). No-smoking rooms. Parking (free). Pool (outdoor). Room service. TV room.

Moderate

Classic Hotel

Viale N Machiavelli 25 (055 229351/fax 055 229353/www.classichotel.it). Bus 11, 36, 37 to Porta Romana. **Rates** €108-€118 single; €156-€166 double; €216 suite. **Credit** AmEx, MC, V.
If you want the convenience of being able to walk into town (or catch a bus), but also like the idea of staying amid a little bit of green, try the very civilised Classic Hotel. Set in a lush garden just five minutes' walk south-west of the old city walls at Porta Romana, this attractive villa has been tastefully refurbished. Breakfast is served either in a basement room or, more pleasantly, in a conservatory leading to a garden full of mature trees and shrubs. Romantics should consider booking the annexe suite with its own terrace, tucked away in a corner of the garden.
Bar. Concierge. Internet (dataport). No-smoking rooms. Parking (free). Room service. TV.

Pensione Bencistà

Via Benedetto di Maiano 4, Fiesole (tel/fax 055 59163/www.bencista.com). Bus 7. **Rates** €76.50-€85 single; €135-€150 double. **Credit** MC, V.

The characterful old Bencistà has taken a few halting steps towards the 21st century in the last couple of years, but it's not taken so many as to destroy the delightful old-world atmosphere of the place. A lift has been installed, all 40 rooms now have bathrooms, credit cards are now accepted and there's even a website (in both Italian and English). Housed in a former convent and run as a *pensione* by the Simoni family since 1925, it has a fabulous setting on the hillside just below Fiesole. Rooms are furnished with antiques; one has a fireplace and shelves stuffed with old books. Bedrooms are off a warren of passageways and staircases. No two are alike – those at the front enjoy unrivalled city views as does the flower-filled terrace. Another improvement: the rather tedious obligatory half-board rule has been lifted.

Bar. Internet (high-speed shared terminal). No-smoking rooms. Parking (free). Restaurant. Room service. TV room.

Hostels

Hostel Archi Rossi

Via Faenza 94r, Santa Maria Novella (055 290804/ fax 055 2302601/www.hostelarchirossi.com). **Open** 6.30am-2am daily. **Rates** €18-€25/person in dormitory. **Credit** MC, V. **Map** p318 A2/3.

The reception of this hostel is covered with garish modern renditions of famous frescoes, all done by guests. The maximum number of beds in the spacious, light rooms is nine, but many are smaller and some have private bathrooms. Being only ten minutes' walk from the station, it's a good choice for early departures or late arrivals. A new floor with 40 beds arranged in rooms sleeping from three to eight is due to open in late 2005. The management allows mixed-sex rooms as long as everyone knows each other. Facilities for the disabled are unusually good, and there's a lovely garden. Dinner is available for a small extra charge.

Bar. Disabled-adapted rooms. No-smoking hostel. Internet (shared terminal). TV room.

Ostello per la Gioventù

Viale A Righi 2-4, Outside the City Gates (055 601451/fax 055 610300/www.iyhf.org). Bus 17A, 17B. **Rates** €16-€17/person in dormitory; €46-€57 bungalow; €66-€70 family room. **Credit** AmEx, MC, V.

If you visit Florence during the torrid summer, head for the hills and this YHA youth hostel, which lies just below Fiesole. It may be some way from the action, but its location, in the impressive (if crumbling) Villa Camerata setting, with a loggia and ranks of lemon trees in its extensive grounds, will keep you cool. Most beds are in dorms, but also available are rooms for families, bungalows sleeping two people and camping facilities. There's a

midnight curfew. You have to be a member of the YHA to join, but if you aren't one already, you can join on the spot for an extra €3 a day.

Bar. Disabled-adapted rooms. Internet (high-speed shared terminal). No-smoking hostel. Restaurant. TV room.

Campsites

Camping Michelangelo

Viale Michelangelo 80, Outside the City Gates (055 6811977). Bus 12, 13. **Open** *Office* 7am-midnight daily. **Rates** €9.50/person; €4.60 concessions; free under-4s; €6 tent; €30.20 house tent; €12 camper van. **Credit** MC, V (minimum €100).

Situated just below Piazzale Michelangelo, this campsite has spectacular views of the city, but it's also just a short walk from the centre of town. There's room on site for 240 tents and caravans, allowing for a maximum capacity of about 950 people. A recent addition are the 150 'house tents', with proper beds for two. There's a bar, a restaurant and a supermarket, but thanks to a disco that stays open until the wee hours, it's also noisy in summer.

Bar. Restaurant.

Camping Panoramico

Via Peramondo 1, Outside the City Gates (055 599069/fax 055 59186/www.florencecamping.com). Bus 7. **Open** *Office* 8am-10pm daily. **Rates** €10-€10.50/person; €15-€15.75 tent; €15-€15.75 camper van. **Credit** AmEx, MC, V (minimum €52).

This 120-pitch site is the most picturesque site within easy reach of Florence (it's about five miles north of the city centre). In addition to the pitches, 21 self-catering bungalows accommodate up to four people, and there are also some caravans to rent. Facilities include a bar, a restaurant, a supermarket and a pool. It gets packed in summer.

Bar. Disabled-adapted bathrooms. Internet (high-speed shared terminal). Pool (outdoor). Restaurant. TV room.

Long-term accommodation

Renting a flat through an agency inevitably involves commission charges, and the minimum stay is usually a week. If you want to avoid these charges, look in the local press – or in the holiday sections of UK newspapers – and phone around to compare prices. The following firms both have English-speaking staff.

Florence & Abroad

Via San Zanobi 58, San Lorenzo (055 487004/ fax 055 490143/www.florenceandabroad.com). **Open** 10am-5pm Mon-Fri. **No credit cards.**

Milligan & Milligan Rentals

Via degli Alfani 68, San Marco (055 268256/fax 055 268260/www.italy-rentals.com). **Open** 9am-noon, 1-4pm Mon-Fri. **No credit cards. Map** p319 A4.

M&M specialises in student-type accommodation and short-term rentals for tourists.

Sightseeing

Introduction

So much to see – where to start?

Sightseeing

See the city with those who know it – **Walking Tours of Florence**. *See p68*.

If you visit Florence in search of art, you certainly don't need to go out of your way to find it. Simply stand still, virtually anywhere in the city, and open your eyes. More than being home to some of the world's greatest galleries and museums, Florence the city *is* one enormous museum and gallery, with more art treasures per square metre than any other town on the planet.

Look up to see hanging gardens with fountains and statues, arched walkways, medieval towers, street-corner tabernacles and huge worn stone crests of ancient noble families. Look down and the river reflects elegant bridges and shell-shaped windows, while exquisite mosaic marble floors appear from behind ornately carved wooden doors and frescoed passageways. Turning practically any corner in the centre of town will yield at least a glimpse of Brunelleschi's dome, with other world-renowned masterpieces – Michelangelo's legendary *David*, Cellini's *Perseus*, the Uffizi's unparalleled collections – only a few minutes' walk away. If all this sounds too daunting, take heart: Florence's churches, chapels and cloisters all make wonderful, low-key alternatives.

ORIENTATION AND GEOGRAPHY

The bell-shaped city centre is compact and easy to get around, with most major sights within walking distance of any other central point. It's practically impossible to get lost, with the often-visible dome of the Duomo and the River Arno and its four central bridges acting as reference points. The majority of the main sights and museums are clustered north of the two central bridges (Ponte Vecchio and Ponte Santa Trinità), in the area around the Duomo. Most of the other important sites are in the areas around this rectangle: Santa Maria Novella, San Lorenzo, San Marco, Santa Croce and Oltrarno zones. We have used these neighbourhood designations throughout this guide, with the rest of the attractions covered in the section called Outside the City Gates.

The main central area of Florence sits in the river valley and so is virtually flat, but the surrounding hills rise steeply on both sides, creating challenging walks and rewarding views that are easily accessible on foot or by bus. For a self-guided walk within the Boboli Gardens, *see p100* **Garden of earthly delights**; for a walk up to the gorgeous church of San Miniato al Monte, *see p106* **Head for heights**.

MUSEUMS AND GALLERIES

During the summer, around Easter and on public holidays, Florence spills over with visitors: the sights are crowded and huge queues can form at the main museums. The best times to visit are the in-between seasons, from January to March (avoiding Easter), and from October to mid December. If you're intending to visit all the main museums, it may be worth going for the week in spring or early summer when state museums give free entrance (*see below and p157*).

Many of Florence's unrivalled museums have private collections at their core, whether that of a mega-family such as the Medici (**Uffizi, Palazzo Pitti**) or of a lone connoisseur (the **Bardini, Horne** and **Stibbert** museums). Other major museums were founded to preserve treasures too precious to expose to the elements (the **Accademia**, the **Bargello** and the **Museo dell'Opera del Duomo**). Administratively, museums fall into three categories: private, state or municipal. The main municipal museums are the **Cappella Brancacci**, the **Cenacolo di Santo Spirito**, the **Museo di Firenze com'era**, the **Palazzo Vecchio** and the **Museo Bardini** (closed for restoration until some time in 2006).

For one week of the year (Settimana dei Beni Culturali), entrance to all the state museums is free. This week is generally in late spring/early summer, but the exact dates vary from year to year (call 055 290832 for details). For general information on the state museums and for booking, call **Firenze Musei** on 055 294883. The state museums are the **Pitti museums**, the **Uffizi**, the **Accademia**, the **Bargello**, the **Museo di San Marco**, the **Opificio delle Pietre Dure**, the **Cappelle Medicee** and the **Museo Archeologico**.

Firenze Musei strongly recommends booking for the Uffizi and the Accademia, and, at busy times of year, for the Pitti museums; this could save you a two-hour wait. At more popular times of the year there are long waits to get tickets for the Uffizi, even by pre-booking, so reserve as soon as you can. Booking costs €3 and tickets are collected from a window beside the normal ticket office, or, in the case of the Palazzo Pitti, from an office in the right-hand wing before you reach the main entrance. Pay when you pick up the tickets. Don't expect to be able to book tickets there directly: you will be told to phone the central number. Last issuing times for tickets vary (and we have given the closing time, not last admission, in our listings). Try to get to the ticket office an hour before the museum closes.

Art lovers should be aware that works of art are often loaned to other museums or to exhibitions, and restoration can be carried out

The best Sights

Outdoor sights

The avenues and lawns in the **Boboli Gardens** (*see p102*); the **Piazzale degli Uffizi** seen from across the river (*see p77*); the panoramic views from the **Campanile** (*see p73*); Alberti's façade of **Santa Maria Novella** (*see p87*); the beautiful **Ponte Santa Trinità** (*see p83*).

Indoor sights

The **Brancacci Chapel** frescoes (*see p103*); Michelangelo's **David** (*see p92*); the models of the Duomo in the **Museo dell'Opera del Duomo** (*see p73*); Botticelli's **Primavera** (*see p82*); **Santo Spirito**'s perfect nave (*see p103*).

Lesser-known sights

The carved ceiling of the **Badia Fiorentina** (*see p77*); Ghirlandaio's frescoes in the chapel of **Santa Trinità** (*see p84*); shoes for all seasons in the **Museo Ferragamo** (*see p83*); the overpass and tabernacle in the **Palazzo dell'Arte della Lana** (*see p77*); the amazing inlays of semi-precious stones in the **Opificio delle Pietre Dure** (*see p94*).

Museo Ferragamo. *See p83.*

Sightseeing

Niche work

The Italian tradition of creating shrines to the Madonna, Jesus or the saints on street corners is particularly strong in Florence. However, it's not that the city has ever been home to a higher than average proportion of devotees: this high concentration of conventicles is partly due to the early 14th-century episodes of armed conflict between the orthodox followers of the Church and the so-called Patarine heretics, a Ghibelline-supported reform movement advocating action against corruption in the clergy and named after the street in Milan from where their most active members hailed.

To prove their devotion (and avoid the potentially nasty repercussions of being branded heretics), many individuals, trades, guilds and confraternities built tabernacles in conspicuous positions, often on the corner of their home or centre. The tabernacle was usually built as an *edicola*, a frame for the icon itself, almost always made of stone. It often came with a protruding 'roof' to protect

the artwork, and a mantle on which to place offerings. The icon itself could be a fresco, painting, panel, relief, sculpture or tile, and sometimes famous artists were hired to create the venerable image and to boost the cachet of the sponsor in the eyes of the Church. The result is an art heritage of sometimes astonishing value. The shrines listed below are among the most noteworthy in the city.

Via Arte della Lana *corner with Via di Orsanmichele.* **Map** p318 C3.
Via della Spada *near San Pancrazio.* **Map** p318 B2.
Via degli Alfani *corner with Borgo Pinti.* **Map** p319 B5.
Via de' Tornabuoni *corner with Via della Vigna Nuova.* **Map** p318 B2.
Piaaza dell'Unità Italiana *corner with Via Sant'Antonio.* **Map** p318 A2.
Via Ricasoli *corner with Via de' Pucci.* **Map** p319 A4.

with little or no notice, so it's always a wise idea to call first if you want to view a specific piece. Otherwise, it's usually possible to pick up a leaflet at the museum ticket office with a list of exhibits that are not currently on show.

Temporary exhibitions are regularly held at a few locations in Florence, among them the Palazzo Vecchio, the Palazzo Medici Riccardi and the Palazzo Strozzi. See *Firenze Spettacolo* magazine, the English-language free paper *The Florentine* or local newspapers for details.

MONDAY BLUES

For residents of larger cities it can be a shock – and a spanner in the planning works – to find that some of Florence's major museums close on Monday. These include the Accademia and the Galleria Palatina in the Palazzo Pitti. If you're lucky and it's the first, third or fifth Monday of the month, you could go to the Bargello or the Museo di San Marco, or if it's the second or fourth, the Cappelle Medicee or some of the museums of the Palazzo Pitti.

TOURIST INFORMATION

Apart from the tourist offices (*see p298*), the city police have permanent information points in Piazza della Repubblica, on Via Calzaiuoli and at the southern end of the Ponte Vecchio, from where they give directions and basic information about the main sights in various

languages. Many of the city's minor sights – churches, *palazzi* and monuments – also have signs posted beside them detailing their history and distinguishing features, making a DIY tour that bit easier. In addition, you'll see big plaques with useful maps mounted in many squares and other strategic positions.

GUIDED TOURS

There's not a great deal to choose between Florence's various tour companies, all of which offer a range of itineraries with English-language options covering the main monuments and museums on foot or by bus. The highly reputable **Association of Tourist Guides** (055 2645217, www.florencetouristguides.com), the **Association of Florentine Tourist Guides** (055 4220901, www.florenceguides.it) and the **Cultural Association of Guides** (055 7877744, www.firenze-guide.com) all have a vast selection of standard tours. Two firms that provide a little more variety are **Walking Tours of Florence** (055 2645033, mobile 329 6132730, www.italy.artviva.com; *see also p186*) and **CAF** (055 283200, www.caftours.com), both offering a wide choice of interesting options.

If you prefer to do it yourself when it comes to sightseeing, the best ways in which to see the city are to hire a bike or moped (*see p285*), or to take a ride on the electric buses that cover the central areas of the city.

Duomo & Around

The awe-inspiring heart of the city.

The immense **Duomo** dominates the centre of Florence. *See p70.*

The geographic, religious and historic hub of the city, the cathedral area stretches from the north side of the Duomo down to the riverbank, bordered by the exclusive designer shops of Via de' Tornabuoni and the heavy, fortified *palazzi* and Gothic pride of Via del Proconsolo.

Around Piazza del Duomo

The glorious **Duomo** (*see p70*) stands at the heart of Florence's historic centre. The cathedral is so huge that there's no spot nearby from which you can see the whole thing, though a walk through the surrounding streets will be punctuated by glimpses of its red-tiled dome.

In Piazza del Duomo, visitors in awe of the cathedral's magnitude gape up at the intricately patterned marble, delicate carvings and the mammoth dome, even more impressive seen in the close proximity forced by the narrowness of the road on its northern flank. The areas outside the entrance and around the south of the Duomo are pedestrianised, while mopeds and buses roar around the north and east sides. Inside the cathedral is the **Crypt of Santa Reparata** (*see p71*), the original church built on this site in

the fifth century, while on the south side of the Duomo is the entrance to the dome itself, the spectacular **Cupola** (*see p71*). The **Campanile** (*see p73*), Giotto's elegant bell tower, is also south of the Duomo, level with its façade.

In Piazza San Giovanni, named after John the Baptist, the octagonal **Baptistery** (*see p73*) faces the main doors of the Duomo. This large square, always thronging with tourists, also houses the tiny **Museo di Bigallo** (*see p73*). West of the Baptistery is Via de' Cerretani, a busy shopping street and traffic thoroughfare that's home to **Santa Maria Maggiore**, an 11th-century parish church. Following the curve of the piazza on the north side of the Duomo, the **Museo dell'Opera del Duomo** (*see p73*), which houses the Duomo's treasures, is on the north-east of the square. Leading south from the façade of the Duomo is Via dei Calzaiuoli, a heaving, pedestrianised shopping street flanked by self-service restaurants, shops and *gelaterie*.

Running down from the south-west corner of the Baptistery is the more upmarket Via Roma, which opens into the pompous **Piazza della Repubblica**. This ungainly square was built in 1882, when the so-called Mercato Vecchio ('old

Campanile. *See p73.*

market', and part of the Jewish ghetto), was demolished and rebuilt in a massive clean-up after a cholera outbreak. The only remnant from before that time is the huge Colonna dell'Abbondanza, a column that used to mark the spot where two principal Roman roads crossed and that was reinstated to its original position after World War II.

Vasari's delightful **Loggia del Pesce**, with its ceramic marine creature *tondi*, was once the central meeting place of the square, but has been moved to Piazza dei Ciompi in Santa Croce (*see p96*). In the medieval period the area covered by the whole of Piazza della Repubblica was given over to a huge market where you could change money, buy a hawk or falcon, pay over the odds for a quack remedy, or pick up a prostitute (distinguished by the bells on their hats and gloves). Further back, the ancient Roman Forum once occupied a quarter of the piazza and the Campidoglio and Temple of Jupiter covered the rest. The sun-trap square is now flanked by pavement cafés, and dominated at night by street artists and strollers.

Duomo

Ufficio del Duomo (055 2302885/www.duomo firenze.it). **Open** 10am-5pm Mon-Wed, Fri; 10am-3.30pm Thur; 10am-4.45pm Sat (except 1st Sat of mth, 10am-3.30pm); 1.30-4.45pm Sun. **Admission** free. **Map** p319 B4.

A hugely successful and expanding wool industry gave the Florentine population such a boost in the 13th century that several new churches had to be built. Santa Croce (*see p97*) and Santa Maria Novella (*see p87*) were among them, but the most important of all was Santa Maria del Fiore, or the Duomo, which replaced the small church of Santa Reparata (*see p71*).

The building was commissioned by the Florentine Republic, which saw it as an opportunity to show off Florence as the most important Tuscan city. The competition to find an architect was won by Arnolfo di Cambio, a sculptor from Pisa who had trained with Nicola Pisano, and the first stones were laid on 8 September 1296 around the exterior of Santa Reparata. Building continued for the next 170 years, with guidance and revision from three further architects, though the church was consecrated 30 years before its completion in 1436.

The rich exterior, in white Carrara, green Prato and red Maremma marbles, shows the huge variation over the time of the building, in the styles of its inlaid patterns. The visionary Francesco Talenti had sufficient confidence to enlarge the cathedral and prepare the building for Brunelleschi's inspired dome. The last significant change came in the 19th century, when Emilio de Fabris designed a neo-Gothic façade. After his death, Luigi del Moro was left with the problem of how to crown the façade: after a referendum, plans for cuspidal spires were cast aside in favour of the flat balustraded balconies.

After the splendid exterior, the interior looks somewhat dull, though decorating the world's fourth largest cathedral was never going to be easy. It's actually full of fascinating peculiarities: notably the clock on the Paolo Uccello inner façade, which marks 24 hours, operates anti-clockwise and starts its days at sunset (it's between four and six hours fast). The clock is surrounded by the so-called *Heads of the Prophets* peering out from four roundels and showing the distinct influences of Ghiberti and Donatello in their perspective.

Also by Uccello is a monument to Sir John Hawkwood, painted in 1436 as a tribute to the English soldier who led Florentine troops to victory in the Battle of Cascina of 1364. The fresco has given rise to debate about whether its perspective and the movement of the horse's right legs are wrong, or the result of Uccello's original treatment of the rules of perspective construction, learned from Masaccio and considered by some to be visionary and even a forerunner to Cubism. Andrea del Castagno's 1456 monument to Niccolò da Tolentino, illustrating the heroic characteristics of a Renaissance man, forsakes perspective play for line. Beyond is Domenico di Michelino's *Dante Explaining the Divine Comedy*, featuring the poet in pink and the new Duomo vying for prominence with the Mountain of Purgatory.

A couple of strides forward and across put you directly underneath the dome, the size of which is even more breathtaking inside than out. The lantern in the centre is 90m (295ft) above you and the diameter of the inner dome is 43m (141ft) across, housing within it one of the largest frescoed surfaces in the world. Brunelleschi had intended for the inner cupola to be mosaic, so it would mirror the Baptistery ceiling. However, interior work only began some 125 years after his death in 1572, when Cosimo de' Medici commissioned Giorgio Vasari to carry out the work; together with Don Vincenzo Borghini, who was responsible for choosing the iconographic subjects, they decided to fresco the surface instead.

The concentric rows of images were started by Vasari, whose subtle treatment of colour and form drew inspiration from Michelangelo's Sistine Chapel, but he died two years later and was succeeded by Federico Zuccari, who worked for a further five years until its completion. Zuccari had a much more flamboyant (and crude) dry-painting style, believing that the distance from which the visitor would view the cupola wasted the delicacy of Vasari's wet fresco technique, especially as his repertoire of faces included some of the best-known personalities of the time and he wanted to make them as visible as possible. Zuccari's most crucial contribution to the cycle is the rendering of Dante's vision of Hell inspired by Signorelli's frescoes in Orvieto Cathedral.

Crypt of Santa Reparata

Open 10am-5pm Mon-Fri; 10am-4.45pm Sat (except 1st Sat of mth, 10am-4pm). **Admission** €3. **No credit cards**. Map p319 B4.

The crypt and some ruins left from the medieval structure of the original fifth-century church of Santa Reparata can still be seen in the Duomo; indeed, the entrance is inside the Duomo itself. The intricate mosaic floor of the church was built only 30cm (12in) above the Roman remains of houses and shops, some of which are on display in the crypt. Also here is the tomb of Brunelleschi, although no trace has ever been found of those of Arnolfo di Cambio and Giotto, both also supposedly buried here. Local legend has it that some of the land needed for the building of the much bigger Duomo was occupied by the Florentine Bischeri family, who, when they continued to refuse the ever-bigger sums of money they were offered to relocate, were unceremoniously kicked out of their palazzo with no compensation. This led to the Florentine expression *bischero* (a gullible fool).

Cupola/Dome

Open 8.30am-7pm Mon-Fri; 8.30am-5.40pm Sat (except 1st Sat of mth, 10am-4pm). **Admission** €6. **No credit cards**. Map p319 B4.

You'll need a little distance in order to appreciate the way in which the Duomo's most celebrated feature towers above the city: it is, as Alberti put it, 'large enough to cover every Tuscan with its shadow'. But the dome isn't just visually stunning: it's an incredible feat of engineering. Brunelleschi had dreamed of completing the cupola since childhood and studied architecture with that ambition in mind. He won the commission with the more experienced Lorenzo Ghiberti, riding on the back of his success with the Baptistery doors, but Brunelleschi soon found that while he was doing the crucial work, Ghiberti was taking the glory. Brunelleschi pulled a sickie, halting work, and got the recognition he deserved.

Brunelleschi first considered designing the classic semi-spherical dome used in existing churches around Italy, but the sheer size of the structure precluded the traditional method of laying tree trunks across the diameter in order to build around them. In the end, a revolutionary design for an elongated dome was followed. Brunelleschi made the dome support itself by building two shells, one on top of the other, and by laying the bricks in herringbone-pattern rings to integrate successive layers that could support themselves. The design was so efficient that it risked becoming a victim of its own success: the ribs around the dome were in danger of 'springing' open at the top, so a heavier lantern than normal was designed to hold them in place.

Just as innovative as the design were the tools used and the organisation of the work. Brunelleschi devised pulley systems to winch materials, and workers, up to the dome. Between the two shells of the dome, he installed a canteen so the workforce wouldn't waste time going to ground level to eat, bringing construction time down to a mere 16 years (1420-36). A separate side entrance gives access to the top of the dome (463 steps, about 20 minutes up and down) with fantastic city views, though the climb is not recommended for the faint-hearted or those with limited mobility.

Campanile

Open 8.30am-7.30pm daily. **Admission** €6.
No credit cards. **Map** p319 B4.

The cathedral's three-floor, 414-step bell tower was designed by Giotto in 1334, though his plans weren't followed faithfully (the original drawing is in the Museo dell'Opera del Duomo in Siena; *see p225*). Andrea Pisano, who continued the work three years after Giotto's death, took the precaution of doubling the thickness of the walls, while Francesco Talenti, who saw the building to completion in 1359, inserted the large windows high up the tower. Inlaid, like the Duomo, with pretty pink, white and green marble, the Campanile is decorated with 16 sculptures of prophets, patriarchs and pagans (the originals are in the Museo dell'Opera del Duomo; *see below*), basreliefs designed by Giotto and artfully executed by Pisano recounting the *Creation and Fall of Man* and his *Redemption Through Industry*; look carefully and you'll make out Eve emerging from Adam's side and a drunken Noah. The steps to the top are steep and narrow, but there are great views of the Duomo and the city from the terrace when you get there.

Baptistery

Open noon-7pm Mon-Sat; 8.30am-2pm Sun.
Admission €3. **No credit cards**. **Map** p319 B4.

For centuries the likes of Brunelleschi and Alberti believed the Baptistery was converted from a Roman temple dedicated to Mars. Other scholars reckoned that the Roman site on which the octagonal church was built was the Praetorium, while still more thought its ancient origins were as a bakery.

In fact, the Baptistery of St John the Baptist was built to an octagonal design between 1059 and 1128 as a remodelling of a sixth- or seventh-century version. In between those times it functioned for a period as the cathedral for Florence (then Florentia) in place of Santa Reparata, the church on whose site the Duomo now stands (*see p71*). The octagon reappears most obviously in the shape of the cathedral dome, but also on the buttresses of the Campanile, which constitute its corners. Today the striped octagon is best known for its gilded bronze doors, though the interior is worth visiting for the vibrant *Last Judgement* mosaic lining the vault ceiling with the 8m- (26ft-) high mosaic figure of *Christ in Judgement* dominating the apse. The mosaics depicting Hell are thought to have inspired Dante's version. Andrea Pisano completed the south doors in the 1330s with 28 Gothic quatrefoil-framed panels depicting stories from the life of St John the Baptist and the eight theological and cardinal virtues.

In the winter of 1400 the Calimala guild of cloth importers held a competition to find an artist to create a pair of bronze doors for the north entrance. Having seen works by seven artists, Brunelleschi among them, they gave the commission to Ghiberti, then just 20 years old. (Brunelleschi later got revenge with superior work on the cupola.) Relief panels on the doors tell the story of Christ from the Annunciation to the Crucifixion; the eight lower panels show the four evangelists and four doctors.

Many scholars believe that these north doors contain the very first signs of Renaissance art with deep pictorial space and an emphasis on figures.

No sooner had the north doors been installed than the Calimala commissioned Ghiberti to make another pair: the even more remarkable east doors, known, since Michelangelo coined the phrase, as the Gates of Paradise. The doors you see are copies (the originals are in the Museo dell'Opera del Duomo; *see below*), but the casts are fine enough that it's not difficult to appreciate Ghiberti's stunning work.

Museo di Bigallo

Piazza San Giovanni 1 (055 2302885). **Open** 10am-6pm Mon, Wed-Sun. **Admission** €2. **No credit cards**. **Map** p318 B3.

The city's smallest museum is housed in a beautiful Gothic loggia built in 1358 for the Misericordia, a charitable organisation that cared for unwanted children and plague victims. The loggia was later renovated for another fraternity, the Bigallo, and the Misericordia moved to Piazza del Duomo (No.19), from where it still works as a voluntary medical service. The main room has frescoes depicting the work of the two fraternities, though the two scenes on the left wall as you enter were damaged while being transferred from the façade in the 18th century. The *Madonna della Misericordia*, a fresco of 1342 from the workshop of Bernardo Daddi, a pupil of Giotto, has the Virgin suspended above the earliest known depiction of Florence, showing the Baptistery, the original Arnolfo façade to the domeless Duomo over the original church of Santa Reparata with its two bell towers, and an incomplete Campanile.

Museo dell'Opera del Duomo

Piazza del Duomo 9 (055 2302885/www.opera duomo.firenze.it). **Open** 9am-7.30pm Mon-Sat; 9am-1.40pm Sun. **Admission** €6. **No credit cards**. **Map** p319 B4.

Baptistery.

The Museum of the Cathedral Works contains tools and machinery used to build the Duomo, the original impressive wood models of the cathedral and its cupola in its various stages of development, and sculptures and artwork from the Duomo complex deemed too precious and vulnerable to be left to the mercy of the elements. It's one of the most interesting museums in the city, despite the fact that the explanatory panels can make for hard reading.

On the ground floor, under the glass roof of the courtyard, are eight of the ten original east Baptistery bronze door panels, the so-called *Porta del Paradiso* (*Gates of Paradise*) sculpted by Lorenzo Ghiberti over the 27 years between 1425 and 1452 and considered by some to be the work of art that initiated the Renaissance. When the two remaining panels have been restored, the doors will be recomposed and displayed in their original splendour. In the first rooms leading to the courtyard are Gothic sculptures from the exteriors of the Baptistery and the original but never-finished Duomo façade, including a classical-style *Madonna* with unsettling glass eyes by Arnolfo di Cambio. There are also pieces from Santa Reparata.

Halfway up the stairs is the *Pietà Bandini*, a heart-rending late work by Michelangelo showing Christ slithering from the grasp of Nicodemus. The sculpture was intended as Michelangelo's tombstone; he sculpted his own features on the face of Nicodemus, showing how his obsession with the story had become too much for him to bear. In true tortured-artist style, frustrated with the piece, he smashed Christ's left arm; it was supposedly left to his servant to pick up the fragments and save the work.

Upstairs, in a new corridor, are the brick stamps and forms, the pulleys and ropes by which building materials (and workers) were winched up to the dome. Donatello was the first artist to free sculpture from its Gothic limitations: in the room at the top of the stairs is an example, albeit a slightly extreme one, of the artist's unprecedented use of naturalism: an emotive wood sculpture of Mary Magdalene, dishevelled and ugly, with coarse, dirty hair so realistic you can almost smell it. The originals of his Prophets from the exterior of the Campanile are also here: notably *Habbakuk*, another work of such realism that Donatello himself is said to have gripped it and screamed, 'Speak, speak, speak!' At the back of the room is a stunning *dossal* (altar-frontal), 400kg of silver, worked on between 1366 and 1480 by several famous artists (Michelozzo, Verrocchio, Antonio del Pollaiolo, Bernardo Cennini).

After the emotion of the Michelangelo and the Donatellos, it's almost a relief to turn to the light, joyful *cantorie* (choir lofts). One is by Donatello, with cavorting *putti* (small, angelic boys); the other, by Luca della Robbia, is full of angel musicians. Beyond are bas-reliefs for the Campanile, most carved by Pisano to Giotto's designs.

Work on a new extension to the museum, doubling its size, is due to start in the next two years. Santiago Calatrava's original plans have been replaced by those of Italian architect Adolfo Natalini.

Around Piazza della Signoria

Florence's civic showpiece square is dominated by the **Palazzo Vecchio** (*see p80*). The crenellated and corbelled building, completed at the end of the 13th century as the seat of the Signoria (the top tier of the city's government), looms down over the piazza and is visible (especially its immense clock tower) from almost any point of the city. The palazzo still houses the main local government offices, but is also home to the imaginative **Museo dei Ragazzi** (*see p79*) and the **Quartieri Monumentali** (*see p80*), the main quarters of the Medicis, who called the palazzo home.

The piazza itself started life in 1268, when the Guelphs regained control from the Ghibellines and demolished their rivals' 36 houses in the area. However, they left the neighbouring houses intact, hence the unusual asymmetrical shape of the square. Over the next few centuries the piazza remained the focus of civic – though not necessarily civilised – activity, life in medieval Florence being beset by political and personal vendettas. It didn't take much to ignite a crowd: on one occasion, in the 14th century, a scrap in the piazza led to a man being eaten by the mob.

It was here that the religious and political reformer Girolamo Savonarola lit his so-called Bonfire of the Vanities in 1497. On to it he threw all the trappings of culture and wealth that he and his followers could gather, many donated by such luminaries as Botticelli and Fra Bartolomeo. Savonarola ended up burned at the stake on 23 May 1498, on the exact spot of his prophetic bonfire (marked by a plaque in front of the Neptune fountain), the fickle folk who had cheered on the book-burning frenzy having turned on him. However, the piazza has also been the seat of civic defence. Whenever Florence was threatened by an external enemy, the bell of the Palazzo della Signoria (known as the *vacca*, or cow, after its mooing tone) was tolled to summon the citizens' militia. Part of their training included playing *calcio* on the piazza; a version of rugby that's still played in Piazza Santa Croce every June (*see p158*).

When, in the mid 1980s, it was decided that the piazza's ancient paving stones should be taken up and restored, the state-run Sovrintendenza dei Beni Archeologici, which oversees the city's archaeological works, took the opportunity to carry out excavations on the area. In the course of the work, the ruins of 12th-century Florence were discovered beneath the piazza, built over the thermal baths of Roman Florentia and parts of the Etruscans' outpost. The authorities ordered further excavation of the ruins, and there was even talk of the site becoming an underground museum. Local government, however, objected, fearing the showpiece piazza would become a building site and so lose valuable tourist income.

The result of this disagreement was an utter shambles. The company engaged to restore the slabs apparently catalogued the position of the stones using nothing more permanent (or, indeed, weatherproof) than chalk, which was washed away on the first rainy day. It

also managed to 'lose' some of the slabs, now rumoured to grace the courtyards of various Tuscan villas. Given that most of Florence lies over the ruins of the Roman city, the decision to replace the paving with artificially aged stones and reseal the Roman site was predictable.

Dominating the piazza are a copy of Michelangelo's *David* (the original is in the Galleria dell'Accademia; *see p92*) and an equestrian bronze of Cosimo I by Giambologna,

Sightseeing

Ponte Vecchio

The **Ponte Vecchio** sits at the Arno's narrowest point within Florence, a crucial fact that might explain why there has been a bridge here – or in the immediate vicinity – since Roman times. The current bridge was constructed by Taddeo Gaddi in 1345, its predecessor having been swept away by floods 12 years earlier.

The higgledy-piggledy buildings on the bridge and the views it affords of the Florentine hills have lent it a reputation as one of the most romantic spots in Italy on which to propose marriage. However, the bridge was far from romantic in the days of the Medici. Back then, the stone workshops were occupied by butchers and tanners, whose trade involved soaking hides in the Arno for eight months before curing them in horse urine. Even though Vasari had built the corridor that runs over the eastern side of the bridge (*see p81* **Corridor of power**), Grand Duke Ferdinando I still grew fed up of retching every time he walked through it above the

bridge. In 1593 he banned all 'vile trades', allowing only jewellers and goldsmiths to conduct business on the bridge.

The Medici Grand Duke's fastidious edict still holds firm. By day the bridge swarms with tourists and locals buying high-quality gold jewellery, and the shops are perhaps more handsome when they're closed, their frontages covered in splendid arched wooden shutters that date back hundreds of years. In deference to its trade, the centre of the bridge is graced by a newly restored 19th-century bust by Raffaello Romanelli of revered sculptor and goldsmith Benvenuto Cellini. The metal theme recently struck a cord with a new generation of visitors, who started an ingenious graffiti craze: bike padlocks, signed, dated and locked one to another in great chains hanging from every available horse-tethering ring or shop bolt. Sadly, the authorities have cracked down on this fad, though you may still see the odd one that's managed to escape the cull.

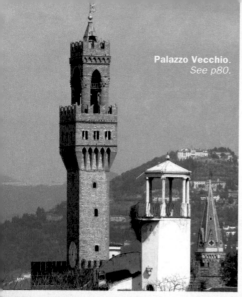

Palazzo Vecchio. *See p80.*

Neptune.

Badia Fiorentina. *See p77.*

notable mainly for the horse cast as a single piece in a purpose-built foundry. Giambologna also created sexy nymphs and satyrs for Ammannati's *Neptune* fountain, a Mannerist monstrosity of which Michelangelo is reputed to have wailed, 'Ammannati, what beautiful marble you have ruined'. Even Ammannati admitted it was a failure, in part because the block of marble used for Neptune lacked width, forcing him to give the god narrow shoulders and keep his right arm close to his body.

Beyond *Neptune* are copies of Donatello's *Marzocco* (the original of this heraldic lion, one of Florence's oldest emblems, is in the Bargello; *see p96*) and *Judith and Holofernes* (the original is in the Palazzo Vecchio; *see p80*).

Like David, Judith was a symbol of the power of the people over tyrannical rulers: a Jewish widow who inveigled her way into the camp of Holofernes, Israel's enemy, she got the man drunk and then sliced off his head. Beyond *David* is *Hercules and Cacus* by Bandinelli, much ridiculed by the exacting Florentines and described by rival sculptor Benvenuto Cellini as a 'sack of melons'. The marble block from which it's carved fell into the river in transit to Bandinelli's workshop, giving rise to the joke that it had tried to commit suicide. On one of the cornerstones at the edge of the Palazzo Vecchio nearest the loggia is the etched graffiti of a hawk-nosed man reputed to be a tongue-in-cheek self-portrait by Leonardo.

Cellini himself is represented by another monster-killer: a fabulous *Perseus*, holding the snaky head of Medusa, standing victorious in the adjacent **Loggia dei Lanzi**. The bronze is testament to the artist's pig-headed determination: most considered it would be impossible to cast the head of the Medusa in Perseus's hands, but after several failed attempts, Cellini finally succeeded by burning his family furniture to fan the furnace. Also in the loggia is Giambologna's spiralling marble *Rape of the Sabine Women* (1582), a virtuoso attempt to outdo Cellini and the first sculpture to have what John Pope Hennessy described as 'no dominant viewpoint'.

The loggia itself, the name of which derives from the *lanzichenecchi* (a private army of Cosimo I), was built in the late 1300s to shelter civic bigwigs during ceremonies. By the mid 15th century, it had become a favourite spot for old men to gossip and shelter from the sun, which, the architect Alberti noted, had a restraining influence on young men engaging in the 'mischievousness and folly natural to their age'. Unfortunately, the loggia is undergoing restoration for the umpteenth time in its recent history, and many of its notable sculptures are likely to be hidden from view until at least 2006.

Leading down to the river from Piazza della Signoria, the daunting Piazzale degli Uffizi is home to the world-renowned **Uffizi** (*see p80*). Also here is the separate entrance to the **Corridoio Vasariano** or Vasari Corridor (*see p81* **Corridor of power**). Halfway down the piazzale on the right, in Via Lambertesca, is the entrance to the **Collezione Contini-Bonacossi** (*see p79*) and the Georgofili library, where a Mafia bomb exploded in 1993.

Turning left from the riverbank leads you to the **Museo di Storia della Scienza** (*see p79*). Via Castellani heads north from the museum to Piazza San Firenze and its imposing law courts; just north of the piazza, in Via Proconsolo, is the entrance to the **Badia Fiorentina** (*see below*), its elegant stone tower visible for the first time in years after a painfully drawn-out restoration. Opposite, on the corner with Via Ghibellina, is the foreboding National Museum, the sculpture-laden **Bargello** (*see p96*). We're now well and truly in Danteland; just behind the Badia is the **Museo Casa di Dante** (*see p79*), while opposite the house is the **Chiesa di Dante**, the delightful little church where Dante's beloved Beatrice is buried.

Back at the river end of the Uffizi and on the right is the landmark **Ponte Vecchio** (*see p75* **Ponte Vecchio**), north of which is the mainly modern architecture of Via Por Santa Maria, much of which had to be rebuilt after the German bombing at the end of World War II.

In a piazza just off the east side of the street is the **Museo Diocesano di Santo Stefano al Ponte** (*see p79*), a tiny church museum.

At the top of Via Por Santa Maria, a busy shopping street, is the **Mercato Nuovo** ('new market', but often called the 'straw market', or Mercato della Paglia), a fine stone loggia erected between 1547 and 1551 on a site where there had been a market since the 11th century. It now houses stalls selling leather and straw goods and cheap souvenirs, but in the 16th century it was full of silk and gold merchants. The market is popularly known as the *Porcellino*, or piglet, after the bronze statue of a boar, a copy of a bronze by Pietro Tacca that in turn was a copy of an ancient marble now in the Uffizi. It's considered good luck to rub the boar's nose and put a coin in its mouth: proceeds go to a children's charity, and the legend goes that the donor is assured a return trip to the city.

A block up Via Calimala (named after the Greek for 'beautiful fleece') on the right is the portico-and-ramparts grandeur of the **Palazzo dell'Arte della Lana**, the Renaissance home to the filthy-rich guild of clothmakers. This fairytale castle is connected by an arched overpass to the church of **Orsanmichele** (*see p79*), the main entrance to which is on Via dei Calzaiuoli, the pedestrian thoroughfare between Piazza della Signoria and the Duomo.

On the corner of the palazzo facing Orsanmichele is the stunning Gothic **Madonna of the Trumpet** tabernacle, complete with spiral columns, a pointed arch, family crest decorations, and a long and complex history. The tabernacle started life in the 13th century on the corner of the Old Market and Calimala, housing the supposedly miracle-working Madonna painting (later destroyed by fire). It was replaced it in 1335 by *Enthroned Madonna and Child, Saints John the Baptist and John the Evangelist and Angels* by Jacopo di Casentino; *Coronation of the Virgin and Saints* by Niccolò di Pietro Gerini was added in 1380. In 1905 the panel was installed on the corner of the Palazzo dell'Arte della Lana.

Badia Fiorentina

Via Dante Alighieri (055 264402). **Open** *Cloister* 3-6pm Mon. *Church* 3-6pm Mon; 6.30am-6pm Tue-Sat. **Admission** donation to Eucharist. **Map** p319 C4.
A Benedictine abbey founded in the tenth century by Willa, the mother of Ugo, Margrave of Tuscany, the Badia Fiorentia was the richest religious institution in medieval Florence. Willa had been deeply influenced by Romuald, a monk who travelled around Tuscany denouncing the wickedness of the clergy, flagellating himself and urging the rich to build monasteries; it was Romuald who persuaded Willa to found the Badia in 978.

When Ugo was a child, his exiled father returned to Florence and invented a novel paternity test by expecting the boy to recognise the father he'd never seen in a room of men. Happily for his mother, Ugo succeeded. The people decided he must have had divine guidance, and he was considered a visionary leader. Like his mother, Ugo also lavished money and land on what was then known as the Badia Florentia, and was eventually buried there in a Roman sarcophagus (later replaced by a tomb made by Renaissance sculptor Mino da Fiesole) that's still housed in the abbey.

It was here in 1274, just across the street from his probable birthplace, that the eight-year-old Dante fell in love at first sight with Beatrice Portinari. He was devastated when her family arranged her marriage, at the tender age of 17, to Simone de Bardi, and absolutely crushed when she died seven years later. Poor Dante attempted to forget his pain and anguish by throwing himself into war.

The Badia has been rebuilt many times since Dante's day, but still retains a graceful Romanesque campanile and an exquisite carved ceiling. The Chiostro degli Aranci dates from 1430 and is frescoed with scenes from the life of San Bernardo. Inside the church Bernardo is celebrated once again, in a painting by Filippino Lippi. The Cappella dei Pandolfini is where writer Giovanni Boccaccio held the first public reading of the works of Dante.

Collezione Contini-Bonacossi

Uffizi, entrance on Via Lambertesca (055 294883). **Open** guided group visits by appt only. **Admission** free. **Map** p318 C3.

An impressive collection donated to the state by the Contini-Bonacossi family in 1974. Exhibits include renderings of the *Madonna and Child* by Duccio, Cimabue and Andrea del Castagno, and a roomful of works by artistic VIPs (Bernini, Tintoretto). El Greco, Velázquez and Goya are among the foreigners considered prestigious enough for the collection.

Museo Casa di Dante

Via Santa Margherita 1 (055 219416). **Open** phone for details. **Admission** €3. **No credit cards**. **Map** p319 B4.

Housed in the building where Dante is thought to have lived, this museum dedicated to the father of the Italian language has been closed for renovation for a long time. It was due to open as this guide went to press, but phone to check first.

Museo Diocesano di Santo Stefano al Ponte

Piazza Santo Stefano 5 (055 2710732). **Open** *Summer* 4-7pm Fri. *Winter* 3.30-6.30pm Fri; also by appointment. Closed mid July-Sept. **Admission** free. **Map** p319 C3.

A tiny, little-known museum hidden from the tourist trail in a square north of the Ponte Vecchio. Among the religious icons and church relics are a few big surprises: a *Maestà* by Giotto, *San Giuliano* by Masolino and the *Quarate Predella* by Paolo Uccello.

Museo dei Ragazzi

Palazzo Vecchio, Piazza della Signoria (055 2768224/www.museoragazzi.it). **Open** times vary. **Admission** €2-€6; €15.50 family. **No credit cards**. **Map** p319 C4.

One for the kids. For children aged three to seven, there's a playroom with a dressing-up corner, a puppet theatre and building blocks, all with a Renaissance theme; for older children (target audience: eight to 88) there's a series of workshops, talks by experts, meetings with historical characters such as Eleonora di Toledo and Cosimo I, visits on 'secret routes', and multimedia activities, all based in the Palazzo Vecchio, the Museo di Storia della Scienza (*see below*) and the Museo Stibbert (*see p105*).

Museo di Storia della Scienza

Piazza dei Giudici 1 (055 2398876/www.imss.fi.it). **Open** *Summer* 9.30am-5pm Mon, Wed-Fri; 9.30am-1pm Tue, Sat. *Winter* 9.30am-5pm Mon, Wed-Sat; 9.30am-1pm Tue. **Admission** €6.50. **No credit cards**. **Map** p319 C4.

Galileo Galilei's scientific instruments are the big draw here, but even without them, this would be one of the most interesting museums in Florence. Galileo's fascinatingly crafted compass and his leather-bound telescope (which, conversely, seems singularly unimpressive) are in the two rooms dedicated to the heretical star-gazer. A morbid reliquary in the shape of his middle right finger is also on display, offering unintentionally ironic echoes to the honour more usually bestowed on saints.

In the next rooms is a collection of prisms and optical games. Art continues to mingle with science in Room 7, devoted to armillary spheres and dominated by a model commissioned by Federico II in 1593. Most of the spheres have the earth placed at the centre of the universe, surrounded by seven spheres of the planets. Look out, too, for the set of spiralling 18th-century thermometers.

The second floor has an eclectic mix of machines, mechanisms and models, including a 19th-century clock (*pianola*) that writes a sentence with a mechanical hand, and a selection of electromagnetic and electrostatic instruments (Room 14). Also interesting are the pneumatic pumps decorated with inlaid wood by Nollet (famous for his globe machine) and the carefully constructed illustration of the mechanical paradox of two spheres ascending a plane. The display of amputation implements and models of foetuses adorning the walls are grisly.

Orsanmichele & Museo di Orsanmichele

Via dell'Arte della Lana (055 284944/284715). **Open** *Church* 9am-noon, 4-6pm daily. *Museum tours* 9am, 10am, 11am daily. Phone to check. Closed 1st & last Mon of mth. **Admission** free. **Map** p318 C3.

With no spire, several distinct floors and no overt religious symbols, Orsanmichele doesn't look much like a church. However, that's precisely what it is, albeit one that melds the relationship between art, religion and commerce.

Sightseeing

In 1290 a loggia intended as a grain store was built to a design by Arnolfo di Cambio, the original architect of the Duomo, in the garden (*orto*) of the Monastery of San Michele (hence, 'Orsanmichele'). The loggia burned down in 1304, along with a painting of the Madonna said to have been invoked to put out a previous fire. The painting had been held in the marvellously elaborate glass and marble tabernacle of Andrea Orcagna, and was replaced by Bernardo Daddi's *Coronation of the Madonna with Eight Angels* in 1347, still in place in the tabernacle.

When the building was reconstructed in the mid 1300s by Talenti and Fioravante, it was first used as a grain market. Two upper floors were added so that monks could use it for religious services. From the outset, the council intended the building to be a magnificent advertisement for the wealth of the city's guilds, and in 1339 each guild was instructed to fill one of the loggia's niches with a statue of its patron saint. Only the wool guild obliged, so in 1406 the council handed the guilds a ten-year deadline.

Six years later the Calimala cloth importers, the wealthiest of all the guilds, commissioned Ghiberti to create a life-sized bronze of John the Baptist. It was the largest statue ever cast in Florence, and its arrival spurred the other major guilds into action. The guild of armourers was represented by a tense *St George* by Donatello (now in the Bargello; *see p96*), one of the first psychologically realistic sculptures of the Renaissance, while the Parte Guelfa guild had Donatello gild their bronze, a *St Louis of Toulouse* (later removed by the Medici in their drive to expunge all memory of the Guelphs).

All the statues in the external niches are copies. However, the originals are on the first floor of the museum, displayed on a platform in the same order in which they appeared around the church. On the second floor is a collection of statues of 14th-century saints and prophets in *arenaria* stone. They were on the external façade of the church until the 1950s, when they were saved from the elements and moved to the Opificio delle Pietre Dure (*see p94*).

Note that the church and museum do not always stick to the opening hours posted, so you're advised to phone to check the hours first before making a special trip.

Palazzo Vecchio
Quartieri Monumentali

Piazza Signoria (055 2768465/www.comune. firenze.it). **Open** 9am-7pm Mon-Wed, Sat, Sun; 9am-2pm Thur. **Admission** €6. **No credit cards**. **Map** p319 C4.

The modern-day home of Florence's town hall, the Palazzo Vecchio was originally built to Arnolfo di Cambio's late 13th-century plans as seat to the Signoria, the city's ruling body as priors of the main guilds of the Medici. The Medici enjoyed their own nine-year stay (1540-49) was brief, and instigated a Mannerist makeover of the palace's interior from 1555 to 1574. However, the rustic stone

exterior of the building and Arnolfo's tower, the highest in the city at 94m (308ft), remained largely intact. The tower, set just off-centre in order to incorporate a previous tower and to fit in with the irregularity of the square, and topped by two of the main symbols of Florence (a lion holding a lily), saw the imprisonment of Savonarola and Cosimo the Elder in a room euphemistically called the Albergaccio ('bad hotel').

From 1565 the Palazzo Vecchio lost some of its administrative exclusivity to the Pitti Palace and the Uffizi. However, it later became the seat of the Italian Government's House of Deputies from 1865 to 1871, when Florence was the capital of the Kingdom of Italy, before returning to its original and current function as town hall. Though it's still a working administrative centre, much of it can be visited.

The Salone dei Cinquecento (Hall of the Five Hundred), where members of the Great Council met, should have been decorated with battle scenes by Michelangelo and Leonardo, not the zestless scenes of victory over Siena and Pisa by Vasari that cover the walls. Frustrated by attempts to develop new mural techniques, Leonardo abandoned the project; Michelangelo had only finished the cartoon for the *Battle of Cascine* when he was summoned to Rome by Pope Julius II. One of the latter's commissions did end up here: the *Genius of Victory*, a statue thought to have been carved, along with the better-known *Slaves*, for the Pope's never-finished tomb.

Off the Salone is the Studiolo di Francesco I, the office where Francesco hid away to practise alchemy. Also decorated by Vasari, it includes a scene from the alchemist's laboratory and illustrations of the four elements. From the vaulted ceiling, Bronzino's portraits of Francesco's parents, Cosimo I and Eleonora di Toledo, look down. Upstairs, the Quartiere degli Elementi contains Vasari's allegories of the elements. The Quartiere di Eleonora, the apartments of the wife of Cosimo I, has two entirely frescoed chapels; the first was partly decorated by Bronzino, who used intense pastel hues to depict a surreal *Crossing the Red Sea*, while the Cappella dei Priori is decorated with fake mosaics and an idealised *Annunciation*.

Beyond here is the garish Sala d'Udienza, with a carved ceiling dripping in gold; more subtle is the Sala dei Gigli, so named because of the gilded lilies that cover the walls. Decorated in the 15th century, it has a ceiling by Giuliano and Benedetto da Maiano, and some sublime frescoes of Roman statesmen by Ghirlandaio opposite the door. Donatello's original *Judith and Holofernes*, rich in political significance, is also here.

Uffizi

Piazzale degli Uffizi 6 (055 23885/www.uffizi. firenze.it). **Open** 8.15am-6.50pm Tue-Sun. **Admission** €6.50; €3.25 concessions. Small extra charge for special exhibitions. *Advance booking* via Firenze Musei (055 294883); booking charge €3. **No credit cards**. **Map** p319 C4.

Corridor of power

We have Cosimo I de' Medici to thank for the presence in central Florence of the **Corridoio Vasariano** (Vasari Corridor). Having moved to the Palazzo Pitti in 1549, Cosimo found that in order to get to work in the Palazzo Vecchio, he'd have to walk among his public, while having his sensibilities offended by the smells, sounds and sights of the butchers' shops and tanneries that lined the Ponte Vecchio at the time. Vasari was commissioned to construct an overhead passageway for Cosimo's near-exclusive use. It sounded like it ought to have been a monumental task, but Vasari completed the job in a lightning-quick five months, just in time for the wedding of Cosimo's son Francesco to Joanna of Austria.

The corridor runs the length of the Uffizi, over the **Ponte Vecchio** (*see p75*), through the interior of **Santa Felicità** (*see p103*) and down to the **Palazzo Pitti** (*see p101*) and the **Boboli Gardens** (*see p102*), where there are two exits, one by Buontalenti's grotto and the other inside the royal apartments of the palace. The 700 paintings lining the walls of the corridor include some veritable masterpieces, among them self-portraits by illustrious artists such as Delacroix, Titian, Bernini, Andrea del Sarto, Artemisia Gentileschi, Raphael, Van Dyck, Velázquez and Rembrandt. Round 'porthole' windows give spectacular views over the river and out to the hills beyond; the smell of privilege emanates from every corner.

Unfortunately, where once the corridor was hallowed ground for dukes and princes

wishing to avoid the medieval mêlée, it's now a holy grail on the tourist trail. Each year the powers-that-be indulge in a fearsome debate about whether to allow mere mortals to visit the fascinating kilometre-long corridor. Limited guided tours were permitted in 2004, but were suspended the following year. It's likely that they will run again but, as this guide went to press, no decision had been taken for future years. For the latest information on access and tours, call the Firenze Musei on 055 294883.

So, this is it: the greatest museum of Renaissance art in the world, the holy grail of Italian art. Every year 1.5 million visitors cram into these handsome, hallowed rooms, lined with Botticellis, Leonardos and Michelangelos.

Time seems to have stood still in this corner of the art world, but changes are afoot. A planned revamp, doubling the gallery's display space, would bring long-hidden works out of storage and into the public domain, as well as making a visit here easier by adding multiple entrances and exits. That said, don't hold your breath: the implementation of Japanese architect Arata Isozaki's plans for a canopy over a new exit was put on ice when excavations revealed the foundations of medieval houses and a boundary wall. As this guide went to press, final decisions had yet to be made, and the scheduled 2006 completion date was looking positively delusional.

In the meantime the queues remain; the best way to jump them is to book a ticket in advance (*see p80*), though even this isn't foolproof: during peak times you need to reserve up to a couple of months in advance. Whether you book in advance or not, aim to arrive either when the museum opens or at lunchtime, when the tour groups are unlikely to be so prevalent. To see the whole collection would take a lot of time and energy: it's best to jump to the rooms in which you're most interested or, better still, to plan a return visit. Allow at least three hours to take in the unmissables. Several groups run guided tours (*see p68*); there are also audio tours in seven languages for €4.65 (single headset) or €6.20 (double headset) from the ticket office.

The building was designed by Vasari in the middle of the 16th century as a public administration centre for Cosimo I (hence 'Uffizi', meaning 'offices').

To make way for the *pietra serena* and white plaster building, inspired by Michelangelo's Laurentian Library in San Lorenzo, most of the 11th-century church of San Piero Scheraggio was demolished (the remains can still be seen beyond the main entrance hall), and the Old Mint, the Palazzo della Zecca, was incorporated into the design.

By 1581 Francesco I had already begun turning the top floor into a new home for his art collection, and the habit caught on. A succession of Medici added to the collection, culminating in the bequest of most of the family's artworks by the last of the family, Anna Maria, on her death in 1743. When the specialist art museums of the city were opened in the 18th and 19th centuries, the silver, sculptures and scientific exhibits were transferred from the Uffizi, leaving the gallery we see today.

Off the corridors, lined with magnificent ancient Greek and Roman wrestlers, flawless Apollos and eminent-looking busts, the chronological collection begins gloriously in **Room 2** with three *Maestàs* by Giotto, Cimabue and Duccio; all were painted in the 13th and early 14th centuries, and all are still part of the Byzantine tradition. **Room 3** is 14th-century Siena, evoked most exquisitely by Simone Martini's lavish gilt altarpiece *Annunciation*. Such delight in detail reached its zenith in the international Gothic movement (**Rooms 5** and **6**) and, in particular, the work of Gentile da Fabriano (1370-1427), whose ornate *Adoration of the Magi*, known as the Strozzi Altarpiece because it was commissioned by Palla di Noferi Strozzi for the sacristy of Santa Trinità, has been restored to its original sumptuous grandeur.

It comes as something of a surprise, then, to find a strikingly contemporary *Virgin and Child with Saint Anne* by Masolino and Masaccio (1401-28) in **Room 7**. Though Masolino was not averse to a little Gothic frivolity, he's restrained here. Masaccio painted the Virgin, whose severe expression and statuesque pose make her an indubitable descendant of Giotto's *Maestà*. In the same room is the *Santa Lucia dei Magnoli* altarpiece by Domenico Veneziano (1400-61), a Venetian artist who had a remarkable skill for rendering the way light affects colour. His influence on pupil Piero della Francesca's work is clear in the younger artist's portraits of the Duke and Duchess of Urbino. Paolo Uccello (1396-1475) is represented by the *Battle of San Romano*: a work of tremendous energy and power, it's part of a triptych; the other thirds are in London's National Gallery and the Louvre in Paris.

Rooms 8 and **9** are dominated by Filippo Lippi and the Pollaiolo brothers. The Madonna in Lippi's *Madonna with Child and Angels* is a portrait of the beautiful Lucrezia Buti, a nun whom he abducted and married after giving up the Carmelite vows, painted with their son Filippino, who was also to become a painter. Antonio, the more talented of the Pollaiolos, was one of the first artists to dissect bodies in order to study anatomy. His small panels of the *Labours of Hercules* demonstrate his familiarity with the skeletal form and musculature.

The two most famous paintings in the Uffizi and in Italy are in **Room 10**. Botticelli's *Birth of Venus*, the epitome of Renaissance romance, depicts the birth of the goddess from a sea impregnated by the castration of Uranus. It's an allegory of the birth of beauty from the mingling of the physical world (the sea) and the spiritual (Uranus). Scholars have been squabbling about the true meaning of Botticelli's *Primavera*, or *Allegory of Spring*, since it was painted in 1482. Many now agree that it was intended to represent the onset of spring (reading from right to left) and to signify the triumph of Venus (centre) as true love, with the Three Graces representing her beauty and Zephyr, on the right, as lust, pursuing the nymph Chloris, who is transformed into Flora, Venus's fecundity. The painting is believed to have been a wedding present from Lorenzo il Magnifico to his cousin Lorenzo di Pierfrancesco de' Medici; many of the 190 different flowers under Flora's feet symbolise marriage.

In **Room 15** are several paintings by Leonardo da Vinci, including a collaboration with his teacher Verrocchio, *The Baptism of Christ* (Verrocchio never painted again, reputedly because his work couldn't match up to Leonardo's). The octagonal **Room 18**, with its mother-of-pearl ceiling, is dominated by portraits by Bronzino, most strikingly that of Eleonora di Toledo, assured, beautiful and very Spanish in an opulent gold and black brocade gown. The oval **Room 24**, originally a treasure chamber, is home to the world's biggest collection of miniatures, including the ebony-framed Medici collection.

In **Room 25**, the gallery makes its transition to Mannerism led by Michelangelo's *Holy Family* (*Tondo Doni*), which shows the sculptural bodies, virtuoso composition and luscious palette that characterised the new wave. Florentine works in the same room include Mariotto Albertinelli's *Visitation*, Elizabeth's saffron-coloured shawl glowing in what was the artist's only masterpiece. Next you'll come to the Pontormo- and Rosso Fiorentino-dominated **Room 27**; once again, Michelangelo's legacy is visible, most notably in *Moses Defends the Daughters of Jethro* by Rosso Fiorentino. Also by the same artist is the *Portrait of a Young Woman*, with the ubiquitous musical angel detail. The works by Titian in **Room 28** include his masterpiece *Venus of Urbino*, whose questionably chaste gaze has disarmed viewers for centuries.

For more Venetian works, skip to **Rooms 31-35**, but don't miss the challenging *Madonna with the Long Neck* by Parmigianino en route in **Room 29**. An Old Masters cherry on the Renaissance cake is provided by **Room 41**, with its classic row of portraits and self-portraits by Rubens, Van Dyck and Velázquez; nearby **Room 43** is home to a particularly grisly rendering of *Judith and Holofernes* by the 17th-century Caravaggio-esque female artist Artemisia Gentileschi. Caravaggio himself is represented by his famous but more shocked-looking than horror-inspiring *Medusa*, and a *Sacrifice of Isaac* that demonstrates his masterly treatment of light.

Note that paintings may be moved or go on loan at any time, so if you've set your heart on seeing a particular masterpiece, you'd be advised to phone first to check they're here.

Around Via de' Tornabuoni

The elegant shopping mecca of Via de' Tornabuoni is dominated by the massive backside of **Palazzo Strozzi** (*see p84*), its gargantuan fortification stones set with horse-tethering rings and embellished with the three crescent-moon motifs of the family crest. The two main entrances are in Via Strozzi, leading from Via de' Tornabuoni towards the Piazza della Repubblica, and in Piazza Strozzi itself. The palazzo is mainly used these days for important art exhibitions; as its courtyard is protected from the sun by perimeter loggias, it's a good place for a breather on hot days. The main street itself sweeps down from Piazza Antinori to Piazza Santa Trinità and the Santa Trinità bridge. It's crowned by Palazzo Antinori, an austere mid 15th-century palace of neat stone blocks that's been inhabited by the Antinori winemaking family since 1506. The rather garish church opposite is the baroque **San Gaetano**.

Heading south towards the river, passing all manner of designer names, you'll come to Piazza Santa Trinità. Just before the square is Via Porta Rossa, with the Renaissance house museum **Palazzo Davanzati** (*see p84*). At the far end of Via Porta Rossa, on the right, the road widens into a square. The ramparts and Gothic leaded windows of the Palagio di Parte Guelfa date back to the 13th century, and have been modified by, among others, Brunelleschi and Vasari. The imposing building, once the headquarters of the Guelphs, is now used as a library and meeting rooms. Running parallel to Via Porta Rossa is Borgo Santissimi Apostoli, a narrow street in the middle of which is Piazza del Limbo; it's so called because it occupies the site of a graveyard for unbaptised babies. The tiny church is **Santissimi Apostoli** (*see p84*).

Piazza Santa Trinità itself is little more than a bulge dominated by the curved ramparts of Palazzo Spini Feroni, home to **Ferragamo** (*see p139*) and the shoetastic **Museo Ferragamo** (*see below*), and by an ancient column taken from the Baths of Caracalla in Rome, a gift to Cosimo I from Pope Pius I in 1560. The statue of Justice on top was designed by Francesco del Tadda. The first palazzo after Via de' Tornabuoni is Palazzo Bartolini-Salimbeni by Baccio d'Agnolo. The architect was savaged by 16th-century critics for creating a design 'more suited to a church

Strolling **Via Strozzi**.

than a palazzo'. Opposite Palazzo Spini Feroni, on the west side of Via de' Tornabuoni, is the church of **Santa Trinità** (*see p84*).

The Ponte Santa Trinità, an elegant bridge with an elliptical arch, links Piazza Santa Trinità with **Oltrarno** (*see pp99-103*). First built in 1252 on the initiative of the Frescobaldi family, it was rebuilt in 1346 and again in 1567. It's this version, built by Ammannati (perhaps to a design by Michelangelo) that stands today; it's considered by many to be the most beautiful bridge in the world. The statues at either end represent the four seasons, and were placed there in 1608 to celebrate Cosimo II's marriage to Maria of Austria. Having been bombed on the night of 3 August 1944 by retreating Germans, the bridge was rebuilt in 1955 in the same position and to the same design. The head of the most famous, *Spring* by Pietro Francavilla, which graces the north-east side of the bridge, remained lost until 1961, when a council employee dredged it up during a routine clean-up and claimed the reward offered for its return years before by a US newspaper.

Museo Ferragamo

Via de' Tornabuoni 2 (055 3360456/www. ferragamo.it). **Open** by appt 9am-1pm, 2-6pm Mon-Fri. Closed Aug & 2wks in Dec. **Admission** free. **Map** p318 C2.

This small museum above Ferragamo's shop in the Palazzo Spini Feroni displays a mere fraction of the company's 10,000 archived shoes, but still affords an opportunity for shoe fetishists to drool over some

Piazza Santa Trinità. *See p83.*

of the world's most beautiful footwear. Born in a small village just outside Naples in 1898, Ferragamo emigrated to the US at 16 and was soon designing shoes for movie stars. In 1927 he moved to Florence to start a factory producing handmade shoes; in 1938 he bought the palazzo in Via de' Tornabuoni, where he had been renting a studio, from the Feroni family. Since then the business, based in the same palazzo but with its production facilities on the outskirts of the city, has continued to flourish.

Palazzo Davanzati/ Museo dell'Antica Casa Fiorentina

Via Porta Rossa 13 (055 2388610/www.polo museale.firenze.it). **Open** 8.15am-1.30pm daily. Closed 1st, 3rd & 5th Mon, 2nd & 4th Sun of mth. **Admission** free. **Map** p318 C3.
After years of renovation, part of the Ancient Florentine House Museum is finally open again. On the first floor are the Sala dei Pappagalli, the Salone Madonnale and the Studiolo, with frescoes, Renaissance furniture and paintings. The building itself is a good example of a 15th-century palazzo for well-to-do Florentines, but the most interesting parts of the museum – the kitchen and the bedrooms – are not due to open for another few years.

Palazzo Strozzi

Piazza Strozzi (Institute Gabinetto Vieusseux 055 288342). **Open** *Library* 9am-1.30pm, 3-6pm Mon, Wed, Fri; 9am-6pm Tue, Thur. *Exhibitions* times vary. **Admission** *Ground-floor courtyard* free. *Exhibitions* vary. **Map** p318 B3.

More than 100 palaces were built in Florence in the 15th century, none more magnificent than this one. Work began on it in 1489 on the orders of Filippo Strozzi, whose family had been exiled from Florence in 1434 for opposing the Medici. However, they'd made good use of the time, moving south and becoming bankers to the King of Naples, and had amassed a fortune by the time they returned to Florence in 1466. Filippo began buying up property in the centre of Florence eight years later, until he had acquired enough real estate to build the biggest palace in the city: he pulled down 15 buildings to make room for it.

An astrologer was asked to choose an auspicious day to lay the foundation stone and came up with 6 August 1489, tying in nicely with the law Lorenzo de' Medici had passed a few months earlier that tax-exempted anyone who built a house on an empty site. When Filippo died in 1491, he left his heirs to complete the project, which eventually bankrupted them. The palace now houses institutions and stages prestigious exhibitions.

Santa Trinità

Piazza Santa Trinità (055 216912). **Open** 7am-noon, 4-7pm daily. **Admission** free. **Map** p318 C2.
This plain church was built in the 13th century over the ruins of two earlier churches belonging to the Vallombrosans. The order was founded in 1038 by San Giovanni Gualberto Visdomini, who spent much of his life attempting to persuade pious aristocrats to surrender their wealth and live a life of austerity. The order became extremely wealthy and powerful, reaching a peak in the 16th and 17th centuries, when its huge fortress abbey at Vallombrosa, in the Casentino countryside north of Arezzo, was built. The church is well worth a visit for the Cappella Sassetti, luminously frescoed by Ghirlandaio with scenes from the life of St Francis, including one set in the Piazza della Signoria and featuring Lorenzo il Magnifico and his children.

Santissimi Apostoli

Piazza del Limbo 1 (055 290642). **Open** 10.15am-noon, 4-7pm Mon-Sat; 10am-noon, 4-7pm Sun. **Admission** free. **Map** p318 C3.
The design of Santissimi Apostoli, like that of the early Christian churches of Rome, is based on that of a Roman basilica, and retains much of its 11th-century façade. The third chapel on the right holds an *Immaculate Conception* by Vasari; in the left aisle is an odd glazed terracotta tabernacle by Giovanni della Robbia. The church holds pieces of flint reputed to have come from Jerusalem's Holy Sepulchre, awarded to Pazzino de' Pazzi for his bravery during the Crusades: he was the first to scale the walls of Jerusalem, though his name, 'Little Mad Man of the Mad Men', suggests his actions may have been more foolish than brave. These flints were used on Easter Day to light the 'dove' that set off the fireworks display at the Scoppio del Carro (*see p156*). Take note: the church has a tendency to close in the afternoon without notice.

Santa Maria Novella

Florence's most intriguing mix of ancient and modern.

Santa Maria Novella is perhaps the most diverse of the central Florentine zones, both in character and design. The area extends from the striking modernist main railway station west to grand residential areas around the **Teatro del Maggio Musicale Fiorentino** (or Teatro Comunale; *see p191*), south towards shopping street Borgo Ognissanti and the imposing riverfront mansions and hotels, and south-east through the parish church square as far as the prestigious Via de' Tornabuoni.

The area's three main streets, which run parallel to each other, are each different in feel. Workaday **Via Palazzuolo** (home to the **Oratorio dei Vanchetoni** at No.17, a beautiful 1602 building that's occasionally open to the public) is sandwiched between elegant **Borgo Ognissanti** and traffic-heavy **Via della Scala**, home to the famous **Farmacia Santa Maria Novella** (*see p152* **Natural selections**).

Dominating the square on which it stands, **Santa Maria Novella station** was designed by Giovanni Michelucci in 1935. Its bold form is not to everyone's taste, but the building is regarded as a masterpiece of modernism. As is the case in most major cities, the area around it (and the adjacent bus terminus) should be approached with wits alert: tourists attract petty thieves. A recent facelift and some better signposting in the shopping mall underpass to and from the station (and the entrance streets to Piazza Santa Maria Novella) have made it a slightly safer option than the rat-run roads above, where an inexplicably complicated design makes crossing Piazza della Stazione something of a trial by traffic.

A short walk south of the station, Leon Battista Alberti's exquisite, precision-built façade for the church of **Santa Maria Novella** (*see p87*) looks out on to the grassy (but scruffy) piazza of the same name; the two turtles, on which rest two marble obelisks, are by Giambologna. Opposite the church, on the southern side of the square, is the newly restored **Loggia di San Paolo**, a late 15th-century arcade built to the model of Brunelleschi's Loggiato degli Innocenti in San Marco (*see p92*) and set with the characteristic glazed terracotta medallions of the della Robbias. This is where the new **Museo di Storia della Fotografia** will open (scheduled for early 2006, but probably later; *see p90*).

Piazza Santa Maria Novella.

Piazza Santa Maria Novella has been the subject of long-running disputes between local residents, hotel owners and the city police, whose opinions over the degree of safety and civic care are, to say the least, at odds with one other. By day the square is a bustling and pretty tourist mecca, but the nights can be dodgier. The opening of smart hotels such as **JK Place** (*see p55*) and adjacent bar **The Lounge** (*see p123* **Hotel cuisine**) has spruced up the eastern side of the square, but problems remain with drug dealers after dark.

In stark contrast, walk a little south of the piazza, where the triangle formed by Via de' Fossi, Via della Spada and Via della Vigna Nuova is not just a friendly, lively area during the day, but also generally safe for night-time window shopping. The area is cluttered with antiques emporia, designer clothes shops, cafés and *trattorie*; next to each other in the centre of the triangle are the fine **Palazzo Rucellai** (not open to the public), the **Capella Rucellai** (*see p86*) and the adjacent modern art museum, the **Museo Marino Marini** (*see p86*).

Alberti had already designed the Palazzo Rucellai in Via della Vigna Nuova for the Rucellai family when he created the façade of Santa Maria Novella. The palazzo's subtle frontage was inspired by Rome's Colosseum: the pilasters that section the bottom storey have Doric capitals, those on the middle level come with Ionic capitals, and those on the top storey are based on the Corinthian style. There's no rustication: Alberti considered it fit only for tyrants, of whom there were plenty at the time. The Rucellai were wool merchants who had grown rich by importing a Majorcan red dye derived from lichen and known as *oricello*, from which their surname derives. The charming Orti Oricellari garden at the far end of Via della Scala was where the family grew their crop.

Up past Piazza Goldoni, Lungarno Vespucci and Borgo Ognissanti open out into Piazza Ognissanti, flanked by swanky hotels and topped by the church of **Ognissanti** (*see p87*), the cloister of which houses the **Cenacolo di Ognissanti** (*see below*). Further up, elegant residential roads lead out on to the main avenues, Porta al Prato and the mammoth park of **Le Cascine** (*see p104*).

Cappella Rucellai

Via della Spada (055 216912). **Open** 10am-noon Mon-Sat. **Admission** free. **Map** p318 B2.

It's not so much a case of blink and you'll miss this tiny chapel; more that if you oversleep or linger over breakfast, you'll already find it closed for the day. Once part of the church of San Pancrazio (now the Museo Marino Marini), the chapel retains the church's charming belltower and contains the tombs of many members of the family of 15th-century wool magnate Giovanni Rucellai, including that of his wife Iacopa Strozzi. It's worth a visit to see Alberti's Temple of the Santo Sepolcro, commissioned in 1467 by Giovanni to be built to the same proportions as the Holy Sepulchre of Jerusalem in an attempt to ensure his own salvation.

Cenacolo di Ognissanti

Borgo Ognissanti 42 (055 2398700). **Open** *Last Supper* 9am-noon Mon, Tue, Sat. **Admission** free. **Map** p318 B1.

The Ognissanti's (*see p87*) lovely cloister, accessed via a separate entrance on Borgo Ognissanti, is painted with frescoes illustrating the life of St Francis. The cloister's main point of interest, however, is Ghirlandaio's most famous *Last Supper*, dated 1480 (*see below*), housed in the refectory. There's also a museum of Franciscan bits and bobs.

Museo Marino Marini

Piazza San Pancrazio (055 219432/www.museomarino marini.it). **Open** *Summer* 10am-5pm Mon, Wed-Fri. *Winter* 10am-5pm Mon, Wed-Sat. Closed Aug. **Admission** €4. **No credit cards**. **Map** p318 B2.

Last Suppers Ghirlandaio

Domenico Ghirlandaio's *Last Supper* (1480), located off the cloister on a refectory wall of the 13th-century church of **Ognissanti** (*see p87*), is one of the artist's most accomplished works. Though his portrayal

of the moment Jesus reveals he will be betrayed by one of his companions is a more serene rendering than many, Ghirlandaio manages to impart a tangible sense of drama with his use of soft colours. As with his work in San Marco (*see p94*), and by request of the Umiliati Benedictine monks who commissioned the fresco, Ghirlandaio used religious iconography to load the work with deeper religious meaning. The peacocks on the tablecloth signify the Resurrection, while the evergreen plants, quails, oranges, cherries and the dove represent other stages of the Passion and Redemption of Christ.

The original Albertian church on this site, San Pancrazio, was redesigned to accommodate the works of prolific sculptor and painter Marino Marini (1901-80). Many of the first-floor sculptures are a variation on the theme of horse and rider; the central exhibit is the 6m (20ft) *Composizione Equestre*. The second floor has a series of other bronze and cement pieces, including the hypnotic *Nuotatore* (Swimmer) and some fabulous colourful paintings of dancers and jugglers.

Ognissanti

Borgo Ognissanti 42 (055 2398700). **Open** 9am-12.30pm, 4-7.30pm daily. **Admission** free.
Map p318 B1.

The church of Ognissanti (All Saints) was founded in the 13th century by the Umiliati, a group of monks from Lombardy. The monks introduced the wool trade to Florence; as the city's wealth was built on the stuff, it can be argued that without them there would have been no Florentine Renaissance. The Umiliati were so rich by the 14th century that they commissioned Giotto to paint the *Maestà* for their high altar; 50 years later, they got Giovanni da Milano to create a flashier altarpiece with more gold. Both works are now in the Uffizi (*see p80*). Ognissanti was also the parish church of the Vespucci, a family of merchants from Peretola (near where the airport now stands) who dealt in silk, wine, wool, banking and goods from the Far East. The family included 15th-century navigator Amerigo, the man who sailed to the Venezuelan coast in 1499 and had two continents named after him.

The church has been rebuilt numerous times and is now visited mainly for paintings by Ghirlandaio, including *St Jerome* and the *Madonna della Misericordia*, which includes a portrait of Amerigo Vespucci: he's the young boy dressed in pink. (To see Ghirlandaio's *Last Supper* (*see p86*) you have to go back outside and through the next door.) Other frescoes include a *St Augustine* by Botticelli and a *St Jerome* by Ghirlandaio. In the Chapel of St Peter of Alcantara, look out for the tomb of Botticelli, marked with his family name of Filipepi.

Santa Maria Novella

Piazza Santa Maria Novella (055 2645184/219257).
Open *Church* 9am-5pm Mon-Thur, Sat; 1-5pm Fri, Sun. **Admission** €2.50. **No credit cards**.
Map p318 A2.

Santa Maria Novella was the Florentine seat of the Dominicans, a fanatically inquisitorial order fond of leading street brawls against suspected heretics and encouraging the faithful to strip and whip themselves before the altar. The piazza outside, one of Florence's biggest, was enlarged in 1244-5 to accommodate the crowds that came to hear St Peter the Martyr: one of the viler members of the saintly canon, Peter made his name persecuting so-called heretics in northern Italy and ended up with one of their axes in his head.

The pièce de résistance of the church is its Alberti façade. In 1465, at the request of the Rucellai family, Alberti incorporated the Romanesque lower storey into a refined Renaissance scheme, adding the triangular tympanum and the scrolls that mask the side nave exteriors in an exercise of consummate classical harmony. The church interior, however, was designed by the order's monks and is fittingly severe, with striped vaults and a peculiar architectural ruse of lowering the height of the arches as they near the altar and adding steps to create a strong horizontal perspective.

The church is also home to the *Crocifisso* by Giotto, a simple, worldly wooden crucifix. It was finally returned to the church in 2001 after a 12-year restoration and was placed in the centre of the basilica where the Dominicans had originally positioned it on its arrival in 1290.

Until Vasari had them whitewashed in the mid 16th century, the church walls were covered with frescoes. Fortunately, Vasari left Masaccio's *Trinità* of 1427 in the third span on the left nave. Here we can see the first ever application of Brunelleschi's mathematical rules of perspective to a painting. The result is a triumph of *trompe l'œil*, with God, Christ and two saints appearing to stand in a niche watched by the patrons Lorenzo Lenzi and his wife. The sinister inscription above the skeleton on the sarcophagus reads: 'I was what you are and what I am you shall be.'

The Dominicans appear to have loosened up over the following decades. In 1485 they let Ghirlandaio cover the walls of the Cappella Tornabuoni with scenes from the life of John the Baptist, featuring lavish contemporary Florentine interiors and a supporting cast from the Tornabuoni family. Ghirlandaio also found the time to train a young man by the name of Michelangelo while working on the chapel. At about the same time, Filippino Lippi was at work next door, in the Cappella di Filippo Strozzi painting scenes from the life of St Philip.

To compare Masaccio's easeful use of perspective with the contorted struggles of Paolo Uccello, visit the Chiostro Verde (green cloister) to the left of the church (via a separate entrance), so-called because of the green base pigment the artist used, which gave the flood-damaged frescoes a deathly hue. Uccello's lunettes can be considered either visionary experiments of modern art before its time or a complete perspective mess, depending on your tolerance of artistic licence. Off the Chiostro you'll find the Cappellone (or Cappella) degli Spagnoli, named after the wife of Cosimo I, Eleonora di Toledo, and decorated with vibrant scenes by Andrea di Bonaiuto celebrating the triumph of Dominicans and the Catholic Church. Look for the odd-looking cupola on the Duomo fresco: it's the artist's own design for the dome, rejected in favour of Brunelleschi's plan.

Also to the left of the church is the Romanesque-Gothic bell tower dating back to 1330; to the right is a cemetery surrounded by the grave niches of Florence's wealthy families. Also here, just off the Chiostro Verde, is the small Museo di Santa Maria Novella, which was designed by Talenti and houses 35 frescoed heads by the Orcagnas.

San Lorenzo

Duck the coach parties and you'll find a buzzy yet historic district.

The original Medici neighbourhood of San Lorenzo is loved and hated in equal measures. A vibrant mêlée of markets, mainstream shopping streets and narrow alleyways, it's always steaming with the smells of bakeries, delis and cafés and doughnut stands, but it's also continuously teeming with tourists.

The central **market** of San Lorenzo is the hub of the area, and spreads its tentacles over a wide area of *piazze*, snaking north from the church of **San Lorenzo** (*see p91*). The street stalls around here sell cheap clothes, mediocre leather goods and tacky souvenirs, though there are richer pickings in the huge covered market.

Roads lead off the *piazze* in a star shape. Head north-east from Piazza San Lorenzo up Via de' Ginori alongside the gardens behind the **Palazzo Medici Riccardi** (*see p91*), and past craft shops up to the corner where Via San Gallo meets Via XXVII Aprile. The Benedictine refectory of **Cenacolo di Sant'Apollonia** (*see p90*) is on the left, while the **Chiostro dello Scalzo** (*see p90*) is situated north of Piazza San Marco on Via Cavour. At the top of Via San Gallo is the old city gate, Porta San Gallo.

Travelling south from Piazza San Lorenzo will lead you past busy shoe and clothes shops in Borgo San Lorenzo to the **Duomo** (*see p70*), while to the north is the main market square, **Piazza del Mercato Centrale**, with the back

entrance to the covered food market, packed with stalls offering fruit and vegetables, fish, cheese and meat (*see p149* **Market forces**). If you head north-west from the **Cappelle Medicee** (*see p90*) in Piazza degli Madonna Aldobrandini at the back of San Lorenzo church, you pass along Via Faenza, with its plethora of one-star hotels. Heading north-east up Via Sant'Antonino takes you past tiny food stores; to the south-west is Santa Maria Novella station.

If you continue up Via Faenza and cross dingy Via Nazionale, you will come to the **Cenacolo di Fuligno** (*see p90*) on the right. South-west down Via Nazionale brings you to Largo Fratelli Alinari, home of the **Museo di Storia della Fotografia** (*see p90*), with its photography museum, archives and shop. Heading in the opposite direction, north-east up Via Nazionale, the roads widen into Piazza dell'Indipendenza, where the grand *palazzi* herald the beginnings of a more genteel area north of the market district. The double square, with a main road running through the middle, a few stone seats scattered round the edges, bald grass and a couple of trees, is a bad excuse for a park. But it does at least take you a step closer to the duck pond and flowerbeds of the gardens of the otherwise unspectacular (albeit massive) **Fortezza da Basso** (*see p105*), on the other side of the traffic-clogged main *viale*.

Sightseeing

San Lorenzo church. *See p91.*

Chiostro dello Scalzo.

Cappelle Medicee

Piazza Madonna degli Aldobrandini (055 2388602).
Open 8.15am-5pm Tue-Sat, 1st, 3rd, 5th Sun & 2nd,
4th Mon of mth. **Admission** €6. **No credit cards.**
Map p318 A3.

Michelangelo's swansong to Florence was this mausoleum, built for the main members of the Medici mob. The floor plan of the Cappella dei Principi (Princes' Chapel) was based on that of Florence's Baptistery and, possibly, of the Holy Sepulchre in Jerusalem; it's inlaid with brilliant *pietra dura*, which kept the workers of the Opificio delle Pietre Dure (*see p94*) busy for decades after Michelangelo himself had been hauled off to Rome to finish the Sistine Chapel. Michelangelo was furious at having to leave the city – 'I cannot live under pressure from patrons, let alone paint' – but he'd worked long enough on the project to leave it as one of his masterpieces.

The Cappella dei Principi, constructed from huge hunks of porphyry and ancient Roman marbles hauled into the city by Turkish slaves, houses six sarcophagi of the Medici Grand Dukes. (It had been hoped that the tombs would be joined by that purported to be of Christ, but the authorities in Jerusalem refused to sell it.) Although it's closed to the public, the recent discovery of the crypt has caused much excitement, especially the sensational unearthing of a stone under the altar that concealed its entrance. Conspiracy theorists were disappointed to learn that many of the Medicis buried there were not poisoned by ambitious relatives but died of malaria.

The Sagrestia Nuova (New Sacristy) is dominated by the tombs of Lorenzo il Magnifico's relatives: grandson Lorenzo, Duke of Urbino, and son Giuliano, Duke of Nemours. The tombs were designed by Michelangelo with the allegorical figures of Night and Day, and, opposite, Dawn and Dusk reclining on top; their gaze directs the visitor's eyes to a sculpture of a Madonna and child on a facing wall. Also here, under the sacristy, is the incomplete tomb of Lorenzo il Magnifico and brother Giuliano. The chapel's coffered dome was designed to contribute to Michelangelo's allegory within the tomb of the inevitability of death, symbolising the 'sun' of salvation.

Cenacolo del Conservatorio di Fuligno

Via Faenza 42 (055 286982). **Open** 9am-noon &
by appointment Mon, Tue, Sat. **Admission** free.
Map p318 A3.

The harmonious fresco on the refectory wall of the ex-convent of St Onofrio was discovered in 1845, and was at first thought to be the work of Raphael. In fact, it is one of the best of Perugino's works: a *Last Supper* dating from about 1490. In the background is a representation of the Oration of the Garden in the characteristically Umbrian landscape, a dead giveaway of the painter's roots: Perugino was a nickname granted to him as he hailed from Perugia.

Cenacolo di Sant'Apollonia

Via XXVII Aprile 1 (055 23885). **Open** 8.30am-
3.30pm Tue-Sat, 2nd, 4th Sun & 1st, 3rd, 5th Mon
of mth. **Admission** free.

The works in this Benedictine refectory, such as the frescoes of the *Passion of Christ*, were covered over during the baroque period and only came to light in the late 19th century. The most important is Andrea del Castagno's *Last Supper* (*see p91*).

Chiostro dello Scalzo

Via Cavour 69 (055 2388604). **Open** 9am-1pm
Mon; by appointment only other days. **Admission**
free. **Map** p319 A4.

The 'Cloister of the Barefoot', so called because the monk holding the cross in the re-enactments of the Passion of Christ traditionally went shoeless, is frescoed with Andrea del Sarto's monochrome chiaroscuro episodes from the life of St John the Baptist. Built to a design by Sangallo around a double courtyard with spindly Corinthian columns, it's a must-see epitome of delicacy and understatement.

Museo di Storia della Fotografia

off Largo Fratelli Alinari (055 23951/www.alinari.it).
Open 9am-1pm, 2.30-6.30pm Mon-Fri; 10am-1pm,
3-7pm Sat. Closed 3wks Aug. **Admission** free.
Map p318 A2.

The Alinari brothers are credited with starting the world's first photography company, and some of their images, such as one of a man in a hat climbing the tiny spiral staircase in the bell tower of Palazzo Vecchio, are nothing short of iconic. The Museum of the History of Photography, currently on a small courtyard off Largo Fratelli Alinari but slated to move to a new Santa Maria Novella site some time in 2006 (*see p85*), documents the history of Florence and other Italian landmark cities by drawing on their collections. The archives and shop will remain in this location.

Palazzo Medici Riccardi

Via Cavour 1 (055 2760340/www.palazzo-medici.it).
Open 9am-7pm Mon, Tue, Thur-Sun. **Admission**
€4. **No credit cards**. **Map** p319 B4.

A demonstration of Medici muscle and subtlety, the
Palazzo Medici Riccardi was home to the Medici
until they moved into the Palazzo Vecchio in 1540.
Not wishing to appear too ostentatious, Cosimo il
Vecchio rejected Brunelleschi's design as too extravagant and plumped for one by Michelozzo, who had
recently proved his worth as a heavyweight architect in the rebuilding of the San Marco convent
complex. Michelozzo designed a façade with a heavily rusticated lower storey in the style of many military buildings. However, the first storey is smoother
and more refined, while a yet more restrained second storey is crowned by an overhanging cornice.

The building was expanded and revamped in
the 17th century by the Riccardi, its new owners,
but retains Michelozzo's charming chapel. Almost
entirely covered with frescoes by Benozzo Gozzoli,
a student of Fra' Angelico, the chapel features a
vivid *Journey of the Magi*, actually a portrait of 15th-
century Medici. In another room, off the Gallery, is
Fra' Filippo Lippi's winsome *Madonna and Child*.

San Lorenzo

Piazza San Lorenzo (055 216634). **Open** 10am-5pm
Mon-Sat. **Admission** €2.50. **No credit cards**.
Map p318 A3.

It may not look like much from the outside, but this
was the parish church of the Medici family, who
largely financed its construction. It was built
between 1419 and 1469 to a design by Brunelleschi,
and was the first church to which the architect
applied his theory of rational proportion. It sprawls,
heavy and imposing, between Piazza San Lorenzo
and Piazza Madonna degli Aldobrandini, with a
dome almost as prominent as that of the Duomo.

Despite the fortune spent on the place, the façade
was never finished, hence the digestive biscuit
bricks. In 1518 the Medici pope Leo X commissioned
Michelangelo to design a façade – the models are in
the Casa Buonarroti (*see p96*) – and ordained that
the marble should be quarried at Pietrasanta, part

of Florence's domain. Michelangelo disagreed, pre-
ferring high-quality Carrara marble. In the end, it
didn't matter: the scheme was cancelled in 1520.

A couple of artworks merit a closer look.
Savonarola snarled his tales of sin and doom from
Donatello's bronze pulpits, but the reliefs are also
powerful: you can almost hear the crowds scream in
the *Deposition*. On the north wall is a *Martyrdom of
St Lawrence* by Mannerist painter par excellence
Bronzino. The work is a decadent affair in which the
burning of the saint is attended by muscle-bound
men and hefty women with red-gold hair, dressed in
pink, green, yellow and lilac. In the second chapel
on the right is another Mannerist work, a *Marriage
of the Virgin* by Rosso Fiorentino, while the north
transept holds an *Annunciation* by Filippo Lippi,
which displays a clarity of line and a depth of perspective that make it perfect for this interior.

Opening off the north transept is the Sagrestia
Vecchia (Old Sacristy): another Brunelleschi design,
it has a dome segmented like a tangerine and proportions based on cubes and spheres, along with a
fabulous painted *tondo* by Donatello. The doors, also
by Donatello, feature martyrs, apostles and Church
fathers; to the left of the entrance is an elaborate
tomb made out of serpentine, porphyry, marble
and bronze containing the remains of Lorenzo il
Magnifico's father and uncle, by Verrocchio.

Reached via the door to the left of the façade,
Michelangelo's architectural classic, the Biblioteca
Mediceo-Laurenziana (Laurentian Library), was built
to house the Medici's large library. It still contains
priceless volumes, papyri, codices and documents,
though not all of them are on permanent display.
The entrance corridor has a stunning red and cream
inlaid mosaic floor, while the library itself displays
Michelangelo's predilection for the human form over
any classical architectural norms. However, it's in the
vestibule leading into the reading room that the true
masterpiece of the library is to be found. The slick
and highly original three-sweep stairwell in *pietra serena* was a ground-breaking design, the first example
ever of the expressive Mannerist style in architecture
and one of the most elegant staircases ever built.

Last Suppers Andrea del Castagno

Andrea del Castagno's masterly *Last
Supper* (1445-50) is one of many works
in the Benedictine refectory of **Cenacolo
di Sant'Apollonia** (*see p90*) that were
discovered only in the 1860s. The
Benedictine nuns had, until this point,
observed a strict *clausura*, and parts of the
frescoes had even been whitewashed during
the baroque period. However, restoration
work revealed the full glory of the *cenacolo*,
now on display to the public.

In his depiction of events, del Castagno
reverts to a 14th-century seating plan:
Judas is alienated on our side of the table,
a dark figure breaking the pure white of the
tablecloth and symbolically portrayed to
resemble a satyr, a Catholic symbol of
evil. The vibrant colours and enclosed
space intensify the scene. Above the *Last
Supper* are a *Crucifixion*, *Deposition* and
Resurrection, also by del Castagno. Ring
the bell for entry.

San Marco

Home to the most famous statue in the world.

Of all Florence's neighbourhoods, visitor-friendly San Marco has the most diverse array of museums, with Renaissance masterpieces jostling with prehistoric gems and Greek ceramics for the attention of the visiting hordes. However, it's far from just a tourist centre: head to the nigh-on perfect porticoed square of Santissima Annunziata, at San Marco's centre, and it'll become apparent that the area also carries a buzzing collegiate feel: the square is invariably busy with crowds of university types from the nearby faculty buildings.

Surrounded on three sides by delicate arcades, the **Piazza della Santissima Annunziata** (abbreviated to SS Annunziata) is dominated by the powerful equestrian statue of Grand Duke Ferdinando I by Giambologna. On the eastern side is the **Spedale degli Innocenti** (*see p94*). Opened in 1445 as the first foundling hospital in Europe, it was commissioned by the guild of silk weavers and designed by architect and guild member Filippo Brunelleschi. The building is one of the most significant examples of early Renaissance construction in the city and marks the advent of Renaissance town planning. Brunelleschi had designed it to fit into his greater plan for a perfectly symmetrical piazza – it was to be modern Europe's first – but the architect died before realising his dream, and the porticoes were continued around two other sides of the square in the 17th century. The powder-blue medallions in the spandrels, each showing a swaddled baby, are by Andrea della Robbia. Unwanted babies, often those of domestic servants, were left in a small revolving door in the wall, where they were collected by the nuns.

Passing under the northernmost arch of the Spedale is Via della Colonna, highlighted by the **Museo Archeologico** (*see p93*). Walking south from the square towards the Duomo will bring you to the **Museo Leonardo da Vinci** (*see p93*). On the western side of the square is upmarket hotel **Loggiato dei Serviti** (*see p56*); the church of **Santissima Annunziata** (*see p94*) is to the north. The street between the two, Via C Battisti, leads west into Piazza San Marco, a hub for local buses and the site of the church of **San Marco** (*see p94*).

Beside San Marco is the **Museo di San Marco** (*see p93*); on the Via Ricasoli corner of Piazza San Marco, the queues reveal the status of the **Galleria dell'Accademia** (*see below*) as one of the city's most popular museums. Round the corner is the **Opificio delle Pietre Dure** (*see p94*), a museum and workshop dedicated to the art of inlaying gems in mosaics. North of the piazza is the mineral department of the city's **Museo di Storia Naturale** (*see p94*), while just around the corner is the perfect resting place after a hard morning of sightseeing, the exotic **Giardino dei Semplici** (*see p93*).

Galleria dell'Accademia

Via Ricasoli 58-60 (055 2388609). **Open** 8.15am-6.50pm Tue-Sun. **Admission** €8. **No credit cards.** **Map** p318 A4.
The Accademia contains a great many magnificent and historic works, but the queues that snake down Via Ricasoli are, in the main, here for one reason above all others. The reward reaped by a wait in line is an eyeful of the most famous statue in the world: Michelangelo's monumental *David* (1501-4), looking fresh from a recent sprucing up. The restoration was controversial, with experts disagreeing over which

Nun shall pass.

method was best for cleaning the marble statue; eventually it was decided that distilled water should be used, rather than a harsher dry-cleaning method.

David started life as a serious political icon portraying strength and resolve, designed to encourage Florentines to support their fledgling constitution. However, having carved it from a narrow, 5m-high (16ft) slab of marble, Michelangelo undoubtedly also considered it a monument to his genius. The artist intended it to be placed on a high column, and so gave *David* a top-heavy shape in order that it would look its best from the beholder's viewpoint a good distance beneath it. However, in 1873, when the statue was moved from Piazza della Signoria (where a copy still stands), the authorities decided to keep the plinth low so that visitors could witness its curves close-up; this is the reason why it seems a little out of proportion (notice the large head).

Other Michelangelo works line the walls of the *David* salon; among them are his *Slaves*, masterly but unfinished sculptures struggling to escape from marble prisons. They were intended for Pope Julius II's tomb, a project that Michelangelo was forced to abandon in order to paint the Sistine Chapel ceiling in Rome. On the right of *David* is the similarly unfinished *Pietà Palestrina*; it's attributed to Michelangelo, although the stilted lines of the figures surrounding Jesus have led many to believe it was taken over halfway through by a student of the master.

The gallery also houses a mixed bag of late Gothic and Renaissance paintings in the rooms on the ground floor, including two of Botticelli's *Madonna*s and bible scenes by Perugino, Fra Bartolomeo and Filippino Lippi. Check the fabulous musical instruments from the Conservatory of Luigi Cherubini on the ground floor, while among the late 14th- and early 15th-century Florentine paintings on the first floor is a moving *Pietà* (1365) by Giovanni da Milano.

Giardino dei Semplici

Via Micheli 3 (055 2757402). **Open** 9am-1pm Mon, Tue, Thur, Fri, Sun; 9am-5pm Sat. **Admission** €3. **No credit cards**.
Set up to cultivate and research exotic plants, the Giardino dei Semplici (literally, the 'garden of samples') was planted in 1545 for Cosimo I, on land seized from an order of Dominican nuns. Essential oils were extracted, perfumes distilled and cures and antidotes sought for various ailments and poisons. A sweet-smelling haven, it's a lovely place to wander.

Museo Archeologico

Via della Colonna 38 (055 23575/www.comune.fi.it/ soggetti/sat). **Open** 2-7pm Mon; 8.30am-7pm Tue, Thur; 8.30am-2pm Wed, Fri, Sun. **Admission** €4. **No credit cards**. **Map** p318 A5.
If the injection of Renaissance art you've been receiving is beginning to feel like an overdose, then Florence's archaeological museum, housed in the cross-shaped Palazzo della Crocetta, is a great antidote. With jewellery, funerary sculpture, urns and bronzes dating from the fifth century BC, this is one of the best places in the country to see important

Etruscan art. The fabulous *Chimera* is here, a mythical beast that's part lion, part goat and part snake; also present is the first-century BC Etruscan bronze *Orator*, famous and historically important because the speaker in question is wearing a Roman toga. The first rooms house Egyptian artefacts from prehistoric eras all the way through to the Copta period (310 AD); one highlight, housed in Room IV, is part of the fabled *Book of the Dead*. On the second floor is a strong collection of Greek ceramics that includes the *Hidria*, a famous water-drawing vase featuring idyllic scenes of fountain maidens.

Museo Leonardo da Vinci

Via dei Servi 66-68r (055 282966). **Open** 10am-7pm daily. **Admission** €7. **No credit cards**. **Map** p319 A4.
Thanks to Dan Brown, interest in Leonardo has never been higher; the new Leonardo da Vinci Museum offers an attractive, interactive insight into the machines that featured in da Vinci's codes. Several of his most extraordinary inventions have been built from studies taken from his drawings: flying machines (suspended from the ceiling on pulleys), a hydraulic saw, a printing machine and even a massive tank, which measures 5.3m by 3m (17ft by 10ft) and weighs two tons. Most of the exhibits can be touched, moved and even dangled from, making the place immensely popular among kids who've long tired of looking at paintings and glass cabinets of priceless old artefacts.

Museo di San Marco

Piazza San Marco 1 (055 2388608). **Open** 8.15am-1.50pm Tue-Fri, 1st, 3rd & 5th Mon of mth; 8.15am-6.50pm Sat; 8.15am-7pm 2nd & 4th Sun of mth. **Admission** €4. **No credit cards**.
Housed in the monastery where he lived with his fellow monks, the Museo di San Marco is largely dedicated to the ethereal paintings of Fra Angelico (known to Florentines as Beato Angelico), one of the most important spiritual artists of the 15th century. You're greeted on the first floor by one of the most famous images in Christendom, an otherworldly *Annunciation*, but the images Fra Angelico and his assistants frescoed on the walls of the monks' white vaulted cells are almost as impressive, with most of the cells on the outer wall of the left corridor by Fra Angelico himself. Particularly outstanding is the lyrical *Noli Me Tangere*, which depicts Christ appearing to Mary Magdalene in a field of flowers, and the surreal *Mocking of Christ*, in which Christ's torturers are represented simply by relevant fragments of their anatomy (a hand holding a whip, one holding a sponge, a face spitting).

The cell that was later occupied by Fra Girolamo Savonarola is adorned with portraits of the rabid reformer, by Fra Bartolomeo. The bell under the portico of the main cloister, rung when Savonarola was arrested, is nicknamed *la piagnona* (the whiner); the term is also a nickname for followers of the puritan Savonarola, who were said to whinge about the depravation and permissiveness of the times.

Sightseeing

On the ground floor, in the Ospizio dei Pellegrini (pilgrims' hospice), are more works by Fra Angelico. *The Tabernacle of the Madonna dei Linaiuoli*, his first commission from 1433 for the guild of linen makers, is here: painted on wood carved by Ghiberti, it contains some of his best-known images, the polichrome musical angels. Also here are a superb *Deposition* and a *Last Judgement* in which the blessed dance among the flowers and trees of paradise while the damned are boiled in cauldrons and pursued by monsters.

To the right, the refectory is dominated by a Ghirlandaio *Last Supper*, where the disciples, by turns bored, praying, crying or haughty, pick at a frugal repast of bread, wine and cherries against a background of orange trees, a peacock, a Burmese cat and flying ducks. The oranges are the fruits of paradise, the peacock symbolises the Resurrection, the cat as a metaphor of evil is near Judas, and the ducks represent the heavens.

Museo di Storia Naturale – Sezione Mineralogia

Via la Pira 4 (055 216936/www.unifi.it/msn). Open 9am-1pm Mon, Tue, Thur, Fri, Sun; 9am-5pm Sat. Admission €4. No credit cards.

This simply arranged and clearly explained collection makes gem lovers drool. It's packed full of strange and lovely stones, including 12 huge Brazilian quartzes. Agates, chalcedony, tourmaline, opals and iridescent limonite sparkle from the cabinets. Also here are glass models of famous stones, such as the Koh-i-noor diamond and treasures from Cosimo III's collection.

Opificio delle Pietre Dure

Via degli Alfani 78 (055 218709). Open 8.15am-2pm Mon-Wed, Fri, Sat; 8.15am-7pm Thur. Admission €2. No credit cards. Map p318 A4.

Pietra dura is the craft of inlaying gems or semi-precious stones in intricate mosaics. The Opificio (workshop) was founded by Grand Duke Ferdinando I in 1588; it's now an important restoration centre (you can see the restorers at work, by appointment), but also provides a fascinating insight into this typically Florentine art, with its mezzanine exhibitions of tools and stones, and its displays of the methods used for the cutting and polishing of the stones through to the inlaying and mosaic techniques.

San Marco

Piazza San Marco (055 287628). Open 8.30am-noon, 4-6pm Mon-Sat; 4-6pm Sun. Admission free. Map p318 A4.

Think the Medici lavished a lot of cash on San Lorenzo (*see p91*)? They spent even more on the church and convent of San Marco. After Cosimo il Vecchio returned from exile in 1434 and organised the transfer of the monastery of San Marco from the Silvestrine monks (who were accused of decadent behaviour) to the Dominicans, he went on to fund the renovation of the decaying church and convent by Michelozzo. (Whether he did so to ease his conscience – banking was still officially forbidden by the Church – or to cash in on the increasing popularity of the Dominicans is uncertain.) Cosimo also founded a public library full of Greek and Latin works, which had a great influence on Florentine humanists; meetings of the Florentine Humanist Academy were held in the gardens. Ironically, later in the 15th century, San Marco became the base of religious fundamentalist Fra Girolamo Savonarola, who burned countless humanist treasures in his notorious Bonfire of the Vanities. The library now houses the monks' tomes, notable especially for their exquisite illuminations.

Note that as of mid 2005 the church was undergoing what was scheduled to be a sustained period of restoration: the forecast completion date as this guide went to press was 2006/7. Don't be surprised to find the interior lined with scaffolding.

Santissima Annunziata

Piazza della SS Annunziata (055 266181). Open 7am-12.30pm, 4-6.30pm daily. Admission free. Map p318 A4.

Despite Brunelleschi's perfectionist ambitions for the square it crowns, Santissima Annunziata (Holy Annunciation), the church of the Servite order, is a place of popular worship rather than perfect proportion. Highlights include a frescoed baroque ceiling and an opulent shrine built around a miraculous Madonna, purportedly painted by a monk called Bartolomeo in 1252 and, as the story goes, finished overnight by angels; it's from this legend that the church derives its name. Surrounding the icon are flowers, silver lamps and pewter body parts, ex-votos left in the hope that the Madonna will cure the dicky heart or gammy leg of loved ones.

Despite its somewhat misleading baroque appearance, the church was actually built by Michelozzo in the 15th century, as can be seen in the light, arcaded atrium. The atrium was frescoed early the following century by Pontormo, Rosso Fiorentino and, most strikingly, Andrea del Sarto, whose *Birth of the Virgin* is set within the walls of a Renaissance palazzo with cherubs perched on a mantelpiece and a festooned bed canopy. There's another del Sarto fresco in the Chiostro dei Morti (Cloister of the Dead), but you need permission from the sacristan to see it.

Spedale degli Innocenti

Piazza della SS Annunziata (055 2037308/www. istitutodeglinnocenti.it). Open 8.30am-2pm Mon, Tue, Thur-Sun. Admission €4. No credit cards. Map p318 A5.

Housed in the recreation room of Brunelleschi's foundlings hospital, this collection received a substantial blow in 1853, when several important works were auctioned off (for a relative pittance) in order to raise money for the hospital. The remaining pieces, a harmonious collection, include an unsurprising concentration of Madonna and Bambino pieces, including a Botticelli and a vivid Luca della Robbia. The high point, however, is Ghirlandaio's splendidly luminescent *Adoration of the Magi*, commissioned for the high altar of the hospital's church.

Santa Croce

Reliquary of history and learning.

The largest of Florence's medieval parochial areas, Santa Croce stretches across the eastern side of the historic centre from Via del Proconsolo and Via de' Castellani to Piazza Beccaria on the main avenue, and north from the river towards Piazzale Donatello. The area, like much of central Florence, carries with it a heady air of history, encompassing the **Sinagoga & Museo di Arte e Storia Ebraica** (*see p98*) in the north, just south of the elegant residential Piazza d'Azeglio, the **Museo di Antropologia e Etnologia** (*see p96*) and Piazza San Firenze, with its imposing ex-prison building (now the **Bargello**; *see p96*), opposite the **Badia Fiorentina** (*see p77*) in the dead centre of the city.

South of the Bargello in Piazza San Firenze, the ornate baroque church of San Firenze now houses the city's law courts. In Via dell'Oriuolo, off Via Proconsolo and east of the Duomo, is the **Museo di Firenze com'era** (*see p96*) stuffed with the city archives, and, nearby, the self-explanatory **Museo Fiorentino di Preistoria** (*see p96*). In Borgo Pinti, east of the Duomo, watch out for the hard-to-find entrance to the church of **Santa Maria Maddalena dei Pazzi** (*see p98*). Just north of the river is **Piazza Santa Croce**, with the imposing Gothic church of **Santa Croce** (*see p97*) and attached **Museo dell'Opera di Santa Croce & Cappella dei Pazzi** (*see p97*). Lining the paved pedestrian square is a mix of shops and restaurants with outside tables. On the south side is the frescoed sepia façade of **Palazzo d'Antella**: decorated in 1620, it now houses smart rental apartments. Outside the church is Enrico Pazzi's 1865 statue of Dante. The sui/homicidal football game *calcio storico* is played here every June (*see p158*).

At the head of Piazza Santa Croce, **Via de' Benci** is dotted with crafts shops and bohemian restaurants running down towards the Arno, past the eclectic **Museo Horne** (*see p97*), to the Ponte alle Grazie. Like most of the bridges in central Florence, this one has a fascinating history; like all but one (the Ponte Vecchio), it was blown up just before the Germans' retreat at the end of World War II and was only rebuilt in 1957. Its own particular irony was that the original stone bridge, built in 1227, had been the only one in Florence to survive a flood in 1333. The bridge once housed several oratories and chapels and a few workshops, before they were demolished in the 19th century. One of these chapels, devoted to Santa Maria delle Grazie, was popular with distraught lovers seeking solace, giving the bridge its name.

Continuing east on Lungarno delle Grazie or Corso dei Tintori (named after the dyers who lived here in medieval times), you'll come across a square dominated by the **Biblioteca Nazionale**. Built to house the three million books and two million documents that were held in the Uffizi until 1935, the national library has two towers with statues of Dante and Galileo. In mock disrespect, Florentines nicknamed the twin towers 'the asses' ears'.

Moon over **Santa Croce church**.
See p97.

Sightseeing

North of the parish square lie myriad winding streets mostly given over to leather factories and tiny souvenir shops. The exception is Borgo degli Albizi, where shops are housed on the ground floors of the dour but grand palazzi that line it. Until recently, the area north of the church of Santa Croce itself, stretching up past the **Casa Buonarroti** (*see below*) in Via Ghibellina to Piazza dei Ciompi, was the rough-and-ready home to rival gangs of bored Florentine youths. Increasingly yuppified, it now yields trendy *trattorie* and wine bars. **Piazza dei Ciompi** was named after the dyers' and wool workers' revolt of 1378, and is taken over by a junk and antiques market during the week and a huge day-long flea market on the last Sunday of the month (*see p149* **Market forces**). It's dominated by the **Loggia del Pesce**, built by Vasari in 1568 for the Mercato Vecchio, which previously occupied the site of Piazza della Repubblica. It was taken apart in the 19th century and re-erected here, and now shelters a book stand.

Further east is the fruit and vegetable market of **Sant'Ambrogio** (*see p149* **Market forces**) and the shops, bars, *pizzerie* and restaurants of Borgo La Croce. Immediately to the south is Piazza Ghiberti, home of the renowned **Cibrèo** restaurant (*see p121*). Borgo La Croce extends as far as Piazza Beccaria and rests at the east city gate, Porta alla Croce, in the middle of the crazed six-lane avenues circling the historic centre of the city.

Bargello

Via del Proconsolo 4 (055 2388606/www.sbas. firenze.it/bargello). **Open** 8.15am-1.50pm Tue-Sat, 1st, 3rd & 5th Mon of mth, 2nd & 4th Sun of mth. **Admission** €4. **No credit cards. Map** p319 C4.
This imposing, fortified building started life as the Palazzo del Popolo in 1250 and soon became the mainstay of the chief magistrate, or *podestà*. The bodies of executed criminals were displayed in the courtyard during the 14th century; in the 15th century law courts, prisons and torture chambers were set up inside. The Medici made it the seat of the *bargello* (chief of police) in the 16th century; it's this history that lends the place its current name.

Officially the Museo Nazionale del Bargello, the museum opened in 1865 and now holds Florence's most eclectic and prestigious collection of sculpture, with treasures ranging from prime pieces – among the most famous works are Michelangelo's *Bacchus Drunk*, Giambologna's fleet-footed *Mercury* and the *Davids* of Donatello – to Scandinavian chess sets and Egyptian ivories. The first-floor loggia in the courtyard has Giambologna's bronze birds, including a madly exaggerated turkey. The loggia leads to the Salone Donatello, which contains the artist's two triumphant *Davids* and a tense *St George*, the original sculpture that once adorned one of the

tabernacles on the outside of Orsanmichele. Also fascinating are the two bronze panels of the *Sacrifice of Isaac*, sculpted by Brunelleschi and Lorenzo Ghiberti for a competition to design the north doors of the Duomo Baptistery.

Casa Buonarroti

Via Ghibellina 70 (055 241752/www.casabuonarroti. it). **Open** 9.30am-2pm Mon, Wed-Sun. **Admission** €6.50. **No credit cards. Map** p319 C5.
Even though Michelangelo never actually lived here, this 17th-century house, owned by his descendants until 1858, has a collection of memorabilia that gives an insight into the life of Florence's most famous artistic son. On the walls are interesting reproductions of scenes from the painter's life, while the pieces collated by the artist's great-nephew Filippo include two important original works: a bas-relief *Madonna of the Stairs* breastfeeding at the foot of a flight of stairs, and an unfinished *Battle of the Centaurs*. Both were created during Michelangelo's adolescence.

Museo di Antropologia e Etnologia

Via del Proconsolo 12 (055 2396449). **Open** 9am-1pm Mon, Wed-Sat, 1st Sun of mth. **Admission** €4. **No credit cards. Map** p319 B4.
Among the eclectic mix of artefacts from all over the world on display here are a collection of Peruvian mummies, an Ostyak harp from Lapland in the shape of a swan, an engraved trumpet made from an elephant tusk from the former Belgian Congo, Ecuadorian shrunken heads complete with a specially designed skull-beating club, and a Marini-meets-Picasso equestrian monument.

Museo Fiorentino di Preistoria

Via Sant'Egidio 21 (055 295159/www.museo fiorentinopreistoria.it). **Open** 9.30am-12.30pm Mon, Wed, Fri, Sat; 9.30am-4.30pm Tue, Thur; guided tours by appointment. **Admission** €3. **No credit cards. Map** p319 B4.
Florence's Museum of Prehistory traces humanity's development from the Paleolithic to the Bronze Age in Italy and the rest of the world, but – predictably, as most evidence is found in caves – it has to content itself with various displays of photographs and illustrations. The first floor follows hominid physical changes, and also examines Italy's prehistoric artistic legacy. The second floor covers the rest of the world and includes a collection of stone implements found by Frenchman Boucher de Perthes, who ascertained that rocks previously believed to have been shaped by weathering and glacial movement were actually the work of prehistoric humans.

Museo di Firenze com'era

Via dell'Oriuolo 24 (055 2616545). **Open** 9am-2pm Mon-Wed, Fri-Sun. **Admission** €2.70. **No credit cards. Map** p319 B5.
This charmingly named museum ('Florence as It Was') traces the city's development through collections of maps, paintings and archaeological discoveries. There are rooms devoted to Giuseppe

Frescoes inside **Santa Croce church**.

Poggi's plans from the 1860s to modernise Florence by creating Parisian-style boulevards; the famous lunettes of the Medici villas painted in 1599 by Flemish artist Giusto Utens; and the history of the region from 200 million years ago to Roman times. New exhibits include a model of 'Florentia' that shows how the city must have been in Roman times, with the Forum right underneath present-day Piazza della Repubblica and a Roman theatre buried below the Palazzo Vecchio. Also interesting is the huge reproduction of the famous *Pianta della Catena*, a 19th-century copy of a 1470 engraving (the original is now in Berlin) showing the first topological plan of Florence. It's possible to pick out the monuments and other features that are still there today.

Museo Horne

Via dei Benci 6 (055 244661). **Open** *June-early Sept* 9am-1pm Mon, Wed-Sat; 9am-1pm, 8.30-11pm Tue. *Late Sept-May* 9am-1pm Mon-Sat. **Admission** €5. **No credit cards. Map** p319 C4.

The 15th-century Palazzo Corsi-Alberti was purchased in the 1800s by English architect and art historian Herbert Percy Horne, who then spent years restoring it to its original Renaissance splendour. When he died in 1916, he left the palazzo and his vast, fabulous, magpie-like collection to the state; it opened as a museum six years later. Objects on the ground floor range from ceramics and Florentine coins to a coffee grinder and a pair of spectacles. Upstairs is a damaged wooden panel from a triptych attributed to Masaccio. Also here is an *Exorcism* by the Maestro di San Severino and, the pride of the Horne collection, a gold-black *Santo Stefano* by Giotto. Other famous works include a limbless statue of an athlete by Giambologna and a painted wedding chest by Filippino Lippi.

Museo dell'Opera di Santa Croce & Cappella dei Pazzi

Piazza Santa Croce 16 (055 2466105/www.operadi santacroce.it). **Open** 9.30am-5.30pm Mon-Sat; 1-5.30pm Sun. **Admission** €4 (incl museum & chapel). **No credit cards. Map** p319 C5.

Brunelleschi's geometric tour de force, the Cappella dei Pazzi was planned in the 1430s and completed almost 40 years later, but it was well worth the wait. The chapel is based on a central square, topped by a cupola flanked by two barrel-vaulted bays with decorative arches on the white walls echoing the structural arches. The pure lines of the interior are decorated with Luca della Robbia's painted ceramic roundels of the 12 apostles and the four evangelists. The chapel opens on to the cloisters of Santa Croce (*see below*), resulting in a calm, almost detached atmosphere.

Across the courtyard is a small museum of church treasures; the collection includes Donatello's pious bronze *St Louis of Toulouse* from Orsanmichele (*see p79*). The backbone of the collection is in the former refectory, with Taddeo Gaddi's imposing yet poetic *Tree of Life* above his *Last Supper* (unfortunately, in particularly bad condition). In equally poor condition is Cimabue's *Crucifixion*, which hung in the basilica until it was damaged in the flood of 1966. There's also a small permanent exhibition of the woodcuts and engravings of the modern artist Pietro Parigi, whose reawakening of Tuscan realism in religious illustrations earned him fame. Access to the museum and chapel is through Santa Croce church.

Santa Croce

Piazza Santa Croce (055 244619). **Open** 9.30am-5.30pm Mon-Sat; 1-5.30pm Sun. **Admission** €4 (incl museum & chapel). **No credit cards. Map** p319 C5.

Known locally as 'the Pantheon' because of its tombs of many of the city's most illustrious historical figures, Santa Croce remains the richest medieval church in the city, with frescoes by Giotto, a chapel by Brunelleschi and the delightful Cappella dei Pazzi (*see above*). The coloured marble façade is impressive, but at first sight the interior seems big and gloomy, with overbearing marble tombs clogging the walls. Not all of them contain bodies: Dante's, for example, is simply a memorial to the writer, who is buried in Ravenna.

Piazza Santa Croce. *See p95.*

In the niche alongside Dante's is the tomb of Michelangelo, by Vasari. The artist had insisted on burial here when the time came, as he wanted 'a view towards the cupola of the Duomo for all eternity', and had worked on his obsession, the *Pietà* (now in the Museo dell'Opera del Duomo; *see p73*) to adorn his tomb. Further into the church are the tombs of Leonardo Bruni by Bernardo Rossellino, Vittorio Alfieri and Count Ugolino della Gherardesca. Back at the top of the left aisle is Galileo's tomb, a polychrome marble confection created by Foggini more than a century after the astronomer's death, when the Church finally permitted him a Christian burial, having previously branded him a heretic.

It's something of a paradox that while the church is filled with the tombs of the great and the grand, it formerly belonged to the Franciscans, the most unworldly of the religious orders. They founded it in 1228, ten years after arriving in the city. A recently established order, they were supposed to make their living through manual work, preaching and begging. At the time, the area was a slum, home to the city's dyers and wool workers, and Franciscan preaching, with its message that all men were equal, had a huge impact on the poor folk who lived there. Indeed, in 1378, inspired by the Franciscans, the dyers and wool workers revolted against the guilds.

As for the Franciscans, their vow of poverty slowly eroded. By the late 13th century, the old church was felt to be inadequate and a new building was planned: intended to be one of the largest in Christendom, it was designed by Arnolfo di Cambio, architect of the Duomo, and the Palazzo Vecchio, who himself laid the first stone on 3 May 1294. The building was financed partly by property confiscated from Ghibellines who had been convicted of heresy.

The church underwent various stages of restoration and modification, with one of Vasari's infamous remodernisations robbing it of the frescoes of the school of Giotto in three naves in favour of heavy classical altars. Fortunately, he left the main chapels intact, though subsequent makeovers completely destroyed the decorations of the Cappella Tosinghi-Spinelli. Among the remaining gems are the fabulous stained-glass windows at the east end (behind the high altar) by Agnolo Gaddi, the beautifully carved marble tomb of Leonardo Bruni and the Cavalcanti tabernacle (both of which are to be found flanking the side door on the south wall).

At the eastern end of the church, the Bardi and Peruzzi chapels, which were completely frescoed by Giotto, are masterpieces. That said, the condition of the frescoes is not brilliant – a result of Giotto painting on dry instead of wet plaster and of them being daubed with whitewash – and were only rediscovered in the mid 18th century. The most striking of the two chapels is the Bardi, with scenes from the life of St Francis in haunting, virtual monotone, the figures just stylised enough to make them otherworldly yet individual enough to make them human. On the far side of the high altar is the Cappella Bardi di Vernio, frescoed by one of Giotto's most interesting followers, Maso di Banco, in vibrant colours.

Santa Maria Maddalena dei Pazzi

Borgo Pinti 58 (055 2478420). **Open** 9am-noon, 5-5.30pm, 6.10-7pm daily. **Admission** €1. **No credit cards. Map** p319 B5.

Tucked away behind an anonymous, un-numbered door is the church and monastery of Santa Maria Maddalena dei Pazzi. It's worth all the counting of street numbers to ensure that you get here, if only for a glimpse of Perugino's luminous fresco, *Crucifixion and Saints* of 1493, which covers an entire wall in the Sala Capitolare (named after the Ionic capitals of its columns).

Sinagoga & Museo di Arte e Storia Ebraica

Via Farini 4 (055 2346654). **Open** *Apr, May, Sept, Oct* 10am-5pm Mon-Thur, Sun; 10am-2pm Fri. *June-Aug* 10am-6pm Mon-Thur, Sun; 10am-2pm Fri. *Nov-Mar* 10am-3pm Mon-Thur, Sun; 10am-2pm Fri. **Admission** €4. **No credit cards. Map** p319 B5.

Built in 1870, following the demolition of the ghetto, this synagogue is an extraordinarily ornate mix of Moorish, Byzantine and Eastern influences, with its walls and ceilings covered in polychrome arabesques. Housed on the first floor, under the copper dome of the main temple, the Museum of Jewish Art and History holds a collection tracing the history of Jews in Florence, from their supposed arrival as Roman slaves to their official introduction into the city as money-lenders on the invitation of the Florentine Republic in 1430. Exhibits include documented stories, jewellery, ceremonial objects and furniture, photos and drawings, many of which depict the ghetto that occupied the area just north of Piazza della Repubblica.

Oltrarno

Escape the crowds and blend in with the locals.

The Oltrarno (literally, 'beyond the Arno')
is Florence's equivalent to the Rive Gauche.
A bustling area that spans the width of the
city centre south of the river, it's awash with
contradictions. Grand *palazzi* run parallel to
dilapidated back streets; wide-eyed tourists
mix with salt-of-the-earth locals, and antique
shops sit by artisans' workshops. The area
tapers south-west to Porta Romana through the
parishes of Santo Spirito and San Frediano; to
the south-east, it encompasses steep picturesque
country lanes that lead via San Niccolò to the
famed **Piazzale Michelangelo** (*see p108*).

Borgo San Jacopo, which backs on to the
river, is an odd mix of medieval towers and
palazzi, shops and '60s monstrosities built to
replace the houses that were bombed in the war.
The street is sandwiched between the antique-
shop-lined Via Maggio and Via de' Guicciardini,
with its expensive paper, crafts and jewellery
shops and the small church of **Santa Felicità**
(*see p103*), and the grandeur of the Medici's
Palazzo Pitti (*see p101*), its rusticated façade
bearing down on its sloping forecourt. Behind
are the **Boboli Gardens** (*see p102*).

South-east of the Ponte Vecchio, snaking
steeply uphill towards the **Forte di Belvedere**
(*see p100*), are the *costas*, pretty narrow lanes.
There are proper sights – **Museo Bardini** (*see
p101*), **Casa Museo Rodolfo Siviero** (*see
below*) – but parallel with Lungarno Serristori
and of greater appeal is **San Niccolò**. The area
feels like a sleepy village until evening, when
the wine bars and *osterie* fill up and the bars on
Via dei Renai overflow on to the riverside Piazza
Demidoff. The edge of San Niccolò is signalled
by Porta di San Niccolò in Piazza Poggi.

West of the Ponte Vecchio are the bohemian
neighbourhoods of **Santo Spirito** and **San
Frediano**. Piazza Santo Spirito is a lively but
low-key space that still belongs to the locals,
whether furniture restorers or restaurateurs.
There's a morning market from Monday to
Saturday; a flea market (second Sunday of
the month) and an organic food market (some
Sundays) also spill across the piazza. The bars
and restaurants are popular meeting places
with the arty, pre-club set; crowds sit on the
steps of the church of **Santo Spirito** (*see p103*)
in summer. To the left of the church on the
square, the refectory houses Andrea Orcagna's
14th-century *Last Supper* fresco (*see p100*).

Giardini di Boboli. *See p102.*

South of the piazza, Via Romana is a narrow
road lined with unusual craft and antique shops
and home to **La Specola** (*see p103*). On the far
side of Via dei Serragli, in San Frediano, things
are even more villagey. Piazza del Carmine, a car
park by day and a social whirl by night, is home
to the **Santa Maria del Carmine** church and
the **Brancacci Chapel** (for both, *see p103*). For
a taste of locals' Florence, walk west into Borgo
San Frediano, with its 18th-century baroque
church, grocery shops and small *trattorie*.

Casa Museo Rodolfo Siviero

*Lungarno Serristori 1-3 (055 2345219/guided tours
055 293007)*. **Open** 9.30am-12.30pm Mon; 3.30-
6.30pm Sat. **Admission** free. **Map** p318 D5.
This was previously the house of government minister Rodolfo Siviero, dubbed 'the James Bond of art'
for his efforts to prevent the Nazis plundering Italian
masters, and for his success in retrieving many that
had been taken. Many of the artists exhibited here
– de Chirico, Annigoni, da Messina – were friends
of Siviero. There are guided tours in English.

Walk Gardens of earthly delights

Most visitors enter the Boboli Gardens from the main Pitti courtyard. To avoid the queues, use the Annalena entrance in Via Romana (opposite the Pensione Annalena at No.34). Immediately ahead of you is a small grotto sheltering statues of Adam and Eve. Head up the hill and, at the top, turn left. Walk up a few yards, take the first lane on the right and then turn immediately left. At the top of the hill and just past a house, turn right. About halfway along this covered path is the entrance to the Botanical Gardens, also known as the Giardino degli Ananassi after the pineapples once grown here. Continue along the same path to the magnificent Viale dei Cipressi (also called 'il Viottolone'), a wide, steeply sloping avenue lined with glorious, lichen-covered statues (at least the ones that haven't been restored) and age-old cypress trees.

At the bottom of the Viale dei Cipressi lies the gorgeous Isolotto, a small island sitting in a circular moat laid out in 1612. In the middle is the *Fountain of Oceanus*, designed by Tribolo for Cosimo II, with its central figure of Neptune a copy of a Giambologna statue. In warm weather the island is filled with orange and lemon trees in 200 huge terracotta pots, but they are taken into shelter in winter. The moat is filled with murky green water evocative of the River Styx, while the stone benches set into the hedge make a sunny spot for a rest.

Beyond the Isolotto is the semicircular, English-style lawn known as the Hemicycle, bordered by plane trees. From here, turn right and join Viale della Meridiana, which follows Via Romana back towards the upper gardens. The path passes the magnificent Orangery, painted in its original green and white; the citrus pots are kept warm and cosy here in winter. At the top, you emerge with the Meridiana wing of Palazzo Pitti on your left and a colossal Roman *vasca* (basin) on your right.

Take one of the steep paths that climb the hill and get splendid views of Florence. Follow the path on the left side of the tree-lined lawn at the top, past a monumental bronze sculpture by Igor Mitoraj. To the right is the top of the Viale dei Cipressi. From here walk straight on past the row of old houses on your right; this will lead to an elegant double stairway that sweeps up to the walled Giardino del Cavalieri, the highest point in the gardens. From here the views are purely rural: villas and the odd crenellated tower, olive groves and cypress trees.

Back at the bottom of the steps, the path immediately to the right brings you to *Abundance*, an enormous statue clutching a sheaf of golden corn. Instead of going with the flow down the steps, walk past *Abundance* and along the path that hugs the walls of Forte di Belvedere until you come to the back gate of the fort (still generally closed as this guide went to press). From here, follow the path opposite down past the pale peppermint green Kaffeehaus, a rococo gem built in 1775 for Pietro Leopoldo, and straight on down a steep path, which brings you out just above the huge amphitheatre and back to the crowds. This faces the rear façade and entrance of the Pitti Palace, where you'll find the *Fontana del Carciofo*, a superb baroque fountain named after the bronze artichoke that once topped it).

Head around to the right, and a wide gravel path (once a carriageway) leads to a small rose garden dominated by *Jupiter*, a statue by Baccio Bandinelli. The little path to the right passes a garden and ends at the small Grotticina di Madama, dominated by

Cenacolo di Santo Spirito

Piazza Santo Spirito 29 (055 287043). **Open** 9am-2pm Tue-Sun. **Admission** €2.20. **No credit cards. Map** p318 D1.

Orcagna's 14th-century fresco *The Last Supper*, housed in a former Augustinian refectory, was butchered by an 18th-century architect, commissioned to build some doors into it so the building could be used as a carriage depot. Only the fringes of the fresco remain, though there's a more complete (albeit heavily restored) *Crucifixion* above it. The museum (the Museo della Fondazione Romano) also houses an eclectic collection of sculptures given to the state in 1946 on the death of sailor Salvatore Romano.

Forte di Belvedere

Via San Leonardo (055 27681). **Open** phone for details. **Admission** free. **Map** p318 D3.

Long-running restoration means that, yet again, this star-shaped fortress has locked gates. The fort was built by Bernardo Buontalenti in 1590 and was originally intended to protect the city from insurgents. It soon became a refuge for the Medici Grand Dukes and a strongroom for their treasures; these days, when open, it's a pleasant stop-off after a walk up the steep hills. Apart from giving a good view of the city, the fort is used for temporary art exhibitions. In summer, it runs an evening cultural programme and, some summers, an open-air cinema (*see p165*).

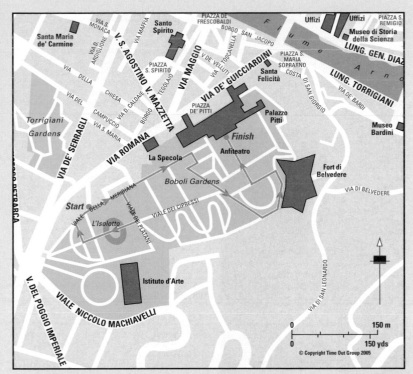

bizarre statues of goats and the first of the several grottoes for which the garden has become famous.

Back at *Jupiter*, follow the railings to the end and go down the steps to the magnificent Grotta Grande or the Grotta di Buontalenti. It's not always possible to walk into the restored series of chambers, but you can see through the railings. The Grotta di Buontalenti was

built between 1557 and 1593 by heavyweights Vasari, Ammannati and Buontalenti, and has casts of Michelangelo's unfinished *Slaves*, an erotic statue of Paris abducting Helen, and, at the back, a luscious Venus emerging from her bath by Giambologna. The last curiosity before heading back to the exit is a famous statue of Pietro Barbino, Cosimo I's pot-bellied, dwarf riding a turtle.

Museo Bardini

Piazza dei Mozzi 1 (055 2342427). Closed until mid 2006. **Map** p319 D4.
Art dealer Stefano Bardini, who built this palazzo in 1881 using salvaged palatial fittings, bequeathed his collection to the city in 1922. When the museum reopens in 2006, it will house the new Galleria Corsi, featuring paintings from the 14th to 19th centuries.

Palazzo Pitti

Piazza Pitti, Via Romana. **Map** p318 D1.
The Pitti Palace was built in 1457 for Luca Pitti, a Medici rival, supposedly to a design by Brunelleschi that had been rejected by Cosimo il Vecchio as too

grandiose. However, it also proved too grandiose for the Pitti, who were forced to sell to the Medici. The palace was more luxurious than the Palazzo Vecchio, and Cosimo I and his wife Eleonora di Toledo moved here in 1549. But it wasn't big enough: Ammannati was charged with remodelling the façade and creating the courtyard. The façade was extended in the 17th century and two further wings added in the 18th. It now holds the vast, opulent Medici collection.

Galleria d'Arte Moderna

055 2388616. **Open** 8.15am-1.50pm (last entry 1.15pm) Tue-Sat, 2nd, 4th Mon of mth & 1st, 3rd, 5th Sun of mth. **Admission** €5 (incl Museo del Costume). **No credit cards.**

The 30 rooms on the top floor of the Pitti were royal apartments until 1920, but today are given over to Florence's modern art museum. The varied collection covers neo-classical to early 20th-century art ('modern' is a relative term here), with highlights including Giovanni Dupré's bronze sculptures of *Cain and Abel* (Room 5) and Ottone Rosai's simple *Piazza del Carmine* in Room 30. Rooms 11, 12, 18 and 19 showcase the Italian impressionist work of the Macchiaioli school, who used dots (*macchie*) to paint, and house works by the most famous artists of the Florentine 'café' scene, Giovanni Fattori and Telemaco Signorini.

Galleria Palatina & Appartamenti Reali

055 2388614. **Open** 8.15am-6.50pm Tue-Sun. **Admission** €6.50. **No credit cards.**

The gallery has 28 rooms of paintings, hung four- or five-high on its damask walls. Linger longest in the five planet rooms, named after Venus, Mercury (Apollo), Mars, Jupiter and Saturn, supposedly in honour of Galileo Galilei. The Sala di Venere (Venus), crowned by a gilded stucco ceiling, is dominated by a statue of Venus by Canova, but also contains Titian's regal *La Bella*. The Sala di Apollo houses the nine Muses and is crowded with works by Rosso Fiorentino and Andrea del Sarto. The Sala di Marte (Mars) houses Rubens' *Four Philosophers*, which contains a suitably detached self-portrait (the standing figure on the left). The best place to look in the Sala di Giove (Jupiter) is up, in order to admire the depiction of Jupiter with his eagle and his lightning. Look, too, for Raphael's lover, the 'baker girl' Margherita Luti, in his *La Velata*. Finally, the Sala di Saturno (Saturn) contains some of Raphael's best-known works: among them is the *Madonna of the Grand Duke*, which shows a distinct Leonardo influence, and his last painting, *Holy Family*, which seems inspired by Michelangelo. The other rooms also follow a classical style, with names such as Allegory, Hercules and Prometheus. The latter includes a beautiful *Madonna and Child* by Filippo Lippi.

Giardini di Boboli

055 2651816/2651838. **Open** *Nov-Feb* 8.15am-5pm daily. *Mar, June-Aug, Oct* 8.15am-8pm daily. *Apr, May, Sept* 8.15am-7pm daily. Closed 1st & last Mon of mth. **Admission** €4 (incl Museo delle Porcellane & Museo degli Argenti). **No credit cards. Map** p318 D1-3.

The only park in central Florence is an oasis on hot summer days, but it's even more pleasant in the quieter months. The gardens were laid out for Eleonora di Toledo and Cosimo I when the Pitti Palace was the Medici stronghold, and the grand avenues, huge fountains and other quirky touches (ice was kept in the round stone structures near the palace) mean that evidence of a life of luxury is never far away.

Far to the left of the main entrance is a fountain showing Cosimo I's obese dwarf as a nude *Bacchus*, heralding the walkway that leads to Buontalenti's grotto with Bandinelli's statues of Ceres and Apollo, casts of Michelangelo's *Slaves* and a second grotto adorned with frescoes of classic Greek and Roman myths and encrusted with shells. The ramps take you to the classical amphitheatre, where Jacopo Peri's and Giulio Caccini's *Euridice* was staged for the Medici in 1600. At the top of the hill is the Museo delle Porcellane (*see p103*), entered through the Giardino dei Cavalieri. The gardens also host summer events. *See also pp100-101* **Gardens of earthly delights**.

Museo degli Argenti

055 2388709. **Open** *Oct-Mar* 8.15am-4.30pm daily. *Apr, May, Sept* 8.15am-6.30pm daily. *June-Aug* 8.15am-7.30pm daily. *Year-round* closed 1st & last Mon of mth. **Admission** €4 (incl Museo delle Porcellane & Boboli Gardens). **No credit cards.**

The name of this extravagant two-tier museum section of the Pitti Palace is a euphemism: the Silver Museum houses not just silver, but a gob-smacking hoard of treasures amassed by the Medici, from tapestries and rock crystal vases to a breathtakingly banal collection of miniature animals.

Museo delle Carrozze
055 2388614. **Open** closed until late 2006.
A collection of carriages that once belonged to the Medici, Lorraine and Savoy houses. Phone for post-renovation opening information.

Museo del Costume
055 2388713. **Open** 8.15am-1.50pm (last entry 1.15pm) Tue-Sat, 2nd, 4th Mon of mth & 1st, 3rd, 5th Sun of mth. **Admission** €5 (incl Galleria d'Arte Moderna). **No credit cards**.
The Costume Museum is next to the Palazzina della Meridiana, which periodically served as residence to the Lorraine family and the House of Savoy, and also houses a permanent exhibition of works by Romantic artists no longer in the Galleria d'Arte Moderna. A large part of the collection comprises Cosimo I and Eleonora di Toledo's clothes, including her sumptuous velvet creation from Bronzino's portrait. In addition, the museum is sometimes used for major exhibitions of fashion and costume history.

Museo delle Porcellane
055 2388709. **Open** as per Boboli Gardens.
Admission €4 (incl Boboli Gardens & Museo degli Argenti). **No credit cards**.
At the top of the Boboli Gardens, this former reception room for artists, built by Leopoldo de' Medici, affords inspiring views over the Tuscan hills. The museum displays ceramics used by the various occupants of Palazzo Pitti and includes the largest selection of Viennese china outside Vienna.

Santa Felicità
Piazza Santa Felicità (055 213018). **Open** 9am-noon, 3-6pm Mon-Sat; 9am-1pm Sun (except 9am & noon services). **Admission** free. **Map** p318 D2.
This church occupies the site of the first church in Florence, founded in the second century AD by Syrian Greek tradesmen. Sadly, there are no traces of its ancient beginnings: the interior is mainly 18th century. Vasari built the portico in 1564 to support the Corridoio Vasariano (*see p81* **Corridor of power**). The main reason to visit is Pontormo's *Deposition* altarpiece in the Cappella Barbadori-Capponi.

Santa Maria del Carmine & Cappella Brancacci
Piazza del Carmine (055 2382195/bookings 055 2768224/2768558). **Open** *Chapel* 10am-5pm Mon, Wed-Sat; 1-5pm Sun. Phone to book. **Admission** €4. **No credit cards**. **Map** p318 C1.
A blowsy baroque church built in 1782, Santa Maria del Carmine is dominated by a huge single nave adorned with pilasters and pious sculptures overlooked by a ceiling fresco of *The Ascension*. It was built to replace a medieval church that belonged to the Carmelites and had burned down the previous decade.

Miraculously, the Brancacci Chapel, frescoed in the 15th century by Masaccio and Masolino, escaped damage. Masolino was a court painter, his graceful style in tune with the decorative international Gothic traditions, while Masaccio had a more realistic and emotive style. Masaccio died aged just 27, but reached his peak with this cycle of frescoes: compare Masolino's elegant Adam and Eve in *The Temptation* with Masaccio's masterpiece, the grief-stricken *Expulsion from Paradise*, or Masolino's dandified Florentines in their silks and brocades with Masaccio's simple saints. There are two themes to the paintings: the redemption of sinners, and scenes from the life of St Peter. Work on the frescoes stopped for 60 years after Masaccio's death and was then taken up again by Filippino Lippi, whose most striking contribution was *The Release of St Peter*. The frescoes were restored in the 1980s, and there are rules about how many people can see them: you must book ahead, and your visit is limited to 15 minutes.

Santo Spirito
Piazza Santo Spirito (055 210030). **Open** *Winter* 8.am-noon, 4-5pm Mon, Tue, Thur, Fri; 8am-noon Wed. *Summer* 8am-noon, 4-6pm Mon, Tue, Thur, Fri; 8am-noon Wed. **Admission** free. **Map** p318 C2.
The simple 18th-century cream façade of Santo Spirito, variously described as the most beautiful in Florence and as a plain slab of marzipan, gives little clue as to the incomparable achievements behind it. One of Brunelleschi's most extraordinary works, its structure is perfectly proportioned, a Latin-cross church lined with a continuous colonnade of dove grey *pietra serena* pilasters sheltering 38 chapels.
There was an Augustinian church on this site from 1250, but in 1397 the monks decided to replace it, eventually commissioning Brunelleschi to design it. Work started in 1444, two years before the great master died; the façade and exterior walls were never finished. Vasari reckoned that if the church has been completed as planned, it would have been 'the most perfect temple of Christianity'. Left of the church is the refectory housing the Cenacolo di Santo Spirito museum (*see p100*). The church is also open on weekends, but only to worshippers.

La Specola
Via Romana 17 (055 2288251/www.specola.unifi.it). **Open** 9am-1pm Mon, Tue, Thur, Fri, Sun; 9am-5pm Sat. **Admission** €4. **No credit cards**. **Map** p318 D1.
La Specola (observatory) is named for the telescope on the roof, but it's actually a zoology museum. The first 23 rooms are crammed with stuffed and pickled animals, but from Room 24 on, the exhibits grow even more stomach-churning. In a Frankenstein-esque laboratory, wax corpses lie on satin beds, each a little more dissected than the last; walls are covered with perfectly realistic body parts crafted as teaching aids between 1771 and the late 1800s. Look out, too, for the gory tableaux devoted to Florence during the plague. A dream day out for older kids with horror fixations, but also, if you keep them from the anatomical wax models, for younger children.

Outside the City Gates

Run to the hills.

Russian Orthodox Church. See p105.

Central Florence, or the area that lies within the boundaries once created by the now mostly defunct medieval city walls, is home to a spectacular concentration of art and sights, which is why most visitors to the city will confine their activities to this relatively small area. Time permitting, however, it's worth widening your horizons in order to take in what lies further afield. Eight of the city's original 16 gates are still standing, and are now more or less linked by the traffic-clogged ring road or *viali*. The efficient ATAF bus network has excellent services to the suburbs: most of the places listed in this chapter are right on a city bus route or a short walk from a bus stop.

One of Florence's unique (and most attractive) physical characteristics is the proximity of the city centre to rural landscape. The hills that surround the city to the north, south and east provide a natural barrier against urban sprawl and mean that, very quickly, you can travel from the town into what feels like

countryside. This is particularly true south of the river, where hills, dotted with villas, cypress and olive trees practically rise from the banks of the Arno; these exclusive residential areas make for some of the city's most expensive real estate. The downside of being situated in a basin is the resulting climate: hot and humid summers, cold and damp winters.

To the north, genteel suburbia extends further before being thwarted by the hills that lead up to Fiesole and Settignano, while to the east, development follows the Arno for some kilometres. Florence isn't, however, immune to suburban ugliness. West and north-west of the centre, unimaginative housing and industrial development have claimed swathes of land, creating urban eyesores such as Brozzi, Campi Bisenzio, Scandicci and Sesto Fiorentino. Firenze Nova, the new satellite city and administrative centre being constructed on reclaimed land to the west of the city, is now well on its way towards completion, and new buildings are appearing above the boundary fence. But even in these areas, once open countryside and now ugly suburban sprawl, you'll find elegant villas and old churches redolent of a quieter, simpler time.

North of the river

A green oasis just beyond the carbon monoxide hell of the *viale* and Porta al Prato to the west, the **Parco delle Cascine** is a 3.5-kilometre- (two-mile-) long public park stretching along the north bank of the Arno, backed by woods that were once full of deer. Its name comes from *cascina*, meaning dairy farm, which is the role the area played under the Medici. It later became a hunting park and, simultaneously, a space for theatre and public spectacles. Shelley wrote his 'Ode to the West Wind' here in 1819, while in 1870 the body of the Maharaja of Kolhapur (who died in Florence) was burned on a funeral pyre at the far end of the park on a spot now marked by an equestrian statue.

These days, the park, which incorporates a riding school, a swimming pool, a horse-race track and tennis courts, is populated by cycling children, rollerbladers, joggers and other Florentines simply out for a stroll. At night, however, it's a little seamier, with transvestites and prostitutes strutting along the parallel *viale*. The Cascine's huge Tuesday-morning market has now been moved further down the park to make way for the new Tramvia (*see p37*), which will link the city centre with the suburbs.

North-east of the Cascine, along Viale Rosselli, is the monstrous pentagonal **Fortezza da Basso** (*see also p89*). Commissioned in 1534 from Antonio da Sangallo by Alessandro de' Medici, who met his death within its ugly walls, it's a prototype of 16th-century military architecture; restored in the 1990s, it's now Florence's main exhibition centre. Five minutes' walk beyond the fortress, among some elegant residential *palazzi*, are the five polychrome onion domes of Florence's exquisite **Russian Orthodox Church** (Via Leone X). Completed in 1904, it's a reminder that the city was once popular with wealthy Russians (Dostoevsky, Tchaikovsky and Gorky, to name but three) as a retreat from the harsh winters back home. You can arrange for a guided tour (available in English or Italian; 055 2477986/290148) or visit during mass (6pm Sat, 10.30am Sun).

Directly north of here is the eccentric **Museo Stibbert** (Via Stibbert 26, 055 475520, www.museostibbert.it, closed Thur, €5). Its bizarre collection, covering everything from arms and armour to snuff boxes, formerly belonged to Frederick Stibbert (1838-1906), a brother-in-arms with Garibaldi. Stibbert was born of an English father and Italian mother, who left him her 14th-century house. He then bought the neighbouring mansion and had the two joined together to house his collection. Among the 50,000 items crammed into the 64 rooms (not all the holdings are open to the public at any one time) are a hand-painted harpsichord, a collection of shoe buckles, chalices, crucifixes and even an attributed Botticelli. The rambling garden is a delightfully cool escape in summer.

Piazza della Libertà, the focal point of northern access to the city, is notable almost exclusively for the massive and rather graceless triumphal arch built to mark the arrival in Florence of the eighth Grand Duke of Tuscany in 1744. A couple of kilometres north-west of here is **Villa della Petraia** (Via della Petraia 40, 055 452691, closed 2nd & 3rd Mon of mth, €2), acquired by the Medici family in 1530. Sitting on a little hill, the villa and grounds stand apart from the surrounding industrial mess. Just down the hill from La Petraia is **Villa di Castello** (Via del Castello 40, 055 454791, closed 2nd & 3rd Mon of the month, €2), another piece of Medici real estate. It's primarily famous for its gardens, which were laid out by Tribolo and which contain Ammanati's famous dripping statue *L'Appennino*, as well as the rather bizarre Grotta degli Animali, a grotto filled with animal and bird statues.

Back down in town and east of Piazza della Libertà is the **Stadio Comunale**, Pier Luigi Nervi's huge football stadium near Campo di Marte. Built in 1932 and enlarged for the 1990 World Cup, it has a capacity of 66,000 and is used for football matches as well as the odd rock concert. It's also one of the few modern buildings in Florence with architectural merit. Not far south-east is the **Museo del Cenacolo di Andrea del Sarto** (Via San Salvi 16, 055 238 8603, closed Mon, free). A refectory-cum-museum, it was part of the Vallombrosan monastery of San Salvi, and is chiefly notable for housing Andrea del Sarto's celebrated *Last Supper* (*see below*). The monastery buildings are now a psychiatric hospital.

Back on the *viale* is the **Cimitero degli Inglesi** (English Cemetery; Piazzale Donatello 38, 055 582608 afternoons, closed Mon

Last Suppers Andrea del Sarto

The glowing colours and theatricality of Andrea del Sarto's huge *Last Supper* fresco have impressed visitors ever since the artist, renowned as a supreme colourist and one of the godfathers of Mannerism, completed the commission in 1527, five years after he started it.

Its setting, in its own museum (*see above*), which was part of the monastery of San Salvi used by the Vallombrosan order, helps its dramatic impact, the lunette-shaped fresco set under an arch decorated with medallions of the Trinity and four Saints, protectors of the Vallombrosan Order.

In 1568 Vasari wrote that del Sarto 'gave such infinite grace, grandeur and majesty to all the figures that I do not know how to praise his *Last Supper* without saying too little, it being so fine that whoever sees it is stupefied'; art critics over the centuries have shared this enthusiasm, declaring it 'the only *Last Supper* not to fade into insignificance after Leonardo's' and even 'one of the most beautiful paintings in the world'. It was only the beauty of the fresco that spared it from the destruction meted out during the siege of Florence in 1529 by rampaging soldiers, who balked at pulling the wall down.

Walk Head for heights

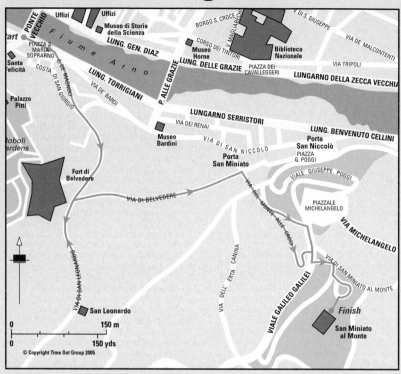

From the southern end of the Ponte Vecchio, with your back to the river, turn left along Via dei Bardi. At Piazza Santa Maria Soprarno, bear right and walk under the arch up Costa de Magnoli, which, after a short distance,

merges into Costa di San Giorgio just opposite the Romanian orthodox church of San Giorgio. This is an enchanting little street, but the ascent is quite steep. A little further on to the left, a fabulous view of the

afternoons, Tue mornings and all day Sat & Sun, admission by donation). The atmospheric graveyard, opened in 1827, is awash with eminently explorable lichen-covered gravestones and tombs, housing the remains of all manner of Anglo-Florentines. Among them are poet Elizabeth Barrett Browning, who died in 1861 and whose tombstone was designed by her husband Robert.

Fiesole & around

The foundation of **Fiesole** precedes that of Florence by centuries. Indeed, without Fiesole there would have been no Florence: this

stubborn Etruscan hill town proved so difficult for the Romans to subdue that they set up camp in the river valley below. When they eventually took Fiesole, it became one of the most important towns in Etruria, remaining independent until the 12th century, when Florence finally vanquished it in battle. It soon found a new role as a refined suburb where aristocrats could escape the heat and hoi polloi of Florence; the road leading up winds by their beautiful villas and gardens. Some 14,000 people live in Fiesole today.

Piazza Mino, the main square, is named after the artist Mino da Fiesole, and lined with cafés and restaurants. It's dominated

Florence skyline suddenly appears in a gap between the buildings. Press on, admiring the tall shuttered buildings and their oversailing rooftops as you go. Galileo's house is on the right at No.19.

Within five minutes' walk from the city centre, you'll hear the first twitters of bird song. At the top of Costa di San Giorgio, pass through the city gates (Porta San Giorgio) and walk a short distance along Via di San Leonardo, which leads straight ahead past the main entrance to Forte Belvedere. After five minutes' walk or so, on your left, is the Chiesa di San Leonardo in Arcetri. This pretty medieval *pieve* (parish church) is guarded by two towering cypress trees and contains, among other things, canvases by Francesco Conti.

Retrace your steps back to the Porta and bear right, down Via di Belvedere, to begin your descent. Hugging the city walls, you'll soon come to the bottom of the hill opposite Porta San Miniato. From here, head up Via del Monte alle Croci, perhaps stopping for a slurp at the picturesque Fuori Porta wine bar (*see p128*). After a short walk, you'll reach the pretty, tree-lined steps of San Salvatore al Monte. Either take this, the express route to the top (past a resident feline community, about 50 metres up on the right), or follow the road on its tortuous journey past olive groves, finally arriving at the busy main road of Viale Galileo Galilei. Directly opposite you is the splendid spectacle of San Miniato al Monte (*see p108*) and the end of your journey. Now all that's left to do is admire the view.

by the immense honey-stone campanile of the 11th-century **Duomo**, inside which sit columns topped with capitals dating from Fiesole's period under Roman occupation. When the nearby **Museo Bandini** (Via Dupré 1, 055 59477, closed Tue in winter, €6.20 incl Teatro Romano & Museo Archeologico) reopens after a spell of restoration and re-organisation, hopefully at the end of 2005, the long-familiar array of Florentine paintings dating from the 13th to the 15th centuries will be joined by two new rooms housing works from the Bandini collection that have never been placed on display before, including a number of Della Robbia terracottas.

Down the hill can be seen more relics of Roman Fiesole at the 3,000-seat **Teatro Romano** (Via Portigiani 1, 055 59477, closed Tue in winter, admission incl in Museo Bandini ticket). Built in 1 BC, the theatre still stages a mix of concerts and plays in summer; a complex here is home to the remains of two temples, partially restored Roman baths and a stretch of Etruscan walls. The **Museo Archeologico** (details as per Teatro Romano above; admission incl in Museo Bandini ticket) houses finds from Bronze Age, Etruscan and Roman Fiesole, and the Costantini collection of Greek vases.

There are some lovely walks around Fiesole, the best of which is down steep, twisting Via Vecchia Fiesolana to the hamlet of **San Domenico**. On the way, you'll pass the **Villa Medici** (to the left), built by Michelozzo for Cosimo il Vecchio and the childhood home of Anglo-American writer Iris Origo. At the bottom of the hill is the 15th-century church and convent where painter Fra Angelico was a monk. It now houses his delicate *Madonna and Angels* (1420), while in the chapter house of the adjacent monastery is one of his frescoes (ring the bell at No.4 for entry). Opposite the church is a lane leading down to the **Badia Fiesolana** (Via Roccettini 9, 055 59155, closed Sat pm & Sun, free), Fiesole's cathedral until 1028. The façade incorporates the original front of the older church, with its elegant green and white marble inlay. Enter via the cloister if the church doors are closed.

The village of **Settignano** lies on the hill to the east of Fiesole. There's no public transport from Fiesole (bus 10 goes from Santa Maria Novella station to Settignano), though the longish walk or drive between the two through woods and cypresses is very pleasant. There's nothing special to see here, but Settignano makes for an almost tourist-free trip out of town, its history littered with eminent names: sculptors Desiderio da Settignano and the Rossellino brothers were born here, and Michelangelo spent part of his childhood at Villa Buonarroti. It's just a pity no one left any art.

South of the river

The hilly area south of the Arno, a short walk from the city centre, is characterised by olive groves, cypresses, the odd farmhouse and a maze of steep lanes lined with high walls and impenetrable gates protecting an array of beautiful villas.

The most famous viewpoint in Florence is probably from **Piazzale Michelangelo**, located up the hill directly above Piazza Poggi.

David gets the best views of all from **Piazzale Michelangelo**. *See p107.*

The Piazzale has always been considered the city's balcony: a large, open square with vistas over the entire city to the hills beyond it. Its stone balustrade is usually crowded with tourists having their photo taken against the spectacular backdrop. Laid out in 1869 by Giuseppe Poggi, it's dominated by a bronze replica of Michelangelo's *David* and crammed all day with coaches. Buses 12 and 13 come here, but the best way up is to walk along Via San Niccolò to Porta San Miniato before climbing Via del Monte alle Croci, winding between handsome villas and gardens. Alternatively, walk up the rococo staircase that Poggi designed to link Piazzale Michelangelo with his piazza below.

From the piazzale it's a short walk to the church of **San Miniato al Monte** (Via delle Porte Sante 34, 055 2342731, free), the façade of which, delicately inlaid with white Carrara and green Verde di Prato marble, looks down on the city. The glittering mosaic dates from the 13th century. There has been a chapel on this site since at least the fourth century; this is also the spot where, legend has it, San Miniato picked up his decapitated head and walked from the banks of the Arno up the hill, where he finally expired. The chapel was replaced with a Benedictine monastery in the early 11th century, built on the orders of reforming Bishop Hildebrand.

The church's interior is one of Tuscany's loveliest, its walls patchworked with faded frescoes and its choir raised above a serene 11th-century crypt. Occasionally, a door from the crypt is opened on to an even earlier chapel. One of the church's most remarkable features is the marble pavement in the nave, inlaid with the signs of the zodiac and stylised lions and lambs. It's worth timing your trip to coincide with the Gregorian chant sung daily by the monks (4.30pm in winter, 5.30pm in summer).

On a nearby hill just above Porta Romana lies the hamlet of **Bellosguardo** ('beautiful view'). It's a 20-minute slog on foot, but you can catch your breath at a viewpoint just before the Piazza di Bellosguardo that affords a glimpse of every important church façade in central Florence. At the top of the hill sits a collection of old houses and grand villas grouped round a shady square. The only sign of modern life, apart from the inevitable cars, is a postbox on a wall. The most impressive of the villas is the **Villa Bellosguardo**, down a little turning to the left. It was built in 1780 for the Marchese Orazio Pucci (ancestor of fashion designer Emilio Pucci) and bought, more than a century later, by the great tenor Enrico Caruso, who lived here for three years before his death in 1921.

About five kilometres south-west of Porta Romana and accessible by bus 36 or 37, the **Certosa del Galluzzo** (Via Buca di Certosa 2, Galluzzo, 055 2049226, admission by donation) looms like a fortress above the busy Siena road. The imposing complex was founded in 1342 as a *certosa* (Carthusian monastery) by Renaissance big-wig Niccolò Acciaiuoli and is the third of six built in Tuscany in the 14th century. Inhabited since 1958 by a small group of Cistercian monks, it's full of artistic interest. The main entrance leads into a large courtyard and the church of San Lorenzo, said to be by Brunelleschi. In the crypt are some imposing tombs. Around the *chiostro grande* (main cloister) are the 12 monks' cells, each with a well, a vegetable garden and a study.

Eat, Drink, Shop

Restaurants & Wine Bars

Feeding Firenze.

Da Mario. *See p119.*

While there are still plenty of rustic eateries that adhere doggedly to the old ways of doing things, changes are most definitely afoot in Florence. OK, so this may not yet have given rise to the cutting-edge gastronomic scene that you find in Rome or Milan, but an increasing number of chefs are employing more creative methods of preparing food. The results, while mixed, have included some genuinely interesting examples of *cucina Toscana rivisitata* (literally, 'revisited'), bringing a fresh approach and new emphases to traditional recipes. Look hard, and you can still find genuine home-style cooking of the sort that *mamma* used to make. But there's more variety here than ever.

THE RESTAURANT

Be warned: Florence is, above all else, a tourist city, and at too many restaurants, sloppy cooking and high prices are the norm. This guide aims to list the very best eateries in and around town, but in addition, a number

of respected Italian restaurant guides give stickers to restaurants they recommend. Look out for windows displaying the approval of Gambero Rosso's *Ristoranti d'Italia*, *Veronelli*, *L'Espresso*, or Slow Food's *Osterie d'Italia*. Failing that, try to pick places where there are plenty of locals, and avoid places that advertise a fixed-price *menù turistico* written in several languages.

Eating out is a very social affair in Florence, especially in the evenings, and restaurants tend to be informal and quite lively. You can wear casual dress in all but the very smartest establishments, and children are almost always welcome. The majority of restaurants are happy to produce a plate of *pasta al pomodoro* to satisfy unadventurous taste buds, and you can also ask for a half portion (*una mezza porzione*). Quite a few restaurants carry high chairs (*una seggiolona*). Booking is advisable, especially at weekends or if you want to dine at an outdoor table in the summer.

THE MENU

An increasing number of more upmarket restaurants now offer some kind of fixed menu (and we're not talking about the ubiquitous *menù turistico* here). Usually called *menù degustazione*, it consists of a series of courses that allows diners to try the house specialities. Such menus tend to represent good value.

THE WINE LIST

The price of your meal will be heavily influenced by the wine you choose: many restaurants and *trattorie* nowadays have more than just a basic choice. While the *liste dei vini* in Tuscany are unsurprisingly dominated by *vini toscani*, other regional wines are now being given more cellar space. For guidelines on choosing wines, *see pp42-45*.

Most budget and moderately priced restaurants offer *vino della casa* (house wine) in quarter-litre, half-litre or litre flasks, usually cheaper than buying by the bottle. The stuff might be anything from ghastly gut-rot to quaffable country wine.

VEGETARIANS

There are few strictly vegetarian restaurants in Florence, but non-meat-eaters, particularly those whose repertoire extends to fish, are better off here than in many parts of, say, France or Poland or Germany. Many waiters look aghast when they hear the words *sono vegetariano* ('I'm vegetarian') and don't really understand the concept. However, most restaurants offer vegetable-based pasta and rice dishes, as well as plenty of salads and vegetable side dishes (*contorni*), while an increasing number of more upmarket places now serve a specifically vegetarian option.

SMOKING

Smoking was banned in public places in Italy in early 2005, and it's now no longer possible to smoke in a restaurant unless it has a separate room with the legally required ventilation system. Few do, so you'll have to go and join the other puffers on the street.

THE BILL

For restaurants and wine bars, we give the average price per person for a three-course meal (*antipasto* or *primo, secondo, contorno* and *dolce*) excluding drinks or extras. The price in a pizzeria covers an average pizza plus a *birra media*. In wine bars where only snacks are on offer, we have not given an 'average'; prices might range from 50¢ for a *crostino* to €12 for a plate of French cheeses.

Bills usually include a cover charge (*pane e coperto*) per person of anything from €1.50 to an outrageous €5; the average is about €2.50.

The best Restaurants

For all-round value for money
Canapone Club (*see p125*); **Cibreino** (*see p121*); **Filipepe** (*see p125*); **Da Mario** (*see p119*).

For designer looks
Borgo San Jacopo (*see p123* **Hotel cuisine**); **Fusion Bar** (*see see p123* **Hotel cuisine**); **The Lounge** (*see p123* **Hotel cuisine**); **Wabi Sabi** (*see p128*).

For fish
L'Arte Gaia (*see p127*); **Borgo San Jacopo** (*see p123* **Hotel cuisine**); **Fuor d'Acqua** (*see p127*); **Pruto** (*see p126*); **Zibibbo** (*see p128*).

For great views
Omero (*see p127*); **Onice** (*see p123* **Hotel cuisine**).

For local colour
I Fratellini (*see p115*); **Nerbone** (*see p119*); **Zanobini** (*see p119*).

For wine buffs
Beccofino (*see p125*); **Enoteca Pinchiorri** (*see p121*); **Il Guscio** (*see p125*); **Pane e Vino** (*see p126*); **Targa** (*see p128*).

If someone else is paying
Cibrèo (*see p121*); **Enoteca Pinchiorri** (*see p121*); **Onice** (*see p123* **Hotel cuisine**).

If you never want to see another plate of *ribollita* in your life
Amon (*see p115*); **Finisterrae** (*see p121*); **Salaam Bombay** (*see p128*); **Wabi Sabi** (*see p128*).

If you're broke
La Mangiatoia (*see p127*); **Da Mario** (*see p119*); **Nerbone** (*see p119*); **Rosticceria Giuliano Centro** (*see p122*); **Salumeria, Vini, Trattoria I Fratellini** (*see p122*); **Il Vegetariano** (*see p119*).

This covers bread, and should also reflect the standard of service and table settings. There's also a service charge, which must by law be included in the bill (though it's sometimes listed separately). Some places now include cover and service in the price of the meal. One consolation is that you're not expected to leave a hefty tip. You can leave ten per cent if you're truly happy with your service, or, in a modest place, perhaps round up the bill by a euro or so.

Eat, Drink, Shop

Il Pizzaiuolo. *See p122.*

holes, which compete with new, upmarket *enoteche* that offer a huge range of labels from all over Italy and beyond and something more sophisticated in the way of food.

Wine bars offer one of several alternatives to full restaurant dining in Florence. *Rosticcerie* (rotisseries) serve everything from *antipasti* and roast meats to desserts; those listed here give the option of eating in or taking away. You can also find traditional tripe stands (*tripperie*) in various parts of the city, dishing up offal options such as tripe itself (in Florence, it's cooked in tomato sauce and sprinkled with parmesan) and *lampredotto* (cow's intestine, often eaten in a *panino* with *salsa verde*). These are stand-up affairs where you can fill up for a few euros.

Duomo & Around

Restaurants

Fusion Bar
See p123 **Hotel cuisine.**

L'Incontro
See p123 **Hotel cuisine.**

Oliviero
Via delle Terme 51r (055 212421). **Open** 7.30pm-midnight Mon-Sat. Closed Aug. **Average** €50. **Credit** AmEx, DC, MC, V. **Map** p318 C3.
Once a favoured haunt of (among others) Sophia Loren and Maria Callas, Oliviero still has a curious retro atmosphere redolent of *La Dolce Vita*: the revolving door, the elderly coat-check lady, the silent grand piano, the red velvet banquettes. The food, however, is not only great but very much in keeping with today's fashion for reinterpreting traditional dishes (in this case, mainly from Tuscany and southern Italy). A glass of complimentary prosecco comes with the menu, where you'll find the likes of bay-spiked duck terrine, cauliflower and ricotta flan, and guinea fowl breast. There's an excellent cheese board and a fine wine list. Service is quite formal.

Wine bars

Cocquinarius
Via delle Oche 15r (055 2302153). **Open** 9am-11pm Mon-Thur; 9am-11.30pm Fri, Sat. *Food served* from noon Mon-Sat. Closed Aug. **Average** €20. **Credit** MC, V. **Map** p318 B3.
A useful address in an area largely devoid of decent places to eat, this cosy little wine bar and café tucked away behind the Duomo is great for a quiet lunch or an informal evening meal: unusually, the full menu is available noon-11pm. Bare brick walls and soft jazz provide the background for good pastas (such as pecorino and pear ravioli), *carpaccio*, imaginative salads and platters of cheeses and meats. The homemade cakes are truly divine.

Although prices have risen horribly since the arrival of the euro, eating out in Florence is still cheaper than in London or New York. The restaurants here have been chosen either for their value for money or simply because the food is great. Some are located out of the centre of town, but the food makes them well worth the journey. For other excellent eateries in Tuscany, *see pp40-41* **Want food, will travel**.

WINE BARS AND ALTERNATIVE EATS
There are various types of wine bar in Florence. Tiny street booths (known as *fiaschetteria*, *vineria* or *mescita*) with virtually no seating, serving basic Tuscan wines and rustic snacks, sit alongside comfortable, traditional drinking

Rosticceria Giuliano Centro. *See p122.*

Frescobaldi Wine Bar

Vicolo dei Gondi, off Via della Condotta (055 284724). **Open** 7pm-midnight Mon; noon-midnight Tue-Sat. Closed 3wks Aug. **Credit** AmEx, MC, V. **Map** p319 C4.

This cosy wine bar – terracotta walls, bright lights – showcases wines from the formidable Frescobaldi estates of Tuscany, Umbria, Friuli and even as far afield as Chile and California, where they collaborate with wine producer Robert Mondavi. Snacks include terrines, pâtés, marinated anchovies, cheeses and salamis, but if you want a more substantial meal, go through to the smart restaurant next door (average €30), where you can sample pumpkin ravioli with an amaretto sauce or *tagliata di manzo* (finely sliced steak) with a potato gratin.

Santa Maria Novella

Restaurants

Cantinetta Antinori

Piazza degli Antinori 3 (055 2359827). **Open** 12.30-2.30pm, 7-10.30pm Mon-Sat. Closed 3wks Aug. **Average** €38. **Credit** AmEx, DC, MC, V. **Map** p318 B2.

Well-heeled tourists rub shoulders with business types and ladies who lunch at this classic restaurant/wine bar. It occupies a vaulted ground-floor room of the 15th-century Palazzo Antinori, the historical home to one of Tuscany's foremost wine-producing families: you can sample all their (often excellent) wines in their original context. Waiters in

PIZZERIA

LIGHT LUNCH

APERITIVO

AFTERDINNER

RISTORANTE

WINEBAR

WINESHOP

LIVE JAZZ

Golden View
OPEN BAR

11.30/02.00
SEMPRE APERTO
TEL.055214502
VIA DEI BARDI 58R (PONTE VECCHIO) FIRENZE
WWW.GOLDENVIEWOPENBAR.COM

PER PRENOTAZIONI
FAX.0552729341

white jackets and black bow ties bring out textbook versions of Florentine classics such as *pappa al pomodoro, salsiccie e fagioli* (sausage and beans), tripe and fillet steak. Very civilised, if a little on the expensive side.

Garga

Via del Moro 48r (055 2398898). **Open** 7.30-10.30pm Tue-Sun. **Average** €50. **Credit** AmEx, DC, MC, V. **Map** p318 B2.

This trattoria is perennially popular despite its high price – so what's the draw? It could be the quirky decor (garish frescoes, cosy rooms filled with an eccentric clutter of objects, chatty staff). It could be the ebullient owner, Giuliano Gargani. Or it could be the well-executed pastas, meats and fish dishes – don't miss the *taglierini del Magnifico*, with a sauce of cream, parmesan, orange and lemon zest – rich yet not sickly. Prices can be high (a few prawns in a peppercorn sauce are not worth €25, we're afraid), so maybe save your pennies for one of the sublime desserts. Co-owner Sharon Oddson also runs cooking classes.

I Latini

Via dei Palchetti 6r (055 210916). **Open** 12.30-2.30pm, 7.30-10.30pm Tue-Sun. Closed last wk Dec & 1st wk Jan. **Average** €35. **Credit** AmEx, DC, MC, V. **Map** p318 B2.

You'll inevitably have to queue (no bookings are taken after 8pm); once inside, it'll be noisy, you'll probably have to share a table, and the food will be no better than average. But there's something about I Latini's boisterous, rustic atmosphere that seems to hold eternal appeal for both Italians and visiting foreigners. Skip the pastas and go for soups and meat: this is a good place for *bistecca*. The Latini are prolific producers of a fine, sludgy-green olive oil, and some decent wines: the house red is very drinkable.

The Lounge

See p123 **Hotel cuisine.**

Nin Hao

Borgo Ognissanti 159r (055 210770). **Open** 6.30-11pm Mon; 11am-3pm, 6.30-11pm Tue-Sun. **Average** €20. **Credit** AmEx, DC, MC, V. **Map** p318 B1.

With the exception of a few places in Calenzano and Prato, home to Chinese communities, Tuscany's Chinese restaurants tend to offer disappointingly tame Asian food. However, Nin Hao is one of the better places to sample tasty dim sum, *gamberoni* (giant prawns) cooked in various ways, duck and fish. Chicken or meat prepared *alla piastra* is brought sizzling to the table on a hot plate.

Wine bars

Cantinetta dei Verrazzano

Via dei Tavolini 18-20r (055 268590/www.verrazzano.com). **Open** *Sept-June* 8am-9pm Mon-Sat. *July, Aug* 8am-4pm Mon-Sat. **Credit** AmEx, DC, MC, V. **Map** p319 B4.

Owned by the Castello da Verrazzano, one of the major wine estates in Chianti, these wood-panelled rooms are continually crowded with smartly dressed Florentines and discerning tourists. On one side is a bakery and coffee shop, while on the other is a wine bar serving (very good) estate-produced wines by the glass or bottle. Snacks include *focaccia* straight from the wood oven (the one with creamy cheese and sweet baby peas is recommended) and unusual *crostini*.

I Fratellini

Via dei Cimatori 38r (no phone). **Open** 8am-8pm Mon-Sat. **No credit cards. Map** p319 C4.

There used to be loads of these hole-in-the-wall *vinai* in Florence; nowadays, I Fratellini, founded in 1875, is one of a very few left. There's nowhere to sit down: just join the locals standing in the road (there's not much traffic) or squatting on the pavement for a glass of cheap and cheerful plonk or something a bit more special. Help it down with a liver-topped *crostino* or a great slab of *porchetta* (rosemary roast pork) on a hunk of bread.

Pizzerie & rosticcerie

Funiculì

Via Il Prato 81r (055 2646553). **Open** noon-3pm, 7pm-1am Mon-Fri; 7pm-1am Sat, Sun. **Average** €14. **Credit** AmEx, MC, V.

With seating for 300, this lively, no-frills place packs in the crowds, who scoff excellent Neapolitan pizzas and various other southern Italian dishes. Four *pizzaiuoli* turn out the puffy-crusted pizzas, using flour, buffalo mozzarella and tomatoes from Naples. Among the options are a simple *regina margherita* (tomato, mozzarella and basil) and a more adventurous *pulcinell'* (mozzarella with asparagus, tomato and porcini mushrooms).

Rosticceria della Spada

Via della Spada 62r (055 218757/www.laspadaitalia.com). **Open** noon-3pm, 7-10.30pm daily. **Average** €18. **Credit** AmEx, MC, V. **Map** p318 B2.

This centrally located *rosticceria* has been selling delicious dishes to go for a good many years, but only recently opened a couple of rooms for those who want to eat on site. The menu is more or less the same whether you choose to eat in or take away, but you'll pay about 50% if you decide to do the latter. There are good pastas (try the lasagne), roast meats and vegetables and a truly delicious *melanzane alla parmigiana*.

Snacks & fast food

Amon

Via Palazzuolo 28r (055 293146). **Open** noon-3pm, 6-11pm Tue-Sat. **No credit cards. Map** p318 B2.

When Amon first started selling Egyptian specialities in 1987, there were few other places in Florence where you could get ethnic food. Amazingly, it has

What's on the menu?

Cooking techniques & descriptions

Affumicato smoked; **al forno** cooked in an oven; **arrosto** roast; **brasato** braised; **fatto in casa** home-made; **griglia** grilled; **fritto** fried; **nostrale** locally grown/raised; **ripieno** stuffed; **ruspante** free-range; **vapore** steamed.

Basics

Aceto vinegar; **burro** butter; **bottiglia** bottle; **focaccia** flat bread made with olive oil; **ghiaccio** ice; **miele** honey; **olio** oil; **pane** bread; **panino** sandwich; **panna** cream; **pepe** pepper; **sale** salt; **salsa** sauce; **senape** mustard; **uovo** egg.

Antipasti

Antipasto misto mixed hors d'œuvres; **bruschetta** bread toasted and rubbed with garlic, sometimes drizzled with olive oil and often topped with tomatoes or white Tuscan beans; **crostini** small slices of toasted bread; **crostini toscani** are smeared with chicken liver pâté; **crostoni** big *crostini*; **fettunta** the Tuscan name for *bruschetta*; **prosciutto crudo** cured ham, either *dolce* (sweet, similar to Parma ham) or *salato* (salty).

Primi

Acquacotta cabbage soup usually served with a *bruschetta*, sometimes with an egg broken into it; **agnolotti** stuffed triangular pasta; **brodo** broth; **cacciucco** thick, chilli-spiked fish soup (Livorno's main contribution to Tuscan cuisine); **cecina** flat, crispy bread made of chickpea flour; **fettuccine** long, narrow ribbons of egg pasta; **frittata** type of substantial omelette; **gnocchi** small potato and flour dumplings; **minestra** soup, usually vegetable; **panzanella** Tuscan bread and tomato salad; **pappa al pomodoro** bread and tomato soup; **pappardelle** broad ribbons of egg pasta, usually served with *lepre* (hare); **passato** puréed soup; **pasta e fagioli** pasta and bean soup; **pici** (thick, irregular spaghetti); **ribollita** literally, a twice-cooked soup of bean, bread, cabbage and vegetables; **taglierini** thin ribbons of pasta; **tordelli/tortelli** stuffed pasta; **zuppa** soup; **zuppa frantoiana** literally, olive press soup – another bean and cabbage soup, distinguished as it's served with the very best young olive oil.

Fish & seafood

Acciughe/alici anchovies; **anguilla** eel; **aragosta** lobster; **aringa** herring; **baccalà** salt cod; **bianchetti** little fish, like whitebait; **bonito** small tuna; **branzino** sea bass; **calamari** squid; **capesante** scallops; **coda di rospo** monkfish tails; **cozze** mussels; **fritto misto** mixed fried fish; **gamberetti** shrimps; **gamberi** prawns; **gefalo** grey mullet; **granchio** crab; **insalata di mare** seafood salad; **merluzzo** cod; **nasello** hake; **ostriche** oyster; **pesce** fish; **pesce spada** swordfish; **polpo** octopus; **ricci** sea urchins; **rombo** turbot; **San Pietro** John Dory; **sarde** sardines; **scampi** langoustines; **scoglio** shell- and rockfish; **seppia** cuttlefish or squid; **sgombro** mackerel; **sogliola** sole; **spigola** sea bass; **stoccafisso** stockfish; **tonno** tuna; **triglia** red mullet; **trota** trout; **trota salmonata** salmon trout; **vongole** clams.

Meat, poultry & game

Agnellino young lamb; **agnello** lamb; **anatra** duck; **animelle** sweetbreads; **arrosto misto** mixed roast meats; **beccacce** woodcock; **bistecca** beef steak; **bresaola** cured, dried beef, served in thin slices; **caccia** general term for game; **capretto** kid; **carpaccio** raw beef, served in thin slices; **cervo** venison; **cinghiale** wild boar; **coniglio** rabbit; **cotoletta/costoletta** chop; **fagiano** pheasant; **fegato** liver; **lepre** hare; **lardo** pork fat; **maiale** pork; **manzo** beef; **ocio/oca** goose; **ossobuco** veal shank stew; **pancetta** like bacon; **piccione** pigeon; **pollo** chicken; **porchetta** roast pork; **rognone** kidney; **salsicce** sausages; **tacchino** turkey; **trippa** tripe; **vitello** veal.

Herbs, pulses & vegetables

Aglio garlic; **asparagi** asparagus; **basilico** basil; **bietola** Swiss chard; **capperi** capers; **carciofi** artichokes; **carote** carrots; **castagne** chestnuts; **cavolfiore** cauliflower; **cavolo nero** red cabbage; **ceci** chickpeas; **cetriolo** cucumber; **cipolla** onion; **dragoncello** tarragon; **erbe** herbs; **fagioli** white Tuscan beans; **fagiolini** green, string or French beans; **farro** spelt (a hard wheat), a popular soup ingredient around Lucca and the Garfagnana; **fave** or **baccelli** broad beans (although *fava* in Tuscany also means the male 'organ', so use *baccelli*); **finocchio** fennel; **fiori di zucca** courgette flowers; **funghi** mushrooms; **funghi porcini** ceps; **funghi selvatici** wild

mushrooms; **lattuga** lettuce; **lenticchie** lentils; **mandorle** almonds; **melanzane** aubergine (UK), eggplant (US); **menta** mint; **patate** potatoes; **peperoncino** chilli pepper; **peperoni** peppers; **pinoli** pine nuts; **pinzimonio** selection of raw vegetables to be dipped in olive oil; **piselli** peas; **pomodoro** tomato; **porri** leeks; **prezzemolo** parsley; **radice/ravanelli** radish; **ramerino/rosmarino** rosemary; **rapa** turnip; **rucola/rughetta** rocket (UK), arugula (US); **salvia** sage; **sedano** celery; **spinaci** spinach; **tartufato** cut thin like a truffle; **tartufo** truffles; **zucchini** courgette.

Fruit

Albicocche apricots; **ananas** pineapple; **arance** oranges; **banane** bananas; **ciliegie** cherries; **cocomero** watermelon; **datteri** dates; **fichi** figs; **fragole** strawberries; **lamponi** raspberries; **limone** lemon; **macedonia di frutta** fruit salad; **mele** apples; **melone** melon; **more** blackberries; **pere** pears; **pesche** peaches; **pompelmo** grapefruit; **uva** grapes.

Desserts & cheese

Cantuccini almond biscuits; **castagnaccio** chestnut flour cake, made around Lucca; **cavallucci** spiced biscuits from Siena; **gelato** ice-cream; **granita** flavoured ice; **mandorlata** almond brittle; **panforte** cake of dried fruit from Siena; **pecorino** sheep's milk cheese; **ricciarelli** almond biscuits from Siena; **torrone** nougat; **torta** tart, cake; **zabaglione** egg custard mixed with Marsala; **zuppa Inglese** trifle.

Drinks

Acqua water, *gassata* (fizzy) or *liscia/naturale* (still); **birra** beer; **caffè** coffee; **cioccolata** hot chocolate; **latte** milk; **succo di frutta** fruit juice; **tè** tea; **vino rosso/bianco/rosato** red/white/rosé wine; **vin santo** dessert wine.

General

May I see the menu? **Posso vedere il menù?** May I have the bill, please? **Mi fa il conto, per favore?**

Enoteca Boccadama

The restaurant is managed by Tony Sasa along with the energetic staff Linda, Ildi, Emanuela and Claudia.
Piazza S. Croce 25, Firenze
055 243 640

Situated in the one of the most beautiful squares in Florence. The menu is small but delightful and consists of home-made Tuscan and Mediterranean cuisine accompanied with some of the best Italian wines.

Wine tasting and sales of more than 800 Italian and international labels

FINISTERRAE
RISTORANTE E BAR MEDITERRANEO

INFO@FINISTERRAEFIRENZE.COM

VIA DE' PEPI 3/5R (PIAZZA S. CROCE) - FIRENZE - TEL. 055 26 38 675
MEDITERRANEAN SPECIALITIES * NEAPOLITAN PIZZERIA * MEZZE Y TAPAS BAR * BEAUTIFUL PRIVATE GARDENS
OPEN EVERY DAY FOR LUNCH - APERITIF - DINNER AND AFTER DINNER

only changed hands once since then and is still going strong in spite of the wide variety of other ethnic options now on offer around the city. Everything is made in house, from pitta breads to veal kebab, and it's all both delicious and cheap (doner kebabs are €3.30, with falafel at €2.80 and sticky Egyptian desserts just €1.30).

San Lorenzo

Restaurants

Da Mario
Via Rosina 2r (055 218550). **Open** noon-3.30pm Mon-Sat. Closed 3wks Aug. **Average** €15. **No credit cards**. **Map** p318 A3.
Be prepared to queue for a table at this tiny, cramped eaterie, in which four generations of the Colsi family have been serving up Florentine home cooking for 50 years. Your fellow lunchers will include stall-holders, businessmen, students and tourists, an egalitarian mix all drawn by a typically Florentine menu: try the earthy *zuppa di fagioli e cavolo nero* (bean and black cabbage soup), a terrific *bollito misto* (mixed boiled meats) served with a biting garlic *salsa verde* and, for a bit more cash, the excellent *bistecca*. It doesn't get much better for the price.

Da Sergio
Piazza San Lorenzo 8r (055 281941). **Open** noon-3pm Mon-Sat. Closed Aug. **Average** €20. **Credit** MC, V. **Map** p318 A3.
If Da Mario (*see above*) is packed, head to this rather less frantic (but slightly dearer) trattoria for Florentine food. Begin with *minestrone di verdura*, *ribollita* or *minestra di farro* (spelt soup), before moving on to a roast or *bistecca alla fiorentina*. There's tripe on Mondays and Thursdays and fresh fish (including superb *seppie in inzimino*, sweet tender squid stewed with Swiss chard) on Tuesdays and Fridays.

Wine bars

Casa del Vino
Via dell'Ariento 16r, San Lorenzo (055 215609/ www.casadelvino.it). **Open** 9am-7pm Mon-Fri. Closed Aug. **Credit** AmEx, MC, V. **Map** p318 A3.
The only seating at this crowded, authentic wine bar, hidden behind the stalls of the San Lorenzo market, is on benches backed up against the wine cabinets. No matter: regardless, punters continue to pile in here regularly for a glass of good wine and some delicious *panini* and *crostini*. Bottles for all budgets sit on lovely old carved wood shelves that line the room; you'll find fairly priced wines from all over Italy, plus labels from further afield and plenty of choice by the glass.

Zanobini
Via Sant'Antonino 47r (055 2396850). **Open** 8am-2pm, 3-8pm Mon-Sat. **Credit** MC, V. **Map** p318 A3.

Squeezed just between the food shops of narrow Via Sant'Antonino, this no-frills stand-up *vineria* has bags of atmosphere. It's usually full of locals propping up the bar, many looking as if they've been propping it up since not long after opening time. The shelves are filled with interesting, well-priced bottles: don't neglect the back room, with its fine selection of *digestivi* and whiskies. It's a good place for a quick slurp (there's nothing to eat) on your way round the market.

Snacks & fast food

Nerbone
Mercato Centrale (055 219949). **Open** 7am-2pm Mon-Sat. Closed Aug. **Average** €10. **No credit cards**. **Map** p318 A3.
This food stall/trattoria, located on the ground floor of the covered central market and dating back to 1872, is a good place to find local colour. From breakfast on, it's packed with market workers: even if you can't face a *lampredotto* (cow's intestine) sarnie and a glass of rough red plonk at 7am, the locals can, and it only costs them €3. Plates of simple pasta and soups (from €3.10) offer alternatives.

San Marco

Restaurants

L'Accademia
Piazza San Marco 7r (055 217343/www.ristorante accademia.it). **Open** noon-3pm, 7-11pm daily. **Average** €28. *Pizza* €13. **Credit** AmEx, DC, MC, V. **Map** p319 A4.
Sure, it's geared towards tourists, but nontheless, L'Accademia is a useful spot in an area where there aren't many good eating choices. There are a few ambitious options on the menu – cold cream of asparagus soup with mixed seafood and a rich mushroom strudel in a parmesan sauce, say – but it's mostly fairly standard fare. The star turn is the tender fillet steak cooked in an intense *brachetto* wine sauce with juniper and glazed shallots. The wine list is surprisingly comprehensive and prices are reasonable.

Il Vegetariano
Via delle Ruote 30r (055 475030). **Open** 12.30-2.30pm, 7.30-10.30pm Tue-Fri; 7.30-10.30pm Sat, Sun. Closed 3wks Aug. **Average** €15. **No credit cards**.
One of only a few dedicated vegetarian restaurants in Florence, Il Vegetariano offers wholesome fare and excellent value for money. Expect the menu to offer plenty of choice, including a variety of ethnic dishes and generous portions all the way around. There's a fabulous salad bar and the wines are all organic. The one drag about a meal here? Actually getting hold of the food is a bit of an ordeal: take your pick from the menu on the blackboard, pay at the desk, get a written receipt and then get your food from the counter.

Olio e Convivium *See p125.*

Santa Croce

Restaurants

Baldovino

Via San Giuseppe 22r (055 241773). **Open** *Apr-Oct* 11.30am-2.30pm, 7-11.30pm daily. *Nov-Mar* 11.30am-2.30pm, 7-11.30pm Tue-Sun. **Average** €27. *Pizza* €15. **Credit** MC, V. **Map** p318 C5.

Scottish restaurateur David Gardner's combination of colourful decor and flexible menus (have a full meal, or snack on a pizza or salad) appeals to everyone from students to tour groups (who tend to eat early and get back on the bus). The food is decent rather than terrific, but prices are reasonable, there's plenty of choice, and the wine list is full and varied. Across the road, the same owners run the smaller, quieter Baldoria, which serves casual, snacky-type food, plus pizzas and pastas.

Boccadama

Piazza Santa Croce 25-26r (055 243640/www.bocca dama.it). **Open** *Summer* 8.30am-11pm daily. *Winter* 8.30am-3pm Mon; 8.30am-11pm Tue-Sun. **Average** €30. **Credit** AmEx, DC, MC, V. **Map** p319 C5.

Under the same management as Finisterrae across the square (*see below*), this inviting restaurant-wine bar is open all day: come here for breakfast or coffee, a glass of wine and a snack, a light lunch (salads, pastas, bruschettas and so on) or a more creative full dinner (beetroot-flavoured pasta with duck and black olive sauce, pork fillet with thyme on a bed of honeyed mushrooms). The wine list contains plenty of interest, including a good range by the glass. Thanks to its location, Boccadama is swamped with tourists (particularly for lunch) during the summer, when the terrace comes into its own.

Cibreino

Via dei Macci 122r (055 2341100). **Open** 12.50-2.30pm, 7-11.15pm Tue-Sat. Closed Aug. **Average** €25. **No credit cards**. **Map** p319 C6.

If your budget won't stretch to Cibrèo (*see below*), nip next door to its trattoria sibling. You can't book (prepare to queue), the atmosphere is rustic and often overcrowded, there are no complimentary extras and the menu has less choice. But the food is the same and the bill will be less than a third of what you would pay in the parent restaurant.

Cibrèo

Via Andrea del Verrocchio 8r (055 2341100). **Open** 12.50-2.30pm, 7-11.15pm Tue-Sat. Closed Aug. **Average** €65. **Credit** AmEx, DC, MC, V. **Map** p319 C6.

Cibrèo has become something of a Florentine institution. The dishes at the flagship of chef/patron Fabio Picchi's little empire comprise a combination of traditional Tuscan and creative cuisines, based on the use of prime ingredients. Flavours are intense, and there is heavy use of fresh herbs and spices. There's no menu, but a chummy waiter sits at your table in the elegant, wood-panelled room and takes you through the options. A series of delicious *antipasti* arrives automatically with a glass of wine, but if you're a pasta fan, you'll be disappointed – there isn't any. Recommended soups include yellow pepper and fish varieties, while *secondi* are divided between meat and fish. Desserts are fabulous, and the wine list is everything you might expect. Cibrèo provokes extreme opinions: some think it's the best restaurant is Florence, while others claim it's overrated and over-full of tourists.

Enoteca Pinchiorri

Via Ghibellina 87 (055 242777/www.enoteca pinchiorri.com). **Open** 7.30-10pm Tue; 12.30-2pm, 7.30-10pm Thur-Sat. Closed Aug. **Average** €250. **Credit** AmEx, MC, V. **Map** p319 C5.

Extensive renovations rather compromised this restaurant's old-world atmosphere, but the cooking didn't slide: the year after Enoteca Pinchiorri reopened in 2003, it won back its third Michelin star. You can choose à la carte, but there are several set menus, including one based on Tuscan traditions and one with more creative options; each involves at least eight or nine tiny but superbly executed courses. Then there's the stellar cellar: Giorgio Pinchiorri has amassed a collection of wines that's second to none. Wherever you eat – inside the palazzo or in the gorgeous, jasmine-scented courtyard – it all looks fabulous; service is elegant and prices are ridiculously high. Note that men are now required to wear jackets.

Finisterrae

Via de' Pepi 3-5r (055 2638675/www.finisterrae firenze.com). **Open** noon-3pm, 7.30-11.30pm Mon-Fri; noon-3pm, 7.30pm-midnight Sat, Sun. Closed 2wks Aug. **Average** €30. *Pizza* €15. **Credit** AmEx, DC, MC, V. **Map** p319 C5.

This gorgeous restaurant occupies the ground floor of an elegant Renaissance palazzo on Piazza Santa Croce. The place itself is lovely – both indoors, where each room is done out to reflect a different country, and out on the beautiful covered terrace at the back. It's a shame that neither the erratic service or the food, which includes dishes from all over the Mediterranean but too often tends towards the bland, lives up to the surroundings. That said, there are some good Neapolitan pizzas, and the tagines, meze, paella and bouillabaisse make a change from *pasta e fagioli*. The lunchtime menu offers a limited (and cheaper) choice of Italian fare.

La Giostra

Borgo Pinti 12r (055 241341/www.ristorantela giostra.com). **Open** 12.30-3pm, 7.30pm-midnight Mon-Fri; 7.30pm-midnight Sat, Sun. **Average** €40. **Credit** AmEx, DC, MC, V. **Map** p319 A6.

It might be run by elderly chef/proprietor Dimitri Miezko Leopoldo, Principe d'Asburgo Loreno, but La Giostra isn't particularly princely: too many tables are squeezed into the rather shabby room, its walls covered by pics of visiting celebs with the host. Still, the atmosphere is good and, while prices are on the high side (especially for wines), the food is very good. *Primi* include pasta generously sauced with seafood or divine ravioli stuffed with pecorino and pears; simple fish and meat dishes (including Wiener schnitzel) feature among the mains. Don't order too much: portions are huge, and there's a generous and complimentary plate of nibbles to start.

Osteria de' Benci

Via de' Benci 13r (055 2344923). **Open** 1-2.45pm, 7.30-10.45pm Mon-Sat. **Average** €23. **Credit** AmEx, DC, MC, V. **Map** p319 C4.

This lively trattoria serves up a well-executed mix of traditional local specialities such as *ribollita* and *trippa alla fiorentina*, plus interesting pasta dishes (tortellini with saffron and rocket, spaghetti with red radicchio and shavings of mullet roe). You'll pay more (€20) for a Chianina fillet, but it'll be worth it – it's vast, cooked over an open fire and served *al sangue* (rare). Desserts are strong – try the excellent chocolate flan with bitter orange marmalade. Service can be brusque when the going gets busy, but such popularity can only be a good sign. If it's sunny, try to nab a table at the outside terrace.

Ruth's

Via Farini 2A (055 2480888). **Open** 12.30-2.30pm, 8-10.30pm Mon-Thur; 12.30-2.30pm Fri. **Average** €20. **No credit cards**. **Map** p319 B6.

Located beside the city's synagogue, Ruth's serves great-value kosher vegetarian food and fish dishes. The dining area is a pleasant, modern and bright room with a full view of the open kitchen. The cooking has palpable Middle Eastern and North African influences, resulting in dishes like falafel and other typical meze, fish or vegetable couscous, and fish *brik* (deep-fried flaky pastry parcels) served with a Tunisian salad, along with pastas and salads.

Simon Boccanegra

Via Ghibellina 124r (055 2001098/www.boccanegra. com). **Open** 7pm-midnight Mon-Sat. **Average** €35. **Credit** AmEx, DC, MC, V. **Map** p319 C4.

The menu at Simon Boccanegra is firmly rooted in local culinary traditions, but isn't without an element of surprise. Seared fresh tuna is sprinkled with sesame seeds and served with hot green radish, rack of lamb is served in a crust with a cocoa sauce, and asparagus and parmesan tart is topped with a lick of saffron cream. The wine list is dominated by Tuscan labels – some good Super Tuscans among them – and the atmosphere is elegant yet relaxed. If you want to spend a little less, pop next door to the rustic Enoteca for a glass of wine and some good cheese, or a simple meal of homespun Tuscan specialities from the same kitchen.

Wine bars

All'Antico Vinaio

Via dei Neri 65r (no phone). **Open** 8am-8pm Tue-Sat; 8am-1pm Sun. Closed Aug. **Credit** AmEx, MC, V. **Map** p319 C4.

This small, no-frills neighbourhood *vineria* is often packed with locals – especially in the evenings, when there's time to mull over the day's proceedings with a *gottino* (a stubby glass) of wine and a delicious artichoke-topped *crostino*. Food comes from the *rosticceria* over the road (the establishments share an owner): soups and hearty pasta in the winter and rice salads and *carpaccio* in summer. The *panini* are also good. As a visitor, you may not be able to join in the chat, but it's a good place to soak up some atmosphere.

Pizzerie & rosticcerie

Caffè Italiano

Via Isola delle Stinche 13r (055 289368/www.caffe italiano.it). **Open** 7.30pm-1am Tue-Sat. Closed 3wks Aug. **Average** €12. **No credit cards**. **Map** p319 C5.

There's almost no choice – marinara, margherita or Napoli – and just four bare tables, but the pizzas at this annexe to the upmarket Osteria del Caffè Italiano are authentic and delicious, their light and puffy bases topped with San Marzano tomatoes and proper *mozzarella di bufala*. After 10.30pm the overflow is seated at the elegant restaurant.

Il Pizzaiuolo

Via de' Macci 113r (055 241171). **Open** 12.30-3pm, 7.30pm-12.30am Mon-Sat. Closed Aug. **Average** €13. **No credit cards**. **Map** p319 C6.

In recent years Florence seems to have favoured Neapolitan-style pizzas (with light, puffy bases) over more traditional local versions (with thin, crisp bottoms), and Il Pizzaiuolo is a good place to sample them. For an authentic taste of Naples, try the pizza topped with *salsiccia e friarelli* – sausage and a kind of bitter greens typical to the Campania region. Delicious Neapolitan pasta dishes include *spaghetti Gaeta* with tomato, olives and capers, or *trofie* with pesto and cherry tomatoes. Finish off with a *babà*. The decor is nothing special: bare tables crowded into a loud, white-tiled room (you may find yourself sharing).

Rosticceria Giuliano Centro

Via dei Neri 74r, Santa Croce (055 2382723). **Open** 8am-3pm, 5-9pm Tue-Sat; 8am-3pm Sun. Closed 2wks July. **Average** €13. **Credit** AmEx, MC, V. **Map** p319 C4.

There's a really appetising display of food on the counter at this *rosticceria*. More unusual dishes include spicy chicken wings and seafood salad, but there's also good lasagne, succulent roasts, grilled veg and some fresh-looking salads. Takeaway food is sold by weight, but you pay only about 15% more to eat in, at the back of the shop.

Salumeria, Vini, Trattoria I Fratellini

Via Ghibellina 27r (055 679390). **Open** noon-3.30pm Mon-Fri. Closed Aug. **Average** €10. **No credit cards**. **Map** p319 C4.

Hotel cuisine

There was a time when the chances of getting a really good meal in one of Florence's hotels were slim. Today, however, some of the city's most interesting eateries are in four- and five-star hotels; all welcome non-residents. Aside from the places reviewed below, the soon-to-open restaurant at the Helvetia & Bristol (*see p51*) ought to be worth a peek.

Borgo San Jacopo

Lungarno Hotel, Borgo San Jacopo 62r, Oltrarno (055 281661/www.lungarnohotels. com). **Open** 7.30-10.30pm Mon, Wed-Sun. Closed Aug. **Average** €40. **Credit** AmEx, DC, MC, V. **Map** p318 C3.

Chef Beatrice Segoni hails from the Adriatic coast; several fish dishes from her home territory feature among the delicious and unfussy food at this classy yet ultimately relaxed eaterie, right on the river. Expect punchy meat choices, such as stuffed duck neck with courgette flowers. A huge arched window offers views of the Arno, and there are four tables on the terrace overlooking the Ponte Vecchio. Prices are surprisingly honest, as long as you go easy on the wine.

Fusion Bar

Gallery Hotel Art, Vicolo dell'Oro 2, Duomo & Around (055 27263). **Open** 11.30am-11.30pm daily. **Average** €40. **Credit** AmEx, DC, MC, V. **Map** p318 C3.

A stylish place to come for a light lunch, an evening cocktail (*see p184* **Night nibbles**) or dinner. During the day there's a help-yourself buffet (€13); in the evening there's a full menu of Japanese and fusion dishes. Go for one of two set menus (€33/€48) or order à la carte (sushi, sashimi, tempura and noodle dishes, plus the likes of satay-marinated saddle of rabbit). There's brunch at weekends.

L'Incontro

Savoy Hotel, Piazza della Repubblica 7, Duomo & Around (055 283313/www.hotel savoy.com). **Open** 12.30-3pm, 7.30-10.30pm daily. **Average** €55. **Credit** AmEx, DC, MC, V. **Map** p318 B3.

Done out in contemporary brasserie style, the Savoy's bar and restaurant have a ringside view of Piazza della Repubblica: try to get a table up front or on the terrace. Food includes Tuscan offerings such as *ribollita* and *baccalà* (salt cod), plus the likes of duck breast in orange sauce with braised red cabbage.

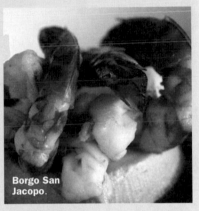

Borgo San Jacopo.

The Lounge

JK Place, Piazza Santa Maria Novella 9-10r, Santa Maria Novella (055 2645282/www. lounge-bar.it). **Open** 12.30pm-midnight daily. Closed 2wks Aug. **Average** €45. **Credit** AmEx, DC, MC, V. **Map** p318 B2.

Though it's annexed to JK Place (*see p55*), The Lounge is intended to be more than just a hotel restaurant: you can order anything from a light lunch on the smart wood-decked terrace to a truffle omelette at midnight. The menu features the best that Italy – especially Tuscany – has to offer in terms of carefully sourced ingredients: renowned butcher Dario Cecchini's *tonno del Chianti*, potato ravioli with guinea fowl sauce, Sicilian tuna fillet, plus mouth-watering puds including ice-cream from Vivoli (*see p133* **Cold comfort**).

Onice

Hotel Villa La Vedetta, Viale Michelangelo 78, Outside the City Gates (055 681631/ www.villalavedettahotel.com). Bus 12, 13. **Open** 12.30-2.30pm, 7.30-10.30pm Tue-Sun. Closed 2wks Aug. **Average** €80. **Credit** AmEx, DC, MC, V.

This Michelin-starred restaurant is kitted out with filmy cerise pink cloths on faux-croc and perspex tables, and silver-painted armchairs. Andrea Accordi's exquisitely presented, Italian-rooted fusion food is fabulous, peppered with zingy oriental flavour. The service doesn't live up to expectations, but a meal here is still worth the expense. Only light lunches are served during the day from Tuesday to Friday. The terrace is popular in summer.

Eat, Drink, Shop

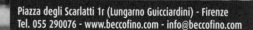

Seemingly caught in a time warp, this atmospheric cross between a grocer's shop, wine bar and *rosticceria* has been run by the Bisazzi family since the 1950s, and is still one of the best bargains in town. Walk through the long, wood-panelled shop to the food counter and real fire, choose what takes your fancy, and either take it away or eat it at one of the wooden tables in the back. *Primi* cost between €3 and €4, while *secondi* (including spit-roasted chicken) will set you back a maximum of €5. Make sure you sample Simona's superbly creamy tiramisù to finish. At €1.30 for 250ml, the house wine is a snip.

Oltrarno

Restaurants

Alla Vecchia Bettola

Viale Ariosto 32-34r (055 224158). **Open** noon-2.30pm, 7.30-10.30pm Tue-Sat. Closed 3wks Aug. **Average** €25. **No credit cards.**
This popular trattoria, situated on a busy ring road, is a real locals' favourite. There's usually a queue, and the noise levels in the single tiled room rise as the evening progresses. The traditional menu includes daily specials alongside such regulars as *penne alla Bettola* (with tomato, chilli pepper, vodka and a dash of cream) and a superb beef *carpaccio* topped with artichoke hearts and shaved parmesan. The *bistecca* is succulent, delicious and vast.

Beccofino

Piazza degli Scarlatti (055 290076). **Open** 7-11.30pm Tue-Sun. **Average** €40. **Credit** MC, V. **Map** p318 C2.
When David Gardner opened Beccofino in 1999, its combination of contemporary decor, innovative food and serious wines was unique in town. Original chef Francesco Berardinelli has now moved on, but his style of modern, Tuscan-based cooking, made with top-quality seasonal ingredients, still anchors the menu and continues to win high praise: try the soft, pillowy potato *gnudi* with *cavolo nero* and crispy bacon, and casserole of pigeon with dried figs in red wine. The menu also runs to fish and vegetarian dishes, while the ample wine list includes an excellent choice by the glass. Be warned: when it gets busy here, it also gets noisy, and service can be slow.

Borgo San Jacopo

See p123 **Hotel cuisine.**

Canapone Club

Via Mazzetta 5A (055 2381729/www.canapone.org). **Open** *Summer* 7-11pm daily. *Winter* 7-11pm Tue-Sat; 12.30-3.30, 7-11pm Sun. Closed 2wks Aug. **Average** €27. **Credit** AmEx, DC, MC, V. **Map** p318 D1.
The short menu at this club – you'll need to pay a €2 membership on your first visit – features fish, meat and vegetable dishes that owe a debt to southern Italian culinary traditions, albeit with variations: the odd Asian flavour creeps in, and specials include sushi on Wednesdays and brunch on Sundays. The food – ravioli stuffed with sea bass and served with

asparagus and ginger, venison braised in Montalcino wine – is punchy and generally top-notch. Service is friendly and, expensive wines aside, it's good value.

La Casalinga

Via dei Michelozzi 9r (055 218624). **Open** noon-2.30pm, 7-9.45pm Mon-Sat. Closed 3wks Aug. **Average** €20. **Credit** DC, MC, V. **Map** p318 D2.
This bustling, family-run trattoria has been part of the Oltrarno scene for decades, managing to maintain its authentic atmosphere in spite of the onslaught of tourists. Prices have remained relatively low and the cooking is wholesome and reliable. Still, some dishes are better than others: avoid the ubiquitous *tortellini alla panna* in favour of such local specialities as *minestrone di riso e cavolo* (thick, warming soup with black cabbage and rice), roast guinea fowl and apple cake.

Filipepe

Via di San Niccolò 39r (055 2001397/www.filipepe. com). **Open** 7.30pm-1am daily. Closed 2wks Aug. **Average** €25. **Credit** AmEx, DC, MC, V. **Map** p319 D5.
Funky chic decor provides a sensual setting for the unusual food at this newish restaurant, one of the best bargains in town. The menu of *sapori mediterranei* (Mediterranean flavours) is split into *freddo*, *crudo* and *caldo* (cold, raw and hot) dishes with no formal structure, so you can mix and match as you wish. The food is beautifully presented on big white porcelain or glass plates: choose *carpaccio* of monkfish with a coriander and orange 'coktail' (sic), or pasta with mussels, courgettes and courgette flower coulis. Desserts are a feast for both eye and palate, and the wine list is interesting and well priced.

Il Guscio

Via dell'Orto 49 (055 224421). **Open** 8-11pm Tue-Sat. Closed Aug. **Average** €30. **Credit** DC, MC, V.
The atmosphere at this popular restaurant is rustic and unpretentious, but the menu is interesting. Alongside Tuscan standards, sample more unusual dishes, such as ricotta ravioli served with an aubergine and ricotta sauce, medallions of beef cooked in *vin santo* and the seafood *padella*, a spicy stew served in its pan. Desserts are good and the wine list is long and varied, offering labels from all over Italy and beyond from just €10.

Olio e Convivium

Via Santo Spirito 4 (055 2658198/www.convivium firenze.com). **Open** *Food served* noon-3pm Mon; noon-3pm, 5.30-10.30pm Tue-Sat. Closed 3wks Aug. **Average** €30. **Credit** AmEx, MC, V. **Map** p318 C2.
Well-heeled locals call into this upmarket grocer to buy delicious food to go (*see p147*), but two cosy restaurant rooms – chequerboard floors, sparkling crystal, shelves stacked with wine, olive oil and other edibles – make a fine spot in which to munch a quiet meal. Specials are chalked up on a board: *taglierini* with lobster, broad bean and pecorino risotto, roast pork with prunes. Wines are expensive.

Zibibbo. See p128.

Pane e Vino

Piazza Cestello 3 (055 2476956). **Open** 7.30pm-
midnight Mon-Sat. Closed 2wks Aug. **Average**
€38. **Credit** AmEx, DC, MC, V. **Map** p318 D5.

Pane e Vino recently relocated to a small former
warehouse near the river, but the food is still good
and prices remain keen. The menu features Tuscan-
based dishes alongside influences from northern
Italy: highlights might include broad bean soup
topped with a sauté of chicory, ravioli stuffed with
potatoes, leeks and speck served with a cheese and
radicchio fondue, and duck breast with red-wine
glazed pear. The five-course set *menù degustazione*
is a very reasonable €30; the honest mark-ups on the
unusual wine list and the late hours are added perks.

Pruto

Piazza Tasso 9r (055 222219). **Open** noon-3pm,
7.30-11pm Tue-Sat. Closed 2wks Aug. **Average**
€30. **Credit** MC, V.

The extrovert ex-proprietor of Stefano's upmarket
fish restaurant in Galluzzo is now at the helm of this
rustic trattoria. Pruto specialises in *pesce azzurro*
(herring, sardines, mackerel, anchovies and so on,
all often rejected by posher fish restaurants), but
there's more besides: prawns, shrimps, tuna, swordfish and lobster, depending on what's at the market.
Try marinated anchovies, swordfish *involtini* stuffed
with pine nuts and raisins, or fresh pappardelle with
lobster; *secondi* include grilled tuna steak and a
mixed grill of *pesce azzurro*.

Il Santo Bevitore

*Via di Santo Spirito 64-66r (055 211264/www.santo
bevitore.com).* **Open** 12.30-3pm, 7.30-11.30pm daily.
Closed 3wks Aug. **Average** €22. **Credit** AmEx, MC,
V. **Map** p318 C2.

Occupying a large, vaulted room with unfortunately boomy acoustics, this restaurant/wine bar is good
both for a quick lunch or a more formal dinner, when
linen replaces paper mats and the menu lengthens.
As well as the ever-present wooden platters laden
with selections of cheeses and cold meats, there's
fresh pappardelle with lamb and artichoke sauce,
potato soufflé with aromatic butter, and tartar of
Chianina beef. The varied and nicely priced wine list
is in the reliable hands of Millesimi (*see p150*).

Trattoria del Carmine

Piazza del Carmine 18r (055 218601). **Open**
noon-2.30pm, 7.30-10.30pm Mon-Sat. Closed 3wks
Aug. **Average** €22. **Credit** AmEx, DC, MC, V.
Map p318 C1.

This pleasantly rustic, good-value neighbourhood
trattoria is a step up, in terms of both food and service, from some of the other budget options in the
area. The clientele is a mix of regular locals and
tourists and the menu is divided between a seasonally inspired *menù del giorno* and a long, fixed menu.
Tuscan standards (*ribollita*, spinach and ricotta ravioli, excellent *bistecca* and so on) are always on offer,
while daily specials might include asparagus risotto or swordfish steaks.

Trattoria 4 Leoni

Via dei Vellutini 1r (055 218562/www.4leoni.com).
Open noon-2.30pm, 7-11pm Mon, Tue, Thur-Sun; 7-11pm Wed. **Average** €30. **Credit** AmEx, DC, MC, V. **Map** p318 C2.

Once a simple local eaterie, the 4 Leoni is trendier these days. The room is now done out in vibrant colours, with exposed brickwork, rustic tables and chairs, and a vaguely intrusive level of background music. Prices have risen accordingly. Still, it continues to buzz with mixed crowds, who chow down on a menu of acceptable Tuscan-based food. In summer, meals are served under big white umbrellas on delightful little Piazza della Passera.

Wine bars

Pitti Gola e Cantina

Piazza Pitti 16 (055 212704). **Open** *Summer* 10am-midnight Tue-Sun. *Winter* 10am-9.30pm Tue-Sun. **Credit** AmEx, MC, V. **Map** p318 D2.

Dark green paintwork and marble-topped tables lend this little wine bar a classy, classic feel. Right opposite Palazzo Pitti (a little terrace gets the full view), it's often packed with tourists and prices are on the high side, but the atmosphere is very pleasant and there's a good choice of wines, heavily weighted towards Tuscany. Snacks include Dario Cecchini's famous *tonno del Chianti*: not tuna fish at all, but pork marinated in white wine and herbs.

Le Volpi e l'Uva

Piazza dei Rossi 1r (055 2398132/www.levolpieluva. com). **Open** 10am-8pm Mon-Sat. **Credit** AmEx, MC, V. **Map** p318 C4.

In winter, there's not much room in this narrow wine bar. You sit up at the bar in the company of local wine aficionados or, in summer, repair to the terrace, which provides much-needed extra space. Much of what's on offer will be unfamiliar to all but the most clued-up oenophiles: owners Riccardo and Emilio search out small, little-known producers from all over Italy, with an eye on value for money. A limited but delicious selection of nibbles includes Italian and French cheeses, cured meats, *panini tartufati* (stuffed with truffle cream), smoked duck and rich pâtés.

Pizzerie & rosticcerie

La Mangiatoia

Piazza San Felice 8-10r (055 224060). **Open** 11.30am-3pm, 7-10.30pm Tue-Sun. **Average** €16. **Credit** AmEx, MC, V.

La Mangiatoia, a combination of *rosticceria* and pizzeria, is popular with a mix of local Santo Spirito residents, students and tourists, thanks in part to the excellent value it offers. Order takeaway food from the counter in the front, or go through to one of a series of rooms behind the shop, where, aside from standard *rosticceria* fare (lasagne, spit-roast chicken, roast meats), there's a daily menu of specials and good pizzas.

Outside the City Gates

Restaurants

L'Arte Gaia

Via Faentina 1 (055 5978498). Bus 1A. **Open** 8-10.30pm Tue, Sun; noon-2.30pm; 8-10.30pm Wed-Sat. Closed 2wks Aug. **Average** €40. **Credit** AmEx, MC, V.

Situated on a small bridge crossing a scruffy tributary of the Arno just below Fiesole, this modern, welcoming restaurant specialises in fresh fish and seafood. Wood floors, crisp white cloths and soft lighting provide the background to colourful and punchy cooking: expect dishes such as *gnocchetti* with red mullet and capers flavoured with mint, citrus-spiked fish kebabs and *polpo Arte Gaia*, deliciously sweet marinated and grilled octopus. At €35 and €39, the four-course set menus are great value.

Bibe

Via delle Bagnese 1r (055 2049085). Bus 36, 37, then taxi. **Open** 7.30-10pm Mon, Tue, Thur, Fri; 12.30-2pm, 7.30-10pm Sat, Sun. Closed last wk Jan, 1st wk Feb & 1st 2wks Nov. **Average** €28. **Credit** AmEx, MC, V.

Occupying an old farmhouse about 3km south of Porta Romana, family-run Bibe is a good place to get the atmosphere of a rustic country restaurant if you don't want to travel too far. From the menu, try deep-fried courgette flowers stuffed with ricotta cheese, or sublime herb-infused *zuppa di porcini e ceci* (porcini mushroom soup with chickpeas). *Secondi* are classic Tuscan dishes; deep-fried chicken, rabbit and brains is a speciality. The puddings and the wine list are several notches above your average rustic eaterie. On the downside, the flower-filled terrace is blighted by mosquitos and traffic noise.

Fuor d'Acqua

Via Pisana 37r (055 222299/www.fuordacqua.com). Bus 6. **Open** 8-11.30pm Mon-Sat. Closed 3wks Aug. **Average** €60. **Credit** AmEx, DC, MC, V.

It's certainly not cheap (and there's a whopping €5 cover charge), but Fuor d'Acqua's fish is as fresh as it gets. Although there is a menu, you're unlikely to see it: the chef prepares what's best from the day's catch with the minimum of fuss, using only olive oil, lemon juice and seasoning. You can order your *antipasti* either *crudo* (raw) or *caldo* (lightly cooked and served tepid). To follow, enjoy *bavette* (flat spaghetti) with prawns and artichokes, and baked catch of the day roasted on a bed of potatoes, cherry tomatoes and olives. Don't get there too early or you'll risk finding that your dinner is still on the boat.

Omero

Via Pian dei Giullari 11r (055 220053). Bus 13, 38. **Open** noon-2.30pm, 7.30-10.30pm Mon, Wed-Sun. Closed Aug. **Average** €40. **Credit** AmEx, DC, MC, V.

The entrance to Omero, located in the quiet, exclusive hamlet of Pian dei Giullari, is on a narrow cobbled street, but if you walk through to the back

Eat, Drink, Shop

of the grocer's that fronts the restaurant, you'll emerge into a sunny room with great views of the rural surroundings; come at lunchtime for maximum effect. (Downstairs is not so nice.) The menu features traditional Florentine food, reliable, if not particularly exciting, and served at high prices. Never mind: you're here for the old-fashioned atmosphere, the respectful service and the wonderful location.

Onice

See p123 Hotel cuisine.

Da Ruggero

Via Senese 89r (055 220542). Bus 11, 36, 37. Open noon-2.30pm, 7.30-10.30pm Mon, Thur-Sun. Closed mid July-mid Aug. Average €25. Credit AmEx, DC, MC, V.

This tiny, family-run trattoria is one of the best places in Florence to eat genuine home cooking. The thing is, everybody knows it, so it's very popular: don't risk the trek to Porta Romana without booking. The menu of local dishes changes with the seasons, but always includes a hearty soup or two and an excellent spicy *spaghetti alla carattiera*. Among the roast meats, try the tasty pigeon or go for the exemplary *bollito misto* (mixed boiled meats) served with tangy, parsley-fresh *salsa verde*.

Salaam Bombay

Viale Rosselli 45r (055 357900). Bus 22. Open 7.30-11.30pm daily. Average €23. Credit AmEx, DC, MC, V.

When you need a spicy change from *pasta e fagioli*, head to one of Florence's few Indian restaurants. Tapestries adorn the walls of the single, galleried room; sit upstairs if you want to look down on the buzzy action below. The menu offers the sort of safe but decently cooked standards found on the menus of most Indian restaurants in Italy: tandooris and mughlai dishes, vegetarian options, great naans and own-made mango chutney. It's good value.

Targa

Lungarno C Colombo 7 (055 677377/www.targa bistrot.net). Bus 31, 32. Open 12.30-2.30pm, 7.30-11pm Mon-Sat. Closed 1st 3wks Aug. Average €45. Credit AmEx, DC, MC, V.

This contemporary but not ultra-hip riverside bistro is a good-looking spot, done out in lots of wood and glass, with low lighting and plenty of greenery. The seasonal menu features homespun Tuscan fare plus some more exciting dishes: gratinée of scallops with leeks and mushrooms, gnochetti with mullet roe and pecorino, and deep-fried salt cod with sweet and sour aubergine. The cheeseboard is impressive and the wine list is superb. If you don't want a full meal, come for pud and a glass of dessert wine to round off an evening, perhaps following it with something from the 127-strong whisky list.

Zibibbo

Via di Terzollina 3r (055 433383/www.zibibbonline. com). Bus 14. Open 12.30-3pm, 7.30-10pm Mon-Sat. Closed Aug. Average €40. Credit AmEx, DC, MC, V.

This bright, sunny restaurant is the domain of Benedetta Vitali, co-founder and former chef at Cibrèo (*see p121*). Her superb, unfussy food finds roots in both Florentine and southern Italian traditions (*zibibbo* is a Sicilian white grape), using only fresh, seasonal ingredients. A faithful and mostly local clientele comes to sample sweet, tender octopus and cannellini bean salad, tagliatelle with duck sauce, *inzimino di calamari* (a fabulous, spicy stew of calamari and Swiss chard) and herby roast pork with apple sauce. Lunchtimes are more casual, and the bill is about a quarter less.

Wabi Sabi

Viale dei Mille 53r (055 587779/www.ristorantewabi sabi.com). Bus 1, 3. Open 11.30am-3pm, 6pm-midnight Tue-Sun. Average €28. Credit AmEx, MC, V.

This stylish opening is one of the more affordable Japanese restaurants in Florence. Tables are arranged in a series of intimate rooms done out in minimalist style; there's also a big terrace. The menu features Japanese standards: sushi and sashimi, teriyaki, tempura (superb, especially the big fat *gamberoni*/prawns), soups and noodle dishes. Sushi aficionados might be a little disappointed, but the rest of the repertoire is very good. Service can be appallingly slow, though it may improve with age.

Wine bars

Fuori Porta

Via Monte alle Croci 10r (055 234 2483/www.fuori porta.it). Bus D. Open 12.30-3.30pm, 7pm-12.30am Mon-Sat. Closed 2wks Aug. Average €20. Credit AmEx, MC, V.

Florence's best known wine bar is situated in a lovely neighbourhood at Porta San Miniato. At any time, there are between 500 and 650 labels on the list, with about 50 available by the glass and carafe (rotating roughly every week). Tuscan and Piedmontese reds dominate, but other Italian regions are also well represented, and there are also formidable choices of grappas and Scotches. The daily menu has pastas, *carpacci* and salads; snacks include delicious *crostoni*. The terrace is popular in warm weather.

Pizzerie & rosticcerie

Santa Lucia

Via Ponte alle Mosse 102r (055 353255). Bus 30, 35. Open 7.30pm-12.30am Mon, Tue, Thur-Sun. Closed Aug. Average €13. No credit cards.

It may be a bit of a trek (a ten-minute walk north-west of Porta al Prato), but many Florentines reckon the pizza at Santa Lucia to be the best in town. It's authentically Neapolitan – light and puffy base, slightly soggy middle, the sweetest tomatoes and the milkiest mozzarella on top – and so is the atmosphere. If you don't want pizza, terrific fish dishes include *spaghetti allo scoglio* (with mixed seafood) and octopus in spicy tomato sauce. Book in advance or prepare to queue.

Cafés & Bars

The bean scene.

Order the wrong kind of coffee at the wrong time of day here, and the natural Florentine haughtiness will turn into pity. The rules are unwritten but they're strict: begin with a cappuccino at breakfast (*never* have one after mid-morning), move on to the concentrated shot of espresso at a bar two or three times later in the day, and knock back a strong hit of sweet black coffee after your evening meal.

Size also matters here. If you want more than a dribble that barely covers the bottom of the cup, ask for a *lungo* (about double the height of an espresso, and thus weaker) or a *caffè americano* (a big cup full of diluted espresso). And if you want milk in your espresso, order a *caffè macchiato caldo* or *freddo* (with a spoon of hot froth or a dash of cold milk). True caffeine hounds could attempt a *ristretto*, an even more concentrated espresso. To perk it up, order your espresso *corretto*, 'corrected' with a shot of your spirit of choice. A final word of advice: many bars serve their cappuccinos tepid, so if you want yours good and hot, ask for it *ben caldo*.

While the etiquette of coffee remains tenaciously inflexible, 2005 brought one major change. New legislation outlawed smoking in public buildings, which covers almost all bars and cafés. Fines are heavy (for both the bar and the customer) and enforcement is strict, so save your smoking for outdoors.

Of course, Florentine café society isn't just about coffee. The 'light lunch' has become a euphemism here for all manner of buffets, gourmet menus and brunch offerings. Tea is a less common affair, though a recent fad for flavoured teas and hot chocolates has brought the biscuits out of the cupboards. Then there's the early-evening *aperitivo* phenomenon, whereby a range of free snacks and home-made dishes are offered to drinkers (*see p184* **Night nibbles**).

A spate of openings, mixing any combination of café, wine bar, restaurant and brasserie, has resulted in a refreshing infusion of design and flexibility to the café scene. However, for all these changes, it's still the simple local bars and cafés that continue to form the real backbone of Florentine life. Classic bars come in several guises, depending on their licence. In café-bars you can usually sit down for a full lunch; in bar-*tabacchi* you can also buy cigarettes, bus tickets and stamps; in *latterie* you can pick up milk and dairy products; and in *drogherie* you can stock up on groceries. In other shops, especially *pasticcerie*, there's also a bar. In bigger bars and cafés you pay for coffee at the till before you order it from the barman with your receipt, unless you want to sit down. And bear in mind that location is everything when it comes to the bill: it usually costs far less if you stand at the bar rather than sit at a table, and you often pay more to sit outside, especially at one of the more touristy spots.

Duomo & Around

Astor Caffè

Piazza Duomo 20r (055 284305). **Open** 6pm-3am daily. **Credit** MC, V. **Map** p319 B4.

Light floods from a central skylight into this vast contemporary chrome-and-glass bar. Perch on a padded bar stool for an *aperitivo* or a freshly made vegetable or fruit juice, or linger for lunch (salads and pasta dishes). There's jazz in the downstairs bar some evenings; upstairs, sip cocktails, eat a full dinner or check your emails at the internet point. *See also p167 and p176.*

Bar Perseo

Piazza della Signoria 16r (055 2398316). **Open** 7am-midnight Mon-Sat. Closed 3wks Nov. **Credit** MC, V. **Map** p319 C4.

Though Perseo's centrepiece is its sculptural art deco chandelier, most eyes are drawn to the mountains of home-made ice-cream topped with cherries,

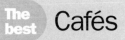

The best Cafés

For jazzy vibes
BZF (Bizzeffe) (*see p132*).

For river views
Capocaccia (*see p132*).

For Old World charm
Caffè Italiano (*see p130*).

For home-made cakes
Coquinarius (*see p130*).

For the creamiest cappuccinos
I Visacci (*see p135*).

Caffè Rivoire.

while upstairs is the salon, in which lunches and home-made cakes are served. *Caffè-choc* (espresso laced with bitter chocolate powder) is a must.

Caffè Rivoire

Piazza della Signoria 5r (055 214412/ www.rivoire.it). **Open** 8am-midnight Tue-Sun. Closed last 2wks Jan. **Credit** AmEx, DC, MC, V. **Map** p319 C4.
The most famous and best loved of all Florentine cafés, Rivoire was founded in 1872 as a chocolate factory. It still sells its own divine chocs, but the coffee is now also up there with the best. Only here does high Florentine society deign to mix with mere tourists, especially at the outside tables, with views of the Palazzo Vecchio and the Loggia dei Lanzi. One downside: your wallet will be hit hard for the privilege.

Caruso Jazz Café

Via Lamberteca 14-16r (055 281940/www.caruso jazzcafe.com). **Open** 9.30am-3.30pm, 6-11pm Mon-Sat. **Credit** AmEx, DC, MC, V. **Map** p319 C4.
Huge papier mâché sculptures of Florentine landmarks and cherubs adorn this vaulted bar, tucked behind the Piazza della Signoria. The artist owner has created a friendly, easy-going atmosphere in this watering hole. As well as the simple lunch and tea menus and the jazz acts who play some evenings (*see p176*), there are four PCs offering net access.

Chiaroscuro

Via del Corso 36r (055 214247). **Open** 7.45am-8.30pm Tue-Fri; 8.45am-9.30pm Sat, Sun. **Credit** MC, V. **Map** p319 B4.
With espresso machines, collectible coffee cups and coffee-bean resin trays (all for sale), Chiaroscuro's window proves it's serious about its java, served by expert barmen but also sold freshly ground. A glass cabinet displays rows and rows of cakes, sweets and savoury dishes. Good news: there's usually room to sit down, even at busy lunchtimes, and in the evening they do a mean *aperitivo*.

Colle Bereto

Piazza Strozzi 5r (055 283156/www.collebereto.com). **Open** *Summer* 8am-midnight Mon-Sat. *Winter* 8am-9pm Mon-Sat. Food from noon. **Credit** AmEx, MC, V. **Map** p318 B3.
Owned by the Tuscan wine producer of the same name, Colle Bereto is a smart bar with a prime location: the outside terrace overlooks the monumental Palazzo Strozzi. The menu is as carefully chosen as its sleek decor, with a daily choice of hot *primi*, a fixed menu of perfect salads and snacks, and – best of all – tiny fruit tarts with whipped yoghurt fillings.

Coquinarius

Via delle Oche 15r (055 2302153). **Open** 9am-11pm Mon-Thur; 9am-11.30pm Fri, Sat. Food from noon. Closed Aug. **Credit** MC, V. **Map** p318 B3.
A vaulted bar with a friendly, home-from-home atmosphere, Coquinarius has an imaginative lunch menu of pastas, salads and smoked fish platters and

berries and chocolate curls. Stand at the bar for an aperitif, or sit outside and admire the bar's namesake: *Perseus*, in the Loggia dei Lanzi.

Caffè Concerto Paszkowski

Piazza della Repubblica 31-35r (055 210236/ www.paszkowski.it). **Open** 7am-1.30am Tue-Sun. **Credit** AmEx, DC, MC, V. **Map** p318 B3.
Formerly a beer hall and a meeting point for artists, Paszkowski was declared a national monument in 1991. While rather grand, its glory days now seem a way off, and the bar now distinguishes itself from others on the square by its questionable summer concerts. Still, it's one of only a few places to remain open after late-night screenings at nearby cinemas.

Caffè Italiano

Via della Condotta 56r (055 291082). **Open** 8am-8pm Mon-Sat (lunch 1-3pm); 11am-8pm Sun. Closed 2wks Aug. **Credit** MC, V. **Map** p319 C4.
Old-world charm abounds at this gem: mahogany cabinets with silver teapots, gourmet chocolates and famous own-brand coffee. The bar sits downstairs,

delicious cakes, all own-made. At teatime, try the exotic range of chais or the speciality hot chocolate with fudge or meringues.

Gilli

Piazza della Repubblica 36-39r (055 213896/ www.gilli.it). **Open** 8am-midnight Mon, Wed-Sun. **Credit** AmEx, DC, MC, V. **Map** p318 B3.

This place is a long-time favourite, and it's easy to see why: the belle époque interior is original, the seasonally themed window displays of sweets, chocolates and pastries are wickedly tempting and the staff are lovely. Don't miss the rich hot chocolates: *gianduja* (hazelnut), almond, mint, orange and coffee. Plus, there's outside seating year-round. Let's hope all this isn't about to change, as rumour has it that Gilli is the latest historic bar to fall into the hands of the designer boutiques. Only time will tell.

Giubbe Rosse

Piazza della Repubblica 13-14r (055 212280/ www.giubberosse.it). **Open** 7.30am-2am daily. **Credit** AmEx, DC, MC, V. **Map** p318 B3.

Dating from the end of the 19th century and an intellectuals' haunt since 1909, when the Futurist manifesto was launched from here, Giubbe Rosse is still popular with the Florentine literati. The outdoor seating provides excellent people-watching opportunities in the piazza. The waiters still sport the red jackets that gave the place its name.

Nova Bar

Via Martelli 14r (055 289880). **Open** 8am-2am Mon-Thur; 8am-3am Fri, Sat; 4pm-midnight Sun. **Credit** MC, V. **Map** p318 B3.

The novelty value of this new café is not just in the funky decor (*see p181* **Designs for (night)life**). The menu is fun to peruse, with speciality teas, alcoholic tea cocktails, hot chocolates, focaccias and cold meat plates, and an early evening buffet with aperitifs.

Procacci

Via de' Tornabuoni 64r (055 211 656). **Open** 10.30am-8pm Mon-Sat. Closed Aug. **Credit** AmEx, MC, V. **Map** p318 B2/C2.

One of the few traditional shops on this thoroughfare to survive the onslaught of the big designer names, the small wood-lined bar and shop is a favourite with nostalgic Florentines and well-heeled shoppers. In season (Oct-Dec), truffles arrive daily at around 10am, filling the room with their soft musty aroma (the speciality is melt-in-the-mouth truffle and butter brioche, delicious with a glass of prosecco).

La Terrazza, Rinascente

Piazza della Repubblica 1 (055 219113). **Open** 9am-8.30pm Mon-Sat; 10.30am-7.30pm Sun. **Credit** AmEx, DC, MC, V. **Map** p318 B3.

The rooftop terrace café at this department store affords some of the most stunning views of the city, the splendour of Brunelleschi's cupola at such close quarters more than making up for the mediocre menu and the churlish service. Come at sundown, when you can experience the city bathed in pink light.

La Terrazza, Rinascente.

Santa Maria Novella

Amerini

Via della Vigna Nuova 63r (055 284941). **Open** 8am-8pm Mon-Sat. Closed 2wks Aug. **No credit cards. Map** p318 B2.

Smart but cosy, with a gravity-defying display of the finest Tuscan wines, Amerini is a lunchtime favourite. Choose from sandwiches such as marinated artichoke or grilled vegetables with brie, or order a bowl of fresh pasta. Breakfast time and afternoons are more relaxing, so you can sample luscious lemon tart and other delights relatively undisturbed.

Bar Curtatone

Borgo Ognissanti 167r (055 210772). **Open** 7am-1am Mon, Wed-Fri, Sun; 7am-2am Sat. Closed 3wks Aug. **No credit cards. Map** p318 B1.

A vast, bustling but stylish café serving a decadent selection of pastries, cakes and savouries. Have a three-course meal (12.30-2.30pm) or sip on a selection of liqueurs and aperitifs.

Indulge in cappuccinos and *crostoni* at **I Visacci**. *See p135.*

Caffè Megara

Via della Spada 15-17r (055 211837).
Open 8.30am-2am daily (lunch noon-3pm).
No credit cards. Map p318 B2.
Always full at lunchtimes, this airy, laid-back bar gets even busier when big matches are on. Two screens ensure a good view from wherever you're sitting; enormous *bruschette* help keep the strength up. Smooth jazzy sounds play out in the evenings; in summer grab one of the tiny tables outside.

Caffè San Carlo

Borgo Ognissanti 32-34r (055 216879/www. caffesancarlo.com). **Open** 7.30am-midnight Mon-Sat. **Credit** AmEx, MC, V. **Map** p318 B1.
If you're not put off by the unwelcoming behaviour of the bar staff, this is a stylish and lively place for lunch. Pre-lunch and dinner aperitifs are the big draws, with culinary quirks pepping up the ubiquitous buffet of snacks. In good weather the canopied outside tables become a miniature socialising hub for catching up on the local gossip.

Capocaccia

Lungarno Corsini 12-14r (055 210751). **Open** noon-2am daily. **Credit** MC, V. **Map** p318 C2.
Thanks to its frescoed salon and doors that open on to a riverbank seating area, Capocaccia is one of the city's most desirable café-bars. Saturday lunch is terrific, with a short 'gourmet' menu, but it's Sunday brunch that's legendary: try eggs benedict, salmon bagels or the 'Babette's feast' buffet. On other days sample pasta or inventive *panini*, washing them down with champagne by the glass. *See also p182.*

Giacosa Roberto Cavalli

Via della Spada 10r (055 2776328). **Open** *Summer* 7.30am-midnight Mon-Sat. *Winter* 7.30am-8.30pm Mon-Sat. Closed 2wks Aug. **Credit** AmEx, MC, V. **Map** p318 B2.

Tagging alongside Florentine designer Cavalli's clothing shop is this café, replete with leopardskin poufs, catwalk shows beamed on to a full-wall screen and plenty of attitude. The outside tables are often frequented by the man himself, so beware of making catty comments about the price-to-value ratio of the scraps of chiffon in the window displays.

Rose's

Via del Parione 26r (055 287090/www.roses.it). **Open** 8.30am-1.30am Mon-Sat (brunch 12.30-3.30pm Sat); 5pm-1.30am Sun. Closed 2wks Aug. **Credit** MC, V. **Map** p318 C2.
This spacious restaurant-bar, its cornflower blue velvet decor modern but soothing, is invariably packed with a young crowd from local shops and offices. Choose from burgers, tacos or classic pastas, risottos and salads for lunch; at night, however, it's one of the hippest sushi bars in town.

San Lorenzo

BZF (Bizzeffe)

Via Panicale 61r (055 2741009/www.bzf.it).
Open 4pm-midnight Tue-Sun. Closed June-Aug. **Credit** MC, V. **Map** p318 A3.
A 13th-century convent, stunningly renovated and now home to a bar, a bookshop, an internet terminal, a jazz venue and an art space. As well as a range of coffees and teas from around the world, there's a strong food menu: try the divine pumpkin soup, the flame-charred tuna carpaccio, cheeseboards or American-style sweets. *See also p167 and p176.*

Nabucco

Via XVII Aprile 28r (055 475087). **Open** 6.30am-10pm Mon-Sat. **Credit** MC, V.
Despite an almost constant influx of students from the nearby university faculties, it's generally easy to get a seat at one of the many tables or bar stools

Cold comfort

Despite strong competition from the personal chefs of Alexander the Great and the dynastic emperors of China, Florentines like to think they have a claim to fame for the first *gelato*. In the 16th century Bernardo Buontalenti, the Medicis' architect, entertained his patrons' guests in the Palazzo Pitti; he's reputed to have fed them frozen desserts made from fruit and zabaglione, with snow and ice from his specially built 'ice-houses' in the Boboli Gardens. Around the same time, Caterina de Medici is believed to have introduced 'cream ice' to the French courts when she moved to Paris to marry Henry II of France.

Delusional they might be about the origins of *gelato*, but the Florentines still work hard to hang on to their reputation, and the city is full of top-class *gelaterie*. If you see *produzione propria*, or *artigianale*, you'll know the ice-cream is home-made. Some of the smaller *gelaterie* that make their own ice-cream are closed for much of the winter. However, it's still easy to find a *gelateria* open on the main thoroughfares, some of which serve the cold stuff with hot chocolate or fudge sauces.

The most famous is **Vivoli** (Via Isola delle Stinche 7r, Santa Croce, 055 292334, closed Mon & most of Aug), whose reputation holds that it's the best in Florence. This is probably true of its *semi-freddi*, creamier and softer than ice-cream, and the divine *riso* (rice pudding) flavour *gelato*. However, the ice-cream at the chocolate shop **Vestri** (Borgo degli Albizi 11r, Santa Croce, 055 2340374, closed Sun; *see also p148*) is even more delicious. The shop only has a few flavours, but what it lacks in variety it makes up for in ingenuity: white chocolate with wild strawberries, chocolate and *peperoncino* (chilli pepper), are topped with spices and spoonfuls of melted gourmet chocolate.

A favourite with the locals is **Perché No!** (Via dei Tavolini 19r, Duomo & Around, 055 2398969, closed Tue in winter), often cited as the best *gelateria* in Florence for *crema* (vanilla), pistachio and chocolate flavours. On summer nights, crowds congregate at the hatch of **Gold** (Piazza Pesce 3-5r, Duomo & Around, 055 2396810, closed Wed in winter), located in a prime position between the Ponte Vecchio and the Uffizi. The house speciality here is exotic fruit flavours: from papaya to lime sorbets, depending on the season. Finally, anyone with a milk intolerance is directed to **Gelateria dei Neri** (Via dei Neri 22r, 055 210034, closed Wed in winter), one of the few parlours in the area to serve soya ice-cream alongside the classic creamy concoctions.

Vivoli.

lining the huge windows of this spacious, pleasant café-wine bar. The lunch and snack menus and evening buffet are arranged around the long wine list. Unusually, just about everything is available by the glass as well as the bottle, and prices are reasonable: there's lots to choose from under €3. Tastings are held on Wednesdays evenings between September and May.

Nannini Coffee Shop
Via Borgo 7r (055 212680). **Open** 7.30am-7.30pm Mon-Fri, Sun; 7.30am-8.30pm Sat. **Credit** MC, V. **Map** p318 B3.
Perennially bustling, Nannini is perfect for coffee and *panforte* (a sticky Sienese nut cake) after a visit to the nearby central market. The Nannini of the name is former racing driver Alessandro; he has a confectionery factory in Siena, and sells his *cantuccini* (almond biscuits), *ricciarelli* (choc-covered marzipan petits fours) and hexagonal *panfortes* here.

Gilli. *See p131.*

Porfirio Rubirosa
Viale Strozzi 18-20 (055 490965). **Open** 7pm-2am Mon-Sat. Closed 2wks Aug. **Credit** MC, V. **Map** p318 B3.
Across from the Fortezza da Basso and overlooking the park, this chic bar was named after a Brazilian playboy and is a monument to hedonism. Lunch on truffle mozzarella or smoked tuna salad, lounge on the balcony mezzanine with a slice of passion fruit cheesecake at teatime, or come back in the evening to make a night of it.

San Marco

Caffellatte
Via degli Alfani 39r (055 2478878). **Open** 8am-8pm Mon-Sat; 10am-6pm Sun. **No credit cards**. **Map** p319 A4.
The lattes in this small café, done out with rustic wooden tables and chairs, are among the best in Florence. But if they're too dull for you, the *cappuccione* comes piping hot in a giant bowl with honey and Turkish cinnamon. The pastries and cakes are made in the café's organic bakery.

Robiglio
Via dei Servi 112r (055 214501). **Open** 7.30am-7.30pm Mon-Sat. Closed 3wks Aug. **Credit** V. **Map** p319 A4.
The sublime hot chocolate here is so thick the spoon stands up in it, and the pastries are a Florentine institution. The sister café in Via Tosinghi (11r, 055 215013) has the same fabulous sweet treats and outside tables in summer.

Zona 15
Via del Castellaccio 53-55r (055 211678/www.zona 15wine.it). **Open** 11am-3am Mon-Fri; 6pm-3am Sat, Sun. **Credit** AmEx, DC, MC, V. **Map** p319 A4.
Looking like a futuristic American diner, this decidedly hip café-cum-wine bar's leather and chrome stools hug a massive central spotlit bar area. Tables filled with posh Florentines line the grey mosaic-tiled walls, crowned by dramatic vaulted ceilings. Splash out on oysters and champagne, or choose from the Mediterranean-inclined menu and over 200 wines.

Santa Croce

Caffè Cibrèo
Via Andrea del Verrocchio 5r (055 2345853). **Open** 8am-1am Tue-Sat (lunch 1-2.30pm). Closed 2wks Aug. **No credit cards**.
This delightful café has exquisite carved wood ceilings, antique furniture, a candlelit mosaic and outside tables, but also a knack for making everything it presents as beautiful as the bar itself. As you'd expect from an outpost of Cibrèo (*see p121*), the savoury dishes are inventive and refined, but the desserts are also truly amazing, notably the dense chocolate torte and the cheesecake with bitter orange sauce.

Caffetteria Piansa

Borgo Pinti 18r, nr Piazza G Salvemini (055 2342362). **Open** 8am-1am Mon-Sat (lunch noon-3pm). Closed 2wks Aug. **No credit cards.** **Map** p319 B5.

Piansa might be the best-known Florentine coffee brand, but it's also a self-service café popular with local students and business folk. It's done out in a rustic canteen style, with wooden benches and shared tables, and is big enough to ensure that finding a seat is rarely a problem – outside the busy lunch period, that is.

La Loggia degli Albizi

Borgo degli Albizi 39r (055 2479574). **Open** 7am-8pm Mon-Sat. Closed Aug. **Credit** MC, V. **Map** p319 B5.

With some of the best pastries and cakes in town, La Loggia degli Albizi is the perfect stop-off after some hard shopping. Try the *torta della nonna* (crumbly pastry filled with baked pâtisserie cream).

I Visacci

Borgo degli Albizi 80r (055 2001956). **Open** 10.30am-2.30am Mon-Sat; 3-10pm Sun. **Credit** MC, V. **Map** p319 B5.

Cosy up in one of the padded alcove sofa seats in this cutesy bar, decked out in different-coloured stripes. The best cappuccinos in the city centre are served here, with froth so smooth it could be whipped cream; the mellow music may also help to lull you into a longer stay. The lunchtime menu hits the right notes: cheap hot *crostoni* (open sandwiches), salads, omelettes and cold meat plates. However, if you're in a hurry, think twice: the wait can be excruciating.

Oltrarno

Cabiria

Piazza Santo Spirito 4r (055 215732). **Open** 8.30am-1.30am Mon, Wed-Sun. **No credit cards.** **Map** p318 C4.

Once a somewhat seedy night-time hangout for grungy types, these days Cabiria has flowers at the outside tables, trendy lighting, and art lining the walls. Hot and cold dishes (including excellent hot focaccias) are available at lunchtime, and the barman shakes up a mean *aperitivo* at midday and at 7pm. Most importantly, though, the coffee is still great. *See also p182.*

Caffè degli Artigiani

Via dello Sprone 16r (055 291882). **Open** May-Sept 8.30am-midnight Mon-Sat. Oct-Apr 8.30am-10.30pm Mon-Sat. **Credit** AmEx, DC, MC, V. **Map** p318 D2.

This charming, laid-back gem of a café is well worth seeking out for its country cottage atmosphere (think low ceilings and fraying, beautifully carved antique chairs), but also for its outside tables, which appear in warm weather on a quiet side street. Staff are friendly and multilingual.

Caffè Ricchi

Piazza Santo Spirito 9r (055 215864/www.caffe ricchi.it). **Open** *Summer* 7am-1.30am Mon-Sat. *Winter* 7am-10pm Mon-Sat. Closed last 2wks Aug, last 2wks Feb. **Credit** MC, V. **Map** p318 D2.

This is a charming setting for alfresco drinking: Ricchi is situated on the traffic-free piazza of the sublime Santo Spirito church. The lunch menu of sandwiches, pastas and speciality *sformati* (hot vegetable terrines) changes daily. If it rains, the side room, plastered with artists' versions of the church façade, is a great place to relax with a coffee and a cake.

Dolce Vita

Piazza del Carmine (055 284595). **Open** *Apr-Oct* 5pm-2am daily. *Nov-Mar* 5pm-2am Tue-Sun. **Credit** AmEx, MC, V. **Map** p318 C1.

The stalwart veteran of hip Florentine bars, Dolce Vita is still known mainly as a pre-club hangout (*see p182*). However, a lunchtime or evening aperitif, sipped outside in the square while shaded from the sun at the canopied tables, is a virtual tradition here.

Hemingway

Piazza Piattellina 9r (055 284781). **Open** 4.30pm-1am Tue-Thur; 4.30pm-2am Fri, Sat; 11.30am-8pm Sun (brunch noon-2.15pm). Closed mid June-mid Sept. **Credit** AmEx, DC, MC, V. **Map** p318 C1.

This charming café has a huge selection of teas, unusual tea cocktails and at least 20 types of coffee, and but it's best known for its chocolate delectables: proprietor Monica Meschini is the secretary of the Chocolate Appreciation Society, and the café's *sette veli* chocolate cake once won the World Cake Championship. Hemingway's high tea (6-7.30pm) tempts with ten different morsels of sweet delights; there's also a Sunday brunch (book in advance).

Il Rifrullo

Via San Niccolò 53-57 (055 2342621). **Open** 8am-2am daily. Closed 2wks Aug. **Credit** MC, V. **Map** p319 D5.

Set in peaceful San Niccolò at the foot of the winding lanes leading up to Piazzale Michelangelo, this long-time favourite of Florentines has had a facelift and is now decked out in pale stained woods and cool greens. The atmosphere is still sleepy and laid-back during the day, but the mood mutates at evening *aperitivo* time, when the music comes on, the back rooms open to accommodate the crowds and plates of snacks and cocktails are served on the charming summer roof garden in warmer weather.

Outside the City Gates

Area 51

Via Bocci 105 (335 8014085/http://www.area51.it). Bus 23. **Open** 24hrs daily. **No credit cards.**

A paradise for computer game freaks, this bar has 40 PCs set up for the latest games, such as Half-Life and Doom III. The bar functions as a members' club (email info@area51.it in advance of a visit) and organises regular games tournaments.

Shops & Services

Note: the chic boutiques and gorgeous gift shops may max out your credit card.

Pucci. See p139.

Florence's look and ambience make shopping a far too tempting prospect. The historic centre of the city is an enticing, concentrated melée of tiny, picturesque, family-run shops, sparkling flagship stores and charming artisans' workshops, unchanged for centuries. On and off the main thoroughfares, bustling markets and delicious-smelling food stores punctuate the central causeways of shops selling clothes, shoes and gifts, all showing off their goods, with characteristic Florentine peacock flair, in their window displays.

The best way to shop in Florence is to let your feet do the walking and keep your eyes peeled. That said, some areas and streets have their own specialities. Swan down **Via de' Tornabuoni** and **Via della Vigna Nuova** to find all the big names in Italian designer clothing. Wander through the backstreets of the **Oltrarno** to watch craftsmen carrying out their age-old skills (marquetry, jewel inlay, gilding, carving, bookbinding, paper-making). See the masterpieces of their ancestors in the wonderful antiques shops lining **Via Maggio** and **Via dei Fossi**. Or marvel at the tiny 16th-century jewellery shops on the **Ponte Vecchio**, which proudly display the past and present work of the Arezzo goldsmiths.

The adoption of the euro in 2002 and the hefty price hikes that followed may have put paid to the status of Florence as a bargain-hunter's paradise, but there are still areas where the speculation has had less of a dramatic impact on the wallet. Head for the spokes leading off the Duomo hub (**Borgo San Lorenzo** is a great street to start), or to **Via de' Neri**, with its small clothes stores and gift shops. Barter for a discount at the **San Lorenzo market**, or make the trip out of town to the designer outlets, where the euro has hardly dented the savings available on top togs.

OUT WITH THE OLD...
For decades the locals have been lamenting the demise of artisan shops in central Florence, which began with the floods of 1966, when many small shops and businesses were destroyed, and some of them found it too hard to pick themselves back up again. More recently, some of the city's best-loved shops and bars have been falling prey to international designer houses prepared to pay huge rents for prized sites. Giacosa, one of the most genteel of Florentine bars, was one of the first casualties, giving way to the jewel-studded jeans of Florentine designer Roberto Cavalli.

But it's not all doom and gloom: for now, at least, there are still plenty of characterful, family-run businesses to make shopping in Florence a pleasant affair.

OPENING HOURS AND INFORMATION

While supermarkets and larger stores in the city centre now stay open throughout the day (*orario continuato*), most shops still operate standard hours, closing at lunchtime and (food shops excepted) on Monday mornings. The standard opening times are 3.30pm to 7.30pm on Monday, and 9am to 1pm then 3.30pm to 7.30pm Tuesday to Saturday, with clothes shops sometimes opening around 10am. Food shops open earlier in the morning and later in the afternoon, and close on Wednesday afternoons. Many of the central stores now stay open for at least part of Sunday; several more open on the last Sunday of the month.

Hours alter slightly in mid June until the end of August, when most shops close on Saturday afternoons. Small shops tend to shut completely at some point during July or August for anything from a week to a month for an annual summer break. Note that the opening times listed here apply most of the year – we have noted closures of more than two weeks whenever possible – but they can vary. In particular, smaller shops may open or close more randomly.

Some shops have a baffling *entrata libera* (free entrance) sign in the window, which just means you're free to browse with no obligation to buy. This may appear to outsiders as though it goes without saying, but there are still a few places – mainly older, family-run shops – where you're expected to tell the assistant what you're looking for as soon as you enter (and you'd better provide a good excuse if you don't like what they offer).

Note that visitors from outside the EU are entitled to a VAT rebate on purchases of goods over €160. Some shops even keep the requisite forms on file: look for the 'Tax-free' signs in the shop window (*see p294*).

Books

Many bookshops stock books in English, but prices are between 15 and 40 per cent higher than in the UK. For children's books, *see p160*.

Alinari

Largo Alinari 15, Santa Maria Novella (055 2395232/www.alinari.it). **Open** 9am-1pm, 2.30-6.30pm Mon-Fri; 10am-1pm, 3-7pm Sat. Closed 3wks Aug. **Credit** AmEx, DC, MC, V. **Map** p318 A2.
The world's first photographic firm, established in 1852, stocks photography books and exhibition catalogues, and can order prints from its archives.

Edison

Piazza della Repubblica 27r, Duomo & Around (055 213110/www.libreriaedison.it). **Open** 9am-midnight Mon-Sat; 10am-midnight Sun. **Credit** AmEx, DC, MC, V. **Map** p318 B3.
This multi-storey superstore sells books, maps, magazines, calendars and CDs. The travel section includes lots of guides in English. Video screens (showing the latest news), internet terminals, a café and a lecture area are further attractions.

Fashion Room

Via dei Palchetti 3-3A, Santa Maria Novella (055 213270/www.fashionroom.it). **Open** 9.30am-1pm, 3-7.30pm Mon-Fri; 10am-1pm, 3-6pm Sat. **Credit** AmEx, DC, MC, V. **Map** p319 A4.
An unrivalled collection of books, catalogues and magazines on interior design, architecture and fashion, including hard-to-find limited editions and coffee-table tomes.

Feltrinelli International

Via Cavour 12-20r, San Marco (055 219524/www.feltrinelli.it). **Open** 9am-7.30pm Mon-Sat. **Credit** AmEx, DC, MC, V. **Map** p319 A4.
This modern bookshop has strong art, photography and comic-book sections, plus a huge selection of titles in English, language-teaching books, original-language videos and a gift section.

Franco Maria Ricci

Via delle Belle Donne 41r, Santa Maria Novella (055 283312). **Open** 3.30-7.30pm Mon; 10am-1pm, 3.30-7.30pm Tue-Sat. **Credit** AmEx, DC, MC. **Map** p318 B2.

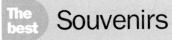

The best Souvenirs

Extra virgin olive oils
From **La Bottega dell'Olio**. *See p147*.

Hand-marbled paper gifts
From **A Cozzi**. *See p141* **The paper round**.

Chocolate Duomos
From **Dolceforte**. *See p147*.

Soft leather gloves in Florentine purple
From **Madova**. *See p145*.

Hand-painted plates
From **La Botteghina del Ceramista**. *See p151*.

Real gold leaf, frankincense and myrrh
From **Bizzarri**. *See p152* **Natural selections**.

Foodie treats and wines
From **Olio e Convivium**. *See p147*.

Eat, Drink, Shop

Art for art's sake, offered at **Franco Maria Ricci**. *See p137.*

This delightful art bookshop and arts and crafts gallery stocks mainly limited editions, numbered prints and handmade stationery.

Libreria delle Donne
Via Fiesolana 2B, Santa Croce (055 240384).
Open 3.30-7.30pm Mon; 9.30am-1pm, 3.30-7.30pm Tue-Fri. Closed Aug. **Credit** MC, V. **Map** p319 B5.
A good reference point for women in Florence, not just for its books – the feminist literature is mostly in Italian – but also for the useful noticeboard that has details on local activities.

Libreria Martelli
Via dei Martelli 22r, Duomo & Around (055 2657603). **Open** 10am-6pm daily. **Credit** MC, V. **Map** p319 B4.
This big, light and airy store has an excellent range of books in various languages, including English. The selection of travel guides is particularly strong. Check out the rooftop terrace.

McRae Books
Via de' Neri 32r, Santa Croce (055 2382456/ www.mcraebooks.com). **Open** 9am-7.30pm daily. **Credit** AmEx, MC, V. **Map** p319 C4.
This excellent bookstore specialises in English titles, stocking everything from travel guides and maps to best-selling novels, art history, cookery and current affairs, plus a small range of compact discs, DVDs and used books. Regular reading groups are a further bonus.

Paperback Exchange
Via Fiesolana 31r, Santa Croce (055 2478154/ www.papex.it). **Open** 9am-7.30pm Mon-Fri; 10am-1pm, 3.30-7.30pm Sat. Closed 2wks Aug. **Credit** AmEx, MC, V. **Map** p319 B5.
A commendable choice of new English-language fiction and non-fiction, particularly art, art history and Italian culture. The noticeboard has information about literary events, courses, accommodation and language lessons. Second-hand books can be traded.

Department stores

COIN
Via dei Calzaiuoli 56r, Duomo & Around (055 280531/www.coin.it). **Open** *Jan-Mar* 10am-7.30pm Mon-Sat; 11am-7.30pm Sun. *Apr-Dec* 10am-8pm Mon-Sat; 11am-8pm Sun. **Credit** AmEx, DC, MC, V. **Map** p318 B3.
Furnishings are the strong point of this mid-range store, especially bright contemporary homewares and regular consignments of Far Eastern goods. Crisp modern fashions, shoes, accessories and gifts all feature. A firm favourite with the locals.

Principe
Via del Sole 2, Santa Maria Novella (055 292764/ www.principedifirenze.com). **Open** 10.30am-7.30pm Mon; 9.30am-7.30pm Tue-Sat. *Sept-June* also 11am-7.30pm last Sun of mth. **Credit** AmEx, DC, MC. **Map** p318 B2.

Stuffy staff run this erstwhile grande dame of department stores, now relegated to a labyrinthine building slightly off the beaten track. Highlights include bedlinens in Egyptian cotton, bath and kitchen accessories and quality toiletries.

La Rinascente
Piazza della Repubblica 1, Duomo & Around (055 219113/www.rinascente.it). **Open** 9am-9pm Mon-Sat; 10.30am-8pm Sun. **Credit** AmEx, DC, MC, V. **Map** p318 B3.
This classic store has casual and designer clothes and the most extensive cosmetics and perfume department in the city, plus a useful lingerie section and smart bedding. The rooftop café, reached via the top floor, has gorgeous views (*see p131*).

Fashion

For sporting clothes and equipment, *see pp185-189.*

Designer

Most of Florence's designer shops are strung along three streets. Via della Vigna Nuova is home to, among others, the stylish **Dolce & Gabbana** (No.27, 055 281003, www.dolce gabbana.it) and lingerie experts **La Perla** (Nos.17-19r, 055 217070, www.laperla.it), while on Via de' Tornabuoni you'll find stylish **Versace** (Nos.13-15r, 055 282638, www.gianni versace.com), cultured **Ferragamo** (Nos.4-14r, 055 292123, www.salvatoreferragamo.com), refined **Armani** (No.48r, 055 219041, www. giorgioarmani.com), chic **Prada** (Nos.51-53r, 67r, 055 283439, www.prada.it) and flashy **Gucci** (No.73r, 055 264011, www.gucci.it). There's also an **Emporio Armani** at nearby Piazza Strozzi (No.16r, 055 284315). Via Roma now has a clutch of designer names, including **Miu Miu** (*see p142*), with **Hugo Boss** on nearby Piazza della Repubblica (No.46r, 055 2399168).

For flashy gear without the prices, both Gucci (Via Aretina 63, Leccio, Reggello, 055 8657775) and Prada (Località SS Levanella, Montevarchi, 055 9196528) have factory outlets out of town.

Ermanno Scervino
Piazza Antinori 10r, Santa Maria Novella (055 2608714/www.ermannoscervino.it). **Open** 3-7.30pm Mon; 10am-1pm, 2-7.30pm Tue-Sat. Closed 2wks Aug. **Credit** AmEx, DC, MC, V. **Map** p318 B3.
The essence of femininity is embodied in Scervino's chiffon mermaid dresses in pinks and translucent whites. For men, there's crisp linen and crumpled silk.

Luisa
Via Roma 19-21r, Duomo & Around (055 217826/ www.luisaviaroma.com). **Open** 10am-7.30pm Mon-Sat; 11am-7pm Sun. **Credit** AmEx, DC, MC, V. **Map** p318 B3.

Renowned for its inventive window displays, this multi-level store features designer collections from Issey Miyake, Roberto Cavalli and others.

Massimo Rebecchi
Via della Vigna Nuova 26r, Santa Maria Novella (055 268053). **Open** 3.30-7.30pm Mon, last Sun of mth; 10am-1.30pm, 3-7.30pm Tue-Fri; 10am-7.30pm Sat. **Credit** AmEx, DC, MC, V. **Map** p318 B2.
Quality cotton and wool jumpers and casual suits, for both men and women.

Pucci
Via de' Tornabuoni 20-22r, Duomo & Around (055 2658082/www.emiliopucci.com). **Open** 10am-7pm Mon-Sat. *Sept-June* also 2.30-7pm last Sun of mth. **Credit** AmEx, DC, MC, V. **Map** p318 C2.
The store may be relatively new, but the polychromatic psychedelic print clothes and accessories have changed little since Emilio Pucci first launched his swirling designs for brave fashion victims in the 1950s.

Raspini
Via Roma 25-29r, Duomo & Around (055 213077/ www.raspini.com). **Open** 3.30-7.30pm Mon; 9.30am-1.30pm, 3.30-7.30pm Tue-Fri; 9.30am-7.30pm Sat. **Credit** AmEx, DC, MC, V. **Map** p318 B3.
A one-stop shop for Romeo Gigli, Armani, Prada, Miu Miu, Anna Molinari, D&G and many others. **Other locations**: Via Por Santa Maria 72r, Duomo & Around (055 213901); Via Martelli 3-7, Duomo & Around (055 2398336).

Roberto Cavalli
Via de' Tornabuoni 83r, Santa Maria Novella (055 2396226/www.robertocavalli.it). **Open** 3-7.30pm Mon, Sun; 10am-7.30pm Tue-Sat. **Credit** AmEx, DC, MC, V. **Map** p318 B2.
Colourful creations for men and women, including the Florentine designer's trademark animal prints.

Spazio A
Via Porta Rossa 107r, Duomo & Around (055 212995/www.aeffe.com). **Open** 3-7pm Mon; 10am-7pm Tue-Sat. **Credit** AmEx, DC, MC, V. **Map** p318 C3.
A light, airy store with friendly assistants. The quirky couture of Jean-Paul Gaultier and Moschino sits oddly with the exquisite designs of Alberta Ferretti, but that doesn't seem to put people off. Mind the step in the centre of the shop.

Womenswear

Aspesi
Via Porta Rossa 81-83r, Duomo & Around (055 287987). **Open** 3-7pm Mon; 10am-2pm, 3-7pm Tue-Sat. **Credit** AmEx, DC, MC, V. **Map** p318 C3.
The funky transfers of Japanese cartoons on Aspesi's shop windows give no clues as to the shop's contents: beautifully coloured, well-made and wearable clothes in crinkle linens and silks, inventive light wool weaves and delicate knits.

Eat, Drink, Shop

BP Studio

*Via della Vigna Nuova 15r, Santa Maria Novella
(055 213243/www.bpstudio.it).* **Open** 3-7pm Mon;
10am-2pm, 3-7pm Tue-Sat. **Credit** AmEx, DC, MC,
V. **Map** p318 B2.
Delicate knitwear, rosebud-edged chiffon skirts and
mohair stoles from young designers are all up for
grabs at this upmarket but youthful store.

Dixie

*Borgo San Lorenzo 5r, San Marco (055 215061/
www.dixie.it).* **Open** 3.30-7.30pm Mon, last Sun of
mth; 10am-7.30pm Tue-Sat. **Credit** AmEx, MC, V.
Map p318 B3.
Fresh, quirky designs at very low prices are Dixie's
forte. Expect to find embroidered jeans, Indochine
chic and flower-power cutesy styles.

Elio Ferraro

*Via del Parione 47r, Santa Maria Novella (055
290425/www.elioferraro.com).* **Open** 3-7.30pm Mon;
9.30am-7.30pm Tue-Sat. **Credit** AmEx, DC, MC, V.
Map p318 B2.
Vintage designer clothes at heart-stopping prices,
sold amid an eccentric selection of original '50s and
'60s furniture and accessories.

Emilio Cavallini

*Via della Vigna Nuova 24r, Santa Maria Novella
(055 2382789/www.emiliocavallini.com).* **Open**
3-7pm Mon; 10am-7pm Tue-Sat. Closed 2wks Aug.
Credit AmEx, DC, MC, V. **Map** p318 B2.
Cavallini's trademark wacky tights, plus a line of
printed lycra and lurex tops and lingerie.

Ethic

Borgo degli Albizi 37r, Santa Croce (055 2344413).
Open 3-8pm Mon, Sun; 10am-8pm Tue-Sat. **Credit**
AmEx, DC, MC, V. **Map** p319 B5.
The clothes at this store are grand, but there are two
added attractions: a cutting-edge range of CDs from
the likes of Kruder & Dorfmeister, De-Phazz and
Boozoo Bajou, and a homewares section.

Expensive!

*Via dei Calzaiuoli 78r, Duomo & Around (055
2654608/www.expensive-fashion.it).* **Open** 10am-
8pm Mon-Thur; 10am-8.30pm Fri, Sat; 11am-8.30pm
Sun. **Credit** AmEx, DC, MC, V. **Map** p318 B3.
The great colour-coded collections at this store
include simple dresses, jackets and accessories, but
the service isn't all it might be.

Il Guardaroba

Via Giuseppe Verdi 28r, Santa Croce (055 2478250).
Open 9.30am-7.30pm Mon-Sat. **Credit** AmEx, DC,
MC, V. **Map** p319 C5.
Il Guardaroba deals in designer end-of-lines and past
seasons' stock. There are some good deals to be had.
Other locations: throughout the city.

Intimissimi

*Via dei Calzaiuoli 99r, Duomo & Around (055
2302609/www.intimissimi.it).* **Open** 10am-8pm
Mon; 9.30am-8pm Tue-Sat; noon-8pm Sun.
Credit AmEx, MC, V. **Map** p318 B3.

The paper round

A gelatine solution made of water and
marine algae is poured into a shallow
tray, coloured inks are dropped into it,
and patterns are made by drawing metal
combs through the liquid. A sheet of
paper is placed on the surface, thereby
absorbing the inks, and is then hung up
to dry. On this relatively straightforward
series of events is built one of Florence's
oldest traditions: the production of brightly
coloured marbled paper.

Unsurprisingly, the city still has a clutch
of old-fashioned paper shops that are
worth a visit if you're hunting for gifts,
or if you simply fancy watching some
bookbinders in action (though not the
marbling, unfortunately). **Giulio Giannini
e Figlio** (Piazza Pitti 37r, Oltrarno, 055
212621), a bookbinding and paper-making
company, was founded in 1856 by the
Giannini family, who still runs it from the
workshop upstairs on the first floor. Among
the items sold these days are marbled
books, leather desk accessories and
unusual greetings cards.

Elsewhere, the old-fashioned **Il Papiro**
chain (Piazza del Duomo 24r, Duomo &
Around, 055 281628; Via Cavour 55r,
San Marco, 055 215262; Piazza Rucellai
8r, Santa Maria Novella, 055 211652)
has an amazing range of marbled paper
products, while at **Il Torchio** (Via dei Bardi
17, Oltrarno, 055 2342862), you can
stock up on handmade paper boxes,
stationery and albums while watching
bookbinders at work. It's a similar story at
A Cozzi (Via del Parione 35r, Santa Maria
Novella, 055 294968), a bookbinder's
workshop and showroom with a wonderful
selection of books, some with swirled
paper covers and others bound in leather.

Cotton lingerie is the speciality at Intimissimi,
though there are also jersey vests and trousers, silk
satin pyjamas and boa-trimmed tops.
Other locations: Via de' Panzani 22, Santa Maria
Novella (055 2608636); Piazza Madonna degli
Aldobrandini 3, San Lorenzo (055 210540).

Liu Jo

*Via Calimala 14r, Duomo & Around (055 216164/
www.liujo.it).* **Open** 3.30-7.30pm Mon; 10am-7.30pm
Tue-Sat; 11am-1.30pm, 2.30-7pm Sun. **Credit** AmEx,
DC, MC, V. **Map** p318 B3.
Net dresses, pretty vest tops, dressy combat gear
and high wooden mules from this hip designer.

Melo e Grano

Via del Giglio 27r, San Lorenzo (055 2654383/ www.meloegrano.it). **Open** 9.30am-1.30pm, 3.30-7.30pm Mon-Sat. Closed 2wks Aug. **Credit** AmEx, DC, MC, V. **Map** p318 A3.
Pay a pittance here for staple wardrobe pieces in crochet, linens and crumpled silks.

Miss Trench

Via Porta Rossa 16r, Duomo & Around (055 287601). **Open** 3.30-7.30pm Mon; 10am-7.30pm Tue-Sat. **Credit** AmEx, DC, MC, V. **Map** p318 C3.
Rock-chick chic, plus a smattering of Miss Sixty accessories such as bags and sequinned belts.

Miu Miu

Via Roma 8r, Duomo & Around (055 2608931/ www.miumiu.com). **Open** 10am-7.30pm Mon-Sat; 10am-7pm Sun. **Credit** AmEx, DC, MC, V. **Map** p318 B3.
Miuccia Prada's concession to the younger, less moneyed fan of her kooky, modern style.

Piazza Pitti Cashmere

Via dello Sprone 13r, Oltrarno (055 283516). **Open** 10am-2pm, 3-8pm Tue-Sat. **No credit cards. Map** p318 C2.
Many pieces at this discount outlet verge on the staid, but you may uncover the odd gem.

Raspini Vintage

Via Calimaruzza 17r, Duomo & Around (055 213901/www.raspinivintage.it). **Open** 3.30-7.30pm Mon; 10.30am-7.30pm Tue-Sat; 2.30-7.30pm Sun. **Credit** AmEx, DC, MC, V. **Map** p318 C3.
This outlet sells previous seasons' stock from the main Raspini stores (*see p139*), with massive savings on designer clothes from major names.

Zini

Borgo San Lorenzo 26r, San Lorenzo (055 289850). **Open** 10am-8pm Mon-Sat. *Sept-June* also 3-7.30pm Sun. **Credit** MC, V. **Map** p318 B3.
Head to Zini for wearable styles from selected young designers, with well-cut jackets, little black dresses and fine knits.

Menswear

AteSeta

Via dei Calzaiuoli 1r, Duomo & Around (055 214959/www.ateseta.com). **Open** 9.30am-7.30pm daily. **Credit** AmEx, DC, MC, V. **Map** p318 C3.
Row upon row of mix 'n' match shirts and ties.

Eredi Chiarini

Via Roma 16r, Duomo & Around (055 284478/ www.eredichiarini.com). **Open** 3.30-7.30pm Mon; 9.30am-7.30pm Tue-Sat. **Credit** AmEx, DC, MC, V. **Map** p318 B3.
A favourite with Florentines, who love its effortlessly stylish polos, softly tailored jackets and cool wool suits. The womenswear store is nearby at Via Porta Rossa 39r.

Gerard Loft

Via dei Pecori 36r, Duomo & Around (055 282491/ www.gerardloft.com). **Open** 2.30-7.30pm Mon; 10am-7.30pm Tue-Sat. **Credit** AmEx, DC, MC, V. **Map** p318 B3.
Trendy clothing, sold by similarly hip assistants to match. The men's and women's lines are by the likes of Marc Jacobs, Chloé and Helmut Lang.

Matucci

Via del Corso 71r, Duomo & Around (055 2396420). **Open** 3.30-8pm Mon; 10am-7.30pm Tue-Sat. **Credit** AmEx, DC, MC, V. **Map** p319 B4.
Collections by Armani, Diesel, Boss and Versace. Womenswear is just down the road at No.46r.

Replay

Via dei Pecori 7-9r, Duomo & Around (055 293041). **Open** 3-7.30pm Mon; 10am-7.30pm Tue-Sat; 2.30-7.30pm Sun. **Credit** AmEx, DC, MC, V. **Map** p318 B3.
Men's and women's casualwear par excellence. **Other locations**: Via Por Santa Maria 27r, Duomo & Around (055 287950).

Sandro P 2

Via dei Tosinghi 7r, Duomo & Around (055 215063). **Open** 3-7.30pm Mon; 10am-1pm, 3.30-7.30pm Tue-Sat. **Credit** AmEx, DC, MC, V. **Map** p318 B3.
Subtitled 'La Vendetta', this is the reincarnation (on new premises) of one of Florence's hippest men's and unisex clothing shops. The shop's famous 'waxwork' mannequin mascot has survived the move, and now finds itself draped with the latest imports from New York and London.

Shoes

Bologna

Piazza Duomo 13-15r, Duomo & Around (055 290545). **Open** 9am-7.30pm Mon-Sat. **Credit** AmEx, DC, MC, V. **Map** p319 B4.
Weird and wonderful men's and women's styles at Florence's favourite shoe store.

Calvani

Via degli Speziali 7r, Duomo & Around (055 2654043). **Open** 9am-7.30pm Mon-Sat; 3-7pm Sun. **Credit** AmEx, DC, MC, V. **Map** p318 B3.
Men's and women's shoes in hip styles and colours from young designers such as Roberto del Carlo, along with sports-casual footwear by Camper.

Divarese

Piazza Duomo 47r, Duomo & Around (055 212890). **Open** 9am-7.30pm Mon-Sat; 11am-6pm Sun. **Credit** AmEx, DC, MC, V. **Map** p319 B4.
Head here for well made, reasonably priced shoes in the latest styles for both men and women.

Fossi

Via del Corso 62r, Duomo & Around (055 212095). **Open** 3.30-7.30pm Mon; 10am-7.30pm Tue-Sat. **Credit** AmEx, DC, MC, V. **Map** p318 B3.
Pretty collections of shoes and boots in seasonal colours, with a distinctly Parisian flavour.

Eat, Drink, Shop

Roberto Cavalli. *See p139*.

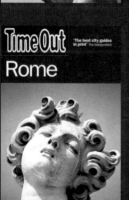
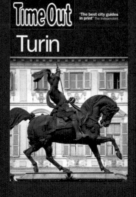
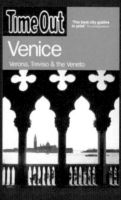

JP Tod's
Via de' Tornabuoni 103r, Santa Maria Novella (055 219423/www.tods.com). **Open** 10am-7.30pm Mon-Sat; 2-7pm Sun. **Credit** AmEx, DC, MC, V. **Map** p318 B2.
Tod's trademark unisex bobbly soles win first prize for comfort on Florence's cobbles.

Marco Candido
Piazza Duomo 5r, Duomo & Around (055 215342). **Open** 3-7.30pm Mon; 10am-7.30pm Tue-Sat; noon-7.30pm Sun. Closed Sun Feb, July, Aug. **Credit** AmEx, DC, MC, V. **Map** p319 B4.
Sexy but stylish modern shoes and boots for women, and classic but modern shoes for men.

Paola del Lungo
Via Cerretani 72r, Duomo & Around (055 280642/ www.genius2000.it). **Open** 9am-7.30pm daily. **Credit** AmEx, DC, MC, V. **Map** p318 B3.
Paola del Lungo's utterly feminine boots and shoes are stocked alongside a tempting range of matching bags and accessories.

Peppe Peluso
Via del Corso 5-6r, Duomo & Around (055 268283). **Open** 2-8pm Mon; 10am-8pm Tue-Sat; 11am-7.30pm Sun. **Credit** AmEx, DC, MC, V. **Map** p319 B4.
A pair of shoes or boots from the vast (men's and women's) ranges here may or may not last the season, but at these bargain prices, who cares? The branch opposite (No.6r) has even cheaper footwear from previous seasons' collections.

Stefano Bemer
Borgo San Frediano 143r, Oltrarno (055 222558/ www.stefanobemer.it). **Open** 9.30am-7.30pm Mon-Sat. Closed Aug. **Credit** AmEx, DC, MC, V. **Map** p318 C1.
Well-heeled Florentine men head here for handmade luxury shoes. The nearby branch at Via Camaldoli 10r does a ready-to-wear line.

Fashion accessories

Jewellery

For traditional gold- and silversmiths, visit Via Por Santa Maria and the Ponte Vecchio (*see map p318 C3*).

Antica Orologeria Nuti
Via della Scala 10r, Santa Maria Novella (055 294594). **Open** 4-7.30pm Mon; 9am-12.30pm, 4-7.30pm Tue-Sat. Closed Aug. **Credit** AmEx, MC, V. **Map** p318 A1/B2.
Fabulous antique and reproduction art deco and art nouveau jewellery and watches, plus an eclectic collection of lantern, long-case, bracket and mantel clocks. Repairs are also undertaken.

Aprosio e Co
Via Santo Spirito 11, Oltrarno (055 290534/ www.aprosio.it). **Open** 9.30am-1.30pm, 3-7.30pm Mon-Sat. **Credit** AmEx, DC, MC, V. **Map** p318 C2.

An aloof dog guards the intricate necklaces, bracelets, earrings, evening bags and belts, all made from tiny glass beads, at this sleek showroom.

Bulgari
Via de' Tornabuoni 61-63r, Santa Maria Novella (055 2396786/www.bulgari.com). **Open** 10am-7pm Mon-Sat. **Credit** AmEx, DC, MC, V. **Map** p318 B2.
The ultimate status-symbol designer jewellery.

Parenti
Via de' Tornabuoni 93r, Santa Maria Novella (055 214438/www.parentifirenze.it). **Open** 3.30-7.30pm Mon; 9am-1pm, 3.30-7.30pm Tue-Sat. Closed Aug. **Credit** AmEx, DC, MC, V. **Map** p318 B2.
Baccarat rings, art deco and '50s Tiffany jewellery.

Pianegonda
Via dei Calzaiuoli 96r, Duomo & Around (055 214941/www.pianegonda.com). **Open** 3.30-7.30pm Mon; 10am-7.30pm Tue-Sat. **Credit** AmEx, DC, MC, V. **Map** p318 B3.
Highly desirable gold and silver pieces set with topaz, citrines and amethysts.

Pomellato
Via de' Tornabuoni 89-91r, Santa Maria Novella (055 288530/www.pomellato.it). **Open** 3-7pm Mon; 10am-7pm Tue-Sat. **Credit** AmEx, DC, MC, V. **Map** p318 B2.
Rings with gems the size and colours of fruit gums, contemporary watches and the famous Dodo line of animal pendants are sold at this stunning showroom.

Leather goods

Il Bisonte
Via del Parione 31r, Santa Maria Novella (055 215722/www.ilbisonte.net). **Open** 9.30am-7pm Tue-Sat. **Credit** AmEx, DC, MC, V. **Map** p318 B2.
A renowned, long-established outlet for top-tier soft leather bags and accessories and rugged cases.

Bojola
Via dei Rondinelli 25r, Duomo & Around (055 211155/www.bojola.it). **Open** 3.30-7.30pm Mon; 9.30am-7.30pm Tue-Sat. **Credit** AmEx, DC, MC, V. **Map** p318 B2.
Top-notch craftsmanship and high-quality hides add up to the city's best classic-style leather goods.

Coccinelle
Via Por Santa Maria 49r, Duomo & Around (055 2398782/www.coccinelle.com). **Open** 10.30am-7.30pm Mon-Sat; 11am-8pm Sun. **Credit** AmEx, DC, MC, V. **Map** p318 C3.
Smart, contemporary leather bags in seasonal colours, crafted in smooth durable leather.

Madova
Via de' Guicciardini 1r, Oltrarno (055 2396526/ www.madova.com). **Open** 9.30am-7.30pm Mon-Sat. **Credit** AmEx, MC, V. **Map** p318 C3.
Madova makes gloves in every imaginable style and colour in its factory, just behind this tiny shop.

Eat, Drink, Shop

Il Parione 35

*Via del Parione 35Ar, Santa Maria Novella
(055 2399770).* **Open** 10am-7.30pm Mon-Sat.
Credit AmEx, DC, MC, V. **Map** p318 B2.
Simple, chic leather bags, wallets and purses in primary, pastel and seasonal colours, from mulberry to turquoise to granite.

Scuola del Cuoio

*Via San Giuseppe 5r, Santa Croce (055 244533/
www.leatherschool.com).* **Open** 9.30am-6pm Mon-Sat; 10am-6pm Sun. **Credit** AmEx, DC, MC, V.
Map p319 C5.
At this leather school inside the cloisters of Santa Croce, you can watch the craftsmen making bags, accessories and gifts. The prices add further appeal.

Tosca Blu

*Via della Vigna Nuova 97r, Santa Maria Novella
(055 218566/www.toscablu.it).* **Open** 3.30-7.30pm Mon; 9.30am-1.30pm, 3.30-7.30pm Tue-Sat. Closed 2wks Aug. **Credit** AmEx, DC, MC, V. **Map** p318 B2.
Head here for quirky lavender, cornflower-blue and candy-pink suede doctor's bags, plus small leather accessories embossed with Betty Boop-style motifs, leather tulips and beaded dragonflies.

Luggage

Mandarina Duck

*Via Por Santa Maria 23-25r, Duomo & Around
(055 210380/www.mandarinaduck.com).* **Open** 9.30am-7.30pm Mon-Sat; 11am-2pm, 3-7pm Sun.
Credit AmEx, DC, MC, V. **Map** p318 D1.
Devotees flock here to snap up the new season's desirable collection of rubber, canvas and leather bags and cases.

Segue

*Via degli Speziali 6r, Duomo & Around (055
288949/www.segue.it).* **Open** 10am-7.30pm Mon-Sat; 1-7.30pm Sun. **Credit** AmEx, DC, MC, V.
Map p318 B3.
The full Benetton range of smart bags and luggage, plus seasonal accessories including funky umbrellas and patterned pink wellies.

Fashion services

Dry-cleaners & laundrettes

Dry-cleaners (*tintorie*) also do washing. All of the following offer reliable, well-priced services.

Lucy & Rita

Via dei Serragli 71r, Oltrarno (055 224536). **Open** 7am-1pm, 2.30-7.30pm Mon-Fri. Closed 2wks Aug.
Credit AmEx, MC, V. **Map** p318 D1.

Tintoria Serena

*Via della Scala 30-32r, Santa Maria Novella
(055 218183).* **Open** 8.30am-8pm Mon-Fri; 9am-8pm Sat. Closed 2wks Aug. **No credit cards**.
Map p318 B2.

Wash & Dry

*Via Nazionale 129r, San Lorenzo (055 580480/
www.washedry.it).* **Open** 8am-10pm daily.
No credit cards. **Map** p318 A3.
Other locations: throughout the city.

Repairs

Il Ciabattino

Via del Moro 88, Santa Maria Novella (no phone).
Open 8am-1pm, 2-7pm Mon-Fri; 8am-12.30pm Sat.
Closed 2wks Aug. **No credit cards**. **Map** p318 B2.
If you don't find the shoemaker in his workshop during opening hours, he'll be on call in the bar on the corner opposite: just ask for *il ciabattino…*

Ferramenta Masini

*Via del Sole 19-21r, 18-20r, Santa Maria Novella (055
212560).* **Open** 9am-1pm, 3.30-7.30pm Mon-Fri; 9am-1pm Sat. **Credit** AmEx, DC, MC, V. **Map** p318 B2.
Two friendly shops, under the same management, with plugs and adaptors, hardware, a key-cutting service and door and lock repairs.

Silvana e Ombretta Riparazioni

*Borgo San Frediano 38r, Oltrarno (mobile 368
7571418).* **Open** 9am-noon, 3.30-6.30pm Mon-Fri.
Closed Aug. **No credit cards**. **Map** p318 C1.
Repairs and alterations to clothes.

Walter's Silver & Gold

*Borgo dei Greci 11Cr, Santa Croce (055 2396678/
www.walterssilverandgold.com).* **Open** 9.30am-5.30pm daily. Closed Nov. **Credit** AmEx, DC, MC, V.
Map p319 C4.
English-speaking Walter does all jewellery repairs.

Florists

Calvanelli

*Via della Vigna Nuova 24, Santa Maria Novella (055
213742).* **Open** 8am-1pm, 3-7.30pm Mon, Tue, Thur-Sat; 7am-1pm Wed. **No credit cards**. **Map** p318 B2.
This lovely shop sells flowers wrapped in pretty crêpe-paper posies. Delivery is free in the city centre.

Al Portico

*Piazza San Firenze 2, Duomo & Around (055
213716/www.semialportico.it).* **Open** 8.30am-7.30pm Mon-Sat; 10am-1pm Sun. **Credit** AmEx, DC, MC, V.
Map p319 C5.
An extraordinary shop in the Renaissance courtyard of a magnificent palazzo, with trees, fountains, huge plants and flowers. The owner is happy to show customers round, even if they don't want to buy.

La Rosa Canina

*Via dell'Erta Canina 1r, Outside the City Gates
(055 2342449/www.larosacaninafioristi.it). Bus 23.*
Open 9.30am-1.30pm, 4.30-9.30pm Tue-Sat; 9.30am-1.30pm Sun. **Credit** V.
On a stroll up to Piazzale Michelangelo, take time to stop off at this shop to admire its wonderful displays of plants and flowers.

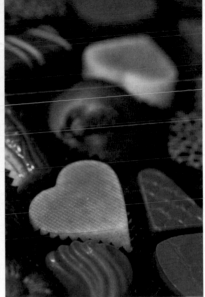

Sweets for my sweet, sugar for my honey: **Dolceforte**.

Food & drink

For food markets, *see p149* **Market forces**.
For *rosticcerie, see p115, p122, p127 and p128*.

Bottega della Frutta

*Via dei Federighi 31r, Santa Maria Novella (055
2398590).* **Open** 8am-7.30pm Mon, Tue, Thur-Sat;
8am-1.30pm Wed. Closed Aug. **Credit** MC, V.
Map p318 B2.
Alongside fruit and veg, this charming shop sells
wines, vintage balsamic vinegars, truffle-scented
oils and speciality sweets. Prepare to queue.

La Bottega dell'Olio

*Piazza del Limbo 2r, Duomo & Around (055
2670468).* **Open** *Oct-Feb* 3-7pm Mon; 10am-1pm,
2-7pm Tue-Sat. *Mar-Sept* 10am-7pm Mon-Sat. Closed
2wks Jan. **Credit** AmEx, DC, MC, V. **Map** p318 C3.
All things olive oil, from soaps and delicacies preserved in the green gold to olive-wood breadboards
and pestles and mortars.

Dolceforte

*Via della Scala 21, Santa Maria Novella (055
219116/www.dolceforte.it).* **Open** 10am-1pm, 3.30-
8pm Mon-Sat. **Credit** AmEx, MC, V. **Map** p318 B2.
Connoisseur chocolates, plus novelty-shaped treats
such as chocolate Duomos. In hot months, melting
stock is replaced with jams, sugared almond flowers
and jars of *gianduja*, a chocolate hazelnut spread.

Mariano Alimentari

*Via del Parione 19r, Santa Maria Novella (055
214067).* **Open** 8am-3pm, 5-7.30pm Mon-Fri; 8am-
3pm Sat. Closed 3wks Aug. **Credit** AmEx, MC, V.
Map p318 C2.

This tiny, rustic food shop-cum-sandwich bar offers
focaccia filled with marinated aubergines and oil-
preserved pecorino cheese, and an array of delicacies.
Have a coffee at the bar or in the vaulted wine cellar.

Olio e Convivium

*Via Santo Spirito 4, Oltrarno (055 2658198/
www.olio.conviviumfirenze.it).* **Open** 5.30-10pm
Mon; 10am-3pm, 5.30-10pm Tue-Sat. **Credit** AmEx,
MC, V. **Map** p318 C2.
A wonderful place for Tuscan olive oils and wines,
sweet and savoury preserves, and other superlative
treats. There's also a restaurant/wine bar (*see p125*).

Pane & Co

*Piazza San Firenze 5r, Duomo & Around (055
2654272/www.paneeco.com).* **Open** 9am-8pm Mon-
Sat. Closed 2wks Aug. **Credit** MC, V. **Map** p319 D4.
Enjoy a glass of wine or a pasta lunch after shopping in this deli, which stages regular wine and
cheese tastings.

Pegna

*Via dello Studio 8, Duomo & Around (055 282701/
www.pegna.it).* **Open** 9am-1pm, 3.30-7.30pm Mon,
Tue, Thur-Sat; 9am-1pm Wed. **Credit** AmEx, MC, V.
Map p319 B4.
This upmarket grocery store/deli has pâtés, coffee,
cheeses, ethnic specialities and general provisions.

Peter's Tea House

*Piazza di San Pancrazio 2r, Santa Maria
Novella (055 2670620/www.peters-teahouse.it).*
Open 3.30-7pm Mon; 10am-1pm, 3.30-7pm Tue-
Sat. Closed 3wks Aug. **Credit** AmEx, MC, V.
Map p318 B2.
Hundreds of teas from around the world, alongside
biscuits to dunk in them and tea-themed gifts.

I Sapori del Chianti

*Via dei Servi 10, San Marco (055 2382071/
www.isaporidelchianti.it).* **Open** 10.30am-8pm daily.
Credit AmEx, MC, V. **Map** p318 B2.
The 'flavours of Chianti' sold here come in the form
of wines, grappas, olive oils and salamis, plus jars
of pesto, condiments and vegetables in olive oil.

Sugar Blues

Via dei Serragli 57r, Oltrarno (055 268378).
Open 9am-1.30pm, 4.30-8pm Mon-Fri; 9am-1.30pm
Sat. *Sept-June* also 4.30-8pm Sat. **Credit** AmEx, DC,
MC, V. **Map** p318 D1.
A great source of organic health foods and produce,
eco-friendly detergents and ethical beauty products.
Other locations: Via XXVII Aprile 46-48r, San
Lorenzo (055 483666).

Vestri

*Borgo degli Albizi 11r, Santa Croce (055 2340374/
www.cioccolateriavestri.com).* **Open** 10am-8pm Mon-
Sat. Closed Aug. **Credit** AmEx, MC, V. **Map** p319 B5.
Handmade chocolates with chilli pepper, cinnamon
and more prosaic fillings. Flavoured hot chocolates
are served in winter, with rich ice-creams the speciality in summer. *See also p133* **Cold comfort.**

Bakeries

Il Forno di Stefano Galli

Via Faenza 39r, San Lorenzo (055 215314). **Open**
7am-8pm daily. **No credit cards. Map** p318 A3.
Great for early-morning pastries and brioches.

Forno Top

*Via della Spada 23r, Santa Maria Novella (055
212461).* **Open** 7.30am-1.30pm, 5-7.30pm Mon, Tue,
Thur-Sat; 7.30am-1.30pm Wed. **No credit cards.**
Map p318 B2.
Tasty sandwiches, hot focaccia, fabulous carrot or
chocolate and pear cakes, and seasonal specialities.
Other locations: Via Orsanmichele 8r, Duomo &
Around (055 216564).

Sartoni

Via dei Cerchi 34r, Duomo & Around (055 212570).
Open 7.30am-8pm Mon-Sat. **Credit** AmEx, MC, V.
Map p319 B4.
A central pit stop stocking slices of delicious hot
pizza, filled focaccia and apple pies.

Ethnic

Asia Masala

*Piazza Santa Maria Novella 22r, Santa Maria Novella
(055 281800/www.ramraj.org).* **Open** 4-8pm Mon;
10am-1.30pm, 3.30-9pm Tue, Wed, Fri; 10am-9.30pm
Thur, Sat, Sun. **Credit** MC, V. **Map** p318 B2.
A wonderful range of Asian foods and spices.

Vivimarket

Via del Giglio 20r, San Lorenzo (055 294911).
Open 9am-2pm, 3-7.30pm Mon-Sat. **Credit** MC, V.
Map p318 A3.

Indian, Chinese, Japanese, Thai, Mexican and North
African specialities, plus good-quality kitchen gear.

Pasticcerie

Most serve breakfast coffee and snacks, plus
takeaway cakes and savouries (*da portare via*).

Dolci e Dolcezze

Piazza Beccaria 8r, Santa Croce (055 2345458).
Open 8.30am-8pm Tue-Sat; 9am-1pm, 4.30-7.30pm
Sun. Closed 2wks Aug. **No credit cards.**
This patisserie is famous for its delectable, flourless
chocolate cake, but you may also be tempted by the
strawberry meringue. Savouries are just as good.

I Dolci di Patrizio Cosi

Borgo degli Albizi 11r, Santa Croce (055 2480367).
Open 7am-8pm Mon-Sat. Closed Aug. **No credit
cards. Map** p319 B5.
A huge range of sweet treats, plus hot doughnuts
(*bomboloni caldi*) served at 5pm.

Dolcissimo

*Via Maggio 61r, Oltrarno (055 2396268/www.
caffeitaliano.it).* **Open** 9am-1pm, 3.30-7.30pm Tue-
Sat; 9am-1pm Sun. **Credit** MC, V. **Map** p318 D2.
The new spot from the owners of Caffè Italiano (*see
p130*) has an unmissable chocolate and pear cake.

Sugar e Spice

Via dei Servi 43r, Duomo & Around (055 290263).
Open 3-7.30pm Mon; 10am-2.30pm, 3.30-7.30pm Tue-
Sat. Closed Aug. **No credit cards. Map** p319 A4.
Home-made, American-style sweets and cakes,
including muffins. There's also a bar here.

Supermarkets

Esselunga

*Via Pisana 130-132, Outside the City Gates
(055 706556/www.esselunga.it).* Bus 6, 12, 13.
Open 8am-9pm Mon-Fri; 7.30am-8.30pm Sat.
Credit AmEx, DC, MC, V.
A wide range of groceries, including an excellent deli
counter, fresh fish, well-priced wines and spirits,
CDs, flowers and newspapers. There's free parking.
Other locations: throughout the city.

Margherita Conad

*Via L Alamanni 2-10r, Santa Maria Novella
(055 211544).* **Open** 8am-7.30pm Mon-Sat.
Credit MC, V. **Map** p318 A1.
A small, well-stocked supermarket by the station.

Natura Si

*Viale Corsica 19-23, Outside the City Gates (055
366024/www.naturasi.com).* Bus 23. **Open** 3.30-8pm
Mon; 9am-7.30pm Tue-Thur, Sat; 9am-8pm Fri.
Credit AmEx, MC, V.
This decent health food store sells mainly fresh,
organic produce, plus all manner of biological fare.
Other locations: Via Masaccio 88-90, Outside the
City Gates (055 2001068).

Market forces

One of the first things visitors will notice after spending a little time in Florence is the abundance of market stalls that seem to show up in even the tiniest of piazzas. A trip to the local market is a way of life for many Florentines: if you know when and where to look, you're in for a treat, especially if you're after a bargain.

The main market of **San Lorenzo** (8.30am-7pm Mon-Sat) covers a cobweb of streets around San Lorenzo church, with stalls selling leather goods, clothes and souvenirs. At its centre is the 19th-century covered market in the **Piazza del Mercato Centrale** (entrances on the piazza itself and on Via dell' Ariento; 7am-2pm Mon-Sat), dedicated to fruit, vegetables, meats, fish and cheeses. The array of goods is highly tempting.

Foodies visiting Florence should also head to the **Sant'Ambrogio** market in Piazza Ghiberti just north of Santa Croce (7am-2pm Mon-Sat) for the freshest and cheapest farmers' produce. Leave time to stop off, on the way back into the centre of town, at the flea market, the **Mercato delle Pulci**, round the corner in Piazza dei Ciompi (9am-7pm Mon-Sat) to browse through the bric-a-brac for that elusive antique find.

The **Mercato Nuovo** (*pictured*), in the covered Loggia del Mercato Nuovo just off Via Calimala (9am-7pm Mon-Sat), is also known as the Mercato del Porcellino in honour of the bronze boar statue whose nose it is *de rigueur* to rub if you want a return visit to Florence. You may not come across anything of value, but the alabaster chess sets, cheap tapestries and lace, stationery, leather goods and scarves make fine souvenirs and gifts.

The town's biggest weekly market, the Tuesday morning affair at the Cascine, is on ice while the new cross-city tramlines are built. However, in the meantime, there's still plenty to browse at the other weekly and monthly markets that spring up in various squares around the city. **Piazza Santo Spirito**, to name but one, is home to a small daily weekday morning market, but is better approached for its antique and flea market on the second Sunday of the month (8am-6pm). You can usually find the odd treasure among the old photos, items of furniture, jewellery and frames. The square also plays host to **Fierucola** on the third Sunday of the month (8am-6pm), a market whose stalls sell organic foods and wines, handmade clothing, cosmetics and natural medicines.

Eat, Drink, Shop

Wine

For more on wine, *see pp42-45*; for wineries out of town, *see pp234-235* **Visiting wineries**.

Alessi

Via delle Oche 27r, Duomo & Around (055 214966/ www.enotecaalessi.it). **Open** 9am-1pm, 4-8pm Mon-Sat. **Credit** AmEx, DC, MC, V. **Map** p319 B4.
This fabulously stocked *enoteca* is piled high with cakes, biscuits and chocolates. Coffee is ground on the spot.

Millesimi

Borgo Tegolaio 33r, Oltrarno (055 2654675/ www.millesimi.it). **Open** 3-8pm Mon-Fri; 10am-8pm Sat, 2nd Sun of mth. Closed 2wks Aug. **Credit** AmEx, DC, MC, V. **Map** p318 D2.

Dolci e Dolcezze. *See p148.*

Home to one of the biggest selections in town, Millesimi has an especially good range of Tuscan wines, plus plenty of bottles from around Italy. Tastings are offered by appointment.

Health & beauty

For more health and beauty options, *see also p152* **Natural selections**.

Profumeria Aline

Via dei Calzaiuoli 53, Duomo & Around (055 219073/www.profumeriaaline.com). **Open** 3-7.30pm Mon; 9am-7.30pm Tue-Sat. **Credit** MC, V. **Map** p319 B4.
A well-stocked perfumery and cosmetics shop, with a prime location on Via dei Calzaiuoli. There's a beauty centre at No.7 (055 2398292). The loyalty card gets you a cumulative discount.
Other locations: Via Vacchereccia 11r, Duomo & Around (055 294976), Piazza San Giovanni 26-27, Duomo & Around (055 212864).

Sephora at Laguna

Via Martelli 10, Duomo & Around (055 2381922). **Open** 9.30am-7.30pm Mon-Sat; 11am-7.30pm Sun. **Credit** AmEx, MC, V. **Map** p319 B4.
This Florentine outlet of the highly regarded French beauty chain is relatively small, but it still sells many other cult labels alongside the famous Sephora own-brand line.

Hairdressers & barbers

Note than all hairdressers in Florence are closed on Mondays.

Bacci

Via delle Oche 26r, Duomo & Around (055 214026). **Open** 8.30am-12.30pm; 3.30-7pm Tue-Sat. **No credit cards. Map** p319 B4.
This old-school Florentine barber is blessed with a very central location.

Gabrio Staff

Via de' Tornabuoni 5, Santa Maria Novella (055 214668). **Open** 9.30am-7pm Tue-Sat. Closed 2wks Aug. **Credit** MC, V. **Map** p318 C2.
This unisex hair and beauty centre is set in an amazing atelier. If your appointment falls in the middle of the day, don't worry about getting hungry: staff dish out buffet snacks to clients at lunchtime. Cuts are €60.

Jean Louis David

Lungarno Corsini 52r, Santa Maria Novella (055 216760/www.jld.com). **Open** 9am-7pm Tue-Sat. Closed 2wks Aug. **Credit** MC, V. **Map** p318 C2.
A women's wash and cut ay Jean Louis David is €35; however, men are also welcome. There's a student discount of 20%. However, if you're adventurous, you can call ahead to book a free haircut in the salon's school.

Health & beauty treatments

Freni
Via Calimala 1, Duomo & Around (055 2396647).
Open 9am-6.30pm Mon-Fri; 9am-12.30pm Sat.
Credit AmEx, MC, V. **Map** p318 A3.
If your feet give out after tramping around all those museums, come here for a pedicure. Facials, manicures and massages are also offered.

Hito Estetica
Via de' Ginori 21, San Lorenzo (055 284424).
Open 9am-7.30pm Mon-Fri; 9am-7pm Sat. **Credit** AmEx, MC, V. **Map** p319 A4.
A range of natural treatments and pampering for men and women, including Ayurvedic techniques. Prices start at around €40 for a facial.

International Studio
Via Porta Rossa 82r, Duomo & Around (055 293393). **Open** 1-8pm Mon; 10am-8pm Tue-Sat.
Credit MC, V. **Map** p318 C3.
A solarium, hair and beauty centre, box office and showcase for objets d'art, all rolled into one.

Opticians

Camera and optical lenses go hand in hand in Italy: photography shops (*see p153*) sell glasses and opticians sell basic photo equipment.

Pisacchi
Via Condotta 22-24r, Duomo & Around (055 214542). **Open** 3.30-7.30pm Mon; 9am-1pm, 3.30-7.30pm Tue-Sat. **Credit** AmEx, DC, MC, V. Closed 2wks Aug. **Map** p319 C4.
As well as providing eye tests, this contact lens specialist sells prescription glasses and sunglasses.

Sbisa
Piazza Signoria 10r, Duomo & Around (055 211339). **Open** 10am-7.30pm daily. **Credit** AmEx, DC, MC, V. **Map** p319 C4.
Frames here come from the likes of Armani, Gucci and Versace. There's also optical and photo gear.

Pharmacies

Farmacia Comunale no.13
Santa Maria Novella train station, Santa Maria Novella (055 216761/289435). **Open** 24hrs daily.
No credit cards. Map p318 A2.
English spoken.

Farmacia all'Insegna del Moro
Piazza San Giovanni 20r, Duomo & Around (055 211343). **Open** 24hrs daily. **Credit** V. **Map** p318 B3.
Some English spoken.

Farmacia Molteni
Via dei Calzaiuoli 7r, Duomo & Around (055 215472/289490). **Open** 24hrs daily. **Credit** AmEx, MC, V. **Map** p318 C3.
English spoken.

Homewares

Home accessories & gifts

Arredamenti Castorina
Via di Santo Spirito 13-15r, Oltrarno (055 212885/ www.castorina.net). **Open** 9am-1pm, 3.30-7.30pm Mon-Fri; 9am-1pm Sat. Closed Aug. **Credit** AmEx, DC, MC, V. **Map** p318 C1.
An extraordinary old shop with all things baroque: gilded mouldings, frames, cherubs, *trompe l'œil* tables and fake malachite and tortoiseshell obelisks.

Arte sì di Paola Capecchi
Via dei Fossi 23r, Santa Maria Novella (055 2645504). **Open** 3.30-7.30pm Mon; 10am-1pm, 3.30-7.30 Tue-Sat. Closed 3wks Aug. **Credit** AmEx, DC, MC, V. **Map** p318 B2.
Capecchi has filled this shop with outlandish design *objets* and furniture pieces: from silvered chairs with pink frosted leather upholstery to Warhol-inspired prints. Hours can be erratic; it's best to call ahead.

Bartolini
Via dei Servi 30r, San Marco (055 211895/ www.dinobartolini.it). **Open** 3.30-7.30pm Mon; 10am-1pm, 3.30-7.30pm Tue-Sat. Closed 2wks Aug.
Credit AmEx, MC, V. **Map** p319 A4.
This charming kitchen shop has extensive selections of cutlery and crockery, plus accessories ranging from garlic mincers to kitchen sinks.

Borgo degli Albizi 48 Rosso
Borgo degli Albizi 48r, Santa Croce (055 2347598/ www.borgoalbizi.com). **Open** 3.30-7.30pm Mon; 10am-1pm, 3.30-7.30pm Tue-Sat. **Credit** AmEx, DC, MC, V. **Map** p319 B5.
Opulent chandeliers and glass pear-drop lamps made with antique or new crystals. You can also order items to your own design.

La Bottega dei Cristalli
Via dei Benci 51r, Santa Croce (055 2344891/ www.labottegadeicristalli.com). **Open** 10am-7.30pm daily. Closed mid Jan-mid Feb. **Credit** AmEx, DC, MC, V. **Map** p319 C5.
A lovely range of Murano and Tuscan-made plates, picture frames, lamps and chandeliers, plus tiny glass 'sweets' and bottles.

La Botteghina del Ceramista
Via Guelfa 5r, San Lorenzo (055 287367/www. labotteghina.com). **Open** 10am-1.30pm, 3.30-7.30pm Mon-Fri; 10am-1.30pm Sat. Closed 2wks Aug.
Credit AmEx, DC, MC, V. **Map** p319 A4.
Superb hand-painted ceramics in intricate designs and vivid colours. Prices start from as little as €15.

Carte Etc
Via de' Cerchi 13r, Duomo & Around (055 268302/ www.carteetc.it). **Open** 10am-7.30pm daily. **Credit** AmEx, MC, V. **Map** p319 B4.
Exquisite glass and stationery, unusual postcards of Florence and handmade greetings cards.

Natural selections

Starting in the 11th century, when Benedictine monks began making alcoholic elixirs, and peaking 500 years later, when Caterina de Medici employed infamous 'perfumer' and herbalist Rene the Florentine as her court doctor in Paris, Florence has been renowned for its knowledge of the therapeutic qualities of herbs. Its fields of lavender and herbs have helped Tuscany maintain its reputation as a centre for alternative remedies, and many locals call at an *erboristeria* rather than a chemist for most minor ailments. Some of these stores are joys to behold even if you're not shopping, though their products double as gorgeous gifts.

The **Erboristeria Inglese** (Via de' Tornabuoni 19, Santa Maria Novella, 055 210628, www.officinadeitornabuoni.com, closed Sun), set in a frescoed 15th-century palazzo, sells handmade gifts, perfumes and candles from Diptyque, plus herbal remedies and goods from famed natural skincare line Dr Hauschka. The **Spezieria Erboristeria Palazzo Vecchio** (Via Vaccchereccia 9r, Duomo & Around, 055 2396055, www.erbitalia.com, closed most Suns), a stone's throw from the Piazza della Signoria's towering landmark, is an old-fashioned and really quite charming frescoed apothecary that specialises in handmade perfumes and floral *eaux de toilette* with such evocative names as Acqua di Caterina de Medici.

The **Officina Profumo-Farmaceutica di Santa Maria Novella** (*pictured*; Via della Scala 16, Santa Maria Novella, 055 216276, www.smnovella.it, closed most Suns), the most famous of the Florentine herbalists' shops, has such power that it hushes visitors into a church-like reverent silence as soon as they walk through its doors. The shop is an ancient herbal pharmacy in a wonderful palazzo with a 13th-century frescoed chapel. Prices aren't cheap, but then you are buying what's reputed to be the best soap in the world. If you think you recognise it from somewhere, it might be from the store's cameo role in the film *Hannibal*. Two other notable shops are **Elisir** (Borgo degli Albizi 70r, Santa Croce, 055 263 8218, closed most Suns), a charming shop with creams, lotions and remedies all made from natural ingredients, and **Bizzarri** (Via Condotta 32r, Duomo & Around, 055 211580, closed Sun), a relic that has shelves of bell jars filled with substances in every conceivable colour. Its herbal concoctions are made to secret, generations-old recipes.

Homeopathy can be sold only in chemists' shops, but some Florentine chemists stock more herbal remedies than pharmaceutical concoctions. **Farmacia Franchi** (Via de' Ginori 65r, San Lorenzo, 055 210565, closed Sun & some Sats) is housed in a stunning vaulted and frescoed room, while **Farmacia del Cinghiale** (Piazza del Mercato Nuovo 4r, Duomo & Around, 055 282128, closed Sun & some Sats), named after the famous wild boar statue in the square opposite, was founded in the 1700s by the herbalist Guadagni and still makes its own herbal remedies and cosmetics. A newcomer by comparison, the charming **Münstermann** pharmacy (Piazza Goldoni 2r, Santa Maria Novella, 055 210660, www.mustermann.it, closed Sun & some Sats) was opened in 1897 and still has its original shop fittings. As well as stocking pharmaceutical and herbal medicines, the mahogany cabinets are filled with unusual hair accessories, jewellery and toiletries.

Frette
Via Cavour 2r, San Marco (055 211369). **Open**
3-7pm Mon; 10am-7pm Tue-Sat. Closed 3wks Aug.
Credit AmEx, DC, MC, V. **Map** p319 A4.
The full range of bedding, towels and robes so
beloved of boutique hotels the world over. Going to
bed has never felt so good.

Passamaneria Toscana
Piazza San Lorenzo 12r, San Lorenzo (055 214670/
www.passamaneriatoscana.com). **Open** 9am-7.30pm
Mon-Sat; 10am-7.30pm Sun. **Credit** AmEx, DC, MC,
V. **Map** p318 B2.
This shop sells all kinds of soft furnishings: every-
thing from rich brocade cushions to embroidered
Florentine crests, wall hangings and tassels.

Rosa Regale
Volta Mazzucconi 3r (off Via Tosinghi), Duomo
& Around (055 2670613/www.rosaregale.it).
Open 3-7.30pm Mon; 10am-1.30pm, 3-7.30pm
Tue-Sat. Closed 3wks Aug. **Credit** AmEx, DC, MC,
V. **Map** p318 B3.
This unusual shop is hidden at the top of a rosebush-
lined vaulted passageway covered in Florentine
crests. Designs include rose-shaped cushions and a
line of floral-themed clothing and accessories.

Sbigoli Terrecotte
Via Sant' Egidio 4r, Santa Croce (055 2479713/
www.sbigoliterrecotte.it). **Open** 9am-1pm, 3-7.30pm
Mon-Sat. **Credit** AmEx, DC, MC, V. **Map** p319 B5.
Handmade Tuscan ceramics and terracotta in tra-
ditional designs are the order of the day here.

Signum
Borgo dei Greci 40r, Santa Croce (055 280621/
www.signumfirenze.it). **Open** 10am-7.30pm daily.
Credit MC, V. **Map** p319 C4.
This delightful shop, housed in an ancient wine
cellar, stocks an appealingly wide range of gifts,
among them miniature models of shop windows and
bookcases, tiny tarot cards, and Murano glass
inkwells and pens.
Other locations: Lungarno Archibusieri 14r,
Duomo & Around (055 289393); Via dei Benci 29r,
Santa Croce (055 244590).

G Veneziano
Via dei Fossi 53r, Santa Maria Novella (055
287925). **Open** 3-7pm Mon; 9am-1pm, 3-7pm
Tue-Sat. Closed Aug. **Credit** AmEx, DC, MC, V.
Map p318 B2.
An upmarket gift shop with flower-embroidered
cushions and tablecloths, lanterns, glass tableware
and jewellery, plus unusual items for the home.

Picture framers

Leonardo Romanelli
Via di Santo Spirito 16r, Oltrarno (055 284794).
Open 9am-1pm, 3-7.30pm Mon-Fri; 9am-1pm Sat.
Closed Aug. **No credit cards**. **Map** p318 C2.
Handmade gilded frames from about €20.

Music

Alberti
Borgo San Lorenzo 45-49r, San Lorenzo (055
294271). **Open** 3.30-7.30pm Mon; 9am-7.30pm
Tue-Sat. **Credit** AmEx, MC, V. **Map** p318 B3.
The oldest record shop in the city has a vast
repertoire of pop, dance, jazz and indie CD recordings, some vinyl, a variety of DVDs and a great
selection of portable DVD and CD players.
Other locations: Via dei Pucci 16r, San Marco
(055 284346).

Data Records
Via de' Neri 15r, Santa Croce (055 287592/
www.superecord.com). **Open** 3.30-7.30pm Mon;
10am-1pm, 3.30-7.30pm Tue-Sat. Closed 2wks Aug.
Credit AmEx, DC, MC, V. **Map** p319 C4.
Data is home to over 80,000 titles, both new and
used, with an emphasis on psychedelia, blues, R&B,
jazz and soundtracks. The have a local reputation
for being able to find the unfindable.

Ricordi
Via Brunelleschi 8r, Duomo & Around (055
214104/www.feltrinelli.it). **Open** 9.30am-7.30pm
Mon-Sat; 3-7.30pm last Sun of mth. **Credit** AmEx,
DC, MC, V. **Map** p318 B3.
Ricordi has the best choice of DVDs and CDs in
town, with original-language films and classical,
jazz, rock and dance sections. Ricordi also sells
instruments, sheet music and scores. The helpful
staff speak English.

Twisted
Borgo San Frediano 21r, Oltrarno (055 282011).
Open 9am-12.30pm; 3-7.30pm Mon-Sat. **Credit**
AmEx, DC, MC, V.
A specialist jazz centre with rare recordings and
more mainstream sounds. The stocked artists span
half a century from 50s trad jazz right though to acid
and nu jazz.

Photography

Bongi
Via Por Santa Maria 82-84r, Duomo & Around
(055 2398811/www.otticabongi.com). **Open** 3.30-
7.30pm Mon; 9.30am-7.30pm Tue-Sat; 10am-7pm
Sun. **Credit** AmEx, DC, MC, V. **Map** p318 C3.
One of the best-stocked photographic shops in
the city centre, with a wide range of new and used
equipment (the latter in good nick). Staff can also do
digital photo repro and print developing.

Foto Ottica Fontani
Viale Strozzi 18-20A, San Lorenzo (055 470981/
www.otticafontani.com). **Open** 2.30-7.30pm Mon;
8.30am-1pm, 2.30-7.30pm Tue-Sat. **Credit** V.
Map p318 B3.
Photography enthusiasts in Florence make a beeline
for this shop, where the prices prices for processing
and developing are the lowest in town. Designer
glasses are also sold here.

Carte Etc. *See p151.*

Stationery & art supplies

Cartoleria Ecologica La Tartaruga
Borgo degli Albizi 60r, Santa Croce (055 2340845).
Open 1.30-7.30pm Mon; 9.30am-7.30pm Tue-Sat.
Credit DC, MC, V. **Map** p319 B5.
Unusual stationery, toys and gifts made of recycled
paper, wood and papier mâché.

Le Dune
*Piazza Ottaviani 9r, Santa Maria Novella (055
214377).* **Open** 9am-7pm Mon-Fri; 9am-1pm Sat.
Closed 2wks Aug. **Credit** AmEx, DC, MC, V.
Map p318 B2.
A small gift and stationery shop with a good choice
of greetings cards. The shop also offers photocopy-
ing, photo developing and faxing services.

Mandragora
*Piazza Duomo 50r, Duomo & Around (055 292559/
www.mandragora.it).* **Open** 10am-7.30pm Mon-Sat;
10.30am-6.30pm Sun. **Credit** AmEx, DC, MC, V.
Map p319 B4.
Decent reproductions by local artists of famous
Florentine works of art on furnishings, scarves, bags
and ornaments, plus great books, cards and prints.

Pineider
*Piazza Signoria 13r, Duomo & Around (055
284655/www.pineider.com).* **Open** 3-7pm Mon;
10am-1.30pm, 2.30-7pm Tue-Sat. **Credit** AmEx,
DC, MC, V. **Map** p319 C4.
Pineider is famous for its high-quality writing paper
and accessories and top-notch office leather goods.

Romeo
Via Condotta 43r, Duomo & Around (055 210350).
Open 9.30am-7.30pm Mon-Sat. **Credit** AmEx, DC,
MC, V. **Map** p318 C4.
The interior of this lovely stationery shop is filled to
the ceiling with Spalding's full range, Aurora pens
and Giorgio Fedon's smart coloured leather bags.

Zecchi
*Via dello Studio 19r, Duomo & Around (055
211470/www.zecchi.com).* **Open** 8.30am-12.30pm,
3.30-7.30pm Mon-Fri; 8.30am-12.30pm Sat. Closed
3wks Aug. **Credit** AmEx, MC, V. **Map** p319 B4.
The best shop in town for art supplies, with everything from pencils to gold leaf.

Ticket agencies

In order to avoid confusion or disappointment,
when booking tickets for events by phone,
ensure that all the arrangements for collection
or delivery are clearly specified.

Box Office
*Via Alamanni 39, Santa Maria Novella (055
210804/www.boxol.it).* **Open** 3.30-7.30pm Mon;
10am-7.30pm Tue-Sat. **Credit** MC, V. **Map** p318 A1.
Box Office sells tickets for concerts, plays and exhi-
bitions in Italy and abroad.
Other locations: Chiasso de Soldanieri 8r, Duomo
& Around (055 293393/219402).

Video & DVD rental

Blockbuster
*Viale Belfiore 6A, Outside the City Gates (055
330542/www.blockbuster.it).* Bus 2, 14, 28.
Open 11am-11pm Mon-Thur, Sun; 11am-midnight
Fri, Sat. **Credit** V.
Stocks some mainstream films in English, plus the
inevitable popcorn and ice-cream.
Other locations: Via di Novoli 9-11, Outside the
City Gates (055 333533).

Punto Video
Via San Antonino 7r, San Lorenzo (055 284813).
Open 9am-8pm Mon-Sat. **Credit** AmEx, DC, MC, V.
Map p318 A2.
Punto has over 500 titles in English.

Eat, Drink, Shop

Arts & Entertainment

Features

Festivals & Events

All the fun of the fairs.

Palio, Siena. *See p158.*

Perhaps the best way to see the Tuscans at play is to time your visit around one of the region's many traditional festivals, which often date back hundreds of years and are still a key part of city, town or village life. Major events, such as Siena's **Palio** (*see p158*), feature hundreds of participants and thousands of spectators; others are much more modest affairs, where the whole village turns out to join in the festivities.

This being Italy, the common denominator in local events is likely to be lots of good food and wine. All year, *sagre* (rites) celebrate seasonal food, from chestnuts to porcini mushrooms. Typically, a *sagra* revolves around the preparation and eating of a particular ingredient: squadrons of village ladies produce huge vats of (for example) wild boar stew, which will be doled out on plastic plates to locals and visitors who share long trestle tables and pay only a few euros for the privilege.

The main problem with festivals in Tuscany and Florence is that few of them are well publicised, particularly from one province to the next. Keep an eye out for posters around neighbourhoods, scour the various provincial websites or contact the tourist board (*see p298*) if you're in need of further information.

Many, but not all, of the following festivals and events are free; call the phone numbers given below for ticket information. Note that the numbers may only be operational during the relevant event, and in the direct run-up to it. For music-only festivals, *see p173* **Seasons in the sun**, *p174 and p177*; for film festivals, *see p165*; for theatre and dance events, *see p192*.

Spring

Festa della Donna
Date 8 Mar.
For International Women's Day, women are traditionally given bunches of yellow mimosa flowers; in the evening, restaurants and clubs, many of which put on male strippers, get packed with girlie gangs.

Holy Week
Date wk leading up to Easter.
Many small Tuscan towns celebrate Holy Week with religious processions, often in Renaissance costume. Some of the larger ones include Buonconvento (near Siena), Castiglion Fiorentino (near Arezzo) and Bagno a Ripoli (just outside Florence). In Grassina and San Gimignano, re-enactments of episodes from the life of Christ are staged on Good Friday.

Scoppio del Carro
Piazzale della Porta al Prato to Piazza del Duomo, Florence. **Date** Easter Sun.
A parade of musicians, flag-throwers and dignitaries escort the *carro*, a tall and heavy wooden cart pulled by four oxen, from the west of Florence to

Piazza del Duomo. At 11am, during mass, a priest lights a mechanical dove, which then 'flies' along a wire from the high altar to the *carro* outside and ignites an explosion of fireworks (*lo scoppio*). If all goes smoothly at the event, which dates to the 12th century, the year's harvest should be good. Piazza del Duomo will be packed, but if you stand outside the tall wooden doors by the Hotel Villa Medici (Via il Prato 2) at 9.30am, you'll get a good view.

Settimana dei Beni Culturali

Florence & throughout Tuscany (055 290832).
Date spring/early summer.
State museums, including the Uffizi, Accademia and Palatina galleries, let the public in free during this week-long event. Queues are not usually that long, maybe because the date is often established at the last minute and few know about it in advance.

Mostra Mercato di Piante e Fiori

Giardino di Orticoltura, Via Vittorio Emanuele 4, Outside the City Gates, Florence (055 2625385). Bus 4. **Date** late 25 Apr/early May, early Oct.
These spectacular plant and flower shows are centred around a grand 19th-century glasshouse, part of a horticultural garden created in 1859. Growers from all over Tuscany exhibit their plants and blooms; the display of azaleas is particularly impressive.

Maggio Musicale Fiorentino

Teatro del Maggio Musicale Fiorentino, Corso Italia 16, Santa Maria Novella, Florence (055 213535/ www.maggiofiorentino.com). **Date** late Apr-late June.
Florence's 'Musical May' festival is a two-month season of opera, concerts and dance performances featuring international artists. It closes with two free jamborees (one ballet, one music), usually held in Piazza della Signoria.

Palio, Magliano in Toscana

Magliano in Toscana (0564 59341). **Date** 1 May.
Though the *palio* (horse race) no longer takes place, this little town in the Maremma still holds an intimate version of the torchlit procession that used to be part of the ritual blessing of the horses on the night before the race.

Artigianato e Palazzo

Palazzo Corsini, Via della Scala, Florence (055 2654589/www.artigianatoepalazzo.it). **Date** wknd in mid May.
An upmarket craft show-cum-market held in the Palazzo Corsini's gorgeous gardens. Artisans from all over Italy exhibit and sell their wares.

Mille Miglia

Florence (030 280036/www.millemiglia.it).
Date Sat in late May.
Some 375 vintage cars take part in this four-day, 1,600-kilometre (1,000-mile) race, which starts and finishes in Brescia (in northern Italy). It passes through Florence on a Saturday afternoon, entering the city through Porta Romana and crossing Ponte Santa Trinità en route to Piazza della Signoria.

Festa del Grillo

Parco delle Cascine, Outside the City Gates, Florence. Bus 17. **Date** Sun in late May/early June.
This ancient symbolic event has become an excuse for a big general market. The crickets that were once sold in hand-painted cages, intended to woo sweethearts and cheer them up during separations, have now been replaced by mechanical versions due to pressure from animal rights activists. Fun for kids.

Cantine Aperte

Throughout Tuscany (0577 738312/www. movimentoturismovino.it). **Date** last Sun in May.
Wine-producing estates, many of which aren't normally open to the public, hold tastings. Pick up a guide from tourist offices.

Summer

Around the end of May, open-air venues emerge from hibernation all over Tuscany, and bars and restaurants move tables out to terraces and gardens. In Florence, outdoor cinemas screen movies (*see p165*), open-air bars double as music venues (*see pp175-184*) and clubs move dancefloors under the stars. Cloisters and squares host classical concerts, as locals take to the city's piazzas and gardens.

Ancient Maritime Republics Boat Race

River Arno, Pisa (050 910393/910506).
Date last Sun in May or 1st Sun in June.
Every year a historic regatta in costume is staged between the four ancient maritime republics of Pisa, Genoa, Venice and Amalfi. The cities take it in turns to stage the event: Pisa next gets to play host in 2006.

Don't miss Festivals

Cantine Aperte
See above.

Carnevale di Viareggio
See p159.

A country *sagra*
See p156.

Luminaria di San Ranieri
See p158.

Mille Miglia
See left.

Palio, Siena
See p158.

Settimana dei Beni Culturali
See left.

Arts & Entertainment

Calcio in Costume

Piazza Santa Croce, Florence (055 290832).
Map p319 C5. **Date** June.

Also known as *calcio storico*, this violent variation on football, played in medieval costume, is one of the most colourful events in the Florentine calendar. Three matches are played in June, one of which is always held on June 24 (*see below* Festa di San Giovanni). Four teams of bare-chested lads representing the city's ancient quarters (Santa Croce, Santa Maria Novella, Santo Spirito and San Giovanni) parade through the streets, before settling old rivalries in a one-hour no-holds-barred match played by two teams of 27. Blood is often spilled.

Luminaria di San Ranieri

Pisa (050 910393/910506). **Date** 16 & 17 June.
Thousands of candles are lit along the Arno for this two-day festival. At 6.30pm on day two, there's a boat race through the town's ancient quarters.

Giostra del Saracino

Piazza Grande, Arezzo (0575 377678/tickets 0575 377262). **Date** penultimate wknd in June; first Sun in Sept.

Run twice a year, this ancient jousting tournament between the four *quartieri* of Arezzo originated in the 13th century; seven centuries later, the stagey rivalries are less fierce, but plenty of fun. The first parade starts at about 10am, with another at 2.30pm. At 5pm, the procession of horses, knights and their escorts arrives in the piazza, and the action begins.

Festa Internazionale della Ceramica

Montelupo (0571 518993). **Date** 8 days in mid-late June.

For centuries, the town of Montelupo has been a ceramics manufacturing centre. This festival celebrates the art with Renaissance music and costumes, and demonstrations of various techniques.

Festa di San Giovanni

Florence. **Date** 24 June.
A public holiday in honour of Florence's patron saint. The highlight is a huge fireworks display near Piazzale Michelangelo.

Il Gioco del Ponte

Pisa (050 910393/910506). **Date** last Sun in June.
A 13th-century 'push-of-war' (a reverse tug-of-war) fought on the Ponte di Mezzo between teams from the two sides of the Arno. Processions start at 4.30pm; the competition begins two hours later.

Palio, Siena

Piazza del Campo, Siena (0577 280551).
Date 2 July & 16 Aug.
The world's most famous bareback horse race has provoked much controversy over the years (mostly to do with fatally injured horses), but for many, it remains Tuscan pageantry at its best. Trial races are run prior to the two main dates, the last at 9am on the days themselves. At 2.30pm, the horses and

jockeys are blessed in their team's church. Two hours later, the procession enters Piazza del Campo; after some flag-throwing, the race (three times around the square) gets going around 7pm and is all over in 90 seconds. It's free to stand, but get there early and take a sun hat. Tickets for balconies overlooking the piazza are sold in the bars and cafés that line it, but they're hard to come by and expensive.

Medieval Festival

Monteriggione (0577 304810). **Date** mid July.
This re-enactment, in period dress, of Monteriggione medieval town life features food, drink and craft stalls, plus music, dancing and other performances. Action focuses on the third weekend of July, but there are events in the ten days leading up to it. Events are lit by torchlight after dark, and visitors must change their cash into medieval currency.

On the Road Festival

Pelago (055 8327301). **Date** mid-late July.
A four-day (Thur-Sun) festival of street performers in a pretty village. The action starts at 6pm.

Giostra dell'Orso

Pistoia (0573 21622). **Date** 25 July.
Pistoia's annual bun fight culminates in the city's main square after a month of concerts, markets and pageantry. The Joust of the Bear dates from the 14th century, and sees 12 knights pitted against a bear (two wooden dummies) dressed in a checked cloak.

Effetto Venezia

Livorno (0586 204611).
Date 10 days in late July-early Aug.
A run of shows and concerts in Livorno's 'Venetian Quarter', so called because of its canals. Restaurants and street stalls serving the local *cacciucco* (spicy fish soup) and other delicacies stay open late.

Tuscan Sun Festival

Cortona (0575 630353/www.tuscansunfestival.com).
Date 1st 2wks Aug.
Writer Frances Mayes is the co-artistic director of this cultural festival, which launched in 2004 and attracts an international line-up. Based in Cortona (which, some say, has been ruined by the tourism resulting from Mayes's twee account of moving here), the programme is slanted towards music, but also includes food and wine events, films, talks and seminars.

Autumn

Florence Marathon

Florence (055 5522957/fax 055 5536823/www.firenzemarathon.it). **Date** late Nov/early Dec.
The route of the Florence marathon winds through the historic centre of the city as well as the western and eastern suburbs. The race starts at 9am in Piazzale Michelangelo and finishes in Piazza Santa Croce. Anybody over 18 can enter, but you have to produce a health certificate. You can apply online, by fax or by post up to the day before the race.

Winter

As the Christmas season rolls around, the Italian love of Nativity scenes reveals itself in numerous ways and places. Many churches set up cribs, some *viventi* (with live animals). The main ones in Florence are at San Lorenzo, Santa Croce, Chiesa di Dante and Santa Maria de' Ricci. Winter's also a season when *sagre* (*see p156*) in country towns and villages celebrate truffles, olive oil and chestnuts.

Christmas

Christmas is marked in Florence mainly by the holy trinity of late-opening shops, decorations and *comune* events. Midnight mass is held in the Duomo. Some restaurants open on Christmas Day, but you'll find more choice on December 26.

New Year's Eve

While many Florentines see in the New Year at home with copious amounts of food and drink, lots of restaurants in the city serve special Cena dell' Ultimo dell'Anno menus. The endless courses traditionally include stuffed pigs' trotters and lentils, for which you'll pay through the nose. Many clubs put on parties.

La Befana (Epiphany)

Date 6 Jan.

Although La Befana is a national holiday, it's celebrated chiefly by kids, who get to open their stockings. As legend has it, the Befana, a ragged old woman riding a broomstick, brings presents to well-behaved children, while naughty ones get just a sock full of dirty coal. Many small towns around the region hold street parties in celebration.

Carnevale

Date 10 days up to Shrove Tuesday.

Many Tuscan towns have *carnevale* celebrations, most of which feature parades of elaborate floats and fancy dress parties. In Florence, children dress up and parade with their parents in the piazzas and along Lungarno Amerigo Vespucci, scattering confetti and squirting anything that moves with foam. Elsewhere in Tuscany, head for Borgo San Lorenzo for kids' events and street performances, Calenzano for medieval revellers or San Gimignano for general festivities.

Carnevale di Viareggio

Viareggio (Fondazione Carnevale Viareggio 0584 962568/www.viareggio.ilcarnevale.com).
Date Feb/early Mar.

Held over four consecutive Sundays, the three before Mardi Gras and the one after, these are the biggest carnival celebrations in Italy outside Venice. Dating back to 1873, they're also the oldest. The first three parades of the carnival start at about 2.30pm, with the last one, an over-the-top procession of gigantic floats, beginning at 5pm and ending around 9.30pm. At the end of it, prizes are awarded for the best floats, before a celebratory fireworks display. You can buy a seat in one of the stands flanking the Lungomare (the route taken by the floats) in advance or at booths in the town from 8am on the day, but it's more fun to be in the enormous crowds. Peripheral festivities include masked balls, street parties and treasure hunts, fireworks displays, sporting and cultural events.

The floats take the best part of a year to assemble, and can be viewed in a series of hangars in the Cittadella del Carnevale on the north side of town; you can just turn up, or book a guided tour.

Let your feathers get ruffled at **Artigianato e Palazzo**. *See p157.*

Arts & Entertainment

Children

Spin the kids on Florence's magic roundabout.

Like the rest of Italy, Florence is an extremely child-friendly place, where restaurateurs welcome young customers with open arms and complete strangers coo over babies at every opportunity. As a result, your only concern as a parent in this art-laden city should be how to make sure your kids have *fun*. The sheer volume of spectacular art leads many parents to try and show their children everything. But burnout is all too common: instead, limit yourself to one or two sights a day and spend the rest of the time exploring the city, watching street entertainers, eating ice-cream and running in the gardens or piazzas.

For a few ideas on how to get your children interested in their surrounds, *see p162* **Bored games**. As a general rule, though, a great way to get kids started is to show them the city from above. Climb to the top of the **Duomo** (*see p70*), or hike up the stairway between Porta San Miniato and **Piazzale Michelangelo** (*see p107*; there's a colony of cats halfway up to the stairs to amuse, and a *gelateria* at the top), from where mini explorers can survey the city: its bridges across the Arno, the crenellated walls, the church towers and the overpowering Duomo.

For something more structured, several museums run dedicated children's programmes, usually in Italian. The best of these is at the **Museo dei Ragazzi** (*see p79*) within the Palazzo Vecchio, which has costumed re-enactments, storytelling and art workshops, plus tours of the palace's secret passages. Phone ahead for details and to book.

Aside from these programmes, however, are many other museums that are magnets for kids by virtue of the collections they house. The **Stibbert Museum** (*see p105*) has a huge array of armour, swords and shields in an old villa north of the city, while the **Museo di Storia della Scienza** (*see p79*) is home to intriguing objects such as Galileo's telescope. Elsewhere, the Palazzo Pitti's **Museo del Costume** (*see p103*) has a beautiful collection of costumes; just behind it are the massive **Boboli Gardens** (*see p102*), where you can run off a little steam. **La Specola** (*see p103*) houses life-size anatomical models of humans (some quite gory), while the **Museo Archeologico** (*see p107*) has Egyptian tombs and mummies. There's also the new **Museo Leonardo da Vinci** (*see p93*), which visitors of all ages will appreciate.

The food markets can likewise be fascinating for kids. Go early to **San Lorenzo market** (*see p149* **Market forces**) to pick up picnic supplies. If children can summon the courage to try out a few Italian words with the vendors, they might be surprised by the extras that get tossed into the grocery bag.

Book & toy shops

Feltrinelli International (*see p137*) also has a large selection of videos, games and books.

BM American British Bookstore
Borgo Ognissanti 4r, Santa Maria Novella (055 294575). **Open** 9.30am-7.30pm Mon-Sat; 10.30am-7pm Sun. **Credit** AmEx, DC, MC, V. **Map** p318 B1.
A tiny shop packed with one of the best collections of English books in Florence, including a wide range of children's books about the Renaissance.

Città del Sole
Via dei Cimatori 21r, Duomo & Around (055 219345/www.cittadelsole.com). **Open** 3.30-7.30pm Mon; 10am-7.30pm Tue-Sat. Closed 2wks Aug. **Credit** AmEx, MC, V. **Map** p319 C4.
Well-made toys, plus board games and puzzles.

Dreoni Giocattoli
Via Cavour 31-33r, San Marco (055 216611/ www.dreoni.it). **Open** 3.30-7.30pm Mon; 9am-1pm, 3.30-7.30pm Tue-Sat. **Credit** AmEx, DC, MC, V. **Map** p319 A4.
The lovely craft toy room at the back here also has costumes for Carnevale and Hallowe'en (celebrated here more and more each year).

Menicucci
Via de' Guicciardini 51r, Oltrarno (055 294934). **Open** 9.30am-8pm daily. **Credit** AmEx, MC, V. **Map** p318 D2/3.
A good all-round toy shop known for its window displays of soft toys and wooden Pinocchios. In the stationery store, there are leather-bound books, feather quills, personalised seals and sealing wax.

Natura e...
Via dello Studio 30r, Duomo & Around (055 2657624/www.natura-e.com). **Open** *Summer* 10am-2pm, 3-7.30pm Mon-Fri; 10am-2pm Sat. *Winter* 3.30-7.30pm Mon; 10am-2pm, 3-7.30pm Tue-Sat. **Credit** MC, V. **Map** p319 B4.
A shop for nature-lovers selling everything from scientific toys, experiments and optical illusions to outdoor trekking gear. It also has pamphlets on WWF activities and parks in Tuscany.

St James's American Church

Via Bernardo Rucellai 9, Santa Maria Novella (Kathy Procissi 055 577527). **Open** *Winter* 10am-noon, 3.30-5.30pm Wed; 10-11am, 12.30-1.30pm Sun. *Summer* times vary; phone to check. **Membership** *Books & videos* €15. **No credit cards. Map** p318 A1.

This place for an extensive selection of English-language books, videos, games and games. On Saturdays before festivals, children come to make decorations and masks; it's on an ad hoc basis, so phone to check it's happening before making a special trip.

Festivals

In addition to **La Befana** (*see p159*), children take the spotlight at a few other festivals. During February's **Carnevale**, especially on Sundays, look for kids in fancy dress in the *piazze* and on Lungarno Amerigo Vespucci. Children can get kitted out in the costume department at **Dreoni Giocattoli** (*see p160*). And for **La Rificolona** in September, Florentine youngsters make or buy paper lanterns, then gather in the evening either in Piazza Santissima Annunziata in San Marco or on the river (keep an eye out for posters). After dark, with lanterns bobbing on the end of long poles, children parade and sing.

Eating out

In general, the best places to look out for are bustling family trattorias with an appealing menu and atmosphere. In particular, try the establishments listed below, which are used to children with less adventurous palates.

Otherwise, just ask for a simple pasta with tomato sauce (*al pomodoro*), or a half portion (*mezza porzione*) of what you're having. Alternatively, stock up on goodies at a market (*see p149* **Market forces**) and head for a park.

Il Cucciolo

Via del Corso 25r, Duomo & Around (055 287727). **Open** 7.30am-8.30pm Mon-Sat. Closed 2wks Aug. **No credit cards. Map** p319 B4.

This bar is known to Florentine children because the *bomboloni* (pastries, plain or filled with cream, chocolate or jam) are made on the floor above and are then dropped down a tube to the bar below and served hot. Go in the morning to catch the action.

Mr Jimmy's American Bakery

Via San Niccolò 47, Oltrarno (055 2480999/ www.mr-jimmy.com). **Open** 9am-7pm Mon-Fri; 10am-1pm, 3-7pm Sat; 10am-1pm, 3-6pm Sun. Closed Aug. **Credit** AmEx, DC, MC, V. **Map** p319 D5.

American-style apple pie, chocolate cake, cheesecake, muffins, brownies and bagels.

Pit Stop

Via F Corridoni 30r, Rifredi, Outside the City Gates (055 4221437). Bus 14, 28. **Open** 12.30-2.30pm, 7pm-1am Mon-Fri; 7pm-1am Sat, Sun. Closed 1wk Aug. **Average** €15. **Credit** MC, V.

The choice is vast at Pit Stop, which offers 128 different *primi* (starters) and 100 types of pizza.

I Tarocchi

Via dei Renai 12-14r, Oltrarno (055 2343912/ www.pizzeriaitarocchi.it). **Open** 12.30-2.30pm, 7pm-1am Tue-Fri; 7pm-1am Sat, Sun. **Average** €12. **Credit** AmEx, DC, MC, V. **Map** p319 D4/5.

Child-friendly portions of pizza and pasta served in a friendly, casual atmosphere. The room with long tables and benches is perfect for boisterous families.

Chocs away! **Parco delle Cascine.** *See p162.*

Sport & leisure

For the pick of the city's swimming pools, *see p189*. Alternatively, go on a one-day bike ride, organised by **I Bike Italy** (055 2342371, open all year, no credit cards). Guides will pick you up from the centre of the city.

Gardens & parks

Boboli Gardens

For listings, *see p102*.

Labyrinths, grottoes, fountains, statues and hiding places make the Boboli a great diversion for children. Their less energetic parents can simply admire the magnificent views of the city.

Parco delle Cascine

Entrance nr Ponte della Vittoria, Outside the City Gates. Bus 17C.

Florence's largest park (west of the city along the river) is the site of regular fairs and markets. It's most animated on Sundays, when groups gather to play football and families stretch out on the grass, lingering over picnics. An early-morning visit often brings views of racehorses being exercised in the Ippodromo (*see p186*). For the energetic, there's also a kiosk where in-line skates can be hired (*see p187*), and many playgrounds dot the park.

Bored games

One creative way to make your children's time more memorable is to make a game out of spotting the many recurring historical, religious and classical images (John the Baptist's tattered camel skin and crossed staff, Hercules' lion skin and club, etc). How many can they spot? Look out, too, for the plaques on the walls that mark the level to which the Arno rose during its two floods, or the tiny doors through which wine was sold and people were fed during the plague. Once children get in the habit of looking, you'll be amazed what else they find. At museums and churches, consider letting your children browse the postcard section of the gift shop first. Let them choose their three favourites, then set them loose to find the artworks or artefacts themselves. Not only will the hunt become a kind of 'I Spy' game, thereby holding their attention for longer, but they will also be more likely to remember the masterpieces themselves, thereby making the whole family's trip to Florence more worthwhile.

Parco Carraia

Entrance off Via dell'Erta Caninna, San Niccolo, Outside the City Gates. Bus 23.

This little-known park surrounded by countryside has swings, picnic benches and plenty of green space. It's a lovely stroll up from Porta San Miniato, with oddly placed but fun climbing structures at the side of the road. The Carraia Tennis Club (*see p189*) is just up the street and offers a variety of activities for children, such as tennis and *calcetto* (football).

Play centres

Canadian Island

Via Gioberti 15, Outside the City Gates (055 677567/www.canadianisland.com). Bus 3, 6, 14. **Open** *June, July, Sept* 8am-5pm Mon-Fri. *Oct-May* 8am-2pm, 3.30-6.30pm Mon-Fri; 9am-1pm Sat. Closed Aug. **Admission** €30/afternoon. **No credit cards.**

Childcare for kids aged between three and 12 by responsible, English- and Italian-speaking adults. The company also organises summer camps on farms and day camps at the Ugolino in Chianti.

Mondobimbo Inflatables

Parterre, Piazza della Libertà, San Lorenzo (055 5532946). **Open** *June-Aug* 10am-1pm, 4.30-11.30pm daily. *Sept-May* 10am-1pm, 3.30-7.30pm daily. **Admission** €5 day ticket. **No credit cards.**

Under-tens can let off steam on huge inflatable castles, whales, dogs and snakes. It's wise to bring spare socks (you can buy some at the entrance).

Theatre

For the children's shows at **Elsinor, Teatro Stabile d'Innovazione**, *see p192*.

Out of town

Outside of Florence, both the coastline and countryside are within easy reach. Olive groves are good for family walks, while the beaches are perfect for a summer day trip.

Giardino Zoologico

Via Pieve a Celle 160, Pistoia (0573 911219/ www.zoodipistoia.it). **Open** *Summer* 9am-7pm daily. *Winter* 9am-6pm daily. Last entry 1hr before closing. **Admission** €9.50; €7.50 3-9s; free under-3s. **No credit cards.**

Giraffes, rhinos, crocodiles, jaguars and Malagasy lemurs are the attractions at this large park.

Parco Preistorico

Peccioli Via Cappuccini 20, Pisa (0587 636030/ 635430/www.parcopreistorico.it). **Open** *Apr-Aug* 9am-7pm daily. *Sep-Mar* 9am-noon, 2-6.30pm daily. **Admission** *Summer* €4. *Winter* €4. Reduced price for children. **No credit cards.**

About 50 km (32 miles) from Pisa, this park has life-size models of dinosaurs, a play area and picnic facilities. Tours (free, in Italian) last an hour.

Film

Florence's cinematic scene is small, but head outdoors or to a festival and you'll be rewarded.

Odeon Original Sound. *See p165.*

Ask ten cine-literate tourists to name a film set in Florence, and nine will offer *A Room With a View*. Although Merchant Ivory's twee piece of eye candy is over two decades old, it strikes a chord with visitors who come here to see Giotto's frescoes or the Ponte Vecchio. The sole remaining cinemagoer will likely cite *Hannibal*, the film that best captures the guts-out dark medieval heart of Florence's complex history.

Much of the big-screen repertoire set in Florence and Tuscany is polarised along similar lines. Nicole Kidman wears 19th-century corsets and frills in *The Portrait of a Lady*, while the *grandes dames* of English cinema take a small boy on a tour in Franco Zeffirelli's autobiographical *Tea with Mussolini*. These sit at the other end of the spectrum from Russell Crowe's *Gladiator*, who discovers the body of his wife, butchered by the Romans, among the incongruously delicious honey colours of the Sienese hill towns.

Florence's cinematic circuit is not generally accessible for non-Italian-speakers. Italians are generally loath to sit through a subtitled film, which is why the country has one of the biggest dubbing industries in the world. Nonetheless, the Odeon Original Sound, for one, shows international films in their original languages (*versione originale*) one or more nights a week. More varied programmes, including many subtitled films, are offered at film clubs (*cineclubs*).

Expect long queues on Friday and Saturday nights for new releases and for blockbusters in their original languages. When the *posto in piedi* light is lit, the tickets sold are standing-room only. If you speak Italian, check the cheaper matinées offered at many main cinemas on weekdays before 6.30pm or all day Wednesday, when it costs €5 instead of the standard €7.20. (The reduction doesn't usually apply to original-language screenings.) For information, check the daily newspapers or 'La Maschera', an information sheet on display at most bars that contains movie and theatre listings. For festivals and other special events, check local listings such as *Firenze Spettacolo*.

Cinemas

British Institute Cultural Programme

Lungarno Guicciardini 9, Oltrarno (055 26778270/ www.britishinstitute.it). **Open** *Lectures* from 6pm. *Screenings* from 8.30pm. **Tickets** €5 plus €5 membership. **No credit cards. Map** p318 C2.

Everybody loves Roberto

'I want to kiss you all!' he said, before clambering over the back of the big-screen bigwigs' seats and French-kissing Sophia Loren on the way to collecting a second Oscar for *Life is Beautiful*, the first Best Actor gong ever awarded to a lead in a foreign film. The irony, of course, is that the ebullient, irrepressible and half-crazed Roberto Benigni, the greatest clown Italy has seen since Totò, won the prize for what is by far his most serious film, the bittersweet story of a father determined to save not just his young son's life but his childish innocence amid the desperation of a Nazi concentration camp.

A true Tuscan by birth and nature, Benigni was born in Misericordia, near Arezzo, and brought up in Vergaio, near Prato. He encapsulates the classic *toscanaccio* character: left-wing, highly cultured yet unapologetically vulgar. His stand-up performances, TV turns and interviews revolve around a tirade of hilarious jibes at Silvio Berlusconi; he can recite Dante's *Divine Comedy* in its entirety; and his film parts, such as Walter Matthau's hard-to-shake *Little*

Devil and a taxi driver detailing his sheep fetish to a shocked priest in *Night on Earth*, are all too convincing.

Buoyed by the popularity brought to him by *Life is Beautiful* both here and abroad, Benigni sunk a mountain of money into his dream project: a live-action version of *Pinocchio*. His love for the tale was nurtured during a childhood spent practically next door to the wooden boy's home town of Collodi; 'I've been waiting for my nose to grow for 20 years,' Benigni quipped. The movie broke box office records in Italy, but its clumsily dubbed version was mercilessly slated abroad; while the film won Best Set and Best Costume Design at the prestigious David di Donatello Italian film festival, Benigni was also awarded the prize for Worst Actor at the 2003 Golden Raspberry Awards. But Benigni is not one to be down for long, and he's already bounced back, appearing in Jim Jarmusch's *Coffee and Cigarettes* (2003), and, due for release in autumn 2005, *La Tigre e la Neve* (The Tiger and the Snow), starring and directed by the man himself.

The British Institute runs a Talking Pictures programme on Wednesday evenings, with a movie sandwiched between an introduction and a discussion, all in English. It also runs courses in Italian cinema; see the website for further details.

Odeon Original Sound

Via Sassetti 1, Duomo & Around (055 214068/www. cinehall.it). **Open** *Box office* times vary. Closed Aug. **Tickets** €7.20. **No credit cards. Map** p318 B3.
Mondays, Tuesdays and Thursdays are big draws for English-speakers at this stunning art nouveau cinema. Films on current release in English are screened, sometimes with English or Italian subtitles; some reach the Odeon before they've been premiered at home. There's a discount of up to 40% with a club card for eight films from a programme of 13 (€36); alternatively, use the voucher from the previous Sunday's *La Repubblica* for 30% off.

Film clubs

Part of the attraction of Florence's film clubs, especially for students, is the value for money they offer. The town's main cinemas sometimes offer discounts for members.

CineCittà

Via Baccio da Montelupo 35, Outside the City Gates (055 7324510). Bus 6. **Shows** 8.30pm Wed-Sun. **Tickets** €4-€5. **Membership** €6. **No credit cards.**
Hollywood action pictures and festivals of obscure Italian films. Some screenings are shown in their original language or with subtitles.

Cineteca di Firenze

Via R Giuliani 374, Outside the City Gates (055 450749/www.cinetecadifirenze.it). Bus 2, 20, 28. **Shows** times vary. **Tickets** €4.50. **Membership** €3. **No credit cards.**
Cycles of films showcasing various actors, some in their original language.

Stensen Cineforum

Viale Don Minzoni 25C, Outside the City Gates (055 576551/5535858/www.stensen.org). Bus 1, 7, 12. **Shows** usually 9.15pm Thur-Sat, but phone to check. **Tickets** prices vary. **No credit cards. Map** p318 B2.
Stensen screens Italian and foreign films, but only for holders of season tickets (prices vary with the number of films). It also runs lectures and debates.

Seasonal cinema

The two major international festivals, where films are usually screened in their original languages, are in Florence and Fiesole. In November or December the **Festival dei Popoli** (055 244778) screens dramas and documentaries in clubs and cinemas throughout Florence. The theme changes each year but always centres around a social issue. The

Premio Fiesole ai Maestri del Cinema (055 597107, www.comune.fiesole.fi.it), held in July/August in Fiesole's open-air Roman theatre, pays homage to the works of one director. In addition, recent years have seen **France Cinema** (055 214053, www.france cinema.it) grow in importance. It's usually held in November at the French Institute (Piazza Ognissanti 2, 055 2398902) and at the Teatro della Compagnia (Via Cavour 50r, 055 217428).

Many cinemas here are air-conditioned and some open throughout the summer. However, a pleasant alternative for Italian-speakers (though international films are sometimes shown in their original languages) or those wanting to sample local life are the area's open-air cinemas, which show recent films from June to September. Shows start as darkness falls – around 9pm to 9.30pm depending on the month – and a couple of cinemas run double-bills, with the second films finishing around 1.30am. Some open-air cinemas have bars and restaurants.

Arena di Marte

Palazzetto dello Sport di Firenze, Viale Paoli, Outside the City Gates (055 293169/www.atelier group.it). Bus 10, 20, 34. **Dates** late June-late Aug. **Open** 8pm (shows 9.30pm & 10pm) daily. **Tickets** €5. **No credit cards.**
One of the two screens at this major outdoor venue shows cult and less mainstream films (some in their original languages with Italian subtitles); the larger screen runs the previous year's major blockbuster movies. There's a good outdoor restaurant too.

Chiardiluna

Via Monte Oliveto 1, Outside the City Gates (055 2337042/218682). Bus 12, 13. **Dates** June-Sept. **Open** 8pm (shows 9.30pm) daily. **Tickets** €5. **No credit cards.**
Surrounded by woodland, Chiardiluna is cooler than the other outdoor cinemas, but you should still take mosquito repellent. The movies are generally recent commercial releases, with some double-bills.

Forte di Belvedere

Via San Leonardo, Oltrarno (055 239169/ www.ateliergroup.it). **Dates** late June-late Aug.
Though restoration work at this star-shaped fortress has finally finished, it's still touch and go whether the summer outdoor screenings will take place. When they do, it's well worth the trek up the steep hill, where films are screened on the breezy terrace.

Raggio Verde

Palacongressi Firenze, Via Valfondo, San Lorenzo (055 239169/www.ateliergroup.it). **Closed for renovation.**
This stunning amphitheatre-style cinema, overlooking a 16th-century villa, runs nightly double-bills during summer. As this guide went to press it was closed for renovation until at least summer 2006; phone ahead for further details.

Arts & Entertainment

Galleries

Botticelli's successors.

Images of art in Florence are inevitably hinged around the likes of Botticelli and Leonardo. Visit one of the modern art fairs in Bologna or Milan, however, and the size of the Florentine contingent in attendance hints at progress.

And so it proves. Contemporary art galleries and centres are increasingly part of the central Florence landscape; all the major players on the scene insist business is booming. Among the more interesting developments of late has been the move into art by **Pitti Immagine**, until now best known for its fashion shows.

Away from the private sector, plans for a major public centre for contemporary art at the former Meccanotessile factory, intended to rival Prato's **Centro per l'Arte Contemporanea Luigi Pecci** (*see p198*), are currently held up by bureaucracy and funding debates. And if past attempts to set up such a centre are anything to go by, there's not much chance of this actually getting off the ground. That said, the recent opening of **Quarter** (*see p167*), which has taken over the festering eyesore site of a co-operative building to the south of the city, proves that it's possible for public and private cash to work together in the name of art.

Gallery spaces

Base

Via San Niccolò 18r, Oltrarno (055 2207281/ 679378/www.baseitaly.org). **Open** 5-8pm Mon-Sat. **No credit cards**. **Map** p319 D4.
A centre of excellence for Tuscany-based artists, many specialising in film, installation and digital art.

La Corte Arte Contemporanea

Via dei Coverelli 27r, Oltrarno (055 284435/www. lacortearte.it). **Open** 4-7pm Tue-Sat. Closed mid July-early Sept. **No credit cards**. **Map** p318 C2.
Old meets new at this tiny gallery, with columns and vaulted church ceilings. The space showcases a diverse range of local artists, with particular emphasis on the experimental scene.

Fondazione Pitti Immagine Discovery

Via Faenza 111, San Lorenzo (055 36931/www. pittimmagine.com). **Open** 9am-1pm, 2-5pm Mon-Fri. **No credit cards**. **Map** p318 A2.
Started in 1999 as a promotional machine, Pitti Immagine now stages major fashion, textiles and interiors shows in Florence. It also offers exhibitions, anything from installations to displays of fashion photography, in the Pitti building on Via Faenza.

Galleria Alessandro Bagnai

Via Maggio 58r, Oltrarno (055 212131/www. galleriabagnai.it). **Open** 10.30am-1pm, 3.30-7.30pm Tue-Sat. Closed Aug. **Credit** AmEx, DC, MC, V. **Map** p318 D2.
Tuscan sculptor Roberto Barni's bronze men sit nonchalantly in the middle of this stately space, while Dormice's bimbos gaze down from canvases.

Galleria Biagiotti Arte Contemporanea

Via delle Belle Donne 39r, Santa Maria Novella (055 214757/www.artbiagiotti.com). **Open** 2-7pm Tue-Sat. Closed Aug. **Credit** AmEx, MC, V. **Map** p318 B2.
Carole Biagiotti runs this stunning 15th-century converted atrium gallery like a fairy godmother. The innovative exhibitions feature works by young artists; pieces often sell to collectors sight unseen.

Galleria Pananti

Via Maggio 15, Oltrarno (055 2741011/www. pananti.com). **Open** 9.30am-1pm, 3-7pm Mon-Fri. Closed Aug. **No credit cards**. **Map** p319 C5.
One of the most important art hubs of the city, this gallery and art auction house hosts major contemporary shows and retrospectives of renowned modern artists, with the emphasis on the Tuscan tradition of figurative photography and painting.

Galleria Il Ponte

Via di Mezzo 42B, Santa Maria Novella (055 240617). **Open** *Sept-June* 4-7.30pm Tue-Sat. *July* 4-7.30pm Mon-Fri. Closed Aug. **No credit cards**. **Map** p319 B6.
Mostly modern and contemporary abstract painters and sculptors feature in major retrospectives at this respected gallery and art publishing house.

Galleria Santo Ficara

Via Ghibellina 164r, Santa Croce (055 2340239/ www.santoficara.it). **Open** 9.30am-12.30pm, 3.30-7.30pm Mon-Sat. Closed Aug. **Credit** AmEx, DC, MC, V. **Map** p319 C5.
The walls of this important city-centre gallery, with its tall vaulted ceilings, are hung with works by established artists with an international market, such as 1950s Gruppo Forma member Carla Accardi.

Galleria Tornabuoni

Via de' Tornabuoni 74r, Duomo & Around (055 284720/www.galleriatornabuoni.it). **Open** 3.30-7.30pm Mon; 9.30am-1pm, 3.30-7.30pm Tue-Sat. **Credit** AmEx, DC, MC, V. **Map** p318 B2.
The prestigious home to artists including Francesco Musante, whose work features on postcards around town. Guiliano Tomaino's rocking horses are also sold.

Poggiali e Forconi.

Isabella Brancolini
Vicolo dell'Oro 12r, Duomo & Around (055 2396263/www.isabellabrancolini.it). **Open** 10am-7.30pm Mon-Fri. Closed Aug. **No credit cards.** **Map** p318 C3.

A pool of a dozen emerging artists from all over the world are chosen for their originality and outlandish styles at this prime riverbank location, part of the Gallery Hotel Art and Lungarno Suites (*see p51*).

Ken's Art Gallery
Via Lambertesca 15-17r, Duomo & Around (055 2396587/www.kensartgallery.com). **Open** 10am-1pm, 3-8pm Mon-Sat. **Credit** AmEx, DC, MC, V. **Map** p318 C3.

Walter Bellini's exciting gallery has several artists in residence. Contemporary pieces, all by Florence artists, include Paolo Staccioli's Etruscan-inspired decorated urns and warrior busts.

Mirabili
Lungarno Guicciardini 21r, Oltrarno (055 294257/ www.mirabili.it). **Open** 3-7.30pm Mon; 9.30am-1pm, 3-7.30pm Tue-Sat. Closed Aug. **Credit** AmEx, DC, MC, V. **Map** p318 C2.

Its slogan is 'Art of Living', and it's easy to see why: the fabulous collections of furniture, *objets* and artworks have been shown at the Pompidou Centre. Artists include Ettore Sottsass and Max Ernst.

Poggiali e Forconi
Via della Scala 35A, Santa Maria Novella (055 287748/www.poggialieforconi.it). **Open** Oct-May 9.30am-1.30pm, 3-7pm Mon-Sat. *June-Sept* 9.30am-1.30pm Mon-Sat. Closed 2wks Aug. **Credit** AmEx, DC, MC, V. **Map** p318 B2.

This series of arched spaces showcases the works of some of Italy's best-known young artists. Shows have featured Livio Scarpella's brash nudes.

Quarter
Viale Giannotti 81, Outside the City Gates (055 6802555). Bus 23, 31, 32. **Open** 4-8pm Tue-Sun; also by appointment. **No credit cards.**

This much-ballyhooed space is a rare example of cooperation between the public and private sectors. The enormous space is far enough from the beaten track to put off all but the most dedicated of visitors; for locals, though, it represents a giant leap forwards.

Consumer art

One of the city's most crucial contributions to modern art comes from the restaurants, bars and hotels that show the work of local artists, often commission-free. Potential customers are normally put in direct contact with the artist.

Astor Caffè
For listings, *see p129*.

Astor's huge central skylight helps create the perfect environment for its regular exhibitions of local photographers and bas-relief sculptors.

BZF (Bizzeffe)
For listings, *see p132 and p176*.

As well as hosting jazz gigs and serving grown-up brunches, BZF runs lectures and shows. Artists include Maria Pecchioli, whose polychromatic visions of youth are in stark contrast to the minimalist surroundings. There's also a bookshop.

Gallery Hotel Art
For listings, *see p49*.

Resident expert Isabella Brancolini (*see above*) organises the innovative two-monthly art cycles at this avant-garde hotel. Shows have included the vivid celluloid images of lens legend David La Chapelle.

Rex Art Bar
Via Fiesolana 25r, Santa Croce (055 2480331/ www.rexcafe.it). **Open** 6pm-3.30am daily. Closed mid May-Aug. **Map** p319 B5.

A backlit bronze wall by artist Giacomo Solfanelli vies for attention with Rex's trademark mosaics and exhibitions of paintings in the Red Room, among them Andrea Orani's colourful abstracts and Marina Lainati's plaintive portraits.

Arts & Entertainment

Gay & Lesbian

Out and about.

Though Florence has been popular with gay writers, artists and travellers for centuries, it was only in 1970 that the city got its first proper gay disco, **Tabasco**, a venue that's still going strong today.

Around the same time, the Fronte Unitario Omosessuale Rivoluzionario Italiano (FUORI – Italian for 'out'), Tuscany's first gay and lesbian organisation, was set up by members of the Radical Party. Other landmarks included the opening of the gay cultural space Banana Moon in Borgo degli Albizi in 1977 and the founding of the regional chapter of ARCIGay/Lesbica, the leading organisation for gay political initiatives in Italy, in the 1980s. In the mid '90s the latter split into two groups: **IREOS** is a social, cultural and information centre, while **Azione Gay e Lesbica** focuses on political issues.

As far as gay etiquette is concerned, in Florence and Tuscany there should be no problem with holding hands in the streets, but anything much more overt than this in public is less acceptable (aside from in the major gay resorts). For gay men there are lots of cruising areas, though some can be dangerous. The **Parco delle Cascine**, for instance, is active from sunset till late at night, but local cognoscenti warn against it. Another popular area is the **Campo di Marte** (in eastern Florence), where most cruising takes place in cars. The park at **Viale Malta** near the football stadium is active too, but subject to frequent incursions from police checking IDs.

The age of consent in Italy is 18, and clubs and bars will check, so bring ID with you. For some venues you will need an ArciGay/Lesbica membership card, which currently costs €14 per year and is available at any of the venues that require it (we have marked these below).

Florence

Bars

BK Bar-Butterfly Kiss
Via Alfieri 95, Sesto Fiorentino, Outside the City Gates (055 4218878). Bus 2, 28. **Open** 7am-2am daily. **Admission** free. **No credit cards.**
This pub may not be centrally located but it's nonetheless highly popular with women, who come for the parlour games, themed performances and photography exhibitions.

Crisco
Via San Egidio 43r, Santa Croce (055 2480580/ www.crisco.it). **Open** 11am-3am Mon, Wed, Thur, Sun; 10pm-6am Fri, Sat. Reduced opening 2wks Feb. **Membership. Credit** MC, V. **Map** p318 B5.
A well-known, long-standing bar with (mostly X-rated) videos, special events, parties and a variety of performances. The exclusively male crowd is mixed but leathermen and bears prevail.

O!O Bar
Piazza Piattellina 7r, Oltrarno (055 212917/ www.oiobarconcucina.it). **Open** 9am-2am daily. **Admission** free. **Credit** AmEx, MC, V.
A new locale in the central San Frediano area, this is a good place for breakfast, lunch and dinner, as well as a Mediterranean-style Sunday brunch, where you can catch chamber music, poetry performances and book presentations.

Monthly party at **Auditorium FLOG**.
See p169.

Piccolo Caffè
Borgo Santa Croce 23, Santa Croce (055 2001057).
Open 6.30pm-2.30am daily. **Admission** free.
Credit AmEx, DC, MC, V. **Map** p318 C5.
Attracting a very mixed crowd, the Piccolo gets especially crowded on Saturdays. Check out the frequent contemporary art exhibitions and live shows.

Yagb@r
Via de' Macci 8r, Santa Croce (055 2469022/ www.yagbar.com). **Open** 9pm-3am daily. **Admission** free. **Credit** AmEx, DC, MC, V. **Map** p318 C6.
This spacious, futurist dance-bar draws a young crowd of both genders. There's internet access and video games, too. It plays the latest music and is a popular first stop on the club-hopping route.

Clubs

Azione Gay e Lesbica at Auditorium FLOG
Via Michele Mercati 24B, Poggetto, Outside the City Gates (055 240397). Bus 4, 8, 14, 20, 28. **Open** 10pm-4am 1st Fri of mth; call for details.
Admission €10. **No credit cards.**
Once a month on a Friday, a megafest of DJs, cabaret acts and bands draws a huge and diverse crowd out to this Poggetto venue in support of Azione Gay e Lesbica. It's also a great place to stock up on literature and information on all the latest goings-on in the local gay community.

Fabrik
Via del Lavoro 19, Calenzano (349 8906645/ www.fabrikfirenze.it). Bus 2, 28. **Open** 4pm-3am Mon-Thur, Sun; 4pm-5am Fri, Sat. **Admission** €8-€10 with ArciGay/Lesbica membership.
No credit cards.
About 15km (nine miles) from Florence, Fabrik is two storeys of post-industrial decor, featuring a video-bar and an open-air garden. There is a cruising area with roomy cabins and a darkroom.

Tabasco Disco Gay
Piazza Santa Cecilia 3r, Duomo & Around (055 213000/www.tabascogay.it). **Open** 10pm-6am Tue-Sun. **Admission** €13 Tue-Fri, Sun; €15 Sat. **Credit** AmEx, MC, V. **Map** p319 C5.
Florence's first gay club, founded more than 35 years ago, Tabasco has stood the test of time and remains popular among tourists and young locals of both sexes. The music is mostly techno, with some '70s-style disco thrown in.

Tenax
Via Pratese 46, Peretola, Outside the City Gates (055 308160/www.tenax.org). Bus 29, 30. **Open** 10pm-4am Sat. Closed mid May-Sept. **Admission** €25 women; €30 men. **Credit** AmEx, MC, V.
Saturday nights at this trendy Peretola club go by the name of Nobody's Perfect. But, hey, that doesn't stop an international fashion crowd going all out to look absolutely flawless – so make sure you dress the part. *See also p177 and p180.*

Saunas

Florence Baths
Via Guelfa 93r, San Lorenzo (055 216050).
Open 2pm-2am Mon-Thur, Sun; 2pm-4am Fri, Sat. **Admission** €13 Mon-Fri; €14 Sat, Sun. **Membership** €6/yr. **Credit** AmEx, MC, V. **Map** p318 A3.
Florence's only sauna offers dry sauna and steam (the steam room is excellent), Jacuzzi (always cold), bar, TV and private rooms. The crowd is mixed and friendly. Best to arrive late afternoon/early evening.

Services

For HIV testing, community information, counselling and other services offered by **Azione Gay e Lesbica** and **IREOS**, *see p289.*

Bed & breakfasts

All the following are gay-friendly options.
For the centrally located **Dei Mori**, *see p54.*

Casa Visconti
Via Santa Maria 3, Oltrarno (055 229019/ www.viscontirooms.it). **Rates** €46 single; €77 double. **Credit** MC, V. **Map** p318 D1.
This small, comfortable B&B offers the experience of life in one of the city's traditional neighbourhoods.

Soggiorno Gloria
Via Nazionale 17, San Lorenzo (055 288147/ www.soggiornogloria.com). **Rates** €40 single; €80-€100 double. **Credit** AmEx, DC, MC, V. **Map** p318 A3.
A pleasant and comfortable hotel with big, bright rooms and generous balconies overlooking the old heart of Florence near the train station.

Tuscany

The **Versilia Riviera** is becoming something of a gay mecca, with loads of gay-friendly and/or gay-owned clubs, bars and beaches. Near Viareggio, **Torre del Lago Puccini** (often just called Torre del Lago) is home to another clutch of clubs, events, concerts and festivals. For a week in mid August it celebrates a 'friendly' Mardi Gras, with music by well-known artists, plus, films, theatre, cabaret and photography exhibitions. The festival is directed by Gay.it (http://it.gay.com), which provides useful information on cultural events, trips and accommodation. In addition, a Friendly Versilia consortium was recently set up, in a bid to unite shops, bars and restaurants in helping to boost the area's gay tourism.
The **Maremma**, too, is growing in importance: in 2004 **Grosseto** held its first Gay Pride, which proved to be an enormous success.

Arts & Entertainment

Florence Baths. See p169.

Maremma

Fiesta!

c/o Coruna Beach, Principina a Mare, Grosseto (338 6119228/www.grossetogay.it). **Open** 11am-4am 1st Sat of mth. **Admission** €10; €7 with ArciGay/Lesbica membership. **No credit cards.**
Fiesta! is held one Saturday night a month for gays, lesbians, transsexuals and bisexuals, with brief performances by male and female dancers and drag queens, and music by DJ Matteo.

Pisa

Absolut

Via Mossoti 10 (050 2201262). **Open** 8pm-late Tue-Sun. **Admission** free with ArciGay/Lesbica membership. **No credit cards.**
Mixed high-tech, DJ bar.

Sauna Siesta Club 77

Via di Porta a Mare 25-27 (050 2200146). **Open** *Mid May-late June* 5pm-1am daily. *Late June-Aug* 8.30pm-1am daily. *Early Sept-early May* 3pm-1am daily. Closed 2wks mid July. **Admission** €12; €10 with ArciGay/Lesbica membership. **No credit cards.**
A bathhouse with sauna, steam, Jacuzzi, video and private rooms.

Pistoia

Montecatini Thermas

Corso Matteotti 121, Pieve a Nievole, Montecatini Terme (0572 81652). **Open** 10pm-4am daily. **Admission** €15, plus €10 membership Mon-Thur; €20, plus €10 membership Fri, Sat. **Credit** V.
New, elegant sauna on two floors. Recommended.

Torre del Lago

Bar Notturno

Via Aurelia 220, Piazza del Popolo (0584 341359). **Open** 7am-3am Mon, Wed-Fri; 7am-6am Sat, Sun. **No credit cards.**
Coffee and breakfast after all-night dancing.

B&B Fate e Folletti

Via Garibaldi 33 (0584 350546/www.fateefolletti. com). **Rates** €34-€46 single; €62-€86 double. **Credit** MC, V.
Located in a beautiful Liberty-style building in the centre of town, with a big flowery garden.

Bed & Breakfast Libano

Via Tabarro 23 (0584 340631). Closed Nov-Jan. **Rates** €40-€65 double for single occupancy; €100-€170 double. **Credit** AmEx, DC, MC, V.
A relaxed B&B situated on the lake. It also organises parties on the premises. Booking essential.

Boca Chica

Viale Europa 30 (0584 350976). **Open** 1pm-2am Tue-Sun. Closed 2wks Nov, 2wks Feb. **Admission** free. **Credit** MC, V.
A seafront bar with music. The garden quickly fills up with a trendy young crowd.

Caffeletti

Via Pardini 34C (347 1964685/www.caffeletti.com). **Rates** €40 single; €80 double. **No credit cards.**
Set in a quiet location amid greenery, this is the closest B&B to the beach, popular gay venues and the Torre del Lago nature reserve.

Frau Marlene

Viale Europa (0584 342282). **Open** 10pm-4am Fri-Sun. **Admission** €15. **Credit** AmEx, MC, V.
Gays and lesbians of all ages consider a stopoff here to be a vital part of any summer night's itinerary.

Hub

Via di Poggio 29 (389 6262642). **Open** 11pm-5am Sat. Closed 1st 2wks June & 1st 2wks Sept. **Admission** €12. **No credit cards.**
A great place for a boogie, with various music zones pumping out house, funk, techno and more.

Mamma Mia

Viale Europa 5 (389 6262642/www.mammamia.tv). **Open** noon-4am daily. Closed Nov-Apr. **Admission** free. **Credit** MC, V.
DJs play to a big and varied crowd at nightly themed parties here. Other attractions include a lounge bar and a terrace overlooking the sea.

Priscilla

Viale Europa (0584 341804/www.priscillacaffe.it). **Open** 10am-5am Tue-Sun. **Credit** MC, V.
Ably managed by Regina, this is a real hotspot, with great music, a pub atmosphere and drag queen performances. It also serves snacks and has net access.

Viareggio

Voice Music Bar

Viale Margherita 63 (0584 45814/www.galleria deldisco.com). **Open** *Summer* 10am-2am daily. *Winter* 9.30am-2am Tue-Sun. **Admission** free. **No credits cards.**
A friendly seafront bar with an electric music selection to match the very mixed crowds who go there.

Music: Classical & Opera

Florence plays it safe, but tunefully.

Zubin Mehta at the **Teatro del Maggio Musicale Fiorentino**. *See p172.*

See p172.

Florence was once at the very forefront of musical culture. Opera was 'invented' in the city, thanks to the work of the Florentine Camerata, a group of intellectuals who experimented with the setting of words to music in the mid 15th century. Pieri and Caccini's *Euridice*, widely considered to be the world's first opera, was performed in the Boboli Gardens in 1600. Florence's musical importance continued into the early 17th century under the last Medicis.

Sadly, the same cannot be said of the musical life in the city at the beginning of the 21st century. Florentines are conservative in their musical tastes – and in many other things, for that matter – and they prefer to stick with familiar territory when it comes to the classical repertoire; as a result, most of the music you'll hear at opera performances and classical concerts will be mainstream. That said, however, there is plenty going on for a small city, and music lovers should find something to keep them happy.

Opera has a special place in the heart of many an Italian, and if you get the chance to catch a production at the **Teatro del Maggio Musicale Fiorentino** (*see p172*), go for it. A performance of a Puccini or Verdi opera by a good Italian orchestra and chorus is almost always a worthwhile experience, and the standards at Florence's municipal theatre are generally high. With the odd exception, however, productions are unlikely to be avant-garde; the Florentines don't take kindly to directors messing with their favourite operas, and any experimenting is likely to be met with slating critiques and disappointing audiences. And given the present financial climate at the Teatro del Maggio, few risks are being taken.

Although programmes suffer from the same tendency towards conservatism, there's lots in the way of symphonic and chamber concerts, with two resident symphony orchestras, a clutch of smaller groups and a world-class chamber music series. Smaller events are promoted on fly posters and in local papers

Orchestra della Toscana. *See p174.*

and listings magazines. From June to October there are concerts in churches, plus outdoor concerts at villas, gardens and museums, some of them free. They're not all well advertised, but tourist offices usually have information. For events outside Florence, *see p173* **Seasons in the sun**.

TICKET INFORMATION

For main ticket agencies, *see p154*. Many hotels and travel agents also book tickets for the biggest venues.

Tickets for the Teatro del Maggio can be hard to come by, as many seats are taken by holders of season tickets. Advance bookings for the opera and concert seasons (Sept-Mar) open around mid September. Tickets for the **Maggio Musicale Fiorentino** (*see p157*) go on sale in early April. You can book online (www.maggio fiorentino.com) using a credit card up to a week before the performance. Phone bookings through the theatre's own ticket office (*see below*) cannot be paid for with credit cards; those made through the call centre (199 112112, only within Italy) can.

If you can't get a seat in advance, turn up on the night for the chance of a return or one of the restricted-vision seats that go on sale an hour before the start of each performance. For chamber concerts and Orchestra Regionale Toscana concerts, tickets are usually available on the door half an hour beforehand, but the safest idea is to go to the box office in good time with cash: not all theatres accept plastic.

TICKET PRICES

At the Teatro del Maggio tickets for the opening night of an opera range from €25 to €35 in the upper circle, and from €55 to €85 for a box or stalls seat. Repeat performances cost a little less. Symphonic concerts cost from €20 to €30 and ballets from €11 to €25. Restricted-view seats are around €11-€25.

Tickets for the Orchestra Regionale Toscana concerts at the Teatro Verdi cost €12-€15, while the Amici della Musica series at the Teatro della Pergola costs €11-€20/€16-€29 Saturday/Sunday per seat.

One-off concerts don't usually cost more than €15, and some outdoor events or concerts in churches are free.

Venues

Accademia Bartolomeo Cristofori

Via di Camaldoli 7r, Oltrarno (055 221646). **Open** by appointment only.

Named after the inventor of the piano, the academy houses a fine private collection of early keyboard instruments, as well as a workshop for restoration and repair. Chamber concerts and seminars are held in a beautiful little hall next door.

Chiesa Luterana

Lungarno Torrigiani 11, Oltrarno (tourist office 055 290832). **Map** p319 D4.

Organ recitals and other chamber music, often involving early repertoire, are held at Florence's Lutheran church all year – and are usually free.

Scuola Musica di Fiesole

Villa La Torraccia, San Domenico, Fiesole (055 597851/www.scuolamusica.fiesole.fi.it). Bus 7 then 10min walk. **Open** 8.30am-8.30pm Mon-Sat.

One of Italy's most famous music schools occupies a 16th-century villa set in beautiful grounds. The annual Festa della Musica, a musical open day with concerts and workshops by pupils, is held on 24 June, while the Concerti per gli Amici series takes place in the 200-seat auditorium from September/October to June.

Teatro Goldoni

Via Santa Maria 15, Oltrarno (055 229651/Teatro Comunale 055 213535). **Open** *Box office* 1hr before performance. **Map** p318 D1.

This divine little theatre in Oltrarno dates from the early 18th century and seats only 400 people. A long-drawn-out restoration was finally finished in the late 1990s and the theatre is now partially under the direction of the Teatro del Maggio (*see below*). It's used – though not regularly enough – for chamber music, small-scale opera and ballet.

Teatro del Maggio Musicale Fiorentino

Corso Italia 16, Santa Maria Novella (box office 055 213535/phone bookings 199 112112 within Italy/ 0424 600458 abroad/www.maggiofiorentino.com). **Open** *Phone bookings* 8am-8pm Mon-Fri; 8am-3pm Sat. *Box office* 10am-4.30pm Tue-Fri; 10am-1pm Sat; 1hr before performance.

Florence's municipal opera house is in deep financial trouble, most immediately due to the reduction of state funding and an increased dependency on private contributions, which are

Seasons in the sun

There's something about hearing music in the setting of a beautiful church or cloister, a historic piazza, an elegant villa or a tiny, restored theatre that is compelling even for people who don't normally 'do' classical music and opera. Tuscany is a great place to indulge such urges, as seasons and festivals spring up all over the place, particularly in the summer months. Some of these events have a high enough profile to be well advertised, while others often go unnoticed by anyone not in the know. So read the local press and posters and search out the smaller, one-off performances, as well as the better-known seasons listed below.

Events worth looking out for include the **Estate Musicale Chigiana** series of concerts in Siena and at such gorgeous venues as the nearby abbeys of San Galgano and Sant'Antimo (July-Aug, 0577 22091); the **Tavernelle Val di Pesa** concerts at the Badia in Passignano monastery (late May, tourist office 055 8077832); the **Barga Opera Festival**, which features productions of little-known operas (July-mid Aug, 0583 723250); the **Incontri in Terra di Siena** chamber music festival based at La Foce in the Val d'Orcia (late July, 0578 69101, www.lafoce.com); the **Puccini Opera Festival**, during which several of the Lucca-born composer's favourite operas are performed on the lakeside near his villa in Torre del Lago (0584 359322); the **Tuscan Sun Festival**, inaugurated in 2003 on the back of Francis Mayes' bestseller *Under the Tuscan Sun*, and featuring high-profile conductors and singers for two weeks of music in Cortona (Aug, 0575 630353, www.tuscansun

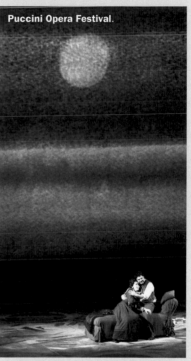

Puccini Opera Festival.

festival.com), and the **International Choral Festival** in Impruneta (June; tourist office 055 2313729).

Local tourist offices can supply further information about these and other events.

inadequate. The theatre has gargantuan overheads: it sustains a full orchestra, chorus and ballet company, plus armies of administrative, technical and domestic staff. Clearly cutbacks need to be made, but the unions make it hard.

Financial worries aside, the theatre has a lot going for it, and plans are being made to build a much-needed new theatre, paid for with a mix of private and public funding. A period of artistic stability and a rise in the number of young orchestra and chorus members have resulted in higher performance standards than for a while. The charismatic Zubin Mehta is nearing retirement, but is currently still in place as principal conductor. When on form, the Teatro del Maggio's resident orchestra and chorus are on a level with La Scala in Milan. However, lack of funds

means that big-name conductors and soloists are often padded out with mediocre unknowns who just don't get the same results. It also means that risks can't be taken in terms of repertoire. A major disappointment in the 2005 Maggio festival was the cancellation of Benjamin Britten's *The Turn of the Screw*. Cash was short and something had to go.

The theatre's performing year is divided roughly into three parts: January to March is the concert season, with performances on Fridays, Saturdays and Sundays (the programme changes each week); October to December is the opera and ballet season, with about four operatic productions, a couple of ballets and the odd concert; and the Maggio Musicale Fiorentino festival (founded in 1933 and one of the oldest in Europe; see p157) runs for two

Arts & Entertainment

months from late April/early May. The latter offers a mix of opera, ballet, concerts and recital programmes, and usually culminates in a free open-air concert in Piazza della Signoria.

The theatre building itself, constructed in 1882 and renovated in 1957, is architecturally unexciting. Of the 2,000-odd seats, the best acoustics are to be had in the second gallery (they are also the cheapest), but if you want to strut your stuff alongside the designer outfits of *Firenze per bene*, you need to fork out for an opening night in the stalls or one of the *palchi* (boxes).

Teatro della Pergola

Via della Pergola 12-32, San Marco (055 2264316/ www.pergola.firenze.it). Open Box office 9.30am-1pm, 3.30-6.45pm Tue-Sat; 10am-12.15pm Sun. **Season** Oct-Apr. **Map** p319 A5/B5.

Inaugurated in 1656, the exquisite, intimate Pergola is one of Italy's oldest theatres. Richly decorated in red and gold and with three layers of boxes, it's ideal for chamber music and small-scale operas. The excellent series of chamber music concerts promoted by the Amici della Musica (*see below*) is held here, while the Teatro del Maggio also uses it for opera during Maggio Musicale (*see p157*).

Teatro Verdi

Via Ghibellina 99, Santa Croce (055 212320/ www.teatroverdifirenze.it). Open Box office 10am-1pm, 4-9pm Mon-Sat. **Season** Sept-June. **Map** p319 C5.

This large theatre has just been revamped. It is the principal venue used for concerts by the Orchestra della Toscana (*see below*).

Tempo Reale

Villa Strozzi, Via Pisana 77, Monte Uliveto, Outside the City Gates (055 717270/www.centrotempo reale.it). Bus 6, 12, 13, 26, 27, 80. **Open** Box office 9am-1pm, 2-6pm Mon-Fri.

Set up by the late Luciano Berio in 1987, this widely renowned centre for contemporary music is dedicated to the research, development and use of new technologies in music. Concerts, workshops and seminars are held.

Performance groups/ promoters

Amici della Musica

055 608420/607440/www.amicimusica.fi.it.
This organisation, founded in 1906, promotes world-class chamber music concerts, most presented at the Teatro della Pergola (*see above*), from September through to late April/early May. Every year the programme includes some of the world's great string quartets and recitalists such as Radu Lupu, Andras Schiff, the English Chamber Orchestra and the Tokyo String Quartet; early music groups appear regularly too. Concerts are usually held on Saturdays and Sundays at 4pm or 9pm.

L'Homme Armé

055 695000/www.hommearme.it.
The repertoire of this small, semi-professional chamber choir ranges from medieval to baroque. It gives about ten concerts a year in Florence (no fixed venue) and runs excellent courses on aspects of early music. Baroque harpist Andrew Lawrence-King makes regular appearances as guest director.

Orchestra da Camera Fiorentina

055 783374/www.orcafi.it.
Under the direction of violinist Giuseppe Lanzetta, this young chamber orchestra plays a season of mostly baroque and classical concerts on Sunday and Monday nights from February to September. The past few seasons have been held in the church of Orsanmichele; standards are generally mixed.

Orchestra della Toscana

055 2340710/www.orchestradellatoscana.it.
If you're looking for something creative, it's well worth trying to catch a concert given by the Orchestra della Toscana. Founded in 1980 with the brief of taking classical music into Tuscany, it has a dynamic management team and artistic director, who are responsible for a wider repertoire than that of the Maggio orchestra. Particular emphasis is given to rarely heard 19th-century music, early 20th-century composers and contemporary works, but there is plenty more besides. International names frequently appear as soloists and conductors, and during the season (November/December-May) the orchestra gives two or three concerts a month in Florence at the Teatro Verdi (*see above*), and up to 40 in other Tuscan towns.

Festivals

In addition to the following, *see also p192* **Estate Fiesolana**, *p157* **Maggio Musicale Fiorentino** and *p158* **Effetto Venezia**, three events with strong musical content. For **Estate Musicale Chigiana**, **Puccini Opera Festival** and **Incontri in Terra di Siena**, *see p173* **Seasons in the sun**.

Christmas Concert

Teatro Verdi (055 2340710/tickets 055 212320). **Map** p318 C5. **Date** 24 Dec.

The concert, staged by the Orchestra Regionale Toscana, has a different programme and conductor every year.

New Year Concert

Teatro Comunale (055 597851). **Date** 1 Jan.
Put on by the Scuola di Musica di Fiesole. Call the above number for free tickets.

Settembre Musica

Teatro della Pergola & other venues (055 608420/ www.amicimusica.fi.it). **Date** Sept.
A month of early music concerts, by young or relatively obscure ensembles with the odd bigger name.

Music: Rock, Roots & Jazz

No need to get the blues: Florence's music scene is livelier than you'd expect.

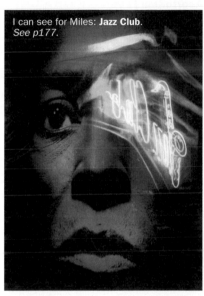

I can see for Miles: **Jazz Club**. *See p177*.

To visual aesthetes, Florence may be just an open-air museum. However, given the city's small size, there's actually quite a lot going on in the way of live music. While the city is a stop on the touring itineraries of only a handful of big international names, it's better for local or low-level live acts, especially for jazz and roots.

One of the best ways to find out what's on when you're in Florence is to drop into one of the city's record shops (*see p153*). The dance music scene thrives through them – many shops are owned by big-name local DJs – but you can also pick up flyers promoting upcoming gigs, festivals and other events. For information on jazz events, contact **Musicus Concentus** (Piazza del Carmine 19, 055 287347), which promotes gigs in Florence and Tuscany and can give information on forthcoming events. Regardless of genre, to book tickets for concerts, call the venue direct or contact the Box Office ticket agency (055 210804, www.boxol.it; *see p154*).

Bigger venues

Palasport Mandela Forum
Viale Paoli, Outside the City Gates (055 678841).
Bus 3. **Tickets** prices vary. **No credit cards.**
This 7,000-capacity hall is where Florence houses major touring artists, both Italian stars like Eros Ramazzotti and international acts such as Elton John. Advance tickets are available from Box Office (*see p153*).

Sala Vanni
Piazza del Carmine 14, Oltrarno (055 287347/
www.musicusconcentus.com). **Tickets** €12-€15.
No credit cards. Map p318 C1.
Sadly under-used, this large warehouse-like auditorium is a great place to hear good progressive jazz and contemporary classical groups. The venue hosts a sparse but excellent series of concerts organised by Musicus Concentus (*see also p263* **And the beat goes on**) during the autumn and winter months.

Saschall-Teatro di Firenze
Via Fabrizio de André, cnr Lungarno A Moro 3,
Outside the City Gates (055 6504112/www.saschall.
it). Bus 14. **Tickets** prices vary. **Credit** AmEx, DC, MC, V.
This tent-shaped, 4,000-capacity venue hosts a variety of mainstream acts from Italy and abroad. The upper balconies have seating, but you should choose

The best Venues

For great acoustics
Saschall-Teatro di Firenze (*see above*).

For cult imports
Tenax (*see p177*).

For jazz with a view
Golden View and **Le Rime Rampanti** (for both, *see p177*).

For serious jazz
BZF (*see p176*) and **Sala Vanni** (*see above*).

For a friendly atmosphere
Caruso Jazz Café (*see p176*).

Arts & Entertainment

the main standing hall downstairs if you're there for sound rather than comfort. Saschall hosts annual events, including a St Patrick's Day knees-up.

Stadio Artemio Franchi
Viale Manfredo Fanti 14, Campo di Marte,
Outside the City Gates (055 667566). Bus 11, 17.
Tickets prices vary. **No credit cards.**
When not even the Palasport Mandela Forum (*see p175*) is big enough – as is the case for acts such as Italian megastar Vasco Rossi – then this football stadium moonlights as a music venue. The covered *tribuna* has the dearest numbered seats; *curva Fiesole* seats are the cheapest (and, it follows, the furthest from the stage).

Auditorium FLOG.

Smaller venues

Admission to all the following venues is free unless otherwise stated.

Astor Caffè
For listings, *see p129*.
Sporadic music nights are held in this sparkling bar. Sounds cover the jazzy spectrum, from Latin and bossa nova via smooth jazz to the blues.

Auditorium FLOG
Via M Mercati 24B, Outside the City Gates
(055 487145/www.flog.it). Bus 4, 8, 14, 20, 28.
Open 10pm-late Tue-Sat (call for details). Closed June-Aug. **Tickets** €8-€13. **No credit cards.**
At FLOG, which has shows Thursday to Saturday, music runs from rock to Tex Mex, with Fridays often dedicated to reggae and ska. A DJ plays after the bands. Dance parties and other theatrical showcases occur earlier in the week; the venue also hosts the Rassegna Internazionale Musica dei Popoli (*see p177*).

Be Bop
Via dei Servi 76r, San Marco (no phone).
Open times vary, but usually 6pm-1am daily.
No credit cards. Map p319 A4.
This sweaty underground cave attracts a brat pack of foreign students, leavened by a handful of brooding arty types. There's music on nearly every night, though it's rarely original (blues tunes, Beatles covers, reggae classics). Drinks are not the cheapest, but on Mondays, when many other clubs are closed, there's a free shot with every beer.

BZF (Bizzeffe)
For listings, *see p132*.
Florence's studiously serious jazz lovers have been blessed with unique surroundings in which to stroke their beards: the vaulted salons of this converted convent are stunning. There's jazz every Tuesday and many Fridays; the bar, restaurant, art space and bookshop keep the mind and mouth busy in between.

Caffè la Torre
Lungarno Cellini 65r, Oltrarno (055 680643/
www.caffelatorre.it). **Open** 10.30am-3am daily.
Credit AmEx, DC, MC, V. **Map** p319 D6.
This riverside café is a fine place for an aperitif or a late snack, but it also stages near-nightly music, anything from polka to Brazilian beats. *See also p182*.

Caruso Jazz Café
For listings, *see p130*.
This cavernous bar is a magnet for talented jazzers, including many famed Italians. Every Thursday, Friday and Saturday, jazz echoes around the bar's brick vaults in a buzzy atmosphere.

Eskimo
Via de' Canacci 12, Santa Maria Novella (no phone).
Open 6pm-4am daily. **Admission** €6 annual membership. **No credit cards. Map** p318 A1.

Tiny Eskimo's communal wooden tables burst with exuberant crowds of Italian university students. Head here to catch local groups – Neapolitan to rock – jamming with Santa Claus-like owner Lalo on the piano. There's live music at about 11pm nightly.

Girasol

Via del Romito 1, Outside the City Gates (055 474948/www.girasol.it). Bus 14. **Open** 8pm-2.30am Tue-Sun. Closed June-Aug. **No credit cards.**
Trying its best to be a Little Havana, Girasol is the best place in town to catch Latin sounds. The dim lighting and flamboyantly fruity cocktails appeal, but while the Latin rhythms might tempt you to your feet, there's scant space for you to get your swerve on. Crowds start arriving around 11pm; aim for 10pm to be sure of a table. Drink prices are a bit steep.

Golden View

Via de' Bardi 58r, Oltrarno (055 214502/ www.goldenviewopenbar.com). **Open** 11.30am-2am daily. **Credit** AmEx, DC, MC, V. **Map** p319 D4.
The uninspiring decor of this restaurant and bar is more than made up for by the direct views afforded of the Ponte Vecchio and Uffizi. The jazz comes from pianist Antonio Figura, who performs on Mondays, Wednesdays and Sundays in duos and trios.

Jazz Club

Via Nuova de' Caccini 3, Santa Croce (055 2479700). **Open** 9pm-2am Mon-Fri; 9pm-2.30am Sat. Closed July, Aug. **Admission** €5 annual membership. **No credit cards. Map** p319 B5.
One of the few places in Florence where you can hear live jazz almost nightly. Performers range from traditional bands to fusion and experimental groups, with evenings dedicated to the likes of blues and flamenco. There's an open session on Tuesdays, a big band on Thursdays and the Jazz Club Gospel choir two Sundays a month. The club's latest initiative of the club is the *jazzperitivo*, the club's own take on the city's *aperitivo* fad taking over the city's early nightlife (*see p184* **Night nibbles**). It's popular with large party groups, but there are a few smaller tables set aside for more intimate conversation.

Loonees

Via Porta Rossa 15r, Duomo & Around (055 212249). **Open** 8pm-3am Tue-Sun. Closed Aug. **No credit cards. Map** p318 C3.
Loonees brims nightly with tipsy foreign students, random punters and locals out on the pull. Sounds range from reggae and rock covers to Italian pop and blues (courtesy of Jeff Jones, who plays Saturdays). Two bars offer free shots with every beer, which may help assuage those with a more critical ear; the two-for-one happy hour (8-10pm) also doesn't do any harm. The vaulted ceiling captures the sound well.

Pinocchio Jazz

Viale Giannotti 13, Outside the City Gates (055 683388/680362/www.pinocchiojazz.it). Bus 23. **Open** 9.30pm-2am Sat. Closed May-Oct. **Admission** €7.50. **No credit cards.**

The quality acts and friendly staff make up for Pinocchio's lack of atmosphere. The joint books international names as well as Italian artists playing in a variety of styles. A mellow, older clientele tends to fill up the small stage area around 9.30pm.

Stazione Leopolda

Fratelli Rosselli 5, Outside the City Gates (055 2638480/2480515). Bus 17, 22. **Tickets** prices vary. **Credit** MC, V.
This huge disused station is beloved of street-chic designers, who host catwalk shows here, but it's also occasionally called into service by dance acts such as Groove Armada. The Fabbrica Europa performing arts festival is held here (*see p192*).

Tenax

Via Pratese 46, Outside the City Gates (055 308160/ www.tenax.org). Bus 29, 30. **Open** 10.30pm-4am Thur-Sat. Closed mid May-Sept. **Tickets** prices vary. **Credit** AmEx, MC, V.
New Order played here in the 1980s, with Basement Jaxx visiting in the '90s, but Tenax's cult-ish line-ups are still strong in the 21st century. The club has a huge raised dancefloor and antechambers stuffed with computers, pool tables and bars for post-gig entertainment. Upstairs are more bars and café-style seating areas with balconies from which to watch the action below. Great acoustics too. *See also p180.*

Universale

Via Pisana 77r, Outside the City Gates (055 221122/ www.universalefirenze.it). Bus 6. **Open** 8pm-3am Wed-Sun. Closed June-Sept. **Admission** €10-€13 incl 1st drink. **Credit** AmEx, MC, V.
Groups often warm up the crowd in this stunning converted cinema. The tone can swing from progressive piano jazz to urban funk , depending on the night's DJ set. *See also p180.*

Summer music venues

From June to September acts play on a variety of open-air stages. Noteworthy are the nightly **Jazz&Co** events in Piazza della Santissima Annunziata (see www.firenzejazz.it) and **Le Rime Rampanti** series at Piazza Poggi on the ramps of San Niccolò (348 5804812), with its jazz and chill-out sounds, plus views over the Arno.

Festivals

Of Tuscany's mixed bag of blues and rock festivals, three major ones stand out. Held over one weekend in mid July, **Pistoia Blues** in Pistoia stages a number of open-air blues/rock concerts. Also in July, the five-day **Arezzo Wave** event features all manner of music styles. For these and others, *see p263* **And the beat goes on.** And in October and November, the **Rassegna Internazionale Musica dei Popoli**, an innovative world music festival, is held at Auditorium FLOG (*see p176*).

Nightlife

Club culture in the city of culture.

While the music has finally made its way into the 21st century, and designer facelifts have nipped away excess fat, it's the traffic that's the driving force of Florentine nightlife. Constant changes to the no-traffic zones and a current ban on night-time driving in the city centre at weekends have given suburban venues a leg-up in the popularity stakes, and mean that only the best central bars and clubs are rocking at weekends. Some owners have thought up novel ways to bring in the crowds: one, **Capocaccia**, has golf carts that pick up punters from various points in the city. Others are content to sit tight and wait for the rules to change. Meanwhile, for the visitor it's a win-win situation, with more likelihood of getting served and seated on Saturday and busier weeknights.

Most clubs have replaced entrance fees with a card system. You're given a card that's stamped whenever you buy drinks or use the cloakroom. You then hand the card in at the till and pay before leaving (there's usually a minimum cost that includes the first drink).

Some smaller clubs are members-only, but will almost always give out free membership.

Note that opening times and closing days of bars and clubs are notoriously vague and erratic, and phones that are answered are the exception, so be prepared to take a chance. Musical genres often vary with the day of the week – check flyers, English-language newspaper *The Florentine* or *Firenze Spettacolo* for information.

SUMMER CLUBBIN'

The hot and humid summer months – from the end of May to the beginning of September – see most Florentine nightlife shift from crowded, overheated underground clubs to outdoor venues in piazzas, gardens and villas. Most have free admission and stay open until well into the small hours. Each summer brings a selection of both new and well-known open-air venues – check the local press for up-to-date details of which venues have been given permission to operate for the season. For riverside seats, head for **Teatro sull'Acqua**

Meccanò. *See p180.*

(Lungarno Pecori Giraldi, 055 2343460) or **Lido** (*see p182*), sprawling bar-cum-clubs on the riverbank. In past summers **Vie di Fuga** at Le Murate (Via dell'Agnolo, 0338 5060253) has been the coolest of the summer bars, with a dancefloor, pizzeria and films (in Italian), plus concerts, theatre and dance events. The biggest summer venue (and again not guaranteed to be open) is **Parterre** (Piazza della Libertà, no phone), a huge indoor and outdoor bar, club and gig venue. Temporary bars set up in streets and squares are also a hot summer phenomenon. **Le Rime Rampanti** (*see also p177*) overlooks the river on the terraces above Piazza Poggi and has live bands and a bar, while for free jazz, **Jazz&Co** (www.firenzejazz.it) has live acts and a bar against the charming backdrop of Piazza Santissima Annunziata. The newest summer venue is at the Cascine park's swimming pool **Le Pavoniere** (Viale della Catena 2), where one of the big names in Florentine nightlife, **Tenax** (*see p180*), holds 'Miami-style' nights around the pool, with a bar, restaurant and pizzeria.

Bear in mind that the local council grants permission to these summer-only venues on a year-by-year basis, and the situation can change at any time. Check the local press for details.

Clubs

Central Park

Via Fosso Macinante 2, nr Ponte di Vittoria, Outside the City Gates (055 353505). Bus 1, 9, 26. **Open** *Summer* 11pm-4am Tue-Sat. *Winter* 11pm-4am Fri, Sat. **Admission** free. **Credit** AmEx, DC, MC, V.
The greatest of summer disco venues, Central Park comes into its own in the hottest weather, when the huge garden areas with bars and outdoor dancefloors provide the perfect environment for sunfrazzled dancing legs. At its best the music is progressive by Florentine standards. You might heed the siren call of garage, drum 'n' bass, deep house classics or techno through the scented summer night. Then again, you might stumble upon mediocre live acts and play-by-rote hits in the four music zones. Thursdays (featuring some of the best drum 'n' bass in Italy) and Fridays are usually good bets. Saturdays see an influx of out-of-towners, while naturally the hip crowd heads for the beach. It can be worth the trek in winter if you're up for a big night, but with the pay-when-you-leave card system, the huge queue for the tills can be excruciating.

Closer

Via Ghibellina 69r, Santa Croce (338 87108383). **Open** 10pm-late Tue-Sun. **Admission** free, but membership required (free). **Credit** AmEx, DC, MC, V. **Map** p319 C4.
A small student-oriented club that vaunts itself as the only place in Florence serving a range of absinthes. Live music sets alternate with DJ nights,

with some music so dire you'll need plenty of stiff shots to survive. The worst are Italian rock nights and Goth revivals, but if you're lucky you might hit a glam-trash, tacky but fun, party night (most Thursdays and Fridays), when the young crowd's wild abandon can be infectious.

Dolce Zucchero

Via Pandolfini 26r, Santa Croce (055 243356). **Open** 11pm-4am Tue-Sun. Closed June-Sept. **Admission** free before midnight. **Credit** AmEx, MC, V. **Map** p319 C5.
Recently refurbished, so obviously planning on sticking around for a while, this stalwart of the local nightlife scene is the most central pure-breed disco in town, and a monument to cheesy fun. Even the hippest Florentines sometimes throw caution to the wind and head here for '70s, '80s or even '90s Italian sounds... just don't expect to hear anything progressive, or you'll be disappointed.

ExMud

Corso dei Tintori 4, Santa Croce (055 2638583/ www.exmud.it). **Open** 11.30pm-4am Tue-Sun. **Admission** €9-€12 (incl 1st drink). **Credit** AmEx, MC, V. **Map** p319 C5.
A warren of passageways and rooms in a stone basement, ExMud is, on a good night, everything a great old-fashioned nightclub should be. Expect hot, sweaty and rocking fun, with a young cosmopolitan crowd boogying to international DJs spinning house, garage, drum 'n' bass or liquid funk. Hit a bad night, on the other hand, and you'll be one of the select few listening to hard-core Italian electronica being played to empty dancefloors.

Faces

Via dei Geppi 3r, Oltrarno (055 293006/www.faces club.it). **Open** 10pm-2am Tue-Sat. Closed June-Sept. **Admission** free before midnight; €10-€15 after midnight (incl 1st drink). **Credit** AmEx, MC, V. **Map** p319 C4.
Tucked away in a nondescript alley near the river, Faces is a tiny club with loyal regulars, so nights have a bit of a house party feel. Saturdays see popular DJ Nate Maestrum lording it with his house, hip hop and R&B set. Other evenings can be anything from '80s to radio anthems – they seem to make it up as they go along.

Full-Up

Via della Vigna Vecchia 25r, Santa Croce (055 293006). **Open** 11pm-4am Tue-Sat. Closed June-Sept. **Admission** free before midnight; €10 after midnight (incl 1st drink). **Credit** AmEx, MC, V. **Map** p319 C4.
A long-running temple to kitsch, and a smoothie's paradise, Full-Up's white piano bar is popular with sugar daddies and miniskirted models looking for a Mercedes ride home. Wednesdays have always been the exception to the steer-clear rule, though, with cool (if flashy) Florentines enjoying funky house. Avoid Thursdays and Fridays at all costs, when it's the very iffy American Sound and Lolly Pop Party.

Restaurant? Bar? Club? **Universale** is a little bit of everything.

Maracana Casa di Samba

Via Faenza 4, San Lorenzo (055 210298). **Open** *Club* midnight-4am Tue-Sun. *Restaurant* 8.30-11.30pm Tue-Sun. Closed June-Aug. **Admission** €10-€20. **Credit** (restaurant only) AmEx, DC, MC, V. **Map** p318 A3.

Give this place a wide berth if you can't stomach middle-aged suits dribbling lecherously over wiggling Brazilian booties – after the restaurant stops serving South American fare, all decorum is shed. The main dancefloor is surrounded by poseur platforms and the balconies assure views of cleavages and bald patches. Exhibitionists will love the shots of themselves on the huge screen.

Meccanò

Viale degli Olmi 1, nr Ponte di Vittoria, Outside the City Gates (055 331371). Bus 1, 9, 16, 26, 27. **Open** *Summer* 11.30pm-4am Tue-Sat. *Winter* 11.30pm-4am Mon-Sat. **Admission** €8-€20 (incl 1st drink). **Credit** AmEx, DC, MC, V.

Meccanò caters to the masses, who come out in force to play in its theme-park atmosphere. It's easy to play hide-and-seek in the labyrinthine tangle of bars and dancefloors, especially when the garden opens in summer. Music is mostly Latin, commercial party and trashy pop, but there's often a sprinkling of hip hop and funky house too.

SottoSopra

Via dei Serragli 48r, Oltrarno (055 282340). **Open** 7pm-2am Mon-Sat. Closed June-Sept. **Admission** free. **No credit cards**. **Map** p318 D1.

This small club's subtitle, *piu sotto che sopra* ('more down than up'), hits the nail on the head: there's a tiny upstairs bar and relatively roomy club area downstairs. Drinks are cheap, the DJs turn out a stream of fine fare and the atmosphere is friendly – so it's not the place to come if you want to sit quietly.

Tenax

Via Pratese 46, Outside the City Gates (055 308160/ www.tenax.org). Bus 29, 30. **Open** 10.30pm-4am Thur-Sat & for gigs. Closed mid May-Sept. **Admission** €10-€15. **Credit** AmEx, MC, V.

The most influential and international of the Florentine clubs is the warehouse-style Tenax in Peretola. Far enough outside the centre to make a night out an adventure, but not too far to be impractical without a car, it's one of the city's best-known nightspots, especially as a live venue for hip international bands and for its DJ exchanges with big-name London clubs. Bands who've played here recently include Zero 7, Thievery Corporation and Scissor Sisters. Nobody's Perfect on Saturday is the hottest night in the city by a long shot, heaving with house, big beat, progressive or drum 'n' bass, depending on the one-nighter DJs hitting the decks (who count Pete Tong, Deep Dish and Ashley Beedle among their illustrious ranks). *See also p177.*

Universale

Via Pisana 77r, Outside the City Gates (055 221122/ www.universalefirenze.it). Bus 6. **Open** *Club* 8pm-3am Wed-Sun. *Restaurant* 8pm-midnight Wed-Sun. Closed June-Sept. **Admission** €7-€18 (incl 1st drink). **Credit** AmEx, MC, V.

A striking club just outside Porta San Frediano, which was converted from a 1950s cinema, Universale is the perfect reward for those who've grown tired of traipsing from one Florentine hotspot to another. It's an all-round emporium of entertainment: there's a restaurant, bar, video screen and club areas, with regular live jazzy music sessions handing over to DJs later on. Restaurant-goers can peer over the balustrade of the magnificent double curved sweeping staircases down towards the flashy central oval bar.

Arts & Entertainment

Yab

Via Sassetti 5r, Duomo & Around (055 215160).
Open 9pm-4am Mon, Tue, Thur-Sat. Closed June-
Sept. **Admission** free (€15 drinks minimum Fri,
Sat). **Credit** AmEx, DC, V. **Map** p318 B3.
Mondays at Yab are an institution among certain
older Florentines. The powerful sound system has
the mammoth dancefloor shimmying with dancers,
while the wall-to-wall bar areas cater to those
with tired feet. Thursdays play deep house, with a
younger crowd letting it all hang out.

Pubs & bars

Art Bar

Via del Moro 4r, Santa Maria Novella (055 287661).
Open 7pm-1am Mon-Thur; 7pm-2am Fri, Sat. Closed
3wks Aug. **No credit cards**. **Map** p318 B2.
Battered French horns hanging from the ceiling and
sepia photos of blues and jazz musicians lend a beat-
nik air to this perennially popular bar. The ambience is cosy but animated, with student types holed
up in the brick cellar sipping their potent piña

Designs for (night)life

Interior design is big news in Florentine
nightlife, with many bar owners splashing out
on state-of-the-art lighting systems and plush
furnishings and fabrics, not to mention big-
name architects and designers. The result
is a feast for the eyes for design-minded
punters. The new **Nova Bar** (Via Martelli
14r, Duomo & Around, 055 289880) has
brightened up the medieval stone palazzo
that houses it with spotlit crimson walls,
scarlet upholstered bar stools, fuschia
pendulum lamps, a glass bar and a full
wall of framed photos. Not to be outdone,
Angels (Via del Proconsolo 29-31r, Duomo
& Around, 055 2398762) boasts illuminated
stone columns punctuating minimalist
high-backed white grosgrain chairs and
white ceiling canopies. **Sèsame** (Via delle
Conce 20r, Santa Croce, 055 2001381)
is an Arabian Nights fantasy. A row of low
burnished tables lines a textured wall with
tiny lit niches framing stone sculptures.
Crimson bolster cushions and organza
drapes soften the look, and lanterns and
chandeliers juxtapose design elements from
east and west. The long arch leads to a
delightful garden with ornate wrought-iron
furniture and a pond.

Sophisticated but laid-back, **L'Incontro** (*see
p123* **Hotel cuisine**) is the Savoy Hotel's bar,
kitted out by the fêted Olga Polizzi, daughter
of hotel mogul Lord Forte and design director
of Rocco Forte Hotels. Sage-green sofas and
zebra-print ottomans are crowned by paintings
of classical goddesses, chocolate leather
bucket seats sit on dark wood floors, while
on the outside platform terrace white cotton
parasols shelter candlelit teak tables. At the
fashionistas' favourite haunt, the Ferragamo-
owned **Fusion Bar** in the Gallery Hotel Art (*see
p123* **Hotel cuisine**), architect Michele Bonan
used square leather sofas and dark wood
coffee tables to give the bar a clean, but

warm, masculine look. Also by Bonan is **The
Lounge**, part of JK Place hotel (*see p123* **Hotel
cuisine**), and an extension of the hotel's neo-
classical calm, with framed black and white
photos, suede seats and a marble fireplace.
Downstairs, the mood changes dramatically,
with all-white square leather banquette seats
and white cushions. All-white, that is, until the
subtle colour-phasing starts, and the whole
room becomes candy pink, then mint green.

Downstairs at **The Lounge**.

coladas. During happy hour (7-9pm) drinks cost a bargain €4; on Mondays and Wednesdays the happiness lasts all night.

Astor Caffè

For listings, see p129.

This huge, lively jazz bar draws an enthusiastic young crowd. The big skylight, soft red lighting and flash chrome bar are a clean backdrop for the regular art exhibitions, while internet points provide distraction from the busy socialising of the main bar.

Cabiria

For listings, see p135.

After a long history as the wildest and grungiest of the pre-club bars, Cabiria has suddenly been spruced up, joining the design revolution of Florentine bars. The clientele has changed to match, and is now a well-behaved, well-to-do genial crowd enjoying the pretty candlelit terrace on Piazza Santo Spirito on warm nights and swaying to soft jazzy sounds from the DJ sets inside.

Caffè la Torre

Lungarno Cellini 65r, Oltrarno (055 680643/ www.caffelatorre.it). **Open** 10.30am-3am daily.
Credit AmEx, DC, MC, V. **Map** p319 D6.
Follow the river to this nice 'n' easy bar. The postclubbing music is mercifully mellow, but if you come earlier you can sway in a dignified and gentle manner to the foot-tapping tunes of the various (almost) nightly live acts. Tapas and pasta are also served.

Capocaccia

For listings, see p132.

Impossibly hip, Capocaccia is the most desired and desirable of central nightspots. The bar is busy on most nights of the year, but positively heaving during the week in summer, when you can join half of cool Florence outside blocking the traffic as you wait to get in. Entry accomplished, sit in the packed bar people-watching and nursing a cocktail, or enjoy the clubby atmosphere with the DJ set pumping out Latin jazz and big beats. Otherwise, you can just chill out in the amazing salon with zebra-skin seating, red walls and a frescoed ceiling. To make sure the new traffic laws banning city-centre motoring don't drive away custom, Capocaccia's powers-that-be send a branded golf cart around various restaurants on the edge of the no-drive zone.

Dolce Vita

For listings, see p135.

Despite the influx of trendy new bars, Dolce Vita is still going strong after years of hegemony in the summer nights-out stakes. Crowds spill out on to the medieval square during warm evenings, making their enjoyment heard to the extent that some neighbours have invested in soundproof windows. Inside, the cold metal and glass bar leads to a cosier salon, with sofas and soft lighting from beautiful crystal lamps, usually inhabited by those too weary to move on to the clubbing scene.

James Joyce

Lungarno Benvenuto Cellini 1r, Oltrarno (055 6580856). **Open** 6pm-2am Mon-Thur; 6pm-3am Fri-Sun. **No credit cards. Map** p319 D6.
The large enclosed garden with long wooden tables makes this one of the best of Florence's pubs in spring and summer. JJ has a high-spirited vibe, especially around happy hour (7.30-9.30pm), when drinks come with free snacks. To go with the name, there's a small bookshop selling paperbacks, some of them in English.

Kilimanjaro

Via Palazzuolo 80-82r, Santa Maria Novella (055 291661). **Open** 7.30pm-midnight Tue-Thur; 1pm-2am Fri-Sun. **Admission** free. **Credit** AmEx, DC, MC, V. **Map** p318 B2.
The most exotic and adventurous venue in central Florence is this new Africa-inspired bar. The leopard-print walls and thatched ceilings give the impression that you're walking into a rather grand hut – one with low-slung tables and a bamboo bar. Music is deep house, with some tribal beats thrown in for good theming.

Lido

Lungarno Pecori Giraldi 1r, Santa Croce (055 2342726). **Open** 12.30pm-2am Tue-Sat; 1pm-2am Sun. *Lunch served* 1-3pm daily. Closed Jan, Feb. **Admission** free. **No credit cards.**
Large glass doors open from this bar to a garden that extends to the riverbank, making it a good bet for hot summer nights, when queues inevitably form. The music is a thumping collection of drum 'n' bass, R&B and the like, though the dancefloor is entirely taken up by the line for the bar. Fridays are stomping deep house. Come early if you want to hire a boat for a quick punt (€8 an hour).

Loonees

Via Porta Rossa 15r, Duomo & Around (055 212249). **Open** 8pm-3am Tue-Sun. Closed Aug. **Admission** free. **No credit cards. Map** p318 C3.
Hugely popular with students, who queue en masse to get in, this mainly live music bar has a relaxed atmosphere that's partly due to the loud music, which leaves punters with little to do but stay and take advantage of the free shot with every pint.

Mayday Lounge Café

Via Dante Alighieri 16r, Duomo & Around (055 2381290/www.maydayclub.it). **Open** 8pm-2am Mon-Sat. Closed 2wks Aug. **Admission** free, but membership required (free). **No credit cards. Map** p319 B4.
That this is the wackiest joint in town is immediately evident from the odd art installations and hundreds of old Marconi radios, some hanging from the ceilings. Mayday is dark and smoky, and the owners gleefully admit they make up the next evening's events as they go along, the only constant being a jazzy edge to the sounds. So a visit could coincide with anything from a 'Japanese porn' night (complete with kinky-shaped sushi) to nu-jazz karaoke.

Arts & Entertainment

Montecarla

Via dei Bardi 2, Oltrarno (055 2340259). **Open**
9.30pm-5am daily. **Admission** free. **No credit
cards. Map** p319 D4.

Montecarla's reputation is built on Chinese whis-
pers, the chief rumour being that it was once a broth-
el (it wasn't, but its low-slung leopard-skin couches,
hidden recesses and oriental drapery encourage the
fantasy). Soft background music plays, a pile of
board games is on hand and service is conspirator-
ial and intimate. The drinks, which are mainly cocktails, come in monster measures.

Moyo

Via dei Benci 23r, Santa Croce (055 2479738).
Open 6pm-2am daily. **Admission** free. **Credit**
AmEx, MC, V. **Map** p319 C5.

Being the first wireless internet bar in Florence is
the main claim to fame for this buzzing new place.
You don't have to be web-savvy to appreciate the
vibe here, though. The cool wood decor and outdoor
seating make for a welcoming year-round environment, and being on the edge of the no-drive zone
means that parking is only a five-minute walk away.
Any wonder that, come *aperitivo* time, it's packed
out with hip Florentines glad of a home in the west.

Negroni

*Via dei Renai 17r, Oltrarno (055 243647/
www.negronibar.com).* **Open** 8am-2.30am Mon-Sat;
6pm-2am Sun. Closed 2wks Aug. **Credit** MC, V.
Map p319 D5.

Named after Mr Negroni himself, who invented the
eponymous cocktail (gin, red vermouth, Campari)
while sitting at a bar that used to be on this site, this
is one of the coolest destinations in town. The
streamlined, sleek, red and black interior is a backdrop for art and photography exhibitions, while the
outside seating in the garden square is crowded on
hot summer nights. The music works around CD
promotions run in conjunction with Alberti record
shop (*see p153*) and showcases the latest releases
from progressive lo-fi bands.

Officina Move Bar

*Via il Prato 58r, Santa Maria Novella (055 210399/
www.officinamovebar.com).* **Open** *Summer* 8am-6pm
Mon-Fri. *Winter* 8am-2am Mon-Fri; 7pm-2am Sat,
Sun. Closed Aug. **Credit** MC, V. **Map** p319 B5.

Expect the unexpected at this low-lit bar, where a
night can bring anything from reggae to hip hop,
techno to nu-jazz, with installation performances,
modern dance shows, interactive multimedia sessions and impromptu live music sets.

Porfirio

Viale Strozzi 38r, San Lorenzo (055 490965). **Open**
11am-2am Tue-Sun. Closed 2wks Aug. **Credit** MC, V.

Once again a heaving hedonists' haven, this hip bar
is named after Brazilian playboy Porfirio Rubirosa.
The roadworks that kept the moneyed Florentine
crowds in their flash cars away for a couple of
years have been completed, and the noblesse and
wannabes are back with a vengeance and making

Mayday Lounge Café. *See p182.*

up for lost time. Weekend traffic restrictions in the
city centre mean Fridays and Saturdays are particularly mobbed, and the outside bar could easily be
mistaken for a car showroom.

Rex Caffè

Via Fiesolana 25r, Santa Croce (055 2480331).
Open 6pm-3.30am daily. Closed June-Aug. **Credit**
MC, V. **Map** p319 B5.

With more of a club than a bar atmosphere, Rex is
the king of the east, filling up with loyal subjects
who bow, scrape and sashay to the sounds of the
session DJs playing bassy beats and jungle rhythms.
Gaudi-esque mosaics decorate the central bar and
columns, wrought-iron lamps shed a soft light and
a luscious red antechamber creates seclusion for
more intimate gatherings. Tapas are served during
the *aperitivo* happy hour (5-9.30pm), and the cocktails are especially good.

Slowly

*Via Porta Rossa 63r, Duomo & Around (055
2645354).* **Open** 7pm-2am Mon-Sat. **Credit** MC, V.
Map p318 C3.

The ultimate chill-out bohemian-chic bar, Slowly is
softly lit by candles in mosaic lanterns, with big soft
sofas in alcoves, laid-back staff and mellow Café del

Night nibbles

The *aperitivo* craze that had Florentines finally abandoning *mamma*'s cooking a few years back is still going strong. The concept is simple: buy a pre-dinner cocktail and, included in the price, the bar provides a buffet of snacks that can be anything from exquisite canapés to full-blown rustic pasta dishes. Since Italians have dinner late, *aperitivo* time starts at around 7.30pm, going on till about 9pm, making it a great way to roll a meal, drink and socialising into one. One of the main highlights of the *aperitivo* world is still **Capocaccia** (*see p182*), which serves up a huge buffet of hot and cold snacks and main dishes in the frescoed salon. When the swarming locusts have consumed every trace, the sweets are rolled out – tiramisù, fruit salads, brownies and cheesecakes. Another favourite with locals is **Slowly** (*see p183*), which treats *aperitivo* time as a chance to show off, with platter after platter of hot and cold delicacies brought to the central pedestal from the bar's own kitchens, and a huge dish of crudités served at your table. **Kilimanjaro** (*see p182*) is Wednesday night's hot *aperitivo* ticket, with unusual filled focaccias, canapés and cold dishes with an African slant. Across the river, **Negroni** (*see p183*) serves couscous, grilled peppers and cold pastas to beautiful people, who wash it all down with its namesake cocktail. Also in Oltrarno, **Dolce Vita**'s (*see p182*) horseshoe bar is loaded with crudités to dip in tiny bowls of olive oil, Tuscan *crostini* and sushi. The **Fusion Bar** (*pictured; see also p123* **Hotel cuisine**) is the oriental *aperitivo par excellence*, with snacks of sushi and tempura, all beautifully presented. **Rex Caffè** (*see p183*) serves up huge trays of cold meats, cheeses and focaccias, followed by hot chocolate fondue with fresh fruit. Drinks cost just €5 from 6.30pm to 8.30pm. In contrast with its modern, minimalist design, **Angels** (Via del Proconsolo 29-31r, Duomo & Around, 055 2398762; *see also p181* **Designs for (night)life**) serves the classic Tuscan dishes *pappa al pomodoro* and *ribollita*, alongside delicate *crostini*, rich pâtés and hot salads.

Mar-style sounds when the DJ gets stuck in. Even the inevitable crowds of pretty young things and hip thirtysomethings can't break the nice 'n' easy spell. The restaurant overlooking the bar serves imaginative global cuisine.

I Visacci

For listings, *see p135*.

The daytime butter-wouldn't-melt style of this small new bar hots up come night-time. On tap are a spicy mix of Latin and salsa beats, steaming coffee and liqueur concoctions, and the sort of regulars that make the polychromatic, holographic striped decor look boring in comparison.

The William Pub

Via Magliabechi 7-11r, Santa Croce (055 2638357). **Open** 6pm-1.30am Mon-Thur, Sun; 6pm-2.30am Fri, Sat. **Credit** AmEx, DC, MC, V. **Map** p319 C5.
British pub culture, complete with photos of English sporting heroes and quaint village scenes, has been transplanted into this most frescoed and Florentine of buildings. The identity crisis extends to the clientele, who run from butch bikers to caressing couples. The downstairs bar is generally packed, while the upstairs bar and the back room have space to sit and relax with a Newcastle Brown and a late-night ploughman's. Just one word of advice: stick to bottled beers rather than draught.

Sport & Fitness

Where to push the boat out, or get pecs like *David*.

Though few people come to Florence for the sports, there are abundant and growing opportunities for the fitness enthusiasts who do decide to partake while here. Each winter the marathon draws a larger and larger international crowd and young Florentines are taking their health more seriously, spawning a plethora of new gymnasiums and spas offering a wider range of services, including yoga and step.

Spectator sports

Car & motorbike racing

Autodromo del Mugello

Nr Scarperia (055 8499111/www.mugellocircuit.it). **Open** Mar-Nov. Closed Dec-Feb. **Tickets** phone for details.

Top-notch racing, including Formula 3 and motor-cycle world championship competitions, are held at this circuit 30km (20 miles) north of Florence. Bikers can live out their Carl Fogarty fantasies on the track (€50 for 20 minutes), but you have to bring your own Ducati. Call 055 480553 for reservations.

Football

Tennis Carraia (*see p189*) also has facilities for *calcetto*, a local variety of football.

Stadio Artemio Franchi

Campo di Marte, Outside the City Gates (055 2625537/www.acffiorentina.it). Bus 11, 17. **Open** Aug-May. **Tickets** approx €20-€140; reduced prices for women. **No credit cards**.

In 2002 Fiorentina, with two championship titles to their credit, found themselves overdrawn elsewhere and went bankrupt amid much scandal. The club was refounded as Florentia but, falling from the Italian league's top division, they were forced to start all over again at the lowest C2 rank. The team later regained its original name, and managed to get back into Serie A.

The season runs from August to May; matches are generally held every other Sunday, with kick-off at 3pm. You can buy tickets directly at the stadium, online (the website also has a list of authorised resellers) or up to three hours prior to a match at Chiosco degli Sportivi (Via Anselmi, near Piazza della Repubblica, Duomo & Around, 055 292363).

Horse racing

Ippodromo Le Cascine
Via delle Cascine 3, Parco delle Cascine, Outside the City Gates (055 353394/4226076/www.ippodromi fiorentini.it). Bus 17C. **Open** *Apr-May, Sept-Oct.*
Admission €4. **No credit cards.**
Florence's *galoppo* (flat-racing) course. Keep an eye out for leading Tuscan jockeys such as Alessandro Muzzi and Claudio Colombi.

Ippodromo Le Mulina
Viale del Pegaso, Parco delle Cascine, Outside the City Gates (055 4226076/www.ippodromi fiorentini.it). Bus 17C. **Open** *Nov-Mar, June-July.*
Admission €4. **No credit cards.**
Florence's racecourse for *il trotto* (trotting), a form of racing where the driver sits in a carriage behind the horse. The Premio Duomo in June is among Tuscany's biggest equine events.

Active sports & fitness

Climbing & trekking

Cave di Maiano
Via Cave di Maiano, Outside the City Gates (no phone). Bus 7.
If you're into free-climbing, this place in Fiesole the place to go. The caves, which are actually old mines, make an ideal rock wall. You'll be on your own, without guides or instructors, so bring equipment.

Galleria dello Sport
Via Pienza 33, Outside the City Gates (055 580611/ www.piugaz.it). Bus 26. **Open** *3-11pm Mon-Fri.*
Rates €6 per day; €50 for 10 days; reduced prices for children. **Credit** AmEx, MC, V.
Galleria dello Sport, a sporting shop based in San Marco, runs a rare climbing facility called Piugaz in Isolotto. With proper gear and a friend to spot you, you can flex your skills or take classes.

Gruppo Escursionistico CAI (Club Alpino Italiano)
Via del Mezzetta 2, Outside the City Gates (055 6120467/www.caifirenze.it). Bus 3, 6, 20. **Open** 3.30-7pm Mon-Fri. Closed Aug. **Rates** vary.
No credit cards.
Guided Sunday treks through the Tuscan countryside, mostly rated easy to moderate. Prices include transport to and from the city centre, but not lunch. In May the Prato section of CAI organises 'Piazza to Piazza', an 84km (52-mile) two-day walk, including overnight arrangements. For more information, get in touch with the Associazione Sportiva Sci CAI Prato, Via Altopascio, Prato (0574 29267).

Guide Alpine
338 9313444/349 7933893/www.ufficioguide.it.
These mountaineering experts organise courses throughout the summer. Phone Ufficio Guide on the above numbers, or check online, for details.

Libreria Stella Alpina
Via Corridoni 14, Outside the City Gates (055 411688). Bus 8, 14, 20, 28. **Open** *Winter* 4-8pm Mon; 9am-1pm, 4-8pm Tue-Sat. *Summer* 9am-1pm, 4-8pm Tue-Fri. **No credit cards.**
This bookshop in Il Romito is a good source of further information on trekking and mountaineering in the whole of Tuscany.

Cycling

Florence by Bike
Via San Zanobi 120r-122r, San Lorenzo (055 488992/www.florencebybike.it). **Open** *Mar-Oct* 9am-7.30pm daily. *Nov-Feb* 9am-1pm, 3.30-7.30pm daily. **Credit** AmEx, DC, MC, V.
Bike rental and organised bike tours. Especially recommended is the one-day tour through Chianti (35km/22 miles), which costs €70 per person and includes bike and helmet rental, an English-speaking guide and lunch in a restaurant. Book in advance, as the maximum number of people in a group is 12.

Walking Tours of Florence
Piazza Santo Stefano 2, Duomo & Around (055 2645033/mobile 329 6132730/www.italy.artviva. com). **Open** *Office* 8am-6.30pm Mon-Sat; 8.30am-1.30pm Sun. *Mobile* 8am-8pm daily. **Credit** MC, V.
Map p318 C3.
Despite the name, this well-regarded company offers just about every kind of tour under the sun, including half-day bike tours of Tuscany. The €40 cost includes a guide, bike, helmet, equipment, snacks and wine. Tours leave from the office, tucked away on a little square off Via Por Santa Maria. *See also p68.*

Golf

Circolo Golf Ugolino
Via Chiantigiana 3, Grassina (055 2301009/ www.golfugolino.it). Bus 31. **Open** *Winter* 8.30am-6.30pm daily. *Summer* 8.30am-7.30pm daily. Closed Jan. **Rates** €60 Mon-Fri; €80 Sat, Sun. **Credit** AmEx, DC, MC, V.
This 18-hole course is the nearest to the city (about 20 minutes south by bus), but it's closed to non-members during the frequent weekend tournaments. It's best to phone or send an email (info@golfugolino.it) for reservations at least a week in advance.

Gyms

Fonbliù
Piazzale di Porta Romana 10r, Outside the City Gates (055 2335385/www.fonbliu.com). Bus 11, 36, 37. **Open** *Winter* 8.30am-8.30pm Mon-Fri; 8.30am-6pm Sat. *Summer* 8.30am-8.30pm Mon-Fri; 8.30am-1.30pm Sat. **Membership** €35 per day; €72 per mth. **Credit** MC, V.
A small, high-tech spa at Porta Romana, with fitness centre and indoor pool. Most of the classes are limited to five people.

Palestra Porta Romana

Via Gherardo Silvani 5, Outside the City Gates (055 2321799). Bus 11, 36, 37. **Open** 10am-10pm Mon-Fri; 10am-1pm Sat. **Membership** €10 per day; €60 per mth. **No credit cards**.

A small gym in Galluzzo, to the south of Porta Romana, specialising in martial arts (women's boxing is particularly popular). There's also a weights room, plus aerobics, step and spinning classes.

Palestra Ricciardi

Borgo Pinti 75, Santa Croce (055 2478462/www. palestraricciardi.it). **Open** 9am-10pm Mon-Fri; 9.30am-6pm Sat; 10am-2pm Sun. Closed Aug. **Membership** €82 per mth, then €10 per day. **Credit** MC, V. **Map** p319 B5.

You'll have probably gathered by now that staying fit in Florence requires exercising your wallet as much as your body. This place is no exception. But at least there's a small garden where you can top up your tan after spinning, step or hip hop classes.

Tropos

Via Orcagna 20A, Outside the City Gates (055 678381/www.troposclub.it). Bus 14. **Open** 8am-9.30pm Mon-Sat. **Membership** €30 trial visit, then various options. **Credit** AmEx, MC, V.

This is a luxurious (and pricey) setting, whether you're splashing about in the aerobics pool, clocking up laps in the main pool or steaming yourself in one of the saunas.

Horse riding

Maneggio Marinella

Via di Macia 21, Outside the City Gates (055 8878066). Bus 28. **Open** 9am-1pm, 3-7pm daily. **Rates** €15 per hr. **No credit cards**.

Phone during the week to book one of the daily rides at this stable in the northern suburbs. Lessons and special or group trips are also organised on request.

Rendola Riding

Rendola, Montevarchi (055 9707045/www.rendolariding.it). **Open** 9am-1pm, 3-6pm Tue-Sun. **Rates** €15 per hr. **No credit cards**.

This stable, run by Jenny Bawtree, is 30 minutes' drive south of Florence on the border with Chianti. It offers one- to five-hour rides through the countryside, lessons, and a package of two hours' riding, lunch and transport to and from the nearest train station. Book at least a day in advance. Two- to three-day trips, with lodging at a neighbouring *agriturismo*, are also available.

Ice skating

Florence sets up a temporary ice-skating rink every winter from December to January. The venue tends to change every year, so contact the APT (055 23320) for the latest information. You pay by the session (there are three or four daily); the last ends at about 11pm.

In-line skating

Le Pavoniere

Viale della Catena 2, Parco delle Cascine, Outside the City Gates (335 5718547). Bus 17C. **Open** 3-8pm Tue-Thur; 10am-8pm Sat, Sun. Closed when raining. **Rates** €5 per hr. **No credit cards**.

Hire in-line skates from this kiosk in the Parco delle Cascine and take advantage of miles of traffic-free paths along the Arno river.

Pool

Gambrinus

Via dei Vecchietti 16r, Duomo & Around (no phone). **Open** 1.30pm-1am daily. **Rates** tables €8 per hr. **No credit cards**. **Map** p318 B3.

The only pool hall in central Florence, Gambrinus offers nine pool tables and eight tables without pockets, where you can try your hand at *boccette* or *cinque birilli*. The clientele here is predominantly serious, though non-hostile, men.

Rowing

Canottieri Comunali

Lungarno Francesco Ferrucci 2, nr Ponte Verazzano, Outside the City Gates (055 6812151/www.canottieri comunalifirenze.it). **Open** 8.30am-9pm Mon-Fri; 8.30am-7pm Sat; 8am-1pm Sun. **Membership** €100-€300 per mth. **No credit cards**.

This club enjoys a delightful location among trees along the Arno – perfect in sunny weather. There's also a full range of lessons and activities, including white-water rafting excursions.

Società Canottieri Firenze

Lungarno Luisa dei Medici 8, Duomo & Around (055 282130/www.canottierifirenze.it). **Open** 8am-8.30pm Mon, Sat; 8am-9.30pm Tue-Fri; 8am-1pm Sun. **Membership** €70 per mth. **No credit cards**. **Map** p318 C3.

Tucked away in the caverns below the Uffizi (you enter the club through a tiny green door on the Lungarno), this fairly exclusive club has boats that go out on the Arno. There's also a gym, indoor rowing tank, sauna and showers.

Running

Most joggers hit the **Parco delle Cascine** along the river, but you can also head for the hills. Your best bet is **Viale Michelangelo**, where there is a wide pavement under trees. Many small, winding roads branch off and will have you in the heart of the beautiful Tuscan countryside within minutes. A word of warning, though: be particularly careful of cars on these back lanes, as they often don't have pavements and locals can take them at fairly high speeds.

Arts & Entertainment

Parco delle Cascine. *See p187.*

Associazione Atletica Leggera

Viale Matteotti 15, Outside the City Gates (055 576616/571401). Bus 8, 80. **Open** 1-6pm Mon, Wed; 9am-1pm Tue, Thur-Sat.

This is Florence's best source for running clubs and meets. Foreigners can only participate in amateur races – phone for further details.

Florence Marathon

Florence (055 5522957/fax 055 5536823/ www.firenzemarathon.it).

Held in late November/early December, the Florence Marathon snakes through the centre of the city and the suburbs. It's open to anyone over the age of 18, provided they can show a certificate of health (you need to apply in advance, especially as the marathon is becoming increasingly popular). *See also p158.*

Skiing

For the Abetone ski area in the province of Pistoia – an easy weekend or day trip from Florence – *see p203.*

Squash

Centro Squash Firenze

Via Empoli 16, San Quirico (055 7323055). Bus 1. **Open** 9.30am-11pm Mon-Fri; 9.30am-6pm Sat. Closed Sat June-Aug. **Rates** €8 per person for 45mins. **No credit cards**.

If you're dying to get some squash practice in while you're in Florence, this is the place to go. In addition, it has a fully equipped gym and a sauna, as well as aerobics, spinning and step classes. Equipment rental is also available.

Swimming

Many swimming pools are open only in the summer. During winter some pools require at least a month's membership and may limit access to a few occasions a week.

Costoli

Viale Pasquale Paoli, Outside the City Gates (055 6236027). Bus 10, 17, 20. **Open** *June-Aug* 2-6pm Mon; 10am-6pm Tue-Sun. *Sept-May* phone for details. **Admission** €6.50; free-€4.50 concessions. **No credit cards**.

Located near the football stadium, this is a swimmer's dream, with Olympic-size, diving and children's pools, surrounded by a lovely green park. Perfect for families.

Hotel Villa Le Rondini

Via Vecchia Bolognese 224, Outside the City Gates (055 400081/www.villalerondini.com). Bus 25. **Open** 10am-7pm daily. Closed Oct-Apr. **Admission** €16 Mon-Fri; €19 Sat, Sun. **No credit cards**.

A small pool beside a chic, hillside hotel at La Ruota just outside of town, surrounded by a lovely lawn and shady trees.

FLOG

Via Mercati 24B, Outside the City Gates (055 484465/www.flog.it). Bus 4, 8, 14, 20, 28. **Open** *June, July* 10am-6.30pm Sat, Sun. *Aug* 10am-6.30pm daily. Closed Sept-May. **Admission** €6; €4 concessions. **No credit cards**.

This small pool in Poggetto is a great place to hang out on a baking hot day. Part of an 'afterwork club' of a metalworking factory, it has a sun terrace and refreshments stand.

NUOTO+

Giovanni Franceschi (0571 9493721/335 6172453/ www.giovannifranceschi.it).

Through this organisation you can book week-long swim camps in locations across Italy. They run during the summer and are open to children, adults and whole families. Instruction at all levels is combined with a relaxing holiday.

Piscina Bellariva (indoor/outdoor)

Lungarno Aldo Moro 6, Outside the City Gates (055 677521). Bus 14. **Open** *Summer* 10am-6pm Mon, Wed, Fri-Sun; 10am-6pm, 8.30-11.30pm Tue, Thur. *Winter* 8.30pm-11pm Tue, Thur; 9.30am-12.30pm Sat, Sun. **Admission** €6.50; €4.50 concessions. **No credit cards**.

A lovely Olympic-size pool in a beautiful green park to the east of town. There's a refreshments stand and a separate pool for small children.

Tennis

ASSI

Viale Michelangelo, Outside the City Gates (055 687858). Bus 12, 13. **Open** *Summer* 8am-10pm daily. *Winter* 8am-6pm daily. **Rates** €10 per hr. **No credit cards**.

Six clay courts beautifully situated overlooking the city on the south side of the River Arno. There are three full-time pros and most of the instructors speak a little English.

Tennis Carraia

Via dell'Erta Canina 26, Outside the City Gates (055 7327047). **Open** phone for details. **Rates** phone for details.

Set in what feels like the countryside, the Carraia courts are located just a ten-minute walk from Porta San Niccolò. There are only three courts, so reservations are needed. There are special programmes for children, and several friendly pros are available for private lessons.

Unione Sportivo Affrico

Viale Fanti Manfredo 20, Outside the City Gates (055 600845). Bus 17, 20. **Open** 9am-10.30pm Mon-Fri; 9am-7pm Sat; 9am-1pm Sun. Closed 2wks Aug. **Rates** €11.50 1hr. **No credit cards**.

Near the football stadium in the east of the city, this down-to-earth tennis club has eight courts. Non-members are allowed to reserve a court up to three days in advance, though unfortunately this has to be done in person.

Arts & Entertainment

Theatre & Dance

Apathy and money worries persist, but the show must go on.

If nothing else, the Tuscan theatre circuit has history on its side. The region is home to around 300 theatres, some of which date back as far as the 15th century. While many have fallen into dereliction, others have benefited from a recent surge of interest in their buildings, resulting in some spectacular restoration projects and the re-establishment of long-abandoned theatre seasons.

Florence itself has two historic theatres: **Teatro della Pergola**, which runs a full season of plays and chamber music concerts, and **Teatro Goldoni**, used principally for dance events, with the odd concert or chamber opera thrown in. **Teatro Verdi** is not as picturesque, but hosts a varied programme. That said, many new productions bypass the region's capital in favour of the **Teatro Manzoni** in Pistoia or the renowned **Teatro Metastasio** in Prato (*see p198*), while others skip Tuscany altogether.

The lack of interest can be explained by the reluctance of funding bodies and producers to stage risky experimental events, something due in no small part to low levels of public curiosity. Middle-of-the-road productions guarantee full houses, which is why they're generally favoured by sponsors; the dedicated few on the fringes are often left with little financial help to get experimental theatre on the stage.

There are bright spots in the general gloom. **Teatro Everest**, a new theatre promoting experimental work, recently opened in Galluzzo. And a major new initiative by ten Florence theatres has meant performances have become far more financially accessible. For €48, the Passteatri gives the holder a ticket to six performances out of a choice of 30 during the season. With a Passteatri, going to the theatre is barely dearer than visiting the cinema; the scheme, unsurprisingly, has been a big success.

Most theatre productions in both Florence and Tuscany – anything from Pirandello and Goldoni to mainstream contemporary productions and radical fringe shows – are in Italian. Don't speak the language? There's also a fair amount of non-verbal theatre. The Tuscan theatre season is short, running from (roughly) September to April.

In contrast to theatre, dance in Florence is in a better state. The scene continues to benefit from public funding, and has a dedicated local following. Full-length classical and contemporary productions by the **MaggioDanza** (which is currently in the midst of a financial crisis) are performed at the **Teatro del Maggio**, while modern work comes from groups such as the **Virgilio Sieni Dance Company**, which performs all year. Elsewhere in Tuscany, look out for groups such as **Motus** (Siena), **Aldes** (Lucca), **Sosta Palmizi** (Cortona), **Micha Van Hoeke** (Castiglioncello), **Compagnia Xe** (San Casciano) and **Giardino Chiuso** (San Gimignano), who perform in festivals such as **La Versiliana** in Marina di Pietrasanta or the **Armunia Festival della Riviera** in Castiglioncello.

In addition to box office hours listed below, theatre venues generally open their ticket offices to personal callers from an hour prior to that night's performance.

Keep an eye out for details of upcoming events in the monthly magazine *Firenze Spettacolo* or other local press.

Venues

Cantiere Goldonetta

Via Santa Maria 23-25, Oltrarno (055 2280525/ www.cango.fi.it). **Box office** 10am-5pm Mon-Fri. **Seasons** Sept-Dec, May-June. **No credit cards**. **Map** p318 D1.

Dance is the main player at this newly restored performance space. Although the project was originally meant to be co-run by several companies, its programme complementing the dance activities at the nearby Teatro Goldoni, the artistic direction has so far been undertaken by the Virgilio Sieni group (*see p192*). The jury is still out on whether the decision was a good one. In addition to the performances (usually free), events include workshops, competitions and promotional platforms.

Florence Dance Cultural Centre

Borgo della Stella 23r, Oltrarno (055 289276/ www.florencedance.org). **Box office** varies. Closed Aug. **Map** p318 C1.

Directed by Marga Nativo and American choreographer Keith Ferrone, this eclectic centre offers a range of dance classes, from children's activities to advanced ballet, through most of the year. It also organises the Florence Dance Festival in July and December (*see p192*). Every couple of months a free performance of new work is staged by Etoile Toy, alongside an art show.

Teatro Cantiere Florida

Via Pisana 111, Outside the City Gates (055 7131783/www.elsinor.net). Bus 6, 26, 27. **Box office** 9am-1pm, 3-6pm Mon-Fri. **Season** late Oct-Apr. **No credit cards.**

Housed in a former cinema, this 288-seat theatre is a handsome space. One of its main objectives is to promote young actors, directors and playwrights, by which it aims to appeal to a young public (there are special family shows on Sundays). Productions range from reworks of Shakespearean classics to experimental pieces. Florida is one of the venues used in the Fabbrica Europa festival (*see p192*).

Teatro Everest

Via Volterrana 4B, Galluzzo, Outside the City Gates (055 2321754/055 2048307). Bus 36, 37, 41. **Box office** 10am-6pm Mon-Fri (055 2321754); 3-7.30pm Tue-Sat (055 2048307). **Season** Oct-Apr. **No credit cards.**

Florence's newest theatre, which occupies a restored 1950s parish hall, generally promotes experimental new works from emerging directors and actors, mixed in with a few established names. The operation is sustained mainly by private funding and the stalwart support of a forward-thinking local priest.

Teatro Goldoni

Via Santa Maria 15, Oltrarno (no phone). **Box office** contact relevant organising body. **Season** varies. **No credit cards. Map** p318 D1.

The delightful and diminutive 18th-century Teatro Goldoni is now used principally for dance events under the programming of three dance bodies: the Florence Dance Company (*see p190*), MaggioDanza (*see p192*) and Versiliadanza (*see p192*).

Teatro della Limonaia

Via Gramsci 426, Sesto Fiorentino, Outside the City Gates (055 440852/www.teatrodellalimonaia.it). Bus 2, 28A. **Box office** 11am-6pm Mon-Fri; 4-7pm Sat. **Seasons** Dec-Apr, May-June. **No credit cards.**

The former lemonery of the Villa Corsi Salviati is the setting for this small, delightful space that wouldn't look out of place in New York City. Shows are mainly alternative: the winter Perle season hosts emerging Italian artists. Look out for the Intercity Festival in June (*see p192*).

Teatro del Maggio Musicale Fiorentino

Corso Italia 16, Santa Maria Novella (055 213535/tickets 199 112112/www.maggiofiorentino.com). **Box office** 10am-4.30pm Tue-Fri; 10am-1pm Sat. **Season** Sept-July. **Credit** AmEx, DC, MC, V.

Home to MaggioDanza (*see p192*), this theatre features mainstream dance in its year-round programme. Maggio Musicale Fiorentino (*see p157*) always includes a free-for-all dance jamboree, usually held in Piazza della Signoria, in its closing days.

Teatro della Pergola

Via della Pergola 12-32, San Marco (055 2264316/www.pergola.firenze.it). **Box office** 9.30am-1pm, 3.30-6.45pm Tue-Sat; 10am-12.15pm Sun. **Season** Oct-Apr. **Credit** AmEx, DC, MC, V. **Map** p319 B5.

A state-controlled theatre, the Pergola presents a full programme of productions from visiting companies. Catch anything from Sophocles to Shakespeare to Woody Allen. *See also p174.*

Teatro Puccini

Piazza Puccini, Outside the City Gates (055 362067/www.teatropuccini.it). Bus 17, 22, 30, 35. **Box office** 3.30-7pm Mon-Fri for in-house productions; contact relevant company for other productions. **Season** Oct-Apr. **No credit cards.**

Inaugurated in 1940 and housed in a large, fascist-style building that has, in the past, been used as a dance hall and cinema, the Puccini hosts light opera, musicals and one-man variety shows. The focus of its programming has always been satire and comedy, and you're just as likely to see an up-and-coming actor as an established name.

Compagnia di Krypton. *See p192.*

Teatro di Rifredi

Via Vittorio Emanuele 303, Outside the City Gates.
(055 4220361/www.toscanateatro.it). Bus 4, 8, 14.
Box office 4-7pm Mon-Sat. **Season** Sept-May.
No credit cards.

Long-term residents Pupi e Fresedde (*see below*) offer
a varied programme devoted mainly to contemporary and fringe shows, many concerned with current
issues and with an emphasis on emerging playwrights and directors. There's also the odd classic
production, plus appearances by guest companies.

Teatro Studio di Scandicci

Via Donizetti 58, Outside the City Gates (055 757348/
www.scandiccicultura.org). Bus 16, 26. **Box office**
4-7pm Mon-Fri. **Season** Oct-June. **No credit cards.**
This small space is a good spot to see alternative
theatre. Artistic director Giancarlo Cauteruccio is a
highly respected name in Florence theatre; his
group, Compagnia di Krypton (*see below*), is the principal resident here. Two other groups also stage performances: Kinkaleri makes big waves with its
shows involving dance, physical theatre and multimedia, while Piccoli Principi performs for children.

Theatre companies

Compagnia di Krypton

055 2345443/krypton@dada.it.
The lighting, stage and sound techniques used by
Krypton were avant-garde when the group started
out in 1982. The company, resident at the Teatro
Studio di Scandicci (*see above*), still experiments with
projections, lasers, microphones and other effects.

Elsinor, Teatro Stabile d'Innovazione

055 7131783/www.elsinor.net.
Resident at the Teatro Cantiere Florida (*see p191*),
Elsinor produces and performs a diverse repertoire
of shows aimed mainly at children and young people.

Pupi e Fresedde

055 4220361/www.toscanateatro.it.
A young company that does a lot of work with
schools and has an eclectic repertoire. It can be con-
tacted via Teatro di Rifredi (*see above*).

Teatro delle Donne

Teatro Manzoni, Via Mascagni 18, Calenzano (055
8876581/www.donne.toscana.it/centri/teatrodonne).
Based at the Teatro Manzoni, this all-female company promotes and performs plays by women.

Dance companies

Compagnia Virgilio Sieni Danza

055 2280525/www.sienidanza.it.
Dancer/choreographer Virgilio Sieni directs one of
the few local avant-garde dance companies to have
achieved global fame. Performances are often col-
laborations with musicians and designers. The company is based at the Cantiere Goldonetta (*see p190*).

MaggioDanza

055 213535/www.maggiofiorentino.com.
The resident group at Teatro del Maggio Musicale
Fiorentino (*see p191*) presents a range of work, from
classics such as *Giselle* to contemporary works by
visiting choreographers. Standards are not always
what they should be, due to ongoing financial problems (the company's future was uncertain as of summer 2005) and frequent staff changes. Performances
are held in the Boboli Gardens in summer.

Versiliadanza

055 350986/www.versiliadanza.it.
Founded in 1993 by dancer/choreographer Angela
Torriani Evangelisti, still artistic director today, this
small company concentrates on contemporary
works, but has worked in the past with a choreographer who specialised in Baroque and Renaissance
dance. The group has been working with German
choreographer Suzanne Linke since 2002.

Festivals

Estate Fiesolana

Teatro Romano, Via Portigiani 1, Fiesole (opera
055 5978308/dance 055 289276/www.estate
fiesolana.it). Bus 7. **Date** mid June-mid Aug.
This festival includes the Florence Dance Festival
summer season, a month-long programme from the
resident Florence Dance Company and guests. At
other times, you can see opera (productions can be
mediocre), concerts and theatre events in Italian.

Fabbrica Europa

Stazione Leopolda, Fratelli Rosselli 5, Outside the City
Gates (055 2480515/www.fabbricaeuropa.net). Bus
17, 22. **Date** May/June.
This big space is well suited to this innovative
festival of theatre and dance. Performances are
also held at the Teatro Cantiere Florida (*see*
p191) and the Cantiere Goldonetta (*see p190*).

Florence Dance Festival

Teatro Romano, Via Portigiani 1, Fiesole (055
289276/www.florencedance.org). Bus 7. **Date** July
& Dec.
The only festival in Tuscany dedicated solely to
dance brings together some of the great names of
contemporary, traditional and classical dance. The
event includes several weeks of performances by
acclaimed companies in Fiesole's Teatro Romano
and dedicates several evenings to up-and-coming
choreographers. A shorter winter edition is held
in the Teatro Goldoni (*see p190*).

Intercity Festival

Date June.
Held in the Teatro della Limonaia (*see p191*), this
festival is a rare opportunity to see contemporary
theatre performed in its mother tongue in Florence.
Each year a European city is chosen as a focus, and
playwrights, actors and theatre companies from the
country concerned are invited to participate.

Tuscany

Getting Started

Hit the beach. Or the hills. Just remember to dodge the crowds.

While Florence's main attractions are its world-renowned, perennially packed museums, Tuscany's appeal is rather more low-key: rolling hills, medieval villages and, outside the cities, a slower pace of life. However, one thing Florence and Tuscany have in common is a turbulent history. Fuelled by endless infighting between its *comuni*, which climaxed between the 13th and 15th centuries, Tuscany gathered commercial strength, mustered military respectability and outpaced its neighbours both artistically and culturally.

The region imposed its language on the rest of the country and produced an unmatched crop of poets, painters, scientists, explorers and architects. Its rulers, though, also had the foresight to amass the greatest artistic wealth anywhere in Europe. To this day, the region has the highest concentration of art in the country and, by extension, the world; Italy, by most accounts, holds over half the planet's artistic treasures. Tuscany's geography also went a long way towards ensuring its overall unity amid constant internal squabbling. More than 90 per cent of its territory is mountainous or hilly, which leaves only small slivers of level ground beside the rivers and along the coast.

AN OVERVIEW

Tuscany's popular image is of sun-drenched and cypress-dotted rolling hills. The Apuan Alps in the north-west and the Appennine peaks to the east set the region apart and provide a plethora of giddy, winding roads, as well as ski resorts and high-altitude trekking. These self-contained, forested valleys – such as the Garfagnana and Lunigiana, which stretch north from Lucca, and the Valtiberina, which branches east from Arezzo – have always provided both the basic ingredients for Tuscany's culinary tradition and the backdrop for many of its paintings.

In the deep south is the Maremma, a large expanse of sparsely populated and previously malarial swampland that was once the region's poorest part but is now a playground for Italy's rich and famous. Etruscan remains are scattered all over this southern part of Tuscany; inland, a series of small, ancient towns, including Pitigliano, cling precariously to hillsides. Towards the northern end of the coast is the modern port of Livorno, Tuscany's historical melting pot, and the Versilia, with its beach

umbrellas and nightspots. But despite all its other attributes, mainland Tuscany is far from ideal for a seaside holiday: its coast is dominated by grey-brown sand, murky water and large crowds (for better beaches you'll have to head to the Argentario peninsula or one of the islands).

The chapters that follow don't aim to provide exhaustive information on the towns and provinces of Tuscany, so much as lead you in the direction of what we consider to be the area's very best elements.

A SENSE OF PLACE

The region's identity, and that of its people, is permeated by a profound sense of belonging known as *campanilismo*: visceral attachment to one's city, town, village or even, as in the case of Siena's *contrade* (*see p221* **Beastly instincts**), one's home district. Having foregone the habit of assaulting one another's walled enclaves, today's Tuscans re-enact their historical enmities mostly verbally, and often colourfully and musically. Florence is generally despised, though this is on account of its historical arrogance and is directed at Florentines as a group rather than individual *Fiorentini*. The capital's two main challengers for regional supremacy have long been Pisa and Siena. While Pisans are also universally

---

Don't miss Tuscany

Best of the country

The unspoilt beauty of the **Parco Naturale della Maremma** (*see p276*); the rugged good looks of **Monte Amiata** (*see p236*); a glug or two at a vineyard (*see p234* **Visiting wineries**); the beaches at **La Giannella** and **La Feniglia** (*see p278*).

Best of the town

Wandering the backstreets in **Siena** (*see p217*); a hot dip in sulphorous waters (*see p215* **Reach for the spas**); **The Leaning Tower of Pisa** (*see p208*); Piero della Francesca's glorious **Legend of the True Cross** in Arezzo (*see p260*); a stroll along the seaside promenade at **Viareggio** (*see p252*).

The old-fashioned way of life on the **Isola del Giglio**. *See p279.*

disliked, it's the Sienese, conscious of being frozen in their medieval glory, who epitomise the idea of identification with place and history.

Prato commands respect for its wealth-generating entrepreneurial spirit, while Pistoia elicits the same for its sense of age. For its part, Montecatini also recalls the past, with its turn-of-the-19th-century parks and grandiloquent bathing establishments. Further west, Lucca, hermetically sealed by its chunky 16th-century walls, always managed to pay off would-be conquerors and now seems to have many more friends – even in Tuscany – than enemies. Bourgeois Arezzo has also kept a high standard of living while falling under Florentine dominion, and working-class Livorno has always been open-minded with loud-mouthed inhabitants and a pioneering spirit.

WHERE, WHEN, HOW

The best overall advice, especially if you only have a week or two, is to concentrate on one or two provinces or parts of the region, such as Siena or Lucca. Unless you want to dedicate your holiday to, say, wine tourism or art and architecture, Tuscany invites you to mix it up a bit. Visit and enjoy ornate churches and galleries in moderation; try not to saturate your days with Tuscan hill towns or devote all your time to long drives around the countryside. Instead, spend a day walking and try to sit down at least once each day to

a Tuscan meal. If you need to recuperate from sightseeing, spend a few hours at one of the region's many thermal spas. Alternatively, build your holiday around a language, cookery or painting course (*see p196*).

In Easter and summer, many places get busy and you have to weigh up whether they're worth the effort. The gorgeous hill town of San Gimignano, for instance, is like honey to the tourist bees: visit in months either side of the rush, such as May or September/October. There are few crowds in winter, but many attractions and restaurants are either shut or are open for limited hours only, and the weather won't be so good. In peak season, book rooms in advance, and even at other times you shouldn't leave it until the last minute.

OUTDOOR PURSUITS

Tuscany offers endless possibilities for walkers. One popular area to hoof it, partly because you can pop into wineries, is to be found among the gentle hills of Chianti. There are more serious walks throughout the Apuan Alps, Monte Amiata and coastal tracks in the Maremma or on the island of Elba. Contact the local tourist offices for further information.

The news for cyclists is mixed. Major roads are a no-no but there are some lovely – if hilly – areas with backroads ripe for exploration, such as Chianti, the Crete Senesi (south-east of Siena) and the Maremma (particularly

Tuscany

inland). A bike is also a good way to get around towns such as Lucca, Montecatini Terme, Pisa and Arezzo.

It's worth considering booking a customised trip or joining a group (*see below*) – having pre-booked accommodation and luggage transfer cuts out a lot of slog.

TOURIST INFORMATION

The general tourist information website for Tuscany is www.turismo.toscana.it. Local tourist offices are listed under the individual towns and areas.

Specialist holidays

Below we list a selection of the best touring and themed holidays. All phone numbers are in the UK unless otherwise stated. For walking and other guided tours within Florence, *see p68*.

Art history holidays

Prospect Art Tours

020 7486 5704/www.prospecttours.com.
Music and art history holidays, including a five-day trip to the Puccini Opera Festival (£995 including accommodation and most meals).

Cookery schools

La Bottega Del 30

0577 359226 within Italy/www.labottegadel30.it.
Popular five-day courses focusing on Chianti cookery. Classes (for up to ten) end with lunch and wine tastings. A wine cellar, library and *videoteca* are also at students' disposal.

Italian Cookery Weeks

020 8208 0112/www.italian-cookery-weeks.co.uk.
Excellent food and wine with daily tuition by an expert chef, accompanied by trips and excursions. Prices start at £1,599 per week including flights.

Farming holidays

WWOOF (Willing Workers on Organic Farms)

01273 476 286/www.wwoof.org.
Working holidays on organic farms, especially during the grape and olive harvests. Food and board are usually provided in exchange for about six hours work a day. It's wise, however, to find out as much as you can about living and working conditions before you go. For a newsletter and a list of farms you need to join WWOOF.

Language schools

See also p296.

Cooperativa 'Il Sasso'

0578 758311 within Italy/www.ilsasso.com.
Two- and four-week language courses for all levels, plus courses in art history and mosaics. Rooms can be arranged in hotels, flats or with families. Prices start at €350 for a two-week course.

Italian Cultural Institute

020 7235 1461/www.italcultur.org.uk.
The Italian Cultural Institute is a good source of information about language courses in Italy.

Painting courses

See also p296.

Simply Travel

0870 166 4979.
Package holidays and city breaks to Florence and Tuscany, staying in private villas and hotels that are off the beaten track. A week-long holiday, including flights, transfers or car hire and accommodation in a villa, starts from £500 per person.

Verrochio Art Centre

020 8869 1035/www.verrocchio.co.uk.
Specialist painting and sculpture courses in a hilltop village. Prices start at £779 for a two-week course (accommodation, breakfast and dinner, excluding flights). Bookings are made through Maureen Ruck on the above number.

Walking & cycling

Alternative Travel Group

01865 315 678/www.atg-oxford.co.uk.
Escorted walking and cycling trips (from £895, excluding flights) in small groups, plus customised unguided walking trips with rooms in family-run hotels (a week from £425 B&B, flights not included).

Ramblers Holidays

01707 331133/www.ramblersholidays.co.uk.
A variety of walking tours, including a week exploring the sights of Florence, from £513 half board, including flights and accommodation.

Villa rentals & *agriturismo*

Many travel companies have a wide range of villas to rent across the region. Our favourites include **James Villas** (UK: 08700 556688, www.jamesvillas.co.uk), **Tuscan House** (US: 1-800 844 6939, 1-251 968 4444, www.tuscanhouse.com) and **Ville in Italia** (Italy: 055 412058, www.villeinitalia.com). Rates vary hugely according to the season and size of property, so call or browse the website.

Agriturismo – whereby farmers let out part of their property – is an increasingly common option. Check www.agriturismo.net for a wide range of properties online.

Florence & Prato Provinces

Leonardo lived here.

Prato's striped **Duomo**.

Florence offers easy access to a clutch of towns and sights in the immediate vicinity. To the west is the province of Prato; the textile industry in the provincial capital and the town's business acumen have made it a place where Florentines go to shop for discount designer wear. There's plenty for culture vultures too, with some magnificent art and one of Tuscany's most prestigious theatres, the historic **Teatro Metastasio** (*see p198*). To the south-west lie the medieval towns of Carmignano, surrounded by vineyards, and Vinci, the birthplace of Leonardo. Also nearby are Montelupo, known for its colourful ceramics, and the enchanting hilltop town of Certaldo Alto. The Mugello, to the north, is a delightful rural escape that is becoming increasingly popular with foreigners.

Work on the man-made but picturesque Lake Bilancino near Barberino di Mugello was finished in 2003 and the lake is now being developed for fishing and windsurfing.

Prato

From a touristic point of view, Prato suffers from its reputation as an industrial suburb of Florence, and few visitors bother to stop off on their way along the A11 motorway to Lucca and Pisa. The Florentines are pretty snotty about it too, dismissing the Pratesi as a bunch of nouveaux riches Rolex-wearers. Maybe it's jealousy; Prato is a lively, prosperous little town with few of the problems suffered by its eastern neighbour. There's a lot less traffic, for a start, and consequently the *centro storico* is not choked by pollution. Housing is much cheaper and the quality of life is high. The city council has been spending squillions in recent years on upgrading Prato's attractions, and there is a range of of good restaurants, bars and clubs.

Hard-working Prato has been renowned for centuries for its production of fine textiles, an industry that is still very much alive today. Some of the world's most famous designers come here for their cloth. The **Museo del Tessuto** (Via Santa Chiara 24, 0574 611503, closed Tue, €4), the Textile Museum, showcases fabrics and looms from the fifth century to the present day.

Like Florence, Prato was a dynamic trading centre in the Middle Ages. Accountancy was virtually invented here in the 14th century by Francesco di Marco Datini, on whose meticulous accounts and private letters Iris Origo based her 1957 novel *The Merchant of Prato*. Prato honours its chief bean-counter with a large 19th-century statue in the Piazza del Comune. You can also visit **Palazzo Datini** (Via Mazzei 33, 0574 21391, closed Sun, admission free), where Datini's documents and records (all 150,000 of them) are stored.

Dedicated to St Stephen, Prato's 13th-century **Duomo** is a striking Romanesque-Gothic building in pinkish brick with a half-finished

Living in a material world: Prato's **Museo del Tessuto**. *See p197.*

green and white striped marble façade. On one corner is the 15th-century Pulpit of the Sacred Girdle (Sacro Cingolo), designed by Michelozzo and carved with reliefs of dancing children and cherubs by Donatello (the originals, now replaced by casts, are in the Museo dell'Opera del Duomo; *see below*). The church houses some very fine art: the pulpit in the nave is by Mino da Fiesole and Antonio Rossellino, while the Chapel of the Sacred Girdle has a magnificent bronze screen and floor-to-ceiling frescoes by Agnolo Gaddi. The choir is decorated with beautiful frescoes by Filippo Lippi; they're under long-term restoration but can be viewed by appointment on Saturdays and Sundays (call the tourist office to book ten days in advance). The city's religious icon, the Sacro Cingolo, is paraded through the Duomo on festival days.

The **Museo dell'Opera del Duomo** (Piazza Duomo 49, 0574 29339, closed Tue, €6 incl Museo di Pittura Murale & Prato castle) is in the Palazzo Vescovile to the left of the Duomo. Exhibits include Donatello's original bas-reliefs for the external pulpit of dancing *putti*, a fresco attributed to Paolo Uccello and works by both Filippo and Filippino Lippi. **Museo di Pittura Murale** (Piazza San Domenico, 0574 440501, closed Tue, admission €4, or €6 with Museo dell'Opera del Duomo) also has works by Filippino and Filippo Lippi, including the latter's *Madonna del Ceppo* (1453), with its portrayal of Prato merchant Datini.

If you still want more culture, check out the **Centro per l'arte Contemporanea Luigi Pecci** (Viale della Repubblica 277, 0574 5317, closed Tue, admission €4-€6), one of Italy's leading centres of contemporary art, and the

historic **Teatro Matastasio** (Via B Cairoli 59, 0574 6084, www.metastasio.it), one of Italy's most prestigious prose venues, which stages everything from Kafka to Shakespeare as well as the Italian classics.

Where to eat

Enoteca Barni (Via Ferrucci 22, 0574 607845, closed lunch Sat & all Sun, average €15 lunch, €50 dinner) stands out. Lunch is informal and cheap-ish, while dinner is a more costly affair and features the likes of roast pigeon with *porcini*. **Il Pirana** (Via Valentini 110, 0574 25746, closed Sat & Sun lunch, average €55) is renowned for its fish and seafood, while **La Vecchia Cucina di Soldano** (Via Pomeria 23, 0574 34665, closed Sun, average €25) is a family-run place serving hearty traditional dishes to the locals. **Osteria Cibbe** (Piazza Mercatale 49, 0574 607509, closed Sun, average €23) is another excellent economical choice.

Where to stay

Hotel Museo (Viale della Repubblica 289, 0574 5787, www.arthotelmuseo.com, doubles €105-€145) is a luxury option out near the Luigi Pecci museum. More central, and cheaper, is the recently renovated **Hotel Flora** (Via Cairoli 31, 0574 33521, www.hotelflora.info, doubles €75-€130). Further out, the **Villa Rucellai** (Via di Canneto 16, 0574 460392, www.villarucellai.it, doubles €80-€90) is a lovely hillside villa with the atmosphere of a slightly faded, grand family home, which indeed it is; the aristocratic Rucellai family has lived here for generations.

Poggio a Caiano, Carmignano & Artimino

Heading west out of Florence on the SS66 through endless ugly suburbs, you pass through the old village of **Poggio a Caiano**, home to one of the most impressive of the Medici villas. Built in 1480 by Giuliano da Sangallo, it was Lorenzo Il Magnifico's favourite country retreat. Today you can visit a number of rooms, including the massive *salone* with its lovely frescoes.

A little further on and just south of the main road, pleasant **Carmignano** is light years away from the hubbub of the city. Its pride and joy is the 1530 *Visitation*, Pontormo's most famous work, housed in the 13th-century church of San Michele e San Francesco.

This area is known for wines that marry sangiovese, canaiolo and cabernet grapes. Nearby estates offering tastings of local wines include **Capezzana** (Via Capezzana 100, Seano, 055 8706005, closed Sun) and **Fattoria di Bacchereto** (Via Fontemorana, 055 8717191, closed 2wks Nov or Jan). Tours are by appointment at both. The latter also has a shop-restaurant called **Cantina di Toia** (055 8717135, closed Mon & lunch Tue, average €35), rooms and apartments.

There are two probable reasons for visiting the delightful little hamlet of **Artimino** nearby: to eat at wonderful **Da Delfina** (*see p40* **Want food, will travel**), or to see the multi-chimneyed Medici Villa known as **La Ferdinanda**. Little seems to have changed by way of the setting here since the villa was built by Buontalenti as a hunting lodge for Fernando I, although there is now an upmarket hotel in what were once the stables. Visits are by guided tour only (055 8718124).

Where to eat & drink

In Carmignano, taste the local wines and have a bite to eat (maybe salt cod with raisins) at **Su Pe' I Canto** (Piazza Matteotti 25, 055 8712490, closed Mon, average €25). Or try **La Barco Reale** (Piazza Vittorio Emanuele II, 055 8711559, closed Tue, average €21), where the traditional dishes include tripe and *stracotto* (beef stewed slowly in local wine).

Vinci

As the birthplace of Leonardo ('da Vinci' tells you where he's from), this quaint little hill town attracts a constant stream of visitors. Models of the fantastic machines and instruments devised by the Renaissance polymath are on display at the **Museo Leonardiano** (0571 56055, admission €5), now housed in two separate buildings. The ticket office is in the new section, Palazzina Uzielli in Via Rossi, while the formidable Castello dei Conti Guidi houses the main body of the collection. A three-kilometre (two-mile) drive or walk up through olive groves brings you to the stone farmhouse (open 9.30am-6pm daily) where Leonardo was born.

Where to eat

Il Ristoro del Museo (Via Montalbano 9, 0571 56516, closed Fri dinner & Sat lunch, average €22) has a panoramic terrace and serves delicious traditional food. The **Cantina di Bacco** (Piazza Leonardo da Vinci, 0571 568041, closed Mon, average €20) is a cute little wine bar that also serves food.

Montelupo

The people of Montelupo have been making beautiful, colourful glazed pottery since the Middle Ages. In 1973 an old public laundry in the Castello district was dismantled to reveal a well that had been filled over the centuries with ceramic rejects and shards. Many are now in the **Museo della Ceramica** (Via Sinibaldi 43-45, 0571 51352, closed Mon, admission €3).

The locals have never forsaken their vocation; the main street of the town is lined with shops selling boldly patterned ceramics, and a big, week-long Festa Internazionale della Ceramica is held towards the end of June.

Certaldo Alto

This picturesque hill settlement's main claim to fame is that Giovanni Boccaccio (1313-75, author of the *Decameron*) was born and died here. Its historic centre monopolises a lovely view over the Val d'Elsa, looking over to Volterra. Don't confuse it with the singularly unattractive new town at the bottom of the hill. During the first week in August the town is bathed in candlelight for the Mercantia, a festival aimed at recreating the atmosphere of the town before the advent of electricity. The **Palazzo Pretorio** (Piazzetta del Vicario, 0571 661219, closed Mon in winter, admission €3) is decorated with the coats of arms of past governors and has beautiful frescoed rooms.

Where to stay & eat

Osteria del Vicario (Via Rivellino 3, 0571 668228, closed Wed in winter, doubles €90, average €40) has rooms and a restaurant with a romantic terrace. The new town may be ugly,

Tuscany

but it's got a great restaurant. Tiny **La Saletta di Dolci Follie** (Via Roma 3, 0571 668188, closed Tue & 2wks in Aug, average €35), at the back of a pastry shop, has excellent wines and good dishes such as risotto with gorgonzola.

The Mugello

The rolling countryside north-east of Florence is known as the Mugello, while the remote Alto Mugello extends up the Appenine passes to the border with Emilia-Romagna. It is a beautiful area of wooded hillsides (which offer great walking) and pastures. The Medici loved its verdant character and built several hunting lodges such as **Castello di Trebbio** and the vast **Villa Cafaggiolo**, both near San Piero a Sieve. The only disturbance is the **Autodromo Internazionale del Mugello** (055 8499411, www.mugellocircuit.it), a racetrack near Scarperia hosting motorcycle racing.

Borgo San Lorenzo is the pleasant, bustling commercial centre of the area, where business has been booming in recent years, partially due to a new, fast train link with Florence. A few kilometres north-west is attractive old **Scarperia**, founded in 1306 as the northernmost military outpost of the Florentine Republic. Because of its strategic location, it enjoyed considerable prosperity until the 18th century, when the main road over the Appennines to Bologna opened further west.

In the spacious central square is the **Palazzo dei Vicari** (055 8468165, closed Mon, Tue June-mid Sept & Mon-Fri mid Sept-May; admission €3), built in the 13th century to designs by Arnolfo di Cambio and reminiscent of the Palazzo Vecchio in Florence. Inside are frescoes dating from the 14th and 16th centuries, and a small museum of cutting tools. The production of traditional bone-handled pocket knives has been practised in the town for centuries. You can visit the factories and watch knives being made or buy the exquisite (and costly) end results from one of the town's showrooms.

Just east of Borgo San Lorenzo, sleepy little **Vicchio** is famous for being the birthplace of Fra Angelico and Giotto. Or for beaches and watersports head west to **Lago di Balancino**.

Where to stay & eat

For Mugello cuisine in Scarperia, try **Il Torrione** (Via Roma 78-80, 055 8430263, closed Mon, average €22) or the more upmarket **Teatro de' Medici** (Località La Torre 14, 055 8459876, closed Mon & 2wks Aug & 2wks Feb, average €40), housed in a mellow old villa on the road to Borgo. In Borgo, enjoy refined versions of local dishes at the delightful

Ristorante degli Artisti (Piazza Romagnoli 1, 055 8457707, closed Wed, average €55), but don't miss the area's best *tortelli* at Giorgione's simple trattoria at **Sagginale** (*see p40* **Want food, will travel**).

The most comfortable hotel in the area is the **Villa Campestri** (Via di Campestri 19, 055 8490107, www.villacampestri.it, closed mid Nov-mid Mar, doubles €140-€165), a lovely old villa set in green hills just above Sagginale between Borgo and Vicchio. If this is too expensive, try **Locanda degli Artisti** (Piazza Romagnoli 2, 055 8455359, www.locanda artisti.it, doubles €90-€110) in Borgo.

Resources

Tourist information

Carmignano *Piazza Vittorio Emanuele II 1-2 (055 8712468).* **Open** *Winter* 9am-noon, 3-5.30pm Tue-Fri & 1st Sun of mth; 9am-noon Sat, Sun. *Summer* 9am-12.30pm, 3.30-7pm Tue-Sun.
Certaldo Alto *Viale Fabiani 5 (0571 656721).* **Open** 9am-1pm, 3.30-7pm daily. Closed Jan-Mar.
The Mugello *Via Togliatti 45, Borgo San Lorenzo (055 845271/www.mugellotoscana.it).* **Open** 9am-1pm Mon, Wed, Fri; 9am-1pm, 3-6pm Tue, Thur.
Prato *Piazza Santa Maria delle Carceri 15 (0574 24112/www.prato.turismo.toscana.it).* **Open** *Summer* 9am-1.30pm, 2.30-7pm Mon-Sat; 10am-1pm, 3-6.30pm Sun. *Winter* 9am-1.30pm, 2.30-6pm Mon-Sat.
Vinci *Via della Torre 11 (0571 568012).* **Open** *Summer* 10am-7pm daily. *Winter* 10am-6pm Mon-Fri; 10am-3pm Sat, Sun.

Getting there

By bus
SITA (800 373760 or 055 294955, www.sita-on-line.it) runs bus services to Borgo San Lorenzo and Vicchio (1hr), with onward connections to Scarperia.

By car
Montelupo is just off the Florence-Pisa-Livorno *superstrada*. To reach Certaldo, turn south off this road on to the SS429 near Empoli. For Vinci, exit at Empoli and head north for Pistoia. Carmignano and Artimino are best reached via the SS66, the Via Pistorese from Florence; there are signs at Poggio a Caiano. For Borgo San Lorenzo take either the SS65 (the Via Bolognese) or the more winding SS302 (the Via Faentina). For Scarperia take the SS65 and pick up the SS503 at San Piero a Sieve. For Vicchio, head for Borgo and turn right on to the SS551.

By train
Carmignano and Montelupo are on the Florence/Empoli/Pisa train line; journey times to Carmignano is 25mins (irregular service); for Montelupo add 5mins. For Certaldo you must change (journey time about 1hr). There's a regular service from Florence to Borgo San Lorenzo and Vicchio – journey time is 45-50mins. For timetable information, call 892021 or consult www.trenitalia.it.

Pistoia Province

Home to thermal spas – and a small wooden boy.

Giardino Garzoni. *See p203.*

The province of Pistoia has much to offer the town-weary visitor. Leave the masses behind in Florence for a few days of cool, green Apennine scenery, spas and sleepy villages; there's even skiing to be had in Abetone. The provincial capital of Pistoia offers some superb art too, but you won't be jostling with thousands of others. If you want glamour (or, indeed, a cure), head to upmarket Montecatini Terme, where you can pamper yourself at one of the swish hotels.

Pistoia

The countryside for miles around Pistoia is characterised by neat rows of dwarf trees and small shrubs. The rich soil has given rise to a lucrative line in plant nurseries, which has become a multi million-euro industry. The quiet old town itself is one of Tuscany's genuine hidden gems, with an almost perfectly intact historic centre encircled by medieval walls and few fellow tourists to spoil your enjoyment.

The architectural style of many of Pistoia's monuments combines Florentine and Pisan elements. The **Cattedrale di San Zeno** has an arcaded Pisan façade and a simple Romanesque interior; the fine campanile has a plain lower section and exotic tiger-striped arcades on top. It houses the famous gold and silver *Altar of St James* within the chapel of the same name (admission €2). Across the square is the octagonal 14th-century, green-and-white, striped Baptistery. The **Museo Civico** (0573 371296, closed Mon, admission €3.50), behind the Duomo, has fine 14th-century paintings on the ground floor and some fairly dreadful late Mannerist works two floors above. The portico of the Ospedale del Ceppo (founded in the 13th century and still a functioning hospital) is decorated with a splendid ceramic frieze in the style of Giovanni della Robbia (1526-9). The nearby church of Sant'Andrea has a magnificent hexagonal stone pulpit (1298-1301) by Giovanni Pisano.

Local events include the Giostra dell'Orso (Joust of the Bear) on 25 July (the live bears have been replaced by wooden dummies) and the Pistoia Blues music festival (May/June); *see also p263* **And the beat goes on**).

Where to eat & drink

La Bottegaia (Via del Lastrone 17, 0573 365602, closed lunch Sun & all Mon, average €26) is a delightful wine bar/restaurant tucked away in a little square behind the Baptistery, which serves great food. The cheap and cheerful **Trattoria dell'Abbondanza** (Via dell'Abbondanza 10, 0573 368037, closed Wed and lunch Thur, average €22) serves hearty Tuscan fare such as *baccalà alla Livornese*. For civilised coffee and cakes, try **Caffè Pasticceria Valiani** (Via Cavour 55, 0573 23034, closed 1st 3wks Aug & Tue in winter). Frescoed walls were uncovered back in 1864 when its foundations were being laid.

Where to stay

Six kilometres (four miles) from town, comfortable **Villa Vannini** (Villa di Piteccio 6, Villa di Piteccio village, 0573 42031, www. volpe-uva.it, doubles €70-€90) has a slightly eccentric country-house atmosphere and superb

Parco di Pinocchio. *See p203.*

from this time. Today the place still has a very civilised air of restrained elegance and thousands of foreign visitors come each year to take the waters and enjoy the town. There are around 200 hotels, but in high season these can be packed, so book ahead. The place all but closes between late November and Easter.

The warm saline waters at Montecatini are supposed to be particularly beneficial for digestive complaints and are taken both internally and externally. The spas are modernising but many are still housed, at least partially, in the original buildings; grandest of all is **Terme Tettuccio**. For information about spas and the treatments on offer, contact the central Terme office at Viale Verdi 41 (www.termemontecatini.it, 800 132538).

On a balmy evening a lovely diversion is to ride the funicular railway (Viale Alfredo Diaz, €3 single, €5 return) up to charming Montecatini Alto and its panoramic views.

Where to eat & drink

On Montecatini Alto's main Piazza Giusti, **La Torre** (0572 70650, closed Tue, average €25) is a good option; you can even try ostrich. Back down in Terme, there's lots of choice. **Il Cucco** (Via del Salsero 3, 0572 72765, closed Tue and lunch Wed, average €45) serves delicious, innovative dishes including pasta with fresh broad beans and courgette flowers. You can get good pizza (dinner only) and pasta at **Egisto's** (Piazza Cesare Battisti 13, 0572 78413, closed Tue, average €23). If you want to try Tuscan wines, staff at **Il Chicco d'Uva Vineria** (Viale Verdi 35, 0572 910300, closed Mon & Feb) are laid-back experts.

Where to stay

Most hotels insist on half or even full board in high season. If you want to stay near Montecatini Alto try the upmarket and tasteful **Casa Albertina** (Via Baccelli, 0572 900238, www.casaalbertina.it, doubles €100), which has glorious views over the Nievole valley from the garden. In town, the **Grand Hotel & La Pace** (Via della Torretta 1, 0572 9240, www.grand hotellapace.com, doubles €294-€440) is set in extensive grounds with two pools and has a sumptuous belle époque atmosphere. The revamped **Metropole** (Via della Torretta 13, 0572 70092, www.hotel-metropole.it, doubles €70) occupies a turn-of-the-century villa and has 40 rooms, while the spotless, family-run **Hotel Savoia & Campana** (Viale Cavallotti 10, 0572 772670, www.hotelsavoiaecampana. com, doubles €50-€82) has an old-fashioned air and 30 pleasant rooms.

food. Another rural option is the five beautifully decorated rooms of *agriturismo* **Tenuta di Pieve a Celle** (Pieve a Celle, 0573 913087, www.tenutadipieveacelle.it, doubles €120). More mainstream is the pleasant and central, if dated, **Hotel Leon Bianco** (Via Panciatichi 2, 0573 26675, www.hotelleonbianco.it, doubles €50-€100). **Hotel Firenze** (Via Curtatone e Montanara 42, 0573 23141, www.hotel-firenze.it, doubles €60-€84) is friendly and good value. There are over 100 farm-stays around Pistoia – call the tourist office for a brochure.

Montecatini Terme

At the start of the 20th century Montecatini Terme was one of the most fashionable destinations in Europe for royalty, aristocracy and the day's political and literary movers and shakers. The monumental thermal buildings, set around the beautiful Parco delle Terme and constructed in a variety of OTT styles, date

Collodi

Collodi, on the SS435 just west of Pescia, is famous for being the birthplace of Pinocchio, Italy's most cherished fairytale character. His 'inventor', the writer Collodi, took his name from the town he visited regularly as a child. This claim to fame brings the tourists to what is an otherwise minor, but not unattractive, town. There's no shortage of signs directing visitors to **Parco di Pinocchio** (0572 429342, www.pinocchio.it, admission €9, €7 under-14s). Opened in 1956, it features a walk-through maze and Pinocchio statues, including one by Emilio Greco, and a colourful mosaic-lined courtyard by Venturino Venturi. Just across the road from the park, **Giardino Garzoni** (Piazza della Vittoria 1, 0572 429590, open 8.30am-7pm daily, admission €7, €5 under-14s; combined ticket with Parco di Pinocchio €12, €9 under-14s) is a baroque garden designed by Romano di Alessandro Garzoni. There's a feeling of faded glory to it, although an ongoing restoration programme is sprucing up the fountains and statues. For the moment, though, it's charming in a crumbly sort of way.

Pescia

Pescia is Italy's capital of flowers. Some three million blooms are exported from this attractive old town every day in summer. It also grows a mean asparagus. Take in the kaleidoscopic colours and head-spinning perfumes between 6 and 8am Mon-Sat at the vast flower market at Via Salvo d'Acquisto 10-12 (0572 440502). Call to let them know you're coming.

The Montagna Pistoiese

The Apennine mountains to the north of Pistoia, known as the Montagna Pistoiese, make a cool, green escape from the heat of the plain in summer; at the top is Abetone, one of Tuscany's two ski destinations (the other is Monte Amiata in Grosseto province; *see p236*). Beautifully-situated San Marcello Pistoiese is a popular summer resort standing 820 metres (2,690 feet) above sea level, while a little further on is the attractive old town of Cutigliano, which also fills up in summer with Florentines fleeing the heat. Reached via a splendid and ancient forest, Abetone stands at nearly 1,400 metres (4,590 feet) above sea level. Just 85 kilometres (53 miles) from Florence, it's easily accessible for a weekend or even a day trip. It gets very crowded at weekends and during the busy *settimana bianca* season (January to March), when parents take kids out of school for a week on the slopes, but its wide runs are ideal for beginners and intermediate skiers. On average, ski-boot hire costs €20 per day and ski passes are €25 per weekday, €29.50 at the weekend.

Where to stay & eat

In Cutigliano, the old-fashioned **Miramonte** (Piazza Catilina 12, 0573 68012, doubles €67 per person full board – obligatory in high season) occupies a 16th-century palazzo on the main square. Up in Abetone, the modest **Noemi** (Via Brennero 244, Località Le Regine, 0573 60168, doubles €26-€52) has ten en suite rooms. Or there's the four-star **Bella Vista** (Via Brennero 383, 0573 60028, www.bellavista-abetone.it, doubles €100-€155). The rustic **L'Osteria** (Via Roma 6, 0573 68272, average €25) in Cutigliano specialises in mushrooms; you can eat them in soups, risottos, pastas or deep fried, while at the **Locanda dello Yeti** (Via Brennero 324, Località Le Regine, 0573 606974, closed Tue, average €28) there's no hairy monsters on the menu, but try the gnocchi with mint pesto.

Resources

Tourist information

Abetone *(tourist information 0573 60231/ ski information 0573 60001)*.
Montagna Pistoiese APT *Via Marconi 70, San Marcello Pistoiese (0573 630145)*. **Open** 8am-2pm Mon-Sat.
Montecatini Terme APT *Viale Verdi 66 (0572 772244)*. **Open** 9am-1.30pm, 3-6pm Mon-Sat; 9am-noon Sun.
Pistoia APT *Piazza Duomo (0573 21622)*. **Open** 9am-1pm, 3-6pm Mon-Sat; also Sun June-Sept.
Pistoia province *www.pistoia.turismo.toscana.it*.

Getting there

By bus

LAZZI (055 363041, www.lazzi.it) runs regular buses from Florence to Pistoia (45mins) and Montecatini Terme (1hr). **CAP** (055 214637) links Pistoia with Florence. From Pistoia, **CAO** operates a service into the mountains (San Marcello, Cutigliano, Abetone). **CLAP** (0583 587897) buses connect Lucca with Pescia (45mins) and less regularly with Collodi. **COPIT/CAP** run daily 'ski buses' from Florence to Abetone in season, but you must change in Pistoia. For timetables call 0573 3630 or 055 214637.

By car

Pistoia, Montecatini and the Montagne Pistoiese are accessible off the A11 *autostrada*.

By train

Regular trains on the Florence-Lucca line service Pistoia (35mins), Montecatini (50mins) and Pescia (60-75mins). For the Montagna Pistoiese, take the train to Pistoia then change to a CAP bus. See www.trenitalia.it or call 892021 for details.

Tuscany

Pisa

So much more than just a tower.

There's a great deal more to Pisa than the sum of its most famous parts, with interesting restaurants, shops and clubs opening all the time. That said, the **Campo dei Miracoli**, where you'll find the **Cathedral**, the **Baptistery** and the **Leaning Tower**, is considered the ultimate Catholic theme park for a reason, so, to make the most of the town, you'd be wise to visit between autumn and spring, when the city is a little quieter.

Pisa is located in a broad flood plain surrounding a loop in the River Arno, ten kilometres (six miles) before it flows into the Tyrrhenian Sea. In ancient times the estuary of the Arno was further inland, creating a lagoon inlet with easy landing for boats. The settlers there soon became traders, initially under the Etruscan sphere of influence, and then, from 27 BC, as a prosperous Roman colony. A few years ago the chance discovery of two dozen 2,000-year-old ships, which had been preserved beneath layers of silt, bore tangible witness to such early clout. The **Arsenale Medicio** on Lungarno Simonelli is being restored and will house the boats and their cargos from 2009.

During the Middle Ages the wealth and power of Pisa increased; by the 11th century it had established itself as a great maritime republic. The accrued wealth paid for urban expansion, including the Campo dei Miracoli, but by the 15th century the city was in decline. It didn't do well under the Medici grand dukes; their successor, Pietro Leopoldo of Lorraine, found it to be 'languid and poor, with insalubrious air, swampy land and widespread misery'. So, in the late 1700s, he set about putting things right.

He did a pretty decent job. By 1844 Pisa was linked to Florence by rail, and had begun to develop the taste for intellectual advancement that it retains to this day. As well as its eminent university and the prestigious Scuola Normale Superiore, it's home to numerous research institutes. The academic population lends the streets a purposeful atmosphere, but also provide a youthful pulse: there are a good number of bars and nightclubs here, as well as events such as June's **Metarock** (*see p263* **And the beat goes on**). The two main local festivals, however, are a little more historic: for the **Luminaria di San Ranieri** (16 June) and the **Gioco del Ponte** (last Sunday in June), for both, *see p158*.

Sightseeing

Campo dei Miracoli

The scale and elegance of the layout of the Duomo, the Baptistery, the Leaning Tower and the Camposanto are undeniable. The 13th-century court astrologer Guido Bonatti argued that the spatial design was symbolic of the cosmos, and the theme of Aries in particular. Get here early if you want to see it at its best: when the crowds descend, as they invariably do, it might not appear quite so attractive. That said, the **Museo delle Sinopie** also gives a fine view of the whole complex.

There are ticket offices in four sites (depicted by yellow triangles on maps and signposts at the Campo), with the tourist office next to the ticket office in the north-east corner. There are several varieties of ticket, including one that offers admission to all the sights (except the Leaning Tower, for which *see p209* **Tilt to last**) for €10.50. Call 050 560547 for information, or check www.opapisa.it.

Baptistery

050 560547/www.opapisa.it. **Open** *Apr-Sept* 9am-8pm daily. *Mar, Oct* 9am-6pm daily. *Nov-Feb* 9am-5pm daily. **Admission** €5. **Credit** MC, V.
The marble Baptistery was designed by Diotisalvi in 1153, with later decorative input by Nicola and Giovanni Pisano. The magnificent pulpit by Nicola Pisano (1260) is still there to be admired in situ, though most of the precious artwork is now kept in the Museo dell'Opera del Duomo (*see p208*). The harmonious, onion-shaped dome was a later addition, from the mid 14th century.

Camposanto

Open *Apr-Sept* 9am-8pm daily. *Mar, Oct* 9am-6pm daily. *Nov-Feb* 9am-5pm daily. **Admission** €5. **Credit** MC, V.
The Camposanto (Holy Field) is a felicitous stylistic misfit, with elements of various styles, including Gothic and Romanesque. Lining the Gothic cloisters around the edge of the field are the gravestones of VIP Pisans buried in holy soil. On the west wall hang two massive lengths of chain that were once strung across the entrance to the Pisan port to keep out enemy ships. An Allied bomb landed on the Campo in 1944, destroying frescoes and sculptures. A fabulous cycle by Benozzo Gozzoli fell victim to it, but a few survived, including, appropriately enough, *Triumph of Death*, *Last Judgement* and *Hell*.

Campo dei Miracoli. *See p204.*

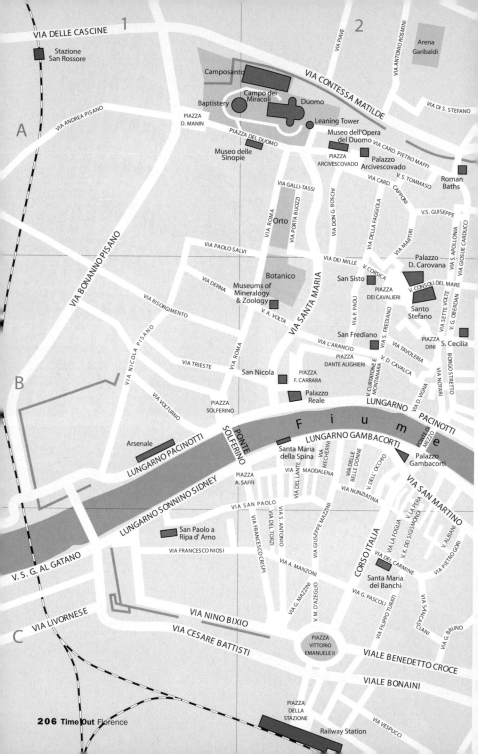

VIA DELLE CASCINE

1
2

VIA PIAVE

VIA ANTONIO ROSMINI

Arena
Garibaldi

Stazione
San Rossore

Camposanto

VIA CONTESSA MATILDE

VIA DI S. STEFANO

VIA ANDREA PISANO

Campo dei
Miracoli

A

PIAZZA
D. MANIN

Baptistery

Duomo

Leaning Tower

Museo dell'Opera
del Duomo

VIA CARD. PIETRO MAFFI

PIAZZA DEL DUOMO

Museo delle
Sinopie

PIAZZA
ARCIVESCOVADO

Palazzo
Arcivescovado

V. S. TOMMASO

VIA CARD. CAPPONI

Roman
Baths

VIA GALLI-TASSI

V.S. GIUSEPPE

VIA ROMA

Orto

VIA PORTA BUOZZI

VIA DON G. BOSCHI

VIA DELLA FAGGIOLA

VIA MARTIRI

V.S. APOLLONIA

VIA GIOSUE CARDUCCI

VIA PAOLO SALVI

VIA DEI MILLE

Palazzo
D. Carovana

VIA S. VOLTE

VIA DERNA

Botanico

V. CORSICA

San Sisto

V. CONSOLI DEL MARE

VIA RISORGIMENTO

Museums of
Mineralogy
& Zoology

PIAZZA
DEI CAVALIERI

V.G. OBERDAN

VIA NICOLA PISANO

VIA SANTA MARIA

V. A. VOLTA

VIA P. PAOLI

Santo
Stefano

VIA BONANNO PISANO

VIA ROMA

VIA L'ARANCIO

San Frediano

V.S. FREDIANO

VIA TAVOLERIA

PIAZZA
DINI

S. Cecilia

BORGO STRETTO

VIA TRIESTE

PIAZZA
DANTE ALIGHIERI

V. D. CAVALCA

B

San Nicola

PIAZZA
F. CARRARA

V. CURTATONE E
MONTANARA

VIA NOTARI

VIA VOLTURNO

Palazzo
Reale

V.D. VIGNA

LUNGARNO
PACINOTTI

PIAZZA
SOLFERINO

F i u m **e**

Arsenale

LUNGARNO PACINOTTI

PONTE
SOLFERINO

Santa Maria
della Spina

LUNGARNO GAMBACORTI

PONTE D.
MEZZO

Palazzo
Gambacorti

VIA MECHERINI

VIA DELLE
BELLE DONNE

VIA DELL'OCCHIO

VIA SAN MARTINO

LUNGARNO SONNINO SIDNEY

PIAZZA
A. SAFFI

VIA DEL LANTE

MADDALENA

VIA NUNZIATINA

VIA SAN PAOLO

VIA S. ANTONIO

VIA DEL TORZI

VIA GIUSEPPE MAZZINI

VIA ALBANI

San Paolo a
Ripa d' Arno

VIA FRANCESCO CRISPI

CORSO ITALIA

VIA LA FOGLIA

VIA LA PERA

V. K. DEI SIGISMONDI

VIA PIETRO GORI

V.S. G. AL GATANO

VIA FRANCESCO NIOSI

VIA A. MANZONI

VIA DEL CARMINE

Santa Maria
del Banchi

VIA SANGSCLANI

VIA G. BRUNO

VIA LIVORNESE

VIA NINO BIXIO

V. M. D'AZEGLIO

VIA G. PASCOLI

VIA FILIPPO TURATI

C

VIA CESARE BATTISTI

PIAZZA
VITTORIO
EMANUELE II

VIALE BENEDETTO CROCE

VIALE BONAINI

PIAZZA
DELLA
STAZIONE

VIA VESPUCCI

Railway Station

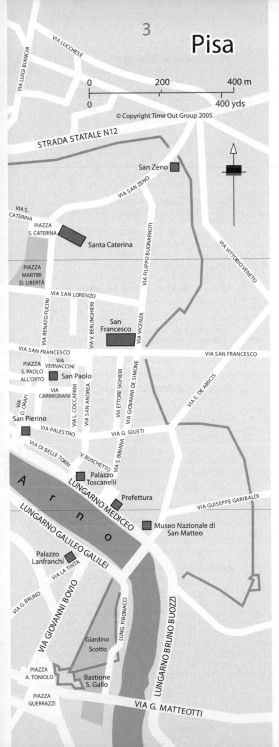

Pisa

3

© Copyright Time Out Group 2005

A. Volta, Via - B2	Lungarno Pacinotti - B1/2
Albiani, Via - C2	Lungarno R. Simonelli - B1, 2
Andrea Pisano, Via - A1	Lungarno Sonnino Sidney - B1, C1
Antonio Rosmini, Via - A2	Maddalena, Via - B2
Belle Donne, Via Delle - B2	Martiri, Via - A2
Benedetto Croce, Viale - C2	Mecherini, Via - B2
Berlinghieri, Via V. - B3	Mille, Via Dei - B2
Bonaini, Viale - C2	Nicola Pisano, Via - B1 .
Bonanno Pisano, Via - A1, B1	Nino Bixio, Via - C1,2
Borgo Stretto - B2	Notari, Via - B2
Buschetto, Via - B3	P. Paoli, Via - B2
Card. Pietro Maffi, Via - A2	Palestro, Via - B3
Card. Capponi, Via - A2	Paolo Salvi, Via - A1
Carmignani, Via. - B3	Piave, Via - A2
Carmine, Via Del - C2	Piazza A. Saffi - B2
Cascine, Via Delle - A1	Piazza A. Toniolo - C3
Cesare Battisti, Via - C1, 2	Piazza Arcivescovado - A2
Consoli Del Mare, Via - B2	Piazza D. Manin - A2
Contessa Matilde, Via - A2	Piazza Dante Alighieri - B2
Corsica, Via - B2	Piazza Dei Cavalieri - B2
Corso Italia - B2, C2	Piazza Del Duomo - A1, 2
Curtatone E Mont., Via - B2	Piazza Della Stazione - C2
D. Cavalca, Via - B2	Piazza Dini - B2
D. Orafi, Via - B3	Piazza F. Carrara - B2
D. Vigna, Via - B2	Piazza Guerrazzi - C3
De Amicis, Via E. - B3	Piazza Martiri D. Libertà - B3
Del Lante, Via - B2	Piazza S. Caterina - A3
Del Torzi, Via - C2	Piazza S. Paolo All'orto - B3
Dell' Occhio, Via - B2	Piazza Solferino - B1
Derna, Via - A2	Piazza Vittorio Emanuele Ii - C2
Di Mezzo, Via - B2	Pietro Gori, Via - C2
Don G. Boschi, Via - A2	Porta Buozzi, Via - A2
Ettore Sighieri, Via - B3	Renato Fucini, Via - B3
Faggiola, Via Della - A2	Risorgimento, Via - B1
Filippo Buonarroti, Via - A3, B3	Roma, Via - A2
Filippo Turati, Via - C2	S. Antonio, Via - B2, C2
Francesco Crispi, Via - C2	S. Apollonia, Via - A2/B2
Francesco Niosi, Via - C1, 2	S. Bibiana, Via - B3
G. Bruno, Via - C2	S. Frediano, Via - B2
G. Giusti, Via - B3	S. G. Al Gatano, Via - C1
G. Matteotti, Via - C3	S. Stefano, Via - A2
G. Oberdan, Via - B2	S. Tommaso, Via - A2
G. Pascoli, Via - C2	San Andrea, Via - B3
Galli-Tassi, Via - A2	San Francesco, Via - B3
Giosue Carducci, Via - A2	San Lorenzo, Via - B3
Giovanni Bovio, Via - C3	San Martino, Via - B2
Giovanni De Simone, Via - B3	San Paolo, Via - B2
Giuseppe Mazzini, Via - B2, C2	San Zeno, Via - A3
Guiseppe Garibaldi, Via -B3	Sancasciani, Via - C2
K. Dei Sigismondi, Via - C3	Santa Maria, Via - A2, B2
L. Coccapani, Via - B3	Sette Volte, Via - B2
La Foglia, Via - C2	Solferino, Ponte - B1/2
La Pera, Via - B2	Strada Statale N12 - A3
La Tinta, Via - C3	Tavoleria, Via - B2
L'arancio, Via - B2	Torri, Via Di Belle -B3
Livornese, Via - C1	Trieste, Via - B1
Lucchese, Via - A3	V. M. D'Azeglio, Via - C2
Luigi Bianchi, Via - A3	Vernaccini, Via - B3
Lung. Fibonacci - C3	Vespucci, Via - C2
Lungarno Bruno Buozzi - C3	Vicenza, Via - B3
Lungarno Galileo Galilei - C3	Vittorio Veneto, Via - A3, B3
Lungarno Gambacorti - B2	Volturno, Via - B1
Lungarno Mediceo - B3, C3	

Duomo

050 560547/www.opapisa.it. **Open** *Mid Mar-Sept*
10am-8pm Mon-Sat; 1-8pm Sun. *Oct* 10am-7pm
Mon-Sat; 1-7pm Sun. *Nov-mid Mar* 10am-1pm, 3-5pm
Mon-Sat; 1-5pm Sun. **Admission** €2. **Credit** MC, V.
Begun in 1063 by Buscheto (who's buried in the wall
on the left side of the façade), Pisa's cathedral is one
of the finest examples of Pisan Romanesque architecture. The delicate, blindingly white marble four-
tiered façade incorporates Moorish mosaics and
glass within the arcades (there are more examples
in the Museo dell'Opera del Duomo; *see below*). The
main entrance facing the Leaning Tower is called
the Portale di San Ranieri and features bronze doors
by Bonanno da Pisa (1180). The brass doors (touch
the lizard for good luck) by the Giambologna school
were added in 1602 to replace the originals, which
were destroyed in a fire in 1595.

After the fire the Medici family came to the rescue
and immediately began restoration work. Sadly, at
the time, nothing could be done to save Giovanni
Pisano's superb Gothic pulpit (1302-11), which was
incinerated and lay dismembered in crates until the
1920s. Legend has it that the censer suspended near
the now-restored pulpit triggered Galileo's discovery of the principles of pendular motion, but it was
actually cast six years later. Crane your neck to
admire the Moorish dome decorated by a vibrant
fresco of the Assumption by Orazio and Girolamo
Riminaldi (1631). Behind the altar is a mosaic by
Cimabue of St John (1302).

Leaning Tower

The south-east corner of the Campo holds Pisa's
most popular attraction, and one of the most famous
curiosities on earth. Begun in 1173 (the commemo-
rative plaque offering 1174 as the start date is incor-
rect), the famous tower started to lean almost as soon
as it was erected, and many years before the top
level, housing the seven bells, was finally added in
1350. In 1989, the last year before the tower was
closed to the public, more than a million visitors
scrambled up its 294 steps. After years of restoration work, it reopened in December 2001, but with
some heavy restrictions: the tower is open only for
guided tours, and then only to groups of 30 willing
to pay €15 a head (plus €2 booking fee). Book online
at www.opapisa.it at least 15 days prior to your visit,
or in person at the ticket office next to the tourist
information booth. Under-8s aren't allowed; children
aged eight to 12s must be hand-held by an adult; and
those between 12 and 18 must be accompanied by a
grown-up. *See also p209* Tilt to last.

Museo dell'Opera del Duomo

050 560547/www.opapisa.it. **Open** *Apr-Sept*
9am-8pm daily. *Mar, Oct* 9am-6pm daily. *Nov-Feb*
9am-5pm daily. **Admission** €5. **No credit cards**.
This museum contains works from the monuments
of the Piazza del Duomo. Among its more interesting exhibits is a series of sculptures from the 12th
to 14th centuries, including a clutch of notable works
by Giovanni Pisano.

Museo delle Sinopie

050 560547/www.opapisa.it. **Open** *Apr-Sept*
9am-8pm daily. *Mar, Oct* 9am-6pm daily. *Nov-Feb*
9am-5pm daily. **Admission** €5. **No credit cards**.
The 1944 bombings and subsequent restoration
work uncovered *sinopie* from beneath the frescoes
in the Camposanto. These reddish-brown prelimi-
nary sketches were meant to be hidden forever after
the artist covered the original *arriccio* (dry plaster
on which the sketches were made) with a lime-rich
plaster called *grassello*. The *sinopie* show what brilliant draftsmen the painters were, but also give the
observer an intriguing sense of scale.

Torre di Santa Maria

Open 10am-6pm daily. **Admission** €2. **No credit
cards**.
Head here for a good overview of the Campo dei
Miracoli and access to a small part of the city walls.

Other sights

Museo Nazionale di Palazzo Reale

Lungarno Pacinotti 46 (050 926539). **Open** 9am-3pm
Mon-Fri; 9am-2pm Sat. **Admission** €5; €6.50 with
Museo Nazionale di San Matteo. **No credit cards**.
Housed in a Medici palace dating from 1583, this
museum shows many works donated by private collectors of Medici pieces. Portrait paintings represent
members of various European dynasties; there's also
traditional Gioco del Ponte gear (*see p158*).

Museo Nazionale di San Matteo

*Piazza San Matteo in Soarta, Lungarno Mediceo
(050 541865).* **Open** 8.30am-7.30pm Tue-Sat;
8.30am-1.30pm Sun. **Admission** €4; €6.50 with
Museo Nazionale di Palazzo Reale. **No credit cards**.
Once a convent, this 12th- to 13th-century building
now contains Pisan and Islamic medieval ceramics,
works by Masaccio, Fra Angelico and Domenico
Ghirlandaio, and a bust by Donatello.

Orto Botanico

Via L Ghini 5 (050 551345). **Open** 8am-5pm
Mon-Fri; 8am-1pm Sat. **Admission** free.
The oldest university garden to be found anywhere
in Europe (it was started by Luca Ghini back in
1543), the Orto Botanico was originally used to
study the medicinal values of plants.

Piazza dei Cavalieri

A focal point of Pisa, this beautiful square houses
the Palazzo dei Cavalieri, the seat of one of Italy's
most prestigious universities: the Scuola Normale
Superiore, established by Napoleon in 1810. In the
16th century Giorgio Vasari designed most of the
piazza's buildings, including the Chiesa dei
Cavalieri, the Palazzo della Conventuale (opposite
the church, erected as home to the Cavalieri of Santo
Stefano), the Palazzo del Consiglio dell'Ordine and
the Palazzo Gherardesca.

The latter occupies the site of a medieval prison
where, in 1288, Count Ugolino della Gherardesca and

Tilt to last

There's always been a certain inclination to Pisa's emblematic campanile. Construction began in 1173, but by the time the fourth storey was under way, the ground had subsided and the tower had begun to tilt. Building was suspended in 1185 and resumed 90 years later, with the distinct southward lean suggesting a rethink of the original design (it was reduced from 70 metres (230 feet) to 55 metres (180 feet) in height). Despit this, the world's most famous leaning tower wasn't completed until the late 14th century.

The quirky tower's popularity as a tourist attraction more than made up for any potential embarrassment it might have caused to Pisans. But while millions made the unnerving climb up its 294 steps, the bell tower continued to tilt until, in 1989, it was deemed in danger of collapse. A complex and expensive rescue operation slowly swung into action, aiming to correct the tilt by 40 centimetres (18 inches). The scheme threatened to fail in 1995 as the lean, far from being harnessed, actually increased by a fraction.

However, by December 2001 the then minister of public works saw fit to declare the €27.5-million project a triumph, with the monument seemingly safeguarded for at least the next 250 years. The supports are now gone and the tower is open to pre-arranged, guided groups (*see p208*). It's quite a climb, but well worth the effort and expense.

three of his male heirs were condemned to starve to death for conducting covert negotiations with the Florentines. His sons and grandsons all died relatively quickly, but Ugolino lasted nine months, after he reputedly kept himself alive by eating his own children. Although that condemned him to hell in Dante's *Inferno*, the poet ensured that Ugolino had a measure of revenge: the Count spent eternity gnawing the head of Archbishop Ruggieri, the man who had betrayed him (Canto XXXIII).

You'll see the Maltese Cross everywhere in this piazza, but nowhere else in Pisa. Cosimo wanted to hammer home the parallel between his new Cavalieri of Santo Stefano and the crusading Knights of Malta. Elsewhere, you're likely to spot the Pisan cross with two balls resting on each point.

San Nicola

Via Santa Maria 2 (tel/fax 050 24677). **Open** 8am-noon, 5-6.30pm Mon-Sat; 9am-noon, 5.30-6.30pm Sun. **Admission** free.

Dating from 1150, this church is dedicated to one of Pisa's patron saints, San Nicola da Tolentino. In one chapel there's a painting showing the saint protecting Pisa from the plague in around 1400. Built on unstable ground, the campanile leans.

Santa Maria della Spina

Lungarno Gambacorti (050 3215446). **Open** *Mar-Oct* 10am-1.30pm, 2.30-6pm Mon-Fri; 10am-7pm Sat, Sun. *Nov-Feb* 10am-2pm daily. Closed late Dec-early Jan. **Admission** €1.50. **No credit cards**.

This gorgeous, tiny Gothic church on the bank of the Arno is finally open again after restoration. Originally an oratory, it took its present form in 1323 and gets its name from the fact that it used to own what was claimed to be a thorn (*spina*) from Christ's crown, brought back by the Crusaders.

Where to eat & drink

Restaurants

Cèe alla Pisana (eels), one of Pisa's culinary assets for centuries, are increasingly hard to find. When they are plucked from the Arno (they're a winter delicacy), the eels are tossed in warm oil, garlic and sage, then sautéed.

Aphrodite

Via Lucchese 33A (050 830248/www.ristorante aphrodite.com). **Open** 6pm-1am Tue-Sun. **Average** €35. **Credit** MC, V.

This exciting new restaurant offers innovative cuisine – and some interesting wines – in a cool, funky setting. Owner Emilio Traina and his chef create dishes that delight both palate and eye. The ample garden comes into its own in summer.

Bruno

Via Luigi Bianchi 12 (050 560818). **Open** noon-3pm, 7-10.30pm Mon, Wed-Sun. **Average** €40. **Credit** AmEx, DC, MC, V.

Bruno concentrates on typical, good-value Tuscan cooking. Try the *ribollita*, supposedly the best this side of the Arno, or pasta with rabbit and wild boar.

Cagliostro

Via del Castelletto 26-30 (050 575413). **Open** 7.45pm-1am Wed, Thur, Sun; 12.45-2.30pm, 8pm-2am Fri, Sat. **Average** €15 lunch, €25 dinner. **Credit** AmEx, DC, MC, V.

Cagliostro is named after a Sicilian count who masqueraded as an alchemist in France and Italy. The extensive wine list complements the menu, which draws on recipes from all over Italy. It's tricky to find; ask for the restaurant, not the street.

Tuscany

La Mescita

Via Cavalca 2 (050 544294/www.lamescita.it).
Open 1-2.15pm, 8-10.30pm Tue-Fri; 1-2.15pm Sat,
Sun. Closed 3wks Aug. **Average** €30. **Credit**
AmEx, MC, V.
Set in the heart of Vettovaglie market, La Mescita is
pretty and tranquil. Try *brandade di stoccafisso* (salt
cod) with tomatoes, but check the window for its cal-
endar of *degustazioni* and creative cooking nights.

Osteria dei Cavalieri

Via San Frediano 16 (050 580858). **Open**
12.30-2pm, 7.45-10pm Mon-Fri; 7.45-10pm Sat.
Closed late July-late Aug. **Average** €30. **Credit**
AmEx, DC, MC, V.
One of Pisa's best eateries, especially for the money.
It serves typical Tuscan dishes with flair: steak with
beans and mushrooms, perhaps, or *tagliolini* with
rabbit and asparagus. The wine list is noteworthy.

Osteria La Grotta

Via San Francesco 103 (050 578105). **Open** noon-
2.30pm, 7-11.30pm Mon-Sat. **Average** €25. **Credit**
AmEx, DC, MC, V.
The new management at this fine spot offers a light
lunch menu and the full works for dinner. The excellent fare is very well presented and there's also a terrific wine list to go with it.

Re di Puglia

Via Aurelia Sud 7 (050 960157). **Open** 8-10pm
Wed-Sat; 1-3pm, 8-10pm Sun. Closed 2wks Jan.
Average €27. **No credit cards**.
Slabs of succulent meat are grilled in front of your
eyes on the open fire at this rustic restaurant a few
kilometres south of Pisa on the Livorno road. While
meat (especially beef, lamb and rabbit) reigns
supreme, the menu also includes five types of
Tuscan *antipasti*. Eat outdoors in summer.

Cafés, bars & *gelaterie*

De Coltelli

*Lungarno Pacinotti 23 (050 541611/www.de
coltelli.com).* **Open** 11am-1am daily. Closed Jan.
No credit cards.
Although the presence of some decidedly strange
varieties – *alle vongole* (clams), for instance – might
scare off some, rest assured that the ice-cream dished
up here is tremendous.

Pasticceria Salza

Borgo Stretto 46 (050 580144). **Open** 7.45am-
8.30pm Tue-Sun. **Credit** MC, V.
This distinguished venue is a real multitasker, with
café tables in the front, a sweet shop further inside
and a restaurant at the back.

Pizzicheria Gastronomia a Cesqui

Piazza delle Vettovaglie 38 (050 580269). **Open**
7am-1.30pm, 4-8pm Mon, Tue, Thur-Sat; 7am-1.30pm
Wed. **Credit** MC, V.
Stock up on cheeses, pastas, wines and snacks at this
deli, while bantering and gossiping with the staff.

Nightlife

For Pisa's best gay bar and sauna, *see p170*.

Borderline

*Via Vernaccini 7 (050 580577/www.borderline
club.it).* **Open** 9pm-2am Mon-Sat. **Admission**
free-€10.50. **No credit cards**.
Good for late drinks or the occasional live gig, with
blues, roots and country music taking centre stage.

Dottorjazz

Via Vespucci 10 (339 8619298). **Open** 9pm-2am
Tue-Sun. Closed June-Sept. **Admission** €5-€10.
No credit cards.
You'll need to look hard to find this jazz venue,
which is located at the far end of what seems like a
warehouse car park and with no sign to give it away.
Once inside, though, it's an attractive place, with
small candlelit tables and pictures of jazz greats on
the walls. Thursday night is blues night.

Mississippi

*Via Livornese 1313, Località San Piero a Grado
(339 1573877/www.mississippi.it).* **Open** from
9.30pm Tue-Sat. **Admission** phone for details.
This out-of-town venue is popular with young people for beer and music (heavy metal, rock and blues).

Teatro Verdi

*Via Palestro 40 (050 941111/542600/www.teatro
dipisa.p.it).* **Open** *Box office* 4-7pm Mon, Tue, Thur,
Sat; 11am-1pm, 4-7pm Wed, Fri; also 1hr before
events. *Phone bookings* 11am-1.30pm Mon-Fri.
Closed Aug. **Credit** MC, V.
An enjoyable venue for dance, drama and music.

Shopping

Pisa's main shopping drag is **Corso Italia**,
but across from the Ponte di Mezzo is a
funkier shopping zone, starting at the *loggia* of
Borgo Stretto. The **Mercatino Antiquario**
takes place where the two meet, on the second
weekend of every month, offering modern arts
and crafts in addition to the expected goodies.
The **Mercato Vettovaglie**, a fruit and
vegetable market, is held every morning. Look
out too for **De Bondt**, one of Italy's foremost
chocolate artisans (Via Turati 22, 050 501896,
www.debondt.it); phone or check the website
first though, as it's planning to relocate.

Where to stay

Accommodation in Pisa can be a bit hit or
miss, with much more of the latter in the budget
categories. To ensure you get a decent room,
reserve in advance during high season and for
major festivals. The tourist information centre
at the Campo dei Miracoli (*see p211*) has a list
of hotels. You'll find the nearest camping in
Marina di Pisa (*see p213*).

Albergo Galileo
Via Santa Maria 12 (tel/fax 050 40621). **Rates**
€45 single; €60 double. **Credit** MC, V.
Though it's illegal to employ Galileo Galilei's full
name for commercial purposes in Pisa, this *pensione*
manages to get away with using half of it. It's worth
asking for one of the five (of nine) rooms that are decorated with 17th-century frescoes.

Amalfitana
Via Roma 44 (050 29000/fax 050 25218). **Rates**
€60-€66 single; €70-€82 double. **Credit** MC, V.
A favourite of visiting Italians seeking central, two-
star accommodation.

Casa della Giovane
Via F Corridoni 29 (tel/fax 050 43061). **Rates**
€38 single; €28 per person double. **No credit cards**.
This college, close to the station, contains a women-
only boarding house. As you'd expect it caters mostly to students and it's often packed in term-time.
Note that there's an 11pm curfew.

Centro Turistico Madonna dell'Acqua
Via Pietrasantina 13 (tel/fax 050 890622).
Bus 3. **Open** *Office* 6pm-midnight. **Rates** *per
person* €21 double; €18 triple; €16 quadruple or
bigger. **Credit** MC, V.
Located in a village a short distance outside the city,
this is the only youth hostel that you'll find in the
Pisa area. There's no point turning up before 6pm:
the hostel doesn't open until then.

Grand Hotel Duomo
*Via Santa Maria 94 (050 561894/fax 050 560418/
www.grandhotelduomo.it).* **Rates** €123 single; €180
double; €205 suite. **Credit** AmEx, DC, MC, V.
Hints of its previous opulence remain, but the Grand
is now, sadly, getting somewhat frayed around the
edges. But if you want somewhere central its location can't be faulted, nor the sweeping views it offers
over the Campo dei Miracoli from its fourth-floor terrace. If you arrive by car, make sure you ask for a
parking permit for Via Santa Maria.

Hotel Repubblica Marinara
*Via Matteucci 81 (050 3870100/fax 050 3870200/
www.hotelrepubblicamarinara.it).* **Rates** €89-€129
single; €129-€199 double. **Credit** MC, V.
The rooms at this new hotel come with all manner
of technological bells and whistles – internet access,
orthopaedic mattresses and various lighting options.

Relais dell'Orologio
*Via della Fagiola 12-14 (behind Piazza dei Cavalieri,
050 830361/fax 050 551869/www.hotelrelais
orologio.com).* **Rates** €225-€235 single; €326-€340
double; €645 suite. **Credit** AmEx, MC, V.
Maria Louisa Bignardi's dream of turning her 13th-
century house into a five-star hotel became a reality a few years back. The 25 rooms are individually
decorated, so the place still has the feel of a private
home. The Peli di Vaglio suite has exposed frescoes.

Royal Victoria
*Lungarno Pacinotti 12 (050 940111/fax 050
940180/www.royalvictoria.it).* **Rates** €108 single;
€128 double. **Credit** AmEx, DC, MC, V.
Situated on the Arno, this hotel was a popular stop
back in the days of the Grand Tour and counts many
illustrious names among its previous guests. In fact,
it acquired its non-Italian title as a result of its many
English visitors. The atmosphere still harks back to
those days, and though the bedrooms have lumber-
ing old furniture, they're full of character. There's
also a pretty roof terrace.

Resources

Hospital
Santa Chiara, Via Roma 67 (050 992111).

Police
Questura, Via Mario Lalli 3 (050 583511).

Post office
Piazza Vittorio Emanuele II 8 (050 5194).
Open 8.15am-7pm Mon-Sat.

Tourist Information
Turistica APT *Campo dei Miracoli (050
560464/www.pisa.turismo.toscana.it).* **Open** 9am-
6pm Mon-Sat; 10.30am-6.30pm Sun.
Other locations: Piazza della Stazione 11
(050 42291); Galileo Galilei Airport (050 503700).

Getting there & around

By air
Galileo Galilei Airport (050 849300) is still
Tuscany's major international airport. The airport
handles flights from all around Europe. There are
frequent buses and regular trains into Pisa and
Lucca from here. For further information, *see p282.*

By bus
LAZZI (Piazza Sant'Antonio, 050 46288, www.lazzi.
it) operates a regular service to Lucca (journey
time 50mins), with onward connections to Florence
(2hrs 30mins), as well as buses to Viareggio
(50mins). **CPT** (Piazza Sant'Antonio, 050 505511,
www.cpt.it) covers the area around Pisa and
runs buses to nearby areas such as Livorno and
Marina di Pisa.

By taxi
There are taxi ranks at Piazza della Stazione
(055 41252) and Piazza del Duomo (050 561878).
Otherwise, call **Radio Taxi** on 050 541600.

By train
Pisa is on a main connecting line to Rome (journey
time 3hrs on Intercity, otherwise 4hrs) and Genoa
(2hrs). There are also frequent trains to Florence
via Empoli (80mins), Lucca (25mins) and Livorno
(15mins); some trains also stop at Pisa Aeroporto
and San Rossore. The train station is Pisa
Centrale, Piazza della Stazione (information
892021, www.trenitalia.it).

Pisa & Livorno Provinces

Escape from the tower to lush hills, quiet beaches and hot springs.

In recent years the stretch of coastline around Pisa and Livorno has become something of an industrial powerhouse. Not that the average holidaymaker would realise this. The activity is all hidden away from the pricey, parasol-stabbed beaches which attract the tourists. But if you look more closely you'll find a few discreet, sandy coves surrounded by dunes and pine groves, where boatyards are producing some of the world's most luxurious and exclusive yachts, many of them custom-designed. Meanwhile, between Bolgheri and Castagneto Carducci, a few minutes from the southern stretch of the coast, what was once a poor farming area now produces some of Tuscany's most prestigious and expensive wines.

The coast is of course the attraction that draws the crowds, but it's not the only reason to visit. Further inland, heading towards the Colline Metallifere to the east, is the northern section of the Maremma; stretching between Cecina and Follonica, this section is known as the Pisan Maremma.

San Giuliano Terme

This small town was built around a magnificent 18th-century residence constructed at the behest of Grand Duke Stephen of Lorraine so that he and his guests could enjoy the healing qualities of the local spa waters. Guests at the very comfortable **Bagni di Pisa** hotel (Largo Shelley 18, 050 88501, www.termesangiuliano. com, *see also p215* **Reach for the spas**), the town's main building, can soak away the aches induced by too much sightseeing, before adjourning to the hotel's fine restaurant for dinner. Indeed, the town is so close to Pisa that it and the hotel make for a handsome alternative base if you'd rather avoid the hordes of tourist tower pushers.

San Miniato

Snaking along the crest of a lofty hill, the town of San Miniato grew prominent on account of its strategic position above the Pisa–Florence road;

it intersects here with the Via Francigena, which brought pilgrims from the north to Rome. The town was fortified in the 12th and 13th centuries and became one of Tuscany's foremost imperial centres, but it succumbed to Florentine power in the mid 1300s. Unfortunately, the interiors of both the 13th-century Duomo and the slightly later church of San Domenico were subjected to some heavy-handed baroque 'improvements'.

The spacious *loggia* of San Domenico is used for an antiques and collectibles fair on the second Sunday of each month (except July and August). The surrounding area is rich in truffles; November weekends are devoted to tasting them as part of the Festa del Tartufo, the truffle festival.

Where to eat

Caffè Centrale (Via IV Novembre 19, 0571 43037, closed Mon, late Aug/early Sept, average €12) serves simple pastas for lunch and has a great view, while just outside town there's **Il Convio** (Via San Maiano 2, 0571 408114, closed Wed, average €30), with more Tuscan favourites, plus a vegetarian menu. As an alternative, try **La Trattoria dell'Orcio Interrato** in nearby Montopoli Valdarno (Piazza San Michele 2, 0571 466878, closed all Mon, Sun dinner in winter, 2wks Aug, 1wk Feb, average €35), which has a summer terrace and an interesting line in modern interpretations of dishes with Renaissance origins.

Tirrenia

Heading south from Marina di Pisa towards Livorno, you'll first come to Tirrenia, home to a US military base but also to a pair of public beaches and several private ones. The main attraction of the area is the flashy, 200-room **Grand Hotel Continental** (Largo Belvedere 26, 050 37031, www.grandhotelcontinental.com, doubles €140-€190), which sits directly on the beach. But if the thought of swimming with the fishes is not appealing there are sanitised waters in the hotel's Olympic-size pool. Book well in advance in summer. For dinner, visit **Dante e Ivana** (Viale del Tirreno 207C, 050 32549), where the kitchen is separated from the dining area by a lobster tank. There's an interesting fish-based menu, plus pasta dishes and a fish fondue. It's worth trying to make it to one of the regular tasting evenings. You can work up an appetite by taking one of the guided walks or bike tours in **San Rossore** park (Via Aurelia Nord 4, 050 525500), though if it's too hot you might prefer to take a leisurely jaunt in a horse-driven carriage.

Casciana Terme

Tucked away in the Pisan hills and less crowded than Montecatini or Saturnia, this spa town, known as Castrum ad Aquas to the Romans, was destroyed in World War II and rebuilt in the 1960s. After taking the waters at **Terme di Casciana** (Piazza Garibaldi 9, 0587 64461) you can relax out front with an espresso at the traditional café. The lush hills between Casciana and the village of Terricciola are ideal camera fodder, resembling nothing so much as a uniformly rolling ocean.

A kilometre east of Calci, the **Certosa di Pisa** (050 938430, closed Mon & Sun afternoon, admission €4) is a vast complex that was used as a monastery on and off from 1366 until 1969, when it was completely abandoned by the Carthusian monks. The interior includes a 14th-century church, various cloisters and gardens, while the former granaries, carpenters' workshops and cellars in the grounds now house the university's **Natural History Museum** (Via Roma 103, 050 2212970, closed Mon, admission €5). Founded in 1591 by Grand Duke Ferdinando I, it's considered one of the top three natural history museums in Italy.

Where to stay & eat

There are several lodging options in the area. Just down the road from the thermal waters is **La Speranza** (Via Cavour 44, 0587 646215, www.hotel-lasperanza.com, doubles €80), which has an attractive little pool and gardens; not too far away is the spacious and inviting **Villa Margherita** (Via Marconi 20, 0587 646113, www.margherita-hotel.it, closed Jan-Easter, doubles €74-€98). **Grand Hotel San Marco** (Via Lischi 1, 0578 764421, doubles €150-€186) is also an attractive option, with a restaurant overlooking the pool and its own beauty centre. Restaurant-wise, go for **Il Merlo** (Piazza Minati 5, 0587 644040, closed Mon, Jan), which has a handsome wine list. A few kilometres and a couple of hamlets further on from Terricciola is the stately, smart **Villa San Marco** (Località San Marco 13, 0587 654054, suites €200-€395). It's housed in a building dating back to the 11th century. More accommodation options are available from the tourist office (Via Cavour 9, 0587 646258).

Volterra

Volterra stands proudly on a 531-metre (1,742-foot) peak between the Cecina and Era valleys in the Pisa province. The surrounding area is rich in mineral deposits (especially iron, copper and silver), which explains why it was settled as early as the Neolithic period. By the 7th century BC the city then known as Velathri had become one of the 12 Etruscan states, with a population of 25,000 and a prosperous trade in iron and alabaster artefacts via the port of Vada to destinations throughout the Mediterranean. It put up a hearty resistance to the expansionist Romans and was the last Etruscan city to fall to the Empire. But fall it did in 260 BC, whereupon it was renamed Volaterrae.

The town, as it appears today, was built in the 12th and 13th centuries; save for patches of the fortified walls that reveal their original foundations, all traces of the Etruscans have been erased. Fortunately, the **Museo Etrusco Guarnacci** (Via Don Minzoni 15, 0588 86347, €8) helps make up for this: among its exhibits, which together make up one of the world's most extensive collections of artefacts related to this mysterious ancient population, is the celebrated 'evening shadow' statuette, a long, thin statue that was found by a local farmer and used as a fire stoker until someone recognised its importance. The €8 ticket also gives you admission to Volterra's other two museums: the **Pinacoteca** (0588 87580, closed afternoons in winter), located in the late 15th-century Palazzo Minucci Solaini and worth a visit purely to see the astounding use of colour in the fabulous Mannerist *Deposition* by Rosso Fiorentino, and the **Museo d'Arte Sacra** (0588 86290, closed afternoons in winter), which also boasts work by the same artist.

The other tangible link to Volaterrae's Etruscan origins is the city's continued trade in goods made from the local alabaster. These days, shops hawk bowls, plates, chess sets, lamps and myriad other items. Unfortunately most of it is pretty kitsch, so it takes a keen eye to dig out the best pieces.

Where to stay & eat

A convent more than five centuries ago, **Hotel San Lino** (Via San Lino 26, 0588 85250, www.hotelsanlino.com, doubles €77-€100) now has its own pool and a shady cloister. Both offer relief from the bustle. Two kilometres outside of Volterra, the 15th-century **Villa Rioddi** (0588 88053, www.hotelvillarioddi.it, doubles €68-€93, €520-€925 weekly for a two-room apartment) also has a pool and a lovely garden. Just outside town, **Il Vecchio Mulino** (Via del Molino, Località Saline, 0588 44060, closed Mon), features both some new guestrooms and a restaurant specialising in Tuscan cuisine with an inventive touch. The town's eating options are otherwise led by the cosy **Trattoria del Sacco Fiorentino** (Piazza XX Settembre, 0588 88537, closed Wed, Jan & Feb, average €25):

located near the Museo Etrusco Guarnacci, it serves seasonal goodies such as gnocchi with spring vegetables, and has good selections of cheese and wine. An elegant alternative is **Del Duca** (Via di Castello 2, 0588 81510, closed Tue, average €35), which has an ancient wine cellar and a charming secret garden.

Livorno

By the 16th century the Arno had silted up, leaving the maritime republic of Pisa shorn of its outlet to the sea. As a remedy, Cosimo I pounced on a tiny fishing village in 1571, with major designs for improving it. A far-sighted constitution set up in 1593 allowed foreigners to reside in the city regardless of nationality and religion, instantly endowing it with a cosmopolitan mentality. Amazingly, it has hung on to it for the last four centuries, so Livorno still has an open-minded attitude.

The **Porto Mediceo**, with the red-brick bastion of the **Fortezza Vecchia** designed by Sangallo the Younger in 1521, has long been the focus of city life. From here the canals of **Venezia Nuova** (or I Fossi) extend, tracing the pentagonal perimeter of Francesco I's late 16th-century plan for an ideal city. Look out for the concerts of the Effetto Venezia that take place in late July. Sadly, bombing during World War II destroyed most of Livorno's historic monuments, and post-war reconstruction finished the job off. Buontalenti's Piazza Grande was cut in two; all that remains of the 16th-century Duomo is Inigo Jones's fine portico.

Where to stay, eat & drink

Osteria da Carlo (Viale Caprera 43-45, no phone, closed Sun & 3wks Sept, average €22) does decent *cacciucco*, the famous spicy fish soup for which Livorno is renowned, while **La Corsara** (Via Mentana 78, 0586 897208, closed Wed, average €25) is also good for fish. Other spots worth trying for local fare include **La Chiave**, across from the Fortezza Nuova (Scali delle Cantine 52, 0586 888 609, closed all Wed, average €40) and **Il Sottomarino** (Via de' Terrazzini 48, 0586 887 025, closed Mon, Tue & 2wks July, average €30). Just out of town at Lari is **Ghiné & Cambri** (Via di Quercianella 263, 0586 579414, closed Mon, Tue Oct-May & 2wks Jan, average €25), which has become something of a cult eaterie with the younger generation for its relaxed atmosphere, friendly service and great meat dishes. For ice-cream, try **La Chiostra** (Lia Cecioni 8, 0586 813564, closed Mon in winter).

Livorno's youth tend to head for the disco-bars on the canals. The **Barge** (Scali delle

Reach for the spas

Heading to Tuscany in the winter? You'd better pack your swimming costume. No Italian region is as rich in spas as Tuscany: the waters are warm, if not hot, and naturally rich with minerals that should ease your aches and uplift your spirits. You can even add a massage for that little bit of extra luxury. Check the websites for opening/closing times, which tend to vary slightly from season to season and year to year.

Just north of Pisa, in San Giuliano Terme, is the very comfortable **Bagni di Pisa** hotel (*see p212*). It has found a measure of fame for its decent restaurant, but it also has a small hot pool, a Turkish bath in a natural grotto and a host of good masseurs. Due south of Pisa, meanwhile, is **Casciana Terme** (0587 64461, www.termedicasciana.it), which has a large, luxurious modern pool and spa facilities fronted by a more traditional café.

At Bagno Vignoni, directly south of Siena, the recently revamped **Hotel Posta Marcucci** (0577 887112, www.hotelpostamarcucci.it) provides another wonderful opportunity for aquatic indulgence. Set in pretty gardens with a magnificent view across the valley, the pool has a thundering cascade that provides a memorable hydro-massage. The water at **Bagni San Filippo** (0577 872982, www.termesanfilippo.it, closed Nov-1wk before Easter), a little further south, is hotter still and more sulphurous, with a 42° cascade that's a real scorcher. Looking over the valley towards Monte Amiata at San

Casciano dei Bagni, the **Terme di San Casciano** (0578 572405, www.fonteverde terme.com), offers upmarket facilities and a pool with a thundering hydro-massage. If it's salty rubs and sea-water cures you pine for, head for Marina di Castagneto Carducci on the coast, where you'll find the **Tombolo Talasso Resort** (Via del Corallo 3, Maria di Castagneto Carducci, 0565 74530, www.tombolotalasso.it), which has five sea water pools and a wellness centre set in pleasant gardens, just a stone's throw from the beach.

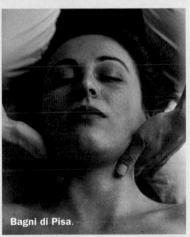

Bagni di Pisa.

Anchore 6, 0586 888320, closed Mon & Sun) has a piano bar, an 'English' bar and canalside tables. Another popular summer disco is **Spianate** at Rosignano (Via Campo Freno Castioncello 15, 0586 752225), though it was closed because of noise pollution as this guide went to press. If you've stayed too late to make it back to Pisa, try the central **Hotel Gran Duca** (Piazza Micheli 16, 0586 891024, www.granduca.it, doubles €98-€154).

Bolgheri, Castagneto Carducci & Suvereto

While Marina di Cecina is a pleasant enough seaside town with a popular windsurfing beach, the inland areas are considerably more attractive. Heading south-east, you'll reach

Bolgheri, a nice little town that has become synonymous with Sassicaia, one of Italy's most prestigious wines: a bottle may set you back several hundred euros. Other wine producers in the area include Michele Satta and Lodovico Antinori, whose Ornellaia is a gem. Bolgheri also has a WWF nature reserve that is a haven for rare ducks, geese and storks.

Further south is **Castagneto Carducci**. Like Bolgheri, it's small and charming, attracting in the summer months the sort of Italian glitterati who spurn the crowded coast. There are many good opportunities for cyclists to stretch their legs in the area; after a day's pedalling, head to **Nettare degli Dei** (Salita San Lorenzo, 0565 765118) to sample the morning's catch, or put your feet up at the **Hotel Ristorante Zi Martino** just

Tuscany

Et tu, Etrusca. **Volterra**. See p213.

outside town at San Giusto (0565 766000, closed Mon in winter & Nov).

From here, proceed south to **Suvereto**, a lovely medieval town surrounded by wooded hillsides. In open countryside, on the other side of the town, is the Petra winery, an imposing pink building featuring a truncated cone with a long flight of steep steps leading up the summit. The building was designed by Swiss luminary Mario Botta, whose work includes the Museum of Modern Art in San Francisco.

San Vincenzo

Back down on the coast, located on the Aurelia fast road, halfway between Livorno and Grosseto, is San Vincenzo, which once acted as a coastal watchtower for Pisa (note the tower itself, which dates from 1304). The attraction here is the Michelin-starred **Gambero Rosso** (see p40 **Want food, will travel**). The creative menu is a departure from the traditional Tuscan norm.

Piombino & around

The appeal of sooty **Piombino** is minimal. Indeed, the town is best approached as a departure point: from here you can catch ferries to **Corsica**, **Elba** (see p280) and **Pianosa**. Far more attractive is the stretch of coastline that runs north of Piombino up to the ruins of Etruscan Populonia. On the way you'll see mystifying rock formations, necropolises,

beaches and unspoilt waters. Follow the signs to Silvoni on the far west of Piombino and keep going until you get to a trail head at Cala Moresca by the car park above the beach, whence a series of tiny trails follow the coastline to the **Golfo di Baratti**.

Populonia, with its Etruscan necropolis, perches high above the little fishing port of Baratti. The historic remains are extensive: allow roughly three hours for a complete tour covering the lush green hillside overlooking the bay. Polyglot guides are available to explain it all; the visitors' centre is across the road from the car park, outside the village. Within the village walls there's a small Etruscan museum.

If you go south from Piombino towards Grosseto, stop at **Castiglione della Pescaia**. This fishing port contains some good hotels and eateries, plus a pleasant town beach. Otherwise, head inland to **Massa Marittima** (see p273).

Resources

Tourist information

Livorno *APT, Piazza Cavour 6 (0586 204611/ www.costadeglietruschi.it)*. **Open** 9am-1pm, 3-5pm Mon-Fri; 9am-1pm Sat.
Piombino *Ufficio di Turismo, Torre Comunale, Via del Ferruccio (0565 225639)*. **Open** 9am-3pm, 5-11pm Mon, Wed-Sun. Closed mid Sept-May.
San Miniato *Ufficio di Turismo, Piazza del Popolo (0571 42745/www.cittadisanminiato.it)*. **Open** *Summer* 9.30am-1pm, 3.30-7.30pm daily. *Winter* 9am-1pm, 3-6.30pm daily.
Volterra *Associazione Pro Volterra, Via Giusto Turazza 2 (0588 86150/www.provolterra.it)*. **Open** *Spring-autumn* 9am-1pm, 3-7pm daily. *Winter* 9am-12.30pm, 3-6pm Mon-Sat.

Getting there

By bus

SITA (800 373760, www.sita-on-line.it) runs buses from Florence to Volterra (1hr 50mins). **LAZZI** (050 46288, www.lazzi.it) connects Livorno with Pisa, Lucca, Viareggio and Florence. Livorno is also a port, with services to Sardinia, Corsica, Capraia and Sicily.

By car

Driving is the easiest option in the area. Livorno is just off the coastal SS1, a 20min drive south of Pisa along the same road. The A12 *autostrada* also runs past the city. The Poggibonsi exit of the Si-Fi (Siena-Florence) *autostrada* quickly gives access to Volterra.

By train

Livorno's main station (on Piazza Dante) is on the Rome/Pisa train line, a 12min journey from Pisa. Trains also run to and from Florence (journey time 1hr 20mins) via Pisa and Empoli. National timetable information is available by calling 892021 or by logging on to www.trenitalia.it.

Tuscany

Siena

Historic rival of Florence, but packed with its own charms.

Though Siena attracts great numbers of visitors all year round, it hasn't sold its soul to tourism. When the throng in Via di Città, the city's main drag, gets too much, there are plenty of quiet spots of great beauty to which you can escape. Indeed, the ideal way to experience Siena is to alternate these two very different atmospheres.

You can do so in the internationally famous, centrally located **Piazza del Campo**, where you can sit and enjoy a quiet drink at one of the cafés overlooking the shell-shaped square. The layout of the piazza and its surrounding architecture act to soften the acoustics, muting the hubbub from the crowds in the centre. By the same token, if a visit to the **Duomo** makes you long for leafy silence, take refuge in the **Orto Botanico**, occupying around five acres of steeply sloping land between Porta Tufi and Porta San Marco.

Wandering around Siena on foot is the best way to savour the city's two personalities. This is the ideal city to get lost in, to explore without a rigid itinerary. Moreover, it's small, so you're never far from a prominent landmark. The tourist board publishes leaflets illustrating some of the hidden corners to be enjoyed *con tranquillità*.

The historic centre of the city is actually divided into three sections. **Terzo di Città** was the original residential nucleus of Siena and includes the Duomo; **Terzo di San Martino** grew around the Via Francigena, the pilgrim route heading south to Rome (St Martin was the patron saint of pilgrims and wayfarers); and the **Terzo di Camollia** contains churches and basilicas on the north side. Piazza del Campo is neutral, but generally connected with Terzo di San Martino. These three sections comprise the 17 *contrade* – city districts that largely define the citizens' perception of their own identity. Each *contrada* has its own visible emblem, proudly affixed to walls and fountains to mark out its patch. The most dramatic manifestation of heightened *contrada* passions is the Palio (*see p158 and p221* **Beastly instincts**), the world-famous horse race held in July and August, when district rivalry reaches its zenith.

If you're planning on seeing all the sights, it's worth visiting the ticket office at the **Museo Civico** (0577 292263; *see p223*), which offers two types of combined ticket. For €10 over a two-day period you can visit the Museo

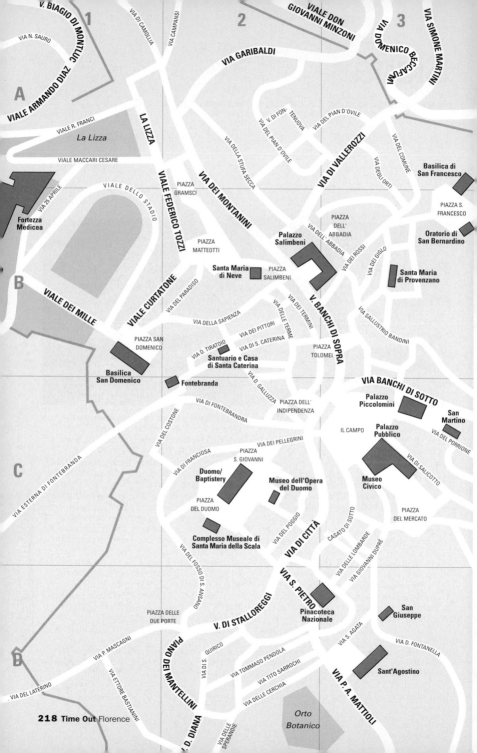

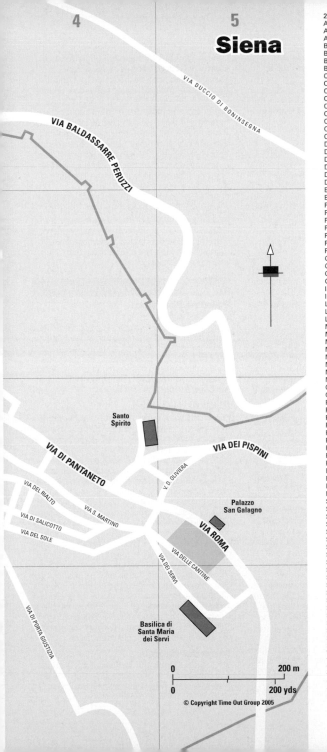

Siena

25 Aprile, Via - A1/B1
Abbadia, Piazza Dell' - B3
Abbadia, Via Dell' - B2/3
Armando Diaz, Viale - A1
Baldassarre Peruzzi, Via - A4/B4/5
Banchi Di Sopra, Via - B2/3
Banchi Di Sotto, Via - C3
Biagio Di Montluc, Via - A1
Camollia, Via Di - A1
Campansi, Via - A2
Cantine, Via Delle - C5/D5
Casato Di Sotto, - C3
Cerchia, Via Delle - D2
Città, Via Di - C2
Comune, Via Del - A3
Costone, Via Del - C2
Curtatone, Viale - B1/2
Diana, Via D. - D2
Domenico Beccafumi, Via - A3
Don Giovanni Minzoni, Viale - A2/3
Duccio Di Boninsegna, Via - A4/5
Duomo, Piazza Del - C2
Duprè, Via Giovanni - C3/D3
Esterna Di Fontebranda, Via - C1
Ettore Bastianini, Via - D1
Federico Tozzi, Viale - B2
Fontanella, Via D. - D3
Fontebranda, Via Di - C2
Fontenuova, Via Di - A2
Fosso Di S. Ansano, Via Del - C2/D2
Franci, Viale R. - A1
Franciosa, Via Di - C2
Galluzza, Via D. - B2/C2
Garibaldi, Via - A2
Giglo, Via Dei - B3
Gramsci, Piazza - A2/B2
Il Campo - C3
Indipendenza, Piazza Dell' - C2
La Lizza - A1
Laterino, Via Del - D1
Lombarde, Via Delle - C3/D3
Maccari Cesare, Viale - A1
Mantellini, Piano Dei - D2
Mascagni, Via P. - D1
Matteotti, Piazza - B2
Mattioli, Via P. A. - D3
Mercato, Piazza Del - C3
Mille, Viale Dei - B1
Montanini, Via Dei - A2/B2
Oliviera, Via D. - C5
Orti, Via Degli - A3/B3
Pantaneto, Via Di - C4
Paradiso, Via Del - B2
Pellegrini, Via Dei - C2
Pian D'ovile, Via - A2/3
Pispini, Via Dei - C5
Pittori, Via Dei - B2
Poggio, Via Del - C2
Porrione, Via Del - C3
Porta Giustizia, Via Di - D4
Porte, Piazza Delle Due - D1/2
Rialto, Via Del - C4
Roma, Via - C5/D5
Rossi, Via Dei - B3
S. Agata, Via - D3
S. Caterina, Via Di - B2
S. Francesco, Piazza - B3
S. Giovanni, Piazza - C2
S. Martino, Via - C4
S. Pietro, Via - D2
S. Quirico, Via Di - D2
Salicotto, Via Di - C3/4
Salimbeni, Piazza - B2
Sallustrio Bandini, Via - B3
San Domenico, Piazza - B1
Sapienza, Via Della - B2
Sauro, Via N. - A1
Servi, Via Dei - C5/D5
Simone Martini, Via - A3
Sole, Via Del - C4
Sperandie, Via Delle - D2
Stadio, Viale Dello - B1
Stalloreggi, Via Di - D2
Stufa Secca, Via Della - A2/B2
Terme, Via Delle - B2
Termini, Via Dei - B2
Tiratoio, Via D. - B2
Tito Sarrochi, Via - D2
Tolomei, Piazza - B2/3
Tommaso Pendola, Via - D2
Vallerozzi, Via Di - A3

Civico, the **Santa Maria della Scala** museum complex and the **Palazzo delle Papesse** centre for contemporary art; for €16 you get a seven-day pass for the above three, as well as the **Museo dell'Opera del Duomo**, the **Battistero** and the **Oratorio di San Bernardino**.

SOME HISTORY

The Sienese hills were inhabited in prehistoric times, but were later settled by the Etruscans, who created an important trading colony with Volterra. (Indeed, it has been suggested that the city was named after the prominent Etruscan Saina family.) In the year 90 BC the city became a Roman colony named Saena Julia, ruled by Emperor Augustus. However, due to its distance from the main Roman roads, development was slow.

What eventually put Siena on the map was the Via Francigena, the pilgrim route leading south from France and spanning the whole of Tuscany. The road was heavily trafficked throughout the Middle Ages, bringing in its wake the trade that provided Siena with commercial and political clout.

The young city had amassed enough self-confidence by 1125 to pick fights with Florence. The hatred between Tuscany's sister cities over the following century was one of history's more malevolent rivalries. Things came to an explosive head on 4 September 1260, when Siena won the bloody Battle of Montaperti. A 15,000-strong Sienese army killed 10,000 Florentine soldiers and captured 15,000 more. The jubilant Sienese danced on the bodies of the fallen Florentines with nails in their shoes to hammer home the victory. But nine years later the two cities clashed again in Colle di Val d'Elsa and this time Florence came out on top. This defeat marked a profound shift in Siena's social and political identity that paradoxically forged the way for its prosperous golden age.

The Sienese then channelled their creative juices into commerce. Gradually, successful merchants and bankers gave rise to a wealthy middle class, while trade with France and England brought in cash and nourished a flourishing wool industry. Siena's civic infrastructure developed. The city's most important public works – much of the Duomo, the Palazzo Pubblico, the Torre del Mangia and Piazza del Campo, among others – were constructed under the Council of Nine, set up in 1287 in friendship with Florence.

Siena's golden age came to an abrupt halt in 1348 with the arrival of the Black Death, which slashed the population from 100,000 to 30,000 in less than a year. The city never fully recovered. Internal fighting brought down the Council of

Nine in 1355; in 1399 Siena fell under the control of Gian Galeazzo Visconti, Grand Duke of Milan, who was followed by Pandolfo Petrucci, a tyrannical, exiled nobleman. Spain's Charles V besieged the city in 1552, but three years later a popular insurrection against the Spanish left Siena open to Cosimo I de' Medici. Reduced to 8,000 inhabitants, the city couldn't defend itself. A group of Sienese nobles tried to keep their republic alive in exile for a few years in nearby Montalcino, but the effort proved fruitless. The definitive end of the Sienese Republic came in 1559.

In 1859 Siena became the first major Tuscan city to join a united Italy. Two years later it was plugged into Italy's budding rail system, allowing faster communication and commerce with the rest of the country. More importantly, it launched a lucrative tourist trade that endures to this day.

Sights

Palazzo Pubblico

Piazza del Campo.
Work on this elegant example of Gothic architecture began in 1288, but the brick and stone building, which houses the town hall and the Museo Civico (*see p223*), wasn't completed until 1342. The palazzo is a symbol of medieval Siena's mercantile wealth; with its she-wolf and Medici balls, its striking façade reads like a history book of the city.

Piazza del Campo

Piazza del Campo is often described as one of Italy's most beautiful squares. Beautiful it is, but square it isn't: the piazza is uniquely shell-shaped. Built on the site of an ancient Roman forum and paved in 1347, it lies at the base of Siena's three hills and curves downwards on the southern side to the Palazzo Pubblico and the Torre del Mangia. Its nine sections pay homage to the city's Council of Nine.

The Fonte Gaia (built 1408-19), designed by Jacopo della Quercia, sits on the north side of the piazza. The eroded marble panels of the basin were replaced by copies in 1868; what's left of the originals can be seen in the loggia of the Palazzo Pubblico. The fountain's basin serves as a terminus for the network of underground wells and aqueducts (a total of 25km/ 16 miles throughout the province) developed by Siena. According to legend, before the Fonte was built, workers uncovered a perfectly preserved antique marble statue of Venus. When the Black Death struck in the middle of the 14th century, the Sienese blamed the treasure, which was smashed to pieces and then buried in Florentine territory.

Torre del Mangia

0577 292263. **Open** *Mid Mar-June, Sept, Oct* 10am-7pm daily. *July, Aug* 10am-11pm daily. *Nov-mid Mar* 10am-4pm daily. **Admission** €5.50 (from Museo Civico ticket office). **No credit cards.**

Beastly instincts

Few cities in Italy appear as stable, compact and cohesive as Siena, something largely due to its historic skill at politely excluding anything potentially disruptive. That includes visitors: you may be treated with respect while you're here, but you'll never feel like a Sienese. Not even Italians who have lived most of their lives here can make such a claim.

The reason for this attitude owes much to the history and structure of the city's 17 *contrade* (districts), membership of which derives automatically from being born within certain borders. Their origins dating back to the 12th century, *contrade* demarcate their territories with their own heraldic signs, forging individual and collective social identities and hosting all the major rites of passage of their members, from baptisms to funerals. The christenings that take place in the *contrada* fountains are often the fruit of careful negotiation. Since membership can also be claimed through descent, even those living in the new residential districts outside the old city walls are accounted for.

Every *contrada* has its own headquarters, museum, chapel and meeting place, along with its own *prior* (director), general council and officers (elected every two years, and no longer an exclusively male prerogative) and even its own micro-economy. And once a year,

between spring and late summer, each *contrada* celebrates the feast day of its patron saint. This involves a solemn reception to which the *priors* of allied *contrade* are invited, followed by a religious service, a colourful open-air dinner around long trestle tables set up in the street, and processions into neighbouring *contrade*.

The famous Palio horse race (*see p158*) that takes place twice a year in the Piazza del Campo is the absolute apotheosis of *contrada* culture. The square itself is divided into sections representing each *contrada*: *Tartuca* (tortoise), *Onda* (wave), *Lupa* (she-wolf), *Oca* (goose), *Nicchio* (shell), *Istrice* (porcupine), *Drago* (dragon), *Civetta* (owl), *Chiocciola* (snail), *Pantera* (panther), *Aquila* (eagle), *Bruco* (caterpillar), *Leocorno* (unicorn), *Montone* (ram), *Giraffa* (giraffe), *Selva* (forest) and *Torre* (tower). The first horse over the line after three circuits of the square wins the race and earns the banner of the Virgin Mary as a trophy, provoking reactions ranging from weeping and hair-tearing (for the losers) to rapturous kissing and embracing. Banquets and festivities sponsored by the winning *contrada* last well into September; animosity between the first- and second-placed teams endures until the following year.

Asked to build their tower as high as possible, architect brothers Minuccio and Francesco di Rinaldo followed their instructions to the letter: when it was completed in 1348, the Torre del Mangia, next to the Palazzo Pubblico, was medieval Italy's tallest tower, checking in at 102m (335ft) and affording views over Siena province. The tower is named after one of its first bell-ringers: the pot-bellied *mangiaguadagni* ('eat-profits'), who bulked up at the local trattoria, despite a daily climb up the tower's 503 steps. These days only 15 visitors are allowed up it any one time, and tickets sell out quickly. At the foot of the tower is the Gothic Cappella di Piazza, finished in 1352 to commemorate the end of the plague.

Churches

Basilica di San Domenico

Piazza San Domenico (0577 280893). **Open** *Nov-Apr* 9am-6pm daily. *May-Oct* 7am-6.30pm daily. **Admission** free.
This soaring brick edifice was one of the earliest Dominican monasteries in Tuscany. Started in 1226 and completed in 1465, it has not been treated

kindly by history: fires, military occupations and earthquakes have all wreaked havoc on it, and the building that remains today is mostly the result of an extensive mid 20th-century restoration. That said, a few historic features have survived intact. At the end of the nave is a *Madonna Enthroned* attributed to Pietro Lorenzetti, while halfway down on the right is the restored chapel of Siena's patron saint, St Catherine. Inside it, in a container, is her head: her body was chopped up by heretics after her death and various Italian cities made off with pieces, but her birthplace got the grand prize.

Basilica di San Francesco

Piazza San Francesco (0577 289081). **Open** 7am-noon, 3.30-7pm daily. **Admission** free.
The Franciscans built this grand, somewhat severe church of Gothic origins in 1326. Precious little of its original artwork survived a big fire in 1655; indeed, even the mock-Gothic façade is a 20th-century addition. However, one work that has lasted through the years is Pietro Lorenzetti's *Crucifixion* (1331), which is housed in the first chapel of the transept. Two frescoes by Lorenzetti's brother Ambrogio are in the third chapel.

Tuscany

Piazza del Campo. *See p220.*

Battistero

Piazza San Giovanni (no phone). **Open** *Summer*
9am-7.30pm daily. *Winter* 10am-1pm, 2.30-5pm daily.
Admission €2.50. **No credit cards**.
Squeezed under the Duomo's apse, the Baptistery is
unusual in its shape: while most are octagonal, this
one is rectangular. The unfinished Gothic façade
includes three arches adorned with human and animal busts, while inside, colourful frescoes by various artists (mainly Vecchietta) fill the room. The
focal point is the central font (1417-34): designed by
Jacopo della Quercia and considered one of the
masterpieces of early-Renaissance Tuscany, it features gilded bronze bas-reliefs by Jacopo, Donatello
and Lorenzo Ghiberti.

Duomo

Piazza del Duomo (0577 47321). **Open** *Summer*
10am-7.30pm Mon-Sat; 2-5pm Sun. *Winter* 10.30am-
1pm, 2-6pm Mon-Sat; 2-4.30pm Sun. **Admission** €3.
No credit cards.
Construction on Siena's Duomo, one of Italy's first
Gothic cathedrals, started in 1150 on the site of an
earlier church, but plans for what was to have been
a massive cathedral had to be abandoned because
of the Black Death of 1348 and technical problems
from an unlevelled foundation. The resulting struc-

ture, Gothic in style but Romanesque in spirit, is
more modest than originally hoped, but it's nonetheless an impressive achievement.
   The black and white marble façade was started in
1226; 30 years later work began on the dome, one of
the oldest in Italy. The lower portion of the façade
and the statues in the centre of the three arches were
designed by Giovanni Pisano and built between
1284 and 1296.
   Inside, the cathedral's polychrome floors are its
most immediate attraction. If, that is, you can see
them: worked on by more than 40 artists between
1369 and 1547, the intricately decorated inlaid boxes
are usually covered by protective planks, but are
generally visible between mid August and mid
September. The most impressive are those beneath
the dome by Domenico Beccafumi, who created 35
of the 56 scenes from 1517 to 1547. In the apse is a
splendid carved wooden choir, built between the
14th and 16th centuries. Above it, back in place after
a restoration-enforced absence, is a stained-glass
rose window (7m/23ft across) made by Duccio di
Buoninsegna in 1288. Probably the earliest example
of a stained-glass window in Italy, it depicts the life
of the Virgin in nine sections. The tabernacle has
Bernini's *Maddalena* and *San Girolamo* statues.
   Another highlight is the pulpit, completed in 1266
by Nicola Pisano with the help of his son Giovanni
and Arnolfo di Cambio, who later made his name by
designing the Duomo in Florence. The Piccolomini
altar includes four statues of saints by a young
Michelangelo (carved 1501-4); above it is a *Madonna*
attributed to Jacopo della Quercia. At the far end of
the left aisle, a door leads to the Libreria Piccolomini
(admission €1.50), built in 1495 to house the library
of Sienese nobleman Aeneas Silvius Piccolomini, the
Renaissance humanist who became Pope Pius II.
This vaulted chamber was constructed at the behest
of his nephew (who became Pope Pius III for 28
days) and frescoed by Pinturicchio (1502-9, his last
work), reportedly assisted by a young Raphael. The
vibrant frescoes depict ten scenes from Pius II's life.

Oratorio di San Bernardino

Piazza San Francesco (0577 283048). **Open**
Mid Mar-Oct 10.30am-1.30pm, 3-5.30pm daily.
Nov-mid Mar phone for appointment. **Admission**
€3. **No credit cards**.
To the right of San Francesco, this oratory was built
in the 15th century on the site where St Bernard used
to pray. On the first floor is a magnificent fresco
cycle (1496-1518) by Beccafumi, Sodoma and their
lesser contemporary, Girolamo del Pacchia.

Museums

Complesso Museale di
Santa Maria della Scala

*Piazza del Duomo 2 (0577 224811/www.santamaria
dellascala.com).* **Open** *Mid Mar-early Nov* 10.30am-
6.30pm daily. *Early Nov-mid Mar* 10.30am-4.30pm
daily. **Admission** €6. **No credit cards**.

Tuscany

This museum in progress is set in a former hospital: Siena was an important stopover for pilgrims on the Via Francigena, and this hospital, founded in the ninth century, was considered the finest of its time. Funded by donations from local noble families, it was one of the first to ensure disinfected medical equipment and bug-free cots. From 1440 to 1443 the Pellegrinaio (Pilgrim's Hall), an emergency care unit, was embellished by, among others, Domenico di Bartolo, with elaborate frescoes depicting the history of the hospital. The hospital was still taking in patients until relatively recently: the author Italo Calvino died here in 1985. However, the complex is now being restored and currently hosts temporary exhibitions. The Museo Archeologico is also housed here and has several rooms devoted to Etruscan and Roman artefacts.

Museo Civico

Palazzo Pubblico, Piazza del Campo (council cultural office 0577 292226/ticket office 0577 292263). **Open** *Mid Feb-mid Mar, 1-late Nov* 10am-6.30pm daily. *Mid Mar-Oct* 10am-7pm daily. *Late Nov-mid Feb* 10am-5.30pm daily. **Admission** €7. **No credit cards**.

The first four rooms of the Museo Civico, accessed through the courtyard of the Palazzo Pubblico and up an iron staircase, house work dating from the 16th to 19th centuries. The Sala del Risorgimento pays homage to the fact that Siena was one of the first cities of the region to embrace a united Italy (1859); in the Sala del Concistorio are frescoed vaults (1529-35) by Domenico Beccafumi and a marble portal sculpted in 1448 by Bernardo Rossellino.

In the Anticappella you can admire a number of frescoes by Taddeo di Bartolo (1362-1422), which reflect his fascination with Greek and Roman antiquity and mythological heroes, plus a *Madonna and Child with Saints* by Sodoma at the altar of the Cappella del Consiglio. The Sala del Mappamondo was decorated by Ambrogio Lorenzetti around 1320-30, its barely visible cosmological frescoes depicting the universe and celestial spheres. This room also houses one of Siena's most cherished jewels: the *Maestà* fresco painted by Simone Martini in 1315. Thought to be one of his earliest works – if not his very first – it's also considered one of the first examples of political art, with the devotion to the Virgin Mary depicted said to represent devotion to the Republic's princes. The faces of the main figures are repaints, after Martini got a second inspiration following a visit to Giotto's masterpiece frescoes in the Basilica di San Francesco in Assisi. The equestrian *Il Guidoriccio da Fogliano* (1328), celebrating a victorious battle in Montemassi, is also attributed to Martini, though this has been disputed by some historians in recent years.

Museo dell'Opera del Duomo

Piazza del Duomo 8 (0577 283048). **Open** *Mid Mar-Sept* 9am-7.30pm daily. *Oct* 9am-6pm daily. *Nov-mid Mar* 9am-1.30pm daily. **Admission** €6. **No credit cards**.

Siena's Gothic **Duomo**. *See p222.*

Occupying the never-completed nave of the Duomo, this museum displays works taken from the cathedral. On the ground floor is a large hall divided in two by a stunning 15th-century wrought-iron gate; along the walls, you can enjoy a better view of Giovanni Pisano's 12 magnificent marble statues (1285-97) that once adorned the façade of the Duomo. In the centre of the room is the bas-relief of the *Madonna and Child with St Anthony* by Jacopo della Quercia, commissioned in 1437 and probably not quite completed when the artist died the following year. On the first floor is the *Pala della Maestà* (1308-11) by Duccio di Buoninsegna, used as the high altar of the Duomo until 1506. The front has a *Madonna with Saints*, while the back depicts 26 religious scenes, all in dazzling colours. A walk up to the unfinished nave affords a beautiful view of the city.

Palazzo delle Papesse

Via di Città 126 (0577 22071/www.papesse.org). **Open** noon-7pm Tue-Sun. **Admission** €5. **No credit cards**.

This new centre for contemporary art operates from within an edifice built in 1460 at the behest of Caterina Piccolomini, whose brother became Pope Pius II. The temporary art exhibitions are well worth looking out for.

Wednesday's general market. *See p225.*

Pinacoteca Nazionale

Palazzo Buonsignori, Via San Pietro 29 (0577 281161). **Open** 8.30am-1.30pm Mon; 8.15am-7.15pm Tue-Sat; 8.15am-1.30pm Sun. **Admission** €4. **No credit cards**.

One of Italy's foremost art collections, this lovely 15th-century palazzo holds more than 1,500 works of art, and is particularly renowned for its Sienese *fondi d'oro* (paintings with gilded backgrounds). The second floor is devoted to Sienese masters from the 12th to 15th centuries, including Guido da Siena and the Lorenzettis (don't miss *A City by the Sea*). The first floor houses works by the Sienese Mannerist school of the early 1500s, including Sodoma and Beccafumi, while the third floor holds the Spannocchi Collection, works by northern Italian and European artists of the 16th and 17th centuries.

Monuments & gardens

Fortezza Medicea

Viale C Maccari.

This vast red-brick fortress just outside the city is a sore reminder of Siena's troubled past. Charles V of Spain forced the Sienese to build a fortress here in

1552; as soon as his reign ended they celebrated by demolishing it, but when Cosimo I de' Medici annexed the city a few years later he demanded the fortress be rebuilt. When Florentine rule finally came to an end, Siena named the square within the fortress walls Piazza della Libertà. These days, with its views over the city, it's a good place for an evening stroll or a glass of wine at the Enoteca Italiana (*see p226*), especially during the *settimana dei vini*, a week-long showcase of regional wines held here in early June.

Orto Botanico

Via Mattioli 4 (0577 232874). **Open** 8am-12.30pm, 2.30-5.30pm Mon-Fri; 8am-noon Sat. **Admission** free.

The Botanical Gardens belong to the university and are a haven of tranquillity, like a microcosm of the Tuscan countryside.

Piazza Salimbeni

A beautiful square flanked by three of Siena's most glorious *palazzi*: Tantucci, Spannocchi and Salimbeni. The latter serves as the headquarters of the Monte dei Paschi di Siena, founded by shrewd Sienese in 1472 to pre-empt the emergence of usury in the wake of developing trade. To this day, by statute, half the bank's profits have to be ploughed back into the community.

Where to eat

Many recipes common to the Siena region today have survived since medieval times, including *pici* (like thick, irregular spaghetti) and *panzanella* (dried bread soaked in water, then made into a bread salad with basil, onion and tomato). Popular desserts include *panforte* (dense slices of nuts, candied fruits and honey) and *ricciarelli* (soft almond biscuits).

Antica Trattoria Botteganova

Via Chiantigiana 29 (0577 284230/www.antica trattoriabotteganova.it). **Open** 12.30-2.30pm, 7.30-10.30pm daily. **Average** €40. **Credit** AmEx, DC, MC, V.

This trattoria is just out of town on the north side, but it's well worth the short taxi ride. The enjoyable food is complemented by a strong wine list.

Caffé Ortensia

Via Pantaneto 95 (0577 40039). **Open** 8.30am-1.30am Mon-Fri; 5pm-1.30am Sat, Sun. **No credit cards**.

A fun bar with a well-stocked bookcase, plus papers, magazines and board games.

Cane e Gatto

Via Pagliaresi 6 (0577 287545). **Open** 8-10.30pm Mon-Wed, Fri-Sun. **Average** €45. **Credit** AmEx, MC, V.

The *menù degustazione* (€65) at this family-run restaurant can teach you everything you could ever wish to know about Sienese cooking. A decadent lunch is served for small groups by arrangement.

Tuscany

Compagnia dei Vinattieri

Via delle Terme 79 (0577 236568). **Open** 11am-1am
daily. **Average** €30. **Credit** AmEx, DC, MC, V.
Cinzia Certosini, a former restaurateur in Chianti,
started this excellent *enoteca* a few years ago, with
an ambition to make wine more approachable. The
admirable list includes a rich array of respectable
Tuscan labels, in addition to products from other
regions and countries. Fine food is also served.

La Costarella

Via di Città 33 (0577 288076). **Open** *Summer*
8.30am-midnight Mon-Wed, Fri-Sun. *Winter*
8am-9pm Mon-Wed, Fri-Sun. **No credit cards**.
If you've made it all the way up the steep hill from
the Fonte Branda, La Costarella's excellent ice-cream
and home-made *cornetti* (similar to sweet croissants)
are a refreshingly indulgent reward.

Enoteca I Terzi

Via dei Termini 7 (0577 44329). **Open** noon-
3.30pm, 6.30pm-1am Mon-Sat. **Credit** AmEx, DC,
MC, V.
This wine cellar, run by the knowledgeable Michele,
also serves various light snacks, including cold cuts,
cheeses and breads.

Fiorella

Via di Città 13 (0577 271255). **Open** 7am-7pm
Mon-Sat. **No credit cards**.
Fabulous coffee, roasted on the spot.

Hosteria Il Carroccio

Via del Casato di Sotto 32 (0577 41165). **Open**
noon-2.30pm, 7.30-10pm Mon, Tue, Thur, Fri.
Average €25. **Credit** MC, V.
Run by Renata Toppi and her children, Hosteria Il
Carroccio is a real deal. Try the *tegamate di maiale*
(pork cooked in a ceramic bowl), based on an old
Sienese recipe that's virtually extinct today.

Da Mugolone

Via dei Pellegrini 8 (0577 283235). **Open** 12.30-
3pm, 7.30-10pm Mon-Wed, Fri, Sat; 12.30-3pm Sun.
Closed 3wks Jan. **Average** €60. **Credit** AmEx, DC,
MC, V.
Many residents consider this one of Siena's best
eateries, with good reason. It's simple yet elegant, and
serves largely meat-based dishes using local ingredients, cooked and presented to unfussy perfection.

Nannini Conca d'Oro

Via Banchi di Sopra 24 (0577 236009). **Open**
7.30am-11pm Mon-Sat; 8am-9pm Sun. **Credit**
AmEx, DC, MC, V.
A good spot for substantial snacks, coffee and pastries, *aperitivi* and *digestivi*.

L'Osteria

Via de' Rossi 79-81 (0577 287592). **Open** 12.30-
2.30pm, 7.30-10.30pm Mon-Sat. **Average** €20.
Credit AmEx, DC, MC, V.
This informal haunt, frequented by neighbouring
university faculty members, serves up simple, well-
cooked Tuscan food at wooden tables.

Osteria Castelvecchio

Via Castelvecchio 65 (0577 49586). **Open** 12.30-
2.30pm, 7.30-9.30pm daily. Closed Sun in winter.
Average €25. **Credit** AmEx, DC, MC, V.
Just a few steps from the Pinacoteca Nazionale
in former horse stables, Castelvecchio offers vegetarian dishes at least twice a week on a menu that is
inventively based on seasonal fare.

Osteria La Chiacchera

Costa di Sant'Antonio 4 (0577 280631). **Open**
noon-3.30pm, 7pm-midnight daily. **Average** €15.
Credit AmEx, DC, MC, V.
A charming place in which to sample traditional
Sienese recipes. Other perks include friendly service
and, just as crucially, a decent house wine.

Osteria Le Logge

Via del Porrione 33 (0577 48013). **Open** noon-
2.45pm, 7.15-10.30pm Mon-Sat. **Average** €35.
Credit AmEx, DC, MC, V.
A popular and conveniently central *osteria* with
good food and a charming setting.

Da Trombicche

Via delle Terme 66 (0577 288089). **Open** 10am-
3pm, 5-10pm Mon-Sat. **Average** €12. **Credit** V.
This tiny, cheerful venue is a good spot for a light
lunch or a casual supper. Expect salads, cold meats,
soups and cheese platters.

Shopping

The main shopping street in Siena is **Via di
Città**, which forks above the Campo: **Banchi
di Sotto** heads down and **Banchi di Sopra**
climbs up to **Piazza della Posta**. Just before
sunset, locals emerge for their evening stroll.
  Siena's fantastic general market (8am-1pm
Wednesday) stretches from Piazza La Lizza to
the Fortezza. Get there early to snag a bargain.
The third Sunday of the month also sees an
antiques market at **Piazza del Mercato**,
behind the Campo.

Aloe & Wolf Gallery

Via del Porrione 23 (0577 283937). **Open** 4-8pm
Mon; 11am-8pm Tue-Sat. **Credit** MC, V.
This gallery/store sells a mixture of items, from con-
temporary art to vintage clothes.

Book Shop

*Via di San Pietro 19 (0577 226594/www.bookshop
siena.com)*. **Open** 10am-7.30pm Mon-Sat. **Credit**
MC, V.
American-born owner Lisa Fallon runs this nice
English bookstore, which hosts interesting book
launches. The selection of wine literature is strong.

Dolci Trame

Via del Moro 4 (0577 46168). **Open** 3.30-7.30pm
Mon; 10am-1pm, 3.30-7.30pm Tue-Sat. **Credit**
AmEx, DC, MC, V.
Hip women's clothing at the back of Piazza Tolomei.

Tuscany

Enoteca Italiana
Fortezza Medicea (0577 288497/www.enoteca-
italiana.it). **Open** noon-8pm Mon; noon-1am Tue-Sat.
Credit AmEx, MC, V.
Italy's only national wine cellar, located in the massive vaults of the fortress, stocks more than 1,000
wines from all over the country (400 from Tuscany).

La Fattoria Toscana
Via di Città 51 (0577 42255/www.lafattoria
toscana.com). **Open** 9.30am-8pm daily. **Credit**
AmEx, DC, MC, V.
La Fattoria Toscana offers an excellent selection of
gastronomic goodies, including wines, oils, sweet-
meats, local truffles and Val d'Orcia saffron.

Libreria Senese
Via di Città 62-66 (0577 280845). **Open** 9am-8pm
Mon-Sat; 10am-8pm Sun. **Credit** AmEx, DC, MC, V.
A family-run bookshop with plenty on local art and
history, including publications in English.

Morbidi
Via Banchi di Sopra 73 (0577 280268). **Open**
8am-8pm Mon-Fri; 9am-8pm Sat. **Credit** V.
A long room full of savoury Tuscan treats, such as
home-made gnocchi and fresh artichokes.

La Nuova Pasticceria di Iasevoli
Via Giovanni Duprè 37 (0577 40577). **Open** 8am-
12.45pm, 5-7.30pm Tue-Sat; 9am-12.30pm Sun.
No credit cards.
A fine selection of Sienese baked confectionery, such
as *cantuccini, pan dei santi* (bread with raisins and
walnuts made for All Saints' Day), *cavallucci* (dry
bread buns spiced with aniseed) and *panforte.*

Where to stay

Siena doesn't have enough hotels to meet the
demand, so booking in advance is advisable.
It's worth contacting the **Hotels Promotion
Service** (0577 288084, www.hotelsiena.com).

Antica Torre
Via di Fieravecchia 7 (tel/fax 0577 222255/
www.anticatorresiena.it). **Rates** €98-€104 double.
Credit AmEx, DC, MC, V.
Set in a nicely restored 16th-century tower, this
eclectic, friendly hotel gets booked up well in
advance: not surprisingly, as there are just two
rooms per floor around the central staircase. Those
on the top two levels boast views over the nearby
rooftops and surrounding countryside.

Certosa di Maggiano
Strada di Certosa 82 (0577 288180/fax 0577
288189/www.certosadimaggiano.com). **Rates**
€400-€1,030 double. **Credit** AmEx, MC, V.
Raised from the ruins of a 13th-century monastery,
Certosa di Maggiano is located just south of the city
and is renowned for its stunning garden and extensive amenities, including tennis courts, swimming
pools and even a heliport.

Chiusarelli
Viale Curtatone 15 (0577 280562/fax 0577 271177/
www.chiusarelli.com). **Rates** (incl breakfast) €65-
€79.50 single; €95-€119 double. **Credit** AmEx,
MC, V.
This three-star hotel sits on the edge of the historic
centre. Rooms are unfussy but comfortable – ask for
a quiet one at the back if possible.

Grand Hotel Continental
Via Banchi di Sopra 85 (0577 56011/reservations
0577 44204/fax 0577 5601555/www.royal
demeure.com). **Rates** €300 single; €480 double;
€637-€1,490 suite. **Credit** AmEx, DC, MC, V.
The area's only five-star hotel is set amid the richly
frescoed interiors of what was once Palazzo Gori
Pannilini. Even if you can't afford to stay here, make
sure you pop in to admire the magnificently ornate
first-floor reception room.

Pensione Palazzo Ravizza
Pian dei Mantellini 34 (0577 280462/fax 0577
221597/www.palazzoravizza.it). **Rates** (incl
breakfast) €160-€230 double. **Credit** AmEx,
DC, MC, V.
Owned by the same family for more than 200 years,
this 17th-century palazzo still has its original furnishings, including lovely frescoes. Many of the 38
rooms overlook a charming, well-kept garden, while
others have a view of the city.

Piccolo Hotel Oliveta
Via Piccolomini 35 (0577 283930/fax 0577 270009/
www.oliveta.com). **Rates** €89 single; €130 double.
Credit AmEx, MC, V.
A stone's throw from Porta Romana, the Piccolo
Hotel Oliveta offers pleasant rooms in what was
once a stone farmhouse. In warm weather breakfast
is served in the garden, whose terrace offers wonderful views over the countryside.

Piccolo Hotel Il Palio
Piazza del Sale 19 (0577 281131/fax 0577 281142/
www.piccolohotelilpalio.it). **Rates** €89 single; €108
double. **Credit** MC, V.
This pleasant small hotel is housed in a building that
dates back to the 15th century. The location is convenient, and the hotel is accessible also by car, which
is unusual for Siena.

Residence Paradiso
Via del Paradiso 16 (0577 222613/fax 0577 220551/
www.residenceparadiso.siena.it). **Rates** €30 single;
€67 double. **Credit** AmEx, MC, V.
Accommodation in 12 furnished mini-apartments in
a historic building, with the use of cooking and laundry facilities. Reductions are offered for longer stays
and in the winter. There are ten more apartments in
similarly historic surroundings in Via del Porrione.

Villa Scacciapensieri
Via di Scacciapensieri 10 (0577 41441/fax 0577
270854/www.villascacciapensieri.it). **Rates** €116-
€130 single; €185-€245 double; €305 suite. **Credit**
AmEx, DC, MC, V.

Grand Hotel Continental.
See p226.

As the name ('banish your thoughts') suggests, you can leave your worries behind as you check into this family-run hotel. It's 3km (two miles) north of the city: follow the signs up a private tree-lined drive to the crest of the hill. There's an excellent restaurant, a tennis court and a pool.

Camping

Colleverde
Strada Scacciapensieri 47 (0577 280044). Closed Nov-Mar. **Rates** €7.75; €4.13 concessions. **Credit** MC, V.
The closest campsite to the city (it's 3km/two miles away) is also one of the more attractive in southern Tuscany. There's a bar, a restaurant and a store, plus a swimming pool (open June to September). Reductions are offered for longer stays.

Resources

Hospital
Viale Bracci, north of the city (0577 586111).

Police
Via del Castoro (0577 201111).

Post office
Piazza Matteotti 37 (0577 214295).

Tourist information
Centro Servizi Informazioni Turistiche Siena (APT) *Piazza del Campo 56 (0577 280551/ www.terresiena.it).* **Open** 9am-7pm daily.

Getting there & around

By bike & moped
For bike hire, contact **DF Bike** (Via Massetana Romana 54, 0577 271905). Mopeds are offered for rent at **Automotocicli Perozzi** (Via del Romitorio 5, 0577 223157).

By bus
If you don't have a car, the bus is the way to go in Siena, especially if you're travelling to or from Florence. Siena's major bus terminal is at the edge of the historic centre at Piazza Gramsci; the main ticket office (0577 204225) is underground. Most buses leave from the adjacent Viale Federico Tozzi or nearby Piazza San Domenico. **Tra-in**, the principal bus company serving Siena and beyond (0577 204225), has departures every 30mins for Florence (direct service takes 75mins), as well as services to Arezzo, Grosseto and most regional towns of interest. The excellent www.comune.siena.it/train gives full timetable information on all services.

By car
The *raccordo* dual carriageway links Florence and Siena, with the journey taking around 45mins. Alternatively, there's the SS2, which weaves its way through the countryside slowly (very slowly if you get stuck behind a tractor). The historic centre of Siena is mainly traffic-free, so you'll have to park on the outskirts and walk in; there are big car parks at the Stadio Comunale and near the Fortezza Medicea, but even these can fill rapidly on weekends and public holidays, and around the time of the Palio. To hire a car, try **Avis** (Via Simone Martini 36, 0577 270305) or **Hertz** (Viale Sardegna 37, 0577 45085).

By taxi
Call **Radio Taxi** (0577 49222), or go to one of the taxi ranks at Piazza Stazione (0577 44504) or Piazza Matteotti (0577 289350).

By train
There are some direct trains to and from Florence, but more often you'll have to change at Empoli (journey time up to 2hrs). For Pisa, change at Empoli. Siena's train station is at the bottom of the hill on the east side of the city (Piazza Fratelli Rosselli, tickets 0577 280115/national timetable information 892021, www.trenitalia.it). From here, a local bus makes the short journey up to Piazza Gramsci, close to the historic centre.

Tuscany

Siena Province

Rolling hills and medieval villages make this a beautiful part of Tuscany.

Siena's Palazzo Pubblico contains some famous frescoes, by Ambrogio Lorenzetti, that portray the effects of good and bad government. The works date back to the 1330s, but they're as relevant today as they were then: good government is illustrated as far-sighted land management, which equates to today's well maintained towns and sustainable agriculture. It's this that accounts for the extraordinary beauty of the area around Siena.

As the cities recede behind you, rest assured that you won't be leaving art behind. Scattered throughout the region is a network of beautifully designed museums housing largely medieval and Renaissance art and Etruscan and Roman archaeology spread out among the smaller towns. They belong to the **Sistema Musei Senesi** (www.museisenesi.org) and are havens of quietude where you can enjoy the great works at your own pace.

gentle slopes are still clad with vines; olive groves abound; and there is plenty of woodland, much of it inhabited by wild boar. The feeling that time has stopped is hard to avoid.

It's an illusion. The way people tend their vines is quite unlike that of the past. The sheep in the fields have increased in number, and are now the gaunt and scraggy Sardinian breed that produces abundant milk for making pecorino cheese. More colourfully, sunflower cultivation gives the farmland a short blast of yellow and a long necrotic stretch of black that were absent from earlier palettes. Yet these transformations are gentle, and the area is so desirable today that there's hardly a barn in sight that hasn't been turned into a holiday home.

Not all of Chianti falls directly in the Siena province. However, for simplicity's sake, we've included such towns as Greve and Panzano in this chapter, despite the fact that they lie just inside the borders of the Florence province.

Chianti

The landscape of Chianti, the hilly area between Florence and Siena, features in much Tuscan art of the Renaissance; it doesn't, on the surface, appear to have changed much since then. The

Greve, Montefioralle & Panzano

Greve makes a pleasant base from which to explore the surrounding area. Its triangular main square, Piazza Giacomo Matteotti, has an arcaded perimeter, and is particularly attractive. On Saturday mornings, its wine bars and food shops heave with gossiping locals.

A tiny road of hairpin bends leads up from Greve's northern side to the ancient walled village of **Montefioralle**, a lovely spot for a quiet lunch. A further seven kilometres (4.5 miles) south is the fortified village of **Panzano**, overlooking the Conca d'Oro valley. The village has found a measure of fame in recent years as the home of the revered traditionalist butcher Dario Cecchini, whose shop on Via XX Luglio has become something of a stage for his opinions on themes from politics to literature.

Where to stay & eat

In Greve itself, you can find delectable meat dishes at the tiny **Mangiando Mangiando** (Piazza Giacomo Matteotti 80, 055 8546372, closed Mon in winter & mid Jan-mid Feb, average €25). If you're looking for a room, the best option is **Albergo Giovanni da Verrazzano** (Piazza Mattoetti 28, 055 853189, closed mid Jan-mid Feb, doubles €105), which has a charming restaurant on its geranium-lined terrace. **Locanda il Gallo** at Chiocchio (Via L Conti 16-18, 055 8572266, www.locanda ilgallo.it, average €25, doubles €80) is an attractive alternative for bed and board (hotel & restaurant closed last 2wks Feb).

Up in Montefioralle, the family-run **La Taverna del Guerrino** is a rustic gem (Via Montefioralle 39, 055 853106, closed Mon, Tue & lunch Wed, 2wks Dec, average €30). In Panzano you can both stay and indulge the palate at **Villa Sangiovese** (Piazza Bucciarelli 5, 055 852461, average €30, doubles €125, restaurant closed Wed, hotel & restaurant closed mid Dec-mid Mar). To the right of the church is the **Enoteca Il Vinaio** (Via Santa Maria 22, 055 852603, closed dinner Thur & all Thur Nov-Mar, average €15), serving classic local fare and a wide selection of local wines.

Resources

Tourist information

Ufficio Turistico Viale G da Verrazzano 59, Greve (055 8546287). **Open** 9.30am-1pm, 2.30-7pm Mon-Sat.

Castellina & around

From Panzano, take the SS222 to the hilltop town of Castellina. Originally an Etruscan settlement, its layout is essentially medieval: the imposing fortifications bear witness to the town's historic role as a bastion of Florentine dominion in its southward expansion towards Siena in the 15th and 16th centuries. The

imposing **Torre** overshadows the main square, Piazza del Comune, and a covered walkway gives a chilly 14th-century feel. There are plenty of places to taste and buy wine; one of Chianti's top wineries, **Castello di Fonterutoli** (*see p234* **Visiting wineries**), is nearby.

Between bibulous sessions, head towards Vagliagli. After eight kilometres (five miles) turn right for Pievasciata; keep an eye out for signs for the **Parco Sculture del Chianti** (0577 357151, www.chiantisculpturepark.it, Nov-Mar by appt only, admission €7.50), which features interesting works created by a variety of artists. If you take the SS429 west from Castellina, on the other hand, you'll reach **Radda**, another jewel in the Chianti crown. In its early days the town was the capital of the medieval League of Chianti, a chain of Florentine defensive outposts against Siena that included Castellina and Gaiole.

Beyond Radda, the Etruscan tomb-rich area around **Volpaia**, seven kilometres (four miles) to the north, is worth a look, as is the town of **Gaiole**, located on the steep eastern edge of Chianti. Back in the Middle Ages it was a busy market town, but it's quieter now and is a pleasant stop on the way to the nearby castles and wineries (*see p234* **Visiting wineries**). One of the latter, **Badia a Coltibuono**, makes a great starting point for anyone up for a hike.

On the other side of Gaiole, taking the SS484 will lead you to the famous **Castello di Brolio**, a 19th-century rendering of a castle wrecked by Spanish troops in 1478 and finished off by the Sienese 50 years later. It was rebuilt by Baron Bettino Ricasoli, who was also responsible for pushing Chianti's wine industry into the major league. The **Barone Ricasoli** winery below the castle (*see p234* **Visiting wineries**) remains one of the region's best, along with nearby Felsina.

Where to stay & eat

In Castellina, pleasant rooms are available at **Palazzo Squarcialupi** (Via Ferruccio 22, 0577 741186, closed Nov-mid Mar, doubles €98-€110). For a verdant setting and a pool, head beyond Fonterutoli on the Siena road and stop at **Belvedere di San Leonino** (Località San Leonino, 0577 740887, www.hotelsanleonino.com, closed Oct-Easter, doubles €120); it has its own restaurant, Il Cortile. **Ristorante Albergaccio** (Via Fiorentina 63, 0577 741042, closed Sun lunch & Wed, Thur lunch in winter & all Nov & 3wks Jan, average €40) offers two 'Taste of Tuscany' fixed menus. **Antica Trattoria La Torre** (Piazza del Comune 15, 0577 740236, closed Fri & last 2wks Feb, 1st 2wks Sept, average €30) is a classic eaterie.

Tuscany

In Radda, you can dine and stay at **Palazzo Leopoldo** (Via Roma 33, 0577 735605, doubles €150-€290), where the **Perla del Palazzo** restaurant has a garden dining area and focuses on local cuisine. Another dining option is the elegant **Ristorante Vignale** (Via XX Settembre 23, 0577 738094, closed Thur & Dec-late Feb, average €40). A similar style is to be found at the **Relais Fattoria Vignale** (Via Pianigiani 8, 0577 738300, closed 2mths in winter, doubles €135-€300) – unsurprising, as it's owned by the same people. The rates at the *agriturismo* **Podere Terreno** (Via della Volpaia, 0577 738312, €90 per person) include an excellent dinner with wine. Near Gaiole, the restaurant at **Badia a Coltibuono** (0577 749031, closed Mon Mar-May, mid Dec-early Mar, average €35) specialises in game; in summer, eat at tables in the beautiful gardens. For lodgings, go south to the hamlet of San Sano, just off SS408, where the friendly **Hotel Residenza San Sano** (0577 746130, closed Nov-Mar, doubles €128-€140) has a pool among old stone houses.

Resources

Tourist information

Castellina *Ufficio Informazioni Turistiche, Via Ferruccio 40 (0577 741392).* **Open** 10am-1pm, 3-7pm Mon-Sat; 10am-1pm Sun.
Gaiole *Pro Loco, Via Antonio Casabianca (0577 749375).* **Open** *Apr-Oct* 9.30am-1pm, 3-6.30pm Mon-Sat. Closed Nov-Mar.
Radda *Piazza Ferucci 1 (0577 738494).* **Open** 10am-1pm, 3-7pm Mon-Sat; 10am-1pm Sun.

West of Siena

The Poggibonsi exit of the Si-Fi (Siena-Firenze) *autostrada* quickly gives access to the western Siena province.

Colle di Val d'Elsa

This attractive, lively town is an ideal base for visiting the whole area, including Siena. The historic centre spans a hilltop (Colle Alta) and the lower-lying Colle Bassa. The river Elsa was channelled for power here as early as the 13th century, giving rise to flourishing industries: first woollen cloths, then paper and, in more modern times, crystal ware. The **Museo del Cristallo** (Via dei Fossi 8A, 0577 924135, www.cristallo.org, closed Mon) is a beautifully designed underground glass museum; for hand-ground and engraved glass, try **La Grotta del Cristallo** (Via del Muro Lungo 20, 0577 924676) up in Colle Alta, but to see a true artisan at work,

visit Giuliano Bandinelli at **BG**, his workshop in Località Belvedere (0577 931879, closed Mon in winter). The **Museo Civico e Diocesano d'Arte Sacra** (Via del Cristallo, 0577 923888, closed Mon, admission €3) and the **Museo Archeologico** (Piazza Duomo, 0577 922954, closed Mon, admission €3) are both worth a visit.

Where to stay & eat

In town, **La Vecchia Cartiera** (Via Oberdan 5-9, 0577 921107, doubles €80) is handily placed, overlooking the entrance to the glass museum; on a hillside, a stone's throw from the centre, is **Relais della Rovere** (Via Piemonte 10, Località La Badia, 0577 924696; www.chiantiturismo.it, closed Nov-Feb, doubles €176-€208), housed in a restored 11th-century abbey set in gardens with a pool. In the nearby village of Strove, **Relais Castel Bigozzi** (Strada di Bigozzi 1, 0577 300000, closed Nov-mid Mar, doubles €80-€200) offers well-appointed apartments of different sizes.

Another good reason for hanging out in Colle is the food. **Da Arnolfo** (Via XX Settembre, 0577 920549, closed Tue & Wed, average €75), carries two Michelin stars, well deserved for its superb ingredients, ingeniously combined. Elsewhere, **Molino Il Moro** (Via della Ruota 2, 0577 920862, closed Mon & lunch Tue, average €28) is located in the renovated mill (the water still courses beneath the dining room), while the **Osteria Vibbò** (Piazza Sant'Agostino 9, 0577 920231, closed Wed & Feb, average €18) is popular with the younger generation. For an *aperitivo* (or, indeed, a handsome snack), try the **14 in Canonica** wine bar (Piazza Canonica 2, 0577 923444, closed Nov-Mar).

San Gimignano

There are 13 stone towers punctuating the skyline of San Gimignano these days, but back in the 12th and 13th centuries, when the town was at its political and financial peak, there were more than five times as many: 72, to be precise. The town's good fortune came from its strategic position on the Via Francigena pilgrim route, which passes through the perfectly preserved medieval city. Tourism has since brought it further wealth: masses of day-trippers now congest its narrow pedestrian streets between the two main squares, though they mostly disappear in the late afternoon.

After visiting the 11th-century **Collegiata**, or cathedral (0577 940316, closed Sun morning & late Jan-early Mar except services, admission €3.50), which features astounding frescoes by the likes of Bartolo di Fredi and Ghirlandaio, the best way to enjoy this delightful town is to

Tuscany

buy an all-in-one ticket (€7.50) for its museums, part of the Sistema Musei Senesi (*see p228*). Up in Piazza del Duomo, in part of the building that houses the Palazzo Comunale (town hall) and the Torre Grossa, is the **Pinacoteca** (0577 990312, average €5): clamber up here for a fine view of the town and surrounding area, but also to check out its collection of 12th- to 15th-century Florentine and Sienese art.

Walk down Via San Matteo from the main square and you'll reach the **Museo Archeologico**, the **Spezzeria di Santa Fina** and the **Galleria d'Arte Moderna e Contemporanea Raffaele De Grada**, all located in what was once the Convent of Santa Chiara (Via Folgore 11, closed Jan-mid Mar, admission €3.50). The archaeology is largely Etruscan, found locally but influenced by the culture of nearby Volterra (*see p213*). The glazed ceramics in the Spezzeria were made for the convent's pharmacy. There's an **Ornithological Museum** (Via Quercecchio, 0577 941388, closed Oct-Apr, admission €1.50) across town. On a less traditional note, works of contemporary sculpture (by Jannis Kounellis, Giulio Paolini, Nick Jonk and Luciano Fabro) are dotted throughout the town.

Where to stay & eat

Perhaps the classiest hotel in San Gimignano is **L'Antico Pozzo** (Via San Matteo 87, 0577 942014, closed 3wks Jan & 3wks Dec, doubles €110-€135); a pleasant alternative is the family-run **Hotel Bel Soggiorno** (Via San Giovanni 91, 0577 940375, closed Jan & Feb, doubles €95-€120), which has a tempting restaurant. Otherwise, head to **Le Renaie** (0577 955044, www.hotellerenaie.com, closed Nov & Dec, doubles €90-€110), in the ancient village of Pancole and home to the Leonetto restaurant.

For regional cooking with a twist, try **Osteria delle Catene** (Via Mainardi 18, 0577 941966, closed Wed, average €25). One of San Gimignano's more elegant places, **Ristorante Dorandò** (Vicolo dell'Oro 2, 0577 941862, closed Mon in winter, average €45) serves food based on a variety of Etruscan, medieval and Renaissance recipes. **Gelateria di Piazza** (Piazza della Cisterna, 0577 942244, closed Nov-Feb) claims to sell the best ice-cream in the world; if the framed photo and letter inside are anything to go by, Tony Blair agrees.

Resources

Tourist information

Pro Loco, Piazza del Duomo 1 (0577 940008/ www.sangimignano.com). **Open** *Summer* 9am-1pm, 3-7pm daily. *Winter* 9am-1pm, 2-6pm daily.

A feline resident of **Colle di Val d'Elsa**. *See p230.*

Abbazia di San Galgano

Located in the Valdimerse, midway between Siena and Roccastrada on the SS73, this abandoned abbey is like something out of a fairy tale. Built between 1218 and 1288, it was a Cistercian powerhouse until the 14th century. Its monks devised complex irrigation systems and sold their services as doctors, lawyers and architects. But the abbey was sacked one time too many and eventually abandoned. The ruins retain an atmosphere of eerie spirituality.

St Galgano Guidotti lived in a hut on a hilltop next to the abbey, where the **Cappella di Montesiepi** now stands. A knight from a local noble family, St Galgano Guidotti renounced his warlike ways to become a Cistercian hermit. When fellow knights persuaded him to revert to his old self in 1180, he defiantly stabbed a stone and his sword slid in. The (alleged) sword in the stone is now on display in the centre of this curious circular Romanesque chapel, which has fading frescoes by Ambrogio Lorenzetti.

Tuscany

Monte Oliveto Maggiore.

South-east of Siena

The landscape south of Siena opens up to reveal rolling hills of open fields interspersed with solitary cypress trees. In the spring it ripples greenly with durum wheat; in the autumn, after ploughing, it's a textured blend of brown and beige. To the east are the Sienese claylands, or Crete Senesi, which helps explain why warm pink brick is a feature of many of the towns in the area. To the west, meanwhile, are a number of well-preserved hill towns to explore.

Buonconvento

If you're heading south in a car, take the SS2 towards Cassia and stop off in Buonconvento to visit the **Museo d'Arte Sacra della Val d'Arbia** (0577 807181, closed Mon, admission €3.50) in the Palazzo Ricci Socini. The collection contains works by Duccio di Buoninsegna.

Where to eat

To refuel after the museum, try **I Poggioli** (Via Tassi 6, 0577 806546, closed Mon & Tue lunch, average €25), which has a very pleasant garden.

Monte Oliveto Maggiore

Up the winding road that leads from Buonconvento towards the lunar landscape of the Crete Senesi is the magnificent abbey of Monte Oliveto Maggiore. Founded in 1313 by Bernardo Tolomei, a scion of one of Siena's richest families, the monastery began as a solitary hermitage in an arid area. However, Bernardo soon drew a large following, and the Olivetan order was recognised by the pope in 1344. Expanded territory brought wealth that was channelled into embellishing the buildings and creating a library (closed to the public since the theft of some volumes) and a fresco cycle in the cloister. Painted between 1495 and 1505, the panels portray *The Stories of St Benedict* and are the work of Giovanni Antonio Bazzi (aka Il Sodoma) and Luca Signorelli. Outside, a Benedictine gift shop sells home-brewed *amaro* drinks, honey and herbal medicines.

San Giovanni d'Asso

The little town of San Giovanni d'Asso has made a heady name for itself through its truffles. It holds two truffle festivals: one in the autumn, featuring the *Tuber Magnatum Pico*, or precious white truffle, and another in March,

Tuscany

when the less heralded but still delectable Marzuolo variety ripens. In the town's castle there is even a multimedia **Truffle Museum** (Piazza Gramsci 1, information 0577 803101, closed Mon-Fri, admission €3) to keep you drooling between events. Moreover, at the rear of the castle sits the **Locanda del Castello** (Piazza Vittorio Emanuele 11, 0577 802939, closed mid Jan-mid Mar, doubles €110-€120), a nice little inn with a good restaurant.

However, the most notable feature here is the **Bosco della Ragnaia**, a magical garden made in a steeply sloping wood, where light flickers through foliage, water plays in the background and all formal geometries are quietly subverted. It's the creation of American painter Sheppard Craige, who is usually to be found on site, spade in hand. The garden is open daily from dawn to dusk, and admission is free.

Montalcino

Montalcino means 'hill of ilex oak'. There was a hilltop town here as early as the 9th century, its first economy based on leather tanning using the tannins from the abundant oak forests. Under Siena's rule in the 13th century, four families dominated the town's political identity, and are represented today in Montalcino's four *contrade* (for an explanation of *contrade*, see *p221* **Beastly instincts**). The **Fortezza** was built by the Sienese in 1362, and in 1555 became the last and short-lived stronghold of the Sienese Republic.

The decline that followed didn't abate until the late 1970s, when careful vine selection and planting, improved cellar techniques and far-sighted marketing put the local **Brunello di Montalcino** red wine on the map (*see p234* **Visiting wineries**). Tourism came in the wake of the red wine, and it's not just Brunello that has benefited: other estates, such as Pacenti Siro, L'Ucceliera and Cupano, all make fine Rosso di Montalcinos, while the production of olive oil and honey has proved an extra boon.

All roads in Montalcino lead to Piazza del Popolo, in the heart of the town. Here you'll find the shield-studded **Palazzo Comunale** (with the tall tower), modelled after Siena's Palazzo Pubblico in 1292. Around the corner, annexed to Sant'Agostino church (built in 1360, with superb frescoes by Bartolo di Fredi), is another admirable example of the Sistema Musei Senesi: the **Museo Civico e Diocesano** (Via Ricasoli 31, 0577 846014, closed Mon, admission €4.50, €6 incl entrance to the Fortezza). Its collection includes works by Simone Martini and Sano di Pietro. Some very early ceramics show how, by the 13th century, the abundant local ilex oak was used for firing kilns.

Montalcino enjoys views that extend all the way to Siena on a clear day. To appreciate them to the full, brace yourself for the climb up to the battlements of the **Fortezza** (0577 849211, admission €3.50, €6 incl entrance to the **Museo** Civico e Diocesano). Following your descent, reward yourself by sampling wines at the well-stocked *enoteca* inside the fortress walls.

Where to stay, eat & drink

On the southern edge of town, the three-star **Hotel Vecchia Oliviera** (Porta Cerbaia, Angolo Via Landi 1, 0577 846028, doubles €120-€150) has a pool, a terrace and lovely views over the valley. In Montalcino itself, the **Albergo Il Giglio** (Via S Saloni 5, 0577 848167, doubles €90) is a family-run place with 12 frescoed rooms in its main building and an additional five (no bath) next door. The **Hotel Residence Montalcino** (Via S Saloni 31, 0577 847188, closed Nov-Apr, doubles €70-€80) has comfortable apartments.

Montalcino's restaurants aren't really up to the fame of its wine. The best is the **Re di Macchia** (Via Saloni 21, 0577 846116, closed Thur, average €20), which has a small, well-thought-out menu. For nicely presented food and great views, head slightly out of town towards Torrenieri until, on your right, you come to **Boccon di Vino** (Località Colombaio Tozzi 201, 0577 848233, closed Tue, average €40). People-watch over a coffee or an *aperitivo* at the **Fiaschetteria Italiana** (Piazza del Popolo 6, 0577 849043, closed Thur in winter). **Bacchus** (Via G Matteotti 15, 0577 847054, closed Mon, Tue, Thur & Sat in winter) is a decent spot for light meals.

Wine connoisseurs are well served here: there are myriad *enoteche* in Montalcino. The most imposing establishment is **Enoteca Osteria Osticcio** (Via G Matteotti 23, 0577 848271, closed Sun, average €20): your samplings may cost a bit, but they come with a priceless view. If you want to buy a bottle or two to take away, try **Montalcino 564** (Via Mazzini 25, 0577 849109, closed Sun in winter), where you may also be tempted by fine glassware and table linens. Another friendly venue at which to sample and stock up is **Enoteca BD** (Via Traversa dei Monti 214, 0577 849019), just outside town beyond the Hotel Vecchia Oliviera.

Resources

Tourist information

Ufficio Informazioni, Costa del Municipio (0577 849331/www.prolocomontalcino.it). **Open** 10am-1pm, 2-5.50pm daily. Closed Mon in winter.

Visiting wineries

Tuscany boasts three of Italy's foremost quality wine appellations: the Chianti area between Siena and Florence, and the vineyards producing Brunello di Montalcino and Vino Nobile di Montepulciano. Tuscan reds outshine the whites, though one or two wineries over on the southern coast (Fattoria di Magliano, for instance) are now producing pleasant whites with Vermentino grapes.

Most wineries are happy to show visitors around, but few are equipped with staff and tasting rooms for proper tours. It's always a good idea to call ahead. Most wineries open their doors for **Cantine Aperte**, held during the last weekend of May. It's an excellent occasion for getting to know some of the smaller wineries that might otherwise be hard to visit. Keep an eye out for the Strada del Vino offices, which can arrange tasting tours relating to the particular DOC they cover.

Listed below are some of the more prominent and worthwhile wineries. For more on Tuscan wines, *see pp42-45*.

Chianti

The heartland of Chianti Classico is best defined by the towns of Radda, Castelnuovo Berardenga, Gaiole, Castellina Greve and Panzano. The wineries below are given in north–south order. Unless otherwise stated, all times listed are for the outlets: visits to the wineries and tastings are by appointment only.

Castello di Fonterutoli

Fonterutoli, Castellina in Chianti (0577 73571/www.fonterutoli.it).
Run by the scions of a family that competes with the Antinori for aristocratic panache. There's a country residence to match. The winery is open to the public, but you must book in advance. Tasting and selling is also done through the Enoteca Fonterutoli (Via G Puccini 4, 0577 741385, Mar-Oct 10am-7pm daily; Nov-Feb 10am-7pm Mon-Fri).

Badia a Coltibuono

Gaiole in Chianti (0577 74481/shop 0577 749479/www.coltibuono.com). **Open** *Mar-Oct* 9am-7pm daily. *Nov, Dec* 9am-7pm Tue-Sun. Closed Jan, Feb. **Credit** MC, V.
Set in the 700-year-old abbey (*see p229*). Visits are held every 45mins 2-5pm Mon-Fri May-July, Sept, Oct, and the rest of the year by request.

Barone Ricasoli

Castello di Brolio, Gaiole in Chianti (0577 730220/www.ricasoli.it). **Open** 9am-7.30pm Mon-Fri; 11am-6.30pm Sat, Sun. **Credit** AmEx, DC, MC, V.
A fine winery below the castle (*see p229*). The shop has informal tastings; guided tastings and cellar visits are available on request.

Riecine

Gaiole in Chianti (0577 749098/www.riecine. com). **Open** 9am-6pm Mon-Fri. **Credit** MC, V.
Run by Sèan O'Callaghan (*see also p44*), this small winery has won widespread international acclaim.

Felsina

SS Chiantigiana 484, nr Castelnuovo Berardenga (0577 355117). **Open** *Mar-Oct* 8.30am-6pm Mon-Fri. *Nov-Feb* 8.30am-12.30pm, 1.30-5.30pm Mon-Fri. **Credit** MC, V.
On Chianti Classico's southernmost border, this winery produces some of Siena's best wines, including the Super Tuscan Fontalloro.

Further information

Consorzio Chianti Classico (055 82285/ www.chianticlassico.com).

Chianti Rufina

This area comprises the towns of Pontassieve and Rufina. Its wineries are protected by low mountains and enjoy a dry microclimate.

Fattoria Selvapiana

Via Selvapiana 43, Rufina (055 8369848/ www.selvapiana.it). **Open** 9am-1pm, 3-7pm Mon-Fri. **Credit** AmEx, DC, MC, V.
The pick of the Rufina wineries.

Montalcino

Brunello di Montalcino (DOCG), one of Italy's top wines, is produced around this hilltop town 40 kilometres (25 miles) south of Siena. There are a number of *enoteche* in town (*see p233*); the output of the 171 producers reflects differences in soil and microclimate within this widespread municipality.

Fattoria dei Barbi

Podere Novi village 170, Montalcino (0577 841111/www.fattoriadeibarbi.it). **Open** 10am-1pm, 2.30-6pm Mon-Fri; 2.30-6pm Sat, Sun. **Credit** AmEx, DC, MC, V.

Barone Ricasoli. *See p234.*

Fine old cellars, with a variety of wines, plus sales of oil, grappa and cheese made on the property. The winery has its own restaurant.

Fattoria del Casato
17 Località Podere Casato (0577 849421/ www.cinellicolombini.it). **Open** 9am-1pm, 3-6pm Mon-Fri; Sat & Sun by appointment. **Credit** MC, V.
Donatella Cinelli Colombini's cellars are manned (as it were) by women. The tour is fun and instructive, and the wines promising.

Further information
Consorzio del Vino Brunello di Montalcino Costa del Municipio 1, Montalcino (0577 848246/ www.consorziobrunellodimontalcino.it).

Montepulciano

In 1981 the Vino Nobile di Montepulciano was among the first Italian wines to achieve the DOCG, hot on the heels of Montalcino.

Avignonesi
Via Colonica 1, Valiano di Montepulciano (0578 724304/www.avignonesi.it). **Open** 9am-6pm Mon-Fri. **Credit** MC, V.
The main Avignonesi vineyard, Le Cappezzine, is approximately 23km (14 miles) outside Montepulciano and has tastings and tours on weekdays. There's also a small cellar in town (Via di Gracciano nel Corso 91).

Poliziano
Via Fontago 1, Montepulciano (0578 738171/www.carlettipoliziano.it). **Open** 8.30am-12.30pm, 2.30-6pm Mon-Fri. Closed Aug & 2wks Dec. **Credit** AmEx, DC, MC, V.
Vineyards on three different sites, producing three different types of Vino Nobile, two of which are single-vineyard *crus*.

Further information
Consorzio del Vino Nobile di Montepulciano Piazza Grande 7, Montepulciano (0578 757812/www.vinonobiledimontepulciano.it).

Tuscany

Monte Amiata

It's a weathervane, a compass, a water source and a furnace supplying the region with hot mineral springs, all rolled into one. Monte Amiata may not have made it yet as a tourist destination, but without it, the Val d'Orcia and the Maremma would never have emerged from insignificance.

The people of southern Tuscany use the handsome mountain of ancient volcanic origin as a point of reference. They orient their whereabouts in relation to the omnipresent mound. When it wears a hat, they know it's going to rain. But the slopes are also worth a visit. There's parkland, plenty of wildlife and some good walking opportunities. Most winters, there's enough snow at the top for some modest skiing. And in summer, once you're above 600 metres (2,000 feet) – the peak is around 2,000 metres (6,500 feet) above sea level – you can breathe again: the daytime sun is hot but the evenings are cool and the air is crisp.

The towns on the east side of the mountain reveal a Sienese influence. **Piancastagnaio** is an attractive village with a good wine bar (the unfortunately named Enoteca Saxa Cuntaria; 0577 784104), while **Abbadia San Salvatore** feels more mountainous; attractions here include an ancient crypt with a forest of carved columns, and plenty of good, inexpensive eateries. Pleasant **Seggiano** is home to a terrific cheesemaker (Roberto Governi at the Caseificio Seggiano; 0564 950991); the town also produces excellent olive oil from the local Olivastro species. A little further up the road is Daniel Spoerri's wonderful sculpture garden (0564 950457); beyond this is the village of **Pescina**, where you'll find the magnificent **Il Silene** restaurant (*see p40* **Want food, will travel**).

On the west side, the towns feel a little more rugged. Great rocky crags punctuate the townscape of Roccalbegna, as though a giant sculptor was working there before the houses were built. The architecture of Santa Fiora is surprisingly imposing, and the town actually sits on what is now a valuable asset: good drinking water, which is piped to much of the province of Grosseto (the mountain straddles the border of both provinces).

Abbazia di Sant'Antimo

The lovely Benedictine abbey of Sant'Antimo lies quietly in a vale beneath the hamlet of Castelnuovo dell'Abate. Its founding is attributed to Charlemagne in 781, though what remains largely dates to the 12th century. The Romanesque interiors feature finely carved capitals, including one portraying Daniel in the lion's den (second column from the right of the nave). A group of French Premonstratensian monks (Cistercian branch) moved here in 1979 and salvaged it from decline. Gregorian chant accompanies many of the day's religious functions, drawing audiences from far and wide.

San Quirico d'Orcia & Bagno Vignoni

Many of Tuscany's foremost building firms hail from **San Quirico d'Orcia**, so it's no wonder they have done such a splendid job in restoring the vast late 17th-century **Palazzo Chigi**. Just opposite is the 13th-century **Collegiata** church, the portals of which are adorned with imaginative creatures carved in stone. Inside, there's a terrific altarpiece by Sano di Pietro.

Down the main street is the main square, which provides dawn-to-dusk access to the 16th-century **Horti Leonini**, a lovely formal garden, at the back of which sits a delightful rose garden. Like many towns in the area, San Quirico has its own traditional olive press, which becomes the focal point of the annual Festa dell'Olio (held around 10 December). It's a convivial, somewhat bibulous opportunity for gorging on *bruschetta* soaked in the excellent freshly pressed oil.

Just south of San Quirico is the tiny hamlet of **Bagno Vignoni**. Piazza delle Sorgenti, the main square, has a large pool of thermal water in its centre flanked by houses and a low Renaissance loggia. Saint Catherine and, later, Lorenzo 'Il Magnifico' came here to ease their aching limbs. Though you can't swim in the historic baths, you can soak blissfully in the thermal pool at **Hotel Posta Marcucci** (*see p215* **Reach for the spas**).

Where to stay & eat

Hotel Casanova (SS146, 0577 898177, closed Nov-mid Mar, doubles €150-€166 half board), just outside San Quirico on the Pienza road, has a traditional style, and both indoor and outdoor

Anyone know the way to the **Bosco della Ragnaia**? *See p233.*

town hall and the pope's palace. If you stand in Piazza Pio II and slowly turn around, you'll notice decorative themes and variations (the *tondo* and the garland) that lend a sense of unity to the different types of building and the materials used. It's pretty astounding to think the whole project was accomplished in four years. The body of the Duomo is in tuff stone and, at the rear, deliberately Gothic in style, as if to fit into the existing urban context. The travertine façade, by contrast, is as Renaissance as it could be, for those days a bold declaration of modernity.

Palazzo Piccolomini (0578 748503, closed Mon & late Feb-early Mar, late Nov-early Dec, admission €3.50), the pope's residence, was modelled after Alberti's Palazzo Rucellai in Florence. There is a delightful hanging garden overlooking the Val d'Orcia that you can view from the gate: it was probably the first garden since antiquity deliberately designed for aesthetic pleasure. You need a ticket for tours of Pius II's lavish private apartments, but access to the courtyard is free.

Pienza's art collection is kept in the **Museo Diocesano** (Corso Rossellino 30, 0578 749905, closed Tue & Mon-Fri Nov-Mar, admission €4.10). The sections devoted to medieval and early Renaissance art are, as you would expect, particularly striking.

Where to stay & eat

Those wanting to stay the night will enjoy the comfort and calm of **Hotel Relais Il Chiostro** (Corso Rossellino 26, 0578 748400, closed early Jan-late Mar, doubles €120-€220), housed in a 15th-century convent overlooking the Val d'Orcia. It has an inviting swimming pool and its own restaurant (closed lunch Mon, average €50). **Camere Gozzante** (Corso Rossellino, 0578 748500, doubles €53-€65) has a handful of pleasant rooms in the main street, while the **San Gregorio Residence** (Via della Madonnina 4, 0578 748059, doubles €80-€120) is a better option for families with small children.

For dining, **La Pergola** (0578 748051, Via dell'Acerto 2, closed Mon & Nov, average €25) is the best restaurant around. **Trattoria Latte di Luna** (Via San Carlo 6, 0578 748606, closed Tue & mid Feb-mid Mar & July average €25) is reliable. Otherwise, head down to the hamlet of Monticchiello, a few miles away, and eat at **La Porta** (Via del Piano 1, 0578 755163, closed Thur & early Jan-early Feb & late June-early July, average €30). Also in Pienza is **Enoteca di Ghino** (Via delle Mura 8, 0578 748057), an excellent, keenly priced wine shop with bottles from Tuscany and beyond.

pools. At the **Hotel Le Terme** (Piazza delle Sorgenti 13, 0577 887150, closed mid Nov-end Dec, doubles €96-€110), right beside the antique baths in the centre, there's fine food and an interesting wine list at the newly renovated **La Terrazza** restaurant. The **Locanda del Loggiato** (Piazza del Moretto 30, 0577 888925, doubles €140) has eight pleasant rooms and provides light meals.

Pienza

Originally called Corsignano, this little town took its current name from the man who remodelled it between 1458 and 1462: Aeneas Silvius Piccolomini, who became Pope Pius II in 1458. The 'Humanist pope', as he was later called, was a close friend of Renaissance genius Leon Battista Alberti, the designer of the façade of the church of Santa Maria Novella in Florence and the author of the *Treatise of Architecture* that was to influence town planning for centuries.

Bernardo Rossellino, Alberti's main assistant, designed the Pienza make-over, creating a central square flanked by the cathedral, the

Resources

Tourist information

Ufficio Informazioni, Palazzo Pubblico, Piazza Dante Alighieri 18 (0578 749071/www.ufficioturistico dipienza.it). **Open** 9.30am-1pm, 3-6.30pm daily.

Montepulciano

Physician and poet Francesco Redi wrote a narrative poem in 1685 entitled 'Bacco in Toscana' that described the imaginary journey, in search of wine, made through the region by Bacchus and Ariadne. After ample libations, their conclusion was clear: 'Montepulciano of all wine is sovereign'.

Though wine has been a mainstay of the local economy for centuries, the town owes its visible substance more to political acumen than viticulture. The buildings suggest the influence of Florentine architects: Montepulciano swore allegiance to Florence as early as 1511, thereby defending itself from the designs of both Siena and Perugia. Among those brought in to rework the town's medieval fabric were Antonio da Sangallo the Elder and Vignola.

The best way to see the town is by tackling the steep Via di Gracciano del Corso, which starts near Montepulciano's northern entrance, Porta al Prato. Along the way, note the Roman and Etruscan marble plaques cemented into the base of **Palazzo Bucelli** (No.73): they were gathered by Pietro Bucelli, an 18th-century collector whose interest in antiquities supplied the Museo Civico with some of its finest items. A bit further up, on Piazza Michelozzo, you can't help but notice the towering **Torre di Pulcinella**, a clock tower topped by a mechanical figure typical of the Neapolitan *Commedia dell'Arte*. It was given to the town by a nostalgic priest from Naples who was long resident in Montepulciano.

Your efforts will eventually be rewarded when you reach Piazza Grande, the town's highest and most beautiful point. The spacious square paved with chunky stones is reminiscent of Pienza's 'ideal city' layout. The **Duomo** was never embellished with a proper façade, and the rough brick front belies the treasures of the interior: the fine *Gothic Assumption* by Taddeo di Bartolo (1401) above the altar; the *Madonna and Child* by Sano di Pietro towards the top of the left of the nave; the marble *Ciborium* sculpted by Vecchietta, one of the artists invited by Pius II to embellish the Duomo in Pienza with a painting; the delicately carved tomb of humanist Aragazzi (1428) by Michelozzo.

Also in the square are Sangallo's Palazzo Tarugi, with *loggia*; the 13th-century Palazzo Comunale, which deliberately echoes the

Mellow yellow

Peppery, warm and aromatic, good saffron lends itself to both sweet and savoury cuisine, enflaming dishes with its deep, reddish yellow and elevating them with a delectable subtlety of taste. In recent years, there has been a return to saffron cultivation in various parts of Tuscany, with the Val d'Orcia taking the lead (see www.crocusbrandi.it for the premium grower). Saffron has always thrived best where a hot Mediterranean breeze rakes across arid ground. Because its cultivation still requires backbreaking labour, its value has not been diminished by the globalised post-industrial economy.

The mauve-flowered *Crocus sativum* grows from a bulb about the size of a small onion that is planted in July and blooms in late October-early November. Harvesting involves protracted bending: each flower must be plucked by hand and gently transported to a dry environment where it will be divested of its deep red stigma. It is these threads, duly dried, that are prized for their depth of flavour and hue. Saffron is sold in tiny packets or jars, with one gram requiring from 100 to 150 stigmas and fetching as much as €25.

Palazzo Vecchio in Florence; and Palazzo Contucci. Not far away and worth a look is the **Museo Civico** in Palazzo Neri Orselli (Via Ricci 10, 0578 717300, closed Mon); its archaeology section is especially strong. Around 20 minutes' walk from Porta al Prato sits the pilgrimage church of **San Biagio**. Designed by Sangallo and built between 1518 and 1545, this Bramante-influenced study in proportion is a jewel of the High Renaissance.

Where to stay & eat

For lodgings, try the **Albergo Il Marzocco** (Piazza Savonarola 18, 0578 757262, doubles €60-€90), just inside the Porta al Prato in a 16th-century palazzo. A few of its spacious rooms have terraces.

For drinks or light snacks, don't miss **Antico Caffè Poliziano** (Via di Voltaia nel Corso 27, 0578 758615, average €35), an art deco institution that's a great place to sample Vino Nobile. In San Biagio there's more substantial food at **La Grotta** (0578 757607, closed Wed, average €40), a former 14th-century staging post where Sangallo ate when working on the church. Another good option is **Le Logge del Vignola** (Via delle Erbe 6, 0578 717290, closed Tue & early Jan-early Feb, average €38), where cover and service charges have been abolished and guests are welcomed with an *aperitivo*.

Resources

Tourist information

Pro Loco, Via del Corso 59A (0578 757341/ www.prolocomontepulciano.it). **Open** *Summer* 9.30am-12.30pm, 3-8pm Mon-Sat; 10am-12.30pm Sun. *Winter* 9.30am-12.30pm, 3-6pm Mon-Sat; 10am-12.30pm Sun.

Chianciano & Chiusi

From Montepulciano, head along the SS146 towards Chianciano and Chiusi. Both of these towns have a pleasant historic district, the appeal of which has been somewhat tapered by some hideous outwards expansion. However, they do both have excellent archeological museums: the **Museo Archeologico delle Acque** at Chianciano (0578 30471, closed Mon Apr-Oct, Mon-Fri Nov-Mar, admission €4) reveals how the healing waters of the town were exploited and embellished back in Roman times, while the much larger **Museo Archeologico Nazionale** in Chiusi (Via Porsenna 7, 0578 20177, admission €4) houses one of the country's most important Etruscan collections.

Where to eat

Chianciano has a good fish restaurant: **Patry** (Viale G Di Vittorio 80, 0578 63014, closed Mon, average €22). In the old part of Chiusi sits the delightful **Osteria il Kantharos** (Via Porsenna 37-39, 0578 21936), great for snacks such as plates of cold cuts (around €5).

Sarteano & Radicofani

Between Chianciano and Chiusi, a turning on the right takes you to **Sarteano**, a delightful, well-preserved and relatively untouristy town. With its collection of Etruscan funerary urns shaped like heads, the tiny **Museo Civico Archeologico** (0578 269261, closed Mon May-Sept, open winter by appt only, admission €2.50) is worth a peek. While you're in the area, wander around **San Casciano dei Bagni**. Nestled in the hillside above the Val di Paglia, it looks over towards Monte Amiata (*see p236*). Before leaving, indulge in a long soak in the hot spring waters of the **Centro Termale Fonteverde** (0578 57241, closed last 3wks Jan, entrance €14-€16).

From Sarteano, head for Celle sul Rigo and beyond until you see the turning on your left for **Radicofani**, a hilltop town perched on what looks like a truncated cone. This stony stronghold is built from the volcanic basalt that must have erupted from Monte Amiata in its fiery prehistoric youth. For the pilgrims of past centuries travelling south to Rome, it must have appeared foreboding, but it's safer than the easier valley route. To reinforce the strategic nature of this location, a **Città Fortificata** (fortress) was built on the summit of the hill to which Radicofani clings. It has now been restored and contains a museum (0578 55905, closed Mon-Fri in winter, admission €3). The top affords amazing views.

Where to stay & eat

In Sarteano, the **Residenza Santa Chiara** (Piazza Santa Chiara 30, 0578 265412, closed Feb, doubles €130), once a convent and now a charming hotel overlooking the town, also has an excellent restaurant (average €30) and an impressive *enoteca* of its own. Down below, opposite the museum, you can eat well at the **Osteria da Gagliano** (Via Roma 5, 0578 268022, closed lunch in winter & Tue year-round, average €20). It's small: book ahead.

In San Casciano, the **Sette Querce** hotel (Viale Manciati 2-5, 0578 58174, closed Jan, doubles €145-€210) offers some classily decorated rooms.

Getting There

By bus

If you decide against car hire, there's a regular **SITA** bus service (800 373760, www.sita-on-line.it) from Florence to Greve (50mins) and Panzano (70mins). Some buses continue on to Radda (90mins) and Gaiole (2hrs). SITA also runs buses from Florence to San Gimignano (Via Poggibonsi, 70mins) via Colle di Val d'Elsa (1hr). In addition, **Tra-in** (0577 204246) operates a regular service between Siena and Montalcino (1hr), and another regular service between Siena and Montepulciano (Via Pienza, 90mins).

By car

The Siena province is best experienced by car. In Chianti, a car will allow you to explore La Chiantigiana and the SS222, which wiggles its way south of Florence to Siena through hilltop towns such as Panzano and Castellina. This section is organised along the north–south route of the SS222.

By train

There are regular trains from Siena to San Gimignano (25mins) and Montepulciano (1hr). For national train information, call 892021 or go to www.trenitalia.it.

Lucca

In a world of its own.

Enclosed by its stout 16th- and 17th-century walls, Lucca has managed to retain its sense of identity, unravaged by outside influences. As soon as you enter the city through one of its six gates, the impression is of a relaxed, prosperous community untouched by the kind of culture-vulture tourism that can be an unpleasant feature of so many other Tuscan cities. That's not to say that tourists aren't welcome – on the contrary, locals are warm and friendly, and whether you decide to join the *lucchesi* strolling on their tree-lined ramparts, congregating in their cafés and restaurants, or even just enjoying a moment's peace in a quiet square or garden, you'll be made to feel very much at home. The flipside, of course, is that you will find fewer major art treasures to admire than in Florence, Siena or Arezzo. But, by the same token, queues are shorter and prices less exorbitant.

Much of Lucca is pedestrianised and the best way to discover the city is on foot. Or do as the locals: spend a day in the saddle – the *lucchesi* prefer bikes to cars. Either way you'll be rewarded with a surprise at nearly every corner. The ornate white façades of the Romanesque

churches – overplayed **San Michele in Foro**, the glistening mosaic of **San Frediano** and the asymmetrical **Duomo di San Martino** – all appear unexpectedly. The colourful **Piazza dell'Anfiteatro**, with its rather touristy bars and cafés, has retained the oval shape of the ancient Roman amphitheatre and is accessed through four arches, while the tree-lined ramparts and the oak-topped **Torre Guinigi** afford splendid views of the cityscape. Another good starting point for an exploration is the huge **Piazza Napoleone**, named after Napoleon's sister, and home to a carousel, but otherwise pretty stark, especially in winter.

Lucca's flatness and relatively simple grid plan make everything easily accessible. A lovely way to get your bearings is to hire a bike and cycle the four kilometres (2.5 miles) along the top of the city walls (*see p251*).

SOME HISTORY

Possibly the site of a Ligurian and then an Etruscan settlement, Lucca acquired political significance as a Roman *municipium* in 89 BC and hosted the signing of the first triumvirate between Pompey, Julius Caesar and Crassus in 56 BC. It was crucially positioned at the crossroads of the Empire's communications with its northern reaches and controlled the Appennine passes along the Serchio valley.

Despite Rome's fall, the city continued to maintain its supremacy in Tuscany, first as capital of Tuscia under Lombard rule and then as the seat of the Frankish Margravate from 774. By the turn of the millennium Lucca had grown into Tuscany's largest city and had become a commercial powerhouse thanks to the wool and silk trades and to its command of a strategic junction of the Via Francigena. Wealth engendered commercial rivalry with its upstart neighbours. This soon turned into open military clashes with Pisa and a gradual loss of political dominance to Florence during the drawn-out Guelph-Ghibelline conflict.

The 14th century was turbulent for Lucca. A short-lived heyday as the capital of a mini-empire in western Tuscany under the helm of the *condottiere* Castruccio Castracani (1320-28) soon gave way to a series of setbacks leading to domination by Pisa from 1342. In 1369 Lucca was granted autonomy and independence by Emperor Charles IV of Bohemia; this was to last, unbroken, until 1799.

Having renounced claims to regional leadership, Lucca moved into relative obscurity and turned in on itself. An oligarchy of ruling families, foremost among them the Guinigi, tightly controlled all public offices and private wealth and set about enlarging the medieval urban nucleus. In 1805 Lucca passed under the direct rule of Elisa Baciocchi, Napoleon's sister, and then in 1817 to the Infanta Maria Luisa di Borbone of Spain. Both did much to recast the city architecturally and patronised a brief but intense period of artistic ferment. In 1847 Lucca was ceded to the Grand Duchy of Tuscany and then joined a united Italy in 1860.

The city's almost uninterrupted history as an opulent, free commune has left it largely unaffected by outside developments, both architecturally and psychologically. Indeed, by very literally minding their own business, the *lucchesi* have stayed both safe and prosperous. In so far as the timing of your visit is concerned, some of the following dates may be worth bearing in mind: the Santa Zita flower show and market (four days at the end of April); a summer music festival in Piazza Anfiteatro (July); the Luminara di San Paolino, a torchlit procession celebrating Lucca's patron saint (11 July); the Luminara di Santa Croce procession of the Volto Santo (13 September); the cultural, religious and sporting events of Settembre Lucchese (September, October); and the Natale Anfiteatro Christmas market.

Sights

Churches

Duomo di San Martino

Piazza San Martino (0583 957068). **Open** *Duomo* Summer 9.30am-5.45pm daily. Winter 9.30am-4.45pm daily. *Sacristy* Summer 9.30am-5.45pm Mon-Fri; 9.30am-6.45pm Sat; 9-9.50am, 11.20-11.50am, 1-5.45pm Sun. Winter 9.30am-4.45pm Mon-Fri; 9.30am-6.45pm Sat; 11.20-11.50am, 1-4.45pm Sun. No entry during services. **Admission** *Duomo* free. *Sacristy* €2; €6 incl Museo della Cattedrale & San Giovanni e Reparata. **No credit cards**.

At first glance Lucca's Romanesque cathedral seems somewhat unbalanced. A closer look reveals why. The oddly asymmetrical façade has the arch and the first two series of *logge* on the right literally squeezed and flattened by the campanile. Nobody is really to blame (or commend) for this as the Lombard bell-tower was erected before the rest of the church in around 1100 and completed just 200 years later. It predates the Duomo, on which work began in earnest only in the 12th century. The asymmetry of the façade, designed by Guidetto da Como, only adds to the overall effect of exuberance and eccentricity.

San Martino's interior is so dimly lit that coin-operated lights are on hand to illuminate paintings such as Tintoretto's *Last Supper,* while restoration work has enhanced the quality of the frescoes in the apse. Midway up the left nave is Matteo Civitali's octagonal marble *Tempietto* (1484), home to a dolorous wooden crucifix known as the *Volto Santo* (Holy Face), which is perpetually surrounded by candle-holding worshippers. The effigy – what we see is a copy – was supposedly begun by Nicodemus and finished by an angel, set on a pilotless ship from the East in the eighth century and brought in to Lucca on a cart drawn by steer. This miraculous arrival quickly spawned a cult following and the relic soon became an object of pilgrimage throughout Europe. Nowadays it is draped in silk and gold garments and ornaments, and marched through Lucca's streets in night-time processions on 13 September.

The Duomo's Sacristy contains the other top attraction: the tomb of Ilaria del Carretto (1408), a delicate sarcophagus sculpted by Sienese master Jacopo della Quercia. It represents the young bride of Paolo Guinigi – Lucca's strongman at the time.

San Francesco

Via della Quarquonia (0583 91175/mobile 338 9433388). **Open** 9-11am daily (phone in advance). Although the Franciscans left in November 2002, this beautifully simple church remains open to visitors in the morning, though you must let the church custodian, Signor Stefanelli, know so he can let you in.

San Frediano

Piazza San Frediano (0583 493627). **Open** 8.30am-noon, 3-5.30pm Mon-Sat; 9-11.30am, 3-6pm Sun; 10.30am-5pm public holidays. **Admission** free.

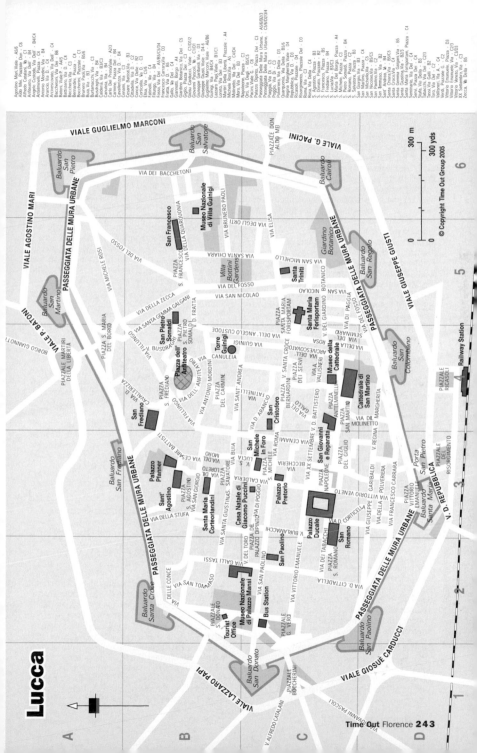

Lucca

VIALE GUGLIELMO MARCONI

VIALE AGOSTINO MARI

VIALE P. BATONI

BORGO GIANNOTTI

VIALE GIUSEPPE GUSTI

VIALE G. PACINI

VIALE LAZZARO PAPI

VIALE GIOSUE CARDUCCI

PASSEGGIATA DELLE MURA URBANE

Baluardo San Pietro
Baluardo San Salvatore
Baluardo San Martino
Baluardo San Frediano
Baluardo Santa Croce
Baluardo San Donato
Baluardo San Paolino
Baluardo San Colombano
Baluardo San Regolo
Baluardo Cairoli

PIAZZALE MARTIRI DELLA LIBERTA

VIA DEI BACCHETONI
VIA DEGLI ORTI
VIA DEL FOSSO
VIA MICHELE ROSI
VIA DELLA QUARQUONIA
VIA SANTA CHIARA
VIA BRUNERO PAOLI
VIA ELISA
VIA SAN MICHELLO
VIA SAN NICOLAO
VIA DI PAGGIA
VIA DEL SEMINARIO
VIA SANTA CROCE
VIA SANTA GEMMA GALGANI
VIA DELLA ZECCA
VIA S. MARIA DEL BORGO
VIA BUSDRAGHI
VIA FILLUNGO
VIA DELL'ANFITEATRO
VIA DELL'ANGELO CUSTODE
VIA GUINIGI
VIA S. PIETRO SOMALDI
VIA D. FRATTA
VIA SAN ANDREA
VIA SANT'ANNA
VIA DELLA CAVALLERIZZA
VIA ANTONIO MORDINI
VIA DEL CARMINE
VIA D. ARANCIO
VIA DEL GALLO
VIA FATINELLI
VIA BERNARDINI
VIA DEL BATTISTERO
VIA DELL'ARCIVESCOVADO
VIA SANTA CROCE
VIA DEI SERVI
VIA MARGHERITA
VIA ELISA
VIA SAN GIROLAMO
VIA DELLA ROSA
VIA DELLA ROSA
VIA D. SEMINARIO
VIA S. MICHELE
VIA V. DI S. CENAMI
VIA BUIA
VIA DEL MORO
VIA DEI CALDERIA
VIA S. LUCIA
VIA S. GIUSTINA
VIA DI POGGIO
VIA GALLI TASSI
VIA DELLE CONCE
VIA SAN GIORGIO
VIA DELLA STUFA
VIA SAN TOMMASO
VIA SAN PAOLINO
VIA DEI BURLAMACCHI
VIA XX SETTEMBRE
VIA DEL TORO
VIA DIPINTA
VIA BECCHERIA
VIA V. VENETO
VIA VITTORIO EMANUELE
VIA DEI TABACCHI
VIA ROMANA
VIA DEGLI ASILI
VIA S. GIUSEPPE GARIBALDI
VIA DELLA POLVERIERA
VIA FRANCESCO CARRARA
VIA DI CITTADELLA
VIA D. CORTICELLA
VIA DEL MOLINETTO
VIA DI SAN PIETRO
VIA REGINA
VIA VITTORIO EMANUELE

Palazzo Pfanner
Sant'Agostino
Santa Maria Corteorlandini
Casa Natale di Giacomo Puccini
Palazzo Pretorio
Palazzo Ducale
San Romano
San Paolino
Museo Nazionale di Palazzo Mansi
Tourist Office
Bus Station
San Frediano
San Francesco
Museo Nazionale di Villa Guinigi
Piazza dell'Anfiteatro
San Pietro Somaldi
Torre Guinigi
Santa Trinità
Santa Maria Forisportam
Museo della Cattedrale
Cattedrale di San Martino
San Michele in Foro
San Giovanni e Reparata
San Cristoforo
Santa Maria Cortelandini
Villa Bottini Gardens
Giardino Botanico
Porta San Pietro
Santa Maria

PIAZZA NAPOLEONE
PIAZZA S. GIOVANNI
PIAZZA DEL GIGLIO
PIAZZA SAN MARTINO
PIAZZA NAPOLEONE
PIAZZA DEL CARMINE
PIAZZA S. FREDIANO
PIAZZA FRANCESCA
PIAZZA S. PIETRO SOMALDI
PIAZZA SAN FRANCESCO
PIAZZA ANTELMINELLI
PIAZZA S. MARIA FORISPORTAM
PIAZZA S. ROMANO
PIAZZA G. VERDI
PIAZZALE S. DONATO
PIAZZALE BOCCHERINI
PIAZZALE DON ALDO MEI
PIAZZALE RICASOLI
PIAZZALE DEL RISORGIMENTO

V. N. D. REPUBBLICA

Railway Station

0   300 m
0   300 yds

© Copyright Time Out Group 2005

A   B   C   D

1   2   3   4   5   6

Time Out Florence **243**

San Frediano's strikingly resplendent Byzantine-like mosaic façade is unique in Tuscany, rivalled only by that above the choir of San Miniato al Monte in Florence. A church was founded on this site by Fredian, an Irish monk who settled in Lucca in the sixth century and converted the ruling Lombards by allegedly diverting the River Serchio and saving the city from flooding. This miracle put the finishing touches on Christianity's hold on Lucca and earned Fredian a quick promotion to bishop, eventually leading to canonisation. A few centuries later, in the 1100s, this singular church was built for him.

Apart from its mosaic, an Ascension in which a monumental Jesus is lifted by two angels over the heads of his Apostles, the façade of San Frediano is in the Pisan-Romanesque style of many of Lucca's other churches and was the first to face east. Inside, immediately on the right, is a small gem: the *fonte lustrale* (or baptismal font) carved by unknown Lombard and Tuscan artists who surrounded the fountain with scenes from the Old and New Testaments. Behind it is a glazed terracotta *Ascension* by Andrea della Robbia. In the chapel next to it is another of Lucca's revered relics, the miraculously conserved though somewhat shrivelled body of St Zita, a humble servant who was canonised in the 13th century and whose mummy is brought out for a close-up view and a touch by devotees on 27 April. Ongoing restoration projects care for San Frediano's frescoes, including those by Amico Aspertini.

San Giovanni e Reparata

Via del Duomo (0583 490530). **Open** *Mid Mar-Oct* 10am-6pm daily. *Nov-mid Mar* 10am-5pm Sat, Sun. **Admission** €2.50; €6 incl Museo della Cattedrale & Sacristy of Duomo di San Martino. **No credit cards**.

Originally Lucca's cathedral, the 12th-century basilica of San Giovanni, now part of the Duomo, is on the site of a pagan temple. Apart from its magnificently ornate ceiling, the church's main draw is the architectural remains uncovered by excavations in the 1970s (included in the ticket price), ranging from a second-century Roman bath to a Paleo-Christian church. Ignore the baffling floor plans and just wander at will.

Santa Maria Corteorlandini

Piazza Giovanni Leonardi (0583 467464). **Open** 8.30am-noon, 4-6pm daily; 8.30am-noon public hols. **Admission** free.

This overwhelming late baroque church is Lucca's odd man out. Its *trompe l'œil* frescoed roofs, abundance of coloured marble, and the gilded and ornamented tabernacle by local artist Giovanni Vambre (1673) provide a break from the stark and grey interiors of the city's other churches.

Santa Maria Forisportam

Piazza Santa Maria Forisportam (0583 467769). **Open** 9am-noon, 3-6pm daily. **Admission** free.

Set on the square known to *lucchesi* as Piazza della Colonna Mozza (referring to the truncated column at its centre), Santa Maria takes its name from its location just outside Lucca's older set of walls. The unfinished marble façade dates mostly from the 12th and 13th centuries, and is a slightly toned-down version of the Pisan-Romanesque style present throughout the city, with lively carvings in the lunettes and architraves above the portals.

San Michele in Foro

Piazza San Michele (0583 48459). **Open** 9am-noon, 3-6pm daily. **Admission** free.

San Michele's façade is a feast for the eyes. Set on the site of the ancient Roman forum, Lucca's consummate take on the Pisan-Romanesque style is one of the city's most memorable sights. Each element lightly plays off against the other: the knotted, twisted and carved columns with their psychedelic geometric designs and the fantastical animals, and fruit and floral motifs in the capitals. The façade culminates in a winged and stiff St Michael precariously perched while vanquishing the dragon. San Michele's façade contrasts sharply with its sombre interior. On the right as you enter is a *Madonna and Child* by Matteo Civitali – a copy of the original is on the church's right-hand outside corner. Further on, you'll find Filippino Lippi's *Saints Jerome, Sebastian, Rocco and Helena*.

San Paolino

Via San Paolino (0583 53576). **Open** 8.15am-noon, 3.30-6pm daily. **Admission** free.

Giacomo Puccini received his baptism of fire here in 1881 with his first public performance of the *Mass for Four Voices*. San Paolino had, in fact, always been the Puccini family's second home, with five generations of them serving as its organists. Built from 1522 to 1536 for Lucca's patron St Paulinus, who allegedly came over from Antioch in AD 65 and became the city's first bishop, and whose remains are buried in a sarcophagus behind the altar, it's Lucca's only example of late Renaissance architecture.

Museums

Casa Natale di Giacomo Puccini

Corte San Lorenzo 9, off Via di Poggio (0583 584028). **Open** *Mar-May, Oct-Dec* 10am-1pm, 3-6pm Tue-Sun. *June-Sept* 10am-6pm daily. Closed Jan, Feb. **Admission** €3; €2 under-14s & groups of 10 & over. **No credit cards**.

Ongoing restorations at the birthplace of Lucca's most famous son, Giacomo Puccini, mean that it's worth phoning ahead just to check that this charming museum is open (if you don't get through, phone the tourist office for information). If it is welcoming visitors, you'll be in for some interesting insights into the artist's sheltered youth, turbulent private life and artistic genius. The rooms of memorabilia include the original librettos of his early operas, his private letters on subjects both musical and sentimental, the piano on which he composed *Turandot* and the gem-encrusted costume used in the opera's American debut in 1926.

Grand designs

The countryside around Lucca is smattered with elegant villas and gardens – some of them open to the public – that were originally the country retreats of wealthy merchants from the city. Elisa Baciocchi, Napoleon's sister, once lived at the 17th-century **Villa Reale** at Marlia (0583 30108, www.parcovilla reale.it, closed Mon & Dec-Feb, admission €6; *pictured*). Although the house is closed, you can visit the lovely garden, which is full of statues and also contains a little theatre. The garden of the 16th-century **Villa Oliva Buonvisi** at San Pancrazio (0583 406462, admission €6) is open from March until November, as is the large English-style park and orangery of the nearby **Villa Grabau** (0583 406098,

closed Mon Easter-Oct & Mon-Sat Nov-Easter, admission €5 garden only, €6 villa and garden). Otherwise, the 17th-century **Villa Mansi** (0583 920234, closed Mon, admission €7) at Segromigno is another fine house, with frescoes of the *Myth of Apollo* by Stefano Tofanelli in the salon. The statue-filled garden was laid out by the Sicilian architect Juvarra; it's partly Italian (geometric) and partly English (not geometric) in style. There are concerts in summer. The **Villa Torrigiani** (0583 928041, closed Tue, admission €6 gardens only, €9 gardens & villa) and its fine park at Camigliano are open from March to November. Inside are some good 16th- to 18th-century paintings and a collection of porcelain.

Museo della Cattedrale
Via Arcivescovado (0583 490530). **Open** *May-Oct* 10am-6pm daily. *Nov-Apr* 10am-2pm Mon-Fri; 10am-5pm Sat, Sun. **Admission** €3.50; €5.50 incl San Giovanni e Reparata. **No credit cards**.
Attractively laid out over various levels, this well-curated modern museum houses many treasures transferred from the Duomo di San Martino (*see p242*) and from nearby San Giovanni (*see p244*). Displays cover everything from the cathedral's furnishings, its gold and silverware to its sculptures, including Jacopo della Quercia's *Apostle*. The free English audio guides are excellent.

Museo Nazionale di Palazzo Mansi
Via Galli Tassi 43 (0583 55570). **Open** 8.30am-7.30pm Tue-Sat; 8.30am-1.30pm Sun. **Admission** €4; free concessions; €6.50 incl Villa Guinigi. **No credit cards**.
Beyond the impressive stagecoach at the entrance to this, Lucca's most remarkable example of baroque exaggeration, is a 16th- to 17th-century palazzo home

to a collection of mostly Tuscan art. While the frescoed Salone della Musica and the neo-classical Salone degli Specchi are light on the eye, over-indulgence climaxes in the Camera della Sposa, an over-the-top bridal chamber with a *baldacchino* bed. The largely uninspiring art includes pieces from the Venetian school with lesser-known works by Tintoretto and Tiziano and some Flemish tapestries. Perhaps best is Pontormo's manneristic portrait of his nasty patron, Alessandro de' Medici. Decorative woven goods made on the original looms are for sale.

Museo Nazionale di Villa Guinigi
Via della Quarquonia (0583 496033). **Open** 8.30am-7.30pm Tue-Sat; 8.30am-1.30pm Sun. **Admission** €4; €6.50 incl Palazzo Mansi; concessions free. **No credit cards**.
This porticoed pink-brick villa (1403-20), surrounded by tranquil gardens and medieval statues, was erected at the height of the rule by Lucca's 'enlightened despot' Paolo Guinigi and now houses art from Lucca and its surrounding region. The first floor of

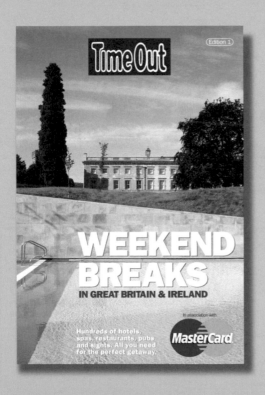

the museum has a selection of Roman and Etruscan finds along with some 13th- and 14th-century capitals and columns by Guidetto da Como, taken from the façade of San Michele in Foro (*see p244*). The rooms upstairs start with a selection of 13th-century painted crucifixes and some wooden tabernacles, but the highlights are Matteo Civitali's *Annunciation*, some impressive altarpieces by Amico Aspertini and Fra Bartolomeo, and the intarsia panels by Ambrogio and Nicolao Pucci.

Monuments

Ramparts

On a good day you'll see Lucchesi of all ages strolling, jogging, picnicking, cuddling and enjoying the views from *le nostre mura* ('our walls'), as the ramparts are lovingly known. Built in the 16th and 17th-centuries, Italy's best-preserved and most impressive city fortifications measure 12m (39ft) in height and 30m (98ft) across, with a circumference of just over 4km (2.5 miles). They are punctuated by 11 sturdy bastions, which were meant to ward off heavily armed invaders. A proper siege, though, never happened and the only real use the ramparts have had was in 1812 when they enabled the city to seal itself hermetically from the floodwaters. Soon after Maria Luisa di Borbone turned the walls into a public park and promenade, dotting them with plane, holm-oak, chestnut and lime trees. Today, cyclists and pedestrians are still making the most of them, not to mention the families who populate the play areas found in almost every *baluardo* (rampart).

Torre Guinigi

Via Sant'Andrea 14 (0583 316846). **Open** *Nov-Feb* 9.30am-4.30pm daily. *Mar, Apr* 9.30am-8pm daily. *May, Oct* 10am-6pm daily. *June-Sept* 9am-midnight. **Admission** €3.50; €2.50 concessions. **No credit cards**.
It's worth the climb to reach the tranquil and leafy summit, with its distinctive cluster of oak trees. From the top of this 14th-century, 44m- (144ft-) high tower, there are spectacular views over Lucca's rooftops to the countryside beyond.

Parks & gardens

Giardino Botanico

Via del Giardino Botanico 14 (0583 442160). **Open** *May, June* 10am-6pm daily. *July-Sept* 10am-7pm daily. *Oct, Mar, Apr* 10am-5pm daily. *Nov-Feb* 9.30am-12.30pm by appointment only. **Admission** €3; €2 concessions. **No credit cards**.
Nestling in the south-east corner of the city walls, the Giardino Botanico makes a relaxed spot for a romantic stroll or a quiet sit-down – as do the gardens of the Villa Bottini just a little further up Via Santa Chiara. The greenhouse and arboretum are planted with a wide and impressive range of Tuscan flora, many of which are rare species, providing Lucca with its greenest and most exotic spot.

Palazzo Pfanner

Via degli Asili 33 (340 9233085). **Open** *Mar-mid Nov* 10am-6pm daily. *Mid Nov-Feb* by appointment. **Admission** €3 for palace and garden; €2.50 for one or the other; free under-8s. **No credit cards**.
These peaceful gardens, overlooked by the tower of San Frediano and the city walls, are a lovely place to stroll. The palace has been restored to its former glory, and features cabinets housing the surgical implements used by Pietra Pfanner (who rose to become mayor of the city and later Knight Commander of the Crown of Italy) beneath impressive frescoed ceilings. Film buffs might remember the gardens from *The Portrait of a Lady*.

Nightlife

Bars & clubs

If you're in Lucca for the nightlife, you'll be disappointed: the big nightspots are out towards the Versilia coast. There are, however, an increasing number of decent wine bars appearing across town. Good choices include **Rewine** (Via Calderia 6, 0583 48427, closed Sun), a red and black bar that also serves decent snacks, **Vinarkia** (Via Fillungo 188, 0583 495336), a laid-back bar with regular wine tastings and free buffet at 6pm and 10pm every night, and **La Corte dei Vini** (Corte Campana 6, 0583 584460, closed Sun), especially known for its cheeses and wines.

Shopping

You'll find plenty of well-known designer and other high-street names on and around Lucca's main shopping artery, **Via Fillungo**. The other main hubs are **Via Vittorio Veneto** (leading off Piazza San Michele) and **Via Santa Croce**. Despite Lucca's staid reputation, there is also a good number of boutiques and shoe shops, in particular along Via Fillungo and Via Vittorio Veneto, selling trendy fashion.

There are excellent delis at each turn, stocked with everything from regional wines and olive oils to cheeses and honeys, and a locally produced salami made with pig's blood and raisins. Two of the best are **La Grotta** (Via dell' Anfiteatro 2, 0583 467595) and **Delicatezze** (Via San Giorgio 5, 0583 492633).

The town's general market is held on **Via dei Bacchettoni** by the eastern wall on Wednesdays and Saturdays, selling clothes, food, flowers and household goods. There's an antiques market in and around **Piazza San Martino** on the third weekend of each month, with everything from coins to jewellery, and a crafts market (*arti e mestieri*) in **Piazza San Giusto** on the last weekend of the month.

Cacioteca

Via Fillungo 242 (0583 496346). **Open** 7am-1.30pm, 3.30-8.30pm Mon, Tue, Thur-Sat; 7am-1.30pm Wed. **Credit** MC, V.

An intense waft of seasoned cheese emanates from this specialist shop. Give your taste buds a treat with the typical dairy products of the Garfagnana.

Gong

Via San Paolino 33 (0583 418786). **Open** 3.30-7.30pm Mon, 9.30am-1pm, 3.30-7.30pm Tue-Sat. **Credit** AmEx, MC, V.

This shop sells an interesting mix of Asian pieces – furniture, slippers, jewellery, ornaments and so on – mainly from Indonesia, though Vietnam, China, Nepal and other countries also get a look-in.

Mercato del Carmine

Off Piazza del Carmine. **Open** 8am-noon, 4-7.30pm daily. **No credit cards.**

Between its fruit and vegetable stalls, fishmongers, butchers and delis, this superb colonnaded covered market offers the best of Lucca's regional produce. There's also a café where you can rest your weary feet and refuel along with the locals.

Vini Liquori Vanni

Piazza del Salvatore 7 (0583 491902). **Open** 4-8pm Mon; 9am-1pm, 4-8pm Tue-Sat. **Credit** AmEx, DC, MC, V.

This *enoteca's* seemingly endless cellar is a treasure for those seeking out Lucca's better vintages. Call ahead and book a wine lesson and *degustazione*, plus a mini-tour.

Where to eat

Restaurants

The nearby Garfagnana valley (*see p254*) contributes many prime ingredients to Lucca's cuisine, including chestnut flour, river trout, olive oil and above all *farro* (spelt grain), which pops up on every menu. The signature pudding is *buccellato* (a doughnut-shaped sweet bread flavoured with aniseed and raisins, and topped with sugar syrup).

La Buca di Sant'Antonio

Via della Cervia 3 (0583 55881). **Open** 12.30-3pm, 7.30-10pm Tue-Sat; 12.30-3pm Sun. Closed 2wks Jan. **Average** €26-31. **Credit** AmEx, DC, MC, V.

A charmingly restored 19th-century hostelry with a few outside tables amid tubs of plants and flowers, La Buca serves traditional food with the occasional innovative touch. You'll need to reserve in advance, but if it's fully booked you could try the sister restaurant, Il Giglio (0583 494058) on Piazza Napoleone.

Da Guido

Via Cesare Battisti 28 (0583 467219). **Open** noon-2.30pm, 7-10.30pm Mon-Sat. Closed 3wks Jan. **Average** €12. **Credit** AmEx, MC, V.

Don't be put off by the appearance of this trattoria: at first glance it looks a bit down-at-heel, but step inside and you're treated to excellent home cooking from the friendly Guido and family. Rich, thick *zuppa di farro* is almost a meal in itself, while the choice of mains features roast meats, pastas and salads. Desserts are home-made and might include *crostate della casa* (jam tarts) or *panna cotta*.

Da Leo

Via Tegrimi 1 (0583 492236). **Open** noon-2.30pm, 7.30-10.30pm daily. **Average** €16. **No credit cards.**

The waiters sing and local families compete to be heard over the din of children, yet despite all this noise and bustle, Da Leo is one of Lucca's mellowest restaurants. You won't be hurried through your meal, which will inevitably be made up of hearty country dishes like roast chicken, grilled steak, *spaghetti alle vongole* and *pappardelle broccoli e salsiccia*. Remember to bring cash, though: in true country fashion, credit cards are not accepted.

Locanda di Bacco

Via San Giorgio 36 (0583 493136). **Open** 12.30-2.30pm; 7.30-10.30pm Mon, Wed-Sun. Closed 2wks Feb & 2wks Nov. **Average** €23. **Credit** MC, V.

This sleek, stylish restaurant is a newcomer to the local restaurant scene, but already a hit with both locals and tourists. The wine list is extensive, with hundreds to choose from. Starters include *crostini* with melted gorgonzola and honey; pasta dishes might include *pappardelle al cinghiale*; and the home-made desserts are irresistible. Service is efficient rather than over-friendly, but this place is well worth a look (try to book in advance as it's popular).

Locanda Buatino

Borgo Giannotti 508, nr Piazzale Martiri della Libertà (0583 343207). **Open** noon-2pm, 7.30-10pm Mon-Sat. Closed 2wks Aug. **Average** €13. **Credit** AmEx, MC, V.

Locanda Buatino is a gem in a busy street leading from the city walls. The feel is low-key but sophisticated, with wooden tables, strings of garlic and rustic paintings. The daily-changing menu includes home-made pasta and enticing meat and fish dishes. On Mondays from October to May, it's jazz night (€25 including a meal with wine). Upstairs are basic rooms for €40 with shared bathrooms.

La Mora

Località Ponte a Moriano, Via Sesto di Moriano 1748, Sesto di Moriano (0583 406402/www. ristorantelamora.it). **Open** noon-2.30pm, 7.30-10pm Mon, Tue, Thur-Sun. Closed 1st 2wks Jan & last 2wks June. **Average** €35. **Credit** AmEx, DC, MC, V.

Culinary heavyweight Sauro Brunicardi has turned this old post-house 10km (six miles) north of Lucca into a regionally renowned *osteria* where you can eat outside in refined surroundings. Try *tagliolini all'anguilla* (with eel sauce), *piccione* (pigeon) and tip-top desserts. La Mora also has a good list of wines from the nearby Lucchese hills.

Pillars of society: Lucca's **Duomo di San Martino**. *See p242.*

Ristorante Puccini

Corte San Lorenzo 1-2, off Piazza Cittadella (0583 316116). **Open** 12.30-2.30pm, 7.30-10.30pm Mon, Thur-Sun; 7.30-10.30pm Wed. Closed Dec-Feb. **Average** €35. **Credit** AmEx, DC, MC, V.

In a quiet courtyard with a secluded terrace, Puccini is widely regarded as Lucca's best fish restaurant. Prices aren't cheap – even a rocket and parmesan salad will set you back €10 – but the tasting menus (€40 for meat, €45 for fish) might be a better bet. Alternatively, in summer you can order a dish at a time for €8.

Vineria I Santi

Via dell'Anfiteatro 29A (0583 496124). **Open** 11am-3pm, 7pm-1.30am Mon, Tue, Thur, Fri, Sun; 11am-3pm, 7pm-2am Sat. **Average** €20. **Credit** AmEx, DC, MC, V.

This superb little *vineria* oozes style – from its modern rustic furniture and delicate light fittings to the discreet wine paraphernalia dotted around its walls. Dishes are short in number but high in imagination; the likes of smoked sea bass with marinated fennel, orange and pine nuts, but simpler dishes (tomato and mozzarella lasagne) also get a look-in. The extensive wine list is its real forte, though.

Cafés & *gelaterie*

Ice-cream parlours, cafés and pretty cake shops abound in Lucca. Those listed below are our favourites.

Caffè di Simo

Via Fillungo 58 (0583 496234). **Open** *Bar* 7.30am-11pm Tue-Sun. *Restaurant* 12.30-2.30pm Mon, Tue, Thur-Sun. Summer also 7-10pm Thur-Sat. **Average** €18. **Credit** MC, V.

Lucca's beautifully preserved belle époque café-*pasticceria* is surprisingly unsnobby. The hot chocolate here is rich and thick, though there are also pastries, ice-creams and posh chocolates should your sweet tooth still need satisfying. More substantial dishes include *zuppa di farro* and other regional fare.

Casali

Piazza San Michele 40 (0583 492687). **Open** *Apr-Oct* 7am-midnight daily. *Nov-Mar* 7am-8.30pm Mon, Tue, Thur-Sun. Closed 20 Jan-06 Feb. **Credit** MC, V.

The perfect spot for watching the crowds, with either an ice-cream or an aperitif in hand.

Tuscany

Caffè di Simo. *See p249.*

Gelateria Veneta

Chiasso Barletti 23 (0583 493727). **Open** *Winter*
11am-8 pm Mon, Wed-Sun. *Summer* 11am-midnight
daily. Closed early Jan-mid Feb. **No credit cards.**
Heavenly ice-creams are sold at this venerated
gelateria. There are some good pavement tables for
those who don't want to walk and lick.
Other locations: Via Vittorio Veneto 74 (0583
467037).

Girovita

Piazza Antelminelli 2 (0583 469412). **Open** 8am-
1am Mon-Fri, Sun; 8am-2am Sat. **Credit** AmEx,
DC, MC, V.
Directly opposite the cathedral, the terrace of this
stylish café-bar is the perfect spot for a morning coffee and pastry or, come cocktail hour, a sundowner
accompanied by a great spread of free nibbles.

Where to stay

Lucca is not known for its abundance of
accommodation – and there are no signs that
this is going to change. The *lucchesi* have no
intention of turning their precious city into an
appendage of the overcrowded Versilia coast.
That said, there are B&Bs cropping up around
town, which are generally nicer than the city's
mediocre hotels. Given Lucca's popularity, it's
always best to book ahead if possible.

As well as the following, **Locanda Buatino**
(*see p248*) also offers basic rooms.

Affittacamere San Frediano

*Via degli Angeli 19 (0583 469630/www.san
frediano.com).* **Rates** €45-€55 single; €55-€70
double. **Credit** AmEx, DC, MC, V.
This friendly bed-and-breakfast receives many
return customers, presumably attracted by its reasonable rates and good location (just off the top end

of Via Fillungo). The cosy rooms have iron bed-
steads and satellite TV, and the top floor of the
building, which dates back to the 16th century, was
recently turned into a lounge for guests.

Alla Corte degli Angeli

*Via degli Angeli 23 (0583 469204/fax 0583
991989/www.allacortedegliangeli.com).* **Rates**
€150 double. **Credit** AmEx, DC, MC, V.
This place is a few notches up from Affitacamere
San Frediano just two doors down (*see above*), and
pricier as a result. Rooms are named after flowers
and decorated to a high standard, with bold colours
and good-quality furniture. All have whirlpool baths
and minibars. A refreshing change from the city's
drab accommodation choices.

La Bohème

Via del Moro 2 (tel/fax 0583 462404/www.boheme.it).
Rates €90-€120 double; extra person €25. **Credit**
MC, V.
A nicely decorated B&B in the heart of town, La
Bohème is a stylish choice if you're thinking of stopping in town, with richly coloured walls, dark wood
furniture, chandeliers and a brightl, airy breakfast
room. Recommended. Cash payers with this guide
get a five per cent discount.

Locanda L'Elisa

*Via Nuova per Pisa 1952, Massa Pisana (0583
379737/fax 0583 379019/www.locandalelisa.com).*
Rates €180 single; €230 double; €390 junior suite.
Credit AmEx, DC, MC, V.
In a league of its own, this elegant four-star hotel
4km (2.5 miles) south of Lucca is one of the area's
best. The villa's current appearance dates back to
1805, when Napoleon's sister and Lucca's ruler, Elisa
Baciocchi, had the interiors and gardens refash-
ioned. Highlights include a restaurant modelled after
an English conservatory, 18th-century furnishings,
revamped gardens and a large swimming pool.

La Luna

Corte Compagni 12 (0583 493634/fax 0583 490021/www.hotellaluna.com). Closed early Jan-early Feb. **Rates** €80 single; €110 double; €175 suite. **Credit** AmEx, DC, MC, V.

La Luna is well priced, given its location at the upper end of busy Via Fillungo. Rooms, housed in two 17th-century *palazzi* facing each other across a courtyard, are comfortable (if plain), with the usual mod cons.

Piccolo Hotel Puccini

Via di Poggio 9 (0583 55421/fax 0583 53487/ www.hotelpuccini.com). **Rates** €60 single; €85 double. **Credit** AmEx, DC, MC, V.

Just a baton's throw from Puccini's boyhood home, this discreet, cosy hotel is excellent value for money. The vibe is friendly and the staff speak English. Highly recommended.

Rex

Piazza Ricasoli 19 (0583 955443/fax 0583 954348/ www.hotelrexlucca.com). **Rates** €65-€80 single; €90-€110 double. **Credit** AmEx, DC, MC, V.

This modern hotel on Piazza Ricasoli has decent facilities, namely air-conditioned rooms, minibars, cable and satellite TV. Like the majority of hotels in Lucca, it won't win any awards for its decor, but it's friendly and has a convenient location, right next to the train station.

Universo

Piazza del Giglio 1 (0583 493678/fax 0583 954854/ www.universolucca.com). **Rates** €120 single; €170 double. **Credit** AmEx, DC, MC, V.

Right beside the elegant Piazza Napoleone, the Universo is the faded old gent of Lucca's hotels. Rooms have recently been given a facelift, but vary hugely in size and decor. The nicest (and priciest) are verging on hip, with wooden beams, blonde wood, cream furnishings and rainfall showers.

Resources

Hospital

Campo di Marte hospital, Via dell'Ospedale (0583 9701).

Police station

Viale Cavour 38, nr train station (0583 455487).

Post office

Via Vallisneri 2, nr Duomo (0583 43351).

Tourist information

Comune di Lucca Tourist Office
Piazzale Giuseppe Verdi, nr Vecchia Porta San Donato (0583 442944). **Open** 9am-7pm daily.
Tourist information offices are also found at Piazza Santa Maria, Viale Luporini, Porta Elisa and inside the Palazzo Ducale.

Getting there & around

By bike

Cycling is a nice way to get around the area, especially during warmer weather (but not too warm). There several bike hire shops here, but the largest concentration of them is in Piazza Santa Maria; for daily or weekly rentals, try **Cicli Bizzarri** at No.32 (0583 496031) or **Poli Antonio** at No.42 (0583 493787, www.biciclettepoli.com).

By bus

The bus station is at Piazzale Giuseppe Verdi. **CLAP** (0583 587897) operates buses to towns in the Lucca province. **LAZZI** runs buses to Florence, Pisa, Bagni di Lucca, Montecatini, La Spezia and Viareggio (0583 584876, www.lazzi.it). At least one bus an hour leaves Florence for Lucca (first 5.58am, last 8.15pm) and from Lucca to Florence (first 6.10am, last 7.45pm). The journey takes around 1hr 15mins.

By car

For car hire try **Europcar** (Via Dante Alighieri 214, 0583 464590), **Hertz** (Via Catalani 59, 0583 418058) or **Nolo Auto Pittore** (Piazza Santa Maria 34, 0583 467960). Within the city walls parking is expensive, except for hotel guests, but there's a spacious free car park just outside the walls past Porta San Donato.

By taxi

There are radio taxi ranks at Piazza Napoleone (0583 492691), the train station (0583 494989), Piazza Verdi (0583 581305), Piazza Sant Maria (0583 494190) and the hospital (0583 950623).

By train

Lucca's train station is at Piazza Ricasoli, two minutes' walk from the southern gate, Porta San Pietro. Trains from Florence to Viareggio stop at Lucca (as well as Prato and Pistoia). The trip from Florence takes about 1hr 20mins, with trains leaving almost every hour from early morning to 10pm. For train information call 892021 or go online to www.trenitalia.com.

Tuscany

Massa-Carrara & Lucca Provinces

Find your marbles.

Life's a beach in **Viareggio**.

Ever wondered where Michelangelo got the marble for his statues? Or how to escape the stultifying heat of a Tuscan summer? Head north from Florence to these two provinces and you'll find the answers. While the Massa-Carrara province creeps up from a coastline of sun-lotioned bodies and pulsating discos to marble quarries and remote villages, the Lucca province is an Alpine wonderland of snow-capped peaks, leafy valleys and medieval towns, where chocolate-box scenery remains largely undiscovered by the tourist hordes.

The Versilia Riviera

Running parallel to the heavy industry and huge unfinished blocks of Carrara marble that lie a few kilometres inland, this belt of sand, bathing spots and hotels welcomes sun-worshippers and pleasure-seekers all the way from the Ligurian border in the north to Viareggio in the south. For Versilia's lively gay scene, *see pp169-170*.

Viareggio

The main attractions of this seaside town are its beach and palm tree-lined promenade flanked by art deco villas and outdoor cafés. On hot summer nights Florence's clubbers desert the city and head here for the mega-clubs that throng the strip between Viareggio and the swanky resort town of **Forte dei Marmi**, ten kilometres (six miles) up the road. By day the *stabilimenti balneari* (bathing establishments) are full of tourists topping up tans. One of Europe's first *stabilimenti*, the **Balena**, was founded in 1827. Long since modernised to include the B2K annex, it offers five pools, an underground sports centre and a wide range of classes and treatments.

The 130-year-old Carnevale, held around February, is one of Italy's wildest (see p159). If you want to see the floats themselves, head to the Cittadella del Carnevale (see p159), in the north of town on Via Santa Maria Goretti (take the exit marked 'Viareggio Nord').

Six kilometres (four miles) south of town is the reed-fringed **Lago di Massaciuccoli**. On its shore is the town of **Torre del Lago Puccini** (or just Torre del Lago), where the composer spent his summers. His villa is open to visitors (0584 341445, closed Mon, admission €7) but contains little of interest except to specialists, who may want a peek at the composer's Förster pianoforte. During July and August the town hosts an outdoor Puccini festival (see p173 **Seasons in the sun**).

Nightlife

Il Giardino (Via IV Novembre 10, Forte dei Marmi, 0584 81462, closed Tue except July & Aug) is a good, though not cheap, spot for pre-club drinks. It's popular with twentysomething *figli di papa* (rich kids who cruise around in daddy's car), but the garden makes up for this. Slick club **Twiga** (Viale Roma 2, Marina di Pietrasanta, 0584 21518, www.twigaclub.it, closed Oct, Nov, & Mon-Thur & Sun Dec-June) is recognisable by its distinctive giraffe logo and hordes of beautiful young things streaming through the doors. **Seven Apples** (Viale Roma 109, Marina di Pietrasanta, 0584 20458, www.sevenapples.it) draws a trendy crowd to its beachside bar with tables straddling a pool and two dancefloors. Otherwise, **La Capannina** (Viale Franceschi, Forte dei Marmi, 0584 80169, www.lacapanninadifranceschi.it) attracts clubbers of all ages. Next to the sea (but without access to the beach), it is Versilia's oldest club, with two dancefloors that are packed all summer. **La Canniccia** (Via Unità d'Italia 1, Marina di Pietrasanta, 0584 745685) has a huge garden, walkways, a lake and a dancefloor.

Where to stay & eat

Although Viareggio has more than 100 hotels, rooms are hard to find in high season. Try Via Vespucci, Via Leonardo da Vinci and Via IV Novembre, which run from the station down to the sea. Stand-outs include **Hotel Garden** (Viale Ugo Foscolo 70, 0584 44025, doubles €107-€156), a glorious Liberty-style building with chandeliers in the foyer, and the swish **Hotel Plaza et de Russie** (Piazza d'Azeglio 1, 0584 44449, www.plazaederussie.com, doubles €90-€310), which offers fin-de-siècle luxury in a refurbished 19th-century building with a roof garden.

On the other side of the marina, affordable fish restaurants such as **La Darsena** (Via Virgilio 150, 0584 392785, closed Sun & late Dec-early Jan, average €30) attract locals to the backstreets behind the boat yards, while further south are the *stabilimenti* and modern bars and restaurants of Viale Europa. If you have time for only one meal in Viareggio, make sure it's at **Ristorante di Giorgio** (Via Zanardelli 71, 0584 44493, closed Wed, average €35). Its yellow walls are cluttered with paintings and there are displays of sea-fresh fish by the door.

Pietrasanta

Carrara is home to the raw material, but Pietrasanta (literally, 'holy stone') is where artists transform the famous marble. Wandering through the backstreets of this relaxed little town, you'll see modern-day Michelangelos with newspaper hats, which absorb sweat but filter fine marble dust, sculpting from marble, bronze and clay. Check out the two busy studios side by side on Via Sant'Agostino (Nos.51 and 53). Small groups wanting in-depth tours of the town's various studios and foundries or the nearby marble quarries should contact Barbara Paci (339 7780379, barbarapaci@inwind.it).

In summer **Piazza del Duomo** becomes an open-air exhibition space for artists against the splendid backdrop of the 13th-century cathedral and the citadel up the hill, **Rocca Arrighina**.

Where to stay & eat

Pietrasanta's accommodation options are fairly limited. The sumptuous 17th-century style of **Albergo Pietrasanta** (Via Garibaldi 35, 0584 793727, www.albergopietrasanta.com, doubles €220-€320) caters to the town's grander visitors, leaving **Hotel Palagi** (Piazza Carducci 23, 0584 70249, www.hotelpalagi.com, doubles €150) and **Hotel Stipino** (Via Provinciale 50, 0584 71448, doubles €68) to mop up the rest.

Of the bars and restaurants dotted among the modern art galleries and clothes shops, **Pizzeria Betty** (Piazza del Duomo 32-33, 0584 71247, closed Mon, average €15) offers good-value food in cool surroundings, while the trendy but relaxed **Enoteca Marcucci** (Via Garibaldi 40, 0584 791962, closed all day Mon, lunch Tue-Sun & all Nov, average €40) serves interesting food accompanied by excellent wine.

Massa & Carrara

Set between the sea and the Apuan Alps, these twin cities are barely distinguishable from the dreary mesh of industry and traffic that congests the area. But where **Massa** is of little

Tuscany

interest, **Carrara** is a marble mecca. The steep ridges of the mountains flanking the town glow brilliant white with the world's largest concentration of pure marble. The ancient Romans built most of their imperial city with it, while Michelangelo considered Carrara's marble the purest and whitest in the world. Its greatest asset, according to artists, is that it reflects light off its thinnest outer layer, giving the stone a translucent, wax-like lustre. Carrara mines less marble these days, but about 1.5 million tonnes are extracted from the nearby hills each year.

If you want to visit the quarries, take the scenic route marked *strada panoramica* towards **Colonnata**, where every second house seems to make or sell the famous *lardo di Colonnata*. If you're peckish, try a meal at the **Locanda Apuana** (Via Comunale 1, 0585 768017, closed Sun dinner & Mon, average €30), where they cure their own *lardo* and make delicious *tordelli* (meat- and vegetable-stuffed ravioli). Three kilometres (two miles) out of town, near the football stadium, is the **Museo Civico del Marmo** (Viale XX Settembre 85, 0585 845746, closed Sun, admission €4.50), which documents marble history and production.

Carrara itself has a lived-in feel. **Piazza Alberica**, its most attractive square, is lined with pastel-coloured buildings. Off the northeast end of the piazza, Via Ghibellina opens up to reveal a seductive view of the 11th-century **Duomo** with its Pisan façade and 14th-century rose window carved from a single slab of marble.

Where to eat

The retro **Caffeteria Leon d'Oro** (8 Piazza Alberica, no phone, closed Sun), overlooking Piazza Alberica, is a nice spot for a drink. A few streets away, the cheap, informal **Pizzeria Tognozzi** (Via Santa Maria 12, 0585 71750, closed Sun) is a good bet for on-the-hop snacks.

Resources

Tourist information
Agenzia per il Turismo APT *Viale Carducci 10, Viareggio (0584 962233/www.versilia.turismo. toscana.it).* **Open** *Summer* 9am-2pm, 3-7.30pm Mon-Sat. *Winter* 9am-1pm, 3-6pm Mon-Sat (also Sun afternoons during Carnevale).

Getting there

By bus
CLAP buses (0584 30996, www.clapspa.it) service Viareggio and link the city several times a day with Pietrasanta and Lucca. **LAZZI** buses (0584 46234, www.lazzi.it) also make the longer journey between Viareggio and Florence (journey time 2hrs).

By car
Both the main A12 coastal *autostrada* and Via Aurelia (SS1, very busy in summer) run through the entire Versilia area. Viareggio, Pietrasanta and Carrara are all accessible via the *autostrada*. Another *autostrada* (A11) in turn links Versilia with Lucca (about 30mins) and other cities inland.

By train
Viareggio is linked to Florence (100-120mins) by regular trains on the Lucca (20mins) line. Trains between Pisa and Genoa also pass through the Versilia area, stopping at Viareggio (20mins from Pisa), Pietrasanta (35mins) and Carrara-Avenza (a bus ride from Carrara, 50mins from Pisa). For information, call 892021 or go to www.trenitalia.it.

The Garfagnana

Just an hour's drive from Lucca, the Garfagnana is a walkers' paradise of snowy peaks and river valleys lined with chestnut trees and wild flowers. Check at the regional tourist office (*see p257*) for information on sporting activities.

Bagni di Lucca

A mood of faded gentility haunts this charming little spa village deep in the bosom of the Lima valley. Its renowned saline and sulphurous thermal waters, together with the less virtuous pleasures of its once glorious casino where roulette is said to have been invented, have attracted many famous names over the decades – everyone from the intellectual elite (Puccini, Shelley, Byron) to Elisa Bonaparte Baciocchi (the Grand Duchess of Tuscany and Napoleon's sister), who had a summer home here (now the Hotel Roma; *see below*).

For healthier indulgences, visit the **Terme Jean Varraud** above the river (Piazza San Martino 11, 0583 87221, www.termebagnidi lucca.it), which offers a range of services, including mud treatments and hydro-massage. But don't go expecting 21st-century gloss: facilities here are purely functional.

On the SS12 from Lucca, six kilometres (four miles) south of Bagni, is a striking sight: the arched spine of the **Ponte della Maddalena** spanning the Serchio river. Nicknamed the Devil's Bridge, it was built in the 11th century by, according to legend, Beelzebub himself in return for the soul of the first person who crossed it. The locals decided to send a dog.

Where to stay & eat

For central accommodation try the beguiling **Hotel Roma** (Via Umberto I 110, 0583 87278, closed mid Oct-Mar, doubles €35-€45), where

The Apuan Alps, viewed from **Barga**.

the cheap, elegant rooms have parquet flooring
and splendid antique furniture. For good
eating there's **Circolo dei Forestieri** (Piazza
Varraud 10, 0583 86038, closed Mon & Tue
lunch & Nov-Jan, average €20) or **Ristorante
Antico Caffè del Sonno** (Viale Umberto I,
146-148, 0583 805080, closed Thur & 4wks Jan
or Feb, average €20) across the street.

Barga

With its perfectly preserved medieval streets
and alleyways threading through the walled
city and up to the 11th-century **Duomo** at its
highest point, Barga is as picturesque as they
come. The cathedral was built in a pale local
stone called *Albarese di Barga*. Its most striking
feature is its pulpit, which was carved by Como
sculptor Guido Bigarelli in the 13th century
and is supported by carved lions and dwarves –
the latter a symbol of crushed paganism. But
there's much more to this town than its history,
since Barga is a lively cultural centre.

Barga's slew of cultural events during
summer include **Barga Jazz** (*see p263* **And
the beat goes on**) and an opera festival (*see
p173* **Seasons in the sun**). For information
on these and more, visit www.barganews.com.

Where to stay & eat

Caffè Capretz (Piazza Salvo Salvi 1, 0583
723001, closed Mon & 2wks Nov) was founded
in 1870; its outdoor tables are set under a wood-
beamed loggia that used to host the town's
vegetable market. Otherwise, there's the low-
key style of **Osteria Angelio** (Piazza Angelio
13-14, 0583 724547, closed Mon, average €16),
which serves excellent Tuscan food, decent
wines, and constant, occasionally live jazz.

Accommodation options vary, but one of the
best is the **Hotel Villa Libano** (Via del Sasso
6, 0583 723774, www.hotelvillalibano.com,
doubles €60), despite its surly staff. The hotel
has quaint rooms and there are mountain views
from its tree-shaded forecourt.

L'Eremo di Calomini

Set on the other side of the Serchio river valley
from Barga, this monastery is built into a
vertical cliff, seemingly hanging in mid air.
To organise a visit, call the parish priest (0583
767003) or the Convent of the Capuchin Fathers
(Monte San Quirico, Via della Chiesa 87, Lucca,
0583 341426).

At its outdoor **Antica Trattoria
dell'Eremita** (0583 767020, closed Nov-Feb,
average €16) there's trout fresh from the
Serchio river, served on the shady terrace
with great views.

Between March and November there's basic
accommodation in the **monastery** (doubles
€20-€23 per night, ask in the trattoria) and
a little shop selling herb syrups and various
medicinal plant extracts.

Grotta del Vento

Seven kilometres (just over four miles) of
hairpin bends and steep ridges from L'Eremo
di Calomini lead to the semi-abandoned town
of **Fornovolasco** and Tuscany's geological
wonder, the Grotta del Vento or 'wind cave'
(0583 722024, www.grottadelvento.com,
admission €7.50-€17), which is packed with
stalactites, stalagmites and underground lakes.
The cold air that blows from the cave's entrance
gave it its name and a practical purpose: it was
used as a refrigerator until the 17th century.

Tuscany

This woman's work: in the studio at **Pietrasanta**. *See p253.*

It wasn't until 1898, when local bullies forced a little girl to go in and she came back out describing the wonders inside, that scientists became aware of its existence. There are one-, two- and three-hour tours.

Castelnuovo di Garfagnana

Garfagnana's capital makes a decent base from which to explore the area. Encased by ancient walls and dominated by a 13th-century castle, its historic centre is a lovely place to refuel.

For daytime and early-evening snacks **Il Vecchio Mulino** (Via Vittorio Emanuele 12, 0583 62192, closed Mon, average €20) is a characterful wine bar with top-notch salamis, cured meats and cheeses. For rooms try **Hotel-Ristorante Ludovico Ariosto** (Via Francesco Azzi 28, 0583 62369, www.hotel ludovicoariosto.com, doubles €45-€62). And just up the street is a must for wine enthusiasts, **La Bottega del Fattore** (Via Francesco Azzi 1A, 0583 62179, closed Mon), where a huge selection of regional and national wines is sold by the glass and bottle.

Parco Orecchiella

This park (0583 619098, 0583 65169, closed Nov-Easter, museum €1.50) is perhaps the loveliest part of the Apuan Alps. Abundant rain gives the area lush forests and meadows, and wildlife includes deer, boar, goats, predatory Appennine wolves and more than 130 species of bird, including the eagles that are Orecchiella's symbol. Hiking and biking paths of varying length and difficulty criss-cross the park, which is best visited in late spring or early autumn.

The Lunigiana

The Lunigiana takes its name from the Luni, the area's aboriginal population. It's Tuscany's least-explored region, as the **Cisa pass** (where the A15 *autostrada* runs) and the area surrounding **Pontremoli** and **Aulla** (the hub for buses and transport to the rest of the area) are way off most tourist itineraries. The people of the Lunigiana don't identify with either Tuscany or nearby Liguria or Emilia Romagna, but are a curious blend of all three – a fact that's reflected in the dialect and cuisine.

Fosdinovo

Lunigiana hasn't always been Tuscany's most isolated corner. For more than ten centuries, from prehistory and the Romans to the heyday of the traffic-heavy Via Francigena trade route, the region was of utmost significance. And with prime location comes fortification. Lunigiana is dotted with scores of castles and towers, of which the **Castello Malaspina** (information 0187 688911, closed Tue, admission €5) in the idyllic feudal town of **Fosdinovo** is a prime example. There are five daily tours of the castle for a minimum of six people or you can simply wander through the pretty sloping streets that surround it and take in some breathtaking views of mountains and sea. Fosdinovo was built by local warlords the Malaspinas; some of their descendants still live here 800 years later.

Fivizzano

Even if it didn't boast gorgeous views and a sleepy pace of life, Fivizzano would be worth a visit just to spend a night in the wonderful family-run **Hotel Il Giardinetto** (Via Roma 151, 0585 92060, doubles €46). Elegant rooms, dark old corridors and day rooms creaking with antiques attract a similarly old-world clientele, while some seriously tasty Tuscan cooking is offered in the restaurant (closed Mon Nov-June & all Oct, average €20).

Just around the corner is **Piazza Medicea** (also called Piazza Vittorio Emanuele), where the main fountain sports four marble dolphins – a gift from Cosimo III in 1683, when the town served as the Medici government's Lunigiana capital. The bell tower belonging to the church of **San Jacopo e San Antonio** and built on the site of a 13th-century church bristles with a Heath Robinson-style collection of giant cogs. On the perimeters of the square is **Caffè Elvetico** (0585 926657, closed Sun in winter), which has tables spilling into the square.

North-east of town on the SS63, the **Castello della Verrucola** was also built by the Malaspinas, who controlled the area from here all the way to Carrara.

Pontremoli

Pontremoli is the Lunigiana's biggest town, though only 11,000 people live here. Its wealth grew from its position as an important station on the Via Francigena trade route and the Cisa pass. These days the route here is more likely to be clogged with packs of cyclists who pit themselves against the steep, winding roads.

Looking down over the pretty arched streets of Pontremoli's old town is the **Castello del Piagnaro**. It houses the **Museo delle Statue Stelle** (Castello di Piagnaro, 0187 831439, closed Mon in winter, admission €3.50), home to 19 prehistoric statues discovered in the area.

In the town itself, the **Duomo Santa Maria del Popolo** (Piazza del Duomo) was designed in 1633 by the Cremonese architect Alessandro Capra. Finished in 1687, it is interesting for its aisleless nave and short transept, but most of all for its notably high, luminous dome. Also worth a look is the 14th-century **Torre del Campanone**, with its beautiful little park and picnic area by the burbling Magra river.

Where to stay & eat

There are plenty of restaurants and trattorias in Pontremoli, but one of the very best is the characterful **Da Bussé** (Piazza del Duomo 31, 0187 831371, closed dinner Mon-Thur, all day Fri & 3wks July, average €27), a wonderfully old-fashioned place where they make fabulous *testaroli*, a local speciality that's is a bit like a pancake smothered in tangy pesto. **Il Caveau del Teatro** (Piazza Santa Cristina, 0187 833328, www.caveaudelteatro.it, average €32) is an altogether more upmarket – but no less charming – option where you can eat creative local dishes and drink fine wines from all over Italy. There are also seven delightful rooms (doubles €90) furnished with antiques.

Resources

Tourist information

Centro Visite Parco Alpi Apuane & Centro di Coordinamento del Turismo Rurale *Piazza delle Erbe 1, Castelnuovo di Garfagnana (0583 65169/garfagnana@tin.it)*. **Open** *June-Sept* 9am-1pm, 3-7pm daily. *Oct-May* 9am-1pm, 3.30-5.30pm daily. The English-speaking staff have information on both the Garfagnana and the Lunigiana, including *agriturismo* accommodation, walking routes and sporting activities in the Apuan Alps.

Getting there

By bus

CLAP (0583 587897, www.clapspa.it) operates buses to Barga and Castelnuovo di Garfagnana from Lucca. LAZZI (0583 584876, www.lazzi.it) runs several buses a day from Lucca to Bagni di Lucca. Neither company runs services to the Lunigiana.

By car

Take the SS12 north out of Lucca; it follows the Serchio river valley and branches off towards Bagni di Lucca just beyond Borgo. At the same intersection you can take the winding hill road (SS445) towards Barga (there's a turn-off after a few kilometres) and Castelnuovo di Garfagnana. This is the main route through the Garfagnana region and smaller roads fan off from it towards highlights such as the Grotta del Vento (turn off near Barga to the south) and the Parco Orecchiella. It also leads, eventually, to the SS63 (and then the SS62), which goes through the Lunigiana region to the far north. The drive through the mountains is very scenic, but you should allow plenty of time (at least a day from Lucca) and perhaps aim to stop over en route.

By train

An irregular but very scenic rail service (892021, www.trenitalia.it) goes through this area between Lucca and Aulla in the north, with stops at Bagni di Lucca (30mins), Castelnuovo di Garfagnana (60mins) and Piazza al Serchio (75mins).

Arezzo

This tidy, historic city is once again on the rise.

Arezzo has got its act together over the past few years. Granted, the industrial outskirts are still extensive and still unattractive, but the largely pedestrian city centre has been nicely restored and injected with a welcome element of fun. Apart from the art and architecture, there are some great little hotels and eateries, a music festival that attracts youthful audiences from all over Italy (**Arezzo Wave**; *see p263* **And the beat goes on**) and a general sense that, at last, Arezzo is growing into a genuinely attractive tourist destination.

All this was unthinkable a decade or so ago, when the *Aretini* (as the locals are known) were too busy manufacturing gold jewellery – which had turned a generation of peasants into millionaires – to devote much attention to their city. They kept to their factories in the suburbs,

Pieve di Santa Maria. *See p260.*

accruing great wealth and occasionally going out for a spin in their Ferraris. Little wonder, then, that tourists beat a retreat after admiring the Piero della Francesca frescoes or looking for bargains at the monthly antiques fair (*see p262*). Happily, a lot has changed in a short time. Just as the city's gold and textile industries face leaner years (though they're undeniably still big businesses), a younger generation has decided to employ its own entrepreneurial acumen outside the confines of the factories. As a result, there's a real buzz about the place.

SOME HISTORY

Strategically built at the intersection of four fertile valleys (the Casentino, Valdarno, Valtiberina and Valdichiana), Arezzo was a flourishing centre of Etruscan culture by the fourth century BC. It was later taken over by the Romans in their northward expansion, becoming a military stronghold and economic outpost. By 89 BC its people were granted honorary Roman citizenship; an amphitheatre, an aqueduct and fortified walls followed. A century later Arezzo's first industry was born: embossed pottery, traded far and wide.

Following the decline of the Roman Empire, the city was overrun by Barbarians. The darkest days came under the Lombards in the sixth century. Yet, gradually, a feudal economic system began to pull the city from its slump. The turning point arrived in 1100, when the emerging merchant class started to question its subservience to Arezzo's clerical-feudal overlords. Secular power began to shift to the budding bourgeoisie, and in 1192 the Commune was established. There was extensive building and Arezzo began to take on its current urban contours. However, another foreign power, this time Florence, set its sights on the city. The two clashed in the Battle of Campaldino in 1289, from which Arezzo never fully recovered. The city eventually succumbed to Florence in 1384.

Fortunately, political submission didn't equal artistic or cultural paralysis: Medici patronage in Florence provided wider scope for those with talent. Foremost among the creative spirits of the time was Giorgio Vasari (1511-74), painter, architect and historian, whose *Lives of the Artists* has enlivened our perception of the Renaissance. However, the boost to local creativity didn't last: the city had become a conservative backwater by the 17th century.

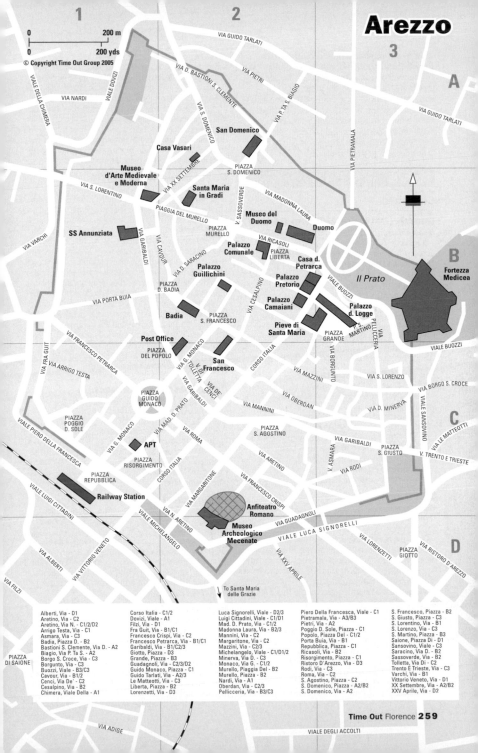

Arezzo

San Domenico

Casa Vasari

Museo d'Arte Medievale e Moderna

Santa Maria in Gradi

SS Annunziata

Museo del Duomo

Duomo

Palazzo Comunale

Casa d. Petrarca

Palazzo Guillichini

Palazzo Pretorio

Badia

Palazzo Camaiani

Pieve di Santa Maria

Palazzo d. Logge

Il Prato

Fortezza Medicea

Post Office

San Francesco

APT

Railway Station

Anfiteatro Romano

Museo Archeologico Mecenate

To Santa Maria delle Grazie

PIAZZA DI SAIONE

VIA ADIGE

VIALE DEGLI ACCOLTI

And so it remained until recently, when the parochial outlook began to be supplanted by more forward-looking policies. Today a younger, better educated generation of entrepreneurs and local administrators seems set on increasing the city's appeal. To those ends, a new parking area just outside the walls on the north side, behind the church of San Domenico, makes access to the city centre far easier and more attractive.

Sights

Churches

Duomo (Cattedrale di San Donato)

Piazza Duomo (0575 23991). **Open** 7am-12.30pm, 3-7pm daily. **Admission** free.
Construction on Arezzo's Gothic Duomo began in 1277, but the finishing touches weren't made until the early 1500s, and it was a further 300 years before its campanile was erected. The overall effect of its size and the vertical thrust of its ogival vaulted ceilings are inspiring, as are the exquisite stained-glass windows (c1515-20) by Guillaume di Marcillat. But the Duomo's real attractions are along the left aisle: Piero della Francesca's *Mary Magdalene* (c1465), and the Cappella della Madonna del Conforto, screened off from the rest of the church.

Pieve di Santa Maria

Corso Italia (0575 22629). **Open** *Oct-Apr* 8am-noon, 3-6pm daily. *May-Sept* 8am-1pm, 2.30-7pm daily. **Admission** free.
A striking example of Romanesque architecture built mostly in the 12th and 13th centuries. Santa Maria's pale stone façade is harmonious, with five arcades surmounted by three increasingly busy orders of *logge*. The ornate columns holding them up, all 68 of which have an eccentric motif, reach a climax in the bell tower *delle cento buche* (of the 100 holes).

San Domenico

Piazza San Domenico (0575 22906). **Open** 8.30am-1pm, 3.30-7pm daily. **Admission** free.
San Domenico was started by Dominicans in 1275 around the same time as their Franciscan brothers were getting under way with San Francesco (*see below*). Facing a simple, open square, it has an attractive quaintness about it that's accentuated by its uneven Gothic campanile with two 14th-century bells. Inside is a magnificent crucifix by Cimabue.

San Francesco

Piazza San Francesco (0575 20630/24001 to reserve tickets). **Open** 8.30am-7pm daily. **Admission** free.
The interior of San Francesco, which was begun by Franciscan friars in the 13th century, was adorned with frescoes, chapels and shrines during the 1500s, thanks to Arezzo's merchant class. By the 19th century it was being used as a military barracks. Happily, however, *The Legend of the True*

Cross (*see also p27 and p28*), Piero della Francesca's magnum opus, survived, and has recently been restored. Considered to be one of the most important fresco cycles ever produced, it was begun in 1453, the year Constantinople fell to the Ottoman Turks, and portrays the fear this induced in the Christian world. A separate ticket (€5.03) gains you an audio guide and access to the chapels (it's best to book in advance in high season), but note that some of the frescoes are too high to be properly appreciated by the naked eye: take a pair of binoculars if you can.

Santa Maria delle Grazie

Via Santa Maria (0575 323140/www.abd.it/santamaria). **Open** 8am-7pm daily. **Admission** free.
On the site of an ancient sacred spring, the Fonte Tecta, the religious complex built around Santa Maria delle Grazie is known, houses the Renaissance's first porticoed courtyard. Started in 1428, the religious buildings were imposed by San Bernardino of Siena on the recalcitrant *Aretini*, who proceeded to march from San Francesco brandishing a wooden cross and destroy the spring site, replacing it with a *Madonna della Misericordia* by local artist Parri di Spinello. The enlightened Antonio da Maiano, one of the Renaissance's foremost architects and the man who created the loggia, reconciled the church's late Gothic, essentially medieval design with the then-emergent classical style.

Museums

Casa Museo Ivan Bruschi

Corso Italia 14 (0575 354126/www.fondazione bruschi.it). **Open** *Summer* 10am-1pm, 3-7pm Tue-Sun. *Winter* 10am-1pm, 2-6pm Tue-Sun. **Admission** €3. **No credit cards**.
Located opposite the Pieve, this was the home of the founder of the Arezzo antiques fair. Today it is full of antiquarian delights, with archaeological pieces, Egyptian artefacts, musical instruments, books, stamps and more.

Casa Vasari

Via XX Settembre 55 (0575 409040). **Open** 9am-7pm Mon, Wed-Sat; 9am-1pm Sun. **Admission** €2. **No credit cards**.
Medici favourite Giorgio Vasari bought and decorated this house in extravagant style before taking up an important post in Florence in 1564. Today the museum houses the Archivio e Museo Vasariano and proudly exhibits a number of Vasari frescoes and other late Mannerist paintings.

Museo Archeologico Mecenate

Via Margaritone 10 (0575 20882). **Open** 8.30am-7.30pm daily. **Admission** €4. **No credit cards**.
This estimable collection of Etruscan and Roman artefacts is located just beside the Roman amphitheatre (*see p261*). The Etruscan bronze votive figurines and jewellery are particularly splendid, as is the Attic bowl decorated by Euphronios (AD 500-510) and the coralline pottery.

Hanging around in **Piazza San Francesco**.

Museo d'Arte Medievale e Moderna
Via San Lorentino 8 (0575 409050). **Open** 8.30am-
7.30pm Tue-Sun. **Admission** €4. **No credit cards.**
Once you realise that *moderna* does not mean
'contemporary', this museum reveals itself to be an
interesting, if uneven, collection of sculpture and
painting from the Middle Ages to the 19th century.
The baroque vestibule on the first floor is dominat-
ed by Vasari's *Wedding Feast of Ahasuerus and
Esther* (1548); past it are rooms containing one of
Italy's finest collections of 13th- to 17th-century
glazed ceramics from the Della Robbia school.
Among the later works are pieces belonging to the
Macchiaioli school.

Museo dell'Oro
*Via Fiorentina 550 (0575 925953/925407/
www.unoaerre.it).* **Open** 9am-6pm Mon-Fri;
9am-1pm Sat. **Admission** free.
Run by Uno A Erre, one of the world's foremost producers of gold jewellery, this museum includes a
unique collection of pieces dating from the 1920s to
the present day.

Landmarks

Anfiteatro Romano
*Accessible from Via Margaritone or Via Crispi (0575
20882).* **Open** *Apr-Oct* 8.30am-7.30pm daily. *Nov-
Mar* 7.30am-6pm daily. **Admission** free.
In the second century this amphitheatre drew
crowds of up to 10,000 people, but its travertine
and sandstone blocks were plundered by Cosimo I
for the Fortezza Medicea (*see below*) in 1531. You can
still make out its elliptical shape and stage, plus
parts of what were probably the stands.

Fortezza Medicea
No phone. **Open** *Summer* 7am-8pm daily. *Winter*
7.30am-6pm daily. **Admission** free.
When the Medici finally decided to turn Arezzo into
a duchy in 1531, they set about improving the city's
defences, and the introduction of cannons prompt-
ed them to embark on another (the eighth) stint of
wall-building. The perimeter is visible in sections
around the city and dominated by the architecturally
revolutionary Fortezza Medicea (1538-60). Its pentagonal form was designed by Antonio da Sangallo
the Elder and required the razing of towers, alleys
and medieval *palazzi* in the hills of San Donato.

Piazza Grande
A visual feast of architectural irregularity, thanks to
its growth from peripheral food market to political
heart of the city. The jumble of styles includes the
arcaded, rounded back of the Romanesque Pieve di
Santa Maria at the square's lowest point, the baroque
Palazzo del Tribunale and, next to it, the Palazzo
della Fraternità dei Laici, designed mostly by
Bernardo Rossellino. Vasari also had a hand in the
Piazza Grande: his is the typically arcaded Palazzo
delle Logge, which presides over the assortment
of medieval homes around the rest of the square.
Like Siena, Arezzo holds its own historic event, the
Giostra del Saracino (*see p158*), in its main square.

Parks & gardens

Il Prato
Arezzo's only park – it's located between the Duomo
and the Fortezza Medicea – has views over the town.
Locals flock to La Casina del Prato (*see p264*) on
summer nights.

Shopping

As you climb Corso Italia, mainstream shops give way to a proliferation of antiques shops around Piazza Grande. On Saturdays a general market sells clothes, food, flowers and household goods, but on the first Sunday of the month (as well as the day before) the city centre is taken over by a huge and important antiques fair. The **APT** (*see p264*) has a handy Italian-English glossary and a map to guide you around the place.

Not surprisingly, there are plenty of shops selling gold jewellery in Arezzo, as well as a store at the **Museo dell'Oro** (*see p261*).

Busatti
Corso Italia 48 (0575 355295/www.busatti.com). **Open** 3.30-7.30pm Mon; 9am-1pm, 3.30-7.30pm Tue-Sat. **Credit** AmEx, DC, MC, V.
Upholstery fabrics and household linens.

Macelleria-Gastronomia Aligi Barelli
Via della Chimera 22B (0575 357754). **Open** 8am-1pm, 4.30-8pm Mon, Tue, Thur, Fri; 8am-1pm Wed, Sat. *Winter* also Sat pm. Closed 3wks Aug. **Credit** DC, MC, V.
This renowned *macelleria* (butcher) has salamis from the Casentino and ready-made meat-based dishes.

Pane e Salute
Corso Italia 11 (0575 20657). **Open** 7.30am-1.30pm, 4-8pm Mon-Sat. Closed Aug. **No credit cards**.
Traditional Tuscan breads such as *schiacciate* (flattened bread with rosemary), plus oven-baked sweets.

Pasticceria de' Cenci
Via de' Cenci 17 (0575 23102). **Open** 9am-1pm, 4-8pm Tue-Sat; 9am-1pm Sun. Closed Aug. **No credit cards**.
This *pasticceria* is full of elegant delights such as *bigné al limone* (lemon cream puff).

Where to eat & drink

Restaurants

Arezzo's culinary specialities draw on the products of the four rich valleys that encircle it. Among the favoured pasta dishes are *funghi porcini* (ceps) and *tartufo nero* (black truffle), while local Chianina steak crops up on many a menu. A couple of newcomers to the scene take their inspiration from further afield.

Il Cantuccio
Via Madonna del Prato 76 (0575 26830/www. il-cantuccio.it). **Open** noon-2.30pm, 7-10.30pm Mon, Tue, Thur-Sun. **Average** €17. **Credit** AmEx, DC, MC, V.
The vaulted cellar here is arguably the city's most rustic. Home-made pasta dishes include *tortelloni alla Casentinese* (with a potato filling).

Pick up a pal at the monthly antiques fair.

Gastronomia Il Cervo
Via Cavour 38-40 (0575 20872). **Open** 7.30am-9pm Tue-Sun. *Meals served* 11am-3pm, 5-9pm Tue-Sun. **Average** €20. **Credit** AmEx, DC, MC, V.
Right opposite San Francesco, this deli prepares a whole range of goodies that you can select and eat at tables on the floor above. Ideal for a light meal.

Miseria e Nobiltà
Via Piaggia di San Bartolomeo 2 (0575 21245/ www.miseriaenobilta.com). **Open** 7-11.30pm Tue-Sun. **Average** €30. **Credit** AmEx, DC, MC, V.
Another universe of culinary creativity, housed in a medieval vault of great architectural impact. The meats, pastas and fish are all recommended.

Sbarbacipolle
Via Garibaldi 120 (0575 299154). **Open** 7.30am-8pm daily. Closed 3wks Aug. **Average** €9. **No credit cards**.
A colourful corner deli with a good choice of *panini* and cold dishes. Immensely popular with the locals.

Trattoria Il Saraceno
Via Mazzini 6A (0575 27644/www.ilsaraceno.com). **Open** 12.30-3pm, 7-11pm Mon, Tue, Thur-Sun. Closed 2wks Jan. **Average** €25. **Credit** AmEx, DC, MC, V.
Fine food, including lamb with rosemary, homemade pasta dishes and wood-oven pizzas.

I Tre Bicchieri
Piazzetta Sopra i Ponti 3-5 (0575 26557). **Open** 12.30-2pm, 7-10.30pm Mon, Tue, Thur-Sun. **Average** €45. **Credit** MC, V.
Tucked into an inner courtyard behind Corso Italia, this excellent restaurant is run by two brothers who opted out of the gold jewellery business to indulge their passion for innovative cuisine. There's also a great wine list.

And the beat goes on

Arezzo is home to one of the region's most established music festivals, **Arezzo Wave** (www.arezzowave.com), a free five-day marathon of pop, funk, jazz, heavy metal, rock and classical music held in early July that also includes theatre, comedy and literature. Two other major musical events in Tuscany are **Pistoia Blues** (www.pistoiablues.com), held over a mid July weekend and featuring musicians both local and international, and the week-long, Pisa-based **Metarock** (www.metamusic.it), now in its third decade.

Jazzers have a good selection of events from which to pick. One of the best known is the **Grey Cat Jazz Festival** (www.toscana musiche.it), which brings big international names to a number of venues in the province of Grosseto in late August. By contrast, **Siena Jazz** (www.sienajazz.it), held in late July and early August, highlights up-and-coming Italian jazzers, albeit with support from musicians of international repute. The concerts at **Barga Jazz** (www.barganews.com/bargajazz), held in the small town north of Lucca in late July/early August, also revolve around young musicians, who are flanked by a professional orchestra.

Music of ethnic origin or inspiration underlies a number of events, among them Florence's **Musica dei Popoli** (*see p177*) and the Carrara-based **Musica e Suoni dal Mondo** (www.eventimusicpool.it) in late July/early August. In mid July, the **Sete Sois Sete Luas** festival (www.7sois7luas.com) explores

musical links between southern Europe and Africa and is held in small towns in the provinces of Pisa and Pistoia.

A few other festivals merit mention. The **Musicpool** festival (www.eventimusicpool.it) embraces jazz, rock, pop and ethnic music in concerts throughout the region from June to August. The Florence-based **Musicus Concentus** (www.musicusconcentus.com; *see also p175*) centres on new music in concerts that span most of the year. And finally the itinerant **On the Road** festival gives street musicians, artists, jugglers and buskers a stage in Pelago in early July.

More information on many of these festivals, and a few others, can be found at www.toscanamusiche.it.

Arezzo Wave.

Bars, enoteche & gelaterie

Wines produced in Arezzo's hinterland are improving: look out for labels from the Sette Ponti estate. Visit the city's numerous wine bars to taste a range of Colli Aretini vintages as well as Tuscany's more acclaimed labels.

La Casina del Prato
Via Palagi 1, Il Prato park (0575 299757).
Open *Summer* 10am-2am daily. *Winter* 10am-2am Mon, Wed-Sun. Closed Dec. **No credit cards**.
An open-air summer hotspot overflowing with the hipper crowd. Some snacks are available.

Enoteca al Canto de' Bacci
Corso Italia 65 (0575 355804/www.cantodebacci. com). **Open** 8am-2pm, 3-8pm Mon-Sat. *Winter* also 1st Sun of mth. **Credit** AmEx, DC, MC, V.
A good selection of wines (some quite unusual), plus other products of local gastronomy. Sample at your leisure at one of the outside tables.

Enoteca La Torre di Gnicche
Piaggia San Martino 8 (0575 352035). **Open** noon-3pm, 6pm-1am Mon, Tue, Thur-Sun. Closed 2wks Jan. **Credit** MC, V.
A tastefully decorated bar with a superb selection of local wines. The hot food is also worth a try.

Fiaschetteria de' Redi
Via de' Redi 10 (0575 355012). **Open** noon-3pm, 7.30-11.30pm Tue-Sun. **Credit** MC, V.
A cosy bustling wine bar just off Corso Italia, with a good wine selection. *Osteria*-style food is served.

Il Gelato
Via de' Cenci 24 (0575 300069). **Open** *Summer* 11am-midnight Mon, Tue, Thur-Sun. *Winter* 11am-8pm Mon, Tue, Thur-Sun. **No credit cards**.
An unassuming, busy *gelateria*. Try *pinolata* (with pine nuts) or *arancello al liquore* (liqueur orange).

Where to stay

La Corte del Re
Via Borgunto 5 (0575 401603/348 6959100/ fax 0575 296720/www.lacortedelre.com). **Rates** €680-€1,000 weekly. **Credit** AmEx, MC, V.
Six fully equipped mini-apartments just a stone's throw from Piazza Grande.

La Foresteria
Via Bicchieraia 32 (tel/fax 0575 370474).
Rates €29-€58 double. **No credit cards**.
A dozen simple rooms in a 14th-century ex-convent. Many of the rooms are frescoed and, although simple, are stylishly furnished. A bargain.

Il Patio
Via Cavour 23 (0575 401962/fax 0575 27418).
Rates €120 single; €160 double. **No credit cards**.
A very nice small hotel featuring comfortable rooms designed with real flair. Original and friendly.

I Portici
Via Roma 18 (0575 403132/fax 0575 300934/ www.hoteliportici.com). **Rates** €130-€155 single; €185-€235 double; €260-€310 suite. **Credit** AmEx, MC, V.
Once a private house, I Portici is now a small upmarket hotel run by the scions of the original owners.

Resources

Hospital
Ospedale San Donato *Viale Alcide de Gasperi 17 (0575 255003).*

Internet
Phone Centre *Piazza Guido Monaco 8B (0575 371245).* **Open** 9am-1pm, 3-8.30pm Mon-Fri; 9am-1pm Sat. Closed 2wks Aug.

Police
Via Poggio del Sole (0575 3181602).

Tourist information
Azienda di Promozione Turistica (APT) *Piazza della Repubblica 28 (0575 377678/ www.apt.arezzo.it).* **Open** *Oct-Mar* 9am-1pm, 3-6.30pm Mon-Sat; 9am-1pm 1st Sun of mth. *Apr-Sept* 9am-1pm, 3-7pm Mon-Sat; 9am-1pm Sun.

Getting there & around

By bus
Bus services from Florence are slow and irregular, so take the train. **LFI** (La Ferrovia Italiana, 0575 39881, www.lfi.it) has direct buses to Siena (90mins) and Cortona (1hr). **SITA** (for Sansepolcro; 0575 74361/743681, www.sita-on-line.it) also covers the region. Buses leave from the terminal opposite the train station. For information and ticket sales for local routes, call ATAM Point in the same square (0575 382651).

By car
Arezzo is a few kilometres off the A1 (Florence-Rome) *autostrada*. Journey time from Florence is around 1hr, though it experiences big jams on summer weekends and public holidays. The SS73 links the city with Siena to the west (about 1hr) and Sansepolcro to the north (30mins).
Parking can be difficult and expensive in Arezzo. The tourist office (*see above*) has a list of free places to park outside the city walls. The new car park on the north side is the best. For car hire there's Avis (Piazza della Repubblica 1, 0575 354232) or Hertz (Via Calamandrei 97D, 0575 27577).

By taxi
Radio Taxi (0575 382626).

By train
Regular Intercity and InterRegionale trains link Arezzo with Florence (50-60mins) and Rome (90mins). The train station is located at Piazza della Repubblica (0575 20553). For national train information, go to www.trenitalia.it or call 892021.

Tuscany

Arezzo Province

How green is my valley?

Cortona. *See p270.*

The province of Arezzo embraces extremes: valley flatlands and mountain peaks; busy highways and quiet paths; industry and crafts; aggregation and solitude.

The balance of modernity and tradition differs considerably among the four valleys that make up the province. Industry predominates in the **Valdarno**, where fast roads connect Arezzo to Florence. Yet even here, to the north, the imposing Pratomagno Appennine range shelters early Romanesque churches that speak of quiet and reflection. By contrast, nature prevails in the **Casentino** area to the north-east. The steep slopes are clad with tall forests, creating the sort of isolation sought by hermits and monks, who chose this area for their sanctuaries. Lower down in the foothills, traditional wood and stone work has survived, as has the production of the thick, rough, hard-wearing Casentino cloth made from wool shorn from the sheep grazing in the meadows.

The **Valtiberina**, Tuscany's easternmost fringe, takes its name from the River Tiber, which flows down from the Appennine peaks.

The inhabitants are proud of the fact that this valley marks the border between a land that produced the likes of Michelangelo and Piero della Francesca and neighbouring Umbria and Le Marche, which they perceive as less sophisticated.

Finally, in the south, is the **Valdichiana**. In previous times this area was swampy and insalubrious. It was first drained and made passable by the Etruscans, only to revert to its previous state following the decline of the Roman Empire. A thousand years passed before the Chiana valley was reclaimed again by the Lorraine Grand Dukes, by which time a layer of humus had formed to create a fertile agricultural plain.

Its name today is synonymous with Chianina beef – large, greyish, white-horned creatures. They are mostly raised organically, producing particularly flavoursome meat. Overlooking the Valdichiana are self-contained outposts such as Monte San Savino and Lucignano, while to the east is a ridge dominated by Castelfiorentino and the lovely sandstone town of Cortona.

Valdarno

Castelfranco di Sopra & Loro Ciuffenna

The Setteponti ('seven bridges') route along the Pratomagno foothills crosses the Arno's tributaries amid olive and chestnut groves. It's less direct than the *autostrada* but more interesting, providing access to towns such as **Castelfranco di Sopra**, which was founded as a Florentine military outpost in the late 13th century. Just outside it is the **Badia di San Salvatore a Soffena**, a 12th-century abbey with a bright interior sporting an *Annunciation* and other pastel-coloured frescoes.

A little further along the same road is **Loro Ciuffenna**, set on the edge of a gorge over the roaring Ciuffenna torrent once used to power flour mills. Loro grew up around an ancient *borgo* (hamlet) and has its own Ponte Vecchio. A couple of kilometres outside Loro, on the Arezzo road, a dirt path twists off towards the stark and simple church of **San Pietro a Gropina**, a Romanesque parish church dating from the ninth century. The carved detail on the capitals and knotted columns on the pulpit, with stylised human figures, grapes, knights and hunting eagles, are a proto-Christian rendition of the circle and knot of life.

The Setteponti's last attraction before Arezzo is **Ponte a Buriano**, a harmonious 13th-century bridge, the Arno's oldest.

Casentino

Poppi & Bibbiena

A delightful small town, **Poppi** slopes down through arcaded streets from the 13th-century **Castello dei Conti Guidi** (0575 520516, closed Mon-Wed Oct-Mar, admission €4 incl audio guide). This castle is well worth a visit, not only for its frescoed rooms, including the chapel, but also for the magnificent view of the Casentino. Dante is said to have stayed here, and there's a noble statue of him outside.

Head out of Poppi towards Pratovecchio and you'll see signs for the **Pieve di Romena**, a 12th-century baptismal church. Inside there are sculpted stone capitals and some remarkable pieces of contemporary art by the local priest.

For **Bibbiena**, a gem of a walled town as yet largely undiscovered by tourists, head in the other direction, leaving the busy road and unprepossessing outskirts and making for the historic centre. There are some fine old *palazzi*

to admire, including the elegant Renaissance **Palazzo Dovizi**, and in the church of **San Lorenzo** you'll find a magnificent della Robbia glazed terracotta, *Adoration of the Shepherds*.

Where to stay & eat

In Poppi, a good base is homely **Albergo Casentino** (Piazza della Repubblica 6, 0575 529090, doubles €65) with its own little enclosed garden and a restaurant (closed Wed, average €16). Otherwise, in the country just beyond Bibbiena you'll find the **Agricola Casentinese** (Località Casanova 63, 0575 594806, www.agricolacasentinese.it, doubles from €55), offering comfortable rooms and an evening meal in the middle of a huge working farm, where you can also ride and trek.

Food-wise, another excellent option in Poppi is the **Antica Cantina** (Via Lapucci 2, 0575 529844, closed Mon, average €21), housed in a cellar dating from the 12th century. There's an excellent wine list, and a number of bottles are available by the glass. In Bibbiena, **Il Tirabusciò** (Via Borghi 73, 0575 595474, www.tirabuscio.it, closed dinner & all Tue) puts together some interesting menus to match particular wines.

Socana, Camaldoli & La Verna

The three destinations that make up this triangle reveal different facets of the spiritual heritage of the area. **Socana**, which is due south of Bibbiena, embodies 2,600 years of history and the votive aspirations of three civilisations: Etruscan, Roman and Christian. Excavation has brought to light a magnificent sacrificial altar and the staircase of a temple dating back to the Etruscan period as well as a cylindrical wall and pilaster strips of Roman origin. The Christians subsequently built three churches on top of the Etruscan temple.

In the wooded hills north-east of Poppi, in the midst of the **Foreste Casentinesi** national park, are the monastery and hermitage of **Camaldoli**. The latter was founded in 1012 by St Romuald. Surrounded by fir trees, the monks' individual cells are visible only through a gate, though Romualdo's original cell, with its wooden panelling and cot, is open to visitors. Three kilometres (two miles) downhill, is the 16th-century monastery that links the Camaldolites to the outside world. Its church contains some early Vasaris, including a *Madonna and Child* and a *Nativity*. The young artist took refuge here from 1537 to 1539, after the murder of his patron, Alessandro de' Medici.

Castello dei Conti Guidi, Poppi.
See p266.

Monte San Savino. *See p269.*

A little further south, close to the town of Chiusi, an even more important monastic complex dominates the surrounding landscape from a rocky outcrop at 1,129 metres (3,670 feet). In 1214 St Francis's vagabondage brought him to this isolated peak, where he and some followers were inspired to build cells for themselves. Ten years later Italy's most famous saint received the stigmata here and, ever since, **La Verna** has been a must-see on the Franciscan trail. The basilica contains a reliquary chapel with the saint's personal effects. The sanctuary also contains a great number of Andrea della Robbia's glazed terracottas. This impressive religious compound of interconnected chapels, churches, corridors and cloisters attracts large numbers of visitors. But on a quiet weekday the sunset over the Casentino inspires meditative silence.

Valtiberina

Sansepolcro

The Valtiberina's largest town, Sansepolcro, gives meaning to the expression 'quality of life'. It is both tranquil and culturally alive, off the beaten track yet welcoming to visitors. Although the outskirts are unprepossessing, the largely pedestrian walled centre is charming.

Sansepolcro is best known as the birthplace of the early Renaissance maestro of perspective and proportion, Piero della Francesca, whose works are prominently displayed in the excellent **Museo Civico** (Via Aggiunti 65, 0575 732218, admission €6.20). Works include

the important *Madonna della Misericordia* (c1445), in which Piero overturns the laws of proportion by depicting an all-encompassing, monumental Madonna dwarfing the faithful and protecting them with her mantle. The artist can't resist placing himself among the Virgin's followers, facing us from the Madonna's left. Another self-portrait appears in *The Resurrection* (c1460), where a muscular Christ steps from his tomb, awakening the somnolent soldiers at his feet. Among them, to the left of Christ, is Piero.

The 14th-century Romanesque **Duomo** contains on its left altar an imposing wooden crucifix known as the *Volto Santo* (Holy Face), probably brought to Sansepolcro from the Orient, and very similar to its better-known equivalent in Lucca's Duomo di San Martino (*see p242*).

Local events include a torch-lit Easter procession on Good Friday and a traditional crossbow tournament, the Palio della Balestra, held on the second Sunday in September.

Where to stay, eat & drink

Central **Albergo Fiorentino** (Via L Pacioli 56, 0575 740350, www.albergofiorentino.com, doubles €50-€70), on the corner of Via XX Settembre, offers perfectly acceptable accommodation, while the **Ristorante da Ventura** (Via Aggiunti 30, 0575 742560, closed dinner Sun, all Mon, average €30) is the best of the classics. For sampling wine together with good food, **Enoteca Guidi** (Via L Pacioli 44, 0575 741086, closed Wed, Sat & lunch Sun) is the place.

Monterchi

This cluster of hilltop homes on the road between Arezzo and Sansepolcro is practically synonymous with Piero della Francesca's *Madonna del Parto*, the famous painting of a pregnant Madonna that once graced a little wayside church and is now the prize possession of the **Museo Madonna del Parto** (Via Reglia 1, 0575 70713, admission €3.10). The rotund Madonna is circled by angels lightly drawing back a canopy. This sublime rendition of a sacred, rustic maternal figure is the only one of its kind in Renaissance art.

Where to eat

For an atmospheric meal, head up to **Ristorante Al Travato** (Piazza Umberto 1, 0575 70111, closed Mon Apr-Oct & 1wk June & Mon-Thur & dinner Fri-Sun Nov-Mar, average €25) in part of Monterchi's fortress.

Anghiari

Perched on a hill overlooking the Valtiberina and Sansepolcro, Anghiari's dominant position and impressive walls made it a stronghold from which Florence controlled the far east of Tuscany, following victory over the Milanese Visconti family in the Battle of Anghiari in 1440. Leonardo consigned the event to posterity in his (unfinished) rendition on display in the Palazzo Vecchio in Florence. Today, with its maze of vaulted alleys and flower-strewn doorways, it's a peaceful place.

The town is also renowned for its wood craft and antique furniture restoration. It hosts the annual Valtiberina crafts market in late April and an antiques fair on the third Sunday of every other month. The **Museo Statale di Palazzo Taglieschi** (Piazza Mameli 16, 0575 788001, closed Mon, admission €2) displays numerous local artefacts, a polychrome terracotta by della Robbia and a striking wooden sculpture of the Madonna by Jacopo della Quercia. Anghiari's other big traditional and commercial draw is its woven and naturally dyed textiles, exemplified by the **Busatti** store-cum-factory (Via Mazzini 14, 0575 788013, closed Sun & Mon morning). Its deafening shuttle looms, some of them almost a century old, produce linens from natural fibres.

Where to eat

The classic local eaterie is **Da Alighiero** (Via Garibaldi 8, 0575 788040, closed Tue, average €25), where regional porcini mushrooms often feature on the menu.

Valdichiana

Monte San Savino

Circular and enclosed, Monte San Savino is a prominent provincial town. Its Renaissance heyday, however, was brief, coinciding with the commercial patronage and religious power exercised by the Di Monte family in the late 1400s and 1500s. The main architectural attractions, both bearing the family's imprint, face each other along Corso Sangallo.

The quintessentially Renaissance Palazzo di Monte, now the **Palazzo Comunale** (designed between 1515 and 1517 by Antonio da Sangallo the Elder), contains an arcaded courtyard, via which you reach hanging gardens and an open-air theatre overlooking a cypress-dotted landscape. Across from it is the **Loggia dei Mercanti**, attributed to architect and sculptor

Andrea Sansovino, Monte San Savino's most eminent son. He also retouched the nearby Piazza di Monte and helped embellish the church of Santa Chiara with two terracottas: the *Madonna* and *Saints Lawrence, Sebastian and Rocco*.

Monte San Savino is known for engraved pottery designed in delicate floral motifs, with examples on display at the **Museo del Cassero** (Piazza Gamurrini, 0575 843098, admission €1.55). The products at **Ceramiche Artistiche Lapucci** (Corso Sangallo 8-10, 0575 844375, closed Sun, ring bell for entry) still reflect this tradition.

The Estate Savinese event in July puts on open-air concerts and films, the Festival Musicale is in the first half of August and the Sagra della Porchetta, an all-you-can-eat roast suckling pig celebration, is in mid September.

Where to stay & eat

For a pleasantly relaxed meal, try the *enoteca-osteria* **La Pecora Nera** (Via Zanetti 4, 0575 844647, www.pecoranera.it, closed Thur, average €20), near Porta San Giovanni. Six kilometres (3.5 miles) west of town, the medieval **Castello di Gargonza** (0575 847021, www.gargonza.it, average €101-€171) has several furnished mini-apartments with modern facilities.

Lucignano

Tiny Lucignano has a curious spiral layout: walk round and up, and you find yourself at the steps of the church of the **Collegiata di San Michele**. Behind it is the 13th-century church of **San Francesco**, barn-like in its simplicity.

Inside the Palazzo Comunale, the **Museo Civico** (Piazza del Tribunale 22, 0575 838001, closed Mon & Wed, admission €3) exhibits Lucignano's symbol, the *Albero di San Francesco*, a late Gothic reliquary representing a plant-like cross, along with panels by Signorelli and a Bartolo di Fredi triptych.

Where to eat

Lucignano has two good restaurants: **Il Goccino** (Via G Matteotti 90, 0575 836707, closed Mon in winter, average €25), which has a good wine list and space for eating outside in the summer; and **La Rocca** (Via G Matteotti 15-17, 0575 836775, closed Tue, average €25), which serves an excellent *zuppa dei tarlati* (chicken soup made with wild fennel and served with croutons). Paradise on a plate here is fried eggs topped with plenty of fresh truffle shavings.

Tuscany

Foiano della Chiana

Foiano's buildings and steeples are distinguished by the warm, reddish tones of their *cotto* bricks. Its oval shape centres on Piazza Cavour, dominated by the Palazzo delle Logge, formerly a Medici hunting lodge. Today, it houses the **Fototeca Furio del Furia**, an engrossing display of early 20th-century photographs of rural life in Italy.

Outside the walls is Foiano's other main draw, the neo-classical **Collegiata di San Martino**. It houses an Andrea della Robbia terracotta, the *Madonna of the Girdle*, and Signorelli's last work, *Coronation of the Virgin* (1523), influenced by Piero della Francesca.

Castiglion Fiorentino

Castiglion Fiorentino is a bustling town set against the lower Appennines and overlooked by its impressive Torre del Cassero, situated on the town's highest point. Its Etruscan origins were reaffirmed by recent excavation of the walls, and the crypt of the Chiesa di Sant' Angelo al Cassero. A sanctuary from the fourth century BC has come to light, and it looks as though there is more to come. The **Museo Civico Archeologico** displays artefacts and building materials from this period. Above this is the **Pinacoteca Comunale** (Via del Cassero, 0575 657466, closed Mon, admission €3), with paintings by Giotto's godson and follower, Taddeo Gaddi, and 15th-century artist Bartolomeo della Gatta.

Castiglion Fiorentino's top spot for views over the Valdichiana is the Loggiato Vasariano in the Piazza del Municipio. Past the Loggiato is the **Panificio Magi Alberto** (Via San Michele 48), which continues the local tradition of alluring baked goodies, including a delicious cheesy bread at Easter called *schiaccia di Pasqua*.

Where to stay & eat

For a friendly, reasonably priced hotel in the country, go for **Villa Schiatti** (Località Montecchio 131, 0575 651481, www.villa schiatti.it, doubles €72-€80), which also serves a pleasant evening meal. It has a pool and plenty of room for children to scamper around in. In town you can also refuel at **Da Muzzicone** (Piazza San Francesco 7, 0575 658403, closed Tue, average €30).

Cortona

In recent years Cortona first revelled, then reeled, at the effects of *Under the Tuscan Sun*, Frances Mayes' idealised picture of the good life in Tuscany. Yet even the hordes of Mayes devotees who dutifully troop to this town to see paradise with their own eyes cannot completely obliterate its beauty. Its jumble of irregular, angular buildings, windswept city walls, layered urban development and its strategic position dominating the Valdichiana distinguish it among central Italy's historic cities.

Cortona grew into an important Etruscan outpost around the eighth century BC and then passed under Roman rule. In this respect the **Parco Archeologico di Cortona**, which extends a way out of town and down into the valley around Camucia, is well worth visiting (pick up a copy of *Gli etruschi in terra di Arezzo* from the Arezzo APT). Nor should you miss the **Museo dell'Accademia Etrusca e della Città di Cortona** in the centrally located Palazzo Casali, devoted to some truly magnificent Etruscan items.

Following depredation by the Goths, Cortona thrived as a free community from the 11th century. Sacked by Arezzo in 1258, it bounced back and was taken over and quickly sold by the King of Naples to Florence in 1411. Since then it has prospered, and today it is the quintessential *città d'arte* with plenty going on: from concerts belonging to the Umbria Jazz Festival in late July to the Sagra della Bistecca in mid August, a convivial feast revolving around sizzling cuts of Chianina beef.

To soak in the atmosphere of the place, head for the steps leading up to the crenellated clock tower of the heavy-set **Palazzo Comunale**, overlooking uneven Piazza della Repubblica. Adjacent is Piazza Signorelli, containing the arcaded Teatro Signorelli. Both honour Cortona's foremost offspring, High Renaissance artist Luca Signorelli (c1445-1523).

The Piazza del Duomo opens on to a picture-postcard view of the valley, while opposite the bland Duomo is the **Museo Diocesano** (0575 62830, admission €5), which is home to Fra Angelico's glorious *Annunciation* and works by Signorelli and Pietro Lorenzetti. For more of Cortona's rewarding sights, climb Via Berrettini towards the Fortezza Medicea. Here is the 15th-century church of **San Nicolò**, with its delicate courtyard and baroque-roofed interior containing a Signorelli altarpiece. Also worth the schlep is the **Chiesa di Santa Margherita**, which has vivid ceilings, and the fort above, with views to Lake Trasimeno.

Where to eat

The **Osteria del Teatro** (Via Maffei 2, 0575 630556, closed Wed, average €30) serves good food in an operatic setting. **Preludio** (Via

Guelfa 11, 0575 630104, closed Mon & lunch Nov-May, average €30) serves great gnocchi with chestnuts or porcini mushrooms. **Tonino** (Piazza Garibaldi 1, 0575 630500, closed Mon dinner & all Tue in winter, average €35) is good for *antipasti* and has lovely views over the valley. For the same view but lighter fare (*bruschette* and omelettes), try its outdoor Belvedere terrace. **Trattoria Dardano** (Via Dardano 24, 0575 601944, closed Wed, average €16) is a locals' haunt that serves home cooking. **La Grotta** (Piazzetta Baldelli 3, 0575 630271, closed Tue) serves excellent home-made pasta dishes.

Where to stay

The **Albergo Athens** (Via Sant'Antonio 12, 0575 630508, doubles €23-€41.50) is the only budget option within Cortona's walls, with dorm-like rooms at unbeatable prices. **Hotel Italia** (Via Ghibellina 7, 0575 630254, doubles €65-€98) has the best quality-to-price ratio, offering rooftop views from top-floor rooms and terrace. **Hotel San Luca** (Piazza Garibaldi 1, 0575 630460, www.sanluca cortona.com, doubles €70-€100) is generic and modern, but has spectacular views over the valley. If you're looking for something central and classy, consider the **Hotel San Michele** (Via Guelfa 15, 0575 604348, www.hotelsanmichele.net, doubles €134-€250), which boasts an 18th-century ceiling in the breakfast room.

For a complete spoil-yourself option, book into the four-star **Hotel Villa Marsili** (Via Cesare Battisti 13, 0575 605252, doubles €132-€310), a beautifully restored 18th-century private residence with its own gardens. Alternatively, three kilometres (two miles) from Cortona, **Relais Villa Baldelli** (Località San Pietro a Cegliolo, 0575 612406, www.villabaldelli.it, doubles €220-€330) offers nice rooms in an 18th century residence. **Il Falconiere** is also about the same distance from town (Località San Martino a Bocena, 0575 612679, www.ilfalconiere.com, doubles €260-€560) and has its own restaurant (average €65) that might be expensive, but that does come with a Michelin star attached.

Resources

Tourist information

Cortona
Via Nazionale 42 (0575 630352/www.apt.arezzo.it). **Open** *May-Sept* 9am-1pm, 3-7pm Mon-Sat; 9am-1pm Sun. *Oct-Apr* 9am-1pm, 3-6pm Mon-Sat.

Sansepolcro
Piazza Garibaldi (0575 740536). **Open** 9.30am-1pm, 3.30-6.30pm daily.

Getting There

By bus

LAZZI (055 9199922, www.lazzi.it) has regular buses linking Montevarchi, Terranuova Bracciolini and Loro Ciuffenna with Arezzo. Irregular LFI buses (0575 39881) serve Camaldoli and Chiusi Verna from Bibbiena station. They run more regular buses between Cortona (from Piazzale Garibaldi) and Arezzo, which also stop in Castiglion Fiorentino. **SITA** (0575 74361, www.sita-on-line.it) runs buses between Arezzo and Sansepolcro (journey time 1hr) that also stop in Anghiari (45mins) and, sometimes, in Monterchi.

By car

There are several driving routes through the Valdarno, including the Florence-Rome *autostrada* (A1), the slower A69, which runs through San Giovanni and Montevarchi and on to Arezzo, or the Settemponti route through the country. By car is the best way to see the Casentino, and there are thrilling mountain roads to explore, but progress is slow, and snow can be a problem between October and April. The region's main arteries are the SS70 and SS71.

To explore the Valtiberina, take the SS73 out of Arezzo, heading north-east towards Sansepolcro. Monterchi and, further on, Anghiari are signposted off this road, a few kilometres before Sansepolcro. The A1 *autostrada* passes right through the Valdichiana, with exits for Monte San Savino and Valdichiana (for Cortona, off the main SS75 to Perugia). From Arezzo, Castiglion Fiorentino and Cortona are reached via the SS71.

By train

Local trains on the Florence–Arezzo line stop at Montevarchi (45mins from Florence, 25mins from Arezzo). Timetable information for this and other routes is available by calling 892021 or by logging on to www.trenitalia.it.

A tiny train line run by **La Ferroviaria Italiana** (LFI) links Pratovecchio (journey time 1hr), Poppi (40mins) and Bibbiena (30mins) to Arezzo, with departures roughly every hour during the day.

Cortona has two train stations: Camucia-Cortona, 5km (3 miles) away, and Terontola-Cortona, 11km (7 miles) from town. Castiglion Fiorentino is on the same line. Trains from Arezzo take 15mins to Castiglion, 22mins to Camucia and 27mins to Terontola. Slow trains between Florence (journey time to Terontola 90mins) and Rome (Terontola 80mins) also pass through all three stations. A regular bus service links Cortona with its two stations.

Tuscany

Southern Tuscany

Escape the crowds in this relatively undiscovered corner of Italy.

Monte Argentario. *See p277.*

Southern Tuscany lacks both the reputation and the popularity of other parts of the region. Development here has been slow, and the area is still slightly cut off from the rest of Tuscany by a lack of major transport arteries. Sure, the region gets crowded at Easter and in the height of summer, especially at Monte Argentario and on the main two island destinations of Elba and Giglio. But at other times it's idyllic, whether your interest lies in trekking through extraordinary wildlife reserves, visiting cosy hill towns or exploring centuries-old Etruscan relics.

Grosseto Province & the Maremma

The coastal and inland area south of Piombino, stretching down to the Tuscan border with Lazio, is known as the **Maremma** (as distinct from the Pisan Maremma; *see p212*). While the island of Elba has been a major destination for

decades, and the coastal area gets its hordes in July and August, much of mainland southern Tuscany is off the tourist map. Count your blessings: the countryside is beautiful in the hilly areas a few miles inland, gently bathed in warm coastal light, even in winter, and the area still has the sort of cosy charm that's disappeared elsewhere.

It's not perfect, mind. Grosseto, the provincial capital, has a historic centre of some charm, but pales into ugly sister mode when compared with other Tuscan cities. Moreover, industry is rare in southern Tuscany, where agriculture embraces viticulture and olive cultivation, animal husbandry and arable farming. For local people, wealth has been harder to come by.

Though the small hilltop towns and villages are not perceived as having the architectural allure of more famous Tuscan destinations, many are pretty and a few truly stunning. The Maremma also has an abundance of lovely landscape, much of it good for trekking: in particular, visit the national Parco Naturale della Maremma, nature reserves and extensive Etruscan necropolises.

Grosseto

The largest Tuscan town south of Siena, Grosseto has had to contend with a lot over the centuries. Though it gained city status in 1138, the surrounding area was so poor and ridden with malaria that the population never thrived. The city was eventually annexed by Siena in 1336, and became part of the Grand Duchy of Tuscany in 1559. Apart from fortifying their new outpost, the Medici clearly didn't feel that Grosseto had much scope, and by 1745 the population has dwindled to a mere 648.

Things didn't pick up until the Lorraine Grand Dukes began reclaiming the surrounding marshlands in the 18th and 19th centuries, before further agricultural improvements came under the Fascist regime in the 1920s and '30s. The strips of pinewood that stretch north and south along the coast are largely the product of this period. Planted to curb the encroaching sea, they also ensured salt water didn't permeate areas now devoted to fish farming.

Although Grosseto got a pasting in World War II, a central area, enclosed by high walls, was partially spared; it's now a nice place for a stroll. Other attractions include the **Museo Archeologico** (Piazza Baccarini 3, 0564 488750, closed Mon), which describes the evolution of the local topography and the importance of Etruscan settlements in the area.

The sea reached further inland in ancient times, almost as far as **Roselle**. This site, a major Etruscan settlement that was later taken over by the Romans, is on a panoramic hilltop about eight kilometres (five miles) east of Grosseto, just off the SS223. Open daily, it gives visitors a real feeling for how an important civilisation could simply be incorporated into a new dominant culture, while also embodying the sense of contemplative mystery that's often a feature of Etruscan sites. Many of the objects found there and at Populonia are now displayed in the Museo Archeologico.

Where to stay & eat

In the pedestrianised part of town, the **Bastiani Grand Hotel** (Piazza Giberti 64, 0564 20047, €146 doubles) is pleasant and slightly old-fashioned. Not far away is one of the town's best eating options: **La Bottega del Vino** (Via Garibaldi 42, 0564 200100, closed lunch in Aug & all Mon, average €25), which has interesting menus, a good wine list and outdoor tables. In the outskirts, towards the airport, sits **Il Pescatore**, a good fish eaterie in an unlikely location (Via Orcagna 62-63, 0564 491035, closed Sun & 1st 2wks Jan & Sept, average €25).

Massa Marittima

Massa dominates the high southern ranges of the Colline Metallifere, a rich source of the iron, copper and other minerals that contributed to its flourishing economy in the Middle Ages. However, when it lost its status as an independent city state and, in 1337, was taken over by Siena, its prosperity began to decline. Half a millennium of neglect followed the plague years of 1348-50, until a small-scale return to mining, along with the draining of the surrounding marshes, turned the tide in the middle of the 19th century. Today Massa has preserved one of the most uniform examples of 13th-century town planning in Tuscany. The **Duomo** harmoniously blends Romanesque and Gothic details and its bare stone interior includes a baptistery, famous for its 13th-century bas-reliefs by Giroldo da Como.

The fountain was the hub of town life in the second half of the 13th century, and it was the saviour of the community when war and extensive surrounding social chaos forced the townsfolk to hole up for extended periods. Named **Le Fonti dell'Abbondanza** ('fountains of abundance'), its basins aren't actually visible, but they are restored and fully functional. Among the town's other diversions

A very big house in the country

Castello di Vicarello.

Luxury is the byword for two new (or, rather old-turned-new) getaways near the Maremma coast. The new co-venture of Alain Ducasse – the first restaurateur in 60 years to hold six Michelin stars at one time – is **L'Andana**, set in 500 hectares of countryside at Tenuta La Badiola, just inland from Castiglione della Pescaia. The former home of Leopold II has been converted into a hotel with 33 stylish rooms and suites, while the estate covers 30 hectares of vineyards and 50 hectares of olive trees. Foodies will be in their element: the menus, overseen by Ducasse himself, feature wines and olive oils produced on the estate, plus other local ingredients. And you can opt into one of the regular cookery classes. There's an outdoor pool and jacuzzi, while a 'gem of a spa' is promised for spring 2006, and a golf course later in the year. Bike rental is also available, plus horse ridding, hiking, birdwatching and other activities.

Further inland to the southeast, on the way to Montalcino, **Castello di Vicarello** is a 12th-century castle on a rocky spur with views down towards the sea. Owners Aurora and Carlo Baccheschi Berti have lovingly restored the castle, using natural materials such as antique stone and terracotta, and furnished with design pieces collected from years of living in the Far East. The result is a peaceful haven surrounded by gardens planted with roses, lavender, jasmine and rosemary (plus the requisite vineyards and olive groves). Guests can stay in one of four suites, or a self-contained villa, while, relaxation-wise, there are two pools (one an infinity pool). All suites have kitchenettes, lunch and dinner can be served on request, and cookery classes are available, using produce from the estate.

L'Andana
Tenuta La Badiola, Località Badiola Castiglione della Pescaia (0564 944800/ fax 0564 944577/www.andana.it).
Rates €320-€615 double; €505-€1,220 suite. **Credit** AmEx, DC, MC, V.

Castello di Vicarello
Poggi del Sasso (0564 990718/www. vicarello.it). **Rates** €270-€380 suite; €500 2-person villa; €700 4-person villa. **Credit** AmEx, DC, MC, V.

L'Andana.

Tuscany

are the **Museo Civico Archeologico** in the 13th-century Palazzo del Podestà on Piazza Garibaldi (0566 902289, closed Mon, admission €3), which has an Etruscan collection and a marvellous 1330 *Maestà* by Ambrogio Lorenzetti, while up Via Moncini is the Città Nuova ('New Town', built in the 14th century). There's a fine Sienese arch here: climb it for a few euros, or walk around the side (for free) in order to take in equally excellent views over the town and countryside.

Another draw is the **Balestro del Girifalco** festival on the fourth Sunday in May: the feast day of San Bernardino of Siena, who was born here. The Renaissance costumes are dazzling, the *sbandieratori* (flag-throwers) are faultless and the final contest, when teams from the town's three *terzieri* attempt to shoot down a mechanical falcon with their crossbows, is fascinating. The town stages concerts in the square in August and a week-long photography festival in July (www.toscanafotofestival.it).

Where to stay & eat

If you fancy staying the night, opt for the three-star **Sole** (Corso Libertà 43, 0566 901971, closed mid Jan-mid Feb, doubles €85), in an old palazzo.

Food-wise, good local dishes such as stewed wild boar with black olives can be had at **Enoteca Grassini** (Via della Libertà 1, 0566 940149, closed Tue & Jan-mid Mar, average €17). Even more atmospheric is **Da Tronca** (Vicolo Porte 5, 0566 901991, closed lunch, all day Wed & mid Dec-mid Mar, average €20), a nearby *osteria* that serves distinctive regional fare. For more inventive cuisine, drive a couple of kilometres north to Ghirlanda to **Bracali** (Via di Perolla 2, 0566 902318, closed all Mon, Tue & lunch Wed, Thur, average €90).

Wine-lovers are in luck: the relatively new Monteregio di Massa Marittima DOC produces some interesting wines, with Morisfarms one of the best producers (call 0566 919135 for tours).

Saturnia & Montemerano

According to legend, Saturn once sent down a thunderbolt that split open the earth, in order to punish those who thought only of war. Steamy water poured forth from the gash; earthlings found solace in it and became calm. That was a while ago; these days, the road to **Saturnia** is well worn by tourists seeking regeneration in the small, sulphurous tributary of the Albenga. The **Hotel Terme** (*see below*) offers mud treatments and massages, as well as its own mineral-rich pool. For a cheaper choice, head down the road and bathe for free in the

pretty **Cascate del Gorello** falls and pools, where the rocks are stained green. It can get crowded, but on a warm, clear and quiet night, it's magical.

Six kilometres (four miles) away sits **Montemerano**, a well-preserved hillside town with a medieval castle. In recent years this has become a favourite spot for those who like the coastal light but not the masses of tourists.

Where to stay & eat

Saturnia's **Hotel Terme** (0564 601061, www.termedisaturnia.it, €360 double) is pretty pricey, but is fitted out with a gym, a golf driving range and tennis courts to go with the mineral-rich pool.

For lunch or dinner, Saturnia's **Bacco e Cerere** (Via Mazzini 4, 0564 601235, closed Wed & 2wks Jan or Feb, average €40) is great for meats. For something cheaper, head up the road to Semproniano, another hill town with four eateries of its own. If you've some cash to splash, make for Montemerano to dine at the renowned **Da Caino** (Via Canonica 4, 0564 602817, closed all day Wed, lunch Thur & mid Jan-mid Feb, average €90), which also has three guestrooms. Otherwise there's **Passaparola nell' Antico Frantoio** (Via delle Mura 21, 0564 602835, closed Thur, 2wks July & 2wks Feb, average €27).

Pitigliano

Perched high on a rocky outcrop, Pitigliano appears to grow from the sheer golden tuff limestone cliffs that fall away on all sides. It's an awesome sight of artefact marrying with nature. The tuff stone from which the town is built is an ideal construction material: strong yet light, and relatively easy to hew.

The dramatic drop into the valley below is accentuated by an immense aqueduct, built in 1545, that connects the lower and upper parts of town. The 1527 church of **Madonna delle Grazie**, on an opposite hill as you approach, provides a vantage point over the town and countryside. During the Middle Ages, Pitigliano was one of the foremost centres of power of the Aldobrandeschi family, who were succeeded by the Orsinis in the 14th century. Both coats of arms are still on display in the Orsini family's palace courtyard on Piazza Orsini.

The Jewish community that was attracted here by increasing Medici tolerance in the 16th century either left or was forced out during World War II. All that's left today is the small **Museo Ebraico**, housed in the former synagogue in Via Zuccarelli (0564 616006, closed Sat, admission €2.50), and a *pasticceria*

This accounts for the development of Sovana, which continued to grow and prosper in Roman times and during the Middle Ages. Today it's a charming little town in which to stay when visiting the wonderfully rich Etruscan necropolises in the immediate vicinity. There's a small museum of local history in the 13th-century **Palazzo Pretorio** (0564 633023, closed Mon, admission €2.50), next door to the arched Loggetta del Capitano; nearby is the church of **Santa Maria** (0564 616532), with its magnificent pre-Romanesque *ciborium*.

Where to stay & eat

Albergo Scilla (Via R Siviero 1-3, 0564 616531, doubles €92) has eight nice, fairly priced rooms and a restaurant, the excellent **Ristorante dei Merli** (0564 616531, closed Tue; average €25), so you can opt for half board. Otherwise, it's worth considering the **Sovana Hotel & Resort** (Via del Duomo 66, 0564 617030, doubles €150), which also owns the fine **La Taverna Etrusca** (Piazza del Pretorio 16, 0564 616183, closed Wed, Jan & Feb, average €25).

Sorano

This village of dark, greyish tufa, perched high above the Lente river as you head north-east from Sovana towards the Lazio border, is a dizzying sight. Sorano was a defence post under the Orsini empire, but at times its geology proved more dangerous than its rampaging enemies, and a series of landslides encouraged a slow but steady exodus. Masso Leopoldino, a giant terraced tufa cliff, peers down on the town.

If you want to stay in a medieval Tuscan fortress, **Della Fortezza** (Piazza Cairoli, 0564 632010, closed Jan & Feb, doubles €100-€130) is comfortable and has amazing views.

Parco Naturale della Maremma

This beautiful, WWF-protected nature reserve, which encompasses the Monti dell'Uccellina, has some great hikes. Birds, both migratory and resident, thrive here: ospreys, falcons, kingfishers, herons and the rare Knight of Italy can all be spotted. The terrain ranges from the mudflats and umbrella pines of the estuary to the untouched woodland of the hills.

The visitors' centre (Via Bersagliere 7-9, 0564 407098, closed afternoons Nov-Apr) has stacks of helpful information, a long list of suggested trails, and details of activities such as canoeing and horse riding. One attraction is the wild and

around the corner, which still makes a local Jewish pastry called *sfratti* ('the evicted'). Follow the delicious waft of baking from down the passageway. Elsewhere, the **Museo Civico Archeologico** (Piazza Orsini, 0564 614067, closed Mon, admission €2.50) has a small but well-presented collection of Etruscan artefacts.

Where to eat

Tucked away in an alleyway is the homely and award-winning **Il Tufo Allegro** (*see p40* **Want food, will travel**). If you can't get in, try a local trattoria such as **Il Grillo** (Via Cavour 18, 0564 615202, closed Tue & July, average €17), **La Chiave del Paradiso** (Via Vignoli 209, 0564 616823, closed Mon & mid Jan-late Feb, average €14) or **Dell'Orso** (Piazza San Gregorio VII 14-15, 0564 614273, closed Thur in winter & mid Jan to mid Feb, average €18).

Sovana

The Etruscans controlled the middle reaches of the Fiora river between the 7th and the 6th centuries BC, and thus also controlled the main communications route between the coast and the mineral rich areas of Monte Amiata (*see p236*).

natural beach at **Marina di Alberese**, the best in mainland southern Tuscany. A train service runs from Grosseto to Marina di Alberese; from the station, take a bus or walk the four kilometres (2.5 miles) to the entrance. The famous *butteri* (Maremma cowboys) put on a show in Alberese on 1 May and 15 August.

The park is open every day from 9am until one hour before sunset. Admission is €5.50-€8. Note that cars aren't allowed in the park: there's a large car park opposite the visitors' centre in Alberese, next to the main entrance.

Where to stay & eat

If you'd like to stay in the park, there are two lodges, which must be booked via the **Poiana Viaggi** travel agent on 0564 412000. Otherwise, head inland to the charming town of Magliano in Toscana to the **Locanda delle Mura** (Piazza Marconi 5, 0564 593057, doubles €80-€100), a classy B&B, or to quiet Talamone, near the southern entrance to the park. Options here include **Hotel Capo d'Uomo** (Via Cala di Forno, 0564 887077, closed Nov-Mar, doubles €110-€130), a three-star hotel overlooking the bay, and **Telamonio** (Piazza Garibaldi 4, 0564 887008, closed Oct-Mar, doubles €90-€130), in the town itself.

Down in Alberese, **Mancini & Caoduro** (Via del Fante 24, 0564 407137, closed Tue & Nov-Feb, average €17) serves simple pastas, pizzas and cold meats. At Alberese Scalo, **La Nuova Dispensa** (Via Aurelia Vecchia 11, 0564 407321, closed Tue in winter & 2wks Jan, average €18) serves local fare such as wild boar *cacciatora* ('hunter style', with tomatoes, herbs, garlic and wine). Booking is advised. **Da Remo** in Santa Maria di Rispecia (Respecsia Stazione 5-7, 0564 405014, closed Wed & late Oct-late Nov, average €30) isn't much to look at, but locals flock here for the quality of the fish. If you're heading back up to Magliano, then go for **Da Sandra** (Via Garibaldi 20, 0564 592196, closed Mon & Feb, average €25), whose wine list features the best of the local Morellino di Scanscano DOC labels. In Talamone, **La Buca di Nonno Ghigo** (Via Porta Garibaldi 1, 0564 887067, closed Mon in winter & Nov, average €25) occupies a cute spot down a tiny street next to the city walls and offers all manner of wonderful fresh seafood.

Orbetello

In the middle of the most central of the three isthmuses that connect Monte Argentario to the mainland, Orbetello has remnants of Spanish fortifications dating from the 16th and 17th centuries, when it was the capital of the Stato dei Presidi, a Spanish enclave on the Tuscan coast. There's a small antiquarium with some rather uninspiring Etruscan and Roman exhibits, and the cathedral has a Gothic façade, but Orbetello is more about atmosphere than sightseeing.

Where to stay & eat

Join the evening *struscio* (a promenade up Corso Italia) before dining on a plate of eels fished from the lagoon at one of the town's simple trattorie. **Osteria del Lupacante** (Corso Italia 103, 0564 867618, closed Tue in winter, average €25) also serves a variety of good spaghetti and shellfish dishes. Another top choice for sea-fresh fish is **I Pescatori** (Via Leopardi 9, 0564 860611, closed Mon-Wed in winter & Mon-Sat lunch in winter, average €20). The best of the town's least expensive hotels is **Piccolo Parigi** (Corso Italia 169, 0564 867233, doubles €68).

Ansedonia

Not much is left that reflects Ansedonia's ancient history, though some Roman ruins from 170 BC overlook the villas with flower-draped walls, and the nearby **Museo di Cosa** (Via delle Ginestre 35, 0564 881421, admission €2) has artefacts from the area.

Daily trains from Grosseto stop at Capalbio station, from where it's three kilometres (two miles) to the beach alongside the picturesque Lago di Burano lagoon (now a WWF reserve). The coastline stretching southwards from Ansedonia offers 18 kilometres (11 miles) of beach, but there's an industrial plant looming through the haze at the far south end, so you're better off on the beaches north of Argentario or heading straight for an island.

Monte Argentario

A mountain rising abruptly from the sea, Monte Argentario is the Tuscan coast at its most rugged. If it looks as though it should be an island, that's because it was – until the 18th century, when the two long outer sand-spits created by the action of the tides finally reached the mainland.

On the south-east corner of Argentario lies the exclusive town of **Porto Ercole**, where Caravaggio died drunk on the beach in 1610. Easter and August holidays see this small bay full to the gills of revellers. **Porto Santo Stefano** is another atmospheric port – you'll almost certainly find fishermen mending nets on the quay – although the vibe is more upmarket during the holidays when the

Tuscany

yachting crowd arrives. You can catch a ferry for the Isola del Giglio here (*see p279*). The tourist office is at Corso Umberto 55A (0564 814208, closed Sun).

Two nice beaches make up the sand-spits that join Monte Argentario to the mainland. To the north, access to **La Giannella** is from the main Talamone-Argentario road (look for any of the little pathways through the pines), while to the south, **La Feniglia** is accessible by parking at the western end; the further you walk, the less crowded it is. Hire a bicycle and cycle through the protected pine woods behind La Feniglia if you fancy a spot of adventure. Both beaches have the odd paid *bagno*, but the rest is free.

Where to stay & eat

In Porto Ercole, the best views are available at the three-star **Don Pedro** (Via Panoramica 7, 0564 833914, closed Oct-Mar, doubles €100-€145), which overlooks the harbour. The charismatic two-star **Hotel Marina** (Lungomare Andrea Doria 23, 0564 833055, doubles €104) is more central; some rooms have balconies with attractive harbour views. Three kilometres (two miles) out of town, **Il Pellicano** (Sbarcatello village, 0564 8581111, closed Nov-Mar, doubles €300-€776) enjoys a private rocky beach and fabulous terraces with sea vistas. There are several seafood restaurants on Porto Ercole harbour, plus **La Lanterna** pizzeria (Lungomare Doria 19, 0564 833064, closed Mon & Jan, average €20). But the best place to eat fish in town has to be the **Osteria dei Nobili Santi** (*see p40* **Want food, will travel**).

It's certainly worth pausing for a meal in Porto San Stefano: particularly at **Dal Greco** (Via del Molo 1-2, 0564 814885, closed Tue & Nov or Jan, average €45), a seafood restaurant with a terrace on the harbour. A little cheaper is **Il Moletto di Amato & Figli** (Via del Molo, 0564 813636, closed Wed & mid Jan-Feb, average €26), in a fantastic location on the end of the quay. A short walk away but removed from the hurly burly is **Da Orlando** (Via Breschi 3, 0564 812788, closed Wed, Nov & Feb, and Mon-Fri in winter, average €35), whose pretty terrace has a nice sea view. The seafront is lined with a string of bars, including the overwhelmingly fashionable **Il Buco** (Lungomare dei Navigatori 2, 0564 818243, closed Tue in winter).

Capalbio

Close to the Lazio border, Capalbio is a magnet for Rome's poets, politicians and musicians (especially during August's Grey Cat Jazz

Festival; *see p263* **And the beat goes on**). The main attraction for tourists is **Il Giardino dei Tarocchi** (0564 895122, closed late Oct-mid May, admission €6.20-€10.50), an amazing walled garden to the south-east of the town. Founded in 1976 by Niki de Saint Phalle, it contains more than 20 huge sculptures that represent the main characters from the tarot deck. Some of the sculptures house four-storey buildings, which you can enter.

Where to stay & eat

Trattoria La Torre da Carla (Via Vittorio Emanuele 33, 0564 896070, closed Mon-Fri in winter & all Thur, average €26) serves robust Tuscan cuisine.

Hotel Valle del Buttero (Via Silone 21, 0564 896097, doubles €45-€130) is a large three-star hotel. **Trattoria da Maria** (Via Comunale 3, 0564 896014, closed Tue spring-autumn, early Jan-early Feb, average €35) also rents double rooms (€52); call in advance. **Ghiaccio Bosco** (Via della Sgrilla 4, 0564 896539, doubles €75-€105) is a nice *agriturismo* with 15 pleasant rooms and a pool.

Grosseto Agenzia Promozione Turismo (APT), Viale Monterosa 206 (0564 462611). **Open** 8.30am-6.30pm Mon-Fri; 8.30am-1.30pm Sat.
Massa Marittima *Ufficio Turistico, Via Todini 3 (0566 904756).* **Open** *Summer* 9.30am-12.30pm, 3-7pm Mon-Sat; 10am-1pm, 4-7pm Sun. *Winter* 9.30am-12.30pm, 3-6pm Mon-Sat; 10am-1pm Sun.
Pitigliano *Ufficio Turistico, Piazza Garibaldi 51 (0564 617111).* **Open** 10.20am-1pm, 3-7pm Tue-Sun.
Saturnia *Consorzio L'Altra Maremma, Piazza Vittorio Veneto 8 (0564 601280/www.laltra maremma.it).* **Open** *Summer* 10.20am-1pm, 3-7pm Mon-Sat. *Winter* 10.20am-1pm, 2-6pm Mon-Sat.

Getting there & around

By bus

There are about 10 buses a day connecting Grosseto and Siena (journey time 90mins). Buses leave from in front of Grosseto's train station. For further information on buses serving regional towns such as Piombino and Pitigliano call **Rama** on 0564 25215.

By car

The main coast road (E80/SS1) links Grosseto with Livorno to the north and the Maremma to the south. The SS223, currently being widened, is the main route down from Siena. The region's most scenic road is the SS74, which branches inland off the SS1, north of Orbetello, and winds towards Manciano and Pitigliano.

Set sail from – or to – the sweet island village of **Giglio Porto**.

By train

Grosseto is on the main train line between Rome and Pisa (90mins from Rome, 80mins from Pisa). Trains on this line also stop at Capalbio and Orbetello (for Monte Argentario) to the south, and San Vincenzo and Cecina to the north. A local train links Grosseto with Siena (2hrs). For national train information, call 892021 or go to www.trenitalia.it.

The Islands

The Tuscan Islands can be a welcome antidote to the area's largely unremarkable coast, particularly tiny, tranquil Isola del Giglio west of Orbetello. Timing is everything, however. Both Elba and Giglio get crowded during Easter, July and August, and their idyllic sands and scenery are best enjoyed in May, June and September. The islands and the sea in which they're set make up the **Parco Nazionale Arcipelago Toscano**, Europe's biggest protected marine park. For information, call 0565 919411 or visit www.islepark.it.

Isola del Giglio

A steep and winding road connects the three villages on this beautiful little island: **Giglio Porto**, where the ferry docks; **Campese**, on the other side; and **Giglio Castello**, on the ridge between the two, with its medieval walls and steep narrow lanes. The main beach is at Campese, but there are other, smaller beaches dotted around elsewhere.

Aside from loafing around on the beach, the two great pleasures here are exploring the virtually uninhabited south and indulging yourself at one of the many good restaurants on the atmospheric quayside in Porto. Most of the hotels on the island are in Porto; there are also a number of rooms to let in local homes.

Where to stay, eat & drink

Overlooking Giglio Porto, the three-star **Castello Monticello** (Via Provinciale, 0564 809252, closed Oct-Mar, doubles €80-€130) occupies a crenellated folly. The **B&B Airone** (Contrada S Maria 12, 0564 806076, doubles €30-€70) has good views. For more sun and sea, head to **Pardini's Hermitage** (Cala degli Alberi, 0564 809034, closed Nov-Mar, doubles €200-€350 full board) in a secluded cove accessible only by foot or by boat (staff will fetch you).

While on the beach in Campese, you can have anything 'from a cappuccino to a lobster' at local stalwart **Tony's** (Via della Torre 13, 0564 806453, closed Nov, €24), on the north end of the beach below the tower.

Tuscany

Resources

Tourist Information

Via Provinciale 9 (0564 809400/www.isoladelgiglio ufficioturistico.com). **Open** 9am-12.30pm, 4-6pm daily. Closed Nov-Easter.

Elba

Part of the Tuscan archipelago, Elba is Italy's third largest island, with 142 kilometres (88 miles) of coastline. Due to its wealth of mineral deposits, it was inhabited in prehistoric times, and later by the Greeks and the Etruscans. The **Museo dei Minerali Elbani** at Rio Marina (Via Magenta 26, 0565 962088, www.parco minelba.it, closed Mon & Nov-Feb, admission €2.50) provides an interesting alternative to lolling on the beach, where things can get a bit crowded at Easter and in the height of summer. The resident population of 30,000 swells to almost a million during the peak season; go in May or late September if you want to catch the island at its best.

Portoferraio is the island's capital and the focus of Napoleonic interest. The **Palazzo dei Mulini**, Napoleon's town residence, is worth a visit for its views and Empire-style furnishings, incongruous in this Mediterranean setting. His summer retreat, the neo-classical **Villa Napoleonica** di San Martino, is roughly six kilometres (four miles) south-west of town, off the road for Marciana.

Choosing between Elba's many village resorts can be tricky. Tiny **Viticcio** overlooks a pretty, secluded bay with some rock and shingle; **Biodola** has a terrific beach, but is dominated by large hotels and the inevitable parasols; **Poggio** has a good portion of free beach but can get very busy; while **Marciana Marina** is an attractive port town.

Up the hill, **Marciana** itself is one of two starting points for an ascent of Monte Capanne. The village of **Sant' Andrea** is relatively quiet and removed, although the beach is pretty tiny. The national park in the north-west is a walker's paradise. Start from Marciana, Poggio or Sant' Andrea if you want to hike around the park and the relatively unexplored western part of the island. The tourist office has a good booklet with a list of trails.

Many of the villages on the south and south-western side of the island have good beaches ranging from rocks and shingle to smooth sand. The pick of the beaches is **Fetovaia**, in a stunning sandy cove only partly devoured by the dreaded parasols. With all the clear water, diving is a popular pursuit around here, and there are numerous centres to satisfy underwater urges.

Where to stay, eat & drink

Rendez-Vous, on Marciana Marina's buzzing Piazza della Vittoria (No.1, 0565 99251, closed Wed in winter, early Nov-early Dec & early Jan-early Mar, average €31) does good grilled fish and steak. In the attractive hill town of Poggio sits **Publius** (Piazza del Castagneto 11, 0565 99208, closed Mon in winter & Jan-Feb, average €25), which has fantastic views, the best cellar on the island and a menu that isn't limited to the usual fish dishes. Nearby is **Luigi** (Località Lavacchio, 0565 99413, closed all Tue & Mon mid June-Aug & Nov-Apr; average €20), offering fresh rustic dishes. In the upmarket port town of Porto Azzurro you'll find **La Lanterna** (Via Vitaliani 5, Porto Azzurro, 0565 958394, closed Mon & Dec-Jan, average €22) and **Delfino Verde** (0565 95197, closed Wed & Nov-Mar, average €18), two of the most renowned seafood restaurants around.

Accommodation-wise, **Casa Lupi**, on the outskirts of Marciana Marina (Ontanelli village, 0565 99143, closed Jan & Feb, doubles €26-€70), is one of the best one-star hotels on Elba. In Viticcio, stay at two-star **Scoglio Bianco** (0565 939036, closed Oct-Easter, doubles €42-€170 half board). More upmarket, in Fetovaia, three-star **Lo Scirocco** is clean, smart and well located (0565 988033, closed Oct-Mar, doubles €79-€120); **Anna** also offers three-star facilities (0565 988032, doubles €58-€110).

Ottone is home to the huge **Rosselba le Palme** (0565 933101, www.rosselbalepalme.it, bungalows €125, tents €13), one of the best camping and bungalow sites on Elba, and **Villa Ottone** (0565 933042, doubles €87-€202 half board per person), a swish hotel with a restaurant open only to hotel guests; both have access to the greyish sandy beach. Alternatively, on the *agriturismo* tip, the **Monte Fabbrello** winery (Schiopparello village, 0565 933324) has rooms at €45-€60.

Resources

Tourist information

Azienda Promozione Turismo Elba, Calata Italia 43, Portoferraio (0565 914671/www.aptelba.it). **Open** 8am-8pm Mon-Sat; 9.30am-12.30pm, 3.30-6.30pm Sun.

Getting there

By boat

Toremar (0564 810803, www.toremar.it) has services from Piombino (*see p216*) to Elba and from Porto San Stefano to Giglio, while **Mareggiglio** (0564 812920, www.mareggiglio.it) runs just the latter service. Ticket outlets can be found at the port.

Directory

Features

Directory

Getting Around

Arriving & leaving

By air

The nearest airport is **Amerigo Vespucci Airport**, west of the city centre at Peretola. However, it only hosts a couple of flights a day to and from London Gatwick. A better bet is Pisa's **Galileo Galilei Airport**, which has more frequent flights to and from the UK. Third choice is Bologna's **Guglielmo Marconi Airport**: it's further, but has good links to the UK. Don't be tempted by Easyjet's flights to Bologna (Forli): they're pretty inconvenient.

Aeroporto di Firenze (Amerigo Vespucci)

055 30615/flight information 055 3061702//www.aeroporto.firenze.it.
About 5km (3 miles) west of central Florence, Amerigo Vespucci is linked to the city by the **Volainbus**, a bus service that runs half-hourly 6am-11.30pm, costs €4 and stops in the SITA station at Via Santa Caterina da Siena 15 (*see p283*). Buy tickets on the bus. A taxi to central Florence costs about €16 (extra for luggage, at night and on public holidays) and will take about 20 minutes.

Pisa International Airport (Galileo Galilei)

050 849111/flight information 050 849300/www.pisa-airport.com.
The direct train service to Florence's Santa Maria Novella (SMN) station from Pisa Aeroporto station takes just over an hour. Buy tickets (€5 each way) at the desk to the right of arrivals in the main airport concourse. Trains run roughly every hour 10.30am-5.45pm, with a two-hour gap at lunchtime. There are few trains after 5.45pm, and none after 10pm-ish. The service via Lucca is less frequent and takes twice as long. Trains run later from Pisa Centrale: the last departure is around 11.30pm. A taxi into Pisa from the airport costs about €8, and the CPT bus 5 leaves for Pisa city centre and train station every quarter-hour.

In the other direction, the first train to Pisa airport from Florence's SMN station is at 11am. Trains run almost every hour until 5.05pm; outside these times, take the train for Pisa Centrale. Call 050 849300 for flight information. Trains to Pisa Aeroporto generally leave Pisa Centrale from Platform 14 (via an underpass), though the indicator boards don't always show this.

A coach service from Pisa airport to Florence train station is run by **Terravision** (06 3244152, www.terravision.it). The coach leaves from outside the arrivals area and from the main steps of Florence SMN train station. Tickets can be bought from the kiosk in the airport, from the BOPA agency on Platform 5 of Florence SMN, online or by phone. If you're intending to take the coach in both directions, it's worth buying a return ticket. A single costs €7.50; a return is €13.50. The journey takes 70 minutes, but the coaches don't always leave on time.

To get to Florence by car, take the Firenze-Pisa-Livorno road (there's direct access at the airport), which goes to the west of the city.

Aeroporto di Bologna (Guglielmo Marconi)

051 6479615/ www.bologna-airport.it.
An airport bus stops outside terminal A (arrivals) and leaves for Bologna train station every 15 minutes. Tickets cost €4.50 from the machine in the terminal building or on board. The trip takes about 30 minutes. A taxi to the station costs about €15.

From Bologna Centrale, trains to Florence are frequent and take 50-90 minutes; prices vary (tell the vendor which train you intend to catch). The fastest and dearest trains are the Eurostars, which run frequently 6.30am-9.45pm daily (7.15am-10.20pm in the other direction). A single ticket is €13.17. Reservations are always required: trains are often sold out at weekends and during rush hour. The Intercities are less regular and cost €10.75.

If you hire a car, the trip to Florence takes about 90 minutes, south on the busy A1 motorway.

Major airlines

Alitalia *055 27881/bookings 848 865642/www.alitalia.it.*
British Airways *199 712266/ 050 501838 (Pisa)/www.british airways.com.*

Easyjet *848 887766/ www.easyjet.co.uk.*
Meridiana *055 2302334/ information & bookings 199 111333/www.meridiana.it.*
Ryanair *050 503770/ www.ryanair.com.*

By rail

Train tickets can be bought from the ticket desks or cash-only vending machines in the station, from **Ticket Point** (*see p283*), from www.trenitalia.com, or from travel agents displaying the **FS** (Ferrovie dello Stato, state railways) logo.

Before boarding any train, stamp (*convalidare*) your ticket and any supplements in the yellow machines at the head of the platforms. Failure to do this will result in a €40 fine payable on the train, unless you go immediately to the train guard and ask him to validate your ticket.

Taxis serve Florence's main **Santa Maria Novella** station on a 24-hour basis; many city buses also stop there. It's a 5-10 minute walk into central Florence. Trains arriving at night go to **Campo di Marte** station to the north-east of the city, where buses 67 and 70 also stop. Note that train strikes are still fairly common.

Details on train services in Italy can be obtained by calling the central information line on 892021 (7.45am-5.15pm daily; some English is spoken) or visiting www.trenitalia.com. Information on disabled access is available at the disabled assistance desk on platform 5 at Santa Maria Novella or on 055 2352275. Both are open 7am-9pm daily; English spoken.

Campo di Marte

Via Mannelli, Outside the City Gates (055 2354136/disabled assistance 055 2352275). Bus 12, 70 (night).
Florence's main station when SMN is closed at night. Many long-distance trains stop here. The ticket office is open 6.20am-9pm.

Santa Maria Novella

Piazza della Stazione, Santa Maria Novella (055 2352061). **Open** 4.15am-1.30am daily. *Information office* 7am-9pm daily. *Ticket office* 5.50am-10pm daily. *Map* p318 A2.

By bus

By coach, you'll probably arrive at either the **SITA** or the **LAZZI** coach stations, both near Santa Maria Novella station (see p282).

Ticket Point LAZZI

Piazza Adua, Santa Maria Novella (055 215155/www.lazzi.it). **Open** 9am-7pm Mon-Sat. **Credit** (train tickets only) AmEx, DC, MC, V. **Map** p318 A2.
Tickets for LAZZI, Eurolines coaches and Ferrovie dello Stato.

SITA

Via Santa Caterina da Siena 15, Santa Maria Novella (800 373760). **Map** p318 A2.
See also p284.

Public transport

While the council continues to consider subway and tram systems, currently the city's only public transport is the fairly comprehensive **ATAF** bus network. Strikes are pretty frequent; weekend and evening waiting times can be very long.

ATAF

Piazza della Stazione, opposite north-east exit of train station, Santa Maria Novella (800 424500/www. ataf.net). **Open** 7am-1.15pm, 1.45-7.30pm Mon-Fri; 7.15am-1.15pm Sat. The main ATAF desk has English-speaking staff, but on the phone you may not be so lucky. At this office, you can buy a variety of bus tickets, and also get a booklet with details of major routes and fares.

Fares & tickets

Except on night buses (see below), drivers cannot sell tickets: they must be bought in advance. Tickets are available from the ATAF office in Piazza della Stazione (except for season tickets), a few machines, *tabacchi*, news-stands and bars displaying an orange ATAF sticker. When you board, stamp the ticket in one of the validation machines. If you are using a ticket for two consecutive journeys, stamp it on the first bus only, but keep it till you complete your journey, and if you go beyond the time limit, stamp another.

Plain-clothes inspectors regularly board buses for spot checks; anyone without a valid ticket is fined €40, payable within 30 days at the main information office or in post offices.
60min ticket (*biglietto 60 minuti*) €1; valid for 1hr of travel on all buses.

Multiple ticket (*biglietto multiplo*) €3.90; 4 tickets, each valid for 60mins.
3-hour ticket (*biglietto tre ore*) €1.80.
24-hour ticket (*biglietto ventiquattro ore*) €4.50; one-day pass that must be stamped at start of first journey.
2-day ticket (*biglietto due giorni*) €7.60.
3-day ticket (*biglietto tre giorni*) €9.60.
7-day ticket (*biglietto sette giorni*) €16.
Monthly pass (*abbonamento*) €31; €20.70 students. The ordinary pass can be bought from the ATAF office at Santa Maria Novella station, or from any outlet with an 'Abbonamenti ATAF' sign. For the student pass, go to the Ufficio Abbonamenti in Piazza della Stazione (open 7.15am-1.15pm, 1.45-7.45pm Mon-Fri; 7.15am-1.15pm Sat) or to Student Point in Via San Gallo (055 2261366) with ID and two passport photos.

A 30-day pass for the electric buses A, B and C (*biglietto bussini trenta giorni*) costs €14 (free for Florence residents).

Daytime services

Most ATAF routes run from 5.30am to 9pm with a frequency of 10-30 minutes. Don't take much notice of the timetables posted on many bus stops : they're over-optimistic, to say the least. After 9pm, there are four night services (see below). The orange and white *fermate* (bus stops) list the main stops along the route. Each stop has its name indicated at the top.

Useful tourist routes

7 from Santa Maria Novella station, via Piazza San Marco to Fiesole.
10 to and from Settignano.
12, 13 circular routes via Santa Maria Novella station, Piazza della Libertà, Piazzale Michelangelo and San Miniato.

ATAF also runs a network of electric buses, which covers four central routes: **A**, **B** and **C**, plus a smaller version of the diesel buses, the **D**. Normal bus tickets or season tickets are valid. These routes are detailed in ATAF's booklet and marked on our map (pp318-319).

Because the best way of getting around the city centre is on foot, we only give bus numbers in listings when the venue/sight is located outside the city gates.

Night services

Three bus routes operate until 12.30am/1am (67, 68 and 71). One, the 70, runs all night: it leaves Santa Maria Novella every hour and passes through the centre of town before heading north, calling at Campo di Marte station and returning to Santa Maria Novella. Tickets are available on board for €1.50, 9pm-6am; you'll need the correct change.

Disabled services

Newer buses (grey and green) share routes 7, 12, 13, 23, 27 and 30 with the old ones (all orange), and are fully wheelchair accessible via an electric platform at the rear door. The small bus route D, which goes through the centre of town, is also fully equipped.

Transport in Tuscany

Driving is the best way of getting around Tuscany, both on well-worn paths (Chianti, the south of Siena province) and off the beaten track. That said, progress on winding country roads can be slow and parking in even the bigger towns is often difficult.

But if you don't have a car, there are few parts of Tuscany that you can't reach by bus. Companies such as **Tra-in** (out of Siena) and **LAZZI** (out of Florence) operate around major towns. Even the region's remotest areas have a bus service, though infrequent: in most villages, buses are timed to coincide with the school day, leaving early and returning at lunchtime. If this is likely to be a problem, combining bus and rail services can make things easier. One useful line links Florence with the cities to its west: from Prato to Lucca and continuing on to Viareggio or, alternatively, Pisa. Services run all day. There are also a variety of small local lines.

Information

For train information, see p282.
Major Tuscan bus companies include:
CAP *Via Nazionale 13, Santa Maria Novella, Florence (055 214627/214537).* **Map** p318 A2.
LAZZI *Piazza della Stazione 4, corner of Piazza Adua, Santa Maria Novella, Florence (055 351061/www.lazzi.it).* **Map** p318 A2.
Rama *Via Topazo 12, Grosseto (0564 454169).*

SITA *Via Santa Caterina da Siena 15, Santa Maria Novella, Florence (055 483651/tickets 055 21472/ international 055 294995).* **Map** p318 A2.
Tra-in *Piazza San Domenico, Siena (0577 204111/www.comune.siena.it/ train).*

Taxis

There are scandalously few taxis in Florence: finding a cab can be tough, especially during rush hour, at night or during trade fairs. Licensed cabs are white with yellow graphics, with a code name of a place plus ID number on the door; 'Londra 6', for example. If you have problems, make a note of this code. You can only get a cab at a rank or by phone: they can't be flagged in the street. For important appointments, book by phone several hours ahead, although this isn't necessarily a guarantee of getting a cab, as you may be told the pre-booking 'quota' has been filled and you'll have to call when you need one.

Fares & surcharges

Taxis here are expensive. When the taxi arrives, the meter should read €2.54 during the day, €4.31 on Sundays and public holidays, and €5.49 at night. The fare increases at a rate of 70¢/km. Lone women pay 10% less after 9pm, but only on request.
There is an overall minimum fare of €3.65, easily reached. Phoning for a cab carries with it a surcharge of €1.71; each item of luggage in the boot is extra, and destinations beyond the official city limits (Fiesole, say) cost a lot more. It also costs more to take a taxi from the airport: the meter starts on €4.91 or €7.86 at night. For details, see the tariff card that cabs are required to display.

Phone cabs

When your call is answered, give the address where you want to be picked up, specifying if the street number is *nero* or *rosso* (for an explanation, *see p287*). If a cab is available, you'll be given its code and a time; for example, '*Londra 6 in tre minuti*'. Otherwise, a pre-recorded message or the operator will tell you to call back.

Taxi numbers 055 4390; 055 4798; 055 4242.

Taxi ranks

Ranks are indicated by a blue sign with TAXI written in white, but this is no guarantee that any cars will be waiting, or will arrive during your lifetime. There are ranks in Piazza della Repubblica, Piazza della Stazione, Piazza Santa Maria Novella, Piazza del Duomo, Piazza San Marco, Piazza Santa Croce and Piazza di Santa Trinità.

Driving in Florence

In a word: don't. Though it can be chaotic, Florence is easily walkable and the bus service is a good complement. Aside from the awful traffic, parts of the centre are off limits, parking is difficult and pricey, and the air quality is so poor that when pollution reaches a certain level, cars on diesel or leaded fuel are banned from within a large radius of the city (hire cars and cars with foreign plates are allowed access to hotels). Digital notices above the main roads into town give notice of these bans, which are also announced on local radio and in the local papers.
In addition, there are the permanent Traffic-Free Zones (ZTL). These areas (lettered A-E) include the old city centre and are gradually expanding. Only residents or permit-holders can enter from 7.30am to 7.30pm, Monday to Saturday. This is usually extended in the summer to exclude cars from the centre in the evenings from Thursday or Friday to Sunday.
On top of this, the city is frequently bringing in new restrictions then revoking them, so if you're in any doubt, your best bet is to check in the local press or with the traffic police (*see p289*).

Breakdown services

It's advisable to join a national motoring organisation such as the AA or RAC in Britain or the AAA in the US before taking a car to Italy. They have reciprocal arrangements with the **Automobile Club d'Italia**

(ACI), which will tell you what to do in case of a breakdown and provide general information on driving in Europe. Even for non-members, the ACI is the best number to call if you have any kind of breakdown, though you will, of course, be charged.

Automobile Club d'Italia (ACI)

Viale Amendola 36, Outside the City Gates (055 24861/24hr information in English 166 664477/ 24hr emergencies 803116). Bus 8, 12, 13, 14, 31. **Open** 8.30am-1pm, 3-5.30pm Mon-Fri.
The ACI has English-speaking staff, and charges reasonable rates. Members of associated organisations are entitled to free basic repairs, and to other services at preferential rates.

Car pooling

Anyone here for several month might be interested in a local car pool initiative, introduced in 2005 in a bid to cut traffic. Subscribers pick up a car from one of the car points, and drop it back there or to another car park. Annual membership is €120, plus a €60 enrolment fee; you then pay between €2.05 and €2.60 an hour, plus 24¢-57¢ per kilometre. For details, see www.carsharingfirenze.it (Italian only).

Car pounds

If your car's not where you left it, chances are it's been towed. Phone the municipal police (*vigili urbani*) on 055 32831, or the central car pound (Depositeria Comunale, Via dell'Arcovata 6, open 24hrs daily) on 055 308249. There is an initial charge for the towing (it varies depending on where it was towed from: the further from the pound, the more it costs), plus a daily charge for the time left at the pound before you retrieve it). In the unlikely event your car was stolen and towed (check first that it has not been towed), it will be taken to Via Circondaria 19 (055 3283944).

Parking

Parking in Florence is a major problem and is severely restricted in the centre of town. Wheel clamping has been introduced and carries a hefty fine: if you find your car has been clamped, the number to call in order to have the clamp removed will be posted on the car.

Most main streets are no-parking zones. Parking is forbidden where you see *passo carrabile* (access at all times) and *sosta vietata* (no parking) signs. In unrestricted areas, parking is free in most side streets. Blue lines denote pay-parking; there will be either meters or an attendant to issue timed tickets, which you should return to them when you get back to your car. Disabled spaces are marked by yellow stripes and are free. *Zona rimozione* (tow-away area) signs are valid for the length of the street.

Most streets are cleaned every one or two weeks, usually in the small hours. Vehicles have to be removed or they'll be towed or clamped. Signs tell you when cleaning takes place.

The safest place to leave a car is in one of the underground car parks (*parcheggi*), such as **Parterre** and **Piazza Stazione**, which both have surveillance cameras.

Garage Europa *Borgo Ognissanti 96, Santa Maria Novella (055 292222).* **Open** 6am-2am daily. **Rates** €3/hr; €30/24hrs; €96-€133/wk. **Map** p318 B1.
Garage Lungarno *Borgo San Jacopo 10, Oltrarno (055 282542).* **Open** 7am-midnight daily. **Rates** €3.50-€5/hr; €22-€37/24hrs. **Map** p318 C3.
Parcheggio Parterre *Via Madonna delle Tosse 9, just off Piazza della Libertà, Outside the City Gates (055 5001994).* Bus *8, 17, 33.* **Open** 24hrs daily. **Rates** €1.50/hr; €15/24hrs; €55/wk.
Parcheggio Piazza Stazione *Via Alamanni 14/Piazza della Stazione 12-13, Santa Maria Novella (055 2302655).* **Open** 24hrs daily. **Rates** €2/hr for 1st 2hrs, then €3/hr. **Map** p318 A2.

Petrol

All petrol stations sell unleaded fuel (*senza piombo*). Diesel fuel is *gasolio*. Stations offer full service during the week; many offer a discount for self-service. Attendants don't expect tips.

There are petrol stations on most main roads leading out of town. Normal hours are 7.30am-12.30pm and 3-7pm daily except Sundays. There are no permanently staffed 24-hour petrol stations in Florence: the nearest are on the motorways. AGIP stations on Via Bolognese, Via Aretina, Viale Europa, Via Senese and Via Baracca have 24-hour self-service machines that accept notes.

Roads

There are three motorways in Tuscany that you have to pay a toll to use: the *autostrade* **A1** (Rome-Florence-Bologna), **A11** (the coast-Lucca-Florence) and **A12** (Livorno-Genova). *Autostrade* are indicated by green signs. As you drive on to one, pick up a ticket from one of the toll booths; hand it in, and pay, when you come off. You can pay with a Viacard (a swipecard available from newsagents and the ACI; *see p284*), cash or credit cards. As an idea of price, it costs €20 to drive the 270km (168 miles) from Rome to Florence.

Car hire

Most major car hire companies are near the station, on or near Borgo Ognissanti. Shop around for the best rates, which vary according to season (as do opening times).

If you don't want to rent a car, there are other decent motor options. **Sunny Tuscany** (055 400652/0335 6052001) provides chauffeur-driven cars for tours of Florence/Tuscany. And in Florence itself, consider renting a golf cart: it might sound eccentric, but it's actually a very practical and pleasant way to see the place. Hire costs €20 for three hours and €5 for each subsequent hour, plus a €10 pick-up/delivery charge. For further information, contact SAVE on 055 7131895/339 8719125.

Avis *Borgo Ognissanti 128r, Santa Maria Novella (055 213629/www.avis.it).* Bus *B.* **Open** 8am-7pm Mon-Sat; 9am-1pm Sun. **Credit** AmEx, DC, MC, V. **Map** p318 B1.
Other locations: Peretola Airport (055 315588); Pisa Airport (050 42028).
Europcar *Borgo Ognissanti 53-55, Santa Maria Novella (055 290437/290438/www.europcar.it).* Bus *B.* **Open** 8am-1pm, 2.30-7pm Mon-Fri; 8am-1pm Sat. **Credit** AmEx, DC, MC, V. **Map** p318 B1.
Other locations: Peretola Airport (055 318609); Pisa Airport (050 41017).
Hertz *Via Maso Finiguerra 33r, Santa Maria Novella (055 282260/www.hertz.com).* Bus *B.* **Open** 8am-8pm Mon-Fri; 8am-5pm Sat; 8am-1pm Sun. **Credit** AmEx, DC, MC, V. **Map** p318 B1.
Other locations: Peretola Airport (055 307370); and throughout the city.
Maxirent Car & Scooter Rental *Borgo Ognissanti 133r, Santa Maria Novella (055 2654207/www.maxirent.com).* **Open** 9am-1pm Mon-Fri; 9am-1pm Sat; by appt Sun. **Credit** AmEx, DC, MC, V. **Map** p318 B1.

Cycling

Cycling in Florence is a form of Russian roulette. There are cycle lanes on the main *viali*, but that's no guarantee they'll only be used by bikes. Watch for doors being opened on parked cars (a bad local habit).

Moped & bike hire

To hire a scooter or moped (*motorino*), you need a credit card, ID and cash deposit. Helmets must be worn on all mopeds. Cycle shops normally ask you to leave ID rather than a deposit. In addition to the following, *see above* **Maxirent**.

Alinari
Via Guelfa 85r, San Lorenzo (055 280500). **Open** 9.30am-1pm, 3-7.30pm Mon-Sat; 10am-1pm, 3-7pm Sun. **Credit** MC, V.
Rental of a 50cc *motorino* for use of one person only is €28/day; 125cc for one or two people is €55/day. A current driver's licence is required.

Florence by Bike
Via San Zanobi 120r, San Lorenzo (055 488992). **Open** 9am-7.30pm daily. Closed Nov-Feb. **Credit** AmEx, MC, V.
Bike hire costs €2.50/hour or €12/day. Guided tours are also available, and English is spoken.

Walking

Even if you're in a hurry, walking is the quickest way to get around this traffic-clogged city: parts of the historic centre (*centro storico*) are totally pedestrianised. Still, watch out for bicycles and mopeds zooming up behind you, and don't be surprised if you meet two-wheeled vehicles coming the wrong way up a one-way street. What's more, don't expect cars to stop instantly at lights, and do expect them to ignore red lights when making right turns from side streets.

Our street maps (*see pp316-319*) cover most of the centre. In addition, a good street map is available free from APT offices. Should you require further coverage, Telecom Italia supplies subscribers with TuttoCittà, a detailed street atlas covering the whole urban area; most bars and hotels keep one. For an overview map of the city, *see p316*.

For suggested guided walks, *see p100 and p106*.

Directory

COLLE BERETO

cocktails and wine bar

Piazza Strozzi 5r Firenze tel/fax +39 055283156

Resources A-Z

Addresses

Addresses in Italy are numbered and colour-coded. Residential addresses are 'black' numbers (*nero*), while most commercial addresses are 'red' (*rosso*). This means that on any one street, there can be two addresses with the same number but different colours; these properties can sometimes be quite far apart. Some houses are both shops and flats and could have two different numbers, one red and one black. Red numbers are followed by an 'r' when the address is written, a practice we have followed throughout this guide.

Note that the name on a business's shop front or awning is quite often different from its official, listed name. We have used the former name wherever possible.

Age restrictions

In Italy, there are official age restrictions on a number of goods and activities. However, it's extremely rare for anyone to be asked to show ID in bars or elsewhere, other than in gay bars and clubs (the age of consent for both gay and heterosexual sex is 18). Beer and wine can be legally drunk in bars and pubs from the age of 16; spirits can be drunk by those 18 and over. It's an offence to sell cigarettes to children under 16. Mopeds (50cc) can be driven from the age of 14; cars from 18; only those over 21 can hire a car.

Attitude & etiquette

In churches, women are expected to cover their shoulders and not wear anything daring. Shorts and vests are out for anyone. Most major museums and galleries forbid the taking of photos with flashes; many even ban non-flash cameras. It's best to check at the ticket desk.

Queues are a foreign concept, but in a crowded shop, customers know who is before them and who's after, and usually respect the order. In shops, say *buongiorno* or *buona sera* on entering and leaving, and bear in mind that it's generally considered rude to walk in, look around and leave without asking for what you are looking for.

When addressing anyone except children, it's important to use the appropriate title: *signora* for women, *signorina* for young women, and *signore* for men.

Business

Conventions & conferences

Firenze Expo *Piazza Adua 1, San Lorenzo (055 26025)*. **Map** p318 A2. This centre includes the Palazzo dei Congressi in the Fortezza da Basso and the Centro degli Affari Firenze. It specialises in hosting international meetings and can accommodate parties of up to 1,000 people.

Copy shops

Centro AZ

Via degli Alfani 20r, San Marco (055 2477855). **Open** 9am-1pm, 3-7pm Mon-Fri; 9am-12.30pm Sat. **No credit cards**. **Map** p319 A4. If you're in need of somewhere to do your admin, Centro AZ is a good bet. Faxes carry a charge of €1 plus the cost of the call. Copies cost 5¢.

Couriers & shippers

All major shipping companies will collect from Florence.

DHL *199 199345/www.dhl.com*. **Open** 24hrs daily. **Credit** AmEx, DC, MC, V.
Federal Express *800 123800/ www.fedex.com*. **Open** 8am-7pm Mon-Fri. **Credit** AmEx, DC, MC, V.
Mail Boxes Etc *Via della Scala 13r, Santa Maria Novella (055 268173/www.mbec.com)*. **Open** 9am-1pm, 3.30-7pm Mon-Fri; 10am-1pm Sat. **Credit** AmEx, MC, V. **Map** p318 B2.
SDA *800 016027/06 665471 from mobiles/www.sda.it*. **No credit cards**.
UPS *800 877877/www.ups.com*. **Open** 8am-7pm Mon-Fri; 8.30am-1pm Sat. **Credit** AmEx, MC, V.

Packing & removals

Oli-Ca *Borgo SS Apostoli 27r, Duomo & Around (055 2396917)*. **Open** 9am-1pm, 3.30-7.30pm Mon-Fri; 9am-1pm Sat. **Map** p318 C3.

Travel advice

For up-to-date information on travel to a specific country – including the latest news on safety and security, health issues, local laws and customs – contact your home country government's department of foreign affairs. Most have websites packed with useful advice for would-be travellers.

Australia
www.dfat.gov.au/travel

Canada
www.voyage.gc.ca

New Zealand
www.mft.govt.nz/travel

Republic of Ireland
www.irlgov.ie/iveagh

UK
www.fco.gov.uk/travel

USA
www.state.gov/travel

Translators & interpreters

Emynet *Lungarno Soderini 5/7/9r, Oltrarno (055 219228/ emynet@emynet.com).* **Open** 9.30am-1.30pm, 3-7pm Mon-Fri. **Map** p318 C1.
Full written and spoken translations in 'all' languages.

Interpreti di Conferenza *Via Guelfa 116, San Lorenzo (055 475165).* **Open** 9am-1pm Mon-Fri. **Map** p318 A2.
Interpreters for business meetings.

Useful organisations

Camera di Commercio Industria, Artigianato e Agricoltura (Chamber of Commerce) *Piazza Giudici 3, Duomo & Around (055 27951).* **Open** 8am-3.30pm Mon-Fri. **Map** p319 C4.
Provides information on all elements of import/export and business in Italy, and on Italian trade fairs.

Commercial Office, British Consulate *Lungarno Corsini 2, Duomo & Around (055 289556).* **Open** 9.30am-12.30pm, 2.30-4.30pm Mon-Fri. *Telephone enquiries* 9am-1pm, 2-5pm Mon-Fri. **Map** p318 C2.
Provides business advice and information to British nationals. Call for an appointment.

Commercial Office, United States of America Consulate *Lungarno A Vespucci 36/38/40, Outside the City Gates (055 211676/ 283780). Bus B.* **Open** 9am-12.30pm, 2-3.30pm Mon-Fri.

Consumer

Most shops are unlikely to take back purchases for a refund, unless the goods are faulty. The best you can hope for is an exchange or credit note. If you feel hard done by, contact the organisation below.

Associazione Italiana per la Difesa Consumatori e Ambiente *Via Ricasoli 28, San Marco (055 216180).* **Map** p319 A4.

Customs

EU nationals don't have to declare goods imported into or exported from Italy for their personal use, as long as they arrive from another EU country. US citizens should check their duty-free allowance on the way out. Random checks are made for drugs. For non-EU citizens, the following import limits apply:

● 400 cigarettes or 200 small cigars or 100 cigars or 500g (17.6oz) of tobacco
● 1 litre of spirits (over 22% alcohol) or 2 litres of fortified wine (under 22%)
● 50 grams (1.76oz) of perfume.

There are no restrictions on the importation of cameras, watches or electrical goods. Visitors are also allowed to bring in up to €10,000 in cash.

Disabled

Disabled facilities in Florence are not great, but they are improving. New laws stipulate that all new public offices, bars, restaurants and hotels must be equipped with full disabled facilities. Currently, the standard of access still varies greatly, though most museums are wheelchair-accessible, with lifts, ramps on steps and toilets for the disabled.

Pavement corners in the centre of town are now sloped to allow for wheelchair access. New buses are equipped with ramps and a wheelchair area (*see p283*). Trains that allow space for wheelchairs in the carriages and have disabled loos have a wheelchair logo on the outside, but there is no wheelchair access up the steep steps on the south side of the station: use the east or north entrance, or call the information office for assistance (055 2352275, English spoken). Taxis take wheelchairs, but tell them when you book.

There are free disabled parking bays all over Florence, and disabled drivers with the sticker have access to pedestrian areas of the city. There are wheelchair-accessible toilets at Florence and Pisa airports and Santa Maria Novella station, as well as in many of Florence's main sights.

The Provincia di Firenze produces a booklet (also in English, available from tourist offices) with disabled-aware descriptions – how many steps on each floor, wide doorways and so on – of venues across Florence province. For more information, call 800 437631 (some English spoken). The official council website (www.comune.fi.it) also has useful sightseeing itineraries suitable for disabled visitors.

Drugs

Drug-taking is illegal in Italy. If you're caught in possession of drugs of any type, you may have to appear before a magistrate. If you can convince him or her that your stash was for purely personal use, then you may be let off with a fine or ordered to leave the country. Anything more than a tiny amount will push you into the criminal category; couriering or dealing can land you in prison for up to 20 years. It is an offence to buy or sell drugs, or to give them away. Sniffer dogs are a fixture at most ports of entry into Italy; customs police take a dim view of visitors entering with even the smallest quantities of any banned substances, and you could be refused entry or arrested.

Electricity

Most wiring systems work on one electrical current, 220V, compatible with British and US-bought products. A few systems in old buildings are 125V. With US 110V equipment, you'll need a current transformer: buy one before you travel as they can be hard to find. Adaptors, on the other hand, can be bought at any electrical shop (look for *elettricità* or *ferramenta*.)

Embassies & consulates

There are no embassies in Florence. However, there are some consular offices, which offer limited services.

Australian Embassy *Via Alessandria 215, Suburbs-North, Rome (06 852721).*

British Consulate *Lungarno Corsini 2, Duomo & Around (055 284133).* **Open** 9.30am-12.30pm, 2.30-4.30pm Mon-Fri. *Telephone enquiries* 9am-1pm, 2-5pm Mon-Fri. **Map** p318 C2.
Out-of-hours, a message will tell you what to do if you need urgent help.

Canadian Embassy *Via GB de Rossi 27, Suburbs-North, Rome (06 445981).*

Irish Embassy *Piazza Campitelli 3, Ghetto, Rome (06 6979121).*

New Zealand Embassy *Via Zara 28, Suburbs-North, Rome (06 4417171).*

South African Consulate *Piazza dei Salterelli 1, Duomo & Around (055 281863).* **Map** p318 C3.
No office. You have to call to make an appointment.

US Consulate *Lungarno A Vespucci 38, Outside the City Gates (055 2398276). Bus B.* **Open** 9am-12.30pm, 2-3.30pm Mon-Fri.
In case of emergency call the above number and a message will refer you to the current emergency number.

Emergencies

Thefts or losses should be reported immediately at the nearest police station (*see p294*), where you should get a crime report for insurance purposes. You should report the loss of your passport to your embassy or consulate (*see above*). To prevent fraud, report the loss of a credit card or travellers' cheques to your credit card company (*see p294*) immediately.

Emergency numbers

Emergency services & state police *Polizia di Stato 113.*
Police *Carabinieri (English-speaking helpline) 112.*
Fire service *Vigili del Fuoco 115.*
Ambulance *Ambulanza 118.*
Car breakdown *Automobile Club d'Italia (ACI) 803 116.*
City traffic police *Vigili Urbani 055 32831.*

Gay & lesbian

For more HIV and AIDS services, *see p290.*

Azione Gay e Lesbica Circolo Finisterrae *c/o SMS Andrea del Sarto, Via Manara 12, Outside the City Gates (055 671298).* **Open** 6-8pm Mon-Fri. Closed 3wks Aug.
As well as running Timida Godzilla parties, this group maintains a library and archive, facilitates HIV testing and provides general community information.

IREOS-Queer Community Service Center *Via de' Serragli 3, Oltrano (055 216907/ireos@freemail.it).* **Open** 5-8pm Mon-Thur, Sat. **Map** p341 C1/D1.
Formerly part of ARCIGay/Lesbica, Ireos hosts a social open house every Wednesday night, and offers referrals for HIV testing, psychological counselling and self-help groups. It also organises hikes and outings.

Queer Nation Holidays *Via del Moro 95r, Santa Maria Novella (055 2654587/www.queernationholidays.com).* **Open** 9.30am-7.30pm Mon-Fri; 10am-6pm Sat. **Credit** MC, V. **Map** p318 B2.
Queer Nation Holidays can organise individual and group travel. It can also make referrals to other gay and lesbian organisations.

Health

Emergency healthcare is available free for all travellers through the Italian national health system. EU citizens are entitled to most treatment for free, though many specialised medicines, examinations and tests will be charged for. To get treatment, you'll need an E111 form (*see p291*).

For hospital treatment, go to one of the casualty departments listed below. If you want to see a GP, go to the state health centre (**Azienda Sanitaria di Firenze**, or ASL) for the district where you are staying, taking your E111 form with you. The ASLs are listed in the phone book and they usually open 9am-1pm and 2-7pm Monday to Friday.

Consulates (*see above*) can provide lists of English-speaking doctors, dentists and clinics. They're also listed in the English *Yellow Pages* (available for purchase from larger bookshops and online at www.paginegialle.it).

Non-EU citizens are advised to take out private health insurance before visiting.

Accident & emergency

If you need urgent medical care, it's best to go to the *pronto soccorso* (casualty) department of one of the hospitals listed below; they're open 24 hours daily. Alternatively, call 118 for an ambulance (*ambulanza*).

To find a doctor on call in your area (emergencies only), phone 118. For a night (8pm-8am) or all-day-Sunday emergency home visit, call the Guardia Medica for your area (west central Florence 055 287788; east central Florence 055 2339456).

Ospedale di Careggi *Viale Morgagni 85, Outside the City Gates (055 4277111). Bus 2, 8, 14C.*

Ospedale Meyer (Children) *Via Luca Giordano 13, Outside the City Gates (055 56621). Bus 11, 17.*

Ospedale Santa Maria Annunziata (known as Ponte a Nicchieri) *Via Antella 58, Bagno a Ripoli, Outside the City Gates (055 24961). Bus 32.*

Ospedale Torregalli *Via Torregalli 3, Outside the City Gates (055 7192447). Bus 83.*

Santa Maria Nuova *Piazza Santa Maria Nuova 1, Duomo & Around (055 27581).* **Map** p319 B4.
The most central hospital in Florence. There's also a 24-hour pharmacy directly outside.

Complementary medicine

Most pharmacies sell homeopathic and other complementary medicines, which are quite commonly used in Italy. Herbalists sell herbal but not homeopathic medicines; some can refer you to alternative health practitioners.

Ambulatorio Santa Maria Novella *Piazza Santa Maria Novella 24, Santa Maria Novella (055 280143).* **Open** 3-7.30pm Mon; 9am-1pm, 3-7.30pm Tue-Fri. **No credit cards. Map** p318 B2.
Ambulatorio Santa Maria Novella is a large group practice at which several homeopathic doctors have consulting rooms and offer a range of alternative health services. Some English is spoken. It's best to call first for an appointment.

Directory

Antica Farmacia Sodini *Via dei Banchi 18-20r, Santa Maria Novella (055 211159).* **Open** 9am-1pm, 4-8pm Mon-Sat. **No credit cards.** **Map** p318 B2.
The English-speaking staff at this homeopathic pharmacy are very helpful. As well as giving advice, they make up prescriptions.

Contraception & abortion

Condoms and other forms of contraception are widely available in pharmacies and some supermarkets. If you need further assistance, the **Consultorio Familiare** (family planning clinic) at your local ASL state health centre (*see p289*) provides free advice and information, though for an examination or prescription, you'll need an E111 form (*see p291*) or insurance. An alternative is to go to a private clinic like those run by AIED.
The morning-after pill is sold legally in Italy; it must be taken within 72 hours, and to obtain it, you'll need to get a prescription (*see below*). Abortion is legal in Italy and is performed only in public hospitals, but the private clinics listed below can give consultations and references.

AIED *Via Ricasoli 10, San Marco (055 215237).* **Open** 3-6.30pm Mon-Fri. **Map** p319 B4.
The clinics run by this private organisation provide help and information on contraception and related matters, and medical care at low cost. Treatment is of a high standard and service is often faster than in state clinics. An examination will usually cost something in the region of €40 plus €15 compulsory membership, payable on the first visit and then valid for a year.

Santa Chiara *Piazza Indipendenza 11, San Lorenzo (055 496312/ 475239).* **Open** 8am-7pm daily by appointment.
This clinic offers gynaecological examinations and general health check-ups. Call for an appointment.

Dentists

The following dentists speak English. Always call ahead for an appointment.

Dr Maria Peltonen Portman *Via Teatina 2, Duomo & Around (055 218594).* **Open** 9.30am-6.30pm Mon-Fri. **Map** p318 B3.
Dr Sandro Cosi *Via Pellicceria 10, Duomo & Around (055 214238/ 0335 332055).* **Open** 9am-1pm Mon-Fri. **Map** p318 C3.

Doctors

Dr Stephen Kerr *Via Porta Rossa 1, Duomo & Around (055 288055/ 0335 8361682).* **Open** *Surgery by appointment* 9am-1pm Mon-Fri. *Drop-in clinic* 3-5pm Mon-Fri. **Credit** AmEx, MC, V. **Map** p318 C3.
This English-speaking GP practises privately in Florence. He charges €30-€60 (standard charge €40) for a consultation in his surgery.

IAMAT (Associated Medical Studio)
Via Lorenzo il Magnifico 59, Outside the City Gates (24hr line 055 475411). Bus 8, 13. **Open** *Clinic* 11am-noon, 5-6pm Mon-Fri; 11am-noon Sat.
A private medical service that organises home visits by doctors. Catering particularly for foreigners, it promises to send an English-speaking GP or specialist out to you within an hour and a half for between €65 and €100. IAMAT also runs a clinic.

Hospitals

For emergencies, *see p289*.
One of the obvious anxieties involved with falling ill when abroad is the language problem. If you need a translator to help out at the hospital, contact:

AVO (Association of Hospital Volunteers) *055 4250126/ 2344567 (24hrs).* **Open** *Office hours* 4-6pm Mon, Wed, Fri; 10am-noon Tue, Thur.
AVO is a group of volunteer interpreters who help out with explanations to doctors and hospital staff in 22 languages. They also give support and advice.

Opticians

For eye tests, prescription glasses and contact lenses, *see p151*.

Pharmacies

Pharmacies (*farmacia*), which are identified by a red or green cross hanging outside, are semi-officially as mini-clinics, with staff able to give informal medical advice and suggest non-prescription medicines. Normal opening hours are 8.30am-1pm and 4-8pm Mon-Fri and 8.30am-1pm Sat, but many central pharmacies are open all day. At other times, there's a duty rota system. A list by the door of all pharmacies indicates the nearest one open outside normal hours, also published in local papers. At duty pharmacies, there's a surcharge of

€2.60 per client (not per item) when only the special duty counter is open – usually midnight-8.30am.
The pharmacies listed on *p151* provide a 24-hour service without a supplement for night service.

Prescriptions

Prescriptions are required for most medicines. If you require regular medication, make sure you know their chemical (generic) rather than brand name, as they may be available in Italy only under a different name.

STDs, HIV & AIDS

Clinica Dermatologica
Via della Pergola 64, San Marco (055 2758684). **Open** 8am-noon Mon, Wed, Thur, Fri; 8-11am Tue, Sat. **Map** p319 A5.
Clinica Dermatologica carries out examinations, tests, treatment and counselling for all sexually transmitted diseases, including HIV and AIDS. Some services are free, while others are state-subsided. An examination costs about €20. Some staff speak English.

AIDS centres

Ambulatorio Malattie Infettive, Ospedale di Careggi *Viale Morgagni, Outside the City Gates (055 4279425/6).* Bus 2, 8, 14C. **Open** 9am-12.30pm, 3-6pm Mon-Fri; 9am-12.30pm Sat.
AIDS centre with information, advice and testing. Call ahead for an appointment. Basic English spoken.

Consultorio per la Salute Omosessuale *Via San Zanobi 54r, San Lorenzo (055 476557).*
Run by the ARCIGay organisation, this centre provides various services relating to AIDS and HIV. Telephone counselling is offered 4-8pm Monday to Friday, and counsellors are also available in person. AIDS tests are carried out on Wednesdays, 4pm-5.30pm. Staffed by volunteers, these services are free. English is spoken.

Helplines

Alcoholics Anonymous
St James' Church, Via Rucellai 9, Santa Maria Novella (055 294417). **Map** p318 A1.
This English-speaking branch of the AA is affiliated to the American Episcopal Church (*see p295*). Meetings are held on Tuesdays and Thursdays at 1.30pm and Saturdays at 5pm. These are also open to anyone with drug-related problems.

Drogatel *840 002244*. **Open**
9am-8pm daily.
A national help centre for drug-
related problems. It also gives advice
on alcohol-related problems.

Samaritans *06 70454444/
06 70454445.*
Staffed by native English speakers.

ID

In Italy, you're required by law
to carry photo ID at all times.
You'll be asked to produce it if
you're stopped by traffic police
(who will demand your driving
licence, which you must have
on you whenever you are in
charge of a motor vehicle).
ID will also be required when
you check into a hotel.

Insurance

EU nationals are entitled to
reciprocal medical care in Italy,
provided they have in their
possession an E111 form.
This form is widely available
in the UK from health centres,
post offices and Social Security
offices. It will cover you for
emergencies, but involves
having to deal with the
Italian state health system,
which can, at times, be
overwhelmingly frustrating.
The E111 will only cover
partial costs of medicines.

Despite this provision,
short-term visitors from all
countries are advised to get
private travel insurance to
cover a broad number of
eventualities (from injury
to theft). Non-EU citizens
should ensure they have
comprehensive medical
insurance with a reputable
company before leaving home.

Visitors should also take out
adequate property insurance
before setting off for Italy.
If you rent a car, motorcycle
or moped, make sure you pay
the extra for full insurance
and sign the collision damage
waiver before taking off.
Check your home insurance
first, though, as it may already
cover you.

Internet & email

It's very easy to find internet
access in Florence. Even most
budget hotels will allow you
to plug your modem into
their phone system; the more
upmarket establishments will
probably have dataports in
every bedroom. Some Italian
phone plugs are different from
US and UK versions: most
have the square plug, though
in modern hotels the standard
US Bell socket is often used.
As usual, it's best to check in
advance with your hotel.

A number of Italian
providers offer free internet
access. These include **Libero**
(www.libero.it), **Tiscali**
(www.tiscalinet.it), **Kataweb**
(www.kataweb.com),
Telecom Italia (www.tin.it)
and **Wind** (www.inwind.it).

Internet access

There are internet points in all
areas of the city centre. Most charge
around €5/hour, and there are often
discounts for students. Remember
to take ID, though: you'll need it to
register, even as a guest user.

Internet Train *Via dei Benci
36r, Santa Croce (055 2638555).*
Open 10am-midnight Mon-Sat;
3-11pm Sun. **Credit** MC, V.
Map p319 B5.
Internet Train was the first internet
shop in Italy: it started off with four
PCs, but now has around a dozen
shops in Florence. The chain has
helpful English-speaking staff.

Intotheweb *Via de' Conti 23r,
San Lorenzo (055 2645628).*
Open 10am-midnight daily.
Credit MC, V. **Map** p318 B3.
This friendly centre has 18 PCs and
Macs, but also sells international
phone cards, sends and receives
faxes and rents out mobile phones.

Netgate *Via Sant'Egidio 10r,
Santa Croce (055 2347967/
www.thenetgate.it).* **Open** *Summer*
11am-9.45pm Mon-Sat. *Winter*
11am-9pm Mon-Sat; 2-8pm Sun.
Map p319 B5.
A spacious centre with 35 computers.
For more branches, see the website.

Virtual Office *Via Faenza 49r,
San Lorenzo (055 2645560).*
Open 10am-midnight Mon-Wed;
10am-1am Thur-Sat; noon-1am Sun.
Credit MC, V. **Map** p318 A3.

Webcams on every PC, DVD
players and a range of office services
on offer, including shipping and
money transfers. Virtual Office also
runs internet courses.

Language

English is spoken in many
central shops and all main
hotels and restaurants,
though in some family-run
businesses, and in the smaller
villages of Tuscany, it may
be trickier to communicate.
Taking a phrase book is a
good idea. For basic Italian
vocabulary, *see p301.*

Left luggage

There's a left luggage point
in Santa Maria Novella train
station on platform 16.

Legal help

Your first stop should be your
embassy or consulate (*see
p289*). Staff will be able to
supply you with a list of
English-speaking lawyers.

Libraries

Biblioteca Marucelliana
*Via Cavour 43-45, San Marco (055
27221/marucelliana@cesit1.unifi.it).*
Open 9am-7pm Mon-Fri; 9am-1pm
Sat. **Map** p319 A4.
A diverse range of books, including
some in English. ID will be needed
to register.

**British Institute Library &
Cultural Centre** *Lungarno
Guicciardini 9, Oltrarno
(055 26778270/library@british
institute.it).* **Open** 10am-6.30pm
Mon-Fri. **Map** p318 C3.
The British Institute's library
requires an annual membership fee
(€56.50, students €38.50), but offers
a reading room that overlooks the
Arno, an extensive collection of art
history books and Italian literature,
and well-informed staff.

**Kunsthistorisches Institut in
Florenz** *Via G Giusti 44, Santa
Croce (055 249111).* **Open** 9am-8pm
Mon-Fri. **Map** p319 A6.
One of the largest collections of art
history books in Florence is held by
the German Institute and is available
to students. You'll need a letter of
presentation and a summary of your
research project.

Directory

angels
res.aurant and american bar

Angels Restaurant and
American bar

Open all year
Business Lunch 12:00 a.m - 3: p.m
Dinner 7:00 p.m – 11:00 p.m
Happy Hour 7:00 p.m - 9:00 p.m
Open all day till 1.30 a.m

via del proconsolo, 29/31 r
50122 Firenze
tel +39 0562398762
fax +39 055 2398123
www.ristoranteangels.it
info@ristoranteangels.it

Lost property

For property lost anywhere other than in planes, trains and taxis, contact the **Ufficio Oggetti Ritrovati**, the council's lost property office. For lost passports, contact the police (*see p294*).

Ufficio Oggetti Ritrovati *Via Circondaria 19, Outside the City Gates (055 3283942/3283943). Bus 23, 33.* **Open** 9am-noon Mon-Sat.

Airports

Aeroporto di Firenze
055 3061302.
Pisa International Airport
050 44325.
Aeroporto di Bologna
051 6479615.

Buses

Check at the council's lost property office (*see above*).

Taxis

If you leave something in a cab, call the taxi company and quote the car's code (place name and number), if you can remember it. Otherwise. contact the *vigili urbani* police (055 212290), where anything left in cabs will be taken by the drivers.

Trains

FS/Santa Maria Novella (SMN) Station *Interno Stazione SMN, Santa Maria Novella (055 2352190).* **Open** 6am-midnight daily.
Map p318 A2.
Articles found on state railways in the Florence area are sent to this office on platform 16, next to the left luggage. Minimal English.

Media

Magazines

Many newsstands in the centre of town sell *Time, Newsweek, The Economist* and other glossy English-language magazines. For Italian speakers, Italian magazines worth checking out include *Panorama* and *L'Espresso*, weekly current affairs and general interest rags, the full-frontal style covers of which do little justice to the high-level journalism and hot-issue coverage found within. There are also some useful booklets with listings of events in Florence:

Firenze Spettacolo A monthly listings and local interest magazine with an English-language section called Florencescope.

Florence Concierge Information Found at tourist offices and most hotels, this freebie gives events, useful information, timetables and suchlike in English.

Newspapers

Foreign dailies

Many newsstands and newsagents sell foreign papers, which usually arrive the next day (the same evening in summer, except Sundays). You'll find the widest range around Piazza del Duomo, Piazza della Repubblica, Via de' Tornabuoni and SMN station.

Local English-language papers

The Florentine Launched in April 2005, this free English-language newspaper is distributed every Thursday in restaurants, bar, hotels, language schools and the main squares. As well as news and events, it includes articles on culture, politics, travel, food and more.

Italian dailies

Only one Italian in ten buys a daily newspaper, so the press has little of the clout of other European countries, and the paper is generally a simple vehicle for information rather than a forum of pressure for change. Most papers publish comprehensive listings for local events. Sports coverage in the dailies is extensive and thorough, but if you're still not sated, the mass-circulation sports papers **Corriere dello Sport** and **La Gazzetta dello Sport** offer even more detail.

Il Giornale Owned by the brother of Silvio Berlusconi, *Il Giornale* takes the expected government line. The Florence edition has a section dedicated to local news.

La Nazione Selling some 160,000 copies daily, this is the most popular newspaper in Tuscany. Founded in the mid 19th century by Bettino Ricasoli, it's also one of Italy's oldest. Basically right-wing and gossipy, it consists of three sections (national, sport and local). Each province has its own edition.

La Repubblica One of the youngest of Italy's major papers. Politically, it's centre-left, with strong coverage of the Mafia and Vatican issues, but it has an unfortunate tendency to pad the news section out with waffle and gossip. The Florence edition has about 20 pages dedicated to local and provincial news.

Il Manifesto A solidly left-wing intellectual paper.

L'Unità The media voice-piece for the far left.

Radio

Controradio (93.6 MHz) Dub, hip hop, progressive drum 'n' bass and indie rock feature heavily on this station.

Nova Radio (101.5 MHz) Run by volunteers and committed to social issues, Nova Radio broadcasts a very good mixture of jazz, soul, blues, reggae, world music, hip hop and rap. Best of all, there are no ads.

Radio Diffusione Firenze (102.7 MHz) This radio station plays mainstream pop, house and club music.

Radio Montebeni (108.5 MHz) Classical music only.

Television

Italy has six major networks. Of these, three are Berlusconi-owned Mediaset channels: **Italia 6** shows familiar US series, Brazilian soaps, Japanese cartoons and adventure films; **Rete 4** spews out an awful lot of cheap game shows and *Columbo* repeats but also shows decent nature documentaries; and **Canale 5** is the top dog, with the best films, quiz programmes, live shows and the most popular programme on Italian TV, the scandal-busting, satirical *Striscia la Notizia*. Programmes are riddled with ad breaks.

RAI channels, which are also basically controlled by Berlusconi, are known for their better-quality programming but generally much less slick presenting, and there is still a relentless stream of quiz shows and high-kicking bikini-clad bimbettes. When these have bored you, there are numerous local stations featuring cleaning demos, dial-a-fortune-teller (surprisingly popular), prolonged adverts for slimming machines and late-night trashy soft porn.

Of the many satellite and cable TV subscription channels, the best are **Stream** and **Telepiù**. Some of their packages include BBC and major US channels. The French channel **Antenne 2** is also accessible in Tuscany.

Money

Italy is in the **euro** (€) zone. There are euro banknotes for €5, €10, €20, €100, €200 and €500, and coins worth €1 and €2, plus 1¢, 2¢, 5¢, 10¢,

20¢ and 50¢ (cents). €1 is equivalent to L1,936.27 old Italian lire. In shops and on receipts, you'll often still see prices listed in both lire and euros.

The introduction of the euro led to price increases in most sectors and total speculation in some; prices remain a lot higher than a few years ago.

ATMs

Most major banks have 24-hour cashpoint (Bancomat) machines, and the vast majority of these also accept cards with the Maestro and Cirrus symbols. To access the cashpoint lobby of some banks, you have to insert your card in the machine outside. Most machines will dispense a daily limit of €250. Your home bank will make a charge.

Banks

Bank opening hours are generally from 8.20am to 1.20pm and from 2.35pm to 3.35pm Monday to Friday. All banks are closed on public holidays; staff also tend to work short hours the day before a holiday, usually closing at around 11am.

Expect long queues even for simple transactions, and don't be surprised if the bank wants to photocopy your passport, driving licence and last exam essay as proof of ID. Staff may even attempt to photocopy credit and debit cards in some banks: refuse if this happens. Many banks no longer give cash advances on credit cards, so check for the signs, or ask before queueing. Branches of most banks are found around Piazza della Repubblica.

Bureaux de change

Changing your money in a bank usually gets you a better rate than in a private bureau de change (*cambio*) and will often be better than in your home country. However, if you need to change money out of banking hours, there's no shortage of bureaux de change (*cambi*). Commission rates vary considerably: you can pay from nothing to €5 for each transaction. Watch out for 'No Commission' signs; the exchange rate at these places will almost certainly be worse. Main post offices also have bureaux de change, where commission is €2.50 for all cash transactions (maximum €1,000). Some large hotels also offer an exchange service, but again, the rate is almost certainly worse than in a

bank. Always take ID for any financial transaction. A few city-centre bank branches have automatic cash exchange machines, which accept notes in good condition in most currencies.

Agency Prime Link *Via Panicale 18r, San Lorenzo (055 291275).* **Open** 9.30am-1.30pm, 3-7pm daily. **Map** p318 A3.
The quickest if not the cheapest way to send money across the world.

American Express *Via Dante Alighieri 14r, Duomo & Around (055 50981).* **Open** 9am-5.30pm Mon-Fri; 9am-12.30pm Sat. **Map** p319 B4.
AmEx also has a travel agency.

Change Underground *Piazza della Stazione 14, interno 37, Santa Maria Novella (055 291312).* **Open** *Summer* 9am-7pm Mon-Sat; 9am-1.30pm Sun. *Winter* 9am-7pm Mon-Sat. **Map** p318 A2.
In the mall underneath the station.

Thomas Cook *Lungarno Acciaiuoli 4/8r, Duomo & Around (055 290278).* **Open** 9am-7pm Mon-Sat; 9.30am-5pm Sun. **Map** p318 C3.
One of the few exchange offices open on a Sunday. No commission for cash withdrawal via MasterCard or Visa.

Chip & PIN

The Chip and PIN system is up and running in Italy. You're advised to remember your PIN number for your debit card, so you can enter it into the terminal instead of signing.

Credit cards

Italians have an enduring fondness for cash, but nearly all hotels of two stars and above, as well as most shops and restaurants, now accept at least some of the major credit cards, though surprisingly few museums do.

Lost/stolen

Most lines are freephone (800) numbers, have English-speaking staff and are open 24 hours daily.

American Express card emergencies *06 72282/gold card holders 06 722807385.*
Diners Club *800 864064.*
Eurocard/CartaSi (including MasterCard and Visa) *800 018548.*
MasterCard *800 870866.*
Visa *800 877232.*

Tax

Sales tax (IVA) is applied to all purchases and services at 1%, 4% and 20% in an ascending scale of luxury, but is almost always

included in the price stated. At some luxury hotels, tax will be added on to the quoted rates, but prices will be clearly stated as *escluso IVA*.

By law, all non-EU residents are entitled to an IVA refund on purchases of €160 and over at shops participating in the 'Tax-free shopping' scheme, identified by a purple sticker. On presentation of your passport, they will give you a 'cheque' that can be cashed at the airport desk on your way home. You'll need to show your passport and the unused goods, and there's a three-month time limit. IVA paid on hotel bills cannot be reclaimed.

Travellers' cheques

Travellers' cheques can be changed at all banks and bureaux de change but are only accepted as payment (in any major currency) by larger shops, hotels and restaurants.

Natural hazards

The sun can be fierce in spring and summer, so take plenty of sunscreen, wear a hat and take to the shade during the hottest parts of the day (*see also p299*). Mosquitoes can be an annoyance in warm weather: bring plenty of repellent.

Police

Italian police forces are divided into four colour-coded units. The *vigili urbani* and *polizia municipale* (municipal police) wear navy blue. The *vigili* deal with all traffic matters within the city, and the *polizia municipale* with petty crime. The two forces responsible for dealing with crime are the *polizia di stato* (state police), who also wear blue jackets but have pale grey trousers, and the normally black-clad *carabinieri*, part of the army. Their roles are essentially the same. The *guardia di finanza* (financial police) wear grey and have little to do with tourists.

In an emergency, go to the tourist aid police or the nearest *carabinieri* post or police station (*questura*); we have listed central ones below, but

courses, many of which have international reputations, the city's student population rivals that of its residents at some times of the year. To study in Florence, you will need a *permesso di soggiorno per studio*. The same requirements apply as for the *permesso di soggiorno* (*see p300*), plus a guarantee that your medical bills will be paid (an E111 form will do), evidence that you can support yourself and a letter from the educational institution.

The courses listed in this section are all generally in English. However, if you don't speak any Italian, double-check before you enrol.

Art, design & restoration courses

Il Bisonte *Via San Niccolò 24, Oltrarno (055 2347215).* **Map** p319 D5.
Located among the artisans' workshops in the former stables of Palazzo Serristori, Il Bisonte has specialist courses and theoretical/practical seminars in the techniques of etching and printing by hand. Contact the school directly for a detailed programme of courses.

Charles H Cecil Studios *Borgo San Frediano 68, Oltrarno (tel/fax 055 285102).* **Map** p318 C1.
The church of San Raffaello Arcangelo was converted into a studio complex in the early 19th century. It now houses one of the more charismatic of Florence's art schools, Charles H Cecil Studios, which is heavily frequented by Brits. It offers a thorough training in the classical techniques of drawing and painting. Twice a week the school runs life-drawing classes for the general public.

Istituto per l'Arte e il Restauro *Palazzo Spinelli, Borgo Santa Croce 10, Santa Croce (055 246001/www.spinelli.it).* **Map** p319 C5.
Widely considered one of the best restoration schools in Italy, Spinelli offers a multitude of courses in the restoration of paintings, furniture, gilt work, ceramics, stone, paper and more; they last between one and three years. One-month courses are run from July to September in the same disciplines.

Oro e Colore *Via della Chiesa 25, Oltrarno (tel/fax 055 229040/www. oroecolore.com).* **Map** p318 D1.
Month- to year-long courses in art restoration, gold leaf restoration and other techniques. No previous experience is needed; however, places on courses are limited and are taught only in Italian.

Studio Art Center International (SACI) *Via San Gallo 30, San Lorenzo (055 486164/info@ saci-florence.org).* **Map** p319 A4.
SACI offers five specific credit programmes for graduates and undergraduates. These include both academic and practical courses in the arts, ranging from museology to batik design. There is an entry requirement for certain courses.

Università Internazionale dell'Arte *Villa il Ventaglio, Via delle Forbici 24-26, Outside the City Gates (055 570216/www.vps.it/ propart/uia). Bus 7.*
Courses at the university cover restoration and preservation, museum and gallery management and art criticism.

Language classes

There are no end of language and culture courses in Florence, including many intensive one- or two-month courses, which should provide an adequate everyday grasp of the language. Prices refer to a standard four-week course with four hours' tuition a day.

ABC Centro di Lingua e Cultura Italiana *Via dei Rustici 7, Santa Croce (055 212001/www.abcschool. com).* **Price** €538. **Map** p319 C4.
ABC offers language teaching at six levels, as well as preparatory courses for the entrance exam to the University of Florence.

British Institute Language Centre *Piazza Strozzi 2, Duomo & Around (055 26778200/www.british institute.it).* **Map** p318 B3.
Short courses in Italian language, history of art, drawing and cooking. For the British Institute's Library & Cultural Centre, *see p291*.

Centro Linguistico Italiano Dante Alighieri *Piazza della Repubblica 5 (055 210808/ www.clida.it).* **Price** €620, plus €80 enrolment fee. **Map** p319 D4.
Eleven language levels; opera and literature courses too.

Istituto Lorenzo de' Medici *Via Faenza 43, San Lorenzo (055 287360/www.lorenzodemedici.it).* **Price** €590. **Map** p318 A3.
Four different courses in Italian as well as classes in cooking, Italian cinema and art history.

others are found in the phone book. Staff will either speak English or be able to find someone who does. If you have had something stolen, tell them you want to report a *furto*. A statement (*denuncia*) will be taken, which you'll need for an insurance claim. Lost or stolen passports should also be reported to your embassy or consulate.

Comando Provinciale Carabinieri *Borgo Ognissanti 48, Santa Maria Novella (055 2061)*. **Open** 24hrs daily. **Map** p318 B1. A *carabinieri* post near the town centre; the best place to report the loss or theft of personal property.

Questura Centrale *Via Zara 2, San Lorenzo (055 49771)*. **Open** 24hrs daily. *Ufficio Denuncie* 8.30a… 8pm daily.
To report a crime, go to the *Uffici Denuncie*, where you will be aske… fill in a form.

Tourist Aid Police *Via Pietr… 24r, Santa Croce (055 20391)* **Open** 8.30am-7.30pm Mon-Fr… 8.30am-1.30pm Sat. **Map** p3… Interpreters are on hand to h… report thefts, lost property a… other problems.

Postal servic…

Improvements have … recently in Italy's … unreliable postal s… you can now be m… sure that the lette… will arrive in rea… though some pr… remain with re… from abroad.

Stamps (*fra…* be bought at … offices. Most … red and hav… la Città (for… Tutte le al… (everywhe… also blue… EU star … Union …

A let… weighi… sent b… addre… and … post… EU… ab…

UK, eigh… equivale… (*posta* … fulfils … withir… days … or fir… A le… less… 60… co… t… r…

● Don't keep wallets i… pockets. This is a pickp… favourite swipe, especia… buses and public transp…
● Wear shoulder bags diagonally and facing aw… from the road to minimis… risk of *scippi* – bag-snatch… from mopeds.
● Never leave bags on ta… or the backs of chairs in ba…
● Keep an eye on valuable… while trying on clothes.

Also, watch out for 'baby-gangs' of children who hang… around the tourist spots and create a distraction by flappi… a newspaper or card while trying to slip their hands into bags or pockets. If you are approached, keep walking, keep calm and hang on to you… valuables.

Serious street crime is rare in Florence, and it remains a relatively safe city to walk in, but take care at night. Stick to the main well-lit streets and, lone women particularly, avoid the station area.

For emergency numbers, see p289. For information on the police, see p294.

Smoking

On 10 January 2005 a law banning smoking in all public places came into force. This includes bars, restaurants and clubs, although there is a clause that allows some venues to set aside a smoking room, as long as it is separated by double doors and adequately ventilated and filtered. Owners who allow customers to smoke are fined heavily, the smoker can also be fined and the law is being scrupulously enforced. Cigarettes are on sale at *tabacchi* and *bar tabacchi*; both are recognisable by the blue/black and white sign outside.

Study

With over 20 US university programmes and countless language schools and art

Directory

C…
B…
(te…
Ti…
Ar…
stu…
cen…
mor…
sch…
whic…
It giv…
class…
oil pa…
hosts…
gener…

L'Isti…
Resta…
Borgo…
Croce (…
Map p3…
Widely…
art resto…
Palazzo S…
of course…
frescoes, …
objects, ce…
glass. The…
three years…
held from J…
same discip…

Scuola Leonardo da Vinci *Via Bufalini 3, Duomo & Around (055 294420/www.scuolaleonardo.com)*. **Price** €500, plus €70 enrolment. **Map** p319 B4.
Versatile languages courses, plus classes in history of art, fashion, drawing, design, cooking and wine.

Scuola Machiavelli *Piazza Santo Spirito 4, Oltrarno (055 2396966/ 280800/www.centromachiavelli.it)*. **Price** €420, plus €30 enrolment fee. **Map** p318 D1.
This small co-op offers Italian, pottery, fresco, mosaic, *trompe l'œil* and book-binding classes.

Universities

To study alongside Florentine undergraduates, contact an Italian consulate to apply to do a *corso singolo*, or one year of study at the University of Florence. You need to register at the *Centro di Cultura per Stranieri* at the beginning of November. The fees for a *corso singolo* (maximum five subjects) are approximately €1,100. To complete a degree course, you must have studied to university level. For details, see www.unifi.it. There are also exchange programmes for EU students.

Several US universities, including Georgetown, Sarah Lawrence, New York, Gonzaga and Syracuse, have Florence outposts open to students from any US university for the semester and summer courses.

Università di Firenze: Centro di Cultura per Stranieri
Via Francesco Valori 9, Outside the City Gates (055 454016/www.unifi.it/ ccs). Bus 8, 10, 11, 13, 17, 20, 33. **Open** 9am-noon Mon-Fri.
Offers language and cultural courses.

Useful organisations

Student Point
Viale Gramsci 9, Outside the City Gates (055 2342857). Bus 8, 12, 13. **Open** 2-6pm Mon, Wed, Fri.
The tourist board has established this office to help foreign students with orientation in Florence. Staff advise on accommodation, getting a *permesso di soggiorno*, study courses, doctors and events.

Council of International Education Exchange (CIEE)
7 Custom House Street, 3rd Floor, Portland, Maine, ME 04101, USA (+1 207 553 7600/www.ciee.org).

Institute of International Education *809 UN Plaza, New York, NY 10017-3580, USA (+1 212 883 8200)*.

Italian Cultural Institute
39 Belgrave Square, London SW1X 8NX, UK (+44 (0)20 7235 1461).

Telephones

Although competition has led to some price cuts for telephone customers, **Telecom Italia**, the biggest and most commonly used Italian telephone company, still operates one of the most expensive phone systems in Europe, particularly for international calls. Some phone companies offer more competitive rates – **Tele 2**, for example – but it can be very difficult to contact them if you have any problems. Tariffs are higher if you're calling from a public phone and usually higher still from a hotel: you're usually better off buying an international phone card, though they don't offer anything approaching the same level of discounts as in the UK or US. Calling from a phone centre costs the same as from a payphone, but it's more convenient.

Dialling & codes

The international code for Italy is 39. To dial in from other countries, preface it with the exit code: 00 in the UK and 011 in the US. All normal Florence numbers begin with the area code 055, for Pisa 050. As with all Italian codes, these must always be used in full, even when you are calling from within the same area, and when dialling internationally.

To make an international call from Florence, dial 00, then the country code (Australia 61; Canada 1; Irish Republic 353; New Zealand 64; United Kingdom 44; United States 1), followed by the area code (for calls to the UK, omit the initial zero) and individual number. The same pattern works to mobile numbers.

All numbers beginning 800 are free lines (*numero verde*). Until recently, these began 167: replace the prefix with 800 or call 12 – directory enquiries – for the new number. For numbers that begin 840 and 848 (147 and 148 until recently), you'll be charged one unit only, regardless of where you're calling from or how long the call lasts. These numbers can be called from within Italy only; some only function within one phone district. Phone numbers starting '3' are mobile numbers; those

with '199' codes are charged at local rates; '167' numbers are billed at premium rates.

Public phones

Since the popular mobile phone revolution, many public phones in Florence have disappeared, especially in less central areas. However, many bars still have payphones. Public phones only accept phone cards with magnetic strips (*schede telefoniche*), not coins; a few also accept major credit cards. *Schede telefoniche* are available from *tabacchi*, some newsstands and some bars, as are the pre-paid phone cards offering access via an 800 number to both domestic and international calls. To use a card phone, lift the receiver and wait for the tone, then insert the card (with the perforated corner torn off) and dial.

Operator services

To make a reverse-charge (collect) call, dial 170 for the international operator in Italy. To be connected to the operator in the country you want to call, dial 172 followed by a four-digit code for the country (hence 172 00 44 for the UK and 172 00 1 for the US) and you'll be connected directly to an operator in that country.

The following services operate 24 hours daily (calls are charged):

Operator and **Italian directory enquiries** *412*.
International operator *170*.
International directory enquiries *176*.
Problems on national calls *182*.
Problems on international calls *176*.
Tourist information *110*.

Phone centres

Telecom Italia *Via Cavour 21r, San Lorenzo (no phone).* **Open** 8am-9.45pm daily. **Map** p319 A4.
At this Telecom Italia office, you're allocated a booth and can either use a phone card or pay cash at the desk after you've finished making all your calls. It also has phone books for all of Europe, information on telephone charges and phone cards.

Telephone directories

All hotels and most restaurants and bars have phone books and *Yellow Pages* (if they're not obviously on display, ask to see the *elenco telefonico* or *pagine gialle*). Telecom Italia has a useful website (www.telecomitalia.it) with an online directory enquiries service under 'Info 412'.

Mobile phones

It's worth considering buying a mobile for longer or business stays or if you visit Italy frequently, since even if your native mobile works here (and it probably will), you'll likely pay very inflated rates.

Pay-as-you-go mobiles can be bought from many phone shops for around €120, including the SIM card and €5 of calls. Top-up cards are available from all bar *tabacchi* and some newsstands; either call the number given on the card, or, if the bar has the electronic top-up facility, tap in your phone number and the amount requested will be credited automatically. One top-up has to be made at least every 11 months to keep the number active. Some internet points hire out phones: try **Intotheweb** or **Internet Train** (*see p291*). Italian mobile phone numbers begin with 3 (no zero).

The mobile phone numbers listed below are located in central Florence.

Il Telefonino (TIM) *Via Pellicceria 3, Duomo & Around (055 2396066).* **Open** 9am-7pm Mon-Fri; 9am-1pm Sat. **Credit** AmEx, MC, V. **Map** p318 C3.

Spazio Omnitel *Via Panzani 33r, Santa Maria Novella (055 2670121).* **Open** 3.30-7.30pm Mon; 9.30am-7.30pm Tue-Sat. **Credit** AmEx, MC, V. **Map** p318 B2.

Faxes

Faxes can be sent from most large post offices (*see p295*), which charge per sheet (€1.30 in Italy, €5.10 for Europe). Faxes can also be sent from some photocopying outlets and internet points, and at most hotels.

Telegrams

Telegrams can be sent from main post offices. The telegraph office at the Posta Centrale (*see p295*) is open 8.30am-7pm Mon-Fri, 8.30am-12.30pm Sat. Alternatively, dictate telegrams over the phone. Dial 186 from a private or hotel phone and a message in Italian will tell you to dial the number of the phone you're phoning from. You will then be passed to a telephonist.

Time

Italy is one hour ahead of London, six ahead of New York and eight behind Sydney. Clocks go forward an hour in spring and back in autumn, in line with other EU countries.

Tipping

The 10-15 per cent tip customary in many countries is considered generous in Florence. Locals sometimes leave a few coins on the counter when buying drinks at the bar and, depending on the standard of the restaurant, will drop €1-€5 for the waiter or waitress after a meal. That said, some larger restaurants are now starting to automatically add a 10-15 per cent service charge on the bill. Tips are not expected in smaller restaurants, although they're always appreciated. Other costs include a small cover charge for bread. Taxi drivers will be surprised if you do more than round the fare up to the nearest €1.

Toilets

Florence has very few public toilets. The most useful are in the Santa Maria Novella train station underpass (open 8am-8pm), Palazzo Vecchio, Palazzo Pitti, the coach park to the west of Fortezza da Basso, inside the Sant'Ambrogio market (open 7am-2pm), and in Piazzale Michelangelo (open 11am-5pm). It's usually easiest to go to a bar (obliged by law to let you use its facilities). Ask for the *bagno*; in some bars you'll be given the key. Bar loos are often kept locked to discourage use by drug addicts.

Tourist information

To be sent an information pack in advance of your visit, get in touch with **ENIT**, the Italian tourist board (UK: 020 7498 1254, www.enit.it; US: 212 245 5618, www.italiantourism.com). Tell staff where and when you're travelling, and whether or not you have any special interests.

Florence's provincial tourist board, the **Azienda Promozionale Turistica (APT)**, and the council-run **Ufficio Informazioni Turistiche** have helpful, multilingual staff who do their best to supply reliable information: not easy, since museums and galleries tend to change their hours without telling them. There's no central information service for the Tuscany region; you have to contact the APT in each area. There is a head office in each provincial capital, then local offices in various towns within the province. Details of tourist offices are listed in this guide under the relevant area.

The English *Yellow Pages*, available from bookshops and online (www.paginegialle.it), lists English-speaking services and useful numbers. For information on maps, *see p285*.

Tourist information offices

Via Cavour 1r, San Lorenzo (055 290832). **Open** 8.15am-7.15pm Mon-Sat. **Map** p319 A4.

Borgo Santa Croce 29r, Santa Croce (055 2340444). **Open** *Summer* 9am-7pm Mon-Sat; 9am-1.45pm Sun. *Winter* 9am-5pm Mon-Sat. **Map** p319 C5.

Piazza della Stazione 4a, Santa Maria Novella (055 212245). **Open** 8.30am-7pm Mon-Sat; 8.30am-2pm Sun. **Map** p318 A2.

Via Portigiani 3, Outside the City Gates (055 5978373). **Open** 9am-1pm Mon-Sat.

Run by the city of Florence, these offices in Fiesole provide maps and other information. There are also offices in Florence and Pisa airports. Hotel bookings can be made by emailing Florence Promhotels on info@promhotels.it, a free hotel-booking service available by email or through the tourist office.

Tourist help

Open *Easter-Sept* 8am-7pm daily. Run by the *vigili urbani* from three vans: one in Piazza della Repubblica, one in Via Calzaiuoli and one just south of the Ponte Vecchio in Via Guicciardini. APT personnel and the municipal police provide help and information. You can also register any complaints you might have about restaurant or hotel charges.

Visas & immigration

Non-EU citizens and Britons require full passports to travel to Italy. EU citizens are permitted unrestricted access to Italy, and citizens of the USA, Canada, Australia and New Zealand do not need visas for stays of up to three months.

In theory, all visitors to Italy must declare their presence to the local police within eight days of arrival. If you are staying in a hotel, this will be done for you by the hotel management. If not, contact the Questura Centrale (*see p295*), the main police station, where they can give you advice along with all the requisite bureaucracy.

Weights & measures

Italy uses only the metric system; remember that all speed limits are in kilometres. One kilometre is equivalent to 0.62 mile, with 1 mile converting to 1.6 kilometres. Petrol, like other liquids, is measured in litres: one UK gallon = 4.54 litres; 1 US gallon = 3.79 litres. A kilogram is equivalent to 2.2 pounds (one

pound = 0.45 kilos). Food is often sold in *etti* (sometimes written *hg*); 1 *etto* = 100 grams (3.52 ounces). In delicatessens, you should ask for multiples of *etti* (*un etto, due etti*, etc).

What to take

Any prescription medicines should always be obtained before leaving. Make sure you have enough to cover the entire period of your stay, as not all US and UK medicines are available in Italy.

When to go

Climate

The hills surrounding Florence mean that it can be cold and humid in winter and very hot and humid in the summer. Between late June and August, temperatures often soar to 40°C (104°F) and rarely fall below 30°C (86°F). During the summer, you should be sure to take the sun seriously: every year, local doctors issue warnings about the number of visitors who are hospitalised with serious burns from spending too much time in the sun and going out in the middle of the day. (Italians stay indoors whenever they can during the hottest hours.)

The short spring and autumn in Florence and Tuscany can be very warm. They're not without risk of rain, though, especially in March, April and September. Between November and February, you can't

rely on good weather: you could find anything from a week of rain to crisp, bright and sometimes even warm sunshine.

Public holidays

On public holidays (*giorni festivi*) virtually all shops, banks and businesses are shut, though most bars and restaurants stay open so you will be able to eat and drink. Public holidays are as follows:

New Year's Day (*Capodanno*) 1 Jan
Epiphany (*La Befana*) 6 Jan
Easter Monday (*Lunedì di Pasqua*)
Liberation Day (*Venticinque Aprile/Liberazione*) 25 Apr
May Day (*Primo Maggio*) 1 May
Republic Day (*Festa della Repubblica*) 2 June
Florence Saint's Day (*San Giovanni*) 24 June
Feast of the Assumption (*Ferragosto*) 15 Aug
All Saints' (*Tutti i Santi*) 1 Nov
Immaculate Conception (*Festa dell'Immacolata*) 8 Dec
Christmas Day (*Natale*) 25 Dec
Boxing Day (*Santo Stefano*) 26 Dec

There is limited public transport on 1 May and Christmas afternoon. Holidays falling on a Saturday or Sunday are not celebrated the following Monday, but if a holiday falls on a Thursday or Tuesday, many locals also take the intervening day off and make a long weekend of it; such a weekend is called a *ponte* (bridge). Beware of the *rientro* or homecoming, when the roads are horrendously busy.

Many people also disappear for a large chunk of August, when *chiuso per ferie* (closed for holidays) signs appear in shops and restaurants detailing dates of closure. These

Average monthly climate

Month	High temp	Low temp	Rainfall	Relative humidity
January	10°C (50°F)	−1°C (30°F)	64mm (2.5in)	75%
February	12°C (54°F)	1°C (34°F)	61mm (2.4in)	72%
March	15°C (59°F)	5°C (41°F)	69mm (2.7in)	72%
April	20°C (68°F)	8°C (46°F)	71mm (2.8in)	72%
May	24°C (75°F)	11°C (52°F)	73mm (2.9in)	71%
June	29°C (84°F)	14°C (57°F)	56mm (2.2in)	64%
July	34°C (93°F)	18°C (64°F)	34mm (1.3in)	66%
August	32°C (90°F)	14°C (57°F)	47mm (1.8in)	71%
September	28°C (82°F)	13°C (55°F)	84mm (3.3in)	76%
October	23°C (73°F)	11°C (52°F)	99mm (3.9in)	81%
November	16°C (61°F)	4°C (39°F)	103mm (4.1in)	81%
December	13°C (55°F)	4°C (39°F)	79mm (3.1in)	73%

Directory

closures are co-ordinated on a rota system by the city council, so there should be something open in each area at any given time. However, if you should find yourself in Florence, or many other Tuscan towns, on the *Ferragosto* (Feast of the Assumption; 15 August), the chances are that your only company will be other tourists wandering the baked streets in search of something to do or somewhere to eat. The Florentines desert the city like rats from a sinking ship, and are likely to stay away for several days either side. You'll find the exceptions to this rule are holiday resorts such as coastal towns where, although shops and public offices may close, the infrastructure doesn't completely collapse. For a calendar of Tuscany's traditional and modern festivals throughout the year, *see pp156-159*.

Women

Although it's not one of the worst places for women travellers, Tuscany still has its hassles. Visiting women can feel daunted by the sheer volume of attention they receive, but most of it will be friendly; men are unlikely to become pushy or aggressive if given the brush-off. It's normally a question of all talk and no action, but be aware of who's around you: it's quite common to be followed. If things get too heavy, go into the nearest shop or bar and wait or ask for help. The notorious bum-pinching is uncommon but not unknown, especially on buses. As in Anglo-Saxon countries, it's an assault and a criminal offence, and recent prosecutions and convictions show that it's taken seriously.

Network
Villa Rossa, Piazza Savonarola 15, Outside the City Gates (contact Jane Fogarty jfogarty.csuitaly@dada.it). Bus 10, 11, 13, 17.
A professional women's organisation geared mainly towards residents whose first language is English. It aims to improve communication, exchange ideas and information among the English-speaking community. Meetings are generally on the second Wednesday of the month. Annual fees are €40, which includes newsletters and mailings.

Women's health

Women who are suffering from gynaecological emergencies should head for the nearest *pronto soccorso* (accident & emergency; *see p289*). Tampons (*assorbenti interni*) and sanitary towels (*assorbenti esterni*) can be bought in supermarkets, pharmacies and some *tabacchi*.

Careggi hospital (*see p289*) has a clinic for women who have suffered a sexual assault, offering them examinations, treatment, counselling and liaison with the police. Some English is spoken.

For information on contraception, abortion and other health matters, *see p290*.

Clinica Ostetrica
Reparto Maternità, Ospedale di Careggi, Viale Morgagni, Outside the City Gates (055 4277111/ 4277493). Bus 2, 8, 14C.
Open 24hrs daily.
Female victims of sexual assault should come to Clinica Ostetrica for medical attention. Legal services and counselling are available 9am-1pm, 3-5pm Monday to Friday at the office at Viale Santa Maria Maggiore 1, Careggi (055 284752).

Working in Florence

Finding a job in Italy is not simple. The country's jobs market isn't known for being mobile and unemployment is fairly high, especially for graduate positions. Most of the jobs that are available are connected to tourism in some way, although there are a few multinationals that occasionally advertise for native English-speakers. The classified ads paper *La Pulce* has job listings; it's also worth checking the local English-language press.

The bureaucracy involved isn't easy. Anyone intending to stay in Italy longer than three months has to acquire a bewildering array of papers in order to get a *permesso di soggiorno* (permit to stay), and if they plan to work, they'll also need a *permesso di soggiorno per lavoro*. While EU citizens should have no trouble getting documentation

once they are in Italy, non-EU citizens, on the other hand, are advised to enquire at an Italian embassy or consulate in their own country before setting off for Italy with the hope of finding employment when they arrive.

All non-EU citizens and EU nationals who are working in Italy should register with the police within eight days of arrival and apply for their permits. There is a useful computer at the Questura Centrale (central police station) that prints out lists (in various languages) of the documents that you'll need for every type of *permesso*. You can also get advice here.

You will need a residency permit to perform certain transactions, including buying a car, although new European laws have eased restrictions and it's possible to buy a car with a Euro plate for the first year. To apply for residency, contact your local *circoscrizione* office. Spot checks will be carried out to ensure that you are, in fact, resident at the address you stated.

Administration & permit offices
Comune di Firenze (Florence town hall), Palazzo Vecchio & Piazza Signoria, Duomo & Around (switchboard 055 27681/800 831133). **Open** 8.30am-1.30pm Mon-Wed, Fri, Sat; 8.30am-6.30pm Thur. **Map** p319 C4.
For residency enquiries, ask for the *Ufficio Circoscrizione*. Given your address, they will then give you the number you need to call to progress further with your application.

Questura Centrale (central police station)
Via Zara 2, San Lorenzo (055 49771). **Open** 24hrs daily. *Ufficio Stranieri* 8.30am-12.30pm Mon-Fri.
To apply for your documents, go to the *Ufficio Stranieri* (foreigners' section) where English-speaking staff are usually available to help. It's advisable to go early in the day to avoid the long queues that can form. There is a number system (take a ticket from the dispenser when you arrive) and applications are dealt with at one of eight desks.

Directory

Vocabulary

Any attempt at speaking Italian will always be appreciated. Indeed, it may well be necessary: away from services such as tourist offices, hotels and restaurants popular with foreigners, the level of English is not very high. The most important thing is making the effort, not whether or not your sentences are perfectly formed with an authentic accent. The key is to take the plunge and not be shy.

Note that it's a myth that you can get by in Italy with Spanish: true, you may well understand some Italian (both written and spoken), but try speaking it and Italians generally won't understand you (unless, of course, they speak Spanish themselves).

Italian is a phonetic language, so most words are spelled as they're pronounced (and vice versa). Stresses usually fall on the penultimate syllable. There are three forms of the second person: the formal *lei* (used with strangers), the informal *tu*, and the plural form *voi*. Masculine nouns are usually accompanied by adjectives ending in 'o', female nouns by adjectives ending in 'a'. However, there are many nouns and adjectives that end in 'e' that can be either masculine or feminine.

Pronunciation

Vowels

a – as in **a**pple
e – like **a** in **a**ge (closed e), or **e** in s**e**ll (open e)
i – like **ea** in **ea**st
o – as in h**o**tel (closed o) or in h**o**t (open o)
u – like **oo** in b**oo**t

Consonants

c – before a, o or u: like the **c** in **c**at; before e or i: like the **ch** in **ch**eck
ch – like the **c** in **c**at
g – before a, o or u: like the **g** in **g**et; before e or i: like the **j** in **j**ig
gh – like the **g** in **g**et

gl – followed by 'i': like **lli** in mi**lli**on
gn – like **ny** in ca**ny**on
qu – as in **qu**ick
r – is always rolled
s – has two sounds, as in **s**oap or ro**s**e
sc – followed by 'e' or 'i': like the **sh** in **sh**ame
sch – like the **sc** in **sc**out
z – has two sounds, like **ts** and **dz**

Double consonants are sounded more emphatically.

Useful words & phrases

hello and goodbye (informal) – *ciao*
good morning, good day – *buongiorno*
good afternoon, good evening – *buona sera*
I don't understand – *non capisco/non ho capito*
do you speak English? – *parla inglese?*
please – *per favore*
thank you – *grazie*
you're welcome – *prego*
when does it open? – *quando apre?*
where is... ? – *dov'è… ?*
excuse me – *scusi* (polite), *scusa* (informal)
open – *aperto*
closed – *chiuso*
entrance – *entrata*
exit – *uscita*
left – *sinistra*
right – *destra*
car – *macchina*
bus – *autobus*
train – *treno*
bus stop – *fermata dell'autobus*
ticket/s – *biglietto/i*
I would like a ticket to... – *vorrei un biglietto per…*
postcard – *cartolina*
stamp – *francobollo*
glass – *bicchiere*
coffee – *caffè*
tea – *tè*
water – *acqua*
wine – *vino*
beer – *birra*
the bill – *il conto*
single/twin/double bedroom – *camera singola/a due letti/ matrimoniale*
booking – *prenotazione*

Days of the week

Monday – *lunedì*
Tuesday – *martedì*
Wednesday – *mercoledì*

Thursday – *giovedì*
Friday – *venerdì*
Saturday – *sabato*
Sunday – *domenica*
yesterday – *ieri*
today – *oggi*
tomorrow – *domani*
morning – *mattina*
afternoon – *pomeriggio*
evening – *sera*
night – *notte*
weekend – *fine settimana, weekend*

The come-on

do you have a light? – *hai da accendere?*
what's your name? – *come ti chiami?*
would you like a drink? – *vuoi bere qualcosa?*
where are you from? – *di dove sei?*
what are you doing here? – *che fai qui?*
do you have a boyfriend/ girlfriend? – *hai un ragazzo/una ragazza?*

The brush-off

I'm married – *sono sposato/a*
I'm tired – *sono stanco/a*
I'm going home – *vado a casa*
I have to meet a friend – *devo incontrare un amico/una amica*

Numbers & money

0 *zero*; **1** *uno*; **2** *due*; **3** *tre*; **4** *quattro*; **5** *cinque*; **6** *sei*; **7** *sette*; **8** *otto*; **9** *nove*; **10** *dieci*; **11** *undici*; **12** *dodici*; **13** *tredici*; **14** *quattordici*; **15** *quindici*; **16** *sedici*; **17** *diciassette*; **18** *diciotto*; **19** *diciannove*; **20** *venti*; **21** *ventuno*; **22** *ventidue*; **30** *trenta*; **40** *quaranta*; **50** *cinquanta*; **60** *sessanta*; **70** *settanta*; **80** *ottanta*; **90** *novanta*; **100** *cento*; **1,000** *mille*; **2,000** *duemila*; **100,000** *centomila*; **100,000** *un milione*.

how much does it cost/is it? – *quanto costa?/quant'è?*
do you have any change? – *ha da cambiare?*
can you give me a discount? – *mi può fare uno sconto?*
do you accept credit cards? – *si accettano le carte di credito?*
can I pay in pounds/dollars/ travellers' cheques? – *posso pagare in sterline/dollari/ con i travellers?*
can I have a receipt? – *posso avere una ricevuta?*
is service included? – *è compreso il servizio?*

Glossary

Annunciation depiction of the Virgin Mary being told by the Archangel Gabriel that she will bear the son of God.

Attribute object used in art to symbolise a particular person, often saints and martyrs.

Baldacchino canopied structure; in paintings holding an enthroned Madonna and child.

Banderuola small forked flag bearing an inscription, held in Renaissance art by angels or *putti*.

Baptistery building for baptisms, usually octagonal to symbolise new beginnings, as seven is the number of completion and eight the start of a new cycle.

Baroque sumptuous art and architectural style from the 17th to mid 18th centuries.

Byzantine spiritual and religious art of the Byzantine Empire (fifth-15th centuries).

Campanile bell tower.

Cartoon full-scale sketch for painting or fresco.

Cenacolo depiction of the Last Supper.

Chiaroscuro painting or drawing technique using shades of black, grey and white to emphasise light and shade.

Classical ancient Greek and Roman art and culture.

Corbel brackets jutting from a roof.

Cupola dome-shaped structure set on a larger dome or a roof.

Deposition depiction of Christ taken down from the Cross.

Diptych painting made of two panels.

Fresco technique for wall painting where pigments bind with wet plaster.

Golden mean Renaissance art theory with division of proportions by a ratio of 8:13. Considered to create perfect harmony.

Gothic architectural and artistic style of the late Middle Ages (from the 12th century) characterised by the integration of art forms, with pointed arches and an emphasis on line.

Grotesque ornate artistic style derived from Roman underground painted rooms (*grotte*).

Hortus conclusus garden around Madonna and child symbolising their uncontaminated world of perfection and contentment.

Iconography study of subject and symbolism of works of art. For example, in Renaissance art: a **dog** symbolises faithfulness to a master, usually the Medici; an **egg** is a symbol of perfection; a **peacock** symbolises the Resurrection; a **giglio** (lily of Florence) is often found in Annunciations to symbolise the purity of the Madonna; a **sarcophagus** (stone or marble coffin) symbolises the death of an important person; and the colour **blue** sometimes symbolises divine peace.

Illumination miniature painted as an illustration for manuscripts.

Loggia covered area with one or more sides open, with columns.

Lunette half-moon painting or semicircular architectural space for decoration or window.

Madonna of Mercy Madonna with her cloak open to give protection to those in need.

Maestà depiction of the Madonna on a throne.

Mandorla almond-shaped 'glory' surrounding depiction of holy person.

Mannerism 15th-century art movement in Italy, defined by exaggerated perspective and scale, and complex compositions and poses.

Medieval relating to the Middle Ages (from the fall of the Roman Empire in the west, in the 5th century, to the 1453 fall of Constantinople).

Modernist (Modernism) the movement away from classical and traditional forms towards architecture that applied scientific methods to its design.

Palazzo (*palazzi*) large and/ or important building, not necessarily a royal palace.

Panel painting on wood.

Panneggio style of folded and pleated drapery worn by figures in 15th- and 16th-century painting and sculpture.

Pietà depiction of Christ lying across the Madonna's lap after the Deposition.

Pietra dura inlaid gem mosaics.

Polyptych painting composed of several panels.

Putto (*putti*) small angelic naked boys, often depicted as attendants of Venus.

Relief sculpted work with three-dimensional areas jutting out from a flat surface.

Renaissance 14th- to 16th-century cultural movement based on the 'rebirth' of classical ideals and methods.

Romanesque architectural style of the early Middle Ages (c500-1200), drawing on Roman Byzantine influences.

Secco the finishing-off or retouching of a fresco, done on dried plaster (*intonaco*).

Sinopia preparatory drawing for a fresco made with a red earth mix or the red paint itself.

Tempera pigment bound with egg, the main painting material from 12th to late 15th centuries.

Tondo round painting or relief.

Triptych painting composed of three panels.

Trompe l'œil painting designed to give the illusion of a three-dimensional reality.

Vanitas objects in art symbolising mortality, such as skulls and hourglasses.

Votive offering left as a prayer for good fortune or recovery from illness, usually as a painting or a silver model of the limb/organ to be cured.

Directory

Further Reference

Books

Non-fiction

Luigi Barzini *The Italians*
A dated yet hilarious portrait.
**Julia Conaway Bondanella
& Mark Musa** *Introduction to the
Major Italian Writers & Influential
Thinkers of the Renaissance*
Famous names and a few surprises.
Thomas Campanello
*A Defence of Galileo, the
Mathematician from Florence*
The life, times and influence of
Florence's most famous heretic.
Leonardo Castellucci
Living in Tuscany
An account of the restoration efforts
that turned Tuscan abbeys, castles,
villas and farmhouses into homes.
Paul Ginsbourg
*A History of Contemporary Italy:
Society and Politics 1943-1988*
Comprehensive modern history.
Frederick Hartt *The History
of Italian Renaissance Art*
The definitive work.
Christopher Hibbert *The Rise
and Fall of the House of Medici*
A very readable history.
Ross King *Brunelleschi's Dome:
The Story of the Great Cathedral*
A fascinating account of the building
of Florence's magnificent dome.
**Monica Larner & Travis
Neighbor** *Living, Studying
and Working in Italy*
Everything you need to know.
Mary McCarthy
The Stones of Florence
A portrait of Florence and its arts.
Iris Origo *Images and Shadows;
The Merchant of Prato*
Autobiographical and biographical
accounts of Florence and Tuscany.
Thomas Paloscia
Accadde in Toscana (Vol III)
A beautifully illustrated who's who
of Tuscany's contemporary artists.
Laura Raison
Tuscany: An Anthology
A collection of writings and
illustrations, classic to contemporary,
about Florence and Tuscany.
Leon Satkowski *Giorgio Vasari:
Architect & Courtier*
A biography of the most famous
Italian art chronicler.
Matthew Spender *Within Tuscany*
A witty account of growing up in an
unusual family in Tuscany.

Fiction

Italo Calvino *The Florentine*
One of Calvino's 'folktales' collections
of short stories. Tells of the misery of
a Florentine who longs to travel.

Jack Dann *The Memory Cathedral:
A Secret History of Leonardo da Vinci*
Mystery and intrigue in Florence.
Michael Dibdin *A Rich Full Death*
An amusing thriller with insight into
19th-century Florence.
Sarah Dunant *The Birth of Venus*
Gender and art in Medici Florence.
EM Forster *A Room with a View;
Where Angels Fear to Tread*
Social comedy from the master.
Robert Hellenga *The 16 Pleasures*
A young American woman goes to
Florence and feels obliged to act out
16 'pleasures' from a book of erotica.
Christobel Kent *Late Season*
Past and present collide for a group
of friends and family on holiday in a
Tuscan farmhouse.
Christobel Kent
A Party in San Niccolò
An eventful week leads up to the 75th
birthday party of an English expat.
W Somerset Maugham
Up at the Villa
Temptation and fate in '30s Florence.
Frances Mayes *Under the Tuscan
Sun, Bella Tuscany*
Ubiquitous *Year in Provence*-style
expat dreams and nightmares.
Magdalen Nabb *Death of
an Englishman*
Murder in the secretive world of
Florentine antiques dealers.
Magdalen Nabb
The Monster of Florence
A thriller based on a serial killer who
murdered 16 campers in the 1980s.
Michael Ondaatje
The English Patient
Booker-winning novel turned Oscar-
winning film, partly set in Tuscany.
Davina Sobell *Galileo's Daughter*
A study of Galileo's life in the context
of his relationship with his daughter.
Sally Stewart
An Unexpected Harvest
London yuppie moves to Tuscany to
help grandparents save family estate.

Food & wine

Leslie Forbes *A Table in Tuscany*
A personal account of Tuscan food,
with recipes from local restaurants.
Claudia Roden *The Food of Italy*
A wonderful book of Italian recipes,
with a section on Tuscany.
Slow Food & Gambero Rosso
Italian Wines Guide
The English edition of reliable
annual guide to Italian wines.

Film

The English Patient (1996)
Tragic World War II story, partly set
in Tuscany, starring Ralph Fiennes
and Juliette Binoche.

Hannibal (2000)
This creepy sequel to *Silence of the
Lambs* shows Anthony Hopkins'
serial killer travelling to Florence.
**Life is Beautiful
(La Vita è Bella)** (1997)
Roberto Benigni's bittersweet
comedy about wartime Arezzo.
Much Ado about Nothing (1993)
Kenneth Branagh's fanciful
interpretation of Shakespeare's
comedy, filmed in Tuscany.
Portrait of a Lady (1996)
Nicole Kidman stars in this version
of Henry James's story about a New
World woman in Old World Italy.
A Room with a View (1985)
Helena Bonham Carter learns of love
and loss in 19th-century Florence in
this Merchant Ivory flick.
Stealing Beauty (1995)
Bernardo Bertolucci's Tuscan-based
film brought us Liv Tyler.
Tea with Mussolini (1998)
Judy Dench and Maggie Smith form
part of an eccentric group of expat
ladies in wartime Florence.
Up at the Villa (2000)
Sean Penn plays a cynical American
who proves innocent in comparison
to his European companions.

Music

Puccini *Gianni Schicchi*
This delightful one-act opera is set in
medieval Fucecchio, west of Florence.
Tchaikovsky *Souvenir of Florence*
The composer wrote this string
sextet while living in Via San
Leonardo in Florence.

Websites

www.boxoi.it
Information and online booking for
concerts and shows.
www.cultura.toscana.it
The official Regione Toscana site has
information on museums, exhibitions
and libraries in Tuscany. Italian only.
http://www.firenze.net
The best local site has information
on cinemas, nightlife, music, art,
traffic and weather in Florence
and Tuscany, plus a booking
service for museums, hotels and
farm holidays.
www.firenzespettacolo.it
The monthly listings mag website
has what's-on information, reviews
and plenty more: you can even order
a pizza here.
www.fol.it
Plenty of links relating to health,
travel, sports, hotels and business.
www.lapulce.it
The online version of the small
ads mag. Italian only.

Index

Index

Advertisers' Index

Please refer to the relevant pages for contact details.

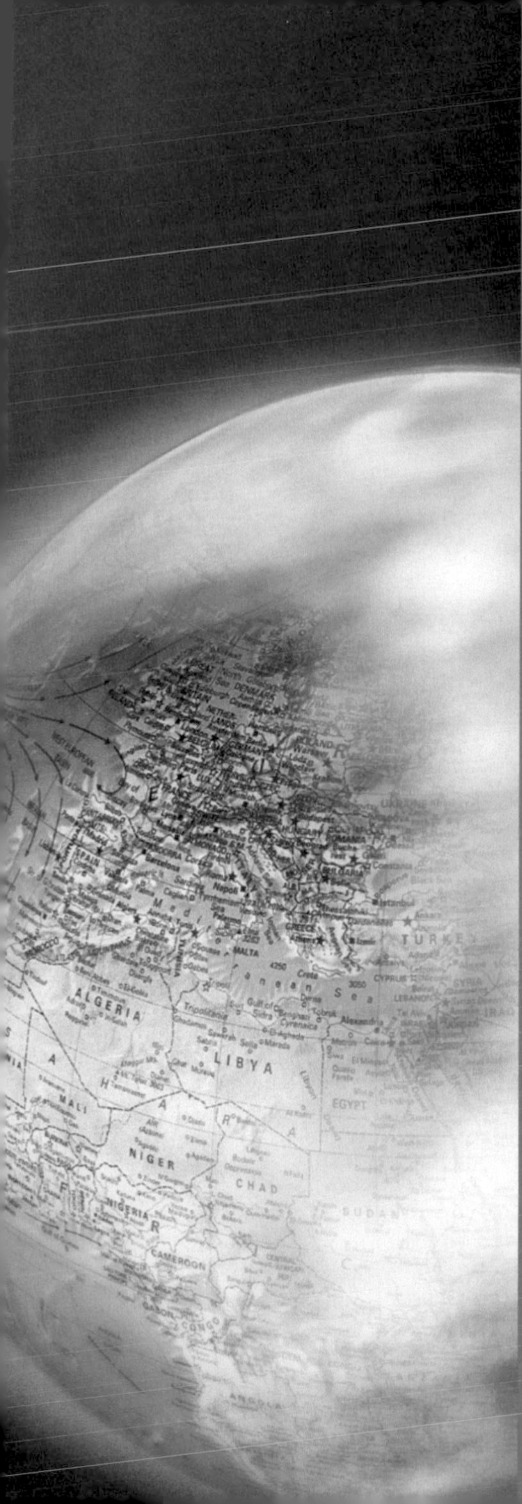

- Regional Border
- Province Border
- Autostrade
- City Wall
- Place of interest and/or entertainment
- Railway station
- Park
- Hospital/university
- Ancient Site
- Car Park — P
- Tourist Information — i
- Predestrianised Area
- Electric Bus Routes — A

Maps

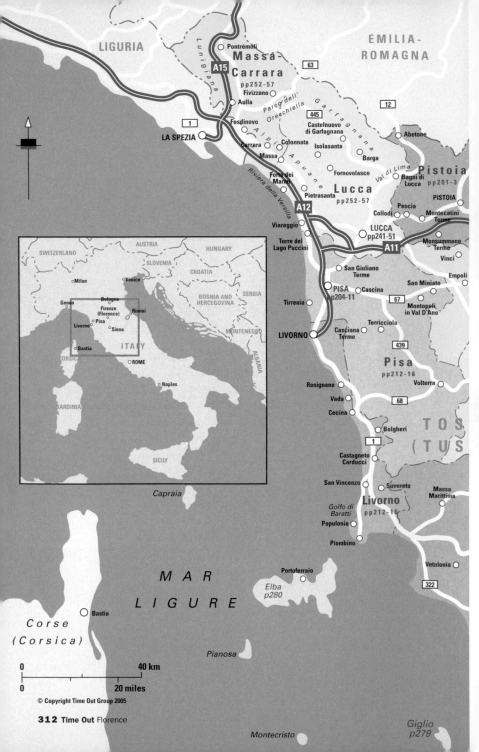

Tuscany

THE WORLD'S YOUR OYSTER

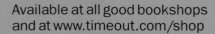

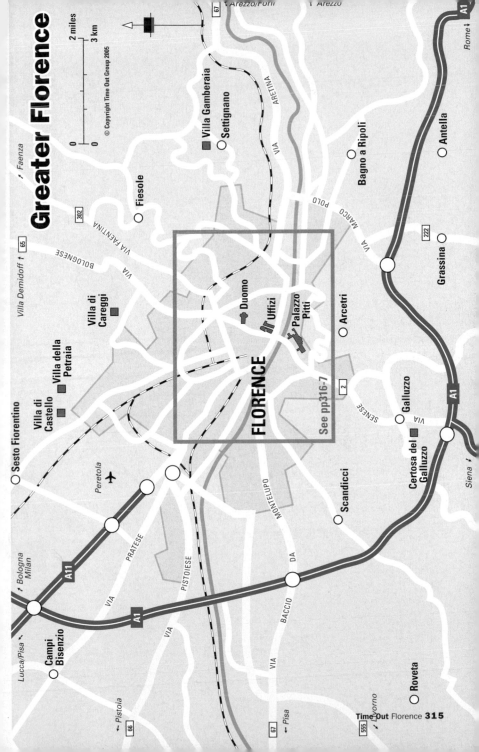

Greater Florence

© Copyright Time Out Group 2005

0   1   2 miles
0   1   2   3 km

↑ Faenza

↑ Arezzo/Forlì   ↑ Arezzo

67

A1

Rome ↓

■ Villa Gamberaia
○ Settignano

○ Fiesole

302

65

Villa Demidoff ↑

VIA FAENTINA

BOLOGNESE

VIA

Villa di
Caready
Careggi ■

Villa della
Petraia ■

Villa di
Castello ■

○ Sesto Fiorentino

A11

↖ Bologna
Milan

VIA PRATESE

Peretola

VIA PISTOIESE

A1

↑ Pistoia

66

Lucca/Pisa ↖

○ Campi
Bisenzio

VIA

↓ Pisa

67

↓ Livorno

555

ARETINA

VIA

○ Bagno a Ripoli

VIA MARCO POLO

○ Arcetri

● Duomo

Uffizi
Palazzo
Pitti

FLORENCE

See pp316-7

222

○ Grassina

2

SENESE

○ Galluzzo

VIA

A1

Certosa del
Galluzzo ■

Siena ↓

MONTELUPO

VIA DA BACCIO

○ Scandicci

○ Roveta

○ Antella

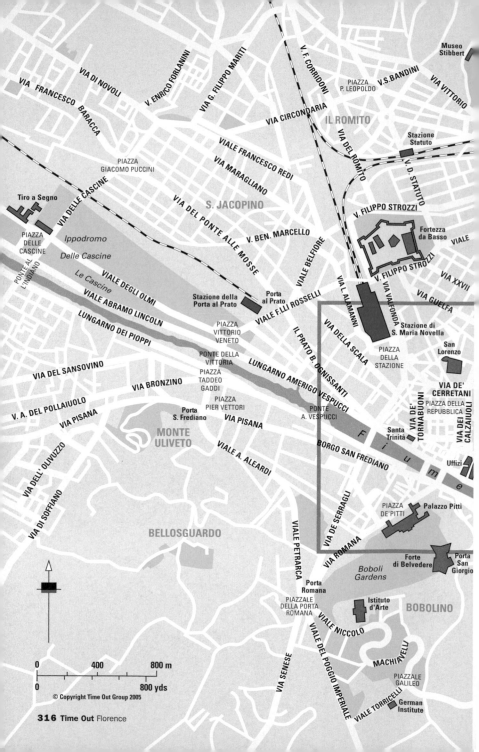

VIA DI NOVOLI

VIA FRANCESCO BARACCA

V. ENRICO FORLANINI

V. F. CORRIDONI

VIA G. FILIPPO MARITI

PIAZZA P. LEOPOLDO

V.S.BANDINI

VIA VITTORIO

Museo Stibbert

VIA CIRCONDARIA

IL ROMITO

VIA DEL ROMITO

Stazione Statuto

PIAZZA GIACOMO PUCCINI

VIALE FRANCESCO REDI

VIA MARAGLIANO

V. D. STATUTO

Tiro a Segno

VIA DELLE CASCINE

S. JACOPINO

VIA DEL PONTE ALLE MOSSE

V. BEN. MARCELLO

V. FILIPPO STROZZI

Fortezza da Basso

PIAZZA DELLE CASCINE

Ippodromo

Delle Cascine

VIALE BELFIORE

VIA L. ALAMANNI

V. FILIPPO STROZZI

VIA VALFONDA

VIA XXVII

VIALE

VIA GUELFA

PONTE AL L'INDIANO

Le Cascine

VIALE DEGLI OLMI

VIALE ABRAMO LINCOLN

Stazione della Porta al Prato

Porta al Prato

VIALE F.LLI ROSSELLI

IL PRATO B. OGNISSANTI

VIA DELLA SCALA

Stazione di S. Maria Novella

San Lorenzo

LUNGARNO DEI PIOPPI

PIAZZA VITTORIO VENETO

PIAZZA DELLA STAZIONE

VIA DE' CERRETANI

VIA DEL SANSOVINO

PONTE DELLA VITTORIA

PIAZZA TADDEO GADDI

LUNGARNO AMERIGO VESPUCCI

VIA DE' TORNABUONI

PIAZZA DELLA REPUBBLICA

VIA DEI CALZAIUOLI

VIA BRONZINO

PIAZZA PIER VETTORI

PONTE A. VESPUCCI

Santa Trinita

V. A. DEL POLLAIUOLO

Porta S. Frediano

VIA PISANA

Uffizi

VIA PISANA

VIALE A. ALEARDI

BORGO SAN FREDIANO

F i u m e

VIA DELL' OLIVUZZO

MONTE ULIVETO

VIA DE' SERRAGLI

PIAZZA DE' PITTI

Palazzo Pitti

VIA DI SOFFIANO

BELLOSGUARDO

VIALE PETRARCA

VIA ROMANA

Forte di Belvedere

Porta San Giorgio

Boboli Gardens

BOBOLINO

Porta Romana

Istituto d'Arte

PIAZZALE DELLA PORTA ROMANA

VIALE NICCOLO

VIALE DEL POGGIO IMPERIALE

MACHIAVELLI

PIAZZALE GALILEO

VIA SENESE

VIALE TORRICELLI

German Institute

0   400   800 m

0   800 yds

© Copyright Time Out Group 2005

Florence Overview

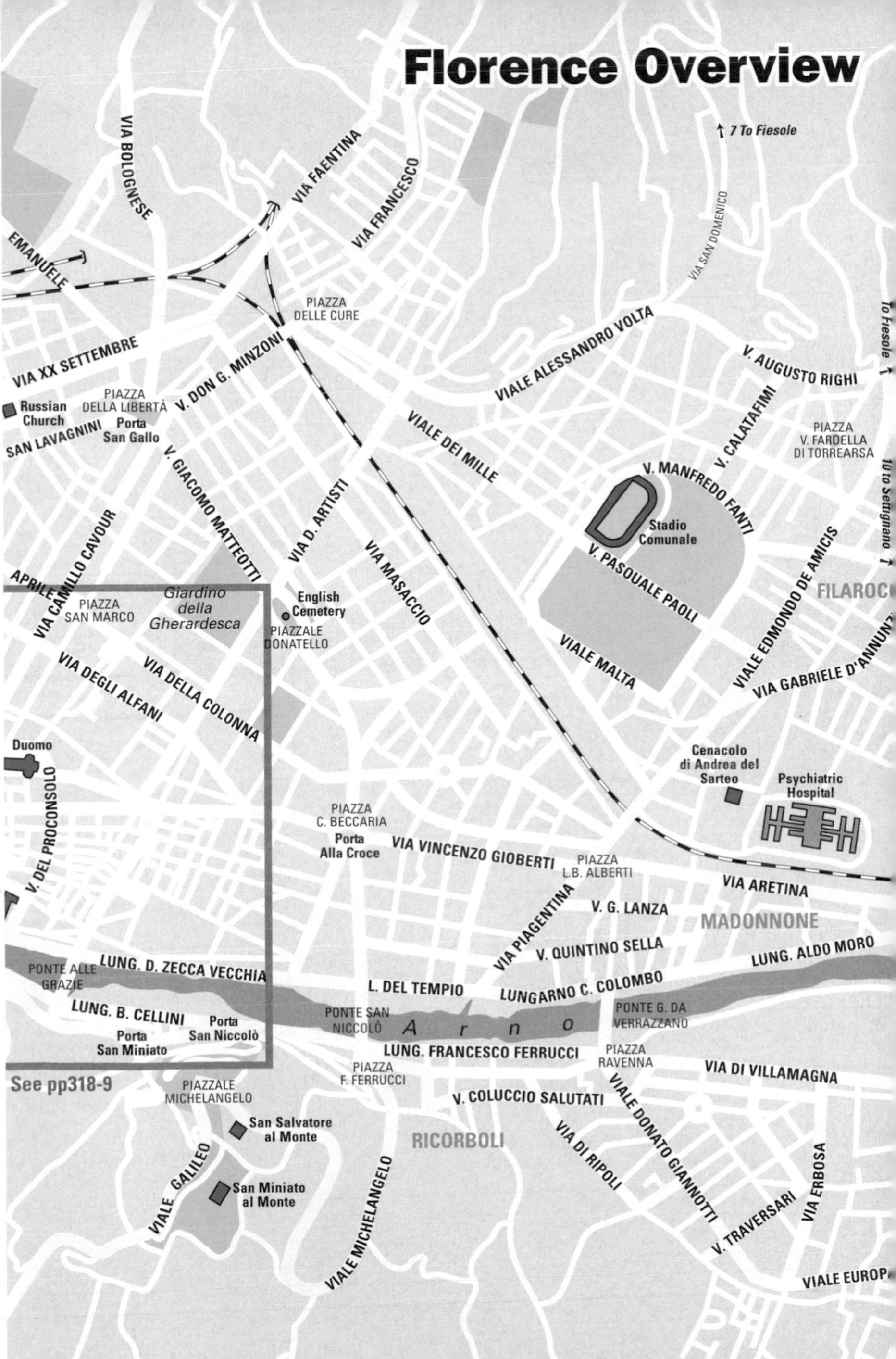

↑ 7 To Fiesole

VIA BOLOGNESE

VIA FAENTINA

VIA FRANCESCO

VIA SAN DOMENICO

To Fiesole ↗

EMANUELE

PIAZZA
DELLE CURE

V. AUGUSTO RIGHI

VIA XX SETTEMBRE

VIALE ALESSANDRO VOLTA

To Settignano ↗

Russian
Church

PIAZZA
DELLA LIBERTÀ

V. CALATAFIMI

PIAZZA
V. FARDELLA
DI TORREARSA

SAN LAVAGNINI

Porta
San Gallo

VIA DON G. MINZONI

VIALE DEI MILLE

V. MANFREDO FANTI

VIA GIACOMO MATTEOTTI

Stadio
Comunale

VIA CAMILLO CAVOUR

VIA D. ARTISTI

V. PASQUALE PAOLI

FILAROC

APRILE

PIAZZA
SAN MARCO

Giardino
della
Gherardesca

English
Cemetery

VIA MASACCIO

VIALE EDMONDO DE AMICIS

VIA DEGLI ALFANI

PIAZZALE
DONATELLO

VIALE MALTA

VIA GABRIELE D'ANNUN

VIA DELLA COLONNA

Duomo

V. DEL PROCONSOLO

Cenacolo
di Andrea del
Sarteo

Psychiatric
Hospital

PIAZZA
C. BECCARIA

Porta
Alla Croce

VIA VINCENZO GIOBERTI

PIAZZA
L.B. ALBERTI

VIA ARETINA

V. G. LANZA

MADONNONE

VIA PIAGENTINA

V. QUINTINO SELLA

LUNG. ALDO MORO

PONTE ALLE
GRAZIE

LUNG. D. ZECCA VECCHIA

L. DEL TEMPIO

LUNGARNO C. COLOMBO

LUNG. B. CELLINI

Porta
San Niccolò

PONTE SAN
NICCOLÒ

A r n o

PONTE G. DA
VERRAZZANO

Porta
San Miniato

LUNG. FRANCESCO FERRUCCI

PIAZZA
RAVENNA

VIA DI VILLAMAGNA

See pp318-9

PIAZZALE
MICHELANGELO

PIAZZA
F. FERRUCCI

V. COLUCCIO SALUTATI

VIALE DONATO GIANNOTTI

San Salvatore
al Monte

RICORBOLI

VIA DI RIPOLI

VIALE GALILEO

San Miniato
al Monte

VIALE MICHELANGELO

V. TRAVERSARI

VIALE ERBOSA

VIALE EUROP

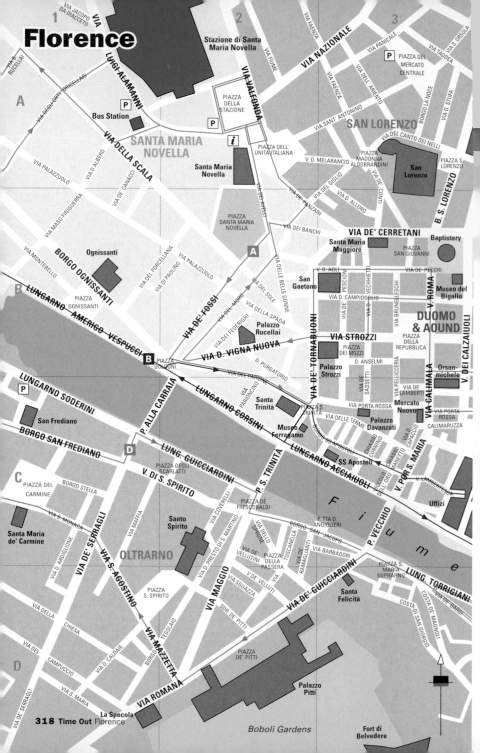

Florence

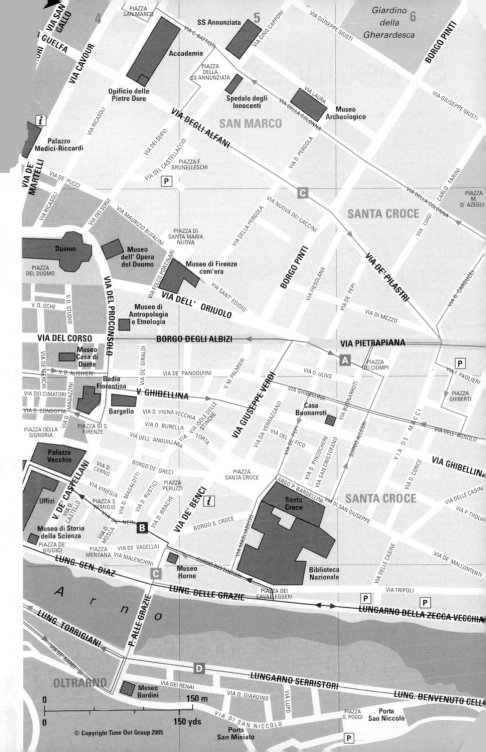

Street Index